FIFTH EDITION

Estate
PLANNING
for Financial Planners

Michael A. Dalton
Thomas P. Langdon

Estate PLANNING for Financial Planners

FIFTH EDITION

Michael A. Dalton
Thomas P. Langdon

YOUR MONEY EDUCATION RESOURCE.™

1000 Riverbend Blvd.
Suite A
St. Rose, LA 70087
888-295-6023

Printed in the U.S.A.

ISBN-10: 0-9801299-5-8
ISBN-13: 978-0-9801299-5-3
Custom Edition for The College for Financial Planning ISBN-10: 0-9801299-4-x
Custom Edition for The College for Financial Planning ISBN-13: 978-0-9801299-4-6

Library of Congress Card Number: 2009921181

ABOUT THE AUTHORS

Michael A. Dalton, Ph.D., JD, CFP®

- Principal of Cobalt Financial Solutions, L.L.C.
- Former Chair of the Board of Dalton Publications, L.L.C.
- Associate professor of Accounting and Taxation at Loyola University in New Orleans, Louisiana.
- Adjunct faculty in Financial Planning at Georgetown University in Washington, D.C.
- Former Senior Vice President, Education at BISYS Group.
- Ph.D. in Accounting from Georgia State University.
- J.D. from Louisiana State University in Baton Rouge, Louisiana.
- MBA and BBA in Management and Accounting from Georgia State University.
- Former board member of the CFP Board's Board of Examiners, Board of Standards, and Board of Governors.
- Former member (and chair) of the CFP Board's Board of Examiners.
- Member of the *Journal of Financial Planning* Editorial Advisory Board and Editorial Review Board.
- Member of the LSU Law School Board of Trustees (2000 - 2006).
- Author of *Dalton Review for the CFP® Certification Examination: Volume I – Outlines and Study Guides, Volume II – Problems and Solutions, Volume III - Case Exam Book, Mock Exams A-1 and A-2* (1st - 8th Editions).
- Author of *Retirement Planning and Employee Benefits for Financial Planners* (1st - 5th Editions).
- Co-author of *Income Tax Planning for Financial Planners* (1st - 2nd Editions).
- Co-author of *Dalton CFA® Study Notes Volumes I and II* (1st - 2nd Editions); Co-author of *Dalton's Personal Financial Planning Series – Personal Financial Planning Theory and Practice* (1st - 3rd Editions) and *Personal Financial Planning Cases and Applications* (1st - 4th Editions).
- Co-author of *Cost Accounting: Traditions and Innovations* published by West Publishing Company.
- Co-author of the *ABCs of Managing Your Money* published by National Endowment for Financial Education.

Thomas P. Langdon, JD, LL.M., CFA, CFP®

- Associate Professor of Business Law, Gabelli School of Business, Roger Williams University, Bristol, RI.
- Principal, Langdon & Langdon Financial Services, LLC (Connecticut-based tax planning & preparation firm).
- Former Professor of Taxation at The American College, Bryn Mawr, PA.
- Former Adjunct Professor of Insurance and Economics at The University of Connecticut Center for Professional Development.
- Former Member (and Chair) of the CFP Board's Board of Examiners.
- Master of Laws (LL.M.) in Taxation from Villanova University School of Law.
- Juris Doctor, from Western New England College School of Law.
- Master of Science in Financial Services from The American College.
- Master of Business Administration from The University of Connecticut.
- Bachelor of Science in Finance from The University of Connecticut, Storrs, CT.
- Chartered Financial Analyst (CFA), Certified Financial Planner (CFP), Chartered Life Underwriter (CLU), Chartered Financial Consultant (ChFC), Accredited Estate Planner (AEP), Certified Employee Benefits Specialist (CEBS), Chartered Advisor in Senior Living (CASL), Registered Employee Benefits Consultant (REBC), Registered Health Underwriter (RHU), Associate in Life & Health Claims (ALHC), and Fellow of the Life Management Institute (FLMI).
- Co-author of *Income Tax Planning for Financial Planners* (1st - 2nd editions).

ABOUT THE CONTRIBUTOR

Phyllis Duhon made a significant contribution to this text by her thoughtful and meticulous reading, rewriting, and editing throughout the book. She provided many valuable suggestions to both the text and instructor materials that significantly improved this edition. We are extremely grateful for her contributions. Phyllis received her J.D. from Loyola University New Orleans College of Law and a B.S. in Business Administration/Finance from the University of New Orleans.

ABOUT THE REVIEWERS

We owe a special thanks to several key professionals for their significant contribution of time and effort with this text. These reviewers provided meticulous editing, detailed calculation reviews, helpful suggestions for additional content, and other valuable comments, all of which have improved this edition.

Allison Dalton McCammon is an attorney and personal financial planner specializing in Small Business Planning and Estate Planning. She received her J.D. from Georgetown University Law Center, an Executive Certificate in Financial Planning from Georgetown University, and a B.A. in International Studies from Rhodes College. She is a contributor to previous editions of this text and to Money Education's *Retirement Planning and Employee Benefits for Financial Planners* and *Income Tax Planning for Financial Planners*.

Kristi M. Tafalla is an attorney and personal financial planner specializing in income tax and estate planning. She teaches estate planning, income tax planning and comprehensive case courses through various CFP Board-Registered Programs as well as comprehensive reviews for the Certified Financial Planner designation. She is a contributor to previous editions of this text and to Money Education's *Retirement Planning and Employee Benefits for Financial Planners*.

Chris White teaches the financial planning program to financial service professionals, attorneys, insurance agents, CPAs, and others working to attain their CFP® certification at Xavier University in Cincinnati. He is also the Vice President of Financial Planning at Provident Financial Advisors, a member of the Financial Planning Association and an instructor for the BISYS Review for the CFP® Certification Examination. Mr. White has an MBA with a concentration in Taxation from Xavier University and a B.S. in Accounting from the University of Cincinnati. After using the 2nd Edition in his estate planning course, he provided invaluable feedback on where improvements could be made for the 3rd edition.

ACKNOWLEDGEMENTS & SPECIAL THANKS

We are most appreciative of the tremendous support and encouragement we have received throughout this project. We are extremely grateful to the instructors and program directors of CFP Board-Registered programs who provided valuable comments on the first, second, third, and fourth edition. We are fortunate to have dedicated, careful readers at several institutions who were willing to share their needs, expectations, and time with us. We also owe a debt of gratitude to all the reviewers and students who have read and commented on the first four editions.

We owe a special thanks to Gregg A. Parish for his significant contribution of time and effort with previous editions of this text. Mr. Parish is a Professor of Estate Planning at the College for Financial Planning. He has a JD from the University of Colorado Law School and a BA from Brown University. His extensive technical knowledge of estate planning was evident particularly in providing feedback on detailed rule specific content throughout the text.

Thanks also to Beth Bracey, Patricia Heckler, and Sherri Knoepfler for their manuscript reviews and thoughtful feedback. Their thorough editing, detailed calculation reviews, helpful suggestions for additional content, and other valuable comments, improved this text. To each of these individuals we extend our deepest gratitude and appreciation.

Developing a textbook that is aesthetically pleasing and easy to read is a difficult undertaking. We would like to pay special thanks to Robin Meyer and Donna Dalton who managed the project, formatted the entire text, performed numerous reviews, and provided invaluable feedback throughout the entire project. This book would not have been possible without their extraordinary dedication, skill, and knowledge.

We have received so much help from so many people, it is possible that we have inadvertently overlooked thanking someone. If so, it is our shortcoming, and we apologize in advance. Please let us know if you are that someone, and we will make it right in our next printing.

PREFACE

Estate Planning for Financial Planners is written for graduate and upperdivision undergraduate level students interested in acquiring an understanding of estate planning from a professional financial planning viewpoint. The text is intended to be used in an Estate Planning course as part of an overall curriculum in financial planning or in a Masters in Tax program emphasizing tax and financial planning. The text can also be used as a reference for practicing professional financial planners.

This text was designed to meet the educational requirements for an Estate Planning Course in a CFP Board-Registered Program. Therefore, one of our goals is to assure CFP Board-Registered Program directors, instructors, students, and financial planners that we have addressed every relevant topic covered by the CFP Board exam topic list and the most recent model curriculum syllabus for this course. The book will be updated, as needed, to keep current with any changes in the tax law, exam topic list, or model curriculum.

Through this text, we hope to convey our knowledge and enthusiasm for estate and financial planning with a user-friendly approach to learning the topic at hand.

Special Features

A variety of tools and presentation methods are used throughout this text to assist the reader in the learning process. Some of the features in this text that are designed to enhance your understanding and learning process include:

- **Key Concepts** – At the beginning of each subsection are key concepts, or study objectives, each stated as a question. To be successful in this course, you should be able to answer these questions. So as you read, guide your learning by looking for the answers. When you find the answers, highlight or underline them. It is important that you actually highlight/underline and not just make a mental note, as the action of stopping and writing reinforces your learning. Watch for this symbol:

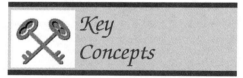

- **Quick Quizzes** – Following each subsection you will find a Quick Quiz, which checks and reinforces what you read. Circle the answer to each question and then check your answers against the correct answers supplied at the bottom of the quiz. If you missed any questions, flip back to the relevant section and review the material. You will also find explanations to the false questions at the end of each chapter. Watch for this symbol:

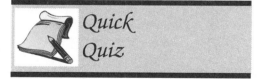

- **Examples** – Examples are used frequently to illustrate the concepts being discussed and to help the reader understand and apply the concepts presented. Examples are identified in the margin with the following symbol:

- **Exhibits** – The written text is enhanced and simplified by using exhibits where appropriate to promote learning and application. Exhibits are identified with the following symbol:

EXHIBIT

- **Key Terms** – Key terms appear in **boldfaced type** throughout the text to assist in the identification of important concepts and terminology. A list of key terms with definitions appears at the end of each chapter.

- **End of Chapter Questions** – Each chapter contains a series of discussion questions and multiple choice problems that highlight the major topics covered in the chapter. The questions test retention and understanding of important chapter material and can be used for review and classroom discussion.

- **Quick Quiz Explanations** – Each chapter concludes with the answers to the Quick Quizzes contained in that chapter, as well as explanation to the "false" statements in each Quick Quiz.

- **Glossary** – A compilation of the key terms identified throughout the text is located at the end of the book.

VISIT OUR WEBSITE AT
WWW.MONEY-EDUCATION.COM
FOR UPDATES TO THE TEXT

NOTE TO USER

We hope to not offend anyone with the use of masculine pronouns throughout the text. However, because of the lack of a proper neuter pronoun and to avoid the use of awkward phrases such as "he or she" and such, the masculine gender is generally used in the text when general reference is made to an individual. We attempted to minimize the impact of gender selection language as much as possible by using both male and female characters in the examples.

To three wonderful young people,
Jordan, Colin, and Cate
in hopes that you are never
affected by transfer taxes.
MAD

To my nephews,
Keegan Patrick, Reilly Kevin,
Ryan Thomas, and Kasey Brendan
my incentive for effective
intergenerational planning.
TPL

Table of Contents

3. TYPES OF PROPERTY INTERESTS

4. THE PROBATE PROCESS

5. GIFT TAX

6. ESTATE TAX

7. TRANSFERS DURING LIFE & AT DEATH

8. TRUSTS

9. CHARITABLE GIVING

10. THE UNLIMITED MARITAL DEDUCTION

11. LIFE INSURANCE IN ESTATE PLANNING

12. SPECIAL ELECTIONS & POST MORTEM PLANNING

13. GENERATION-SKIPPING TRANSFERS

14. BASIC ESTATE PLAN

APPENDICES

Introduction to Estate Planning

INTRODUCTION

Many philosophers and great thinkers have contemplated the inevitability of death and taxes. Benjamin Franklin is known for his famous saying that "in this world nothing is certain but death and taxes." Despite Mr. Franklin's words of wisdom, there is often uncertainty when it comes to both death and taxes. While no one likes to plan for death, the fact remains that no one lives forever. Unless we prepare for our deaths, there is uncertainty as to where our assets and liabilities will end up when we die. The best way to eliminate some of that uncertainty is through a properly prepared estate plan that incorporates planning for the accumulation, protection, and disposition of wealth.

Estate planning is complex. Among other things, it is about planning for risks, including the risks of untimely death and its consequences, ill health, artificially sustaining life, inability to manage property, immaturity of heirs, and application of state intestacy rules that may be totally inconsistent with a person's wishes. In large measure, estate planning is about the transfer of property, either during life or at death, the methods of effecting those transfers, and the risks associated with those transfers. It is also about the process of growing old, or not, and the planning for financial consequences of each possible outcome.

If we knew exactly what we would face in the future, we would arrange our financial affairs, prepare our families and loved ones, get our financial records in order, identify who is to receive what property, advise our relatives what to do if we are unable to make our own decisions, select someone to make critical healthcare decisions for us, confide in someone about our funeral and burial wishes, select someone to care for our children, provide for our children's education, and provide for our spouse. We would evaluate whether we could, in good conscience, leave money or property outright to particular heirs or whether we need to have someone else protect them from themselves and others.

Consider what would happen if you knew you would die in exactly five years. The question that you would face is "what do I do?" As an individual, you may be young, middle age, or older. You may be married, single, or divorced. You may have no children, minor children, adult children, or a combination of both. You may have a low net worth, medium net worth, or high net worth. You may require small or large amounts of money for consumption over the next five years. You may be very healthy right now or in poor health. You may prefer a traditional burial or cremation. You may wish to exhaust your entire financial estate on artificially sustaining your life or prefer no artificial sustainment of life. You may wish to provide for your spouse and heirs if you have any or you may not wish to provide for anyone's support. You may wish to leave money to charities or not. You may be tax averse or indifferent to taxes. If you give some thought to the above demographics, attitudes, and goals, there are an endless number of permutations. Estate planning is concerned with addressing the different demographics that each of us face and the risks associated with them, our goals and the risks and likelihood of achieving them, and various attitudes toward planning and our motivations and consequences. Estate planning involves developing a plan that fits the particular individual and meets the individual's goals and objectives.

It is easy to make the case that everyone needs estate planning. However, most people concentrate on developing a good financial plan for life. In financial planning, there is an unstated, underlying assumption that people will live to their full life expectancy. Unfortunately, many do not. The next step most people take is to plan for the financial risks that exist during life. They buy life insurance, health insurance, disability insurance, long-term care insurance, property insurance, and liability insurance to mitigate against these financial risks. Assuming that all of those risk management techniques are adequate, individuals then turn their attention to saving and investing to achieve both short and long-term financial goals. While estate planning is incorporated into all of these tasks, it also concerns itself with the individual person. Anyone can become unable to make their own healthcare decisions. Anyone can become unable to care for themselves physically, financially, or psychologically.

Estate planning involves the transfer of property, which will be addressed throughout this text, but it is about so much more. Estate planning is about being prepared for the expected and the unexpected while taking into consideration the individual client's demographic and family profile, their assessment and an objective assessment of risks, their goals, their values, and their attitudes about property, heirs, taxation, charities, and life itself. A well-designed estate plan will be very much an individual plan, considering all of the issues mentioned as applied to each particular person.

Estate Planning Reform

The Economic Growth and Tax Relief Reconciliation Act of 2001 (herein referred to as EGTRRA 2001) was signed by President George W. Bush in June of 2001 resulting in a $1.35 trillion tax cut. While EGTRRA 2001 repeals the estate and generation-skipping transfer tax in 2010, the repeal was phased in over a nine year period (2001 - 2009). Financial advisors must be familiar with the provisions of EGTRRA 2001 because of the law's sunset provision. This provision dictates that the 2001 estate tax rules, rates, and exemptions return in 2011, assuming no new changes to the tax law are made between now and 2010. This text presents current law, and where applicable, the impact of future changes in the law.

ESTATE PLANNING DEFINED

Estate planning may be broadly defined as the process of accumulation, management, conservation, and transfer of wealth considering legal, tax, and personal objectives. Estate planning is financial planning in anticipation of a client's inevitable death. The goal of estate planning is the effective and efficient transfer of assets. An **effective transfer** occurs when a person's assets are transferred to the person or institution intended by that person. An **efficient transfer** occurs when transfer costs are minimized consistent with the greatest assurance of effectiveness. Some estate planning experts define estate planning more narrowly to include only conservation and transfer, ignoring the accumulation factor in the broader definition above.

GOALS, OBJECTIVES, AND RISKS OF ESTATE PLANNING

Common goals and objectives of estate planning include transferring (distributing) property to particular persons or entities consistent with client wishes; minimizing taxes (income, gift, estate, state inheritance, and generation-skipping transfer taxes); minimizing transaction costs associated with the transfer (costs of documents, lawyers, accountants, and the **probate process** - the legal process of changing title to the decedent's assets from the decedent to the heirs and legatees); maximizing the transfer of assets to heirs and providing the estate of the decedent with sufficient liquidity to pay for costs that commonly arise upon or around one's death, such as taxes, funeral expenses, and final medical costs.

ESTATE PLANNING GOALS AND OBJECTIVES

EXHIBIT 1.1

- Fulfill client's property transfer wishes.
- Minimize transfer taxes.
- Minimize transfer costs.
- Maximize net assets to heirs.
- Provide needed liquidity at death.
- Fulfill client's healthcare decisions.

Key Concepts

Underline/highlight the answers to these questions as you read:

1. What is estate planning?

2. Explain the differences between an efficient and effective transfer.

3. What are the common goals of estate planning?

4. Why do people avoid estate planning?

5. Identify the risks associated with failing to plan for estate transfer.

Everyone needs a basic estate plan to address health care issues, property management, and the ultimate transfer of property according to their wishes. Typically, the most important estate planning objective is to assure that the decedent's property is transferred to the person, persons, or entities consistent with the decedent's wishes.

The process of estate planning requires us to face the inevitability of mortality. Clients tend to delay estate planning decisions for both emotional and practical reasons. Some people find contemplating their own mortality too morbid a task to engage in effective planning. Others are simply unaware of the value of their assets and may lack sufficient knowledge about the **transfer costs** (the costs of avoiding taxes), such as the cost of document preparation, planning, and other professional fees and taxes. Still others may not realize that alternative transfer devices exist, and that each alternative transfer device bears its own costs and risks. Whatever the reason, failing to plan for estate transfer is itself a risky proposition.

The risks associated with failing to plan for an estate transfer include the transfer of property contrary to the client's wishes, insufficient financial provision for the client's family, and the emergence of liquidity problems at the time of death. Any one of these risks could be catastrophic for the decedent's **heirs** (those who inherit under state law) and family. For example, the disposition of a decedent's assets could be delayed for many years in the probate court if that decedent has no will or if conflicts arise among the heirs. Another risk of not preparing an effective estate plan is exposure to excessively high transfer tax rates. The gift and estate tax structure is progressive, and rises to 45 percent for a decedent whose taxable estate exceeds $3,500,000 (in 2009).

EXHIBIT 1.2	RISKS IN FAILING TO PLAN AN ESTATE

- Client's property transfer wishes go unfulfilled.
- Transfer taxes are excessive.
- Transfer costs are excessive.
- Client's family not properly provided for financially.
- Insufficient liquidity to cover client's debts, taxes, and costs at death.

Quick Quiz 1.1

Highlight the answer to these questions:

1. Estate planning is the process of accumulation, management, conservation, and transfer of wealth considering only the estate tax consequences.
   a. True
   b. False

2. The Economic Growth and Tax Relief Reconciliation Act of 2001 completely repeals the estate tax after 2010.
   a. True
   b. False

3. An effective transfer occurs when a person's assets are transferred to the person or institution intended by that person.
   a. True
   b. False

False, False, True.

WHO NEEDS ESTATE PLANNING

Everyone needs estate planning. While each person's place in life, family status, and net worth may be different, one characteristic all persons share is mortality. Estate planning allows individuals to minimize taxes, ensure that their loved ones receive their property, and arrange for the care of loved ones. Estate planning ensures that each person's wishes are carried out when they die.

WHY THE INTEREST IN ESTATE PLANNING

There is significant interest in the topic of estate planning for two primary reasons. The first reason is the onerous excise taxes that are charged for transfers during life or at death (up to 45% in 2009). The second reason is that everyone has an interest in making sure that when they die, their worldly possessions are transferred to the persons or institutions that they so desire. When considering asset transfer, there are three primary recipients of a person's assets: heirs and legatees (family and friends), institutions (charities), or the government (in the form of taxes). Transfers to qualified charities are not taxed but transfers to family and friends exceeding certain thresholds are ultimately subject to transfer taxes. Because the transfer tax rates are substantial, the interest in tax avoidance and planning is also substantial.

TOOLS FOR WEALTH PROTECTION

Since estate planning primarily focuses on wealth transfer, protecting current and projected wealth is often an important consideration in estate planning. There are many insurance products designed to protect current wealth and future income, including life insurance, disability insurance, long-term care insurance, and business disability insurance, to name a few. The government even provides some of this protection through Medicare and the provision of Social Security disability benefits. Having sufficient insurance coverage to hedge against the risks facing the client is one of the basic elements of an effective estate plan.

THE ESTATE PLANNING PROCESS

THE SIX BASIC STEPS

There are six basic steps in the estate planning process:

1. Establish the client/planner relationship.
2. Gather client information, including the client's current financial statements and establish the client's transfer objectives, including family and charitable objectives.
3. Determine the client's financial status.
4. Develop a comprehensive plan of transfers consistent with all information and objectives.
5. Implement the estate plan.
6. Review the estate plan periodically and update the plan when necessary (especially for changes in family situations).

The first two steps will be discussed in this chapter and the remaining steps will be discussed in detail in Chapter 14.

Key Concepts

Underline/highlight the answers to these questions as you read:

1. Identify the six basic steps of the estate planning process.

2. What is usually the most important estate planning client objective?

3. Who are the members of the estate planning team, and what are their roles?

4. Why must financial planners be concerned with the unauthorized practice of law?

ESTABLISH THE CLIENT/PLANNER RELATIONSHIP

The client/planner relationship may arise in several different ways, but clients are often reluctant to seek out a planner to plan their estate. This reluctance may stem from several causes including concern about the expense associated with estate planning, the belief that estate planning is only for the extremely wealthy, or the desire to avoid the inevitability of the client's own mortality. Therefore, the opportunity to discuss the issue of estate planning generally arises when the planner is meeting with the client for financial planning matters other than estate planning.

The estate planning engagement is the same as any other financial planning engagement. The planner should meet with the client, detail the services to be provided and the expectations of both the client and the planner. The financial planner should then send an engagement letter to the client detailing the information discussed in the meeting.

COLLECTING CLIENT INFORMATION AND DEFINING TRANSFER OBJECTIVES

Collecting a client's information is essential to gain a complete financial and family picture of the client and to assist the client in identifying their financial risks. Information about prospective **heirs** (those who inherit under state law) and **legatees** (those who receive property under a will) needs to be collected to properly arrange for any transfer that the client wants to make.

To begin the estate planning process, the planner should collect:
- Current financial statements (Balance Sheet and Income Statement).
  - A detailed list of assets and liabilities, including, for each asset, the fair market value, adjusted basis, expected growth rate, how title is being held, and the date acquired.
- Family information (information about parents and children).
  - Age and health.
- Copies of medical, disability, and long-term care insurance policies.
- Copies of all current life insurance policies identifying the owner of each policy, the named insured, and the designated beneficiaries.
- Copies of annuity contracts.
- Copies of wills and trusts.
- Identification of powers of attorney and general powers of appointment.
- Copies of all previously filed income tax, gift tax, and estate tax returns.
- Identification of assets previously transferred to loved ones.

After collecting the client and family information, the client's transfer objectives must be determined. Usually the client's most important objective is to transfer his assets as he wishes (an effective transfer). Next, the client generally wishes to maximize the net transfers to his heirs while minimizing the reduction in his or her estate due to taxes and transfer cash. Exhibit 1.3 provides a list of common transfer objectives, many of which will be covered in more detail throughout this text.

EXHIBIT 1.3	COMMON TRANSFER OBJECTIVES

1. Transfer property as desired and minimize estate and transfer taxes to maximize the assets received by heirs.
2. Avoid the probate process.
3. Use lifetime transfers – gifts.
4. Meet liquidity needs at death.
5. Plan for children.
6. Plan for the incapacity of the transferor.
7. Provide for the needs of the transferor's surviving spouse.
8. Fulfill the transferor's charitable intentions.

THE ESTATE PLANNING TEAM

The estate planning team commonly consists of an attorney, Certified Public Accountant (CPA), life insurance consultant, trust officer, and financial planner. The typical role of the financial planner is to help integrate the work of the estate planning team in developing the overall estate plan.

The estate planning process is complex and can be somewhat confusing to the client. A licensed attorney is almost always a part of the team, as the process requires drafting numerous legal documents. A CPA is usually involved as a member of the estate planning team because the process requires the identification of assets, the calculation of the related adjusted basis, as well as other tax issues. A life insurance specialist is usually involved to help assure liquidity at death, provide asset protection, and provide guidance on the use of insurance to fulfill many of the client's transfer objectives. A trust officer manages the assets of trusts used in the estate plan. The financial planner serves as the team captain and assists in data collection, identification of goals and objectives, analysis, and investment decisions.

While each member of the planning team is often knowledgeable in estate planning, each specialist brings a particular and unique perspective, the combination of which is likely to produce a better result for the client. The financial planner, unless also a licensed attorney, should be careful not to engage in acts that could be considered the unauthorized practice of law.

Quick Quiz 1.2

Highlight the answer to these questions:

1. A financial planner should consult with CPAs, attorneys, trust officers and insurance professionals throughout the estate planning process.
   a. True
   b. False

2. A financial planner should collect client information, analyze the information, and present an estate plan to the client to minimize estate transfer taxes.
   a. True
   b. False

3. To reduce the cost of estate planning, a financial planner should always draft and review all of his client's wills.
   a. True
   b. False

True, False, False.

THE UNAUTHORIZED PRACTICE OF LAW

To practice law an individual must be a licensed attorney in the jurisdiction where he or she is practicing. Simply being educated or knowledgeable in law is not sufficient to give legal advice; licensing is required by that jurisdiction (state). Certain activities are clearly reserved for a licensed attorney, such as the drafting of legal documents. A professional who is not a licensed attorney should avoid offering legal advice on any matter as this is considered the **unauthorized practice of law**. Consequently, if a matter arises that requires legal advice, the planner should refer the client to a licensed attorney. Each state determines the requirements necessary to become a licensed attorney in their state and also defines the activities that constitute the practice of law. Planners should have an understanding of their applicable state laws before engaging in activities that may be construed as the practice of law.

Key Terms

Effective Transfer - A transfer of a person's assets to the person or charitable institution intended by that person.

Efficient Transfer - A transfer in which costs of the transfer are minimized consistent with the greatest assurance of effectiveness.

Estate Planning - The process of accumulation, management, conservation, and transfer of wealth considering legal, tax, and personal objectives.

Heir - One who inherits under state law.

Legatee - One who inherits under the will.

Probate Process - The legal proceeding that serves to prove the validity of existing wills, supervise the orderly distribution of decedent's assets to the heirs, and protect creditors by insuring that valid debts of the estate are paid.

Transfer Costs - Includes the gift and estate taxes and the costs of avoiding taxes, such as the cost of documents, planning, trusts, and other professional fees.

Unauthorized Practice of Law - The proffering of legal advice or services by one who is not a licensed attorney.

DISCUSSION QUESTIONS

1. Define estate planning.

2. Explain the estate and generation-skipping transfer ramifications of the Economic Growth and Tax Relief Reconciliation Act of 2001.

3. What is an effective transfer?

4. What is an efficient transfer?

5. List three common goals of estate planning.

6. List some of the reasons people avoid estate planning.

7. Discuss some of the risks associated with failing to plan for estate transfer.

8. List the six basic steps of the estate planning process.

9. What is usually the most important client objective?

10. List the members of the estate planning team and describe their roles.

11. Why must a financial planner be concerned with the unauthorized practice of law?

1. Which of the following is included in the definition of estate planning?

    1. Asset management.

    2. Accumulation of wealth.

    3. Asset preservation.

      a. 1 only.

      b. 1 and 2.

      c. 2 and 3.

      d. 1, 2, and 3.

2. Which of the following statements is the best definition of estate planning?

    a. Estate planning is the process of accumulation, management, conservation, and transfer of wealth considering legal, tax, and personal objectives.

    b. Estate planning is the management, conservation, and transfer of wealth considering estate tax transfer costs.

    c. Estate planning is the management, conservation, and transfer of wealth considering legal, tax, and personal objectives.

    d. Estate planning is the process of accumulation, management, conservation, and transfer of wealth considering estate and generation-skipping transfer tax costs.

3. Which of the following does not need estate planning?

    a. Charles, age 30, married with two minor children, and a net worth of $375,000.

    b. Sheila, age 35, never been married, one severely disabled son.

    c. Cynthia, age 45, single, has a net worth of $450,000 and two dogs.

    d. All of the above need estate planning.

4. The first step in the estate planning process includes:

    a. Meeting with the client and discussing the client's assets, family structure, and desires.

    b. Prioritizing the client's goals.

    c. Developing a formal written estate plan.

    d. Identifying key areas of concern in relation to the client's plan - taxes, cash on hand, etc.

5. Of the following, who should be a member of the estate planning team?

    1. Attorney.

    2. Certified Public Accountant (CPA).

    3. Life insurance consultant.

    4. Loan officer.

        a. 1 and 2.

        b. 1 and 4.

        c. 1, 2, and 3.

        d. 1, 2, 3, and 4.

6. Who on the estate planning team usually calculates the adjusted basis of assets and addresses tax issues?

        a. Licensed attorney.

        b. Certified Public Accountant (CPA).

        c. Financial planner.

        d. Trust officer.

7. Which of the following tasks is typically performed by a financial planner who is not a licensed attorney or accountant?

        a. Drafting wills, trust documents, and powers of attorney.

        b. Calculating asset basis.

        c. Preparing financial statements.

        d. Collecting data and assisting with investment decisions.

8. Joe is a financial planner in the state of Iowa. Although he attended one year of law school, Joe is not a licensed attorney. Which of the following actions would be considered the practice of law?

        a. Drafting wills, trust documents, and powers of attorney.

        b. Reviewing wills, trust documents, and powers of attorney.

        c. Directing a client to seek legal advice from a licensed attorney.

        d. Acting as trustee for a client's trust.

9. Which of the following statements correctly describes the impact of the Economic Growth and Tax Relief Reconciliation Act of 2001 (EGTRRA 2001)?

    a. EGTRRA 2001 repeals the estate tax after 2010.

    b. EGTRRA 2001 repeals the estate and generation-skipping transfer tax before 2010.

    c. EGTRRA 2001 repeals the estate and generation-skipping transfer tax during 2010.

    d. EGTRRA 2001 repeals the estate and generation-skipping transfer tax after 2010.

10. Which of the following statements concerning the practice of law is correct?

    a. The practice of law is defined by each state.

    b. Special circumstances are sometimes given to financial planners to enable them to draft wills, trust documents, and other legal documents.

    c. Reviewing wills to ensure client goals are being addressed is considered practicing law.

    d. A licensed attorney can give anyone the right to practice law as their agent.

11. Joann contacts you on the phone. She is 65 and has accumulated over $3,000,000 in assets. She informs you that she is not married, and wants to leave all of her assets equally to her three adult children. She agrees to come meet with you, but asks what she should bring. Which of the following items would be least important for her to bring if the topic of discussion is estate planning?

    a. Copy of her will and any codicils.

    b. Copy of children's birth certificates.

    c. Copy of life insurance policies.

    d. Copy of latest bank statements.

12. Jimmy would like to meet with you regarding his estate plan. Jimmy is 55 years old, and currently has an estate that would be subject to estate tax. His wife died of lung cancer last year. Jimmy has three children, ages 23, 26, and 32, and one grandchild, age 4. He does not have any dependents. Which of the following options would be the least likely reason for Jimmy to have an estate plan?

    a. Minimize estate and transfer taxes.

    b. Minimize costs.

    c. Plan for his children.

    d. Plan for his incapacity.

13. Don does not want to write a will. It upsets him to contemplate his own death and he simply desires to avoid the estate planning process. All of the following are risks Don's estate may face due to Don's inaction, except:

    a. Don's property transfers contrary to his wishes.

    b. Don's estate may face liquidity problems.

    c. Don's estate faces increased estate administration fees.

    d. Don's estate faces increased debt payments for outstanding debts at death.

14. Which the following is a risk of failing to plan for the estate?

    1. Property transfers contrary to the client's wishes.

    2. The client's family may not be provided for financially.

    3. The estate suffers liquidity problems at the client's death.

    4. The estate may bear higher transfer costs.

        a. 2 only.

        b. 2 and 3.

        c. 1, 3, and 4.

        d. 1, 2, 3, and 4.

Quick Quiz Explanations

Quick Quiz 1.1

1. False. To result in an effective transfer of assets, estate planning must first consider the goals and objectives of the client. Given the overriding goals of the client, his or her affairs should be arranged to minimize estate taxes and other transfer costs.
2. False. EGTRRA 2001 has a sunset provision that revives the estate tax rates in effect in 2001 after 2010 (beginning in 2011).
3. True.

Quick Quiz 1.2

1. True.
2. False. In addition to minimizing taxes, the planner must ensure that the client's wishes for asset transfers are achieved.
3. False. Unless the financial planner is a licensed attorney, he or she should not draft the client's will, since this would be considered the unauthorized practice of law.

Basic Estate Planning Documents

BASIC DOCUMENTS INCLUDED IN AN ESTATE PLAN

Effective estate planning usually requires the execution of some basic estate planning documents. These documents effectuate the transfer of property at the death of the testator, grant powers to others for both property and health care decisions, and direct doctors and hospitals on matters concerning the artificial sustenance of life. The basic documents that are used in estate planning include:

- wills,
- side letters of instruction,
- powers of attorney for property,
- durable powers of attorney for health care,
- living wills or advance medical directives, and
- do not resuscitate orders.

This chapter will describe each of these documents, discuss their importance and clarify why an estate plan is incomplete having given each consideration.

WILLS

A **will** is an essential part of any estate plan. A will is a legal document that gives the **testator** (will-maker) the opportunity to control the distribution of his property at death and thus avoid his state's intestacy laws (the distribution scheme provided by each state for those individuals that die without a valid will). A will may be amended or revoked by the testator at any time prior to his death provided that the testator is competent. In addition, the provisions of a will are not invoked until the death of the testator. Any assets that do not automatically transfer upon the testator's death under state contract laws, state property titling law, or state trust law (such as retirement benefits with a designated beneficiary, jointly owned property, and life insurance policies) will become part of the probate estate, which is normally distributed according to the will. The will is the voice of the decedent directing how probate assets should be administered and distributed through the probate process.

INTESTACY

A decedent who has a valid will is said to die "**testate**." To die "**intestate**" is to die without a valid will. A decedent who dies with a will that does not dispose of all property is said to die "partially intestate." An individual may not have a valid will for several reasons, including failure to write a will, or perhaps the will is invalid under state law. A will may be invalid under state law if:

- the decedent did not comply with the testamentary requirements of the domiciliary state at the time of the execution of the will;
- if the decedent moved to another state of domicile and failed to update his will to meet the new state law requirements (however, if the will is valid in a previous state of domicile, then it may be held to be valid in a new domicile); or
- the decedent did not satisfy the necessary requirements (such as testamentary competence) to execute a will.

In the case of intestacy, the laws of the decedent's state of **domicile** (the place where a person votes, lives, pays taxes, etc.) at the time of his death, determines how the decedent's personal property will be distributed. Personal property is distributed according to the will or the laws of intestacy in the state of domicile of the decedent. Real property, on the other hand, is distributed based on the laws of the state in which the property is actually located (the **situs**). Non-domiciliary states achieve this by applying that state's intestacy laws in the absence of a valid will or non-probate transfer. A probate process in a state other than the state of domicile is called **ancillary probate.**

The 1990 Uniform Probate Code is a model set of rules that serves as a guideline for many states' probate laws. Although state intestacy laws vary greatly from state to state, approximately 18 states have adopted at least part of this uniform code. Under the Uniform Probate Code, close relatives receive the decedent's assets. Close relatives include the surviving spouse, lineal descendents, parents, descendents of the decedent's parents (siblings, nieces, and nephews), grandparents, and descendents of the decedent's grandparents (aunts, uncles, and cousins). The Uniform Probate Code treats adopted descendents in the same manner as biological descendents and treats relatives of the half blood in the same manner as relatives of whole blood. In cases where no person is considered qualified to receive the assets, the property by default transfers to the decedent's state of domicile, or if real property is held outside the state of domicile, to the state of its situs. Exhibit 2.1 provides an example of how a state's intestate succession law may be phrased. Practitioners should review their own state's intestacy laws, and be aware of its provisions.

The old adage "one size does not fit all" applies to state intestacy laws since they may not distribute property in the manner that the client would like their property to be distributed. For example, in certain states, a surviving spouse's legal statutory share of the decedent spouse's estate under intestacy laws is equal to a child's share. In these states, the surviving spouse's share who has one child would be one-half, but a surviving spouse who has nine children would only receive a one-tenth share. Other states provide the surviving spouse with a life estate (discussed in Chapter 3) with the remainder beneficiaries being the children. Under other state laws, the surviving spouse may be forced to share with the deceased spouse's parents or siblings when there are no children. In addition, although each child's needs may be quite different, children are usually treated equally and, therefore, not necessarily equitably.

Intestacy requires the appointment of an **administrator** (an estate representative appointed by the probate court), as opposed to an **executor** (an estate representative appointed by the decedent through the will). In most states, the individual with the largest share in the estate is entitled to be appointed an administrator. The probate court must approve the administrator of the estate and the administrator typically has to furnish a surety bond. In contrast, an executor is chosen by the decedent and although he must be approved by the probate court, the executor is generally not required to furnish a surety bond, thus reducing the overall cost of administering the estate. This topic will be discussed more fully in Chapter 4.

SAMPLE STATE INTESTATE SUCCESSION LAW

EXHIBIT 2.1

If any part of a decedent's estate is not effectively disposed of by will, the intestate share will generally be distributed in the following order and manner:

1. A surviving spouse is generally first in line to get any assets from the intestate estate. However, the amount to which a surviving spouse is entitled varies as follows:
   - A surviving spouse is entitled to the entire intestate estate if the decedent is not survived by lineal issue (i.e., descendents such as children and grandchildren).
   - If the decedent is survived by issue, a surviving spouse gets the first $50,000, plus one-half of the remaining property in the intestate estate.

2. Any part of the intestate estate not passing to the surviving spouse as indicated above, or the entire intestate estate if there is no surviving spouse, passes as follows to the first applicable group:
   - Decedent's issue, taking by representation (per stirpes, as discussed later in this chapter).
   - Decedent's surviving parent or parents equally.
   - Issue of decedent's parents, taking by representation (brothers, sisters, nieces, and nephews).
   - If none of the above relatives are available, but the decedent is survived by one or more grandparents or immediate issue of grandparents (i.e., decedent's aunts and uncles), half of the estate passes to the paternal grandparents if both survive, or to the surviving paternal grandparent or to the issue of the paternal grandparents (taking by representation) if both are deceased. The other half passes to the maternal relatives in the same manner. If there is no surviving grandparent or issue of grandparent on either the paternal or maternal side, the entire estate passes to the relatives on the other side in the same manner as the half portion would. For purposes of this category, issue of grandparents does not include issue more remote than grandchildren of such grandparents.
   - Great-grandchildren of decedent's grandparents, split one-half to the great-grandchildren of the paternal grandparents side and one-half to the great-grandchildren of the maternal grandparents side, with per capita distributions to each side. If there are no great-grandchildren of grandparents on one side, the whole amount goes to the other half (still split per capita).

3. If there is no taker under any of the above provisions, the intestate estate passes (escheats) to the state.

ADVANTAGES OF WILLS

A properly drafted will can eliminate many of the problems that arise from dying intestate. An effective will also provides other benefits to the testator, including the ability to:

- select an executor as the decedent's personal representative to administer the estate;
- transfer assets that do not automatically transfer at death via contract or operation of law;
- designate a guardian for minor children and/or dependents;
- transfer assets to a designated charity;
- maximize the utilization of the marital deduction;
- direct that certain people do not receive any inheritance (disinheritance);
- implement provisions to minimize the estate tax burden; and
- direct the payment of the estate's share of the estate tax burden as well as the designation of the source of funds to pay such estate taxes.

LIMITATIONS OF WILLS

Although a will can provide many benefits and advantages, it also has limitations. Some of these limitations include:

- The potential for a will contest, particularly if the decedent disinherits potential beneficiaries. The estate may have to litigate if the will is contested, which will increase costs (attorney fees) and delay distribution to other heirs or legatees.
- The possibility that courts may invalidate certain restrictions and/or sections in a will that put impermissible conditions on the receipt of assets or that have too many constraints on the transfer of assets. For example, a will that requires a beneficiary/heir to commit an illegal act in order to receive the asset will be deemed invalid.
- Assets that pass automatically by contract or by law supersede the transfers provided for under the will. Property that passes by beneficiary designee (retirement plans, life insurance policies), through payable/transfer on death clauses (bank accounts and brokerage accounts), through trust, or through property titled with a survivorship feature will be transferred directly to those named beneficiaries or joint tenants and will not be a part of the probate process or distributed according to any will provisions or intestacy laws.
- A poorly drafted will that contains conflicting transfers, reference to deceased heirs, or nonexistent property may become invalid or the testator's wishes may not be understood.

TYPES OF WILLS

In most states, the only requirements necessary to execute a valid will are:

1. the will must be in writing, and
2. the will must be signed at its logical end by the testator.

The three basic forms of wills include statutory, holographic, and nuncupative. While most wills are statutory wills (professionally drafted by an attorney), some states continue to recognize the other two types of wills.

- **Statutory wills** are drawn by an attorney, and comply with the statutes for wills of the domiciliary state. Statutory wills are generally witnessed and attested. Statutory wills must be typed or be in writing, be signed by the testator (generally in front of witnesses), and be signed by the witnesses. Typically, a statutory will includes a self-proving affidavit which aids in the institution of probate proceedings when the testator dies.

- **Holographic wills** are handwritten (not typed) by the testator and include the material provisions of a will. The holographic will must be dated and signed by the testator, but most states do not require a witness. Holographic wills are valid in most states.
- **Nuncupative wills** are oral, dying declarations made before a sufficient number of witnesses. In some states, nuncupative wills may only be effective to pass personal property, not real property, and the dollar amount transferred by this method may be limited. The use of nuncupative wills is restrictive and is not valid in most states. In states where such wills are permitted, the witnesses must generally submit an affidavit declaring the testator's final wishes.

Wills may also be classified based on the function or characteristics of the will. For example, two individuals may sometimes execute identical wills that leave all assets to the other person. This type of will is generally used by spouses who want all assets to go to the other spouse at death. This type of simple will may be referred to as a **mutual** or **reciprocal will** and if executed by spouses it may be called a "**sweetheart**" **will** or an "I Love You" will. Reciprocal wills, like all other wills, are not permanently binding on the individuals and can be changed at any time.

In some instances, two or more individuals, usually spouses, will execute one will, called a **joint will**, that transfers their common interest in property to one individual. When the first party dies and the will is probated, the will contractually binds the surviving party to dispose of their assets in the manner set forth in the joint will. The intent of this type of will is for two or more individuals, usually spouses, to agree who will receive the property in advance and contractually bind the survivor to the agreement. This type of will is recognized in many states and is often used in situations where an individual enters into a second marriage and wants to protect children from a previous marriage. This type of arrangement is generally not recommended because it binds the surviving spouse to dispose of property without considering future events (including future tax law changes) and there are other devices that will more appropriately achieve the desired objective.

Quick Quiz 2.1

Highlight the answer to these questions:

1. A nuncupative will is a handwritten will dated and signed by the testator.
   a. True
   b. False

2. A will controls the distribution of all property.
   a. True
   b. False

3. A decedent who dies without a will cannot appoint an executor.
   a. True
   b. False

4. The intestacy laws vary from state to state.
   a. True
   b. False

5. A holographic will is drawn by an attorney, complying with the statutes for wills of the domiciliary state.
   a. True
   b. False

False, False, True, True, False.

LEGAL CAPACITY TO EXECUTE A WILL

To execute a valid will, the testator must have sufficient legal capacity. A will is considered valid when the will maker is the age of majority in his domiciliary state, or is an emancipated minor, and when the will maker has legal testamentary capacity. A testator has legal testamentary capacity if he has sufficient mental capacity to:

- understand the consequences of writing the will;
- understand the nature and extent of the property being disposed of by the will; and
- recognize the natural objects of his or her bounty (those friends and relatives who have any claim to the testator's assets).

It is often said that the testator must be of "**sound mind**." The "sound mind" mental capacity rules that apply to wills are not as rigorous as the capacity rules that are required to form contracts. In other words, a person who may not have the legal capacity to form a contract may nonetheless have sufficient legal capacity to execute a will to transfer his assets at death, provided that the conditions specified above are met.

All or part of a will may be invalidated by the probate court if the will was executed by a testator who did not have sufficient capacity. Invalidation may occur when an individual, usually an heir-at-law that has been excluded from the will, successfully contests the will. A will contest typically includes a claim that the testator did not have the capacity to create a will or that the testator was subject to undue influence from another person. Undue influence occurs when the decedent was susceptible to influence from a third party (such as a caregiver), the third party had the means and opportunity to exercise influence over the decedent and the decedent made a disposition because of such influence. To avoid the appearance of undue influence, attorneys and financial planners should avoid drafting wills or assisting in distribution planning where the professional is a legatee, particularly in instances where the professional is not a related party. In some instances, attorneys and financial planners may feel obligated to assist related parties with their estate planning, but in these cases, extra caution should be taken to avoid future will contests.

COMMON CLAUSES IN WILLS

All wills are unique, but certain common provisions or clauses appear in most wills. These common clauses, found in even the simplest of attorney-prepared (statutory) wills, include:

- An **introductory clause** to identify the testator. The testator's full name and residence, the state of domicile where the will is executed, and the identification of the next of kin will all serve to identify the testator.

- A **declaration clause** which states this is the last will and testament of the testator. The will should clearly and specifically (by date) revoke all previous wills and codicils (discussed in more detail later in this chapter) of the testator. This clause serves to eliminate any confusion and possible discord in the future by clearly identifying this will as the most current will and, therefore, the proper will to submit to probate.

A typical introduction containing the above two clauses may say, "I, Angelica Marie Steed, living at 1000 Lovers Lane, Houston, Texas, do hereby declare this is my last will and testament. I hereby revoke all prior wills, including the will written on January 14, 1987, as well as any other papers, documents, oral declarations, writings, or anything else that may have been or could be construed as a last will and testament. I have been married only once, and then to Ryan Arthur Steed, and have two children from that marriage, namely, Delano Trey Steed and Sammy Ann Steed. I have neither adopted any children, nor has anyone adopted me."

EXAMPLE 2.1

- A specific **bequest clause** directs the distribution of specific property, whether cash, tangible personal property, or real estate. If multiple legatees are to inherit then there may be multiple bequests clauses, generally grouped together in one section of the will.

A typical bequest clause may say, "To my daughter, Sammy Ann Steed, I leave my prized doll collection and $100,000 in cash."

EXAMPLE 2.2

- A **residuary clause** transfers assets not previously distributed to specific individuals or to charitable institutions through a specific bequest clause. Without a residuary clause, some assets may remain undistributed, which will pass under the laws of intestacy. When this occurs, the decedent is said to die partially testate and partially intestate.

A typical residuary clause may say, "I leave all remaining property owned by me, not previously provided for in this document, herein referred to as my residuary estate, to my wonderful husband, Ryan Arthur Steed."

EXAMPLE 2.3

- An **appointment of executor clause** identifies the executor and any successor executor. This clause may also define the extent of the executor's powers and may grant specific or general powers. For example, this clause may direct the executor to pay the estate taxes and any debts of the estate out of specific assets or to use assets at the executor's discretion (tax-apportionment clause). This clause may also waive the surety bond requirement discussed in Chapter 4, and may give the executor the option to be paid for services rendered or to decline compensation. Executor compensation is governed by state law, but typically ranges between two and five percent of the gross estate value. An executor may elect to forfeit an executor fee when the executor is also a legatee and would prefer to receive an inheritance instead of taxable compensation.

A typical executor clause may say, "I name Ryan Arthur Steed as my Executor. In the event Ryan is unable or unwilling to serve as executor, I name Delano Trey Steed as Executor. I grant my executor the power to direct my estate as he deems reasonable to the full extent of the law. I waive any surety bond requirement imposed by any party. At my exec-

EXAMPLE 2.4

utor's discretion, he may be compensated for his services in the amount of 5% of the fair market value of my gross estate."

- A **guardianship clause** allows the testator to identify an individual to raise minor children or legal dependents. The testator often selects successor guardians, in the event that the testator's original choice is unwilling or unable to serve as the guardian. The probate court will generally need to approve the appointment of guardians. Individuals who have few financial assets but have minor children should execute a will so that they can choose the person who will raise their children. The testator's choice will almost always be preferable to a family court determination of guardianship for minor children.

<table>
<tr><td>EXAMPLE 2.5</td><td>A typical guardianship clause may say, "In the event that my children are minors, as defined by state law, at the time of my death, I appoint my husband, Ryan Arthur Steed, as guardian of our children. In the event he is unable or unwilling to serve as guardian, I appoint my sister, Cheryl Conn, as guardian."</td></tr>
</table>

- A **tax-appointment clause** directing which assets will bear the payment of any debts and estate taxes. Often this clause is included as part of the residuary clause, but only when the residuary estate is directed to bear the payment of the estate taxes and debts.

<table>
<tr><td>EXAMPLE 2.6</td><td>A typical tax-appointment clause may state, "I direct that debts and taxes be paid out of my residuary estate."</td></tr>
</table>

- An **attestation clause**, or witness clause, is a provision at the end of the will that is signed by at least two qualified witnesses (some states require three witnesses) who certify that the document is the testator's will bearing the testator's signature and that the testator was competent and not under any kind of duress at the time the will was executed. As discussed previously, beneficiaries should not serve as a witness, as it could jeopardize their right to receive a bequest under the will.

<table>
<tr><td>EXAMPLE 2.7</td><td>A typical attestation clause may say, "On this 15th day of June, 2005, the testator declared this his last will and testament and signed in our joint presence and by us in his presence."</td></tr>
</table>

- A **self-proving clause** involves the notary signing a declaration that he witnessed the testator and witnesses sign the will. The self-proving clause eliminates the need for the witnesses' live testimony during the opening of the probate process (discussed in Chapter 4).

EXAMPLE 2.8

A typical self-proving clause may say, "In witness whereof, I have hereunto subscribed my name and affixed my seal on this 15th day of June, 2005, in the presence of the subscribing witnesses.

OTHER CLAUSES

More sophisticated wills often have additional clauses that dictate specific wishes regarding the administration of the estate. Additional clauses may include:

- **A simultaneous death clause** establishes a presumption regarding which individual died first in the event that both individuals die in the same event (such as in a plane crash, car accident, fire, etc.) when it is impossible to determine which person died first. The simultaneous death clause overrides any state law presumption determining who died first and allows the decedent's estate to move directly to probate without the possibility of the other deceased individual inheriting the estate. Many states now have incorporated simultaneous death clauses into state law which requires individuals to live a defined period, generally one to five days in order to take from the estate of a prior decedent. These state imposed rules can be superseded by including a simultaneous death clause in the testator's will. The simultaneous death clause establishes the guidelines for the disposition of the assets, eliminates the expense of two probate proceedings including identical assets, and most importantly, ensures the fulfillment of each individual's transfer desires. The simultaneous death clause also eliminates the possibility that competing heirs will fight over who died first.

EXAMPLE 2.9

Kerner, age 65, is married to Kelly, age 32. They have no children. In the event Kerner dies, he wants all of his assets to go to Kelly, but if Kelly dies first, he plans to leave his assets to his only sibling, Pam. Kelly plans to leave all of her assets to Kerner, but if Kerner dies first, she plans to leave her assets to her brother, Jeff, who Kerner has always disliked. Assume that Kerner and Kelly die in a tragic car accident and it is impossible to determine who died first but doctors believe that Kelly may have survived Kerner by a few minutes. Without a simultaneous death clause, the heirs of Kerner and Kelly would be left to fight over which person died first. If Jeff could show that Kerner died first all of Kerner's assets would initially transfer to Kelly's estate which would then transfer to Jeff. Under this scenario, Jeff inherits both Kelly's estate and Kerner's estate. Kerner never intended that his assets would immediately transfer to Jeff. He only wanted his assets to transfer to his wife, if she were alive and expected to live for a substantial period.

If Kerner and Kelly had each included simultaneous death clauses in their wills, each including the presumption that the other died first (Kelly's simultaneous death clause assumes Kerner dies first and Kerner's simultaneous death clause assumes Kelly dies first), Pam would receive Kerner's estate and Jeff would receive Kelly's estate. In this case, both Kerner and Kelly's transfer desires would have been fulfilled.

- A **survivorship clause** is an alternative to, and sometimes eliminates the need for, a simultaneous death clause. A survivorship clause requires that a beneficiary/heir must actually survive the decedent for a specified period of time to receive the identified inheritance or bequest. Similar to the simultaneous death clause, the survivorship clause prevents property from being included in two different estates in rapid succession and ensures that a decedent's transfer objectives are met. For transfers to a surviving spouse to qualify for the unlimited marital deduction (discussed in Chapter 10), the survival period included in the survivorship clause for a spouse cannot exceed six months. If the survivorship clause requires the surviving spouse to live beyond six months, the transfer will occur if the surviving spouse outlives the defined period, but the transfer will not qualify for the unlimited marital deduction. A survivorship clause overcomes problems with simultaneous death issues or close death issues and, therefore, often eliminates the need for a simultaneous death clause.

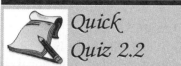

| EXAMPLE 2.10 |

Assume in the example above that Kerner dies immediately and Kelly survives the car accident but is critically injured. She remains in intensive care for over a month and then dies. The simultaneous death clause is not relevant because of the time frame involved as it is clearly identifiable which individual died first. However, a survivorship clause would solve this problem. Assume Kerner's will had a survivorship clause which stated that in order to inherit under the will Kelly must survive him by three months. If Kelly died within the three month period, Kerner's estate would go to his sister, as he intended if his wife was not alive. Had the survivorship clause not been included in his will, Kerner's estate would have transferred to Kelly and subsequently (in one month) at Kelly's death, to her brother, Jeff.

Had Kelly outlived the survivorship clause and received the property, the value of the property would have qualified for the marital deduction because the clause did not require Kelly to live beyond six months after Kerner's death.

- A **disclaimer clause** reminds heirs that they can disclaim a bequest, while still allowing the testator to direct the distribution of disclaimed property. Some states have specific statutory provisions that deal with who receives disclaimed property. When an heir disclaims all or part of his interest in an estate, the disclaimed property will generally pass to the designated heirs, or will default to the residuary estate, as if the disclaiming party was not alive. To be effective:
  1. the disclaiming party cannot benefit from the property (with the exception, in certain circumstances, of the surviving spouse);
  2. the disclaiming party must not direct who receives a future interest in the property;
  3. the disclaiming party must disclaim the property within nine months of the decedent's date of death; and
  4. the disclaimer must be in writing.

When a bequest is disclaimed the property avoids the gift tax that would have otherwise been incurred if the disclaiming party received the property and then transferred it to the intended beneficiary. Disclaimers are used to reallocate interests so that the property passes without gift tax consequences and to ensure that a decedent's estate is not **overqualified** (i.e., the taxable estate is less than the applicable estate tax credit amount). In such cases, disclaiming property can be an effective tool in estate planning.

> Arline leaves $500,000 to Brian in her will. Arline's will states that if Brian is unable or unwilling to take the $500,000, then the money goes to Brian's daughter Shelby. When Arline dies, Brian is still alive, but does not need the money and would prefer Shelby to have it. He properly disclaims his inheritance and Shelby receives the $500,000. Because Brian properly disclaimed his inheritance, the money passes directly to Shelby and thus avoids a gift tax on the constructive transfer from Brian to Shelby. However, the transfer will be subject to generation skipping transfer tax which is discussed in Chapter 13.

EXAMPLE 2.11

- Because legatees may predecease the decedent, die within the survivorship clause period, or disclaim property bequeathed to them, the will generally has a **contingent legatee clause**. The contingent legatee clause allows the testator to determine in advance how their property should be distributed in the event the original legatee is no longer able to inherit under the will because of death or disclaimer. This clause may specifically designate an alternate legatee or may allow the assets to be distributed to the original legatee's heirs. Frequently, broad language will be used to allow the will to meet the client objectives over time as both the client and their objectives change.

A typical contingent legatee clause may say, "In the event any legatee is unable or unwilling to accept such property, either that the legatee predeceased me, did not survive the six month survivorship requirement, or disclaims the bequeathed property, that legatee's share will pass to that legatee's then living heirs in equal shares, per stirpes."

The contingent legatee clause may employ one of two common methods, per capita or per stirpes, to determine how the proceeds will be divided with relation to the deceased heir and their descendents. The **per capita** method, sometimes called "by the head" allows the deceased person's heirs to move into the generational slot of the deceased heir and inherit accordingly. Alternatively, the **per stirpes** method, sometimes called "by the roots" directs that the deceased person's designated share flow to their heirs. Per stirpes is also referred to as taking by representation.

Andy has two children, Betty and Charles. Betty has 2 children, David and Greg, and Charles does not have any children. Andy's will leaves all of his assets to his children and states that in the event that one of his children predecease him then his estate should be distributed between his remaining child and grandchildren per capita. If Betty and Charles are living when Andy died then they would both receive 1/2 of Andy's estate.

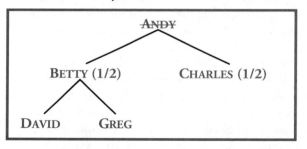

Assume Betty died many years ago. Under the per capita method of distribution, David and Greg would replace Betty in her generational slot and now the estate would be split three ways, with David receiving 1/3, Greg receiving 1/3 and Charles receiving 1/3.

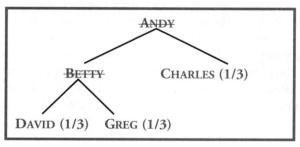

EXAMPLE 2.15

Assume now that Betty died many years ago and the will used a per stirpes method instead of the per capita method. Now the per stirpes method would direct that Betty's 1/2 would transfer to her two children. So in this instance Charles would receive 1/2 of the estate and David and Greg would share their mother's one half interest, giving them each 1/4 of Andy's estate.

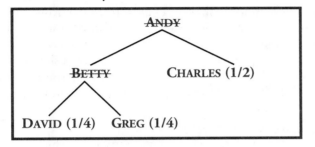

- **A no-contest clause** (sometimes called an *in terrorem* clause) attempts to discourage disappointed heirs from contesting the will by substantially decreasing or eliminating a bequest to them if they file a formal, legal contest to the will. In the event that the disappointed heir is able to successfully have the will invalidated the no-contest clause will not apply. The key when designing a no-contest clause is to make sure that the token bequest is sufficient to create the incentive not to contest. Although no-contest clauses generally discourage contests to the will, they may not discourage disinherited parties or those who have little to lose. The no-contest clause can be broad or specific, but if the clause is too general, it may be subject to various interpretations. Enforcement of the no-contest clause depends on the interpretation of specific state laws.

EXAMPLE 2.16

Fred has two children, Chris and Steven. Fred was widowed many years ago and has amassed substantial wealth. The last few years before his death Fred required around the clock in home nursing care. During this time Fred became very fond of his young, beautiful nurse, Jane. A few months before his death, Fred changed his will so that Jane was the sole beneficiary of his fortune instead of his two children. The will, which was drafted by Jane's brother, Pete, included a no-contest clause because Pete suspected that Chris and Steven would contest. Because of the circumstances, Chris and Steven were furious when the will was produced by Jane and they announced their intention to contest the will based on undue influence. In this instance, the no-contest clause does not provide any incentive for Chris and Steven to not contest the will. If they are unsuccessful in court then they lose nothing because they don't currently stand to inherit anything. If they are successful in court then they get everything.

EXAMPLE 2.17

Assume instead, that the will gives Steven and Chris $1,000,000 each and Jane $10,000,000. Now the no-contest clause may incentivize the children not to contest because if they lose in court then they each forfeit their right to $1,000,000, a risk they may not be willing to take.

SAMPLE WILLS

Two examples of actual wills follow. Since probate is a public process, anyone can look up a will to see what a testator has done with his or her assets. The examples that follow are of Chief Justice Warren Burger and Elvis Presley's wills.

EXHIBIT 2.2 **LAST WILL AND TESTAMENT OF WARREN BURGER**

Source: Courtroom Television Network, LLC

The Will of Warren Burger

LAST WILL AND TESTAMENT OF WARREN E. BURGER

I hereby make and declare the following to be my last will and testament.

1. My executors will first pay all claims against my estate;

2. The remainder of my estate will be distributed as follows: one-third to my daughter, Margaret Elizabeth Burger Rose and two-thirds to my son, Wade A. Burger;

3. I designate and appoint as executors of this will, Wade A. Burger and J. Michael Luttig.

IN WITNESS WHEREOF, I have hereunto set my hand to this my Last Will and Testament this 9th day of June, 1994.

[Signed by Warren E. Burger]

The Will of Elvis Presley

Known as "The King," Presley sold more than 45 million records and starred in 33 motion pictures. He left much of his vast fortune to members of his family.

Last Will And Testament Of Elvis A. Presley, Deceased Filed August 22, 1977

I, Elvis A. Presley, a resident and citizen of Shelby County, Tennessee, being of sound mind and disposing memory, do hereby make, publish and declare this instrument to be my last will and testament, hereby revoking any and all wills and codicils by me at any time heretofore made.

Item I - Debts, Expenses and Taxes

I direct my Executor, hereinafter named, to pay all of my matured debts and my funeral expenses, as well as the costs and expenses of the administration of my estate, as soon after my death as practicable. I further direct that all estate, inheritance, transfer and succession taxes which are payable by reason under this will, be paid out of my residuary estate; and I hereby waive on behalf of my estate any right to recover from any person any part of such taxes so paid. My Executor, in his sole discretion, may pay from my domiciliary estate all or any portion of the costs of ancillary administration and similar proceedings in other jurisdictions.

Item II - Instruction Concerning Personal Property: Enjoyment in Specie

I anticipate that included as a part of my property and estate at the time of my death will be tangible personal property of various kinds, characters and values, including trophies and other items accumulated by me during my professional career. I hereby specifically instruct all concerned that my Executor, herein appointed, shall have complete freedom and discretion as to disposal of any and all such property so long as he shall act in good faith and in the best interest of my estate and my beneficiaries, and his discretion so exercised shall not be subject to question by anyone whomsoever.

I hereby expressly authorize my Executor and my Trustee, respectively and successively, to permit any beneficiary of any and all trusts created hereunder to enjoy in specie the use or benefit of any household goods, chattels, or other tangible personal property (exclusive of choses in action, cash, stocks, bonds or other securities) which either my Executor or my Trustees may receive in kind, and my Executor and my Trustees shall not be liable for any consumption, damage, injury to or loss of any tangible property so used, nor shall the beneficiaries of any trusts hereunder or their executors of administrators be liable for any consumption, damage, injury to or loss of any tangible personal property so used.

Item III - Real Estate

If I am the owner of any real estate at the time of my death, I instruct and empower my Executor and my Trustee (as the case may be) to hold such real estate for investment, or to sell same, or any portion therof, as my Executor or my Trustee (as the case may be) shall in his sole judgment determine to be for the best interest of my estate and the beneficiaries thereof.

Item IV - Residuary Trust

After payment of all debts, expenses and taxes as directed under Item I hereof, I give, devise, and bequeath all the rest, residue, and remainder of my estate, including all lapsed legacies and devices, and any property over which I have a power of appointment, to my Trustee, hereinafter named, in trust for the following purposes:

(a) The Trustees is directed to take, hold, manage, invest and reinvest the corpus of the trust and to collect the income therefrom in accordance with the rights, powers, duties, authority and discretion hereinafter set forth. The Trustee is directed to pay all the expenses, taxes and costs incurred in the management of the trust estate out of the income thereof.

(b) After payment of all expenses, taxes and costs incurred in the management of the expenses, taxes and costs incurred in the management of the trust estate, the Trustee is authorized to accumulate the net income or to pay or apply so much of the net income and such portion of the principal at any time and from time to time to time for health, education, support, comfortable maintenance and welfare of: (1) My daughter, Lisa Marie Presley, and any other lawful issue I might have, (2) my grandmother, Minnie Mae Presley, (3) my father, Vernon E. Presley, and (4) such other relatives of mine living at the time of my death who in the absolute discretion of my Trustees are in need of emergency assistance for any of the above mentioned purposes and the Trustee is able to make such distribution without affecting the ability of the trust to meet the present needs of the first three numbered categories of beneficiaries herein mentioned or to meet the reasonably expected future needs of the first three classes of beneficiaries herein mentioned. Any decision of the Trustee as to whether or not distribution, to any of the persons described hereunder shall be final and conclusive and not subject to question by any legatee or beneficiary hereunder.

(c) Upon the death of my Father, Vernon E. Presley, the Trustee is instructed to make no further distributions to the fourth category of beneficiaries and such beneficiaries shall cease to have any interest whatsoever in this trust.

(d) Upon the death of both my said father and my said grandmother, the Trustee is directed to divide the Residuary Trust into separate and equal trusts, creating one such equal trust for each of my lawful children then surviving and one such equal trust for the living issue collectively, if any, of any deceased child of mine. The share, if any, for the issue of any such deceased child, shall immediately vest in such issue in equal shares but shall be subject to the provisions of Item V herein. Separate books and records shall be kept for each trust, but it shall not be necessary that a physical division of the assets be made as to each trust.

The Trustee may from time to time distribute the whole or any part of the net income or principal from each of the aforesaid trusts as the Trustee, in its uncontrolled discretion, considers necessary or desirable to provide for the comfortable support, education, maintenance, benefit and general welfare of each of my children. Such distributions may be made directly to such beneficiary or to the guardian of the person of such beneficiary and without repsonsibilty on my Trustee to see to the application of nay such distributions and in making such distributions, the Trustee shall take into account all other sources of funds known by the Trustee to be available for each respective beneficiary for such purpose.

(e) As each of my respective children attains the age of twenty-five (25) years and provided that both my father and my grandmother are deceased, the trust created hereunder for such child care terminate, and all the remainder of the assets then contained in said trust shall be distributed to such child so attaining the age of twenty-five (25) years outright and free of further trust.

(f) If any of my children for whose benefit a trust has been created hereunder should die before attaining the age of twenty- five (25) years, then the trust created for such a child shall terminate on his death, and all remaining assets then contained in said trust shall be distributed outright and free of further trust and in equal shares to the surviving issue of such deceased child but subject to the provisions of Item V herein; but if there be no such surviving issue, then to the brothers and sisters of such deceased child in equal shares, the issue of any other deceased child being entitled collectively to their deceased parent's share. Nevertheless, if any distribution otherwise becomes payable outright and free of trust under the provisions of this paragraph (f) of the Item IV of my will to a beneficiary for whom the Trustee is then administering a trust for the benefit of such beneficiary under provisions of this last will and testament, such distribution shall not be paid outright to such beneficiary but shall be added to and become a part of the trust so being administered for such beneficiary by the Trustee.

Item V - Distribution to Minor Children

If any share of corpus of any trust established under this will become distributable outright and free of trust to any beneficiary before said beneficiary has attained the age of eighteen (18) years, then said share shall immediately vest in said beneficiary, but the Trustee shall retain possession of such share during the period in which such beneficiary is under the age of eighteen (18) years, and, in the meantime, shall use and expend so much of the income and principal for the care, support, and education of such beneficiary, and any income not so expended with respect to each share so retained all the power and discretion had with respect to such trust generally.

Item VI - Alternate Distributees

In the event that all of my descendants should be deceased at any time prior to the time for the termination of the trusts provided for herein, then in such event all of my estate and all the assets of every trust to be created hereunder (as the case may be) shall then distributed outright in equal shares to my heirs at law per stirpes.

Item VII - Unenforceable Provisions

If any provisions of this will are unenforceable, the remaining provisions shall, nevertheless, be carried into effect.

Item VIII - Life Insurance

If my estate is the beneficiary of any life insurance on my life at the time of my death, I direct that the proceeds therefrom will be used by my Executor in payment of the debts , expenses and taxes listed in Item I of this will, to the extent deemed advisable by the Executor. All such proceeds not so used are to be used by my Executor for the purpose of satisfying the devises and bequests contained in Item IV herein.

Item IX - Spendthrift Provision

I direct that the interest of any beneficiary in principal or income of any trust created hereunder shall not be subject to claims of creditors or others, nor to legal process, and may not be voluntarily or involuntarily alienated or encumbered except as herein provided. Any bequests contained herein for any female shall be for her sole and separate use, free from the debts, contracts and control of any husband she may ever have.

Item X - Proceeds From Personal Services

All sums paid after my death (either to my estate or to any of the trusts created hereunder) and resulting from personal services rendered by me during my lifetime, including, but not limited to, royalties of all nature, concerts, motion picture contracts, and personal appearances shall be considered to be income, notwithstanding the provisions of estate and trust law to the contrary.

Item XI - Executor and Trustee

I appoint as executor of this, my last will and testament, and as Trustee of every trust required to be created hereunder, my said father. I hereby direct that my said father shall be entitled by his last will and testament, duly probated, to appoint a successor Executor of my estate, as well as a successor Trustee or successor Trustees of all the trusts to be created under my last will and testament.

If, for any reason, my said father be unable to serve or to continue to serve as Executor and/or as Trustee, or if he be deceased and shall not have appointed a successor Executor or Trustee, by virtue of his last will and testament as stated -above, then I appoint National Bank of Commerce, Memphis, Tennessee, or its successor or the institution with which it may merge, as successor Executor and/or as successor Trustee of all trusts required to be established hereunder.

None of the appointees named hereunder,including any appointment made by virtue of the last will and testament of my said father, shall be required to furnish any bond or security for performance of the respective fiduciary duties required hereunder, notwithstanding any rule of law to the contrary.

Item XII - Powers, Duties, Privileges and Immunities of the Trustee

Except as otherwise stated expressly to the contrary herein, I give and grant to the said Trustee (and to the duly appointed successor Trustee when acting as such) the power to do everything he deems advisable with respect to the administration of each trust required to be established under this, my last will and Testament, even though such powers would not be authorized or appropriate for the Trustee under statutory or other rules of law. By way of illustration and not in limitation of the generality of the foregoing grant of power and authority of the Trustee, I give and grant to him plenary power as follows:

(a) To exercise all those powers authorized to fiduciaries under the provisions of the Tennessee Code Annotated, Sections 35-616 to 35-618, inclusive, including any amendments thereto in effect at the time of my death, and the same are expressly referred to and incorporated herein by reference.

(b) Plenary power is granted to the Trustee, not only to relieve him from seeking judicial instruction, but to the extent that the Trustee deems it to be prudent, to encourage determinations freely to be made in favor of persons who are the current income beneficiaries. In such instances the rights of all subsequent beneficiaries are subordinate, and the Trustee shall not be answerable to any subsequent beneficiary for anything done or omitted in favor of a current income beneficiary may compel any such favorable or preferential treatment. Without in anywise minimizing or impairing the scope of this declaration of intent, it includes investment policy, exercise of discretionary power to pay or apply principal and income, and determination principal and income questions;

(c) It shall be lawful for the Trustee to apply any sum that is payable to or for the benefit of a minor (or any other person who in the Judgment of the Trustee, is incapable of making proper disposition thereof) by payments in discharge of the costs and expenses of educating, maintaining and supporting said beneficiary, or to make payment to anyone with whom said beneficiary resides or who has the care or custody of the beneficiary, temporarily or permanently, all without intervention of any guardian or like fiduciary. The receipt of anyone to whom payment is so authorized to be made shall be a complete discharge of the Trustees without obligation on his part to see to the further application hereto, and without regard to other resource that the beneficiary may have, or the duty of any other person to support the beneficiary;

(d) In Dealing with the Trustee, no grantee, pledge, vendee, mortgage, lessee or other transference of the trust properties, or any part thereof, shall be bound to inquire with respect to the purpose or necessity of any such disposition or to see to the application of any consideration therefore paid to the Trustee.

Item XIII - Concerning the Trustee and the Executor

(a) If at any time the Trustee shall have reasonable doubt as to his power, authority or duty in the administration of any trust herein created, it shall be lawful for the Trustee to obtain the advice and counsel of reputable legal counsel without resorting to the courts for instructions; and the Trustee shall be fully absolved from all liability and damage or detriment to the various trust estates of any beneficiary thereunder by reason of anything done, suffered or omitted pursuant to advice of said counsel given and obtained in good faith, provided that nothing contained herein shall be construed to prohibit or prevent the Trustee in all proper cases from applying to a court of competent jurisdiction for instructions in the administration of the trust assets in lieu of obtaining advice of counsel.

(b) In managing, investing, and controlling the various trust estates, the Trustee shall exercise the judgment and care under the circumstances then prevailing, which men of prudence discretion and judgment exercise in the management of their own affairs, not in regard to speculation, but in regard to the permanent disposition of their funds, considering the probable income as well as the probable safety of their capital, and, in addition, the purchasing power of income distribution to beneficiaries.

(c) My Trustee (as well as my Executor) shall be entitled to reasonable and adequate compensation for the fiduciary services rendered by him.

(d) My Executor and his successor Executor and his successor Executor shall have the same rights, privileges, powers and immunities herein granted to my Trustee wherever appropriate.

(e) In referring to any fiduciary hereunder, for purposes of construction, masculine pronouns may include a corporate fiduciary and neutral pronouns may include an individual fiduciary.

Item XIV - Law Against Perpetuities

(a) Having in mind the rule against perpetuities, I direct that (notwithstanding anything contained to the contrary in this last will and testament) each trust created under this will (except such trust created under this will (except such trusts as have heretofore vested in compliance with such rule or law) shall end, unless sooner terminated under other provisions of this will, twenty-one (21) years after the death of the last survivor of such of the beneficiaries hereunder as are living at the time of my death; and thereupon that the property held in trust shall be distributed free of all trust to the persons then entitled to receive the income and/or principal therefrom, in the proportion in which they are then entitled to receive such income.

(b) Notwithstanding anything else contained in this will to the contrary, I direct that if any distribution under this will become payable to a person for whom the Trustee is then administering a trust created hereunder for the benefit of such person, such distribution shall be made to such trust and not to the beneficiary outright, and the funds so passing to such trust shall become a part thereof as corpus and be administered and distributed to the same extent and purpose as if such funds had been a part of such a trust at its inception.

Item XV - Payment of Estate and Inheritance Taxes

Notwithstanding the provisions of Item X herein, I authorize my Executor to use such sums received by my estate after my death and resulting from my personal services as identified in Item X as he deem necessary and advisable in order to pay the taxes referred to in Item I of my said will.

In WITNESS WHEREOF, I, the said ELVIS A. PRESLEY, do hereunto set my hand and seal in the presence of two (2) competent witnesses, and in their presence do publish and declare this instrument to be my Last Will and Testament, this 3 day of March, 1977.

[Signed by Elvis A. Presley]
ELVIS A. PRESLEY

The above examples highlight the differences in the length and detail that can be covered in wills. Elvis Presley's will contains many of the important clauses discussed in this chapter, while Chief Justice Warren Burger's will is practically void of any of those clauses. Fortunately, the length and the number of clauses mean very little to estate planning if proper planning is not completed. Exhibit 2.4 details that Elvis only passed 27 percent of his ten million dollar estate to his heirs, while Warren Burger passed 75 percent of his $1,800,000 to his heirs.

EXHIBIT 2.4	CELEBRITY ESTATE TAX CONSEQUENCES

Source: www.stricklen.com

	Estate	Taxes & Costs	Net Estate	% Passed to Heirs
Henry Kaiser Jr.	$55,910,373	$1,030,415	$54,879,958	98%
Warren Burger (estimated)	$1,800,000	$450,000	$1,350,000	75%
Walt Disney	$23,004,851	$6,811,943	$16,192,908	70%
Humphrey Bogart	$910,146	$274,234	$635,912	70%
Gary Cooper	$4,948,985	$1,520,454	$3,454,531	70%
Al Jolson	$4,385,143	$1,349,066	$3,036,077	69%
Cecil B. DeMille	$4,043,607	$1,396,064	$2,647,543	65%
Hedda Hopper	$472,661	$165,982	$306,679	65%
Earle Stanley Gardner	$1,795,092	$636,705	$1,158,387	65%
W.C. Fields	$884,680	$329,793	$554,887	63%
Clark Gable	$2,806,526	$1,101,038	$1,705,488	61%
Henry J. Kaiser Sr.	$5,597,772	$2,488,364	$3,109,408	56%
William Boeing	$22,386,158	$10,589,748	$11,796,410	53%
William Frawley	$92,446	$45,814	$46,632	50%
Marilyn Monroe	$819,176	$448,750	$370,426	45%
Frederick Vanderbilt	$76,838,530	$42,846,112	$33,992,418	44%
Alwin Ernst (CPA)	$12,642,431	$7,124,112	$5,518,319	44%
Charles Woolworth	$16,788,702	$10,391,303	$6,397,399	38%
John D. Rockefeller	$26,905,182	$17,124,988	$9,780,194	36%
J.P. Morgan	$17,121,482	$11,893,691	$5,227,791	31%
Elvis Presley	$10,165,434	$7,374,635	$2,790,799	27%

Key Concepts

Underline/highlight the answers to these questions as you read:

1. How is a will revoked or changed?

2. What is a side instructional letter?

3. What are some of the statutes that affect wills and how do they affect them?

4. How can will contests be avoided?

REVOKING AND CHANGING WILLS

Unfortunately, creating a will is not the ultimate and final step in estate planning. Due to the passage of time, heirs are born and die, property is bought and sold, and preferences regarding distributions change, wills need to be reviewed and updated periodically. Attorneys drafting statutory wills, try to draft wills that will be flexible over time through use of broad language but, nonetheless, wills may need to be changed at some point in time. The testator may change or update his will by revoking the previous will and creating a new one, or by executing a codicil (an amendment or supplement to the existing will).

Revocation

Revoking a will is very simple. The testator can destroy the will, either by shredding it or burning it. The testator can also create a new will specifically revoking the previous will. In some states, the testator can revoke the will by writing "cancel" across the will. Other states provide that any defacing of the will, such as crossing out one provision, constitutes revocation of the will. The testator's state law may also provide other acceptable methods of revoking a will. When revoking and creating new wills, clients should be cautioned not to write new provisions on a previously executed will, as some state probate courts have interpreted the new handwritten provisions to be valid alterations to the will, superseding the original provisions. Any writings clients make regarding their will distribution choices should be labeled "draft" to avoid courts interpreting these documents as a last will and testament.

Codicil

A codicil is an amendment, or supplement, to a will. It is a separate document or attachment to the will and must meet all of the legal requirements of a will. A codicil may be executed like a statutory will, which must be signed, properly witnessed, and notarized as discussed previously. If the state allows, the codicil may also be in the form of a holographic, or handwritten, document attached to the will. The purpose of a codicil is to modify, explain, or amend a will. A codicil may be used, for example, to include additional children born after the drafting of the original will or when additional property is acquired after the drafting of the will. When admitted to probate, the codicil becomes part of the will.

Because codicils are attached to the will, they can be inadvertently or intentionally separated from the will and lost. If this happens, the testator's ultimate desires may not be fulfilled. If the codicil addresses an important issue, or addresses many issues, redrafting the will may be wiser than adding a codicil. A sample codicil is displayed at Exhibit 2.5.

SIDE INSTRUCTION LETTER

Another separate document from the will, the **side instruction letter,** or personal instruction letter, details the testator's wishes regarding the disposition of specific tangible possessions (such as household goods), as well as funeral and burial wishes. The side instruction letter exists separately from the will, to avoid cluttering the will with small details that may create conflicts among heirs and is not binding in the probate process. In many states, burial is required before probate can begin, and the side letter of instruction gives specific instructions to the heirs. This letter, which is given to the executor, may contain information regarding the location of important personal documents, safe deposit boxes, outstanding loans, and other personal and financial information that the executor will use to administer the decedent's estate. While the letter has no legal standing, the executor will generally carry out the wishes of the decedent.

EXHIBIT 2.5 **SAMPLE CODICIL**

SAMPLE CODICIL

I, _____ being of sound mind and body and free will, and having full testamentary intent and capacity, do hereby voluntarily make, publish and execute this document as a codicil to my Last Will and Testament which was made on the _____ day of _____ , 20___.

I hereby amend and modify the provisions of my Last Will and Testament identified above as follows:

        1.

        2.

        3.

Except as expressly modified by this codicil, all remaining terms and provisions of my Last Will and Testament identified above shall remain in full force and effect.

IN WITNESS WHEREOF, I have signed this document as a codicil to my Last Will and Testament identified above on this _____ day of _____, 20___.

_____
Your Signature

The foregoing codicil of _____ , dated this _____ day of _____ , 20___, was signed and published in our presence as a codicil to his/her Last Will and Testament. We declare that the maker was of sound mind and body and free will at that time, and we have hereto signed our names as witnesses in the presence of the maker and of each other.

_____   _____
(Name & Address of Witness)   *(Name & Address of Witness)*

Subscribed and sworn to before me by said
(testatrix, testator) and the said witnesses,
this _____ day of _____ , 20___.

_____
Notary Public
My Commission expires:

STATUTES AFFECTING WILLS

Over the course of time, state legislatures have enacted statutes designed to protect both testators and natural heirs during the probate process. These statutes may in many instances override the preferences set forth in the will. Particular attention should be paid to the statutes in the testator's domiciliary state to determine how these statutes will affect the testator.

Forced Heirship

While the concept may be termed differently, some states have statutes requiring a certain portion of the estate to be transferred to the decedent's children. **Forced heirship** in the United States derives from French law, but the concept of forced heirship is common in civil law jurisdictions throughout the world.

Marital Share

The marital share is somewhat similar to that of forced heirship in that both require a decedent to provide for certain people. State laws concerning the marital share require the decedent to provide for his surviving spouse under certain circumstances.

Felonious Homicide Statutes

Substantial wealth has, on occasion, served to encourage heirs to intentionally participate in the death of their so called loved one. Because of this, many states now have **felonious homicide statutes** that prevent legatees and heirs who have been convicted of intentionally killing the decedent from inheriting from the decedent's will or through the intestate process. If a will has been executed, the probate court will invalidate any provisions relating to the legatee. Likewise, if a will has not been executed, the probate court will distribute assets under the intestacy scheme, pretending that the convicted heir is dead. If the testator's state does not have such a statue, a clause in the will indicating the testator's desire to exclude those individuals who intentionally caused their death will typically create the same result.

Divorce Statutes

Many times divorcing spouses fail to revise their wills in a timely fashion. To protect such individuals, many states now have statutes that invalidate any provisions in a will that leave assets to a former spouse. In the event that a testator does wish to leave assets to a former spouse clear indication should be made in the will to prevent the clause from being stricken by the probate court. These statutes do not apply, however, to property passing by contract, such as life insurance, pension plans, and annuities. After a divorce, the beneficiary designations on these instruments should be changed to ensure the former spouse does not receive these assets. Be aware, however, that not all states have statutes that invalidate bequests to former spouses. To effectively serve their client's estate, planners must know the specifics of their state's laws.

Anti-Lapse Statutes

Some states have statutes that will presume that if a close relative, like a child or sibling, is not alive when the testator dies the testator would have wanted bequests to those individuals to pass directly to their heirs. Anti-lapse rules generally do not apply to gifts to friends, or distant relatives. In those instances, the law generally presumes the testator would have wanted the assets to go to the residuary estate. Obviously, a well drafted will can overcome these presumptions.

Quick Quiz 2.3

Highlight the answer to these questions:

1. When additional property is acquired after writing a will, a codicil can amend the will without having to rewrite the entire will to include provisions that dispose of the new property.
    a. True
    b. False

2. By using a side instruction letter, specific bequests are left out of the will and avoid probate.
    a. True
    b. False

3. Will contests can always be eliminated by using a no-contest clause.
    a. True
    b. False

True, False, False.

AVOIDING WILL CONTESTS

Unfortunately, will contests cannot be totally prevented. No-contest clauses may be used to discourage contests but, nonetheless, cannot stop them. Will contests often occur in nontraditional relationships, such as same-sex relationships or relationships where there is a substantial age difference between the partners. They also occur in cases where individuals leave substantial fortunes to nontraditional churches or other charitable organizations. Sadly, they can occur in any family. Will contests result in added time and expense incurred in estate administration. Testators can and should take action to avoid will contests. Being open and honest with heirs before death regarding will choices may alleviate some of the disagreements that may occur after the decedent's death. In addition, detailed and well-drafted wills can, in some cases, prevent will contests. For non-traditional bequests, the testator may consider lifetime gifts, trust options, or property titling as a means of avoiding will contests.

Some states allow the testator to have the will validated before death. In such cases, the testator notifies all interested parties that a hearing will be held and if they would like to challenge the will they should attend the hearing. The court will evaluate any claims and provide a judgment on the validity of the will. While this may prevent will contests, it can be expensive and time consuming as a new hearing will be needed each time the will is altered.

POWERS OF ATTORNEY AND POWERS OF APPOINTMENT

People frequently need a trusted person to make decisions or sign papers for them regarding their property or health. A **power of attorney** is a legal document that authorizes a trusted person to act on one's behalf. It grants a right to one person, the **attorney-in-fact** (sometimes called the power holder or agent), to act in the place of the other person, the **principal** (the grantor of the power). Generally, any person who is legally capable to act for himself may act as an attorney-in-fact for another. The principal must have reached the age of majority, defined in most states as 18 years old, and be legally competent in order to grant the power. All powers are revocable by the principal and all powers granted cease at the principal's death. A power of appointment is sometimes included in a power of attorney. A power of appointment is a power to appoint the assets of one person to another and may be either general or limited.

Key Concepts

Underline/highlight the answers to these questions as you read:

1. What is a power of attorney?

2. Identify and discuss the parties to a power of attorney.

3. Identify a reason to use a power of attorney.

4. What is a durable power of attorney and why are they used?

5. What is a springing durable power of attorney?

GENERAL POWER OF ATTORNEY

The broadest power a person can give another is a general power of attorney. The person who is given the power of attorney will be able to act in the principal's place as though he is the principal. Essentially the general power of attorney gives the agent the power to do anything that the principal could do. The general power of attorney may be revoked by the principal by giving notice, usually with a revocation form, to the agent and is automatically revoked at the principal's death.

Although the general power of attorney grants the agent the right to do anything the principal could have done, some states require certain powers, such as the power to make gifts or to engage in self-dealing, to be specifically granted. The ability for the agent to appoint assets to himself, to his estate, his creditors, or his estate's creditors is considered a general power of appointment over the property covered by the power of attorney. Although a power of appointment or the ability to appoint assets in a general or limited way, is traditionally associated with trusts, it functions similarly when included in a power of attorney. Power of appointments will be discussed in more detail later in the text. The following exhibit illustrates the general characteristics of Powers of Attorney and Powers of Appointment.

POWER OF ATTORNEY VS. POWER OF APPOINTMENT

EXHIBIT 2.6

POWER OF ATTORNEY	POWER OF APPOINTMENT
• A stand alone document that allows an agent to act for the principal and may include the power to appoint assets	• A power, usually included in a trust or power of attorney, allowing the power holder to direct assets to another
• Power to act	• Power to transfer assets
• Ends at the death of the principal	• May survive the death of the grantor
• May be general or limited	• May be general or limited
• May be revoked at any time by the principal	• May be revoked by the principal during life or at death (via last will and testament)

General Power of Appointment

If the agent dies before the principal and is holding a general power of appointment over assets of the principal, the agent's gross estate will include the fair market value of the principal's assets over which the agent held the power of appointment regardless of whether the power has been invoked. Therefore, a general power of appointment should be granted sparingly.

Most states presume that agents do not have the power to gift assets to themselves, their estates, or pay to their creditors unless such power is expressly provided for in the power of attorney. If a principal wants the holder to have this kind of power, he should be sure to have the appropriate language included in his power of attorney.

LIMITED POWER OF ATTORNEY

A limited power of attorney, also referred to as a special power of attorney, gives the agent very specific, detailed powers. The power granted in a limited power of attorney may be extremely narrow, only authorizing the agent to act on a specific matter. For example, if the principal were purchasing a new home and was unable to attend the actual closing because he was out of the country, he can give a power of attorney to someone else specifically authorizing them to sign his name at the act of sale. Other uses for a limited power of attorney include situations where a principal gives an agent the authority to act on his behalf to pay his bills, or handle a specific business transaction.

As a written document, the limited power of attorney should state the agent's name and the powers granted to the agent. Although the powers granted under most limited power of attorney documents are quite narrow, the power granted may be more broad if the principal desires. For example, a very broad power will still be considered limited if the agent is authorized to do anything the principal can do, except appoint assets to the agent (himself), to the agent's creditors, to the agent's estate, or to the agent's estate's creditors.

Exhibits 2.7 and 2.8 graphically depict the differences between the special/limited power and general power of attorney and appointment.

Limited Power of Appointment

Like a general power of appointment, a limited power of appointment is the power to affect the beneficial enjoyment of property. Unlike a general power of appointment, a limited power of appointment is limited in some way. One of the ways in which a power of appointment can be limited is by the application of an ascertainable standard. According to the Internal Revenue Code, a power is limited by such a standard if the extent of the holder's duty to exercise and not to exercise the power is reasonably measurable in terms of his needs for health, education, maintenance, or support (or any combination of them). If a power of appointment is limited by an ascertainable standard, then the property subject to the power will not be includible in the gross estate of the power holder. Furthermore, the use of an ascertainable standard allows the principal to give the power holder the ability to appoint assets to himself without creating a general power of appointment.

EXAMPLE 2.18	John gives Allison the power to appoint the $1,000,000 in his bank account to herself or her mother. John has given Allison a general power of appointment. If Allison dies while holding the power of appointment, the $1,000,000 bank account will be included in her gross estate.
EXAMPLE 2.19	John gives Allison the power to appoint the $1,000,000 in his bank account to herself or to her mother, but only for educational expenses. Even though Allison can appoint the assets to herself (which would usually create a general power of appointment), she has a limited power of appointment because she is limited by the fact that the assets can only be used for educational expenses. Therefore, if Allison dies while holding the power, the value of John's bank account will not be included in her gross estate.

In determining whether a power is limited by an ascertainable standard, it is immaterial whether the beneficiary is required to exhaust his other income before the power can be exercised.

GRAPHICAL DEPICTION OF POWERS OF ATTORNEY

EXHIBIT 2.7

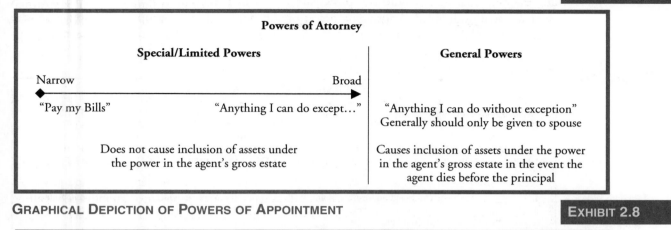

GRAPHICAL DEPICTION OF POWERS OF APPOINTMENT

EXHIBIT 2.8

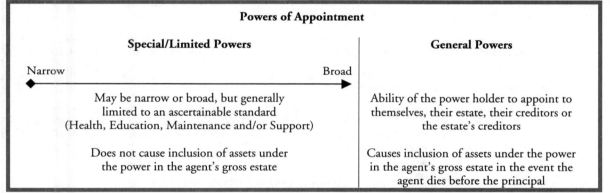

DURABLE FEATURE

When a power of attorney is "durable," the agent's power does not expire upon the principal's incapacity or disability but rather expires only at the principal's death. Because the power remains in effect even after the principal becomes incapacitated, it is considered to be durable. The durability feature, which allows the agent to maintain the power granted even after the principal's incapacity, should be included if the principal intends the power to survive his incapacity or disability. The durable power of attorney is especially appropriate where the principal anticipates the need for someone to manage his affairs in the near future. For example, an elderly parent about to enter a nursing home may need to appoint his adult child to manage his existing home affairs or make health care decisions.

SPRINGING POWER

When a power of attorney is structured as a **springing power**, the agent's authority to act "springs" into existence upon some defined event or determination (i.e., at the disability of the principal). In this case even though the principal has signed the power of attorney, the agent cannot exercise the powers granted to him until the specific event occurs. Generally, the power springs upon disability or incapacity and lapses if the principal recovers. The power is always revocable by the principal, provided that the principal is competent at the time of revocation.

The purpose of a springing power of attorney is to make sure that someone has the power to act for the principal and handle the principal's affairs in the event that the principal becomes incapacitated or disabled. A springing power of attorney would be appropriate for someone who is currently able to handle their own affairs but would like to plan for possible future incapacity.

| EXHIBIT 2.9 | **POWER OF ATTORNEY EXAMPLE** |

STATUTORY DURABLE POWER OF ATTORNEY (Texas)

NOTICE: THE POWERS GRANTED BY THIS DOCUMENT ARE BROAD AND SWEEPING. THEY ARE EXPLAINED IN THE DURABLE POWER OF ATTORNEY ACT, CHAPTER XII, TEXAS PROBATE CODE. IF YOU HAVE ANY QUESTIONS ABOUT THESE POWERS, OBTAIN COMPETENT LEGAL ADVICE. THIS DOCUMENT DOES NOT AUTHORIZE ANYONE TO MAKE MEDICAL AND OTHER HEALTH-CARE DECISIONS FOR YOU. YOU MAY REVOKE THIS POWER OF ATTORNEY IF YOU LATER WISH TO DO SO.

I, _____ (insert your name and address), appoint _____ (insert the name and address of the person appointed) as my agent (attorney-in-fact) to act for me in any lawful way with respect to all of the following powers except for a power that I have crossed out below.

TO WITHHOLD A POWER, YOU MUST CROSS OUT EACH POWER WITHHELD.

Real property transactions; Tangible personal property transactions; Stock and bond transactions; Commodity and option transactions; Banking and other financial institution transactions; Business operating transactions; Insurance and annuity transactions; Estate, trust, and other beneficiary transactions; Claims and litigation; Personal and family maintenance; Benefits from social security, Medicare, Medicaid, or other governmental programs or civil or military service; Retirement plan transactions; Tax matters.

IF NO POWER LISTED ABOVE IS CROSSED OUT, THIS DOCUMENT SHALL BE CONSTRUED AND INTERPRETED AS A GENERAL POWER OF ATTORNEY AND MY AGENT (ATTORNEY IN FACT) SHALL HAVE THE POWER AND AUTHORITY TO PERFORM OR UNDERTAKE ANY ACTION I COULD PERFORM OR UNDERTAKE IF I WERE PERSONALLY PRESENT.

SPECIAL INSTRUCTIONS:

1. Special instructions applicable to gifts (initial in front of the following sentence to have it apply):

    I grant my agent (attorney in fact) the power to apply my property to make gifts, except that the amount of a gift to an individual may not exceed the amount of annual exclusions allowed from the federal gift tax for the calendar year of the gift.

2. ON THE FOLLOWING LINES YOU MAY GIVE SPECIAL INSTRUCTIONS LIMITING OR EXTENDING THE POWERS GRANTED TO YOUR AGENT.

    _____

    _____

3. UNLESS YOU DIRECT OTHERWISE ABOVE, THIS POWER OF ATTORNEY IS EFFECTIVE IMMEDIATELY AND WILL CONTINUE UNTIL IT IS REVOKED.

    CHOOSE ONE OF THE FOLLOWING ALTERNATIVES BY CROSSING OUT THE ALTERNATIVE NOT CHOSEN:

    (A) This power of attorney is not affected by my subsequent disability or incapacity.

    (B) This power of attorney becomes effective upon my disability or incapacity.

    YOU SHOULD CHOOSE ALTERNATIVE (A) IF THIS POWER OF ATTORNEY IS TO BECOME EFFECTIVE ON THE DATE IT IS EXECUTED.

    IF NEITHER (A) NOR (B) IS CROSSED OUT, IT WILL BE ASSUMED THAT YOU CHOSE ALTERNATIVE (A).

If Alternative (B) is chosen and a definition of my disability or incapacity is not contained in this power of attorney, I shall be considered disabled or incapacitated for purposes of this power of attorney if a physician certifies in writing at a date later than the date this power of attorney is executed that, based on the physician's medical examination of me, I am mentally incapable of managing my financial affairs. I authorize the physician who examines me for this purpose to disclose my physical or mental condition to another person for purposes of this power of attorney. A third party who accepts this power of attorney is fully protected from any action taken under this power of attorney that is based on the determination made by a physician of my disability or incapacity.

I agree that any third party who receives a copy of this document may act under it. Revocation of the durable power of attorney is not effective as to a third party until the third party receives actual notice of the revocation. I agree to indemnify the third party for any claims that arise against the third party because of reliance on this power of attorney.

If any agent named by me dies, becomes legally disabled, resigns, or refuses to act, I name the following (each to act alone and successively, in the order named) as successor(s) to that agent: _____.

Signed this ___ day of _____, 20__.

_____
(your signature)

State of _____

County of _____

This document was acknowledged before me on _____ (date) by _____ (name of principal).

_____
(signature of notarial officer)

(Seal, if any, of notary)

_____
(printed name)

My commission expires:_____

THE ATTORNEY IN FACT OR AGENT, BY ACCEPTING OR ACTING UNDER THE APPOINTMENT, ASSUMES THE FIDUCIARY AND OTHER LEGAL RESPONSIBILITIES OF AN AGENT.

DISCUSSION OF EXHIBIT 2.9

Exhibit 2.9 is an example of a durable, general power of attorney. Because it is a general power of attorney, the Internal Revenue Code dictates that the agent must include the fair market value of the principal's assets that are under the power in his gross estate if the agent predeceases the principal. Had the principal limited the power as follows: "the agent cannot appoint assets to himself or to anyone else for his own benefit," this power would have become a special power of attorney (albeit a broad power) and forego the risk of inclusion in the agent's gross estate if the agent predeceases the principal. The power of attorney is also effective as of the date of writing unless the principal chooses to make the power springing.

POWER OF ATTORNEY FOR PROPERTY

A **power of attorney for property** is a special power of attorney designed for a specific purpose. It provides an agent with the power to manage a principal's property and finances. The power of attorney for property may be durable to provide for continuity in the management of property affairs in the event of the principal's disability and/or incapacity. It is an inexpensive and relatively easy way for the principal to ensure that his finances will be managed by a trusted person of his choosing.

A durable power of attorney for property enables the principal to select a particular person or financial institution to act on his behalf and manage financial tasks that may arise in the event of incapacity. Examples of these tasks include paying bills, making bank deposits, handling insurance issues, and managing property and investments. In most cases, a durable power of attorney is the most practical way to handle such situations. A durable power of attorney for property may also be used to manage a business.

Consequences of Not Having a Durable Power of Attorney for Property

- A durable power of attorney eliminates the necessity of petitioning a local court to appoint a guardian of the estate to make property decisions for a person who is incapacitated or disabled. These proceedings can be expensive and embarrassing for those involved, as court proceedings are a matter of public record. If relatives disagree over who should be the guardian of the estate, the proceedings can become lengthy and costly.
- Although a spouse may have some authority over jointly owned property, there are limits to a spouse's right to sell jointly owned property. In most states, both spouses must agree to the sale of jointly owned property. Because an incapacitated

spouse cannot consent, the other spouse without a durable power of attorney for property may be limited in what he can do with the property.

Quick Quiz 2.4

Highlight the answer to these questions:

1. A power of attorney is generally granted to a relative or person whom an individual would trust making decisions for them if they become incapacitated, disabled, or cannot perform a needed task. A power of attorney does not survive death.
   a. True
   b. False

2. If someone dies holding a general power of appointment over someone else's assets, the agent's gross estate will include the value of all of the assets under the general power of appointment.
   a. True
   b. False

3. Durable powers of attorney are irrevocable.
   a. True
   b. False

True, True, False.

EXAMPLE 2.20

Eric and Jessica have been married for 35 years. Their home is owned in both their names as joint tenants. Their only other major asset is stock that Eric bought prior to their marriage and is titled in his name only. Even if Eric becomes incapacitated and requires expensive medical treatment, without a durable power of attorney for property Jessica cannot legally sell the stock to pay for medical costs without a local court's approval.

DISADVANTAGES OF A POWER OF ATTORNEY

- The agent possessing a power of attorney can abuse the powers granted to him, so the principal should give serious consideration in choosing the person to hold such a power. Unfortunate as it may be, agents may take advantage of their position for their own interest after the principal is incapacitated or disabled.
- In most cases, a person possessing a limited/special power of attorney is not permitted to make gifts to himself or other family members. In addition, if the power to gift to charitable or noncharitable donees is a desirable feature, such powers should be separately and explicitly stated in the instrument.
- In the case of a general power of attorney, if the agent dies before the principal and is holding a general power of appointment over the principal's assets, such power will cause the inclusion in the agent's gross estate of the value of the principal's assets over which the agent had a power.

DIRECTIVES REGARDING HEALTH CARE

Directives regarding health care are probably the most controversial and difficult documents to discuss with your client. Individuals tend to have strong feelings regarding their health care and the ability of others to make health care decisions for them. This section discusses some of the alternative documents available in most states.

Key Concepts

Underline/highlight the answers to these questions as you read:

1. What is a durable power of attorney for health care and why are they used?

2. What is a living will and why are they used?

3. What is a DNR and why are they used?

DURABLE POWER OF ATTORNEY FOR HEALTH CARE

A **durable power of attorney for health care**, also called a medical power of attorney or health care proxy, is a legal document that appoints an agent (someone with authority to act on behalf of another) to make health care decisions on behalf of a **principal** who is unable to make those decisions for him/herself. Unlike the living will, which states the person's wishes regarding the sustainment of life, the durable power of attorney for health care puts health care decision making in the hands of a third person.

The durable power of attorney for health care may provide direction in terminal and nonterminal situations, such as disclosure of medical records, blood transfusions, cardiac resuscitation, organ transplants, and selection of medical support staff, but generally does not provide the right to end life-sustaining treatment. (Note that in some states a power of attorney for health care may provide the right to withhold or end life-sustaining treatment.) The durable power of attorney for health care eliminates the necessity of petitioning a local court to appoint a guardian to make health care decisions for a person who is incapacitated or disabled.

The durable power of attorney for health care is typically a springing power of attorney. As discussed previously, this feature only allows the agent to act on behalf of the principal when the principal becomes incapacitated. It also lapses the power when the principal recovers from the disability. In some states, it is assumed that the power of attorney for health care is a springing power.

The advantage of the document is that it is less costly to prepare in advance than to have a guardian seek court approval at a time when a health care decision needs to be made. The durable power of attorney for health care is recognized in almost every state, although each state has different laws governing the drafting of such documents.

A durable power of attorney for health care is distinguished from a regular power of attorney (discussed above) in two ways. First, the power is specific to health care decisions, and second, the document entitles the power holder to do exactly what may be needed if the principal is incapacitated or disabled to the extent that the principal cannot make his own health care decisions.

An example of a health care power of attorney is shown in Exhibit 2.10.

MEDICAL POWER OF ATTORNEY DESIGNATION OF HEALTH CARE AGENT (Texas)

I, _____ (insert your name), appoint:

Name:_____
Address:_____
Phone:_____

as my agent to make any and all health care decisions for me, except to the extent I state otherwise in this document. The medical power of attorney takes effect if I become unable to make my own health care decisions and this fact is certified in writing by my physician.

LIMITATIONS ON THE DECISION-MAKING AUTHORITY OF MY AGENT ARE AS FOLLOWS:
Insert any limitations here.

DESIGNATION OF ALTERNATE AGENT.
If the person designated as my agent is unable or unwilling to make health care decisions for me, I designate the following persons to serve as my agent to make health care decisions for me as authorized in this document, who serve in the following order:

A. First Alternate Agent
Name:_____
Address:_____

B. Second Alternate Agent
Name:_____
Address:_____

The following individuals or institutions have signed copies:
Name:_____
Address:_____

DURATION.
I understand that this power of attorney exists indefinitely from the date I execute this document unless I establish a shorter time or revoke the power of attorney. If I am unable to make health care decisions for myself when this power of attorney expires, the authority I have granted my agent continues to exist until the time I become able to make health care decisions for myself.

(IF APPLICABLE) This power of attorney ends on the following date: _____.

PRIOR DESIGNATIONS REVOKED.
I revoke any prior medical power of attorney.

ACKNOWLEDGMENT OF DISCLOSURE STATEMENT.
I have been provided with a disclosure statement explaining the effect of this document. I have read and understand that information contained in the disclosure statement.

I sign my name to this medical power of attorney on __ day of _____ (*month, year*) at [it may be prudent to include at this point: _____ (time).]

_____
(City and State)

_____
(Signature)

LIVING WILLS/ADVANCE MEDICAL DIRECTIVES

A **living will**, also known as an **advance medical directive** or in some states, a Natural Death Declaration or Instruction Directive, is not a will at all, but rather a legal document expressing an individual's last wishes regarding sustainment of life under specific circumstances. The living will establishes the medical situations and circumstances in which the individual no longer desires life-sustaining treatment in the event he is no longer capable of making those decisions. The document only covers a narrow range of situations, and is usually limited to decisions concerning administering artificial life support treatments when there is no reasonable expectation of recovery from extreme physical or mental disability. Almost every state has legislation in place that disregards the living will if the patient is pregnant.

The purpose of the living will is to allow individuals who are terminally ill to die on their own terms, or as it has been coined, "die with dignity." Many states have adopted Natural Death Acts stating that the withholding or

discontinuance of any extraordinary means of keeping a patient alive, or the withholding or discontinuance of artificial nutrition and hydration, shall not be considered the cause of death for any civil or criminal purpose, nor shall it be considered unprofessional conduct, thus allowing terminal individuals the right to choose the healthcare provided to them.

The living will is also used to avoid the expense of sustaining life artificially and thus to preserve assets for the decedent's heirs. The living will is prepared in advance of an illness to (1) explicitly state the client's wishes, and (2) avoid the necessity for heirs to seek court approval for life-sustaining or termination decisions. The document, though authorized in all states, must meet the specific requirements of the individual's state statute. If the document is not drafted by a competent attorney, problems may arise with vagueness or ambiguities in drafting. Some states have developed a computerized registry of those who have filed living wills so if a person is alive solely because of life-sustaining treatments, the institution providing care can determine if the document exists, and thus comply with the wishes of the registrants. In addition, privately administered national registries have also increased in popularity in the wake of the highly publicized case of Terri Schiavo in 2005. Schiavo's case highlights the importance of having a living will regardless of age or current health. An example of a living will can be found at Exhibit 2.11.

Many health care providers suggest that all people, regardless of age or health, should have a living will and a durable power of attorney for health care. In addition, individuals should discuss with their loved ones their feelings regarding natural death as well as anatomical gifts (the donation of organs and tissue). A desire to make anatomical gifts can usually be declared through the state board of motor vehicles as an election printed on the driver's license, or through a notarized declaration. In addition, family members may be able to elect organ donation for an individual at death.

Do Not Resuscitate Order (DNRs)

Individuals may also have a document called a "DNR" which stands for Do Not Resuscitate. These documents declare the principals wish to avoid having cardiopulmonary resuscitation (CPR) performed in the event their heart stops beating. This is not generally prepared as part of an overall estate plan unless the individual is already terminally ill. These types of orders are generally prepared once an individual has already been admitted to the hospital and is near death, and are commonly used by patients with advanced cancer or kidney damage, or patients suffering from significant ailments relating to old age.

DNRs are generally executed on a form provided by the state and may be filed with the patient's medical records. Some states also provide statewide registries allowing these documents to be placed on file for easy access. Some states provide medical bracelets to patients with DNRs that have been sent home to spend their remaining days. The bracelet notifies emergency personnel of the individual's wish to decline CPR.

It is crucial to understand that DNRs only apply to CPR and do not apply to any other medical treatment. DNRs are not sufficient to avoid other life sustaining treatment. As the application of DNRs vary by state, a thorough understanding of the individual state law is imperative when working with DNRs.

EXHIBIT 2.11   LIVING WILL EXAMPLE

ADVANCE MEDICAL DIRECTIVE (Texas)

DIRECTIVE made this _____ day of _____ (month, year).

I, _____, being of sound mind, willfully and voluntarily make known my desire that my life shall not be artificially prolonged under the circumstances set forth in this directive.

1. If at any time I should have an incurable or irreversible condition caused by injury, disease, or illness certified to be a terminal condition by two physicians, and if the application of life-sustaining procedures would serve only to artificially postpone the moment of my death, and if my attending physician determines that my death is imminent or will result within a relatively short time without the application of life-sustaining procedures, I direct that such procedures be withheld or withdrawn, and that I be permitted to die naturally.

2. In the absence of my ability to give directions regarding the use of those life-sustaining procedures, it is my intention that this directive shall be honored by my family and physicians as the final expression of my legal right to refuse medical or surgical treatment and accept the consequences from that refusal.

3. If I have been diagnosed as pregnant and that diagnosis is known to my physician, this directive has no effect during my pregnancy.

4. This directive is in effect until it is revoked.

5. I understand the full import of this directive and I am emotionally and mentally competent to make this directive.

6. I understand that I may revoke this directive at any time.

Signed:

_____

City, County and State of Residence:

_____

I am not related to the declarant by blood or marriage. I would not be entitled to any portion of the declarant's estate on the declarant's death. I am not the attending physician of the declarant or an employee of the attending physician. I am not a patient in the health care facility in which the declarant is a patient. I have no claim against any portion of the declarant's estate on the declarant's death. Furthermore, if I am an employee of a health facility in which the declarant is a patient, I am not involved in providing direct patient care to the declarant and am not directly involved in the financial affairs of the health facility.

Witness: _____

Witness: _____

NEED FOR DOCUMENTS

Everyone needs some or all of the documents discussed in this chapter. Individuals often do not realize the necessity of having these documents until it is too late. Consider the following example which illustrates several different scenarios and the need for documents in each case.

Bill, age 42, is married to Marsha and they have three small children. Bill also has an older child from his first marriage to Cindy. Bill has a net worth of $200,000. On his way home from work one day, Bill is in a serious accident that leaves him comatose and terminally ill where his only means of survival are life-sustaining procedures provided by the hospital. Bill does not have any of the documents discussed in this chapter. Due to the extent of Bill's injury and the means needed to keep him alive, he quickly meets his health insurance policy's maximum lifetime benefit. Thus, his own funds are then needed to continue to maintain his life. Studies show that a hospital stay where life-sustaining procedures are needed costs between $5,000 and $14,000 per day.

In this instance, Bill's family is faced with many dilemmas. Since Bill did not have a living will, his family will have to consider when, or if, to end life sustaining treatment and will likely need a court order to do so. Assume it takes one month after medical benefits run out for Bill's family to consider and obtain the authorization to end life-sustaining treatment and his hospital cost is $5,000 per day. By the end of this first month, Bill's assets will have been reduced from $200,000 to $50,000. If instead, the cost was on the high end of the estimate at $14,000 per day, his assets would be completely depleted and his estate would owe the hospital $220,000. The following chart illustrates this scenario.

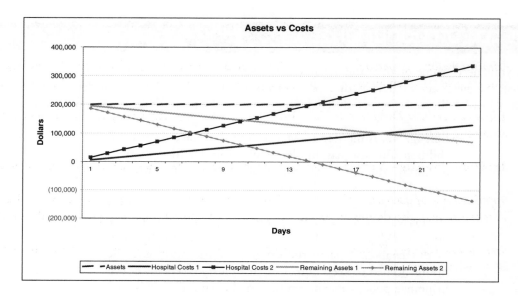

Unfortunately, this is just one of the possible negative situations. Recall that Bill does not have a Power of Attorney either. If Bill is in a common law (separate property) state (see Chapter 3) and holds all of his assets in a separate account, his family may not have access to his funds during his hospital stay. Assuming that Marsha is not employed and all funds are held in an account titled in Bill's name only, Marsha will not have immediately accessible funds. She may have to seek a court order to access his funds for his use, and for their family's use. Unfortunately, this takes time. Again, we see that poor planning on Bill's part has negatively impacted his family.

Let's now assume that Bill dies the day after his accident and his $200,000 in assets are left intact. The fact that he does not have a will may result in his assets not being distributed as he would have wished. In Bill's case this is a concern because of the blended family (i.e., the presence of a child from his first marriage). In some states, the children would inherit most, or all, of the assets with the current spouse retaining a small interest for life. This may leave Marsha with very little assets, or in some cases, the need for her to account for the assets she holds interest in on a regular basis. Such distributions can lead to animosity within the extended family.

All adults should have the documents discussed in this chapter as part of their estate plan. While use of these documents is important to the estate planning process, they are just one of the factors involved in proper estate planning.

Key Terms

Administrator - A person, usually a relative of the deceased, appointed by the probate court to oversee the probate process when an executor is not named in the will.

Advance Medical Directive/Living Will - Legal document expressing an individual's last wishes regarding life sustaining treatment.

Ancilliary Probate - A probate process conducted in a state other than the state of the decedent's domicile.

Appointment of Executor Clause - A clause in a will that identifies the executor and any successor executor. This clause may also define the extent of the executor's powers and may grant specific or general powers.

Attestation Clause - Witness clause stating that the testator is of sound mind and that he signed the document in the witness' presence.

Attorney in Fact - Agent or power holder of a power of attorney.

Bequest Clause - Directs the distribution of property, whether cash, tangible property, intangible property or real property.

Codicil - A document that amends a will. A codicil is prepared subsequent to and separate from the will to modify or explain the will.

Contingent Legatee Clause - A clause in a will that names a secondary person to inherit if the original legatee is dead or disclaims the property.

Declaration Clause - A clause in a will which states this is the last will and testament of the testator.

Disclaimer - An heir or legatee's refusal to accept a gift or bequest. The disclaimer allows assets to pass to other heirs or legatees without additional transfer tax.

Domicile - Where a person lives, the location of their home.

Durable Feature - Allows a power of attorney to survive incapacity and/or disability.

Durable Power of Attorney Issued Either for Health Care or for Property - A written document enabling one individual, the principal, to designate another person(s) to act as his "attorney-in-fact." A durable power of attorney survives the incapacity and/or disability of the principal.

Executor - Estate representative designated in the will by the decedent. An executor may serve without bond if the bond is waived by the decedent.

Key Terms

Felonious Homicide Statutes - Statute that prevents heirs who feloniously participated in the decedent's death from inheriting via the will or state intestacy laws.

Forced Heirship - A state requirement that a certain portion of the decedent's estate be transferred to a spouse and, in some instances, children.

Guardianship Clause - A clause in a will which allows the testator to identify an individual(s) to raise any minor children.

Holographic Will - Handwritten will.

Intestacy - To die without a valid will or to die with a will that does not distribute all property.

Introductory clause - A clause in a will which identifies the testator.

Joint Will - One will executed by two or more individuals jointly that transfers their common interest in property.

Living Will/Advance Medical Directive - Legal document expressing an individual's last wishes regarding life sustaining treatment.

Mutual Will - Two or more identical wills that leave all assets to the reciprocal party.

No-Contest Clause - A clause in a will that discourages heirs from contesting the will by substantially decreasing or eliminating bequests to them if they file a formal legal contest to the will.

Nuncupative Will - Oral will consisting of dying declarations.

Overqualified - A decedent's taxable estate is less than the applicable estate tax credit equivalency, usually the result when too many assets pass to a surviving spouse.

Per Capita - Sometimes called "by the head" allows the deceased person's heirs to move into the generational slot of the deceased heir and inherit accordingly.

Per Stirpes - Sometimes called "taking by representation" directs that the deceased person's designated share of an estate is transferred to his heirs.

Power of Attorney - Legal document that authorizes an agent to act on a principal's behalf.

Principal - The grantor giver of a power of attorney.

Key Terms

Reciprocal Will - Two or more identical wills that leave all assets to the reciprocal party.

Residuary Clause - A clause in a will which directs the transfer of the balance of any assets not previously bequeathed or distributed.

Self Proving Clause - A clause in a will which involves the notary signing a notarized declaration that he/she witnessed the testator and witnesses sign the will.

Side Instruction Letter - Also known as a personal instruction letter, details the testator's wishes regarding the disposition of tangible possessions (household goods), the disposition of the decedent's body, and funeral arrangements. A side instruction letter is not legally binding, but generally followed.

Simultaneous Death Clause - A clause in a will that establishes a presumption of which person died first in simultaneous death situations.

Situs - The place, generally referring to the state, where property is located.

Sound Mind - A person's mental capacity.

Springing Power - The agent's power "springs" into existence upon some defined event or determination.

Statutory Will - A will meeting state statutes generally drawn up by an attorney and signed in the presence of witnesses.

Survivorship Clause - A clause in a will requiring that the legatee survive for a specific period in order to inherit under the will. The bequest will qualify for the marital deduction if the property transfers to the surviving spouse and the time period of the survivorship clause is six months or less.

Sweetheart Will - Two wills executed by spouses that leave all assets to the other spouse.

Tax-Appointment Clause - A clause in a will directing which assets will bear the payment of any debts and estate taxes.

Testate - When a decedent dies with a valid will.

Testator - Writer of a will.

Will - A legal document that provides the testator, or will maker, the opportunity to control the distribution of property, appoint an executor and avoid the state's intestacy law distribution scheme.

1. List the basic documents used in estate planning.

2. What problems arise for someone who dies intestate?

3. Briefly define the types of wills.

4. List the common provisions in a valid will.

5. Briefly list and define at least three other additional clauses found in wills.

6. What is a living will?

7. Why should a living will be prepared in advance?

8. Identify a reason to use a living will.

9. What is a power of attorney?

10. Identify and discuss the parties to a power of attorney.

11. Identify a reason to use a power of attorney.

12. What is a durable power of attorney?

13. What is a springing durable power of attorney?

14. What is a side instruction letter?

15. Identify some examples of instructions included in a side instruction letter.

1. Carl is married and owns and manages several rental properties. He is concerned that if he became incapacitated, the properties would not be properly managed and his tenants would be upset. Of the following arrangements, which one could fulfill Carl's desire to plan for the management of his rental properties in the case of his unanticipated physical or mental incapacity?

    a. A durable power of attorney.

    b. Owning the property as joint tenancy.

    c. Owning the property as tenancy by the entirety.

    d. All of the above.

2. Donald drafted his own will utilizing the "Will-Maker" software that he purchased at the local office supply store and sends it to you for a review. In your first review of the will, you look for which of the following most common provisions?

    a. A left-over clause.

    b. A statement of the domicile of the testator.

    c. A primary clause.

    d. A specific bequest of property owned tenancy by the entirety.

3. After listening to a popular radio financial planning talk show, Deborah decided to grant a durable power of attorney to her neighbor, Jimmy. All of the following statements regarding the durable power of attorney are correct except?

    a. At the creation of the durable power of attorney, Deborah must be at least 18 years old and competent.

    b. The power can spring at a certain age or event.

    c. After Deborah's death, the power remains in force.

    d. If Deborah becomes disabled, the power remains in force.

4. Claudette's cousin John gave her a general power of appointment over his assets. Disregarding any fidicuary problems, which of the following is not true regarding the power?

    a. Claudette can pay for her own groceries with her cousin's money.

    b. Claudette can pay for John's groceries with John's money.

    c. Claudette's gross estate will include John's assets if Claudette dies before John.

    d. The general power of appointment only allows Claudette to appoint John's assets for expenditures related to health, education, maintenance, or support.

5. Which of the following documents appoints a surrogate decision-maker for health care?

    a. Durable power of attorney for health care.

    b. General power of appointment.

    c. Life insurance beneficiary designation.

    d. All of the above.

6. Which type of will is handwritten and does not generally require a witness?

    a. Holographic.

    b. Oral.

    c. Nuncupative.

    d. Statutory.

7. Which type of will complies with the statutes of the domiciliary state and is drawn by an attorney?

    a. Holographic.

    b. Oral.

    c. Nuncupative.

    d. Statutory.

8. While he was in the hospital, Emile told his wife that if he died he wanted to give his fishing tackle to his son, Joseph; his golf equipment to his son, Joshua; his truck to his daughter, Abigail; and everything else to her (his wife). Emile died the next day without writing anything that he told his wife, but a nurse and another patient were in the room and heard his declarations. What type of will does Emile have, if any?

    a. Holographic.

    b. Nuncupative.

    c. Statutory.

    d. Emile does not have a will.

9. Of the following, which is not a clause commonly found in a will?

    a. Introductory clause.

    b. Payment of debts clause.

    c. Payment of taxes clause.

    d. Conclusory clause.

10. Which of the following clauses are commonly found in a will?

    1. Residuary clause.

    2. Secondary clause.

    3. Witness attestation clause.

    4. Simultaneous death clause.

       a. 1 only.

       b. 2 and 3.

       c. 1, 3, and 4.

       d. 1, 2, 3, and 4.

11. Which of the following clauses in a will would detail the required amount of time a beneficiary must live following the death of the decedent to receive a bequest?

       a. Survivorship clause.

       b. Living clause.

       c. Remaining life clause.

       d. Simultaneous death clause.

12. Jenny's will leaves her car to her brother, her boat to her sister, and her vacation home to her cousin. Her will directs the remainder of her assets to be divided equally among her two children. Jenny's will directs all debts and taxes to come from the children's assets. Of the following, which are included in Jenny's will?

    1. Residuary clause.

    2. Specific bequests.

    3. Payment of debts and taxes clause.

       a. 1 only.

       b. 3 only.

       c. 1 and 3.

       d. 1, 2, and 3.

13. Glen's will leaves all of his property to his wife. If she does not survive him by more than eight months, the property will transfer to Glen's only son. Glen dies on April 13 and his wife dies the following January 12. Of the following statements, which is true?

       a. Glen's property will transfer to his son.

       b. Glen's property will not transfer to his wife.

       c. Glen's property will transfer to his wife, but the property will not be eligible for the unlimited marital deduction in Glen's estate.

       d. Glen's property will transfer to his wife and the property will be eligible for the unlimited marital deduction in Glen's estate.

14. Jorge spent four hours with his attorney drafting his will and ensuring that the will accounted for everything. The will was signed, witnessed, and notarized before it was filed away in the attorney's safety deposit box. Two years later, Jorge reviews the will and determines that he had forgotten to account for grandchildren not yet born at the time the will was written. Which of the following would be the least expensive way for Jorge to add in this new language?

    a. Write a codicil.

    b. Add a generation-skipping transfer clause to his current will.

    c. Revoke the prior will and write a new will.

    d. Issue a disclaimer indicating his intentions.

15. Maxine is terminally ill. Her doctors gave her twenty-four months to live thirty-six months ago. Maxine has decided that she does not want to be placed on life support. Which document will direct Maxine's doctors to refrain from putting her on life support?

    a. Living will.

    b. Power of attorney.

    c. Durable power of attorney.

    d. General power of appointment.

16. Donald agreed to sell his house to his brother, but could not attend the closing date of the sale (act of sale). Of the following options, which would allow Donald's mother to attend the closing and sign the necessary documents on Donald's behalf?

    a. Living will.

    b. Advanced real estate directive.

    c. Power of attorney.

    d. Side instruction letter.

17. As part of his military duties, Matthew has been called to active duty. Six years ago, in anticipation of being called to service, Matthew gave his brother a power of attorney over all of his property that should only be effective when Matthew is on active duty. Of the following, what should this power of attorney include?

    1. Springing powers.

    2. Durable powers.

    3. Limited powers.

    4. General powers.

        a. 4 only.

        b. 1 and 2.

        c. 3 and 4.

        d. 1, 2, and 3.

18. Martin has given his father, Edward, a springing durable power of attorney over his real estate holdings. The power of attorney springs if Martin is ever out of the country. Of the following statements regarding this power, which is not true?

    a. If Martin becomes disabled while travelling in Italy, Edward can continue making decisions regarding the real estate.

    b. If Martin dies while travelling in Taiwan, Edward can continue making decisions regarding the real estate under the power of attorney.

    c. Martin can revoke the power at any time.

    d. Edward can do anything that Martin can do with respect to the real estate.

19. Bob has been a party animal his entire life. Many times, after his late night partying, Bob has been heard telling his friends that when he dies he wants his friends to throw a party in his honor. He tells them that he has even set aside some funds in his estate to pay for the party. If Bob is serious, in what document should he include this type of information?

    a. Will.

    b. Living will.

    c. Side instruction letter.

    d. Durable power of attorney.

20. Match the following characteristics:

_____ Survives incapacity	A. Durable power of attorney
Survives death	B. Nondurable power of attorney
_____ Can be revoked by a competent party	C. Both
	D. Neither

Quick Quiz Explanations

Quick Quiz 2.1

1. False. Noncupative wills are oral, not written, wills.
2. False. While it is possible to a will to control the disposition of all property, it is common to have some property pass by contract or by law.
3. True.
4. True.
5. False. Holographic wills are drawn by the testator and are in the testator's own handwriting.

Quick Quiz 2.2

1. True.
2. False. If a survivorship clause applies to a spouse and requires the spouse to survive the decedent by more than six months, transfers to the spouse will not qualify for the marital deduction.
3. False. While a survivorship clause often eliminates the need for a simultaneous death clause, a simultaneous death clause does not eliminate the need for a survivorship clause.

Quick Quiz 2.3

1. True.
2. False. Side letters of instruction are not binding in the probate process, but the property transfers that are covered in the side letter of instruction are probate transfers.
3. False. Will contests can never be eliminated although use of no-contest clauses can minimize the likelihood that they will occur.

Quick Quiz 2.4

1. True.
2. True.
3. False. All powers of attorney may be revoked at any time by a competent principal.

Quick Quiz 2.5

1. False. A durable power of attorney for health care does not typically direct the termination of life-sustaining treatment, although this is allowed in some states.
2. True.
3. False. A living will is concerned with the provision or withholding of life-sustaining treatment. It does not direct the transfer of property during life.

Types of Property Interests

OWNERSHIP AND TRANSFER OF PROPERTY

INTRODUCTION

In our legal system, all property interests are classified into one of three categories: (1) real property, (2) tangible personal property, or (3) intangible personal property. **Real property** (realty) includes land and anything permanently attached to the land (such as buildings, trees, and items permanently affixed to buildings, called fixtures). **Tangible personal property** consists of all property that is not realty (not affixed to the land and generally movable) and that has physical substance. **Intangible personal property** is property that is not real property and is

Key Concepts

Underline/highlight the answers to these questions as you read:

1. Identify the three types of property and examples of each.

2. Identify the characteristics of fee simple ownership.

without physical substance (such as stocks, bonds, patents, and copyrights). Some types of property require a state title as proof of ownership. Examples of titled property include real estate, automobiles (assuming the state has a motor vehicle title law), stocks, bonds, bank accounts, and retirement accounts. Other property, such as household goods, may not have a specific title. State law determines the forms of ownership interest available as well as the ways in which property interests can be transferred from one person to another during lifetime or at death.

Alternative types or forms of property interest vary from state to state. Thus, financial planning professionals need a working knowledge of the various forms of property interests and how each is transferred. Depending on the client's objectives and the way in which the client intends to transfer the property during life or at death, clients need to be properly advised as to the appropriate ownership form.

PROPERTY INTERESTS (TITLE AND OWNERSHIP)

State law classifies the interest an owner has in property based on how the property is held (referred to as legal form of ownership) by the owner. Common among these legal forms of ownership are fee simple, tenancy in common, joint tenancy, tenancy by the entirety, and community property. In addition, some ownership interests in property represent less than complete ownership and are referred to as partial interests. Partial interests in property include life estates, usufruct interests, and term interests.

SOLE OWNERSHIP - FEE SIMPLE

Fee simple ownership is the complete ownership of property by one individual who possesses all ownership rights associated with the property, including the right to use, sell, gift, alienate, convey, or bequeath the property. The key characteristic of fee simple ownership is that the owner has the unfettered right to transfer his ownership interest in the property during lifetime (gift, sale) or at death (will). Fee simple ownership is the most common way to own property interests today.

The ability to use, consume, or dispose of one's property in the form of fee simple is often referred to as fee simple absolute. The entire fair market value of a fee simple property interest is included in the owner's gross estate for federal estate tax purposes. When a person dies owning fee simple property, that property is passed to the decedent's heirs (or whomever else the decedent specifies) through the probate process (discussed in Chapter 4) by virtue of the will or, where no will exists, by virtue of the state intestacy laws. If, however, real property is located in a state that is not the **residence domiciliary** (decedent's state of residence) of the decedent, it will be subject to **ancillary probate** (probate in a state where the owner is not domiciled) in the state of situs.

Quick Quiz 3.1

Highlight the answer to these questions:

1. Examples of real property are land, automobiles, and stocks.
   a. True
   b. False

2. In a fee simple ownership, the joint tenants must agree to sever.
   a. True
   b. False

3. Fee simple property owned by a decedent is included in the owner's gross estate for federal estate tax purposes.
   a. True
   b. False

False, False, True.

When someone owns property in fee simple, he can mortgage that property and use it in any way he desires. Of course, jurisdictional restrictions may place reasonable limits on the use of property. For example, if someone owns land in the middle of an urban area, certain zoning laws may prohibit the owner from using the land to hunt, conduct outdoor concerts, or engage in other types of activities that could endanger others or interfere with the rights other people have to the quiet enjoyment of their own property.

EXHIBIT 3.1

Number of Owners	Only 1
Right to Transfer	Freely
Automatic Survivorship Feature	No, transfers at death via will or intestacy laws
Included in the Gross Estate	Yes, 100%
Included in the Probate Estate	Yes, 100%

TENANCY IN COMMON (TIC)

Tenancy in common is an interest in property held by two or more related or unrelated persons. Each owner is referred to as a tenant in common. Tenancy in common is the most common type of joint ownership between non-spouses. Each person holds an undivided, but not necessarily equal, interest in the entire property. Each co-owner does not own a designated portion of the property, instead he owns an interest in the entire property. For example, if Jim and Bill own a two story home together, Jim does not own the top floor and Bill does not own the bottom floor. Instead, they each own a percentage of the entire house, and both are entitled to use the entire property.

The property interest is treated as if it were owned outright and each owner's interest can be used, sold, donated, placed in trust, willed, or transferred via the state intestacy laws at the owner's death (unless restricted by contract or agreement). On its own, property held as tenancy in common does not avoid probate. Each party shares in the income and expenses of the property in proportion to his interest.

Usually, co-owners are not liable for the debts of the other co-owners. Thus, a creditor of one co-owner is unable to seize the entire property to satisfy a debt of one particular owner. The creditor is only able to seize the portion of the property that corresponds to the ownership interest of that debtor.

Key Concepts

Underline/highlight the answers to these questions as you read:

1. Identify the characteristics of tenancy in common ownership.

2. Identify the characteristics of joint tenancy with right of survivorship.

3. Identify the characteristics of tenancy by the entirety.

4. Identify the characteristics of community property.

EXAMPLE 3.1

Naomi and Andrew, who are not married, own a tract of land together, held as tenants in common. The property is worth $100,000 and each of them owns 50% of the property. Andrew recently defaulted on a personal loan that was not associated with the property and the creditor has placed a lien on his property. The creditor will only be able to seize Andrew's 50% interest in the tract of land. Except in exceptional circumstances, the creditor will not be able to seize Naomi's portion. If the creditor ultimately forces Andrew's 50% interest in the property to be sold to satisfy the debt, Naomi will have a new co-tenant in the property.

EXHIBIT 3.2   **TENANCY IN COMMON OWNERSHIP SUMMARY**

Number of Owners	2 or more
Right to Transfer	Freely without the consent of other co-tenants
Automatic Survivorship Feature	No, transfers at death via will or intestacy laws
Included in the Gross Estate	Usually the FMV of ownership percentage
Included in the Probate Estate	Yes, fair market value of interest
Partitionable	Yes, with or without consent of joint owner

Tenancy in common does not imply an automatic right of survivorship. At the death of a tenant in common, the other tenant in common does not automatically receive the decedent's interest. When an owner of a tenancy in common interest dies, his interest will pass through the probate process and will be retitled in accordance with his will or the state intestacy laws. The fair market value of a tenant in common's ownership interest is included in his gross estate for federal estate tax purposes. If an owner transfers his interest to a new owner, the new owner receives the transferor's share of ownership, and holds the property with the other tenants in common.

If tenants in common cannot agree on the management of the property or no longer want to own the property jointly, they can partition, or sever, the property. If all tenants in common do not agree to sever, the right to partition can be requested of a court without the permission of the other tenants in common. Once the property has been severed, each former tenant in common will own a piece of the original property in fee simple.

Usually, each tenant in common will have an interest proportional to his financial contribution. On occasion, however, a tenant in common's share of ownership in the property will be of greater proportional share than his pro rata contribution. In such a case, a gift has been made from one party to another.

EXAMPLE 3.2

If Carla and Brian agree to purchase property for $100,000, and Carla pays $60,000 and Brian pays $40,000, but they agree to own the property tenancy in common 50% each, Carla has made a gift to Brian of $10,000 (the value of a 10% interest in the property).

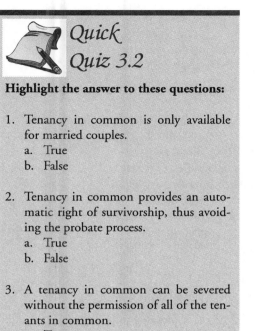
Property owned tenancy in common is included in the tenant's gross estate to the extent of the tenant's ownership percentage.

Kayli and Brody own a tract of land, titled tenancy in common. Kayli contributed $75,000 and Brody contributed $25,000. Assuming Brody died today, the value of the jointly held property included in his gross estate is 25% of the fair market value of the property. If Kayli died she would have included 75% of the fair market value in her gross estate. In this example, it is irrelevant whether they are married; the answer will be the same.

EXAMPLE 3.3

JOINT TENANCY WITH RIGHT OF SURVIVORSHIP (JTWROS)

Joint tenancy is an interest in property held by two or more related or unrelated persons called joint tenants. Each person holds an undivided, equal interest in the whole property. Each joint tenant shares equally in the income and expenses of the property in proportion to his interest.

A right of survivorship is normally implied with this form of ownership, and at the death of the first joint tenant, the decedent's interest transfers to the other joint tenants outside of the probate process according to state titling law. Because of this right of survivorship, joint tenancy is often called joint tenancy with right of survivorship (JTWROS).

Unlike tenancy in common, in some instances co-owners may be liable for the debts of the other co-owners to the extent of the property held in joint tenancy. Thus, a creditor of one co-owner may be able to seize the entire property to satisfy a debt of one particular owner.

EXAMPLE 3.4	

Naomi and Andrew own a tract of land together, held JTWROS. The property is worth $100,000 with each of them owning 50% of the property. Andrew recently defaulted on a loan and the creditor has placed a lien on his property. The creditor may be able to seize the entire piece of property to satisfy Andrew's debt depending on the state law.

In the event joint tenants cannot agree on the management of the property, or no longer want to own the property jointly, any joint tenant can sever his interest in the property without the consent of the other joint tenants. After the property is severed, each former joint tenant will hold his interest in fee simple if the property has been divided and there is no longer joint ownership, or tenancy in common, if joint ownership remains.

Quick Quiz 3.3

Highlight the answer to these questions:

1. Because of the implied right of survivorship, only related parties can enter into a joint tenancy.
   a. True
   b. False

2. The actual contribution rule does not apply to married persons where the married couple owns property JTWROS.
   a. True
   b. False

3. Tom created a joint checking account for himself and his cousin, Bill, with a $50,000 deposit. Because Bill has every right to withdraw the money at anytime, for federal gift tax purposes Tom has made a gift to Bill.
   a. True
   b. False

False, True, False.

EXHIBIT 3.3	JOINT TENANCY WITH RIGHT OF SURVIVORSHIP OWNERSHIP SUMMARY

Number of Owners	2 or more
Right to Transfer	Freely without consent
Automatic Survivorship Feature	Yes, transfers at death to other owners
Included in the Gross Estate	Yes, FMV times the % contributed
Included in the Probate Estate	No
Partitionable	Yes, with or without consent of joint owner

While JTWROS property avoids the costs and delays of probate, it is still included in the decedent's gross estate to the extent of the decedent's original contribution percentage. This rule, sometimes known as "the **actual contribution rule**," does not apply to spouses who are named as joint tenants. Spouses named as joint tenants are legally deemed to have each contributed 50 percent of the financial consideration to purchase the property regardless of the actual source of funding.

Tom purchased a piece of real estate and titled the property JTWROS with his son, Paul. Paul did not make any financial contribution to the purchase of the property. When this transaction occurred Tom made a gift to Paul of one-half of the value of the property. When Tom dies, 100 percent of the value of this property will be included in Tom's gross estate even though he made a gift of 50%.

EXAMPLE 3.5

Even though Tom only had a legal right to 50% of the property, and had made a gift to Paul for the other 50%, 100% of the value of the property is included in his federal gross estate due to the actual contribution rule. If Paul died first he would initially be presumed to include 100% of the value of property in his gross estate, but when his executor provides proof that Paul did not contribute to the purchase price, none of the value of the property will be included in his gross estate.

Assume instead that Tom purchased a piece of real estate and titled the property JTWROS with his wife, Pauline. Again, Pauline made no financial contribution towards the purchase of the property. In this transaction Tom is deemed to have contributed only 50% because he and Pauline are married. When Tom dies only 50% of the value of the property will be included in his gross estate.

EXAMPLE 3.6

In this example, Pauline gains ownership rights to the property (50%) without ever having contributed to the overall price of property. While a gift has been made to Pauline, the unlimited gift tax marital deduction prevents it from being subject to gift tax (provided that Pauline is a U.S. citizen).

An exception to "the actual contribution rule" exists for gifts of a joint interest in a bank account or Series H bond. In these situations, a completed gift is not made until the non-contributing joint account owner takes a withdrawal from the account for his own personal benefit.

If Tom creates a joint checking account for himself and his son, Paul, by contributing $10,000, Tom has not made a gift to Paul at the date of the contribution. However, if Paul later withdraws any of the money for his own personal benefit, Tom will be deemed to have made a gift to Paul equal to the amount withdrawn at the date of withdrawal.

EXAMPLE 3.7

TENANCY BY THE ENTIRETY (TE)

Tenancy by the entirety is very similar to joint tenancy between a husband and wife. To understand this form of ownership it is important to remember the following four key components:

1. tenancy by the entirety applies to joint ownership only between married couples,
2. neither tenant is able to sever their interest without the consent of the other tenant (spouse),
3. property ownership interest is automatically transferred to the surviving spouse upon death, and
4. it may involve the ownership interest of either real or personal property.

In most respects, tenancy by the entirety is simply a JTWROS that can only occur between a husband and wife. Tenancy by the entirety exists throughout the length of the marriage and terminates upon divorce or death. Upon divorce, the tenancy by the entirety form of ownership ceases to exist, thus transforming the ownership interests of both parties to some form of joint ownership, usually tenants in common.

In most states, neither tenant (spouse) is able to sever their interest in property titled tenancy by the entirety without the consent of the other tenant (spouse). If either husband or wife wishes to transfer their share of interest in the property to a third party (through sale or gift), both parties must join (or consent) in a mutual transfer of the property. This stipulation helps to prevent any termination of the other spouse's right of survivorship by transfer of property to a third party. In such cases, the interest in the property between the remaining tenant (spouse) and the new third party owner becomes a joint tenancy or tenancy in common. Spouses may choose to convert their tenancy by the entirety ownership into a tenancy in common or a joint tenancy. The form of property ownership is simply changed without triggering any gift tax consequences.

EXHIBIT 3.4   **TENANCY BY THE ENTIRETY OWNERSHIP SUMMARY**

Number of Owners	2 - spouses only
Right to Transfer	Need consent of other spouse
Automatic Survivorship Feature	Yes, transfers at death to other spouse
Included in the Gross Estate	Yes, always 50% of FMV
Included in the Probate Estate	No
Partitionable	Not without consent of spouse / joint owner

For property held as tenancy by the entirety at the death of the first tenant, the decedent's property ownership is passed to the surviving spouse according to state law titling requirements.

Because the state law provides for retitling upon presentation of a certified death certificate, there is no need for this property to go through the probate process to be retitled in the name of the surviving spouse. Like property owned as JTWROS between spouses, 50 percent of the value of the property held as tenants by the entirety is included in the gross estate of the first spouse to die, regardless of the amount the deceased spouse contributed to the purchase price of the property.

COMMUNITY PROPERTY AND SEPARATE PROPERTY IN COMMUNITY REGIMES

Community property is a civil law originating statutory regime under which married individuals own an equal undivided interest in all property accumulated during their marriage. During marriage, the income of each spouse is considered community property. Property acquired before the marriage and property received by gift or inheritance during the marriage retains its status as separate property. However, if any separate property is commingled with community property, it is often assumed to be community property. The states following the community property regime are Arizona, California, Idaho, Louisiana, Nevada, New Mexico, Texas, Washington, and Wisconsin (see Exhibit 3.5). In addition, Alaska allows residents and nonresidents to enter into community property agreements permitting in-state property to be treated as community property. Community property regimes may vary slightly from state to state; thus, a thorough understanding of a client's state laws is needed for proper planning.

EXHIBIT 3.5

COMMUNITY-PROPERTY STATES

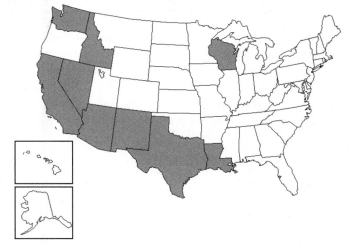

Community property does not usually have an automatic right of survivorship feature although some states, including Texas and California, have a survivorship option. When the first spouse dies, one half of the value of the property will pass through the probate process for retitling per the direction of the decedent's will or the state intestacy law. Each spouse's one-half interest will also be included in their own federal gross estate.

Community property status can be dissolved by death, divorce, or by agreement between the spouses. Specifically, one spouse can gift his half of the community property to the other spouse, thereby creating separate property owned entirely by the donee spouse. Because there is an unlimited marital deduction for gift taxes (as discussed in Chapter 5), such a gift would not create any gift tax liability. This type of gift may occur when a couple moves from a community-property state to a common law (separate property) state in which the couple intends to make their permanent domicile. Otherwise, community property retains its community property status.

When a couple moves from a common law (separate property) state into a community-property state, the property acquired before the move retains its separate property status, unless the couple agrees to treat the property as community property. Any property acquired subsequent to the couple's move into the community-property state is considered community property unless statutory law allows, and the couple chooses, to formally opt out of the state's community property regime.

EXHIBIT 3.6	COMMUNITY PROPERTY OWNERSHIP SUMMARY

Number of Owners	2 - spouses only
Right to Transfer	Need consent of other spouse
Automatic Survivorship Feature	No, transfers via will or intestacy law
Included in the Gross Estate	Always 50% of community property + 100% of separate property
Included in the Probate Estate	Always 50% of community property + 100% of separate property not retitled otherwise
Partitionable	Not without consent of spouse / joint owner

In certain community-property states, a **quasi-community property** regime is recognized for a couple moving from a common law (separate property) state to that community-property state. Quasi-community property is property that would be community property had the couple been living in the community-property state at the time of acquisition. Quasi-community property is treated just like community property at the death of either spouse, or at the time of divorce. Aside from treating the property as community property at death or divorce, quasi-community property is treated as separate property.

As will be discussed in Chapter 6, a decedent's property is valued for federal estate tax purposes as of his date of death or the alternate valuation date (six months after death). Upon distribution of the property, the decedent's heirs will receive an adjusted basis equal to the value used in the federal estate tax calculation (date of death or alternate valuation date). When property owned jointly is included in a decedent's gross estate, the individual who receives such property will generally receive a new tax basis in the inherited portion equal to the fair market value at the date of death or the alternate valuation date (if elected) and the other joint owners will retain their original adjusted basis in the portion they owned originally.

By contrast, community property provides that at the death of the first spouse both halves of community property are stepped to fair market value even though the decedent only owned 50 percent of the property. Generally, this new tax basis is higher than the old tax basis and will thus reduce future capital gains. Only property owned as community property is afforded this tax basis treatment. Recall that in certain situations, a married couple can own property, even within a community-property state, as separate property. Such separate property would only receive a new tax basis at the death of the separate property owner.

EXAMPLE 3.8

Ann and Bill have lived in a community-property state all 32 years of their marriage. Ann and Bill purchased a home 20 years ago for $120,000 (each would have a deemed $60,000 adjusted basis in the home). The value of their home has appreciated to $2,000,000. When Bill dies, his executor will include 1/2 of the value of the home, equal to $1,000,000, in Bill's gross estate for federal estate tax purposes. Bill's heirs (not necessarily Ann - community property does not have an automatic right of survivorship) will have an adjusted basis in 1/2 of the home of $1,000,000. Ann will also receive a new income tax basis equal to $1,000,000 for her 1/2 of the home.

In this example, it is important to remember that Bill can bequeath his share of community property to whomever he wishes (assuming there are not any state statutes limiting his ability to do so). However, Bill could have bequeathed his 1/2 to Ann and she would then own the entire house with an adjusted basis of $2,000,000.

EXAMPLE 3.9

If Bill and Ann had lived in a common law (separate property) state and owned the property tenancy in common, only Bill's heirs would receive a new basis in 1/2 of the home. Ann would continue to own her 1/2 of the home with a tax basis equal to her original $60,000 adjusted basis.

EXAMPLE 3.10

Jim and Carol lived in Illinois (a common-law state) since their marriage in 1978. In 1982, Jim and Carol purchased a vacation home in California for $50,000 and titled the property joint tenancy with right of survivorship. In 2001, Jim and Carol moved to California, but did not declare all property community property. When Jim died in 2002, Jim's executor included 1/2 of the value of the California vacation home in Jim's federal gross estate at $150,000 (the home was valued at Jim's date of death at $300,000). Because of the right of survivorship, Carol is the beneficiary and receives Jim's 1/2 of the home with a tax basis of $150,000. Because the property was not community property, Carol does not receive a new tax basis for her original 1/2 of the home, but keeps her old tax basis of $25,000 ($50,000/2). Carol now owns 100% of the home but with an income tax basis equal to $175,000 ($25,000 + $150,000 = $175,000). Had Carol and Jim declared all the property community property, Carol would have received a new tax basis on her 1/2 of the home and would have a tax basis equal to $300,000 in the property. An increase in tax basis could greatly affect any capital gains tax on a future sale of the property.

OTHER OWNERSHIP TOPICS

PARTIAL OWNERSHIP INTERESTS

Certain planning scenarios call for the creation, or transfer, of less than a full and complete ownership of property under state law. Three of the most common types of property titling that represent partial ownership interests are the life estate, the usufruct, and the term interest.

Life Estate

A **life estate** is an interest in property that ceases upon the death of the owner of the interest and provides the owner of such interest with a right to the income or the right to use property, or both. Upon termination of the life estate (at the death of the life tenant), the property is transferred to the remainder beneficiary (who owns the underlying property and any right to income or use at the death of the life estate owner). Life estate interests are generally excluded from the life tenant's taxable estate, since they have no disposition powers associated

with the property. A common example of a life estate is when one person leaves another person the use of their beach property for the life of the other person. For example, if John bequeathed his vacation home to his mother for the rest of her life and then to his brother at his mother's death, John's mom would have a life estate in the property, and his brother would have a remainder interest.

Usufruct

A **usufruct** is a civil law concept (only available in Louisiana) similar to a life estate under common law rules. A usufruct provides the holder with the right to use property and/or the right to income from property similar to a life estate. At the death of the usufructuary (the person who owns the usufruct interest), the property passes to the naked owners (remaindermen) in full ownership interest. For example, when Steve dies he leaves his home to his children subject to a usufruct on behalf of Steve's mother. Steve's mother can enjoy the property for her life, but the children own the home. Upon the death of Steve's mother, the complete interest in the home will pass to his children.

Term Interest

A **term interest** is an interest in property that grants the holder the right to use the property for a definite term (number of years). A term interest may grant a right to income or use of the property or both. At the end of the term interest, the property is transferred to the remainderman.

LEGAL VS. EQUITABLE OWNERSHIP

Legal ownership implies that a party has title to the property. Generally, the legal owner possesses all rights, duties, responsibilities, and privileges associated with the property. Only the person with legal ownership of property can convey that property to others.

Equitable ownership is the economic right to enjoy the benefits of the property. Equitable ownership is a form of ownership that is typically associated with use of the property. Even though a person possessing legal ownership holds absolute title to the property, an equitable owner holds temporary title to the property for as long as he has legal use of the property. This holds true even though the absolute title may be in the name of someone else. The equitable owner reaps the rewards of property ownership through the use of the property. Benefits associated with the use of the property include:

- the right to possess the property,
- the right to enjoy the property,
- the right to use the property, and
- the right to receive income from the property.

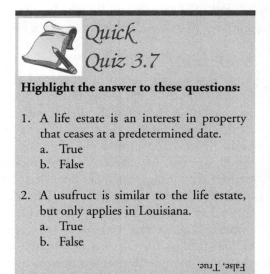

Quick Quiz 3.7

Highlight the answer to these questions:

1. A life estate is an interest in property that ceases at a predetermined date.
   a. True
   b. False

2. A usufruct is similar to the life estate, but only applies in Louisiana.
   a. True
   b. False

False, True.

A common example of a technique that splits legal and equitable title is a trust. In the case of trusts, the trustee has the legal title to the property held in trust and acts as a fiduciary for the holder of the equitable interest or the beneficiary of the trust. We will explore this in more detail in Chapter 8.

CUMULATIVE SUMMARY AND EXAMPLE

As described in this chapter, each property ownership type has a unique combination of features and characteristics. The five most important planning questions concerning the various property ownership forms are:

1. What value or percentage of value is included in a decedent's gross estate?
2. Is the property included in the decedent's probate estate?
3. Does the property have an automatic right of survivorship?
4. Will the value of the property qualify for the unlimited marital deduction?
5. Can an interest in the property, if jointly held, or an interest in community property, be partitioned without the consent of the other joint or community owner?

FEE SIMPLE

Fee simple is full outright ownership by one person. The fair market value of property owned as fee simple is fully included in a decedent's gross estate, but if the property is transferred to the surviving spouse, the fair market value of the property is eligible for the unlimited marital deduction. Also, because fee simple property does not automatically pass to another person at the decedent's death, the full fair market value of fee simple property is included in the decedent's probate estate.

TENANCY IN COMMON

Tenancy in common is a joint interest in property between two or more individuals who can choose to partition their interests without the consent of the other owners. The fair market value of a decedent's ownership interest in tenancy in common property is included in the decedent's gross estate. If the property is transferred by probate to the decedent's surviving spouse, the fair market value of the decedent's interest in the property is eligible for the unlimited marital deduction. The decedent's interest in tenancy in common property does not automatically transfer, but must pass through probate for retitling.

JOINT TENANCY WITH RIGHT OF SURVIVORSHIP

Joint tenancy with right of survivorship is an equal joint interest in property between two or more individuals who can choose to partition their interest without the consent of the other joint tenants even when the joint tenant is a spouse. At the death of one joint tenant, his interest automatically passes to the surviving property owners, and therefore the property is not included in a decedent's probate estate. The fair market value of the decedent's interest (as determined under the actual contribution rule) in the property is included in the decedent's gross estate, but if the property is owned with the spouse as joint tenancy with rights of survivorship the value of the property is eligible for the unlimited marital deduction. In the case of a spousal joint tenant, the contribution rule will always assume a 50 percent contribution from each spouse, regardless of the amount that was actually contributed by each spouse.

TENANCY BY THE ENTIRETY

Tenancy by the entirety is joint ownership of property between a husband and wife that cannot be partitioned without the consent of the other spouse. At the death of the first spouse, the property is automatically transferred to the surviving spouse, and therefore does not go through probate. Fifty percent of the fair market value of the property is included in a decedent's gross estate as there is a deemed 50 percent contribution rule. Because the property automatically transfers to the surviving spouse, the value of the property is eligible for the unlimited marital deduction.

COMMUNITY PROPERTY

Community property is a property ownership form available only to spouses. Like tenancy by the entirety, each spouse is deemed to have contributed, and to own, 50 percent of the property. A community property interest cannot be partitioned without the consent of the other party. However, unlike the tenancy by the entirety property ownership form, community property does not have an automatic right of survivorship to the surviving spouse, and therefore the decedent's interest is included in the probate estate. Fifty percent of the value of the property is included in the decedent's gross estate, and if the property is transferred to the surviving spouse by will or intestacy, the value of the property transferred to the spouse is eligible for the unlimited marital deduction.

Exhibit 3.7 summarizes and contrasts these five key features and characteristics of each of the different property ownership types.

| EXHIBIT 3.7 | PROPERTY OWNERSHIP KEY FEATURES (SUMMARY) |

Property Ownership Type	Value Included in Gross Estate	Included in Probate Estate	Automatic Survivorship Feature	Qualifies for the Unlimited Marital Deduction	Is the Property Partitionable without Consent?
FEE SIMPLE	100%	Yes 100%	No	Yes, if spouse is the beneficiary	Not applicable
TENANCY IN COMMON	% Owned	Yes % Owned	No	Yes, if spouse is the beneficiary	Yes
JOINT TENANCY WITH RIGHTS OF SURVIVORSHIP	Actual Contribution Rule* % Owned	No	Yes	Yes, if spouse is the beneficiary	Yes
TENANCY BY THE ENTIRETY	50% Deemed Contribution Rule	No	Yes	Yes	No
COMMUNITY PROPERTY	50% Deemed Contribution Rule	Yes 50% of value	No	Yes, if spouse is the beneficiary	No

*Follow the actual contribution rule except when property is jointly owned with a spouse who is always deemed to have contributed 50% of the property's purchase price.

Using the fact pattern below fill in the chart assuming the personal residence was owned using each alternative ownership type. When you are done, check your answers on the next page.

Mandy and Steven had been married for six years. Three years ago, after having their only daughter, Carol, they bought their first home for $250,000. Last year, Steven was killed in a car accident. His will left everything to his daughter. The value of the home at Steven's death was $400,000. Referring to the notes below, complete the following table.

EXAMPLE 3.11

Property Ownership Type	Amount Included in Gross Estate? (Steven)	Amount Included in Probate Estate? (Steven)	Who receives Steven's ownership in the home?	Mandy's income tax basis after Steven's death?	Carol's income tax basis after Steven's death?	Qualifies for Unlimited Marital Deduction
Fee Simple*						
Tenancy in Common**						
Joint Tenancy with Rights of Survivorship with Spouse**						
Tenants by the Entirety**						
Community Property***						

* Assume that Steven had purchased the home with his separate funds for $250,000.

** Assume, at the purchase of the home Steven contributed $150,000 and Mandy contributed $100,000 and held in corresponding percentages unless the method of titling assumes otherwise.

*** Assume the home was purchased with community funds.

The correct answers are provided on following page.

Solution to Example 3.11

Property Ownership Type	Amount Included in Gross Estate? (Steven)	Amount Included in Probate Estate? (Steven)	Who receives Steven's ownership in the home?	Mandy's income tax basis after Steven's death?	Carol's income tax basis after Steven's death?	Qualifies for Unlimited Marital Deduction
Fee Simple*	$400,000	YES $400,000	CAROL	N/A	$400,000	NO
Tenancy in Common**	$240,000	YES $240,000	CAROL	$100,000	$240,000	NO
Joint Tenancy with Rights of Survivorship with Spouse**	$200,000	NO $0	MANDY	$325,000	N/A	YES
Tenancy by the Entirety**	$200,000	NO $0	MANDY	$325,000	N/A	YES
Community Property***	$200,000	YES $200,000	CAROL	$200,000	$200,000	NO

*Assume that Steven had purchased the home with his separate funds for $250,000.

** Assume, at the purchase of the home Steven contributed $150,000 and Mandy contributed $100,000 and held in corresponding percentages unless the method of titling assumes otherwise.

*** Assume the home was purchased with community funds.

Fee Simple: The full fair market value of the property, $400,000, is included in Steven's gross estate because Steven was the full, outright owner of the property. The property is included in Steven's probate estate because fee simple ownership does not provide a right of survivorship and will transfer to Carol as directed by the will. A legatee receives fee simple property at an adjusted basis equal to the fair market value of the property at the decedent's date of death, which, in this case is $400,000. Mandy does not receive any interest in the property, but may have a claim to continue living in the home or some other right granted by her state because she is a spouse.

Tenancy in Common: The full ownership percentage is included in the gross estate thus 60 percent (or the ratio of the Steven's contribution to the original purchase price over the full original purchase price, $150,000/$250,000) of the fair market value at Steven's date of death is included in his gross estate, $240,000 (60% of $400,000). Per the direction of the will, Steven's interest in the property will transfer through the probate process to Carol. Carol will receive the property with an adjusted basis equal to the value reported on Steven's estate tax return, or $240,000, and Mandy will retain her original adjusted basis, equal to her original cash contribution at the purchase date, or $100,000.

Joint Tenancy with Rights of Survivorship (JTWROS): When property is owned JTWROS between a husband and wife, each is assumed to have contributed 50 percent of the value of the property at the original purchase date. Accordingly, Steven's gross estate will include 50 percent of the fair market value of the property at his date of death, or $200,000. With the right of survivorship, the property automatically transfers to Mandy and does not transfer through the probate process. Accordingly, Carol does not receive any interest in the property. Mandy has an adjusted basis in the property equal to her original deemed contribution, $125,000, plus the fair market value included in Steven's gross estate, $200,000, for a total adjusted basis equal to $325,000.

Tenancy by the Entirety: Property owned tenancy by the entirety is just like property owned JTWROS between a husband and wife for all of the matters addressed. A key point to remember, however, is that property owned tenancy by the entirety requires the consent of both spouses to partition the interest, whereas property owned JTWROS, even between spouses, can be partitioned without the consent of the other spouse.

Community Property: If the home is community property, 50 percent of the value, or $200,000, would be included in Steven's gross estate, and his interest would pass through probate to Carol per the direction of the will. Mandy would retain her 50 percent interest and would receive an increased adjusted basis equal to the fair market value of her interest at Steven's date of death, $200,000. Carol's adjusted basis in her 50 percent interest would also be the fair market value at Steven's date of death, $200,000.

Key Terms

Actual Contribution Rule - The value of a decedent's joint interest in property is based on the actual percentage of the original purchase price contributed by the decedent - not the decedent's ownership percentage.

Ancillary Probate - Concurrent second probate process conducted in a non-domiciliary state in which the decedent owns property, which often requires the services of an attorney from that state, and separate court fees.

Community Property - A regime in which married individuals own an equal undivided interest in all of the property accumulated, utilizing either spouse's earnings, during the marriage.

Equitable Ownership - Possession of the economic right to property.

Fee Simple - The complete individual ownership of property with all the rights associated with outright ownership.

Intangible Personal Property - Property that cannot truly be touched such as stocks, bonds, patents, and copyrights.

Joint Tenancy (with right of survivorship) - An undivided interest in property held by two or more related or unrelated persons, generally includes a right of survivorship.

Legal Ownership - Possession of legal title to the property.

Life Estate - An interest in property that ceases upon the death of the owner of a life interest or estate and provides a right to the income or the right to use property or both.

Quasi-Community Property - Property that would be community property had the married couple been living in the community-property state at the time of acquisition (applies to married couples who move from a common law (separate property) state to a community-property state).

Real Property - Property that is land and buildings attached to the land.

Residence Domiciliary - An individual's legal state of residence.

Tangible Personal Property - Property that is not realty and may be touched.

Tenancy by the Entirety - A JTWROS that can only occur between a husband and wife.

Tenancy in Common - An undivided interest in property held by two or more related or unrelated persons.

Term Interest - An interest in property that ceases after a defined period of time.

Usufruct - A Louisiana device similar to a life estate which provides the holder with the right to use property and/or the right to income from the particular property.

DISCUSSION QUESTIONS

1. List and define the three major types of property.

2. List at least three types of property ownership.

3. Define fee simple property ownership.

4. Discuss what happens when a person dies owning property fee simple.

5. Define tenancy in common.

6. Discuss what happens at the death of a tenant in common.

7. Can a tenancy in common be partitioned? If so, how?

8. Discuss the consequences of two people owning property as a tenancy in common with equal interests, but one contributes 70% to the initial purchase price.

9. Define joint tenancy.

10. Define right of survivorship.

11. Can a joint tenancy by partitioned?

12. Discuss the contribution rule and how it affects inclusion in the decedent's gross estate.

13. Define community property.

14. List three common ways to own separate property in a community-property state.

15. Which states recognize community property?

16. Discuss what happens at the death of the first spouse to die when property is held as community property.

17. How can a married couple convert community property into separate property when property is held as community property?

18. Discuss the implications when a married couple moves from a community-property state to a common law (separate property) state.

19. What is quasi-community property?

20. Define life estate.

21. Define usufruct.

22. Who is a remainderman?

23. Define interest for term.

MULTIPLE-CHOICE PROBLEMS

1. Twenty-two years ago, James and Kevin began dating, and 19 years ago, they began living together. Last year, James inherited over $9,000,000 from his grandfather. He wants to ensure that if he dies first, Kevin will be taken care of for the rest of his life. Despite your insistence, James does not have a will, and you have advised him previously that state intestacy laws do not protect same-sex partners. Which of the following asset ownership options would fulfill James' goal of transferring assets to Kevin at his death?

   a. Community property.
   b. Tenancy in common with each other.
   c. Joint tenancy with rights of survivorship.
   d. Tenancy by the entirety.

2. Jim has been married to Rebecca for six years. They are about to buy their first home and have come to you with some questions that they have regarding titling of the home. In your explanation of the different property ownership arrangements, which of the following titling structures can only be entered into by spouses?

   a. Tenancy by the entirety.
   b. Tenancy in common.
   c. Joint tenancy with rights of survivorship.
   d. Fee simple.

3. Which of the following statements regarding joint tenancy with rights of survivorship is correct?

   a. Each tenant may bequeath their interest in the property at their death.
   b. Joint tenancy with rights of survivorship is the same as community property.
   c. Only spouses can establish joint tenancies.
   d. Each tenant under a joint tenancy with rights of survivorship has an undivided interest in the property.

4. Which of the following statements regarding joint tenancy with rights of survivorship is not correct?

   a. At the death of a joint tenant, his interest in the property will transfer to the beneficiary listed in his will.
   b. Property owned JTWROS transfers by operation of law.
   c. Each tenant owns the same fractional share in the property.
   d. During his life, each joint tenant has the right to sever his interest in the property without consent.

5. Which of the following statements regarding community property is not correct?

    a. If one spouse inherits property during the marriage, that property is generally not considered community property.

    b. Assets acquired by either spouse before marriage generally become community property upon their marriage.

    c. Community property assets are included in probate.

    d. If one spouse utilizes his paycheck from work performed during the marriage to purchase property, the property is community property.

6. Of the following types of ownership, which is available for married couples?

    1. Tenancy by the entirety.

    2. Tenancy in common.

    3. JTWROS.

    4. Tenants by marriage.

    a. 1 only.

    b. 1 and 3.

    c. 1, 2, and 3.

    d. 1, 2, 3, and 4.

7. At the death of either partner, a same-sex couple would like to ensure that all property, insurance policies, and retirement plans transfer to the surviving partner. Which of the following will NOT accomplish the couple's goal?

    a. Each partner is listed as the beneficiary of the other partner's life insurance policy.

    b. Each partner is listed as the beneficiary of the other partner's qualified pension plan.

    c. Each partner is a joint tenant in all of the couple's property owned joint tenancy with rights of survivorship.

    d. State intestacy laws.

8. Kim and Tommy have lived in Arizona since their marriage. Kim received an inheritance from her father during their marriage. Kim and Tommy are moving to Massachusetts for a new job and have some questions regarding their move to a common law (separate property) state from a community-property state. Which of the following statements is correct?

   a. When a couple moves from a community-property state to a common law (separate property) state, separate property will generally remain separate property.

   b. When a couple moves from a common law (separate property) state to a community-property state, separate property will generally become community property.

   c. Community property avoids probate at the death of the first spouse and automatically passes to the surviving spouse by operation of law.

   d. To get the step-to fair market value in basis at the death of the first spouse, a couple who lives in a common law (separate property) state can elect to treat their separate property as community property.

9. Dara has owned 100% of the stock of Dara's Baked Goods, a corporation, for 22 years. In the current year, she gifted 50% of the business to her daughter, Sheila, who lives in California. Sheila does not work at the business and reinvests any income in the company. With respect to the transfer of the business interest, which of the following statements is/are correct?

   a. Sheila's 50% interest in Dara's Baked Goods is community property, owned equally by Sheila and her husband.

   b. If Sheila's husband dies tomorrow, both his share of Dara's Baked Goods and Sheila's share of Dara's Baked Goods would receive a step-to fair market value in basis.

   c. Sheila owns 50% of Dara's Baked Goods outright, and the interest will not be considered community property.

   d. If Sheila dies tomorrow, the executor of her estate would include 25% of the value of Dara's Baked Goods in her gross estate.

10. If Paula died with the following property interests, which would not be included in her probate estate?

   a. Community property.

   b. Property held tenants in common.

   c. Death proceeds of life insurance payable to her daughter.

   d. Property owned fee simple.

11. Which of the following statements regarding joint tenancy is correct?

    a. Joint tenancies may only be established between spouses.

    b. Tenancy by the entirety is a special form of joint tenancy only available to residents of Louisiana.

    c. Joint tenancies can only be severed with the permission of a court.

    d. Each joint tenant in a joint tenancy has an undivided, equal interest in the property.

12. Which of the following is considered real property?

    1. Stocks.

    2. Automobile.

    3. House.

    4. Land held for investment.

        a. 3 only.

        b. 1 and 2.

        c. 3 and 4.

        d. 1, 2 and 3.

13. Which of the following is considered tangible property?

    1. Stocks.

    2. Automobile.

    3. Rental house.

    4. Land.

        a. 2 only.

        b. 1 and 2.

        c. 3 and 4.

        d. 1, 2, 3, and 4.

14. Which of the following is considered intangible property?

    1. Stocks.

    2. Patents.

    3. Bonds.

    4. Land held for investment.

        a. 4 only.

        b. 1 and 2.

        c. 2 and 4.

        d. 1, 2, and 3.

15. Which of the following statements regarding fee simple ownership is not true?

    a.   Fee simple ownership is the complete individual ownership of property with all rights associated with outright ownership.

    b.   Property owned as fee simple passes through probate at the death of the owner.

    c.   Property owned as fee simple is excluded from the federal gross estate of the owner.

    d.   Fee simple ownership allows the owner to use, sell, gift, alienate, convey or bequeath the property without others' approval.

16. Erica has come to you for estate planning advice. She has been in a long-term relationship with Judy. Because Erica's family is not aware of the relationship between Judy and Erica, Erica is concerned that at her death, Judy will be overlooked by Erica's family. Of the following recommendations, which would you least likely recommend to fulfill Erica's goal of transferring assets to Judy at Erica's death?

    a.   Transfer the ownership of Erica's real estate investments into Tenancy by the Entirety.

    b.   Name Judy as the beneficiary of Erica's retirement plan.

    c.   Advise Erica against creating a will, specifically bequeathing her property to Judy.

    d.   Name Judy as the beneficiary of Erica's life insurance policy.

17. Three years ago, brothers Darren and Andy, purchased real property and titled it as joint tenancy with right of survivorship. At the time of the purchase, Darren did not have any cash, so Andy paid the $50,000 purchase price himself. Over the next five years, Darren and Andy allocated the income and expenses of the property equally, and luckily for them the value of the property increased to $350,000. If Andy dies this year, how much will his executor include in his federal gross estate as the value of this real property?

    a. $50,000.

    b. $175,000.

    c. $300,000.

    d. $350,000.

18. Three years ago, Jack and Mary, having been married for 3 years, agreed to purchase some real property and titled it as joint tenants with right of survivorship. At the time of the purchase, Mary did not have any cash, so Jack paid the $50,000 purchase price himself. Over the next five years, Jack and Mary allocated the income and expenses of the property equally, and luckily for them the value of the property increased to $350,000. If Jack dies this year, how much will his executor include in his federal gross estate as the value of this real property?

    a. $50,000.

    b. $175,000.

    c. $300,000.

    d. $350,000.

19. Mike travels quite often and wants his daughter to have access to his checking account while he is out of town. For this reason, on October 3, 2006, Mike deposited $100,000 in a checking account. Several years passed and Mike used the funds for normal living expenses, but his daughter never accessed any of the funds. On May 2, 2009, Mike's daughter needed an extra $35,000 to purchase the car of her dreams so she made a withdrawal from the account with full intentions of reimbursing the account. At what date has Mike made a gift to his daughter?

    a. October 3, 2006.

    b. December 31, 2006.

    c. May 2, 2009.

    d. May 31, 2009.

20. Timmy and Bryan agree to purchase a condo at the beach for $200,000 as tenants in common. Bryan will contribute $150,000 of the price, and Timmy will contribute the remaining $50,000. They have agreed to split all income and expenses at 75%/25%, the same as their ownership percentages. What is the gross gift from Bryan to Timmy for the year relating to this property?

    a. $0.

    b. $50,000.

    c. $150,000.

    d. $200,000.

Quick Quiz Explanations

Quick Quiz 3.1

1. False. Automobiles and stocks are examples of tangible and intangible personal property. Land is real property.
2. False. If property is held in fee simple, there are no joint owners / joint tenants.
3. True.

Quick Quiz 3.2

1. False. Tenancy in common ownership is available for spouses, related individuals, and unrelated individuals.
2. False. A tenancy in common interest is a probate asset. It does not have an automatic survivorship feature.
3. True.

Quick Quiz 3.3

1. False. Related and unrelated individuals may enter into a joint tenancy with right of survivorship.
2. True.
3. False. For gift tax purposes, Tom is not deemed to make a gift to Bill until Bill withdraws money for his own use. A gift does not result when the money is deposited into the account.

Quick Quiz 3.4

1. False. A tenancy by the entirety is essentially a joint tenancy with right of survivorship between spouses that cannot be severed without the consent of both spouses.
2. True.

Quick Quiz Explanations

Quick Quiz 3.5

1. False. Only the half interest in the property held as tenants in common that passes through the decedent's estate receives a step-up in basis. The surviving co-tenant's half interest in the property retains its original basis.
2. True.
3. False. As a general rule, there is no right of survivorship associated with community property. Some states, like Texas and California, have passed legislation to allow this.
4. False. Since community property does not typically have a survivorship feature attached to it, the only portion of community property that will qualify for the estate tax marital deduction is that portion that actually passes to the surviving spouse.
5. True.
6. False. When moving from a common law to a community-property state, property either retains its character as separate property or is considered quasi-community property depending on the laws of the state to which the married couple is moving.

Quick Quiz 3.6

1. True.
2. True.
3. False. Quasi-community property is property that was acquired during marriage in a common-law state after a married couple has moved to a community-property state.

Quick Quiz 3.7

1. False. A life estate is an interest in property that ceases upon the death of the owner of the interest.
2. True.

The Probate Process

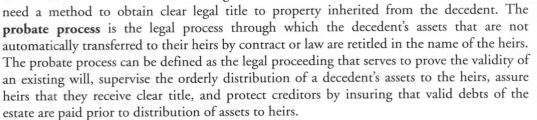

INTRODUCTION

THE PROBATE PROCESS DEFINED

When a person dies, there are many things the survivors must do. Relatives and friends must be notified, funeral and burial arrangements must be made, and the survivors must begin to pick up the pieces and rebuild their lives without the decedent. After facing the emotional distress that naturally occurs upon the death of a loved one, the survivors must begin to look at their financial security and the process of transferring the decedent's assets from the decedent's estate to the heirs. Surviving heirs

Key Concepts

Underline/highlight the answers to these questions as you read:

1. Define the probate process.

need a method to obtain clear legal title to property inherited from the decedent. The **probate process** is the legal process through which the decedent's assets that are not automatically transferred to their heirs by contract or law are retitled in the name of the heirs. The probate process can be defined as the legal proceeding that serves to prove the validity of an existing will, supervise the orderly distribution of a decedent's assets to the heirs, assure heirs that they receive clear title, and protect creditors by insuring that valid debts of the estate are paid prior to distribution of assets to heirs.

TESTATE VS. INTESTATE SUCCESSION

Chapter 2 discussed in detail the basic estate planning documents including wills and their applicable provisions. The preparation of the will is often considered the first step in an overall estate plan, since it expresses some or all of the decedent's transfer wishes regarding property. In theory, every person who dies has an estate plan. If the decedent did not establish his own estate plan by executing a will, the state in which he is domiciled has created one for him under the state intestacy laws. The state intestacy laws specify to whom assets will be transferred for a person who does not validly transfer assets by will, contract law, state titling law, or trust law.

A person who dies with a valid will is said to die testate, whereas a person who dies without a valid will is said to die intestate. A person named in a will to receive property is referred to as a **legatee**, while a person who receives property under the state intestacy laws is called an **heir**. In addition, the term devisee is used to refer to a person who inherits real property under the will. Historically, the term heir was reserved only for those individuals who received property under the intestacy laws, but the term is now used more loosely and may refer to any individual who inherits property from the decedent, even under a will. A planner should understand these distinctions since there are legal differences in some states, but realize that clients and non professionals may not use the terminology appropriately in practice.

TRANSFER OF ASSETS

Assets may be transferred and retitled through the probate process, by contract law, by state titling law, or by state trust law.

ADVANTAGES OF PROBATE

Transferring assets through the probate process has several advantages over transferring assets outside of probate. The central advantage to the probate process is the protection of the individuals involved in the probate process. The advantaged parties include the decedent, the decedent's named heirs, unnamed heirs, and creditors. The following is a discussion of the more common advantages of the probate process.

Protect the Decedent

When individuals die testate (with a valid will), they are considered to have given great consideration to whom and how their assets will pass. The probate court will generally honor the wishes set forth by the decedent in the will. The exceptions include instances of proven fraud or undue influence by a legatee or third party regarding the decedent or in cases where the decedent lacked the mental capacity to execute a will. Since the probate process is the legal process used to implement the disposition objectives of the testator, the testator is assured that his desires will, for the most part, be followed.

Quick Quiz 4.2

Highlight the answer to these questions:

1. The probate process often requires the executor or administrator to advertise the upcoming probate for a statutory period of time in legal newspapers to give interested parties notice to enter into the process.
   a. True
   b. False

2. The probate process protects the decedent's creditors by ensuring that the debts of the estate are paid prior to distributions to heirs.
   a. True
   b. False

True, True.

Protect the Legatees and Heirs

The legatees and heirs are generally the parties with the largest interest in the probate process. The probate process provides for an orderly administration of the decedent's assets. Thus, it prevents one legatee or heir from having priority over another of equal rank. The following example illustrates this point.

EXAMPLE 4.1

Sarah has two children, Ruth and Matthew. Ruth has lived with Sarah for many years and is known by the family to take advantage of her mother. Matthew lives far away, but has often helped both his mother and sister financially. When Sarah dies, Ruth believes that she can take all of her mother's belongings, sell them, and keep the profits for her own use, even though her mother's will bequeaths the assets equally to Ruth and Matthew. Ruth is mistaken. The probate process will protect Matthew by requiring the assets be marshalled and accounted for (as discussed below).

Transfer of Clear Title

The probate process also provides clear title to heirs or legatees. When the heirs or legatees receive property, they want to receive the property free of creditor claims and other competing ownership interests. Thus, the probate process assists the estate in satisfying creditor claims and clarifying competing ownership interests.

EXAMPLE 4.2

Joelle dies leaving her car to her son, Don. Without the probate process, Don would be responsible for determining if there are any liens on the vehicle and also for clearing the liens. If Joelle did not bequeath other property or cash to Don, he would have to clear the title with his own funds. The probate process eliminates these responsibilities on the part of Don. The probate process clears all liens and provides Don with clear title to the vehicle.

The probate process provides for an orderly administration of the decedent's assets and increases the chances that all parties of interest have notice of the proceeding and, therefore, an opportunity to be heard. The probate process generally requires the executor or administrator of an estate to advertise the upcoming probate proceeding for a statutory period of time in legal newspapers and a newspaper of general circulation in the county where the decedent was domiciled. This gives interested parties notice of the death of the decedent and an opportunity to participate in the probate process. It also allows heirs and creditors that may not have been recognized or absent legatees the opportunity to present themselves and take property under the will or via the state intestacy laws.

<table>
<tr><td>EXAMPLE 4.3</td><td>Dylan and Kali were married for many years but never had children. Dylan, who was not always faithful in the marriage, had an affair with Chelsea while travelling to Chicago on business. After several months of carrying on the affair, Dylan broke off the affair. Unknown to Dylan, Chelsea gave birth to a boy, Blake, after Dylan ended the affair. Chelsea was certain that Dylan was Blake's father but kept it to herself. On her death bed, Chelsea revealed to Blake that Dylan was his father. When Blake finally came to grips with this knowledge, he began to seek out his father. Unfortunately, Dylan died days before Blake found him. Dylan died intestate and the probate process had already begun. The probate process may permit Blake to join the proceedings and establish his right as the biological son of Dylan, thus allowing Blake to take property under the intestate laws of the state.</td></tr>
</table>

Protect the Creditors

When a person dies they often have outstanding debts. The creditors would like to be paid the money owed to them and the probate process protects these creditors by insuring that the debts of the estate are paid before distributions are made to heirs or legatees.

EXHIBIT 4.1	**ADVANTAGES OF PROBATE (SUMMARY)**

1. Implements disposition objectives of testator.
2. Provides for an orderly administration of assets.
3. Provides clean title to heirs or legatees.
4. Increases the chance that parties of interest have notice of proceedings and, therefore, a right to be heard.
5. Protects creditors by insuring that debts of the decedent are paid.

DISADVANTAGES OF THE PROBATE PROCESS

The probate process also has certain disadvantages. While the advantages of probate center around protecting individuals, the disadvantages center around the losses individuals may face. The losses include time (delays), money (costs), and privacy (publicity).

The Time Cost of Probate (Delays)

The probate process is a complex legal process that takes time to complete. In order to protect the individuals involved, legal notices must be posted, hearings must be scheduled, and asset valuations must be conducted. Delays are frequently caused by the difficulty in locating and identifying property, time needed to value assets, time needed for the identification of creditors and heirs, court delays, and the filing of tax returns. All of these processes take time, with probate proceedings typically averaging from six to 24 months to complete. In addition, probate also ties up the decedent's probate assets during administration of the estate.

EXAMPLE 4.4

Imagine a nonworking spouse whose working spouse dies. The surviving spouse does not have the funds to buy food for the family because the working spouse's assets are tied up in the probate process. Frequently, surviving spouses have serious financial hardships in the immediate period after their spouse's death because they have less income while many of their expenses remain fixed and they cannot use assets that are tied up in the probate process to meet daily living needs.

Monetary Cost of Probate (Costs)

Probate may also have a large monetary cost. The legal notice requirement, attorney's fees, and court costs are just a few of the expenses that are included in the probate process. The average probate process generally consumes five to 10 percent of an estate in legal fees and administrative costs, with some estates losing up to 20 percent. This can result in a significant reduction in the total dollar value of assets that will pass to the decedent's heirs. In addition, real property located in a state outside the testator's domicile requires a separate ancillary probate in the **situs** state. **Ancillary probate** is a concurrent probate process conducted in the nondomiciliary state. It often requires an attorney in that nondomiciliary state and additional, separate court fees, thus further reducing the overall value of the estate which passes to the heirs.

Quick Quiz 4.3

Highlight the answer to these questions:

1. Because of the orderly administration, the probate process is private.
   a. True
   b. False

2. Because of the orderly administration, the probate process is quick.
   a. True
   b. False

False, False.

EXAMPLE 4.5

Chance recently died in a bizarre fishing accident. He died leaving his $1,000,000 estate to his wife Laurie. Let's assume first that the probate process goes rather smoothly and only 5% of the estate is consumed by fees and other costs. In this instance, $50,000 would be used to pay these expenses, leaving Laurie with $950,000 of Chance's $1,000,000. Instead, let's assume that Andi, an old friend of Chance's, claims her newborn son, Rowdy, is the biological child of Chance. Although the claim proves to be false, the estate's legal fees and administrative costs are 20% of the estate. Now Laurie would only receive $800,000 of Chance's $1,000,000 estate. As illustrated, the heirs could suffer a substantial loss of assets during the probate process.

Privacy (Publicity)

One of the biggest disadvantages of the probate process is the loss of privacy. The probate process is an open court proceeding, and like any other court proceeding, the documents filed and hearings held are open to the public. Since the files are public records, anyone can access the probate documents. In Chapter 2, Elvis Presley's and Warren Burger's wills are reprinted as examples because each document is part of a public record and open to public scrutiny.

EXAMPLE 4.6	A golfer dies with a will directing the disposition of all of his assets. Because the golfer was famous, the news media and tabloids are covering the funeral and stories of his death blanket the television every evening. Soon, reporters scouring through publicly available probate court documents begin reporting the location and value of all of his homes, cars, and investment accounts. Had his assets been titled under other methods, such as a trust arrangement or property titling with survivorship, the golfer's assets could have remained confidential, and the news media would not have had access to the information.
	Now assume the deceased person is you and instead of the media and the tabloids, the snoopers are your nosy neighbor and the annoying busybody at work. Now imagine that the public probate documents are yours that they are scouring. It's your home's valuation they want to know and how much you had in your investment accounts. This example illustrates why many individuals do not want to go through the probate process.

EXHIBIT 4.2	**DISADVANTAGES OF PROBATE SUMMARY**

1. Can be complex and excruciatingly slow - Delays
2. Can result in substantial monetary costs - Costs
3. The process is open to public scrutiny - Publicity

NONTRADITIONAL RELATIONSHIPS

Nontraditional relationships require additional considerations in transferring assets, especially at death. A nontraditional relationship includes not just couples of the same sex, but also unmarried couples with extensive age gaps and other nonmarried couples living together. Additionally, nontraditional relationship planning may apply to any couple where there is an anticipated will contest from family members.

From an estate planning point of view, it is advisable that nontraditional relationships avoid probate if the goal is to pass assets to the nontraditional partner. There have been a number of cases where family members of the decedent contested the will based on undue influence by the nontraditional partner. Some courts have held the will of the first deceased partner to be invalid, thus leaving the nontraditional surviving partner without the assets the decedent intended.

Key Concepts

Underline/highlight the answers to these questions as you read:

1. Identify the risks associated with the probate process for individuals who are in a nontraditional relationship.

EXAMPLE 4.7

One of the most famous examples of a nontraditional party will contest occurred in the estate of Robert Kaufmann. Robert had inherited substantial wealth and was the major stock holder in his family's business, Kay Jewelers. Robert had a long-term relationship with Walter Weiss from 1948 until Robert died in 1959. As part of his will, Robert left a letter to his family describing why he left his amassed fortune to his "dearest friend" Walter. The family, who had always suspected a homosexual relationship and were unhappy about the purported relationship, managed to convince two juries and an appellate court that Walter had manipulated Robert through undue influence. The end result was that Walter did not receive the assets Robert wanted him to have. Individuals in nontraditional relationships, whether they be same sex or not, should consider avoiding the probate process.

Quick Quiz 4.4

Highlight the answer to these questions:

1. If a partner of a nontraditional couple wishes to pass assets to the surviving partner, he should plan to avoid probate.
   a. True
   b. False

True.

Fortunately, nontraditional partners can ensure that transfers will be made to each other in other ways. An annual gifting program up to the annual exclusion amount ($13,000 in 2009) may be an appropriate place to start. Additionally, non-traditional partners should make use of transfer devices that pass property outside of the probate process, such as transfers by contract, titling with survivorship features, and trusts. Each of these alternative methods offer advantages over transfers through probate for nontraditional relationships. For example, the use of JTWROS may be appropriate for nontraditional partners where one partner is not concerned about relinquishing some control over the property during life. Alternatively, a revocable living trust may be a better alternative if the wealthier partner is concerned about relinquishing control because such a trust can be revoked by the principal at any time before death. Automatic retitling mechanisms reduce the risk of challenges from blood relatives of the decedent and increase the probability that the decedent's assets will be left as desired.

Financial planners should focus not just on the appropriate transfer devices for nontraditional partners, but also the tax consequences of each device, including the income, gift, estate and generation-skipping transfer taxes involved. It is important to realize that nonmarried nontraditional partners will not be able to make use of the unlimited marital deduction, and that substantial age gaps may trigger a generation skipping transfer tax. Some states do have domestic partnership acts that offer some protection for nontraditional relationships. As various transfer devices are discussed throughout this book, keep in mind how they may apply to nontraditional relationships.

THE PROBATE PROCESS

STATE PROBATE LAWS

The probate process varies among states. The discussion below focuses on the more general aspects of the probate process in order to explain how the process works.

BEGINNING THE PROBATE PROCESS - PRODUCING THE WILL

Once a person dies, the first step in the probate process is producing a will, if one can be found. Any person can begin the probate process by presenting the will to the probate court. Generally, clients should be advised to let a trusted individual, usually the executor, know where the will is located. If the will is in a safe deposit box, banks will generally open the safe deposit box for the sole purpose of removing the will after receiving proof of death. If individuals plan to keep the will in a safe deposit box it is wise to make a copy of the will and give this to the executor with a note stating the actual will's location. This will expedite the retrieval of the will. At this point, it is also advisable for the family to obtain multiple certified copies of the death certificate for insurance, Social Security, probate, and other purposes.

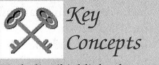

Key Concepts

Underline/highlight the answers to these questions as you read:

1. Distinguish between an executor and an administrator.

2. Identify how the probate process begins.

3. Determine which individuals must post a surety bond.

4. Distinguish between letters testamentary and letters of administration.

THE PROBATE COURT

Once the will has been found or it is determined that the decedent did not have a will, then the interested parties must go to the probate court to open the **estate administration** or **succession** (a term for passing property) process. The appropriate probate court in which to bring a petition will depend on the type and location of assets owned by the decedent. For a majority of individuals, the appropriate probate court will be the court where the person was domiciled at death. A person's **domicile** is the place where the person has made their home, is registered to vote, has a drivers license, filed a resident state income tax return, etc. In the event that a person holds real property located outside the city or state of their domicile, then an additional probate court must be consulted. This process is called ancillary probate. In most cases, a majority of the process is completed with the initial probate court, with only a few documents being filed in the ancillary probate court to change title for the real property sitused in that jurisdiction.

To begin the probate process, the petitioner (generally the executor) must provide the court with certain information, including a certified copy of the death certificate, the last will (if available), a list of the names and addresses of the decedent's heirs, and a list of the known creditors. Depending on the state, this can be rather easy. Generally the state will have a short document that can be filled out and submitted to the probate court with the necessary documents attached. A hearing will then be scheduled for interested parties to appear. The known creditors of the estate should be notified of the date of the hearing. In addition, the date of the hearing should be publicized in the appropriate legal and community newspapers. Assuming all paperwork is in order and there are no disputes among the heirs, then the hearing will be rather short. The court will accept the will, it will be filed in the public records and the court will officially open the probate process. The court will then appoint a personal representative, as is discussed below.

As mentioned in Chapter 2, if the will is a statutory will and has a self proving affidavit, then the will is considered valid on its face without the need for witnesses to testify that the decedent did indeed sign the will and was mentally competent. If the will does not have a self proving clause, then witnesses will be needed at the initial hearing to validate the will.

PERSONAL REPRESENTATIVE - EXECUTORS AND ADMINISTRATORS

When the probate process begins, a personal representative will be appointed to administer the estate. Depending on whether the decedent had a will or not, the personal representative is called the **executor** or **administrator**. When females were appointed they were historically referred to as the executrix or administratrix, but today many people use the generic terms executor/administrator. In addition, some states now use the generic all encompassing title of personal representative and do not distinguish between an executor or administrator.

In the case of a valid will in which an executor is named, the probate court usually accepts the appointed individual as executor and provides that person with powers called letters testamentary. A grant of **letters testamentary** empowers the executor to act as the agent of the court. In the event of intestacy, or where an executor cannot be appointed by the probate court, the court will appoint an administrator (generally a family member of the decedent who has the largest interest in the estate). The court provides individuals appointed as administrator with powers called **letters of administration**. The primary difference between an executor and an administrator is that the decedent chooses the executor, and the probate court names the administrator. In some states, administrators may have to formally close the estate before the probate court while an executor may be able to close informally. Letters testamentary or letters of administration are essentially equal in power and provide the holder with the legal authority to perform the functions of executor or administrator. Exhibit 4.3 identifies the primary duties of an executor or administrator in the probate process.

EXHIBIT 4.3   COMMON DUTIES OF EXECUTOR AND/OR ADMINISTRATOR

When the Decedent Dies Testate (with a will)	When the Decedent Dies Intestate (without a will)
The Executor:	The Administrator:
• Locates and proves the will.	• Petitions court for his or her own appointment.
• Locates witnesses to the will.	• Receives letters of administration.
• Receives letters testamentary from court.	• Posts the required bond.

Duties of the Executor or Administrator

- Locates and assembles all of the decedent's property.
- Safeguards, manages, and invests property.
- Advertises in legal newspapers that the person has died and that creditors and other interested parties are on notice of the death and opening of probate.
- Locates and communicates with potential beneficiaries of the decedent.
- Pays the expenses of the decedent.
- Pays the debts of the decedent.
- Files both federal and state income, fiduciary, gift tax, and estate tax returns (such as Forms 1040, 1041, 709, and 706 for federal tax purposes) and makes any required tax payments.
- Distributes remaining assets to beneficiaries according to the will or to the laws of intestacy.
- Closes the estate formally or informally.

Surety Bonds

If an administrator is appointed by the court, then the administrator must generally post a bond called a **surety bond**. Some states also require a bond to be posted if the will names an individual as executor, unless a provision of the will waives the bond requirement. Although the surety bond requirement can be waived by the will or by the heirs and legatees, states generally will not allow the bond to be waived if an executor is named that is not a resident of the state in which the probate process is occurring. The purpose of the surety bond is to protect the creditors, heirs, and legatees of the estate from financial loss in the event that the administrator or executor engages in a wrongful act. In the event that the administrator or executor misappropriates assets of the estate or is negligent and causes a loss to the estate, the surety bond company will reimburse the estate for the loss. An administrator will need a formal discharge of the surety bond before closing the estate.

MANAGING AND DISTRIBUTING THE ESTATE

Once appointed, the executor or administrator identifies and takes control of the decedent's assets. This is referred to as "marshalling the assets." After the assets have been marshalled, the personal representative compiles an inventory list of the decedent's property. The property is then valued by a valuation specialist or appraiser. Depending on the type of assets, the valuation may be relatively inexpensive or substantial in both cost and time.

The personal representative must then identify and list all debts owed by the decedent. This includes notifying potential creditors regarding the death and requesting final payoff balances. Most importantly, the personal representative must file the necessary federal and state tax returns and pay any taxes due. Remember that the personal representative must be paid (unless compensation is waived) and the court-approved advisors to the executor or administrator must also be paid. Once the debts and taxes have been paid, the probate court will generally allow the assets to be distributed to the heirs or legatees. At this point, if ancillary probate is required, then the court order allowing disposition of property is filed in the ancillary probate court to allow title to change in that jurisdiction as well.

The personal representative will first distribute the specific personal property bequests to specific legatees (e.g., a particular piece of jewelry is left to the decedent's daughter) and then the specific real property bequests to specific legatees. Only after all debts, taxes, and costs have been paid and all specific legatees have been satisfied will the residuary heir or legatee take the remaining property. After all of the assets have been distributed, the court will officially close the probate proceedings.

POTENTIAL PROBLEMS IN DISTRIBUTION

Probate is not simple. One common problem is that assets specifically bequeathed to legatees may have been disposed of prior to the decedent's death. In these cases, unless the testator has provided some alternative asset, the legatee is not entitled to any replacement asset. This extinction of the legacy is called **ademption**.

Quick Quiz 4.5

Highlight the answer to these questions:

1. The probate court provides an appointed administrator with certain powers represented by letters testamentary.
   a. True
   b. False

2. All executors are chosen by the probate court.
   a. True
   b. False

3. Court-appointed administrators must generally post a bond.
   a. True
   b. False

4. Letters testamentary provide the holder with the legal authority to perform the functions of executor.
   a. True
   b. False

5. In the event a decedent dies without a valid will, the probate court appoints an administrator.
   a. True
   b. False

False, False, True, True, True.

> In Mike's will, he leaves a 1986 convertible to Joe. When Mike dies, he has a 1999 convertible, which he acquired when he traded in his 1986 convertible. Joe receives nothing under the will, and his gift is said to adeem.

EXAMPLE 4.8

Another frequently encountered problem during the probate process occurs when there are not enough assets in the estate to satisfy all of the decedent's specific bequests. If the estate is too small to satisfy all bequests, the court will generally reduce the amounts given to the legatees. This reduction is called **abatement**.

EXAMPLE 4.9

Len leaves $100,000 to each of his four brothers, but when he dies, Len only has $250,000. If Len has not decided who takes what and in what priority, the probate court will ascertain the likely wishes of the decedent. In this case, since all four brothers have equal standing, the court would likely award each 25% of the total.

Even if there are sufficient assets to satisfy all specific legatees and create a residuary, there remains a question as to who will bear the cost of debts and federal estate taxes and state inheritance taxes of the estate. Should each specific legatee pay his own taxes pro rata or should the residuary legatee bear the entire burden of state and federal taxes? Most states have a default presumption if the testator fails to specify, but any presumption may or may not be consistent with the testator's wishes.

EXAMPLE 4.10

Karen and Teddy were married and had two children, Josh and Kerstin. Teddy died with an estate valued at $400,000. Teddy's will left $100,000 to each child and the remainder of his estate to his wife Karen. His will did not specify how taxes should be paid, so assume the state law dictates that the estate taxes should be paid out of each bequest based on the percentage the assets bear to the estate. Also, assume the taxes were $10,000. In this instance each person will pay based on the pro rata share they received. Since Karen received $200,000 of the $400,000 estate, one half of the estate taxes will be paid from her proceeds (($200,000/ $400,000) x $10,000 = $5,000)). Each child's net proceeds are reduced by one fourth of the tax due because they are each receiving one-fourth of the estate (($100,000/ $400,000) x $10,000 = $2,500 per child). Thus Karen will receive a net amount of $195,000 and each child will receive a net amount of $97,500.

Now assume that the will stated that the state estate taxes are paid from the residuary portion. Since Karen is receiving the residuary, her portion will be reduced by the full amount of all taxes paid. Therefore, she will receive a net amount of $190,000 and each child will receive $100,000. The point is that the will should be written in a clear way so as to avoid any possible ambiguity. The will is the voice of the decedent and the decedent's desires should be clearly expressed.

PROPERTY PASSING THROUGH PROBATE

Property passing through probate includes property that can be disposed of by a will, such as fee simple property, the decedent's share of property held as tenancy in common, the decedent's share of community property (as discussed in Chapter 3).

Recall that fee simple is outright ownership and does not provide for automatic retitling. Therefore, this type of property must pass through the probate process to be retitled. Similarly, there are no provisions for property held as tenancy in common or community property to automatically transfer title once the owner dies and therefore the property must be retitled through the probate process at the time of death.

Key Concepts

Underline/highlight the answers to these questions as you read:

1. Determine which types of assets go through probate.

2. Determine which types of assets do not go through probate.

In addition to real property, other tangible and intangible property also passes through probate for retitling. For example, automobiles and household goods are often disposed of through a will and must pass through probate for retitling. Finally, the probate process also retitles property owned at the time of death, but not disposed of through the will, such as intestate property resulting from the failure of the decedent to include a residuary clause in his will.

PROPERTY PASSING OUTSIDE OF THE PROBATE PROCESS

Property that passes outside of the probate process includes property that passes by state contract law, state property titling law, and state trust law. All of these transfers reduce the probate estate and therefore reduce probate transaction costs and may improve liquidity for the named heirs and legatees.

STATE CONTRACT LAW

Transfers that avoid probate by contract allow the client to select a designated beneficiary to whom the property will be transferred. The selected beneficiary will directly receive title to the property at the death of the owner. However, before the death of the owner, the selected beneficiary does not have any rights to the property; since the owner of the property can, at any time, change, amend, or revoke any revocable beneficiary selection. In all situations, if a named beneficiary is not chosen, the property is included in the decedent's probate estate. If a beneficiary or successor beneficiary that was named predeceased the testator, and there is not a living contingent beneficiary, then the property will transfer through the probate process to be retitled. In addition, if the decedent had named his estate as the beneficiary of a contract, then the proceeds would also transfer through the probate process.

| **EXAMPLE 4.11** | Jaime owns a life insurance policy on his life with his wife Barbara named as the beneficiary. At Jamie's death the death benefit will be paid directly to Barbara, thus avoiding the probate process. |

| **EXAMPLE 4.12** | Jamie owns a life insurance policy on his life. He does not have a named beneficiary. At Jamie's death, the death benefit will be paid to his estate and thus will be transferred through the probate process to his heirs. |

| **EXAMPLE 4.13** | Jamie owns a life insurance policy on his life. The named beneficiary is his wife Barbara, who died last year. At Jamie's death the proceeds will be paid to Jamie's estate because Barbara is deceased. Thus, the death benefit will transfer through Jamie's probate estate. |

| **EXAMPLE 4.14** | Jamie owns a life insurance policy on his life with his estate as the named beneficiary. When Jamie dies the assets will be paid directly to the estate and thus will transfer through the probate process. |

Naming a beneficiary does not trigger any gift tax consequences. These contractual beneficiary designators are easy and efficient mechanisms to avoid the probate process, as there is no need for the asset to be retitled, since title is transferred automatically to the named beneficiary. The following are typical devices that use beneficiary designations to transfer property at the death of the owner under state contract law.

Life Insurance

Life insurance is a contract that allows the owner of the policy to name a beneficiary. The life insurance company contracts with the owner of the policy and agrees to pay the death benefit to the named beneficiary upon the death of the insured. The insurance company is thus acting as agent of the owner. For the beneficiary to collect the proceeds of life insurance, he simply has to provide a certified copy of the death certificate obtained from the local coroner's office to the insurer. Life insurance thus offers a fairly quick solution to help meet the many immediate liquidity needs that arise when someone dies.

Annuities

Annuities are contracts, similar to life insurance, where a named beneficiary can be selected by the owner of the annuity. At the death of the owner of the annuity, the named beneficiary will receive the annuity death benefit, which may come in the form of an annuity for life, annuity for term, or a cash payment. In some cases, the death benefit settlement option has been pre-selected by the owner, or if not pre-selected the beneficiary may choose any one of the settlement options allowed under the contract.

IRAs, SEPs, SIMPLEs, and Qualified Retirement Plans

Retirement plans also allow the owner to name a beneficiary. At the death of the account owner, the named beneficiary receives the assets from the retirement account. The custodian of the plan or account has a contract with the owner of the account and is directed upon the owner's death to pay the beneficiary upon receipt of a certified death certificate.

Totten Trusts, Pay-on-Death (POD) Accounts and Transfer-on-Death (TOD) Accounts

Totten Trusts, named after the legendary 1904 Totten case (*In re Totten*, 179 N.Y. 112, 71 N.E. 748), are not really trusts at all, but are instead accounts designated as "held in trust for another." Totten Trusts are not joint accounts, and the named beneficiary does not have any rights to the account while the owner was alive. Instead, they are merely bank accounts with beneficiary designations. At the death of the account owner, the bank transfers the assets in the account to the named beneficiary. Most states have now codified the historical Totten Trust into what is now called **Pay-on-Death (POD) Bank Accounts** or **In Trust For (ITF) Accounts**. In addition, many states have statutorily created **Transfer-on-Death (TOD) Accounts** for investment accounts with named beneficiaries.

Most states have adopted PODs/ITFs for bank accounts and/or TODs for investment accounts to allow these types of accounts the same advantages as other beneficiary-designated accounts. The beneficiary designation is similar to naming a beneficiary for a retirement account or IRA and generally completed in a similar fashion. All but two states now have a similar transfer device for either bank accounts or investment accounts, with over half of the states having transfer devices for both types of accounts. State laws vary and a full understanding of applicable state law is needed when selecting such designations.

STATE TITLING LAW

Property held as a joint tenancy with rights of survivorship (JTWROS), or as a tenancy by the entirety (TE) pass outside of the probate process because of the automatic retitling mechanism of the survivorship feature. At the death of a joint tenant, his or her interest passes automatically to the surviving tenant, or in the case of TE, to the surviving spouse. The surviving joint tenant must produce a certified death certificate of the decedent in order to transfer title.

STATE TRUST LAW

As discussed in Chapter 8, all trust property will pass outside of the probate process per state trust law. Property in trust has already been retitled because when the grantor of the trust transferred the property into the trust, it had to be retitled as trust property. Even in the case of a revocable trust, the trust becomes irrevocable upon the grantor's death. Property in trust is managed and distributed according to the specific provisions of the particular trust and has no further need to be retitled. Exhibit 4.4 illustrates various assets and how they pass through and around probate.

EXHIBIT 4.4   **ASSETS PASSING THROUGH AND AROUND THE PROBATE PROCESS**

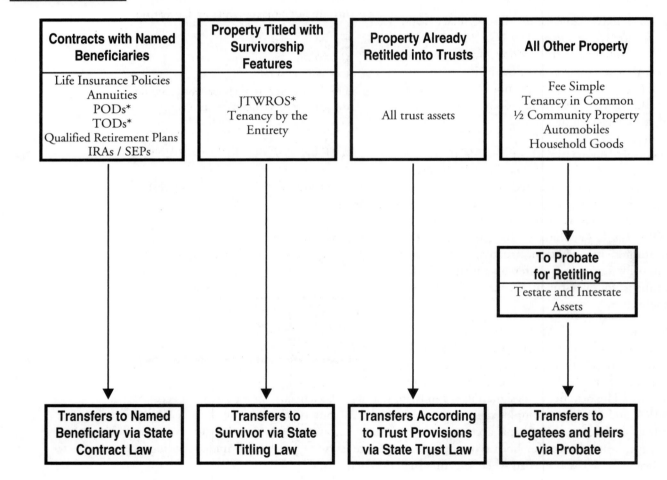

*PODs - Pay-on-death bank account with named beneficiaries.
*TODs - Transfer-on-death investment accounts with named beneficiaries.
*JTWROS - Joint tenancy with right of survivorship.

CALCULATING THE PROBATE ESTATE

Calculating the value of the probate estate is important and should be fairly easy if you can identify which assets are and which are not included in the probate estate. We will use the following example to work through the concepts that have been discussed in this chapter.

Cody and Reese were married years ago and had one child, Amber. Cody and his longtime friend, Kandi, were recently flying in Kandi's new plane. For a brief period Kandi was distracted and lost control of the plane. Unfortunately, the plane crashed and Kandi died instantly and Cody died a few days later as a result of the injuries sustained during the crash. When Cody died he and Reese owned the following property:

- Home valued at $500,000 held tenancy by the entirety.
- Car 1 valued at $10,000 held fee simple by Cody.
- Car 2 valued at $15,000 held Joint Tenancy with Rights of Survivorship by Cody and Amber.
- Diamond ring valued at $50,000 held fee simple by Reese.
- Boat valued at $20,000 held tenancy in common by Cody and Amber.
- Life Insurance Policy 1 on Reese's life, owned by Cody. The fair market value of the policy was $100,000 and the death benefit was $200,000. The beneficiary is Amber.
- Life Insurance Policy 2 on Cody's life, owned by Cody. The fair market value of the policy was $85,000 and the death benefit was $500,000. The only beneficiary is Kandi.
- IRA account valued at $2,000,000 owned by Cody with Amber as the beneficiary.
- Irrevocable Trust by Cody for the benefit of Amber created five years ago. The trust is valued at $500,000, and Amber is the beneficiary at Cody's death.

Calculate Cody's probate estate in the box below. Unless otherwise stated, assume equal contributions were made by all parties for jointly owned property. The first asset has been completed for you. Answers are provided on the next page.

Asset	FMV at Date of Death	FMV of Cody's Interest	Included in the Probate Estate
Home	$500,000	$250,000	$0
Car 1			
Car 2			
Diamond Ring			
Boat			
Life Insurance 1			
Life Insurance 2			
IRA			
Trust			
Total			

ANSWERS:

Asset	FMV at Date of Death	FMV of Cody's Interest	Included in the Probate Estate
Home	$500,000	$250,000	$0
Car 1	10,000	10,000	10,000
Car 2	15,000	7,500	0
Diamond Ring	50,000	0	0
Boat	20,000	10,000	10,000
Life Insurance 1	100,000	100,000	100,000
Life Insurance 2	500,000	500,000	500,000
IRA	2,000,000	2,000,000	0
Trust	500,000	0	0
Total	**$3,695,000**	**$2,877,500**	**$620,000**

HOME

The home is owned tenancy by the entirety. Therefore, Cody owns one half and Reese owns one half. Since the property is held tenancy by the entirety, the property automatically has a survivorship feature, thus it will not pass through probate.

CAR 1

Car 1 is held fee simple by Cody; therefore, he owns the entire asset outright. Since there is no survivorship feature associated with fee simple, the property will pass through probate.

CAR 2

Car 2 is owned JTWROS by Cody and Amber. Thus Cody owns one half of the property. Since the property will pass via state titling law because of the survivorship feature, the asset will not pass through probate.

DIAMOND RING

The ring belongs to Reese (she owns it fee simple) and there is no effect on Cody regarding this asset.

BOAT

The boat is held tenancy in common and Cody owns one half. Since there is no survivorship feature, his half of the asset will pass through the probate process. Note that while only half of the value of the boat is included in the probate estate, the amount included in the gross estate for estate tax purposes will be determined by the percentage of contribution rule, since Cody owned the boat with his daughter. This illustrates one of the common differences between the probate and gross estate calculations.

LIFE INSURANCE POLICY 1

Cody owns the policy on Reese's life. When he dies the value of the policy will transfer through his probate estate. The ownership of the policy is like any other asset in that it must be transferred to someone else. Because the death benefit is not currently payable (the policy is on Reese's life) only the FMV of the policy is included in Cody's gross estate.

LIFE INSURANCE POLICY 2

There was a named beneficiary, but the beneficiary was Kandi who died in the crash shortly before Cody. Since the beneficiary is dead, the property will transfer through the probate process like any other asset unless a contingent beneficiary had been named.

IRA

The IRA has a designated beneficiary, Amber, who is living. Therefore, the property passes by the operation of contract law and will not transfer through the probate process.

IRREVOCABLE TRUST

The trust is not part of Cody's assets and is therefore not part of Cody's probate estate. The assets in the trust pass via state trust law.

Key Terms

Abatement - The reduction in assets transferring to a legatee because the estate has insufficient assets to satisfy all of the legatees.

Ademption - Extinction of a legacy because an asset, specifically bequeathed to a legatee, has been disposed of prior to death.

Administrator - A person, usually a relative of the deceased, appointed by the probate court to oversee the probate process when an executor has not been named.

Ancillary Probate - Concurrent second probate process conducted in a non-domiciliary state in which the decedent owns property, which often requires the services of an attorney from that state, and separate court fees.

Domicile - Where a person lives, the location of their home.

Estate Administration or Succession - The passing of property at death to surviving heirs/legatees.

Executor - Estate representative designated in the will by the decedent. An executor may serve without bond if the bond is waived by the decedent.

Heir - One who inherits under state law.

Legatee - One who inherits under the will.

Letters of Administration - A legal document that affirms the power of the administrator to act as the agent of the probate court.

Letters Testamentary - A legal document that affirms the power of the executor to act as the agent of the probate court.

Pay-on-Death Account (POD) - A bank account utilizing a beneficiary designation.

Probate Process - The legal proceeding that serves to prove the validity of existing wills, supervise the orderly distribution of decedent's assets to the heirs, and protect creditors by ensuring that valid debts of the estate are paid.

Situs - The place, generally referring to the state, where property is located.

Surety Bond - A bond posted by the administrator or the executor of the estate to protect creditors, heirs, and legatees from losses created by the administrator or executor.

Totten Trust - Not a trust, but rather a bank account with a beneficiary clause.

Transfer-on-Death Account (TOD) - An investment account utilizing a beneficiary designation.

DISCUSSION QUESTIONS

1. Describe the probate process.

2. Describe at least three advantages and three disadvantages of the probate process.

3. Identify alternatives to probate regarding the disposition of property.

4. Discuss the main differences between an executor and an administrator.

5. List the duties of the executor and/or administrator.

6. Define pay-on-death and transfer-on-death accounts.

7. Identify assets that pass outside of probate by contract law.

8. Identify assets that pass outside of probate by titling or trust law.

1. If Paula died with each of the following property interests, which will be excluded from her probate estate?

    a. Property owned as community property.

    b. Property held tenancy in common.

    c. Death proceeds of life insurance payable to a living stranger.

    d. Property owned fee simple.

2. Many planners believe that the best estate plan excludes as many assets as possible from the probate estate. Which of the following statements justifies these planners' belief?

    a. The probate assets are not subject to creditors.

    b. The probate estate is filed with the court and can become public knowledge.

    c. The more excluded assets from the probate estate, the more expensive the administration is likely to be.

    d. The more assets that go through the probate process, the faster the heirs are likely to receive the assets.

3. Which of the following is generally included in a decedent's probate estate?

    a. Revocable trust with a named living beneficiary.

    b. Fee simple ownership specifically bequeathed in a decedent's will.

    c. Life insurance with a named living beneficiary.

    d. Transfer-on-death investment account with a named living beneficiary.

4. Craig's attorney has advised him to set up trusts to avoid probate. Which of the following statements regarding the probate process is not correct?

    a. The distribution of probate assets can be delayed.

    b. Through the probate process heirs and/or legatees are given clear title to the property.

    c. Creditors are protected through the probate process.

    d. The probate process is confidential.

5. Which of the following property interests of a decedent will avoid probate?

    a. Proceeds of life insurance payable to the decedent's estate.

    b. Community property.

    c. Property owned tenants in common with decedent's father.

    d. Proceeds of life insurance payable to the decedent's living son.

6. Which of the following is a disadvantage of the probate process?

    a. The decedent's heirs and/or legatees are given clear title to property.

    b. The probate process requires several court filings.

    c. The probate process provides for an orderly distribution of the decedent's assets.

    d. The decedent's creditors are protected.

7. Which of the following is considered an advantage of the probate process?

    a. The probate process creates delays.

    b. The probate process is costly.

    c. Heirs receive property with clear title.

    d. Information that is filed with the court becomes public information.

8. Ramona inherited the property listed below from her father upon his death. Which of the following property interests passed to her through probate?

    a. A 2005 Porsche titled and held within a revocable living trust.

    b. Ramona's father's community property share of a vacation property.

    c. A $300,000 distribution to Ramona, as listed beneficiary, from her father's 401(k) plan.

    d. Title to a Manhattan condo previously owned within a trust with Ramona listed as the beneficiary at her father's death.

9. Tom died owning the following property. Which would not be included in Tom's probate estate?

    1. A certificate of deposit, in Tom's name, at the local bank.

    2. An interest in commercial investment real estate held tenancy in common with a son of the decedent.

    3. Retirement plan proceeds made payable to Tom's daughter.

    4. A mountain vacation home Tom owns jointly (JTWROS) with his wife.

        a. 1 only.

        b. 3 and 4.

        c. 1, 2, and 3.

        d. 1, 2, and 4.

10. Which of the following items will pass through probate?

    a. Retirement plan with someone other than the decedent listed as the beneficiary.

    b. Investment real estate held JTWROS.

    c. Personal residence held tenancy by the entirety.

    d. Life insurance policy with no designated beneficiary.

11. Carol's executor has located all of her property. Given the following property listing, what is the total value of Carol's probate estate?

Life Insurance	Face	$1,000,000	Beneficiary is James, Carol's son.
401(k)	Balance	$350,000	Beneficiary is Carla, Carol's Daughter
Vacation Home	Value	$460,000	Titled Tenancy by Entirety with Jim
Automobile	Value	$24,000	Owned by Carol

    a. $24,000.

    b. $484,000.

    c. $834,000.

    d. $1,024,000.

12. Krista would like to reduce the risk of public scrutiny of her assets at her death. Which of the following would not help Krista accomplish this goal?

    a. Place all property in trust.

    b. Retitle property so that it is titled with a survivorship feature.

    c. Include a specific bequest of each and every item Krista owns in her will.

    d. Use items such as annuities, PODs and TODs.

13. Eric owns the following property:

Property	Joint Owner	Titling
Home	None	Fee Simple
Stock in ABC Corp	Brother, Jim	Tenancy in Common
Beach House	Wife, Rebecca	Tenancy by the Entirety
Checking Account	None	Pay-on-Death to Son

Which of the following is included in Eric's probate estate?

    a. Home and stock in ABC Corp.

    b. Home, beach house, and checking account.

    c. Stock in ABC Corp and checking account.

    d. Home only.

Quick Quiz Explanations

Quick Quiz 4.1

1. True.
2. True.

Quick Quiz 4.2

1. True.
2. True.

Quick Quiz 4.3

1. False. Probate is a public process and is open to public scrutiny.
2. False. The probate process typically takes six to twenty-four months to complete.

Quick Quiz 4.4

1. True.

Quick Quiz 4.5

1. False. An administrator receives letters of administration. An executor receives letters testamentary.
2. False. Executors are appointed by the decedent in a validly executed will. Administrators are appointed by the court when the decedent died without a will, or failed to name an executor in his will.
3. True.
4. True.
5. True.

Quick Quiz 4.6

1. True.
2. True.
3. True.
4. False. Tenancy by the entirety has automatic survivorship feature and will therefore pass to the surviving spouse by operation of law and will not pass through the probate process.
5. True.

Gift Tax

THE GIFT TAX SYSTEM

HISTORICAL BACKGROUND AND PURPOSE

The gift tax is an excise tax on the right to transfer assets gratuitously to another person during life. Like the federal estate tax, the gift tax exists as a method of raising revenue for the federal government and functions as a method of social reallocation of wealth by taxing large masses of wealth transferred from one generation to subsequent generations. The gift tax is paid from the taxpayer's wealth to the federal government and thus is reallocated to other members of society through the social programs and other expenditures of the federal government.

The gift tax system was established in 1932 to prevent individuals from avoiding the income tax, which existed as early as 1862, and the estate tax, which was enacted in 1915. Before the gift tax system, some individual transferors (donors) would transfer income producing property with no transfer tax cost to their family members (donees) who were in lower income tax brackets for the purpose of reducing the overall family income tax burden. Others would transfer property during life to family members to avoid the imposition of the estate tax at their death. Congress, being ever mindful of the resolve and ingenuity with which some taxpayers avoid income and estate taxes, established an excise tax for gifts during life. Initially, the gift tax rates were lower than the estate tax rates, and as such, individuals continued transferring property during life, paying the lower gift tax rates, and avoiding the higher estate tax rates at their death.

In 1976, Congress unified the gift and estate tax rate schedules to discourage taxpayers from transferring assets during life to avoid the higher tax on the transfer of property at death. Essentially, the unified gift and estate transfer tax system taxed the transfer of property at the same tax rates regardless of the time of transfer of property, during life (gifts) or at death (bequests). Despite the equal tax rate systems, there were some major differences between transfers made during life and those made at death. This unified system ended after 2003, when the **Economic Growth and Tax Relief Reconciliation Act** of 2001 (herein referred to as EGTRRA 2001), repealing the estate tax over a nine year period ending in 2010, took force.

ESTATE AND GIFT TAX REFORM

EGTRRA 2001 was signed by President George W. Bush in June of 2001 designed to provide a $1.35 trillion tax cut. Under the law, the gift and estate tax systems continue using the same tax rate schedules through 2009 (See Exhibit 5.1), but each year until 2007, the highest marginal tax rate decreased by one percent (See Exhibit 5.2). In addition, EGTRRA 2001 eliminates the unified transfer tax system by increasing the applicable exemption amount for transfers at death over the 2001 to 2009 period, while the applicable exclusion amount for lifetime gifts will remain level at $1,000,000 (See Exhibit 5.2). The difference in the applicable exemption amounts allows an individual to transfer more assets, without incurring transfer tax, at death than during life. This effectively causes the transfer cost of transferring assets greater than $1,000,000 during life to be more expensive than transfers at death. However, that does not mean that advantages resulting from lifetime transfers do not continue to exist.

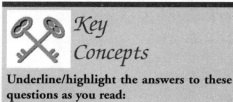

Key Concepts

Underline/highlight the answers to these questions as you read:

1. How does EGTRRA 2001 affect the estate tax rates over the next ten years?

2. Explain how EGTRRA 2001 "sunsets."

| EXHIBIT 5.1 | TAX RATE SCHEDULE FOR GIFTS AND ESTATES (FOR 2007-2009) |

Over $0 but not over $10,000	18% of such amount.
Over $10,000 but not over $20,000	$1,800 plus 20% of the excess of such amount over $10,000
Over $20,000 but not over $40,000	$3,800 plus 22% of the excess of such amount over $20,000
Over $40,000 but not over $60,000	$8,200 plus 24% of the excess of such amount over $40,000
Over $60,000 but not over $80,000	$13,000 plus 26% of the excess of such amount over $60,000
Over $80,000 but not over $100,000	$18,200 plus 28% of the excess of such amount over $80,000
Over $100,000 but not over $150,000	$23,800 plus 30% of the excess of such amount over $100,000
Over $150,000 but not over $250,000	$38,800 plus 32% of the excess of such amount over $150,000
Over $250,000 but not over $500,000	$70,800 plus 34% of the excess of such amount over $250,000
Over $500,000 but not over $750,000	$155,800 plus 37% of the excess of such amount over $500,000
Over $750,000 but not over $1,000,000	$248,300 plus 39% of the excess of such amount over $750,000
Over $1,000,000 but not over $1,250,000	$345,800 plus 41% of the excess of such amount over $1,000,000
Over $1,250,000 but not over $1,500,000	$448,300 plus 43% of the excess of such amount over $1,250,000
Over $1,500,000 but not over $2,000,000	$555,800 plus 45% of the excess of such amount over $1,500,000
Over $2,000,000 but not over $3,500,000	$780,800 plus 45% of the excess of such amount over $2,000,000
Over $3,500,000	$1,455,800 plus 45% of the excess of such amount over $3,500,000

Exhibit 5.2 identifies the highest marginal estate and gift tax rates for each tax year (2004-2010).

Calendar Year	Applicable Estate and GST Tax Exclusion Amount	Applicable Gift Tax Exclusion Amount	Highest Estate, GST, and Gift Tax Rates
2004	$1.5 million	$1 million	48%
2005	$1.5 million	$1 million	47%
2006	$2 million	$1 million	46%
2007	$2 million	$1 million	45%
2008	**$2 million**	**$1 million**	**45%**
2009	**$3.5 million**	**$1 million**	**45%**
2010	Estate Tax Repealed	$1 million	35% (Gift Tax Only)

By reducing the highest marginal rate over the nine-year period, the law also phases in the repeal of the estate and generation-skipping transfer taxes in 2010. The gift tax remains in force throughout, but the top gift tax rate will be decreased to 35 percent (the highest individual income tax rate as provided by the Jobs and Growth Tax Relief Reconciliation Act of 2003) for transfers subject to gift tax made during 2010.

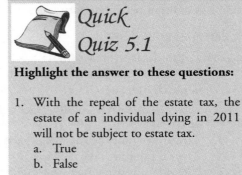

Quick Quiz 5.1

Highlight the answer to these questions:

1. With the repeal of the estate tax, the estate of an individual dying in 2011 will not be subject to estate tax.
   a. True
   b. False

False.

EGTRRA 2001 "sunsets" in 2011, at which time the estate, gift, and generation-skipping transfer tax rules, rates, and exemptions revert back to the rules, rates and exemptions in effect in 2001. Before 2011, Congress will most likely address the estate, gift, and generation-skipping transfer taxes again, so it is unlikely that all of the provisions of EGTRRA 2001 will remain in effect as currently written. Most experts believe that a federal estate tax will continue to be a reality but probably with an increased applicable exclusion amount.

INTRODUCTION TO GIFTS

While the gift tax system is replete with rules, exceptions, and exemptions, the overall scheme of gift taxation can be understood by asking four basic questions:

1. Disregarding all other factors, is the transfer a taxable gift?
2. Is the gift nontaxable because of an available exemption, exclusion, or due to legislative grace?
3. If the gift is taxable, what is the tax due and how is it reported?
4. Is the gift appropriate considering the objectives and goals of donor and donee?

This chapter will discuss each of these issues presenting both the rules and application of those rules.

CHARACTERISTICS OF A GIFT

The first step in the gift tax system is to determine if a transfer is a gift. This section covers the elements and types of gifts.

PARTIES

There are two parties involved in a gift transfer. The **donor** is the person who makes the gift. The **donee** is the person who receives the gift.

DEFINITION OF A GIFT

A **gift** is a voluntary transfer, for less than full consideration, of property from one person (a donor) to another person or entity (a donee).

ELEMENTS OF A GIFT

In general, the elements of a gift are:
1. The donor must have the intent to make a voluntary transfer.
2. The donor must be competent to make the gift.
3. The donee must be capable of receiving the gift.
4. The donee must take delivery.
5. The donor must actually part with dominion and control over the gifted property.

Key Concepts

Underline/highlight the answers to these questions as you read:

1. List the elements of a gift.

2. List the various types of gifts.

3. How can an incomplete gift become a complete gift?

4. What is a gift loan?

5. How are real estate and securities valued for gift tax purposes?

Donative intent implies that the donor had a conscious desire to make a gift to the donee. The element of donative intent differentiates gifts from transfers received in return for consideration. Whether or not the requirements of donative intent have been met is a frequent subject of litigation in the courts. Transfers that lack donative intent include quid-pro-quo transfers, transfers occasioned by lost or stolen property, and transfers resulting in a poor economic arrangement for one or both parties.

Competence to make a gift implies that the donor has:
1. attained the legal age of majority,
2. has the mental capacity to make the gift, and
3. owns the property that is the subject of the gift. One who does not own property cannot give that property to someone else, unless he/she is acting pursuant to a valid power of appointment.

To receive a gift, the donee (an individual or organization) must be identifiable at the time of the gift. The requirements of legal age and mental capacity are not necessary, provided that the gift is made in trust or to a guardian for the benefit of a person who has not attained legal age or does not have the capacity to manage his/her property. For the gift to be complete, the donee (or, if necessary, the donee's trustee or guardian) must take delivery of the gift, requiring the donor to relinquish dominion and control over the property.

EXAMPLE 5.1

Bob transfers $10,000 to his grandson, and his grandson has not worked for, sold, or transferred anything to Bob in return for the $10,000. Bob has made a $10,000 gift to his grandson.

EXAMPLE 5.2

Bob transfers $15,000 to Jerry and Jerry in turn transfers the title to his vehicle, with a fair market value of $15,000, to Bob. Bob has not made a gift to Jerry, even if Bob later discovers that the vehicle is worth less than $15,000 because of a bad engine that neither Jerry nor Bob knew of at the date of the sale. Bob did not have any intent to transfer an amount greater than the fair market value of the vehicle to Jerry.

CONSIDERATION

Consideration is the value of property transferred in return for other property. A gift arises whenever an exchange of property occurs and one of the parties does not receive full and fair consideration for their property or services. One of the parties could have made a poor economic deal, but in evaluating suspect transactions, it is always prudent to look closely at the relationship of the parties (especially if they are related) to determine if there was a lack of consideration and/ or any donative intent.

EXAMPLE 5.3

If Father transfers a house to his Son, and Son pays Father $1, Father has made a gift to Son of the difference between the fair market value of the house and $1. This is not a bona fide sale because adequate consideration was not paid for the house.

TYPES OF GIFTS

Gifts can be classified into several categories, including direct, indirect, complete, incomplete, reversionary interests, and net gifts.

Direct Gifts

A direct payment of cash or transfer of property to a donee is a **direct gift**. When a donor makes a direct gift, control of the property is transferred to the donee, and the donor does not retain any control over the property after the transfer.

EXAMPLE 5.4

A transfer from George to Robin of $10,000 cash without consideration is a direct gift from George to Robin.

Indirect Gifts

Indirect gifts can take many forms, and generally occur with intrafamily transactions. One of the most common ways an indirect gift occurs is through the payment of another's debt.

EXAMPLE 5.5

Joann pays her friend Susan's automobile note. While Joann has not transferred any property directly to Susan, she has made an indirect gift to Susan equal to the payment made.

Indirect gifts also occur when one person titles property in joint tenancy with another and the other person has not paid for their ownership share. Recall from Chapter 3 that certain exceptions apply when titling checking accounts and savings bonds; in this instance the gift is not yet complete until money is withdrawn by the non-contributing party (discussed later in this chapter).

<table>
<tr><td>EXAMPLE 5.6</td><td>April buys a vacation home and titles it joint tenancy with right of survivorship with her brother Billy. If Billy has not paid anything towards the purchase of the vacation home, April has made an indirect gift to Billy equal to one-half of the equity in the vacation home.</td></tr>
</table>

An interest-free or below-market loan (also known as a gift loan) is also an indirect transfer. Interest-free loans and below-market loans have special income tax treatment that requires the lender to impute the interest income as if the arrangement was a bona fide interest-bearing market loan. Imputed interest creates phantom income for the lender. The interest is included in income even though the lender did not actually receive any money. In addition to the income tax consequences, the lender is also deemed to make a gift to the borrower in the amount of the imputed interest. When calculating the gift tax consequences of the transfer the gift of the imputed interest may be eligible for the annual gift tax exclusion (discussed below).

Although the income tax consequences of below-market loans are covered more thoroughly in an income tax course, the rules have been restated here. In general, loans of less than $10,000 are exempt from both income tax and gift tax consequences. Loans of $100,000 or less are exempt from income tax and gift tax consequences when the borrower has net investment income of less than $1,000 from any source. Loans in excess of $10,000 but up to and including $100,000 where the net investment income of the borrower (donee) exceeds $1,000 require the donor (lender) to impute interest income for income tax purposes equal to the lesser of the donee's (borrower's) net investment income or the applicable federal rate (AFR) times the loan balance. Any imputed interest will also be considered a gift for gift tax consequences. For loans in excess of $100,000 the lender imputes an amount equal to the AFR times the loan balance for income tax purposes and includes the same amount for gift tax purposes. If any loan has a stated interest rate below the AFR, the imputed interest is the difference between the AFR and the stated rate. Exhibit 5.3 summarizes the rules for imputed interest on gift and below market loans.

EXHIBIT 5.3	SUMMARY OF IMPUTED INTEREST ON GIFT AND BELOW MARKET LOANS

Loan	Imputed Interest
$0 ≤$10,000	$0
$10,001 ≤$100,000	The lesser of: <ul><li>Net investment income, or</li><li>Interest calculated using AFR less interest calculated using stated rate of the loan</li></ul> If borrower's net investment income < $1,000, $0 imputed interest
> $100,000	Interest calculated using AFR less interest calculated using stated rate of the loan.

In some planning scenarios, individuals will make below-market or interest-free loans and then later forgive the debt. Forgiving such debt is also an indirect gift even if there was a bona fide debt transaction.

Complete and Incomplete Transfers

As discussed previously, a gift is complete when the donor releases control over the asset to a donee who can be identified at the date of the gift. Naming an individual as a revocable beneficiary of an account, or transfers to a revocable trusts (See Chapter 8) are **incomplete transfers** and are not considered to be gifts for gift tax purposes. Since incomplete gifts allow the donor to choose the ultimate disposition of the property, the donor has not released control of the property, so the true donee cannot yet be determined. If the transferor effectively renounces his retained or reversionary interest, or the trust becomes irrevocable by election, by death of the transferor, or by direction of the trust document, the transfer would, at that time, become a **completed gift** for gift tax purposes.

> James transfers title on his Ferrari to his friend, Randy, without receiving anything in return. Randy becomes the fee simple owner of the car. The transfer of the property is complete because James did not retain any interest in the car, and it is clear that Randy is the ultimate donee of the transfer.

EXAMPLE 5.7

> Warren transfers his home to a revocable living trust. Warren retains the right to live in his home for the rest of his life, and at his death, the home will transfer to his daughter, Sara. Because this is a revocable trust, Warren can revoke the trust at any time and ownership of the home will return to him. Also, Warren could change or add a beneficiary to the trust at any time. This gift to the trust is incomplete, and not considered to be a gift for gift tax purposes because Warren retains control over the asset. Since this is not a complete gift for gift tax purposes, there is no gift tax consequence on the day of transfer.

EXAMPLE 5.8

The creation of joint bank accounts and the purchase of U.S. Savings Bonds are treated differently from other joint gifts. A completed gift does not occur until the noncontributing party withdraws money for their own benefit. The reasoning is simple; the contributing party could have withdrawn all of the money at any time prior to a withdrawal by the noncontributing party. A gift does not occur upon the creation of the joint account nor upon the notification that the joint account has been created. The gift occurs only upon a withdrawal by the noncontributing party for their own benefit.

> On February 14th, Barbara deposited $40,000 into a joint banking account titled with her daughter, Jessica. On April 30th, Jessica withdraws $10,000 from the joint bank account to purchase a diamond ring. The gift was not complete until Jessica withdrew the $10,000 because anytime between February 14th and April 30th Barbara could have

EXAMPLE 5.9

withdrawn the entire $40,000 and Jessica would not have been able to access any of the money.

Reversionary Interests

Reversionary interests are interests that have been transferred and subsequently revert back to the grantor. A reversionary interest has both gift and estate tax consequences. The value of the gift to the donee is not the full fair market value of the property. Rather, it is the present value of the right to use. The value of the reversionary interest is determined using statutory tables found in the Treasury Regulations. As will be discussed in Chapter 6, a reversionary interest also has certain estate tax consequences.

EXAMPLE 5.10

Chuck transfers property to a trust for five years for the benefit of Robbie. At the end of the five years the property reverts back to Chuck. Since the property reverts back to Chuck, his interest is a reversionary interest and the value of the gift is less than the full value of the property.

Net Gifts

Ordinarily, the donor is responsible for gift tax associated with a taxable transfer. A **net gift** is a gift made on the condition that the donee pay gift tax due when a net gift is made. The donor will report taxable income to the extent that any gift tax paid by the donee exceeds the donor's adjusted basis in the gifted property. Since the taxable gift is calculated by subtracting the actual gift tax paid by the donee from the gross gift, the calculation of a net gift and its associated gift tax is a circular calculation.

EXAMPLE 5.11

Assume Brianna gifts property worth $400,000 to Kenny on the condition that Kenny pay the gift tax. Brianna's adjusted basis in the property is $100,000. Because Kenny must pay the gift tax, the gift is considered a net gift, and the gift tax is calculated on $400,000 less the gift tax that Kenny must pay, assumed to be $116,000 ($400,000/(1+.41)). In this example, Kenny would pay the gift tax of $116,000, the taxable gift would be $284,000 and Brianna would be required to recognize taxable income of $16,000 ($116,000 - $100,000) on the gift.

VALUATION OF A GIFT

The value of a gift for gift tax purposes is equal to the fair market value of the gifted property on the date of the gift. For real estate, an appraisal is usually necessary to determine the fair market value of the property. Publicly traded securities are valued at the average of the high and low trading price for the day. The fair market value of a bond is the present value of the expected future payments. Treasury Regulations 25.2512-1 through 25.2512-8 provide detailed guidelines to calculate the fair market value of certain types of property. Valuation discounts are allowed for lack of marketability, lack of liquidity, and lack of control. A more thorough discussion of valuation as it is related to particular assets and the availability and application of valuation discounts is covered in Chapter 6.

EXCLUSIONS AND EXEMPTIONS

Once a transfer is determined to be a gift, the donor should determine whether an exclusion or exemption applies making the transfer a nontaxable transfer. The next two sections cover the annual exclusion and lifetime exemption, and the related rules and devices to ensure applicability.

THE ANNUAL EXCLUSION

All individuals may gift, transfer-tax free, up to $13,000 (2009) per donee per year to a related or unrelated party. This **annual exclusion** is a de minimis rule set by Congress to help reduce the reporting requirements for small gifts. The annual exclusion will offset the fair market value of the total gifts to each donee by $13,000. To qualify for the annual exclusion, the gift must be of a present interest (discussed in the next section). If the gift is of a future interest, it normally does not qualify for the annual exclusion and will be reported as a taxable gift.

Key Concepts

Underline/highlight the answers to these questions as you read:

1. How much can an individual transfer, gift tax free, each year?

2. What are the requirements of utilizing the annual exclusion?

3. How is the gift-splitting election an advantage?

4. Why was gift-splitting enacted?

5. What is the lifetime gift tax applicable exclusion amount?

The $13,000 annual exclusion is indexed using the Consumer Price Index (CPI) rounded down to the nearest $1,000. The annual exclusion is available and expires at the end of each calendar year. Any annual exclusion a taxpayer might have for a particular year is lost forever if not used. For 2010, the annual exclusion is expected to remain at $13,000. Gifts equal to or less than the annual exclusion are also exempt from generation-skipping transfer taxes. There is a special annual exclusion for noncitizen spouses equal to $133,000 (as indexed) for 2009. For citizen spouses there is an unlimited deduction for gifts. In addition to the annual exclusion, each person has a $1,000,000 lifetime applicable gift tax exclusion (resulting in a gift tax applicable credit of $345,800 for 2002 - 2009).

EXAMPLE 5.12

Carolyn makes a present interest gift of property with a fair market value of $13,000 to Bobby. This was the only gift Carolyn made during the year. Because the gift is for property of a present interest, the transfer will qualify for the annual exclusion, and Carolyn will not owe any gift tax on the transfer to Bobby nor will Carolyn be required to file a gift tax return.

EXAMPLE 5.13

Early this year, Mary made a present interest gift to Emile with a fair market value of $14,000. Later in the year, Mary made another present interest gift to Emile for $6,000. As the annual exclusion applies on a per year, per donee basis, Mary has made a taxable gift equal to $7,000 ($14,000 + $6,000 - $13,000) to Emile during this year and will be required to file a gift tax return.

SPLIT GIFT ELECTIONS

As will be discussed later in this chapter, gift tax returns are filed on a per donor basis, which creates some interesting issues for married individuals. If both spouses each gave one donee $13,000, then each donor spouse would use their annual exclusion, and would not be required to file a gift tax return. In many cases, one spouse would like to give property to a donee but the other spouse does not. In this case, the donor spouse, with the consent of the non-donor spouse, could use both the donor and the non-donor spouse's annual exclusion and gift $26,000 of separate property to the donee. This concept is called gift-splitting.

Therefore, if a donor is married at the time of the gift and joins with his spouse to use both annual exclusions for a particular donee, the exclusion is effectively increased to $26,000, double the annual exclusion, per donee, per year. Since the exclusion per donee expires annually, the donor spouse is essentially using the non-donor spouse's annual exclusion right for this particular donee, this particular year, even though the non-donor spouse would not have used it. When one

Quick Quiz 5.3

Highlight the answer to these questions:

1. A donor's gross estate will not include the fair market value of lifetime gifts that qualify for the annual exclusion.
   a. True
   b. False

2. If the annual exclusion is not used during the year, it does not carryover to the following year.
   a. True
   b. False

3. If a donor gifts $14,000 of community property to his niece, the donor must file a gift tax return.
   a. True
   b. False

4. An individual who gifts a total of $100,000 split equally between eleven donees is not required to file a gift tax return.
   a. True
   b. False

5. The amount of annual exclusion for transfers to a noncitizen spouse is $133,000 for 2009.
   a. True
   b. False

True, True, False, True, True.

donor makes the gift, and the donor's spouse consents to use their annual exclusion for that donee, then the gift is called a **split gift**.

A gift tax return (Form 709) is required for all split gifts, and both spouses are required to sign the gift tax return (the non-donee spouse signs an election to split gifts on the return). If no taxable gift is made during the year, (because all gifts are under the annual exclusion due to gift-splitting), only the donor who actually gifts property is required to file a gift tax return. If an election to split gifts is made, the election applies to all gifts made from both spouses during the year, regardless of the identity of the donees. If the couple married during the year, any property gifted after their marriage may be considered a split gift, but the couple cannot elect to split gifts made prior to their marriage. In addition, if they are divorced during the year and are not remarried at the end of the year then the split gift election can be used only for gifts given while married. A split gift election can also be made for gifts made in the year in which one spouse dies, but only for those gifts made while the spouse was alive.

EXAMPLE 5.14

Jennifer gifts $15,000 of her separate property to her son, Alex. Jennifer's husband, Robbie, consents to split. The gift to Alex is the only gift made by Robbie or Jennifer during the year. Neither Jennifer nor Robbie will have a taxable gift as both annual exclusions, totalling $26,000, can offset the $15,000 gift. Because of Robbie's election to split the gift, Jennifer will be required to file a gift tax return and Robbie will be required to sign her gift tax return to make the gift splitting election.

GIFTS OF COMMUNITY AND JOINT PROPERTY

Gifts of community property do not require gift-splitting, since each spouse is deemed to own one-half of any community property. Therefore, any gift of community property is a joint gift not subject to gift-splitting. Gift-splitting was enacted as a way to equalize to impact of the gift tax rules in community and non-community-property states. Since gifts of community property are not considered split gifts, the donor(s) are not required to file a gift tax return unless the gifts constitute taxable gifts. A comparison between gifts of separate property and gifts of community property is presented in the following example.

EXAMPLE 5.15

Gift-Splitting Comparison:

Peter and Reagan, who are married, made the following gifts during the current year:

Donees	Donor From Peter	Donor From Reagan	Total
To daughter, Amber	$50,000	$3,000	$53,000
To daughter, Nicole	$50,000	$3,000	$53,000
To niece, Victoria	$30,000	$3,000	$33,000
	$130,000	$9,000	$139,000

If the gifts were from community property:

Gifts of Community Property			
	From Peter	From Reagan	Total
To daughter, Amber	$26,500	$26,500	$53,000
To daughter, Nicole	$26,500	$26,500	$53,000
To niece, Victoria	$16,500	$16,500	$33,000
Total Gross Gifts	$69,500	$69,500	$139,000
Less Annual Exclusions			
To daughter, Amber	$13,000	$13,000	$26,000
To daughter, Nicole	$13,000	$13,000	$26,000
To niece, Victoria	$13,000	$13,000	$26,000
Total Exclusions	$39,000	$39,000	$78,000
Equals Current Taxable Gifts	$30,500	$30,500	$61,000

If the gifts were from separate property and without gift splitting:

Gifts of Separate Property without Gift Splitting			
	From Peter	From Reagan	Total
To daughter, Amber	$50,000	$3,000	$53,000
To daughter, Nicole	$50,000	$3,000	$53,000
To niece, Victoria	$30,000	$3,000	$33,000
Total Gross Gifts	$130,000	$9,000	$139,000
Less Annual Exclusions			
To daughter, Amber	$13,000	$3,000	$16,000
To daughter, Nicole	$13,000	$3,000	$16,000
To niece, Victoria	$13,000	$3,000	$16,000
Total Exclusions	$39,000	$9,000	$48,000
Equals Current Taxable Gifts	$91,000	$0	$91,000

If the gifts were from separate property and gift splitting was elected:

Gifts of Separate Property with Gift-Splitting			
	From Peter	**From Reagan**	**Total**
To daughter, Amber	$26,500	$26,500	$53,000
To daughter, Nicole	$26,500	$26,500	$53,000
To niece, Victoria	$16,500	$16,500	$33,000
Total Gross Gifts	$69,500	$69,500	$139,000
Less Annual Exclusions			
To daughter, Amber	$13,000	$13,000	$26,000
To daughter, Nicole	$13,000	$13,000	$26,000
To niece, Victoria	$13,000	$13,000	$26,000
Total Exclusions	$39,000	$39,000	$78,000
Equals Current Taxable Gifts	$30,500	$30,500	$61,000

Notice in the above example where the gifts are from community property, Peter and Reagan have the same gift tax consequences as if the property were separate and they elected to split gifts.

Electing to split gifts in the above example results in a decrease in the total taxable gifts from $91,000 to $61,000. The $30,000 difference is a result of Reagan not making full use of her annual exclusion for gifts.

THE APPLICABLE CREDIT AMOUNT

In addition to the annual exclusion, there is a lifetime gift tax applicable credit amount of $345,800. This applicable credit amount shelters up to $1,000,000 of cumulative lifetime taxable transfers, in excess of the annual exclusion amount, from transfer taxes. The applicable exclusion amount of $1,000,000 (also known as the applicable credit equivalency amount) is defined as the fair market value of taxable property that can transfer without creating a gift tax greater than the applicable credit against transfer taxes. For gifts in excess of the annual exclusion, there is a mandatory reduction in the applicable credit amount.

EXAMPLE 5.16

A couple with two children who had made no previous gifts could gift a total of $2,052,000 during 2009 (one-half to each child) and not pay any gift tax by fully using each parent's annual exclusion and applicable transfer credit (2 donors x $13,000 x 2 donees = $52,000 + 2 x $1,000,000). They could gift each child another $26,000 each subsequent year to use their annual exclusions, but since the applicable gift tax credit is not increasing, any future transfer in excess of the annual exclusion would require the payment of gift tax. At the death of either parent, the applicable credit against estate taxes will allow additional property to transfer free of estate tax.

EXAMPLE 5.17

Celeste transfers a present interest in property with a fair market value of $32,000 to Raymond in 2009. This transfer is the only gift that Celeste has ever made and the only gift made to Raymond for the year. It qualifies for the annual exclusion because it is a gift of a present interest. $13,000 of the $32,000 is excluded under the annual exclusion and the tax on the remaining $19,000 reduces Celeste's available applicable credit ($345,800) resulting in no gift tax payable.

EXAMPLE 5.18

Zeke gifts a total of $2,052,000 ($1,026,000 to each of his two children). Zeke is married to Debbie. Debbie allows Zeke to use her annual exclusion and her lifetime applicable gift tax credit by signing a split gift election. Assuming no previous taxable gifts, there would be no gift tax payable. The couple would use their annual exclusions for the year for these donees and would have exhausted each of their applicable gift tax credits ($345,800 or $1,000,000 credit equivalency).

For tax years beginning before December 31, 2003, the applicable credit for transfers during life is equal to the applicable credit for transfers at death. However, EGTRRA 2001 increased the applicable credit against estate taxes for years after 2003, while the applicable credit against gift taxes for years after 2003 remains at the same level. Since the credit amounts are no longer unified, we will refer to the credit against gift taxes as the "applicable gift tax credit" and the credit against the estate tax as the "applicable estate tax credit." The exhibit below illustrates the differences in the applicable credits against gift and estate tax.

APPLICABLE GIFT AND ESTATE TAX CREDITS AND EXCLUSION AMOUNTS

EXHIBIT 5.4

Year of Death	Applicable Estate Tax Credit	Applicable Estate Tax Credit Equivalency	Applicable Gift Tax Credit	Applicable Gift Tax Credit Equivalency
1997	$192,800	$600,000	$192,800	$600,000
1998	$202,050	$625,000	$202,050	$625,000
1999	$211,300	$650,000	$211,300	$650,000
2000	$220,550	$675,000	$220,550	$675,000
2001	$220,550	$675,000	$220,550	$675,000
2002	$345,800	$1,000,000	$345,800	$1,000,000
2003	$345,800	$1,000,000	$345,800	$1,000,000
2004	$555,800	$1,500,000	$345,800	$1,000,000
2005	$555,800	$1,500,000	$345,800	$1,000,000
2006 - 2008	$780,800	$2,000,000	$345,800	$1,000,000
2009	**$1,455,800**	**$3,500,000**	**$345,800**	**$1,000,000**
2010	REPEALED	REPEALED	$345,800	$1,000,000
2011	$345,800	$1,000,000	$345,800	$1,000,000

Note: Under EGTRRA 2001, the applicable gift and estate tax credits and exclusion amounts will revert to the law in effect in 2001 in 2011.

GIFTS OF A PRESENT AND FUTURE INTEREST

PRESENT INTEREST GIFT

A gift can be a gift of a **present interest** or a gift of a future interest. Only a present interest gift will qualify for the annual exclusion. A present interest is an unrestricted right to the immediate use of property. Gifts of cash, property, etc., where title passes immediately to the donee are common examples of gifts of a present interest. A gift in trust must be a gift of a present interest to qualify for the annual exclusion. Gifts to minors in trust under 2503(b) or 2503(c) are deemed to be gifts of a present interest and will be discussed in detail in Chapter 8.

Key Concepts

Underline/highlight the answers to these questions as you read:

1. What is the difference between a future interest gift and a present interest gift?

2. How does the Crummey provision convert an otherwise future interest gift to a present interest gift?

3. How can the problem with the 5/5 Lapse rule be solved?

EXAMPLE 5.19

Erin transfers her car to her brother, Aaron. All necessary title transfers are filed with the state. This is a gift of a present interest equal to the fair market value of the car because Aaron can benefit from the car and has control over it at the date of the transfer. The gift is eligible for the annual exclusion.

EXAMPLE 5.20

Randy transfers $14,000 to Christie's individual bank account. Christie has full and complete control over the current use of the money so it is a gift of a present interest. The gift is eligible for the annual exclusion.

FUTURE INTEREST GIFT

A **future interest** is an interest in property that comes into being at a future date or time. The donee's right to control the property will materialize upon some future date or the passage of time. Generally, gifts in trust are considered to be future interests. However, a present value gift of a mandatory income interest in a trust is considered to be a present, not a future, interest. A gift of a future interest does not qualify for the annual exclusion.

EXAMPLE 5.21

Cheryl gives Billy a vacation home, but reserves for herself the right to use the property for a term of 10 years. Because Billy cannot benefit from the property at the time of the transfer, the interest transferred to Billy is a gift of a future interest.

EXAMPLE 5.22

Catherine assigns (transfers) a life insurance policy on her life to an irrevocable life insurance trust and names Frank as the beneficiary of the trust. Frank cannot benefit from the transfer until Catherine dies (some time in the future) so this is a gift of a future interest.

EXAMPLE 5.23

Gaynelle made a gift of a future interest to Skip with a fair market value of $9,000. Because the gift is for property of a future interest, the transfer does not qualify for the annual exclusion and Gaynelle will have made a taxable gift on the transfer to Skip. Gaynelle must therefore file a gift tax return.

EXAMPLE 5.24

Jacklyn made the following gifts in the current year:

Gift	Donee	Value
Cash	Sarah	$25,000
Car	Bailie	$7,000
Bonds	Mikayla	$9,000
Stock in trust with a life estate to:	Bailie	$22,000
Stock in trust with the remainder to:	Mikayla	$25,000
Total		$88,000

Jacklyn's total taxable gifts for the current year equal $53,000 as determined below:

Donee	FMV	Less Annual Exclusion	Total Taxable Gifts
Sarah	$25,000	$13,000	$12,000
Bailie	$29,000	$13,000	$16,000
Mikayla -Present Interest	$9,000	$9,000	$0
Mikayla -Future Interest	$25,000	$0	$25,000
Total	$88,000	$35,000	$53,000

Each of Jacklyn's gifts qualified for the annual exclusion except the gift to Mikayla consisting of the remainder interest in a trust. Because Mikayla is unable to currently use the gift, it is not a gift of a present interest and therefore does not qualify for the annual exclusion. All of the other gifts qualify for the annual exclusion since they are gifts of a present interest.

THE CRUMMEY PROVISION

Historically, individuals struggled with a desire to limit access to gifted property by placing gifted assets into a trust while wanting the gift to qualify for the gift tax annual exclusion. A famous court case, *Crummey v. U.S.*, 397 F.2d 82 (9th Cir. 1968) eliminated this struggle to some extent. A **Crummey provision**, as it is now called, is the explicit right of a trust beneficiary to withdraw some, or all, of any contribution to a trust for a limited period of time, generally 30 days, after the contribution. A Crummey provision does two things:
1. it qualifies the transfer as a present interest gift, and
2. it creates a general power of appointment for estate tax purposes.

A Crummey provision typically limits the withdrawal right to an amount equal to the annual exclusion or less, thus, converting what might have been a gift of a future interest in trust to a gift of a present interest, which will then qualify for the annual exclusion. If the Crummey power limits the withdrawal right to an amount less than the annual exclusion, only the amount under the Crummey power is considered a present interest gift and is eligible for the annual exclusion. It is important to understand that the donee does not actually have to withdraw the money; the mere right to withdrawal creates the present interest.

Jeff created an irrevocable trust in 2009 for the benefit of his son, Joe. The trust document prohibits distributions to Joe until he reaches the age of 26. Included in the trust document, however, is a Crummey provision which allows Joe to take a withdrawal from the trust equal to the lesser of the annual exclusion or the amount contributed to the trust each year. In 2009, Jeff contributed $6,000 to the trust and in 2010, Jeff contributed $15,000 to the trust. Even though Joe cannot benefit under the trust document until he reaches the

EXAMPLE 5.25

age of 26, and thus his interest is a future interest, the Crummey provision creates a present interest for the lesser of the contribution or $13,000 each year. As such, in 2009, Joe has the right to withdraw $6,000 from the trust which will qualify for the annual exclusion. In 2010, the $15,000 contribution to the trust is offset by the annual exclusion of $13,000 to determine the taxable gift of $2,000. Note that the present interest is created by virtue of the fact that Joe has the right to withdraw. Joe does not actually have to withdraw for the present interest to apply. In fact, grantors who make gifts to Crummey trusts do not want the beneficiaries to exercise the withdrawal right.

THE 5/5 LAPSE RULE

A Crummey provision basically gives a beneficiary the power to appoint to him/herself property for a limited time. In most cases, the beneficiary will allow the power provided by the Crummey provision to expire, or lapse, without exercising it. If a trust has more than one beneficiary, the **5/5 Lapse Rule** must be applied to determine if the lapse causes a taxable gift from the beneficiary holding the Crummey power to the other beneficiaries of the trust. Under the 5/5 Lapse Rule, a taxable gift is deemed to have been made when a power to withdraw an amount in excess of the greater of $5,000 or 5 percent of the trust assets has lapsed, or not been used by a beneficiary. These numbers are not adjusted for inflation. The 5/5 Lapse Rule does not come into play for gift tax purposes (but may cause estate tax consequences for the beneficiary) when a trust only has a single beneficiary because any lapse of a power to withdraw would only result in the beneficiary essentially making a gift to himself. In a trust with multiple beneficiaries, however, the lapse of one beneficiary's power to withdraw assets in excess of $5,000 or 5 percent results in a taxable gift to the other beneficiaries, thus requiring the filing of a gift tax return. Since the taxable gift treatment from a lapse of the 5/5 amount is a gift of a future interest it does not qualify for the annual exclusion.

EXAMPLE 5.26

Harry and Wendy transfer $72,000 to an irrevocable trust and name their three children, Adam, Billy, and Christopher, as beneficiaries. The trust provisions include a right to withdraw an amount equal to one-third of any contribution for 30 days for each beneficiary up to the annual exclusion limit for both spouses ($26,000 for 2009). After 30 days, Adam has allowed his power to withdraw $26,000 to lapse. Allowing the power to withdraw $26,000 to lapse violates the 5/5 Lapse Rule because $26,000 exceeds $5,000. In this case the lapse of the power to withdraw $26,000 also exceeds 5% of the value of the assets of the trust, or $3,600 (5% of $72,000).

To determine the taxable gift that Adam made to Billy and Christopher as a result of the lapse, first determine the total amount of the lapse, which in this case is $26,000. However, only the amount of the lapse that exceeds the greater of $5,000 or 5% of the trust ($26,000 - $5,000 = $21,000) is reported as a taxable gift. Divide $21,000 by the total number of beneficiaries, which in this case is three. Therefore, Adam has made a taxable gift to Billy and Christopher of $7,000 ($21,000 ÷ 3 = $7,000). Note that Adam has also technically made a gift to himself of $7,000, but this is not reported as a taxable gift. Adam's gifts to Billy and Christopher as a result of the lapse are gifts of a future interest and therefore do not qualify for the annual exclusion.

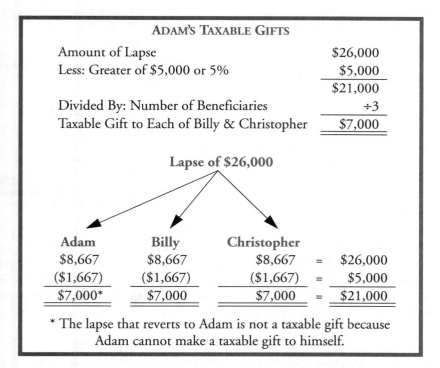

ADAM'S TAXABLE GIFTS

Amount of Lapse	$26,000
Less: Greater of $5,000 or 5%	$5,000
	$21,000
Divided By: Number of Beneficiaries	÷3
Taxable Gift to Each of Billy & Christopher	$7,000

Lapse of $26,000

Adam	Billy	Christopher		
$8,667	$8,667	$8,667	=	$26,000
($1,667)	($1,667)	($1,667)	=	$5,000
$7,000*	$7,000	$7,000	=	$21,000

* The lapse that reverts to Adam is not a taxable gift because Adam cannot make a taxable gift to himself.

Harry and Wendy could have created a separate trust for each beneficiary or included a 5/5 lapse provision in the trust in order to avoid these intra-beneficiary gift problems. The 5/5 lapse provision would limit the withdrawal amount to the greater of $5,000 or 5% of the trust assets.

TRANSFERS RESULTING IN NO GIFT TAX

Transfers to political organizations, qualified transfers, payments for legal support, payments between divorcing spouses, and transfers within a business setting are types of gifts that are not subject to gift tax. Other transfers, such as gifts to spouses and gifts to charities, are subject to the gift tax regime but generally result in no gift tax due to their unlimited deduction.

TRANSFERS TO POLITICAL ORGANIZATIONS

Under Section 2501(a)(5) of the Internal Revenue Code, gifts made to political organizations are exempt from gift tax. The term "political organization" means a party, committee, association, fund, or other organization (whether or not incorporated) organized and operated primarily for the purpose of directly or indirectly accepting contributions or making expenditures, or both, for an exempt function. Under IRC Section 527(e)(2), exempt functions include influencing or attempting to influence the selection, nomination, election, or appointment of any individual to any Federal, State, or local public office or office in a political organization, or the election of Presidential or Vice-Presidential electors, whether or not such individual or electors are selected, nominated, elected, or appointed.

QUALIFIED TRANSFERS

Certain transfers, called **qualified transfers**, are not subject to transfer taxes. A qualified transfer is a payment made directly to a qualified educational institution (a qualified educational institution is an educational organization which maintains a regular faculty and curriculum and normally has a regularly enrolled body of students in attendance) for tuition (this does not include room and board, books, supplies, and other similar expenses which do not constitute direct tuition costs) or a payment made directly to a medical care provider for qualifying medical expenses of someone else. Qualifying medical expenses include physician expenses for the

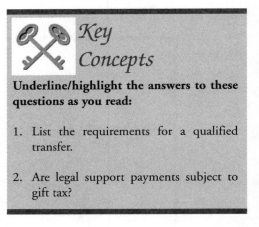

diagnosis, cure, mitigation, treatment or prevention of disease, as well as the cost of prescription drugs (generally expenses that would be deductible to the benefited taxpayer for income tax purposes if actually paid for by the taxpayer). The exclusions does not apply to the payments for unnecessary cosmetic surgery. These qualified transfers allow taxpayers to effectively transfer wealth to others (no relationship between the donor and the donee is necessary) without being subject to transfer tax. To qualify, the payments must be paid directly to the specific institution or provider.

Since qualified transfers are not subject to gift tax and there is no limitation on the amount of the qualified transfer, individuals can provide assistance to other individuals without worrying about transfer taxes. This exclusion is not limited to family members. Qualified transfers do not reduce the grantor's annual exclusion and do not reduce the applicable lifetime credit. Qualified transfers can be used to minimize the overall transfer tax within a family. For example, grandparents can pay for their grandchildren's college tuition instead of making gifts to the grandchildren's parents, which may be taxable.

EXAMPLE 5.27

Jennifer, who is single, gave an outright gift of $60,000 cash directly to her friend, Tiffany, who used the money to pay for her medical expenses. Because the gift was paid to Tiffany, instead of directly to the medical institution, it is not a qualified transfer. However, the gift is of a present interest and qualifies for the $13,000 annual exclusion. Therefore, Jennifer made a taxable gift of $47,000 and must file a gift tax return to report the gift. If Jennifer had paid Tiffany's medical expenses directly to the medical institution, the entire $60,000 would have escaped gift taxation. In addition, Jennifer would have been able to gift Tiffany an additional $13,000 during that year that would have qualified for the gift tax annual exclusion.

PAYMENTS FOR SUPPORT

Legal support payments or obligations are transfers to, or for, children or dependents and can be interpreted broadly. Payments of support obligations are exempt from the gift tax rules. Support obligations take many forms and do not necessarily stop at age 18 (the age of majority in most states).

EXAMPLE 5.28

Graduate or professional education and the living expenses incurred while pursuing a graduate or professional education paid for by the parent of the student may or may not qualify as legal support depending on state law regarding the definition of legal support obligations.

PAYMENTS BETWEEN DIVORCING SPOUSES

Payments made from one spouse to another pursuant to a divorce or separation decree are not gifts. Rather, they are either nontaxable property settlements with a carryover basis or alimony payments deductible for income tax by the payor and includible for income tax by the payee. A property transfer is deemed to be pursuant to a divorce decree if it occurs within one year of the termination of the marriage or is related to the cessation of the marriage.

TRANSFERS WITHIN A BUSINESS SETTING

Any transfer within a business setting between business people is presumed to be compensation for services rendered and is not a gift. De minimis type gifts are excepted from this presumption and because of the size of their amount are generally not subject to gift tax. Examples of such de minimis gifts would include token gifts at retirement or as part of a service reward program.

GIFTS TO SPOUSES

An unlimited marital deduction allows for unlimited tax-free transfers between spouses during life provided that both spouses are U.S. citizens. This is because the Internal Revenue Code considers a married couple to be a single economic unit. Note that to be eligible for this unlimited marital deduction, the donee spouse must be a citizen of the United States.

EXAMPLE 5.29

Travis gifts his wife $1,000,000. Travis' wife is a U.S. citizen. With the marital deduction, Travis will not owe any gift tax on the transfer to his wife.

Noncitizen spouses do not receive an unlimited marital deduction. However, a citizen spouse may transfer $133,000 annually (2009) to their noncitizen spouse with no transfer tax consequences. This annual exclusion is sometimes refereed to as the "spousal super annual exclusion."

CHARITABLE GIFTS

There is an unlimited gift tax charitable deduction for transfers to the following organizations:

1. Federal, state, or local government for public use;
2. Section 501(c)(3) corporations operated exclusively for religious, charitable, scientific, literary, or education purposes;
3. Section 501(c) fraternal or veterans organizations.

Quick Quiz 5.5

Highlight the answer to these questions:

1. Qualified transfers are limited to the annual exclusion amount.
   a. True
   b. False

2. If a payment is made directly to an educational institution, the portion of the payment that applies to room and board is not excluded from gift tax.
   a. True
   b. False

3. Reimbursing an individual for medical expenses that he paid directly to the hospital is a qualified transfer.
   a. True
   b. False

4. To be eligible for the unlimited marital deduction, the donee spouse must be a citizen of the United States.
   a. True
   b. False

False, True, False, True.

EXHIBIT 5.5 **TRANSFERS EXEMPT FROM GIFT TAX**

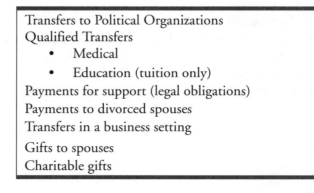

Transfers to Political Organizations
Qualified Transfers
  • Medical
  • Education (tuition only)
Payments for support (legal obligations)
Payments to divorced spouses
Transfers in a business setting

Gifts to spouses
Charitable gifts

THE GIFT TAX RETURN

FORM 709

Any donor who makes a gift during a calendar year must file a gift tax return, unless all of the gifts are less than or equal to the annual exclusion, or are not subject to gift tax, such as qualified transfers, transfers to spouses, or transfers to charities. If a split gift election is made, a gift tax return must be filed by the spouse who makes the gift, or both spouses if both make a gift, even if after the split, the gift is under the annual exclusion. Individuals in a community-property state do not split gifts when using community funds as any gift of community property is a joint gift and therefore deemed to be one-half owned by each spouse. Thus, spouses making community property gifts would only file a gift tax return if the value of the total community property gift exceeds $26,000.

The gift tax return (Form 709) must be filed by the donor by April 15 following the year of the gift. The filing date can be extended simply by extending the donor's income tax return, but similar to income tax, the time to pay is not extended and penalties will apply. In the event the donor dies in the year of the gift, the gift tax return must be filed no later than the due date, including extensions, of the estate tax return. The donor is primarily liable for the payment of gift tax, but if the donor does not or cannot pay the tax due, the IRS will seek to collect the tax from the donee.

STATUTE OF LIMITATIONS

The **statute of limitations** for the IRS to assess any additional gift tax is three years, unless the gift is not adequately disclosed on a filed gift tax return. If the gift is not adequately disclosed, the statute of limitations will never expire. It is important to file a gift tax return where a valuation discount (e.g., a minority interest stock) may be subject to reasonable differences of opinion. When the gift tax return is filed, the statute of limitations will begin, whereas the failure to file (even when the proposed value is less than the annual exclusion) would subject the valuation to argument from the IRS without the protection of the statute of limitations.

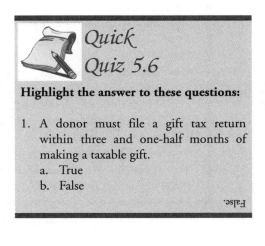

CALCULATION OF THE GIFT TAX

The following steps are used to determine the gift tax liability for a particular donor:

1. Sum the total gifts for the calendar year;
2. Subtract the total exclusions and deductions (annual exclusions, marital deduction, charitable deductions);
3. Add the donor's taxable gifts for the calendar year (total gifts less exclusions and deductions) to the donor's previous taxable gifts for all prior calendar years;
4. Calculate the gift tax from the unified estate and gift tax rate schedule;
5. Reduce the gift tax by the gift tax deemed paid and the lesser of the applicable gift tax credit ($345,800 for all years until 2010) or the calculated gift tax. (The gift tax deemed paid is the amount of tax that would have been paid if the donor had made the gift today. The deemed paid amount and the actual amount paid will vary in years when there has been a change in the marginal transfer tax rates.)

Until the donor makes cumulative taxable gifts greater than $1,000,000, he will have no gift tax liability. The following example demonstrates the gift tax calculation.

EXAMPLE 5.30

Tracy gave his daughter Skylar outright $611,000 in 2005, $712,000 in 2006 and $813,000 in 2009. An abbreviated schedule detailing the gift tax due each year is shown below. (Note: the schedule provided has been simplified to ease illustration. Form 709 is more extensive.) The annual exclusion is $11,000 for 2005, $12,000 for 2006, and $13,000 for 2009.

YEAR 2005 GIFT TAX CALCULATION

Total Gifts	$611,000	
Less Annual Exclusion	($11,000)	
Taxable Gifts	$600,000	
Plus Previous Taxable Gifts	$0	
Total Taxable Gifts	$600,000	
Tax	$192,800	($155,800 + (37% x 100,000))
Less Gift Tax Previously Paid	$0	
Less Applicable Credit Previously Used	$0	
Less Applicable Credit Remaining*	($192,800)	**
Gift Tax Due	$0	

* Credit remaining before transfer = $345,800.
** Do not exceed the tax due.

YEAR 2006 GIFT TAX CALCULATION

Total Gifts	$712,000	
Less Annual Exclusion	($12,000)	
Taxable Gifts	$700,000	
Plus Previous Taxable Gifts	$600,000	($600,000 in 2005)
Total Taxable Gifts	$1,300,000	
Tax	$469,800	($448,300 + (43% x 50,000))
Less Gift Tax Previously Paid	$0	
Less Applicable Credit Previously Used	($192,800)	
Less Applicable Credit Remaining*	($153,000)	
Gift Tax Due	$124,000	

* Credit remaining before transfer = $153,000 ($345,800 - $192,800).

YEAR 2009 GIFT TAX CALCULATION

Total Gifts	$813,000	
Less Annual Exclusion	($13,000)	
Taxable Gifts	$800,000	
Plus Previous Taxable Gifts	$1,300,000	($600k in 2005 and $700k in 2006)
Total Taxable Gifts	$2,100,000	
Tax	$825,800	($780,800 + (45% x 100,000))
Less Gift Tax Previously Paid	($124,000)	
Less Applicable Credit Previously Used	($345,800)	
Less Applicable Credit Remaining*	$0	
Gift Tax Due	$356,000	

* Credit remaining before transfer = $0.

Notice that each year the previous taxable gifts are added to the taxable gifts and the tax is recalculated. This is to prevent individuals from escaping the progressive increase in the gift tax rate schedule by gifting in multiple years. Therefore, over the years Tracy paid a total of $480,000 ($124,000 + $356,000) in tax and gave $2,100,000 ($600,000 + $700,000 + $800,000) in taxable gifts and $2,136,000 ($611,000 + $712,000 + $813,000) in total gifts including those subject to the annual exclusion.

Assume instead that Tracy gave his daughter Skylar $2,113,000 in 2009 and had not made any previous taxable gifts. Notice that the total taxable gifts is equal to the total taxable gifts over the three years given by Tracy in the previous example. In addition, the total tax paid equals the total tax Tracy paid over the years in the example above. The only difference between the examples is that Tracy was only able

EXAMPLE 5.31

to use one annual exclusion rather than three in the previous example.

YEAR 2009 GIFT TAX CALCULATION - SAME TAXABLE GIFTS AS PREVIOUS EXAMPLE

Total Gifts	$2,113,000	
Less Annual Exclusion	($13,000)	
Taxable Gifts	$2,100,000	
Plus Previous Taxable Gifts	$0	
Total Taxable Gifts	$2,100,000	
Tax	$825,800	($780,800 + (45% x 100,000))
Less Gift Tax Previously Paid	$0	
Less Applicable Credit Previously Used	$0	
Less Applicable Credit Remaining*	($345,800)	
Gift Tax Due	$480,000	

* Credit remaining before transfer = $345,800.

If Tracy gave the same amount of total gifts, $2,136,000, as he had given over the three years but within 2009, then he would have paid $10,350 more transfer tax because of his failure to use the annual exclusion for the previous two years. Note, however, that the planner must consider the potential appreciation in the property to determine if making a gift in one installment (and foregoing some annual exclusions) makes sense. If the appreciation over the proposed transfer period exceeds the additional gift tax that is incurred by making the transfer in one year, it may make sense to incur the additional tax if the client is engaging in long-term planning.

YEAR 2009 GIFT TAX CALCULATION - SAME TOTAL GIFTS AS PREVIOUS EXAMPLE

Total Gifts	$2,136,000	
Less Annual Exclusion	($13,000)	
Taxable Gifts	$2,123,000	
Plus Previous Taxable Gifts	$0	
Total Taxable Gifts	$2,123,000	
Tax	$836,150	($780,800 + (45% x 123,000))
Less Gift Tax Previously Paid	$0	
Less Applicable Credit Previously Used	$0	
Less Applicable Credit Remaining*	($345,800)	
Gift Tax Due	$490,350	($10,350 greater than before)**

* Credit remaining before transfer = $345,800.
** The $10,350 is equal to 45% of the $23,000 annual exclusion not claimed.

Form **709**	**United States Gift (and Generation-Skipping Transfer) Tax Return**	OMB No. 1545-0020
Department of the Treasury Internal Revenue Service	(For gifts made during calendar year 2008) ► See separate instructions.	20**08**

Part 1—General Information

1 Donor's first name and middle initial	2 Donor's last name	3 **Donor's social security number**
4 Address (number, street, and apartment number)		5 Legal residence (domicile)
6 City, state, and ZIP code		7 Citizenship (see instructions)

		Yes	No
8	If the donor died during the year, check here ► ☐ and enter date of death ...., ...		
9	If you extended the time to file this Form 709, check here ► ☐		
10	Enter the total number of donees listed on Schedule A. Count each person only once. ►		
11a	Have you (the donor) previously filed a Form 709 (or 709-A) for any other year? If "No," skip line 11b .		
b	If the answer to line 11a is "Yes," has your address changed since you last filed Form 709 (or 709-A)?		
12	**Gifts by husband or wife to third parties.** Do you consent to have the gifts (including generation-skipping transfers) made by you and by your spouse to third parties during the calendar year considered as made one-half by each of you? (See instructions.) (If the answer is "Yes," the following information must be furnished and your spouse must sign the consent shown below. **If the answer is "No," skip lines 13–18 and go to Schedule A.)**		
13	Name of consenting spouse	14 SSN	
15	Were you married to one another during the entire calendar year? (see instructions)		
16	If 15 is "No," check whether ☐ married ☐ divorced or ☐ widowed/deceased, and give date (see instructions) ►		
17	Will a gift tax return for this year be filed by your spouse? (If "Yes," mail both returns in the same envelope.)		
18	**Consent of Spouse.** I consent to have the gifts (and generation-skipping transfers) made by me and by my spouse to third parties during the calendar year considered as made one-half by each of us. We are both aware of the joint and several liability for tax created by the execution of this consent.		

Consenting spouse's signature ►   Date ►

Part 2—Tax Computation

1	Enter the amount from Schedule A, Part 4, line 11	1	
2	Enter the amount from Schedule B, line 3	2	
3	Total taxable gifts. Add lines 1 and 2	3	
4	Tax computed on amount on line 3 (see *Table for Computing Gift Tax* in separate instructions) .	4	
5	Tax computed on amount on line 2 (see *Table for Computing Gift Tax* in separate instructions) .	5	
6	Balance. Subtract line 5 from line 4	6	
7	Maximum unified credit (nonresident aliens, see instructions)	7	345,800 00
8	Enter the unified credit against tax allowable for all prior periods (from Sch. B, line 1, col. C) .	8	
9	Balance. Subtract line 8 from line 7	9	
10	Enter 20% (.20) of the amount allowed as a specific exemption for gifts made after September 8, 1976, and before January 1, 1977 (see instructions)	10	
11	Balance. Subtract line 10 from line 9	11	
12	Unified credit. Enter the smaller of line 6 or line 11	12	
13	Credit for foreign gift taxes (see instructions)	13	
14	Total credits. Add lines 12 and 13	14	
15	Balance. Subtract line 14 from line 6. Do not enter less than zero	15	
16	Generation-skipping transfer taxes (from Schedule C, Part 3, col. H, Total)	16	
17	Total tax. Add lines 15 and 16	17	
18	Gift and generation-skipping transfer taxes prepaid with extension of time to file	18	
19	If line 18 is less than line 17, enter **balance due** (see instructions)	19	
20	If line 18 is greater than line 17, enter **amount to be refunded**	20	

Sign Here

Under penalties of perjury, I declare that I have examined this return, including any accompanying schedules and statements, and to the best of my knowledge and belief, it is true, correct, and complete. Declaration of preparer (other than donor) is based on all information of which preparer has any knowledge.

May the IRS discuss this return with the preparer shown below (see instructions)? ☐ Yes ☐ No

▶ _____
Signature of donor   Date

Paid Preparer's Use Only

Preparer's signature ▶	Date	Check if self-employed ☐	Preparer's SSN or PTIN
Firm's name (or yours if self-employed), address, and ZIP code ▶			EIN
			Phone no. ( )

Attach check or money order here.

For Disclosure, Privacy Act, and Paperwork Reduction Act Notice, see page 12 of the separate instructions for this form.   Cat. No. 16783M   Form **709** (2008)

SCHEDULE A	**Computation of Taxable Gifts** (Including transfers in trust) (see instructions)

A Does the value of any item listed on Schedule A reflect any valuation discount? If "Yes," attach explanation . . . . . Yes ☐ No ☐

B ☐ ◄ Check here if you elect under section 529(c)(2)(B) to treat any transfers made this year to a qualified tuition program as made ratably over a 5-year period beginning this year. See instructions. Attach explanation.

Part 1—Gifts Subject Only to Gift Tax. Gifts less political organization, medical, and educational exclusions. (see instructions)

A Item number	B • Donee's name and address • Relationship to donor (if any) • Description of gift • If the gift was of securities, give CUSIP no. • If closely held entity, give EIN	C	D Donor's adjusted basis of gift	E Date of gift	F Value at date of gift	G For split gifts, enter ½ of column F	H Net transfer (subtract col. G from col. F)
1							

Gifts made by spouse—*complete **only** if you are splitting gifts with your spouse and he/she also made gifts.*

Total of Part 1. Add amounts from Part 1, column H . . . . ►

Part 2—Direct Skips. Gifts that are direct skips and are subject to both gift tax and generation-skipping transfer tax. You must list the gifts in chronological order.

A Item number	B • Donee's name and address • Relationship to donor (if any) • Description of gift • If the gift was of securities, give CUSIP no. • If closely held entity, give EIN	C 2632(b) election out	D Donor's adjusted basis of gift	E Date of gift	F Value at date of gift	G For split gifts, enter ½ of column F	H Net transfer (subtract col. G from col. F)
1							

Gifts made by spouse—*complete **only** if you are splitting gifts with your spouse and he/she also made gifts.*

Total of Part 2. Add amounts from Part 2, column H . . . . ►

Part 3—Indirect Skips. Gifts to trusts that are currently subject to gift tax and may later be subject to generation-skipping transfer tax. You must list these gifts in chronological order.

A Item number	B • Donee's name and address • Relationship to donor (if any) • Description of gift • If the gift was of securities, give CUSIP no. • If closely held entity, give EIN	C 2632(c) election	D Donor's adjusted basis of gift	E Date of gift	F Value at date of gift	G For split gifts, enter ½ of column F	H Net transfer (subtract col. G from col. F)
1							

Gifts made by spouse—*complete **only** if you are splitting gifts with your spouse and he/she also made gifts.*

Total of Part 3. Add amounts from Part 3, column H . . . . ►

(If more space is needed, attach additional sheets of same size.)   Form **709** (2008)

Part 4—Taxable Gift Reconciliation

1	Total value of gifts of donor. Add totals from column H of Parts 1, 2, and 3	**1**	
2	Total annual exclusions for gifts listed on line 1 (see instructions)	**2**	
3	Total included amount of gifts. Subtract line 2 from line 1	**3**	

Deductions (see instructions)

4	Gifts of interests to spouse for which a marital deduction will be claimed, based on item numbers _____ of Schedule A . .	**4**			
5	Exclusions attributable to gifts on line 4	**5**			
6	Marital deduction. Subtract line 5 from line 4	**6**			
7	Charitable deduction, based on item nos. _____ less exclusions .	**7**			
8	Total deductions. Add lines 6 and 7			**8**	
9	Subtract line 8 from line 3			**9**	
10	Generation-skipping transfer taxes payable with this Form 709 (from Schedule C, Part 3, col. H, Total)			**10**	
11	**Taxable gifts.** Add lines 9 and 10. Enter here and on page 1, Part 2—Tax Computation, line 1 . . .			**11**	

Terminable Interest (QTIP) Marital Deduction. (See instructions for Schedule A, Part 4, line 4.)

If a trust (or other property) meets the requirements of qualified terminable interest property under section 2523(f), and:

a. The trust (or other property) is listed on Schedule A, and

b. The value of the trust (or other property) is entered in whole or in part as a deduction on Schedule A, Part 4, line 4,

then the donor shall be deemed to have made an election to have such trust (or other property) treated as qualified terminable interest property under section 2523(f).

If less than the entire value of the trust (or other property) that the donor has included in Parts 1 and 3 of Schedule A is entered as a deduction on line 4, the donor shall be considered to have made an election only as to a fraction of the trust (or other property). The numerator of this fraction is equal to the amount of the trust (or other property) deducted on Schedule A, Part 4, line 6. The denominator is equal to the total value of the trust (or other property) listed in Parts 1 and 3 of Schedule A.

If you make the QTIP election, the terminable interest property involved will be included in your spouse's gross estate upon his or her death (section 2044). See instructions for line 4 of Schedule A. If your spouse disposes (by gift or otherwise) of all or part of the qualifying life income interest, he or she will be considered to have made a transfer of the entire property that is subject to the gift tax. See *Transfer of Certain Life Estates Received From Spouse* on page 4 of the instructions.

12 Election Out of QTIP Treatment of Annuities

☐ ◄ Check here if you elect under section 2523(f)(6) **not** to treat as qualified terminable interest property any joint and survivor annuities that are reported on Schedule A and would otherwise be treated as qualified terminable interest property under section 2523(f). See instructions. Enter the item numbers from Schedule A for the annuities for which you are making this election ► _____

SCHEDULE B   Gifts From Prior Periods

If you answered "Yes" on line 11a of page 1, Part 1, see the instructions for completing Schedule B. If you answered "No," skip to the Tax Computation on page 1 (or Schedule C, if applicable).

A Calendar year or calendar quarter (see instructions)	B Internal Revenue office where prior return was filed	C Amount of unified credit against gift tax for periods after December 31, 1976	D Amount of specific exemption for prior periods ending before January 1, 1977	E Amount of taxable gifts

1	Totals for prior periods	**1**			
2	Amount, if any, by which total specific exemption, line 1, column D, is more than $30,000		**2**		
3	Total amount of taxable gifts for prior periods. Add amount on line 1, column E and amount, if any, on line 2. Enter here and on page 1, Part 2—Tax Computation, line 2		**3**		

(If more space is needed, attach additional sheets of same size.)   Form **709** (2008)

DONEE'S ADJUSTED BASIS OF GIFTED PROPERTY

In general, when a donor makes a gift of property other than cash to a donee, the donee's basis in the property will equal the donor's adjusted basis. The holding period of the donee will include the holding period of the donor for purposes of subsequent transfers and the determination of long or short-term capital gains.

EXAMPLE 5.32

On April 13, 2009, Roman gifts a painting to Leroy with a fair market value of $35,000. Roman's adjusted basis in the painting was $4,000 and Roman had purchased the painting on January 1, 1987. Leroy's adjusted basis in the painting is $4,000 and his holding period began on January 1, 1987.

Assume, in the above example, Leroy sold the painting on May 12, 2009 for $31,000. Because Leroy receives a carry-over basis from Roman, his basis in the property would be $4,000 and his holding period would include Roman's holding period. As such, Leroy would have a long-term capital gain of $27,000 ($31,000 - $4,000).

EXCEPTIONS

Certain exceptions apply to the general basis rule stated above. The first exception occurs when the fair market value of the property at the date of the gift is less than the donor's adjusted basis. In this case, the donee will have one basis for gains and one basis for losses, sometimes referred to as the **double-basis** (or bifurcated basis) rule. The basis for losses is the fair market value as of the date of the gift (the lower value) and the basis for gains is the donor's adjusted basis (the higher value). If the donee subsequently sells the property for an amount between the two bases there is no gain or loss. Due to the application of the double-basis rule, if a donor gives away property that has a loss attached to it, he/she would have been better off selling the property, taking the capital loss against taxable income, and gifting the cash proceeds from the sale to the donee. When loss property is gifted, and is sold by the donee at a price less than the donor's basis, the difference between the donor's basis and the sale price will never be recovered in the form of a capital loss. When a donee must use the double-basis rule to determine his adjusted basis in gifted property, the holding period for the determination of long or short-term capital gains is determined as follows (1) if the gain basis is used, the holding period of the donor is included with the holding period of the donee, but (2) if the loss basis is used, the holding period of the donee begins at the date of the gift.

Key Concepts

Underline/highlight the answers to these questions as you read:

1. Generally, what is a donee's adjusted basis in property?

2. What are the exceptions to the general basis rules?

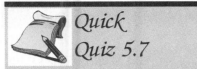

Quick Quiz 5.7

Highlight the answer to these questions:

1. If at the date of a gift, the fair market value of the gifted property is greater than the donor's adjusted basis in the gifted property, the donee's basis in the property received will be the fair market value at the date of the gift.
   a. True
   b. False

2. If at the date of a gift, the fair market value of the gifted property is less than the donor's adjusted basis in the gifted property, the donee will be subject to the double-basis rule.
   a. True
   b. False

False, True.

TJ transfers stock to Angela with a fair market value at the date of the gift of $250,000. TJ's adjusted basis in the stock was $400,000 and he had held the stock for seven months. Because TJ has gifted Angela stock with a fair market value lower than his adjusted basis, Angela must follow the double-basis rule for the stock. If Angela subsequently sells the stock six months after the gift for $440,000, she will have a long-term capital gain of $40,000. If she were to subsequently sell the stock for $300,000, Angela would not recognize a gain or loss. If Angela were to subsequently sell the stock six months after the date of the gift for $200,000, she would recognize a short-term capital loss of $50,000.

EXAMPLE 5.33

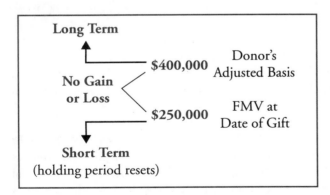

The second exception to the general basis rule occurs when the donor gives property with a fair market value in excess of his adjusted basis and the donor pays gift tax. (If gift tax has been paid, realize that the entire applicable gift tax credit of $345,800 has already been used, implying that the donor has made cumulative taxable gifts of at least $1,000,000 over his/her lifetime.) The gift tax associated with the appreciation is added to the donor's original adjusted basis to determine the donee's basis. The holding period for the donee in this case will always include the holding period of the donor.

$$\text{Donor's Adjusted Basis} + \left(\frac{\text{Appreciation}}{\text{FMV}} \times \text{Gift Tax Paid} \right) = \text{Donee's Adjusted Basis}$$

If the annual exclusion applied to the gift, the denominator for the gift tax paid adjustment is the fair market value less the annual exclusion used.

$$\text{Donor's Adjusted Basis} + \left(\frac{\text{Appreciation}}{\text{FMV} - \text{Annual Exclusion}} \times \text{Gift Tax Paid} \right) = \text{Donee's Adjusted Basis}$$

EXAMPLE 5.34

Jimmy gave Lou 400 shares of ABC Corporation stock with a fair market value of $100,000 and Jimmy did not use his annual exclusion for this transfer. Jimmy's adjusted basis in the stock was $40,000, and he paid $5,000 of gift tax on the transfer. Lou's adjusted basis will be a carryover basis from Jimmy plus an allocation of the gift tax paid on the appreciation of the stock calculated as follows:

$$\$40,000 + \left(\frac{\$60,000}{\$100,000} \times \$5,000 \right) = \$43,000$$

EXAMPLE 5.35

On March 3, 2009, Mr. Hawkins gifted rare art with a fair market value of $25,000 to his son, Derek. Mr. Hawkins' adjusted basis in the rare art was $38,000 and he paid $5,000 of gift tax on the transfer. Derek's basis in the rare art is subject to the double-basis rule. If he sells the rare art for an amount greater than $38,000, Mr. Hawkins' adjusted basis, Derek's adjusted basis is $38,000. If he sells the rare art for an amount less than $25,000, the fair market value at the date of the transfer, Derek's adjusted basis is $25,000. Finally, if Derek sells the rare art at a price between $25,000 and $38,000, he will not have a gain or loss. In this case, when the fair market value is less than the donor's adjusted basis, gift tax paid is not allocated to the donee's adjusted basis since none of the gift tax paid was associated with appreciation in the value of the gift.

EXAMPLE 5.36

Prior to 2009, Mike has made taxable gifts of $1,000,000. In 2009, Mike gave a piece of real estate with a fair market value of $513,000 to Kristi. He allocated his 2009 annual exclusion of $13,000 to the transfer. Mike's adjusted basis was $225,000 and he paid gift tax of $210,000 at the time of the gift ($1,500,000 total taxable gifts = $555,800 - $345,800 credit = $210,000 gift tax paid). Kristi's adjusted basis in the real estate is:

$$\$225,000 + \left(\frac{\$513,000 - \$225,000}{\$513,000 - \$13,000} \times \$210,000 \right) = \$345,960$$

GIFT STRATEGIES

ACHIEVING CLIENT GOALS WITH DIRECT GIFTS

Recall that one of the estate planning objectives mentioned earlier in the text was the effective and efficient transfer of property. Nothing could be more effective or efficient than a direct gift during life from the client to a loved one. With a direct gift, the transferor can assure the completion of the gift, see the beneficial effect and joy the gift brings to the donee, and enjoy the pleasure of making the gift. Furthermore, a direct gift has low transaction costs, (usually only a fee to change the title to the asset, such as a state fee charged to retitle a car to the name of the donee). Unfortunately, whenever a donor makes a direct gift, the client loses control of the gifted asset, and any future income and/or appreciation derived from the gifted asset, because the asset becomes the property of the donee at the date of the gift. Also, there is some risk that the donee may not act or use the gift in the manner intended by the transferor. The donor can do little, if anything, to change any outcome after the gift has been completed. Even with these noted disadvantages, lifetime direct gifts remain a cornerstone of estate planning.

GIFTS OF APPRECIATING PROPERTY

If the overall objective of the client is federal gross estate reduction, the client should gift property that has the greatest potential for future appreciation, rather than transferring cash or fully-appreciated property. A gift of property is valued for gift tax purposes at the fair market value as of the date of the gift. Therefore, any future appreciation on the transferred property will belong to the transferee (donee) and, thus, is excluded from the transferor's federal gross estate. Property, which commonly experiences substantial future appreciation includes, but is not limited to (1) business interests, (2) real estate, (3) art or other collections, (4) investment securities (stocks and bonds), and (5) other intangible rights (patents, copyrights, royalties). Thus, the selection of property for gifting requires careful financial and estate planning consideration. Usually, if the donor's objective is restricting or decreasing the growth of the federal gross estate, cash is not necessarily the most appropriate gift.

GIFTS TO SPOUSES

Gifts to citizen spouses are not subject to gift tax and may be in any amount. Frequently, large gifts are made to a spouse so that the spouse will have an amount equal to the applicable exemption amount for estates ($3,500,000 for 2009). Spousal gifts can be made outright or in a qualified trust. If the wealthier spouse simply wants to use the lifetime exemption of the non-wealthy spouse they can make use of the split gift election to gift assets to a junior generation and thus use the spouse's credit equivalency. Recall that gifts to noncitizen spouses are limited to an annual exclusion amount of $133,000 (2009) and there is no unlimited marital deduction for transfers at death unless certain requirements (discussed in the marital deduction chapter) are met.

GIFTS TO MINORS

Gifts to minors, excepting small amounts, are usually made either in trust or through a custodian type account. The Uniform Gifts to Minors Act (UGMA) provides that gifted property is transferred to a named custodian under the state UGMA. Permissible gifts include cash, securities, life insurance, and annuities. The custodian is permitted to spend money on behalf of the minor and serves without posting a bond and normally without the need to file accounting with the probate court. The Uniform Transfers to Minors Act (UTMA) was designed to replace UGMA. The UTMA expands the kind of property that can be transferred to minors to almost any type of asset including real estate and partnership interests. UGMAs and UTMAs are less expensive than establishing trusts and transfers to either are considered gifts of a present interest. The only caution is that UGMAs and UTMAs cannot be used to provide what would otherwise be legal support. There could also be estate tax consequences for the donor if the donor serves as guardian of the UGMA/UTMA account (discussed in more detail in Chapter 6). Gifts in trust to minors under 2503(b) and 2503(c) of the Internal Revenue Code will be covered in Chapter 8.

SINGLE PARTY GIFT STRATEGIES

One of the most common donor objectives in establishing a gifting program is to reduce the overall gross estate of the donor. To achieve this goal, it is generally never wise to gift cash. Rather, the donor should prepare a current balance sheet with a forecast of which property is likely to experience the greatest appreciation. Once this is determined, the donor should select from those assets which are expected to appreciate the most. This strategy will remove highly appreciating assets from the donor's gross estate and future appreciation will occur in the hands of the donee. Unless the donor is very close to death, this strategy will be superior to receiving a step-up in basis for transfers at death (since the highest marginal gift and estate tax rates are 45 percent and the long-term capital gain rate for income tax purposes is 15 percent).

EXAMPLE 5.37

If the objective is to reduce the gross estate, which of the following assets would be the most appropriate to transfer?

	Assets	FMV	Adjusted Basis	Expected Appreciation
Public Stock	A	$100,000	$20,000	5%
Cash	B	$100,000	$100,000	3%
Public Stock	C	$100,000	$50,000	12%
Public Stock	D	$100,000	$75,000	11%
Public Stock	E	$100,000	$125,000	3%
Closely Held Company Stock	F	$100,000	$0	15%

The intent is to determine the best asset to transfer considering current earnings, potential gains and losses, and future appreciation. The most appropriate assets to transfer (in order) are closely held company Stock F, then Stock C, and then Stock D (because assets that are expected to appreciate the most should be transferred first). One should not transfer Stock E by sale to a related party or gift the asset because the income tax loss would be disallowed. Stock E should be sold so the donor may recognize the capital loss (only the donor can recognize the economic value of the loss).

MULTIPARTY GIFT STRATEGIES

If one of the purposes of gifting is to minimize future income and transfer taxes for the donor, and if there are multiple donees, it is wise to consider which assets to give to which donee. Here is a general set of guidelines:

1. Never gift property when the fair market value is less than the adjusted basis. Rather, sell the property and let the donor recognize a capital loss for income tax. The donor can then gift the cash proceeds to the donee who can then purchase the property with the proceeds.

2. Consider gifting property with the greatest appreciation potential to the youngest donee available who has the most time for the asset to appreciate.

3. When making gifts to charities, always gift appreciated property to avoid the capital gain taxes on the difference between the fair market value and the donor's adjustable taxable basis. For such property, the donor may able to deduct the fair market value as a charitable deduction, subject to the income tax limitations.

4. Gift income-producing property to the donee in the lowest marginal income tax bracket so that the income is subject to the lowest possible income tax.

EXAMPLE 5.38

Assume that Arthur wants to make equal dollar value gifts to four parties: his mother, his son, his favorite charity, and a lifelong friend who is about the same age as Arthur. In determining what assets he should give to these various donees, Arthur should consider income tax issues, income needs of the recipient, and the actual and potential appreciation of the property. Specifically, Arthur should consider his basis in each piece of property, the potential for a charitable income tax deduction, the potential for avoidance of capital gains tax on appreciated property, and future income tax.

Donor	Arthur, age 65
Donee 1	Mother, age 85, (Low Marginal Rate Taxpayer)
Donee 2	Son, age 40
Donee 3	Charity
Donee 4	Lifelong friend, age 60

Assume Arthur has the following assets:

Assets	FMV	Adjusted Basis	Yield	Future Appreciation
Stock A	$35,000	$5,000	1%	3%
Stock B	$35,000	$26,000	0	11%
Stock C	$35,000	$35,000	2%	5%
Bond D	$35,000	$35,000	6%	+/- 1%
Bond E	$35,000	$50,000	4%	0

Who should receive which asset?

Asset with Loss	Highly Appreciated Assets	Highly Appreciated Assets	Highest Income Property	Other
Bond E	Stock A	Stock B	Bond D	Stock C
Arthur should retain or sell for capital loss	To charity to avoid capital gain and receive charitable income tax deduction	To youngest, noncharitable party to receive greatest compounding	To oldest party, Mom	By default to similar age friend

Summary Solution:

- Arthur should keep the loss property, Bond E. He should sell it and recognize the capital loss.
- Gift the most appreciated property to the charity to get the charitable contribution deduction.
- Gift the property with the highest potential for appreciation to the son who is the youngest donee.
- Gift income producing property to Mom who is in the lowest marginal income tax bracket.
- By default, Arthur's friend should get Stock C.

BASIC STRATEGIES FOR TRANSFERRING WEALTH THROUGH GIFTS **EXHIBIT 5.7**

Generally, if the objective of the transferor is to reduce the size of the transferor's gross estate, the transferor can use the following lifetime gifting techniques to achieve a lower gross estate at death:
1. Make optimal use of qualified educational transfers (pay tuition for children and grandchildren from private school through professional education).
2. Pay medical costs for children, grandchildren, and heirs directly to provider institutions.
3. Make optimal use of the $13,000 annual gift exclusion ($26,000 if the gift is made jointly with the spouse). Example: John is married to Joan and has 3 adult children who all have stable marriages and there are 7 grandchildren. John and Joan can gift $338,000 per year without coming into the gift tax system. ($26,000 x 13 transferees, including 3 children, 3 spouses, 7 grandchildren)
4. A spouse may make unlimited lifetime gifts to their spouse who is a U.S. citizen.
5. If the above four (1-4) are completely exhausted, the transferor can begin using his/her lifetime applicable gift tax credit equivalency amount ($1,000,000 in years 2002 - 2011) while still paying no gift tax until the summation of lifetime taxable gifts exceeds the applicable exclusion amount.
6. Any gift tax paid on gifts prior to three years of death will also reduce the estate of the transferor. This is discussed below.

ADVANTAGES OF LIFETIME GIFTS VS. BEQUESTS

While at first glance it may appear that transfers during life or at death are subject to the same transfer taxes because the gift and estate tax system use the same tax rate schedules, there is a big difference between lifetime and testamentary gifts. Lifetime gifts have significant advantages from a transfer tax point of view compared to testamentary, or at death, transfers (bequests).

Key Concepts

Underline/highlight the answers to these questions as you read:

1. List the advantages of making lifetime gifts.

First, any appreciation on a gifted asset occurring after the date of the gift is excluded from the donor's gross estate. Second, any gift tax paid on a taxable gift is excluded from the donor's gross estate if the gift was made more than three years prior to the donor's death. Third, the cash used to pay the estate tax is included in the decedent's federal gross estate. Fourth, gifts during life, unlike bequests at death, qualify for the annual exclusion which transfers $13,000 (2009) free of transfer taxes. Fifth, any gift of income producing property transfers the income from the donor to the donee after the date of the gift and reduces the donor's gross estate. Finally, payments of support obligations and the expenses that would be considered qualified transfers during life are excluded from the calculation of gift tax. The estate tax calculation includes the transfers for future support and future qualified transfers. The following chart provides a summary of the advantages listed above.

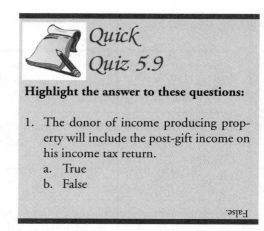

Quick Quiz 5.9

Highlight the answer to these questions:

1. The donor of income producing property will include the post-gift income on his income tax return.
   a. True
   b. False

False.

EXHIBIT 5.8 **ADVANTAGES OF LIFETIME GIFTS VS. BEQUESTS**

Transfers	Gifts and Lifetime Transfers effect on Gross Estate	Bequests at Death effect on Gross Estate
Support payments	Excluded from gross estate	Not Applicable
Qualified transfers	Excluded from gross estate	Not Applicable
Annual exclusion	Applicable	Not Applicable
Future appreciation on assets transferred	Excluded from gross estate	Included in gross estate
Future income on transferred assets	Excluded from gross estate	Not Applicable
Transfer tax paid for gifts made more than three years before death	Excluded from gross estate	Not Applicable
Cash used to pay estate taxes	N/A	Included in gross estate

Key Terms

Annual Exclusion - An exclusion from gift taxes for present interest transfers less than or equal to $13,000 per year per donee.

Consideration - Payment or transfer of property in return for other property.

Crummey Provision - The right of a trust beneficiary to withdraw some or all of any contribution to a trust for a limited period of time after the contribution. A Crummey provision converts what otherwise would have been a gift of a future interest (not eligible for the annual exclusion) to a gift of a present interest, eligible for the annual exclusion.

Direct Gift - A direct payment of cash or transfer of property to a donee.

Donee - The person who receives the gift.

Donor - The person who gives the gift.

Economic Growth and Tax Relief Reconciliation Act of 2001 (EGTRRA 2001) - Tax act signed by President George W. Bush in June of 2001. The act phases in a repeal of the estate and generation-skipping transfer tax. It also creates separate applicable credits for gift tax and estate tax.

Future Interest - An interest which is limited in some way by a future date or time. A gift of a future interest does not qualify for the annual exclusion.

Gift - A voluntary transfer, without full consideration, of property from one person (a donor) to another person (a donee) or entity.

Incomplete Transfer - Any transfers that include a revocable beneficiary designation or a transfer to a revocable trust. Incomplete transfers are not considered gifts for gift tax purposes.

Indirect Gift - A payment, or transfer, to a third party on behalf of a donor for the benefit of the donee.

Net Gift - A gift that requires the donee to pay the gift tax. The gift tax is based on the value of the transfer less the gift tax.

Present Interest - An unrestricted right to the immediate use of property. A present interest gift qualifies for the annual exclusion.

Qualified Transfers - A payment made directly to a qualified educational institution for tuition, excluding room and board, or a payment made directly to a medical institution for the qualified medical expenses of someone else. Qualified transfers are excluded from gift tax.

Key Terms

Reversionary Interest - Interests that have been transferred and subsequently revert back to the transferor. Also includes a possibility that the property transferred by the decedent may return to him or his estate and a possibility that property transferred by the decedent may become subject to a power of disposition by him.

Split Gift Election - An election available to a donor of separate property which allows him to utilize his spouse's annual exclusion and transfer up $26,000 per year per donee without incurring gift tax.

DISCUSSION QUESTIONS

1. Explain the Gift and Estate Tax reforms created by EGTRRA 2001.

2. List the elements of a gift.

3. List and define the various types of gifts.

4. List the imputed interest rules for no-interest loans and below-market loans.

Loan	Imputed Interest
$0 ≤ $10,000	
$10,001 ≤ $100,000	
> $100,000	

5. How is the creation of a joint bank account where one party contributes the entire amount treated for gift tax purposes?

6. Discuss the requirements and limitations of the annual exclusion.

7. Explain the advantage of using the election to split gifts.

8. Explain the use of the Crummey provision.

9. Qualified transfers allow certain indirect gifts to be excluded from gift taxation. Explain these gifts and the requirements to exclude them from gift taxation.

10. How are gifts to spouses treated for gift tax purposes?

11. What is the due date to file Form 709, the United States Gift (and Generation-Skipping Transfer) Tax Return?

12. Who must file Form 709, the United States Gift (and Generation-Skipping Transfer) Tax Return?

13. List the steps in calculating the gift tax.

14. A donee's adjusted basis of gifted property is generally the donor's basis. List the two circumstances when this is not true.

15. List three advantages of making lifetime gifts as compared to transfers at death.

MULTIPLE-CHOICE PROBLEMS

1. Grandmother Jones contributed $2,500,000 to a revocable trust. She has a life expectancy of 24 years and she will receive an 8% per year annuity from the trust. At her death, the corpus will be paid to her granddaughter, Lisa. What is Grandmother Jones' taxable gift?

    a. $0.
    b. $2,094,752.
    c. $2,489,000.
    d. $2,500,000.

2. Crystal loans Holly $650,000, so that Holly can buy a home. Holly signs a note, with a term of 5 years, promising to repay the loan. The home is the collateral, but because Crystal and Holly have been friends since childhood, Crystal does not charge Holly interest. Of the following statements which is true?

    1. The imputed interest is considered a taxable gift from Crystal to Holly.
    2. The imputed interest is taxable income on Crystal's income tax return.
    3. The imputed interest is an interest expense deduction for Crystal.
    4. Holly can deduct the imputed interest on her income tax return.

        a. 2 only.
        b. 2 and 4.
        c. 1, 2, and 4.
        d. 1, 2, 3, and 4.

3. Timothy made the following transfers to his only daughter during the year:

    1. A bond portfolio with an adjusted basis of $130,000 and a fair market value of $140,000.
    2. 2,000 shares of RCM Corporation stock with an adjusted basis of $126,000 and a fair market value of $343,000.
    3. An auto with an adjusted basis of $15,000 and a fair market value of $9,000.
    4. An interest-free loan of $2,000 for a personal computer on January 1st. The applicable federal rate for the tax year was 8%.

    What is the value of Timothy's gross gifts for this year?

        a. $271,000.
        b. $492,000.
        c. $494,000.
        d. $498,000.

4. In the current year, Jerry loaned his daughter, Charisse, $15,000 to purchase a new car. The loan was payable on demand, but there was no stated interest rate. The applicable federal rate for the current year was 10%, and Charisse had $900 of net investment income for the year. For gift tax purposes with regards to this loan, how much has Jerry gifted Charisse during the current year?

    a. $0.

    b. $900.

    c. $1,500.

    d. $15,000.

5. Pedro has begun a program of lifetime gifting. All of the following statements regarding lifetime gifts are true, except?

    a. Appreciation on property after the date of the gift will not be subject to gift tax and will not be included in the donor's gross estate.

    b. Payments directly to his grandchildren for their education over the annual exclusion amount will not be taxable.

    c. Annual exclusion gifts will not be subject to the gift tax and will not be included in the donor's gross estate.

    d. The donee of income producing property will have to recognize the post-gift income from the property on the donee's income tax return.

6. Carlos would like to make a gift to his son, but does not want the value of the gift and the associated gift tax to total an amount greater than $100,000. Carlos' cousin has told him about the net gift, but Carlos has come to you for clarification. Which of the following statements from Carlos' cousin is correct?

    a. A net gift does not qualify for the annual exclusion because it is a gift of a future interest.

    b. Carlos must prepay the gift tax due when he makes a net gift.

    c. A net gift requires Carlos' son to disclaim the interest in the gift.

    d. Carlos will have taxable income to the extent the gift tax paid is greater than his adjusted basis in the gifted property.

7. Which of the following is eligible for the annual exclusion?

    a. Frank designates his daughter, Holly, beneficiary of his 401(k) plan.

    b. Frank designates his wife, Betty, as beneficiary of his life insurance policy.

    c. Frank funds an irrevocable trust with $1,100,000 for the benefit of his son. The terms of the trust allow a payout at the discretion of the trustee.

    d. Frank funds an irrevocable life insurance trust with the amount necessary to pay the premiums of the policy. The beneficiaries can take a distribution equal to the contribution each year.

8. After reading an estate planning article in a popular magazine, Vaughn has decided to take action to reduce his gross estate by making annual gifts to his 4 kids, 8 grandchildren, and 4 great-grandchildren. Vaughn has discussed the gifting strategy with his wife, Rebecca, and provided it does not result in use of any of her applicable gift tax credit, she has agreed to split each gift. Vaughn does not want to use his applicable gift tax credit either. If Vaughn carries the plan out for 5 years, how much can he gift in total while meeting Rebecca's requirement? (Assume the 2009 exclusion amounts.)

    a. $208,000.

    b. $1,040,000.

    c. $2,080,000.

    d. $3,120,000.

9. Mary and Emile would like to give the maximum possible gift that they can to their son without having to pay gift tax. Mary and Emile have never filed a gift tax return and live in a community-property state. How much can they transfer in 2009 to their son free of gift tax?

    a. $26,000.

    b. $345,800.

    c. $1,013,000.

    d. $2,026,000.

10. Celeste and Raymond have been married for 29 years. Last year, Raymond sold his extremely successful automotive repair shop and his net worth now exceeds $10 million dollars. Celeste and Raymond have twin daughters, Kelly and Shelly, who will be 35 next month. Celeste and Raymond, neither of whom have given any gifts in the past, would like to give their daughters the maximum amount of cash possible without paying any gift tax. How much can Celeste and Raymond give to Kelly and Shelly during 2009?

    a. $13,000.

    b. $26,000.

    c. $1,026,000.

    d. $2,052,000.

11. Deborah provides the following list to her CPA who is preparing her gift tax return. Which of the following will Deborah's CPA include as a taxable gift on Deborah's gift tax return?

    a. Payment to grandmother of $20,000 to help her with her medical bills.

    b. Payment to Doctor's Hospital for $35,000 to cover the medical bills of a friend.

    c. Payment to Northshore Medical School for $17,000 to cover nephew's tuition.

    d. Payment to child of $6,000 that represents legal support.

12. Celeste made the following transfers during 2009:

    1. Her friend, Paul, needed $23,000 to begin law school. Celeste gave Paul the cash.
    2. An alimony payment of $14,000 to her ex-husband.
    3. She paid $15,000 to Diamond Shores Hospital for her friend Jackie's medical bills.

    What is the amount of Celeste's taxable gifts?

    a. $10,000.
    b. $12,000.
    c. $27,000.
    d. $50,000.

13. While completing Joelle's tax returns, Joelle's CPA asked her if she made any gifts during the year. Joelle faxed her the following information. Of the following, which would not require the filing of a gift tax return?

    a. Joelle created a revocable trust under the terms of which her son is the income beneficiary for his life and her grandson is the remainder beneficiary. Joelle created the trust with a $6,000,000 contribution and the trust made an income distribution in the current year.

    b. Joelle opened a joint checking account in the name of herself and her sister with $75,000. The day after Joelle opened the account, her sister withdrew $35,000 to purchase a car.

    c. Joelle created an irrevocable trust giving a life estate to her husband and a remainder interest to her daughter. Joelle created the trust with a $1,000,000 contribution.

    d. Joelle gave her husband one-half of an inheritance she received from her uncle. The inheritance was $3,000,000.

14. During 2009, Janice made the following transfers. What is her total taxable gifts for 2009?

    1. Janice gave $10,000 to her boyfriend so he could buy a new car.
    2. Janice's neighbor Judy needed $15,000 to pay for her knee surgery. Janice paid Doctors-R-Us Hospital directly.
    3. Her nephew began attending Georgetown Law School this year. Janice made the initial yearly tuition payment of $25,000 directly to Georgetown Law School during 2009.

    a. $0.
    b. $13,000.
    c. $14,000.
    d. $50,000.

15. Brent and his wife live in a common law (separate property) state. Each year, Brent makes gifts equal to the annual exclusion to his three children. During the year, he comes to you looking for a way to transfer more than $39,000 each year to his kids without using his applicable gift tax credit or paying any gift tax. All of the following statements regarding gift-splitting, are true, except:

    a. If Brent's wife would agree to elect gift splitting, Brent could transfer $78,000 per year to his kids without utilizing his applicable gift tax credit or paying any gift tax.

    b. Even if Brent's wife elected to split gifts, only Brent's gifts would be split.

    c. Even though all of the gifts are less than the annual exclusion, and not taxable, Brent will have to file a gift tax return if his wife agrees to gift split.

    d. If a couple elects to split gifts, all gifts made during the year (while the couple is married) by either spouse must be split.

16. During the year, Sean made the following gifts to his daughter:

    1. An interest-free loan of $6,000 to purchase an SUV. The applicable federal rate was 6%. The loan has been outstanding for two years.

    2. A corporate bond with an adjusted basis of $14,000 and a fair market value of $16,000.

    3. A portfolio of stock with an adjusted basis of $10,000 and a fair market value of $25,000.

Sean's wife agrees to elect gift-splitting for the year, but she did not make any gifts of her own. What is the amount of total taxable gifts made by Sean during the year?

    a. $7,500.

    b. $30,000.

    c. $41,000.

    d. $41,360.

17. Donna and Daniel have lived in Louisiana their entire marriage. Currently, their combined net worth is $4,000,000 and all of their assets are community property. After meeting with their financial advisor, Donna and Daniel begin a plan of lifetime gifting to reduce their gross estates. During 2009, they made the following cash gifts:

Son	$80,000
Daughter	$160,000
Republican National Committee	$75,000
Granddaughter	$15,000

What is the amount of the taxable gifts to be reported by Donna?

    a. $59,000.

    b. $94,000.

    c. $196,000.

    d. $255,000.

18. Jason and his wife, Maria, live in Texas with their two minor children. All of their property is owned as community property. During the year, Jason gave his brother a $13,000 car, his friend a $4,000 watch, and his dad a $45,000 fishing boat. What is the total amount of gifts attributable to Maria if she elects to split gifts?

    a. $0.

    b. $16,000.

    c. $31,000.

    d. $62,000.

19. Which of the following statements regarding the rules of the federal gift tax return is incorrect?

    a. James made a gift to his brother of $20,000 from his separate property. Even though Carly, James' wife, agreed to elect gift-splitting, only James will be required to file a gift tax return.

    b. Carly made a gift to her sister of $18,000 from the community property. Because it is community property, Carly and James are each deemed to have made a gift of $9,000.

    c. A gift tax return is due 3 and 1/2 months (excluding extensions) after the end of the donor's year-end.

    d. Carly and James filed an extension to file their federal income tax return. To extend any gift tax returns due for the year, Carly and James must file a gift tax return extension.

20. Randy transferred property with a fair market value of $56,000 to his brother, Robbie. Randy's adjusted basis in the property was $23,000. Of the following statements related to this transfer, which is correct?

    a. Robbie has an adjusted basis in the property of $0.

    b. Randy must recognize a capital gain on this transfer of $33,000.

    c. If Robbie subsequently sells the property for $60,000, he will have a capital gain of $4,000.

    d. Randy has a taxable gift to Robbie of $43,000.

21. Stephanie received 100 shares of ZYX Corporation from her aunt with an adjusted basis of $60,000 and a fair market value of $30,000 on the date of the gift. Her Aunt paid $1,500 of gift tax. Stephanie sold the stock for $45,000. What is her recognized gain or loss?

    a. No gain or loss.

    b. $15,000 gain.

    c. $15,000 loss.

    d. $13,500 loss.

22. Jack gave his nephew, Stephen, 1,000 shares of ABC Corporation. Jack had an adjusted basis of $10,000 for all 1,000 shares and the fair market value at the date of the gift was $45,000. Jack paid gift tax of $9,000 on the gift to Stephen. If Stephen sells the stock three days after receiving the gift for $46,000, what is his capital gain/loss? (Assume Jack had already made transfers to Stephen during the year to utilize the annual exclusion.)

    a. No gain or loss.

    b. $1,000 gain.

    c. $29,000 gain.

    d. $36,000 gain.

23. Landon has several pieces of property valued at $30,000 that he wants to give away. He wants to make gifts that make sense for both himself and for the recipient. He wants to give gifts to his father, Preston (who is in a low marginal income tax bracket), his sister, Tabitha, his daughter, Kelcie, and to the United Way. Match the properties to the best recipient considering he would like to keep one asset.

    a. Stock with an FMV of $30,000 and an adjusted basis of $12,000. The stock has a dividend yield of 3% and is expected to appreciate 9%.

    b. Stock with an FMV of $30,000 and an adjusted basis of $25,000. The stock has a dividend yield of 7% and is expected to appreciate 14%.

    c. Stock with an FMV of $30,000 and an adjusted basis of $45,000. The stock has a dividend yield of 0% and is expected to appreciate 4%.

    d. Real Estate with an FMV of $30,000 and an adjusted basis of $27,000. The real estate is expected to appreciate 8%.

    e. Bond with an FMV of $30,000 and an adjusted basis of $30,000. The bond has a dividend yield of 7% and is expected to appreciate 0%.

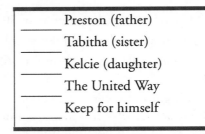

_____	Preston (father)
_____	Tabitha (sister)
_____	Kelcie (daughter)
_____	The United Way
_____	Keep for himself

Quick Quiz Explanations

Quick Quiz 5.1

1. False. While EGTRRA 2001 repealed the estate tax in 2010, the sunset provisions of the legislation brings the 2001 estate tax system back beginning in 2011.

Quick Quiz 5.2

1. True.
2. True.
3. False. The donor of a gift is primarily liable for any gift tax due.
4. True.

Quick Quiz 5.3

1. True.
2. True.
3. False. Community property is deemed to be owned equally by both spouses. Since a total of $14,000 was gifted, each spouse is deemed to make a gift of $7,000, which is below the annual exclusion.
4. True.
5. True.

Quick Quiz 5.4

1. False. Gifts of remainder interests in trusts are gifts of future interests, and therefore, do not qualify for the annual exclusion. A gift of a mandatory income interest in a trust is a present interest gift, and would qualify for the annual exclusion.
2. True.

Quick Quiz 5.5

1. False. Qualified transfers are available in addition to the annual exclusion, and there is no limit on the amount of the transfer.
2. True.
3. False. Qualified transfers must be made directly to the provider of the services, reimbursement of expenses will not qualify.
4. True.

Quick Quiz 5.6

1. False. The donor must file a gift tax return by April 15th of the year following the gift.

Quick Quiz Explanations

Quick Quiz 5.7

1. False. This statement is not always true. In some cases, when gift tax has been paid by the donor, the donee's basis will equal the donor's basis plus the portion of the gift tax paid attributable to appreciation in the property.
2. True.

Quick Quiz 5.8

1. False. When the overall objective is a reduction in the gross estate, gifts of appreciating property, as opposed to cash, would be more appropriate.

Quick Quiz 5.9

1. False. Once a completed gift is made, income generated by the property that was the subject of the gift will be reported by the donee, not the donor.

Estate Tax

INTRODUCTION

When a citizen or resident of the United States dies, an estate tax is imposed on the decedent's right to transfer property to his heirs. The gift tax system imposes a transfer tax on transfers during life. The generation-skipping transfer tax system (discussed in Chapter 13) taxes transfers made during life, or at death, to skip persons.

The estate tax applies to all transfers at death of property owned by the decedent or property over which the decedent had a sufficient interest to require inclusion in the gross estate. The estate tax is coordinated with the gift tax by including taxable gifts (at the fair market value on the date of the gift) in the estate tax calculation. This approach is used because of the progressive rate structure of both the estate and gift tax regimes.

All property owned directly or indirectly by the decedent, in whole or in part, at the time of death is included in the decedent's estate at the fair market value as of the date of death (or the alternative valuation date, if elected). Several questions arise when considering what property should be included in a decedent's estate, including: (1) whether the decedent had a sufficient ownership interest to require inclusion, and (2) whether or not property can be transferred at the decedent's death. In some cases, the decedent's rights to the property may be limited, and will therefore not require inclusion in the estate (e.g., property transferred in trust to the decedent that imposes specific limitations on his/her right to access the property). If, however, the decedent possessed a general power of appointment, property not owned by the decedent may be included in his/her estate. Furthermore, interests in property that expire at death (e.g., a single life annuity owned by the decedent) will not be included in the decedent's gross estate.

The federal estate tax is applied to the estate tax base and the decedent's estate is liable for the payment of estate taxes. The manner in which property is transferred (e.g., by probate, intestacy, joint titling, trust, contract, TOD, POD) is generally irrelevant to the calculation of estate tax provided that the decedent's property is being transferred at death.

The estate tax applies to both citizens and residents of the United States and to nonresidents of the United States. For U.S. citizens and residents, estate tax is imposed on worldwide assets. Non-U.S. citizens and non-U.S. residents only pay estate tax on assets located within the United States.

It is particularly important when studying the estate tax to understand the differences between gross estate, adjusted gross estate, taxable estate, and tentative tax base. Exhibit 6.1 will help to gain a perspective of each of these terms which are described in detail throughout this chapter.

EXHIBIT 6.1 **THE ABBREVIATED ESTATE TAX FORMULA**

(1)	Gross Estate		$ _____	Gross Estate
	Less Deductions from the Gross Estate:			
(2)	Last Medical Expenses	$ _____		
(3)	Administrative Expenses	$ _____		
(4)	Funeral Expenses	$ _____		
(5)	Debts of the Decedent	$ _____		
(6)	Losses During Estate Administration	$ _____	$ _____	Total Deductions from GE
(7)	Equals: Adjusted Gross Estate		$ _____	Adjusted Gross Estate
(8)	Less: Unlimited Charitable Deduction	$ _____		
(9)	Less: Unlimited Marital Deduction	$ _____	$ _____	
(10)	Equals: Taxable Estate		$ _____	Taxable Estate
(11)	Add: Previous (post 1976) Taxable Gifts		$ _____	Post-1976 Gifts
(12)	Equals: Tentative Tax Base		$ _____	Tentative Tax Base
(13)	Tentative Tax		$ _____	Tentative Tax
	Less: Allowable Credits			
(14)	Credit for Previous Gift Tax Paid	$ _____		
(15)	Applicable Estate Tax Credit	$ _____		
(16)	Credit for Tax Paid on Prior Transfers	$ _____		
(17)	Foreign Death Tax Credit	$ _____	$ _____	Total Allowable Credits
(18)	Equals: Federal Estate Tax Liability		$ _____	Federal Estate Tax Liability

Note: An additional credit may be available for gift tax paid before 1977. The state death tax credit may be available for years before 2005. In years after 2004 a deduction is available for state death taxes.

THE GROSS ESTATE

The starting point for determining the estate tax due is to calculate the value of a decedent's gross estate. The decedent's **gross estate** is defined as the fair market value of all interests owned by the decedent at the time of death. However, a decedent's gross estate may also include certain property interests the decedent transferred during his lifetime, as well as the decedent's interest in any jointly held property and, in some cases, the proceeds of life insurance on the decedent's life.

A financial planner must have a clear understanding of the current and projected value of the client's gross estate in order to develop a meaningful estate plan. The value and types of interests included in the gross estate will directly determine which planning techniques should be considered for implementation.

THE ABBREVIATED ESTATE TAX FORMULA - GROSS ESTATE

EXHIBIT 6.2

(1)	Gross Estate		$	Gross Estate
	Less Deductions:			
(2)	Last Medical Expense	$		
(3)	Administrative Expenses	$		
(4)	Funeral Expenses	$		
(5)	Debts of Decedent	$		
(6)	Losses During Estate Administration	$	$	Total Deductions from GE
(7)	Equals: Adjusted Gross Estate		$	Adjusted Gross Estate

Property interests included in a decedent's gross estate are defined in Sections 2033-2042 of the Internal Revenue Code. Each of these code sections are discussed below to explain the full scope and the many nuances of asset inclusion in the decedent's gross estate.

EXHIBIT 6.3 FEDERAL ESTATE TAX SECTIONS OF THE IRC

IRC SECTION	PROPERTY DESCRIPTION
2033	Property owned by the decedent or in which the decedent had an interest at his date of death.
2034	Dower and curtesy interests.
2035	Gift tax paid on gifts made within three years of the decedent's date of death. Gifts of an interest described under 2036, 2037, 2038, 2042, made within three years of the decedent's date of death.
2036	Property transferred prior to the decedent's date of death in which the decedent retained a life interest.
2037	Property transferred prior to the decedent's date of death in which the decedent retained a reversionary interest.
2038	Property transferred prior to the decedent's date of death in which the decedent retained the right to amend, revoke, or alter the transfer.
2039	Annuities.
2040	Jointly owned property.
2041	Powers of appointment.
2042	Proceeds of life insurance receivable by the decedent's estate, or in which the decedent possessed any incidents of ownership at his death.
2044	Property for which a QTIP marital deduction was previously allowed.

Furthermore, additional rules may be applicable to transactions before 1947, thus subsequent research is needed for client transactions before this date. Exhibit 6.3 outlines the major sections of the Internal Revenue Code related to the calculation of a client's gross estate and the topics detailed in each section.

PROPERTY OWNED BY THE DECEDENT (IRC SECTION 2033)

IRC Section 2033 requires the value of all property in which the decedent held an interest at his death to be included in the gross estate. Examples of the types of assets included in the decedent's gross estate by this section include: cash, stocks, bonds, retirement accounts, notes receivables, residences, automobiles, clothes, household furnishings, art collections, and income tax refunds due. In many estates, most of the assets included in a decedent's gross estate will consist of Section 2033 assets.

Some property owned by a decedent and included in the estate under Section 2033 may not be immediately apparent. For example, rental payments that have accrued and are receivable before the decedent's death on rental property will be included in the decedent's gross estate. Also, the interpolated terminal reserve (which is approximately the cash surrender value) or the policy's replacement cost (if the policy was paid up) of a permanent life insurance policy owned by the decedent on the life of someone else is included in a decedent's gross estate. Additionally, state income tax refunds due at the decedent's date of death are included in the decedent's gross estate. Medical insurance reimbursements due to a decedent are also included in the gross estate. These reimbursements usually occur when a decedent has paid hospital, doctor, or other medical bills and, subsequently, an insurance company reimburses the expenses.

A court award for pain and suffering the decedent experienced as the result of a fatal automobile accident caused by another person would also be included in the decedent's gross estate. Even though the court award may be paid to the decedent's surviving spouse or heirs, its value is included in the decedent's gross estate because the cause of action was personal to the decedent. In contrast, a court award for wrongful death paid to the decedent's family will be excluded from the decedent's gross estate. Since a wrongful death suit is based on the family's loss of the decedent's future earnings, it is an interest that arises after death. Therefore, it is not included in the decedent's gross estate. Exhibit 6.4 lists most of the asset types that are included in a decedent's gross estate under Section 2033.

ABBREVIATED LIST OF ASSETS INCLUDED IN THE GROSS ESTATE UNDER IRC SECTION 2033

EXHIBIT 6.4

Cash
Stocks and bonds
Retirement accounts
Notes receivable
Personal residences
Other real estate
Household goods
Automobiles
Business interests
Life insurance on someone else's life
Collectibles (art, wine, jewelry)
Vested future rights
Outstanding loans due from others
Income tax refunds owed to the decedent
Patents/copyrights
Pain and suffering award
Damages owed to the decedent
Dividends declared and payable
Income in respect of decedent (Wages receivable)
Any other tangible personal property

DOWER AND CURTESY INTEREST (IRC SECTION 2034)

The common law concepts of dower and curtesy were developed to require that a surviving spouse receive a statutory share of their deceased spouse's estate. The curtesy right is a husband's right to receive a life estate at his wife's death in the land she owned in fee simple if the couple had at least one child. The dower right was traditionally a wife's right to a life estate in one third of the land her husband owned in fee simple at his death. Dower rights later evolved to be more consistent with curtesy rights by giving the wife a life estate in all property owned at death, not just one third. In the United States, dower and curtesy rights have been replaced in many states with a statutory right of election in favor of the surviving spouse. A statutory right of election prevents a decedent from disinheriting a spouse by allowing a surviving spouse to elect against the deceased spouse's testamentary estate plan and take between 1/3 and 1/2 of the deceased spouse's assets (depending on state law). IRC Section 2034 includes the fair market value of any property subject to dower, curtesy, or elective share rights in a decedent's gross estate.

| EXAMPLE 6.1 | Marguerite's will bequeaths all of her property to her son Jeff. However, Marguerite's state of residence allows her surviving husband to take 1/2 of Marguerite's assets (elective share right) regardless of the will provision. In either case, Marguerite's estate will include the full fair market value of her assets, that pass to her husband. Her husband's elective share right does not alter the inclusion of the assets in her gross estate. As will be discussed below, the property passing to her husband may be eligible for the unlimited marital deduction. |

GIFTS MADE WITHIN THREE YEARS OF DEATH (IRC SECTION 2035)

Section 2035 of the IRC includes a lookback provision that requires the value of certain lifetime transactions to be included in a decedent's gross estate. Specifically, IRC Section 2035 requires a decedent's gross estate to include (1) any gift tax paid on gifts made within three years of the decedent's date of death, (2) the value of any property gifted within three years of the decedent's date of death if the property would have been included in the decedent's gross estate under IRC Sections 2036, 2037, or 2038, and (3) the death proceeds of any life insurance policy insuring the decedent's life that was gifted within three years of the decedent's date of death.

Gift Tax Paid Within Three Years of Death

Any gift tax paid on gifts made within three years of a decedent's date of death must be added to the gross estate. This is called the gross-up approach and is designed to prevent the amount of the gift tax paid from escaping the gross estate and ultimately transfer tax. The actual value of the gifts made within three years of the decedent's date of death are NOT included in the decedent's gross estate, but only the gift tax paid. The value of the gifts themselves are added to the taxable estate just like any other post-1976 taxable gifts. The effect of the gross-up rule is to require the decedent to pay estate tax on amounts used to pay gift tax for lifetime transfers.

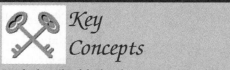

Key Concepts

Underline/highlight the answers to these questions as you read:

1. Identify the types of property that are included in the gross estate.

2. Describe the applicable code sections related to the gross estate and the inclusion rules associated with these sections.

On March 13th of the current year, Travis gave his brother a tract of land valued at $1,000,000. Travis had already used his applicable gift tax credit and accordingly paid gift tax of $450,000 on this transfer to his brother. Fifteen months after the gift to his brother, Travis died. Consequently, Travis' gross estate will include $450,000 relating to the gift tax paid on the transfer to his brother within three years of his death.

EXAMPLE 6.2

The inclusion required by IRC Section 2035 only applies to actual gift tax paid (i.e., cash paid by the decedent). Gifts shielded from gift tax by the applicable gift tax credit, marital deduction, or annual exclusion will not trigger the application of the gross-up rule.

On February 2nd of the current year, Richard gave his three daughters $60,000 each. Richard has not made any previous gifts during his lifetime and as such no gift tax was due on the transaction because of the application of his applicable gift tax credit. Six months after the gifts, Richard died. Richard's gross estate will not include any amounts related to these gifts to his daughters because gifts are not included in the gross estate and there was no gift tax paid.

EXAMPLE 6.3

Property Gifted Within Three Years of Death

IRC Section 2035 also requires inclusion of the value of property gifted by the decedent within three years of his death which would otherwise have been included in the decedent's gross estate under Sections 2036 (transfers with a life estate), 2037 (transfers taking effect at death), or 2038 (revocable transfers). These IRC sections are referred to as the retained interest provisions of the Code. They include partial transfers of property and are premised on the notion that since the decedent made a gift of property but retained a certain degree of control and enjoyment over the property, the value of the property should be included in his gross estate if he dies within three years of the transfer. Each of these sections is discussed in detail below.

Transfer of a Life Insurance Policy Within Three Years of Death

Under Section 2035, the proceeds of a life insurance policy on the life of the decedent will be included in the decedent's gross estate if, within three years of the decedent's death, the decedent made a gratuitous completed transfer of the policy.

John was the sole owner of a paid-up whole life insurance policy on his own life with a death benefit of $3,000,000. On April 3, 2007, the policy had a replacement cost of $232,000 and John gave the policy to his son Oscar. Since John had already used his applicable gift tax credit and his annual exclusion for his son Oscar, he paid $95,120 of gift tax on the transfer. Unexpectedly, John died on May 30, 2009. Because John gratuitously transferred the life insurance policy to Oscar within three years of his death, John's gross estate will include the death benefit of the policy trans-

EXAMPLE 6.4

ferred of $3,000,000. John's estate will get credit for the gift tax paid.

If the decedent continued to pay premiums on a policy gifted within three years of death the premiums payments would be a gift eligible for the annual exclusion (if they are considered a present interest transfer), and any gift tax paid on the gift may be included in the decedent's gross estate under Section 2035.

EXAMPLE 6.5	If, in the above example, John's whole life insurance policy had not been paid up, and John gave money to Oscar to pay policy premiums, the additional premiums would be treated as gifts eligible for the annual exclusion. Any gift tax paid within three years of his death on the premium payments would be included in John's gross estate.

Chapter 11 of this text is completely devoted to estate planning with life insurance and its gift and estate tax consequences. See Chapter 11 for additional discussion of life insurance.

TRANSFERS WITH A RETAINED LIFE ESTATE (IRC SECTION 2036)

A decedent's gross estate includes the value of any interest in property transferred by the decedent in which he retained some interest in the property during his life. A transferred interest is treated as having been retained if, at the time of the transfer, there was an understanding, expressed or implied, that the interest or right would later be conferred. Three basic situations cause the fair market value of the property at the decedent's date of death to be included in the decedent's gross estate: an interest retained for life, an interest retained for a period only ascertainable by death, and a retained interest held at death.

Interest Retained for Life

A decedent who retains or reserves an interest in transferred property for his life must include the value of that property in his gross estate under IRC Section 2036. An example of this situation is when the decedent transfers property but retains the income, use or enjoyment, or the right to exercise voting rights over such property for his life.

EXAMPLE 6.6	Sally conveys her home to her three children and relinquishes any legal ownership in the home. At the time of the transfer, the value of the home was $200,000. The titling document indicates that Sally retained the right to live in the home for the remainder of her life. Because Sally retained the right to live in the home, the full fair market value of the home at her date of death will be included in her gross estate.

Interest Retained for a Period Only Ascertainable by Death

A decedent who retains an interest in property for any period not ascertainable without reference to the decedent's death must include the fair market value, determined at the decedent's date of death, of the property in his gross estate under IRC Section 2036.

Andy transferred his bond portfolio to his favorite son Jackson, but reserved the right for himself to receive quarterly bond income payments. The transfer agreement also stated that the income payable for the period between the last quarterly payment and Andy's date of death was to be payable to Jackson. Even though Andy's right to the interest terminated before his death, the fact that the termination of his interest was not determinable without reference to Andy's death requires inclusion of the fair market value, at Andy's date of death, of the bond portfolio in Andy's gross estate.

EXAMPLE 6.7

Retained Interest Held at Death

When a decedent transfers property and retains or reserves an interest for any period of time, and that interest does not in fact end before the decedent's death, the fair market value of the property at the decedent's date of death must be included in his gross estate. The inclusion also applies when the decedent retains the use, possession, right to the income, other enjoyment of the transferred property, or the right, either alone or with another person, to designate the person, or persons, who shall possess or enjoy the transferred property or its income.

Haley transferred the ownership interest in her home to her son, but retains the right to live in the home for the following 10 years. Haley died 5 years after the transfer. Since Haley died during the 10-year period in which she retained the interest, the fair market value of the property at Haley's date of death is included in her gross estate under IRC Section 2036.

EXAMPLE 6.8

If a decedent retained an interest in property transferred by him, the amount to be included in his gross estate under Section 2036 is only a corresponding proportion of the property less the value of any outstanding income interest which is not subject to the decedent's interest or right and which is actually being enjoyed by another person at the time of the decedent's death.

TRANSFERS TAKING EFFECT AT DEATH (IRC SECTION 2037)

A decedent's gross estate also includes the fair market value at the decedent's date of death of any interest in property transferred by the decedent if the transfer was conditioned on all of the following:
* possession or enjoyment of the property can be obtained only by surviving the decedent, and
* the decedent has retained a reversionary interest in the property, and
* the value of such reversionary interest immediately before the death of the decedent exceeds five percent of the value of such property.

IRC Section 2037 applies whether the interest is held in a trust or is held outright, but it will not apply to property transferred for full and adequate consideration.

EXAMPLE 6.9

Jon transferred $1,000,000 to a trust with the income payable to his wife Wanda for her life with the remainder payable to himself, but if he is not living at his wife's death, then to his daughter, Kayla, or her estate. Jon died while Wanda was still living and the value of his reversionary interest immediately before death was greater than 5% of the value of the trust. Since Kayla cannot obtain possession or enjoyment of the property without surviving Jon, the value of the property, less the value of Wanda's outstanding life estate, is included in Jon's gross estate.

Reversionary Interest

A **reversionary interest** is any interest which includes a possibility that the property transferred by the decedent may return to him or his estate or the possibility that property transferred by the decedent may become subject to a power of disposition by him. A reversionary interest does not include any of the following interests:

- A transferor's right to income only, such as the right to receive the income from a trust after the death of another person; however, this right may cause inclusion in the gross estate under Section 2036.
- The possibility that the decedent, during his lifetime, might have received in return an interest in transferred property by inheritance through the estate of another person. Similarly, a statutory right of a spouse to receive a portion of whatever estate a decedent may leave at the time of his death is not a reversionary interest.

EXAMPLE 6.10

Lucas transferred $100,000 to a trust which will pay the income interest to Lucas for the following ten years and the remainder to Lucas' daughter Rebecca. Lucas does not retain any other rights to the transferred property. If Lucas died twelve years after making the transfer, his gross estate will not include any amount related to the transfer because he had only retained an income interest payable for a period that ended before his death. Had Lucas died within the 10-year income payment period, the full fair market value of the transferred property at his date of death would be included in his gross estate under IRC Section 2036.

The fair market value of a decedent's reversionary interest is calculated as of the moment immediately before his death, and election of the alternate valuation date (discussed below) is not available. The fair market value is determined using recognized valuation principles for determining the fair market value for estate tax purposes of future or conditional interests in property. These valuation principles are beyond the scope of this text.

Five Percent of the Value of the Property

To determine whether or not the decedent retained a reversionary interest in transferred property of a value in excess of five percent, the fair market value of the reversionary interest in the property is compared with the fair market value of the transferred property, including interests in the property which are not dependent upon survivorship of the decedent.

EXAMPLE 6.11

Keith transferred stocks into a trust with the income payable to Austin for life with the remainder payable to Channing. If Austin predeceases Keith, then the property will revert back to Keith. If Keith dies before Austin, then the value of the reversionary interest immediately before his death is compared with the value of the trust corpus. If Keith had retained a reversionary interest in only one-half of the trust corpus, the value of his reversionary interest would be compared with the value of one-half of the trust corpus.

REVOCABLE TRANSFERS (IRC SECTION 2038)

A decedent's gross estate includes the fair market value at the decedent's date of death of any interest in property transferred by the decedent if the enjoyment of the interest was subject, at the date of the decedent's death, to any change through the exercise of a power by the decedent to alter, amend, revoke, or terminate the gift, or if the decedent relinquished these powers in contemplation of death.

It is immaterial in what capacity the power was exercisable by the decedent or by another person or persons in conjunction with the decedent. Whether the power was exercisable alone or only in conjunction with another person or persons, whether or not the power can only be exercised in conjunction with a person having an adverse interest, and at what time or from what source the decedent acquired his power does not affect the property's inclusion in the gross estate. Section 2038 is applicable to any power affecting the time or manner of enjoyment of property or its income, even though the identity of the beneficiary is not affected.

EXAMPLE 6.12

Nellie places property in a trust for Jesse. The trust is an irrevocable trust and both the income and remainder are payable to Jesse. Nellie retains the right to accumulate or distribute earnings and the right to change the income beneficiary. Even though Jesse will receive the property at termination of the trust, Nellie's right to change the income beneficiary causes inclusion of the fair market value of the trust assets in Nellie's gross estate.

Section 2038 does not apply:
1. To the extent that the transfer was for full and adequate consideration in money or money's worth, or
2. If the decedent's power could be exercised only with the consent of all parties having an interest (vested or contingent) in the transferred property, and if the power adds nothing to the rights of the parties under local law, or
3. To a power held solely by a person other than the decedent. But, for example, if the decedent had the unrestricted power to remove or discharge a trustee at any time and appoint himself trustee, the decedent is considered as having the powers of the trustee.

However, this result would not follow if he only had the power to appoint himself trustee under limited conditions which did not exist at the time of his death.

ANNUITIES (IRC SECTION 2039)

A **straight single life annuity** is an annuity paid to the annuitant until his death. A decedent who owned a straight life annuity before his death will not include any amount related to the annuity in his gross estate since the annuitant's interest in the contract terminated at his death. A **survivorship annuity** is an annuity that provides payments to one person, and then provides payments to a second person upon the death of the first. When the first annuitant dies, the value of a comparable policy on the second annuitant is included in the first annuitant's gross estate. If the second to die has contributed to the purchase of the policy, then only the proportionate value of the annuity is included in the gross estate of the first to die.

EXAMPLE 6.13	Steve purchases a straight single life annuity. When he dies, the annuity is not included in his gross estate because the annuity extinguishes upon Steve's death.
EXAMPLE 6.14	Steve purchases a survivorship annuity. Steve dies and his companion, Erin, becomes the annuitant. The value of a comparable annuity, based on Erin's age, is included in Steve's gross estate.
EXAMPLE 6.15	Steve and Erin purchase a survivorship annuity together. They each pay half of the premiums. When Steve dies, only one half of the value of Erin's survivorship annuity will be included in his gross estate since he contributed only one-half of the premiums.

Under Section 2039, the value of the survivorship annuity included in a decedent's gross estate is based on the ratio of the decedent's contributions to the survivorship annuity's total cost to the total cost of the survivorship annuity. This ratio is then multiplied by the value of the annuity at the decedent's date of death.

$$\text{Gross Estate Inclusion} = \left(\text{Value of annuity at decedent's death} \times \frac{\text{Decedent's cost basis}}{\text{Total annuity cost basis}} \right)$$

EXAMPLE 6.16	Louis and Margie each contributed $15,000 to the purchase price of a survivorship annuity contract. The annuity will pay an annuity over their joint lives and will continue the annuity for the survivor's life. Assume that the value of the survivorship annuity at the first death is $20,000. Since the decedent contributed one-half of the cost of the annuity contract, the amount to be included in his gross estate under Section 2039 is $10,000. ($20,000 x ($15,000 ÷ $30,000))

Recall that this will not apply to a single life annuity as the value of single life annuity will not be included in a decedent's gross estate.

JOINT INTERESTS (IRC SECTION 2040)

Section 2040 requires the following jointly held interests to be included in a decedent's estate:

- Property held by the decedent and any other person as joint tenancy with rights of survivorship,
- Property held by the decedent and spouse as tenants by the entirety,
- A deposit of money, or a bond or other instrument owned by the decedent, but held in the name of the decedent and any other person, which is payable to either the decedent or a survivor.

A decedent's gross estate includes the fair market value at a decedent's date of death of any property jointly held by the decedent and another person with a right of survivorship. To the extent that the property was acquired by the decedent and the other joint owner or owners by gift, devise, bequest, or inheritance, the value of the decedent's fractional share of the property is included in his gross estate. In all other cases, the value of the property is included based on the actual contribution rule as discussed in Chapter 3. The actual contribution rule requires the full fair market value of the property less any amount attributable to, and actually paid for by another joint owner or owners, to be included in the decedent's gross estate.

The value attributable to the other joint owner or owners only considers the portion of their ownership which is not attributable to money or other property acquired by the other joint owner from the decedent for less than a full and adequate consideration. For example, a surviving joint owner would not be credited with any value for any portion of the property acquired as a gift from the decedent. In such a case, the decedent would include the full fair market value of the property even though he may own less than 100 percent of the property. Recall from Chapter 3, the actual contribution rule does not apply to spouses who are named as joint tenants. In such cases, each spouse is deemed to have contributed exactly fifty percent of the financial consideration for the property.

To prove that the entire value of jointly held property does not have to be included in a decedent's gross estate, the executor must submit facts sufficient to show that property was not acquired entirely with consideration furnished by the decedent, or was acquired by the decedent and the other joint owner or owners by gift, bequest, devise, or inheritance.

The application of this section may be explained in the following examples, each of which assumes that the other joint owner or owners survived the decedent.

At Mario's death, he was the joint owner with his son, Richard, of a building that had a fair market value of $130,000. Six years ago at the time the building was purchased, Mario paid the full purchase price of $60,000 to the seller. Richard received his interest in the property as a gift from his father four years prior to Mario's death. Because Mario contributed the full amount towards the purchase price of the building,	**EXAMPLE 6.17**

the full fair market value of the building as of his date of death is included in his gross estate. As such, Mario's gross estate will include $130,000 with regard to the jointly owned building.

EXAMPLE 6.18

Assume the same facts as above except that at the purchase of the building, Mario and Richard each contributed $30,000 towards its purchase price. Because Richard actually contributed 50% of the purchase price of the building, 50% of the value at Mario's date of death is attributable to Richard. Accordingly, Mario's gross estate will include 50% of the fair market value of the building or, $65,000, in relation to the jointly owned building.

EXAMPLE 6.19

Assuming the same facts as above except that Mario and Richard had both received their ownership interested as gifts from Mario's father, Mario would only include the fair market value attributable to his ownership interest of 50%, or $65,000, in his gross estate.

EXAMPLE 6.20

Don and his wife Diane own a tract of land joint tenancy with rights of survivorship. The tract of land has a fair market value of $600,000 at Diane's date of death. At the time the tract of land was purchased, Don paid the full purchase price of $120,000. Diane's gross estate will include 50%, or $300,000, related to the tract of land because the actual contribution rule does not apply to property owned jointly between spouses.

POWERS OF APPOINTMENT (IRC SECTIONS 2041 AND 2514)

A decedent's gross estate includes the value of property over which the decedent possessed, exercised, or released certain powers of appointment. As discussed in Chapter 3, a **Power of Appointment** is the power to decide who will enjoy or own property.

The parties to a grant of a power of appointment are the donor, the holder, and the appointee. The donor grants the power. The holder receives the power. The appointee is the person whom the holder appoints to enjoy the property.

Powers of appointment can be general or limited. A general power of appointment is a power in which the holder can appoint the property to any one of the following (1) to the holder, (2) to the holder's estate, (3) to the holder's creditors, or (4) to the creditors of the holder's estate. When the holder of the power can exercise the power in any of these ways, he has the right to enjoy the property if he should choose to appoint the property to himself, his creditors, his estate, or his estate's creditors. A general power of appointment should usually only be given to a spouse because of the potential for estate tax consequences for the holder of the power (discussed below). A limited power of appointment is any power that is not a general power. A limited power is also called a "special" power.

The gross estate of a decedent includes any assets over which the decedent held a general power of appointment at the time of his death. Exercise or non-exercise of the power does not change the estate tax result, but there are several exceptions. If the right to exercise a general power of appointment is subject to an ascertainable standard (health, education, maintenance, or support), then the power is not a general power of appointment and the property is not included in the decedent's gross estate. If the right to exercise requires approval of the holder and someone else (who is termed an adverse party – someone who has an interest in the property), then the power of appointment is not included in the decedent's gross estate.

EXAMPLE 6.21

Jill is the beneficiary of a trust established by her husband, Jeff. The trust is funded with assets valued at $100,000. The trust includes a power of appointment clause allowing Jill to appoint up to $20,000 to herself each year. Jill dies before exercising her power in the current year. $20,000 will be included in Jill's gross estate under Section 2041, regardless of the fact that she did not exercise the power.

EXAMPLE 6.22

Jill is the beneficiary of a trust established by her husband, Jeff. The trust is funded with assets valued at $100,000. The trust includes a power of appointment clause allowing Jill to appoint up to $20,000 to herself each year for educational expenses. Jill dies in the current year. Nothing is included in Jill's gross estate under Section 2041 because her power of appointment was limited by an ascertainable standard.

If the right to exercise is limited to the greater of $5,000 or five percent of the aggregate value of the property each year, referred to as a "5-and-5" power, and the power lapses before the decedent's death, then the power of appointment is not included in the decedent's gross estate. The "5-and-5" power is designed to limit the withdrawal right to a de minimis amount and penalize those withdrawals that exceed the de minimis amount.

EXAMPLE 6.23

Mary Sue is the beneficiary of a trust established by her deceased husband, Dennis. The trust includes a power of appointment clause allowing Mary Sue to appoint to herself the greater of $5,000 or 5% of the trust principal each year. If Mary Sue does not exercise her right to withdraw this year, she cannot take an extra $5,000 or 5% out of the trust principal next year, and the power is said to have lapsed.

EXAMPLE 6.24

Mary Sue is the beneficiary of a trust established by her deceased husband, Dennis. The trust includes a power of appointment clause, allowing Mary Sue to appoint to herself the greater of $5,000 or 5% of the trust principal each year. Before exercising the 5-and-5 power for the current year, Mary Sue died before her right to withdraw expired. The trust balance at the time of her death was $500,000. Mary Sue will include the value of her power of appointment in her gross estate (which, in this case, is $25,000, or 5% of $500,000).

The assets subject to a limited power of appointment are not included in the power holder's gross estate at death.

PROCEEDS OF LIFE INSURANCE (IRC SECTION 2042)

As will be discussed in Chapter 11, IRC Section 2042 includes the death benefit proceeds of a life insurance policy on the life of the decedent in the decedent's gross estate if, at the decedent's death, either the proceeds were receivable by the decedent's estate or the decedent possessed any incident of ownership in the policy (discussed below). Section 2042 also requires inclusion of the death benefit of a split-dollar life insurance policy on the life of the decedent where the insured possessed an incident of ownership in the policy even though a part of the proceeds may be payable to a third party, usually the employer.

Inclusion Under Other Sections of the IRC

Generally, the amount to be included in a decedent's gross estate under Section 2042 is the full death benefit payable from the life insurance policy. If the proceeds of the life insurance policy are made payable to a beneficiary in the form of an annuity for life, or for a term of years, the amount to be included in the decedent's gross estate is the value of the available lump sum payment at the decedent's death, or if no lump sum option was available, the amount used by the insurance company to determine the annuity payment.

If under the terms of the life insurance policy, the proceeds payable to a beneficiary are subject to the beneficiary's obligation to pay taxes, debts, or other charges enforceable against the estate from the life insurance policy proceeds, then the amount of such proceeds required for the payment of the beneficiary's obligation is includible in the decedent's gross estate. Similarly, if the decedent purchased a life insurance policy in favor of another person or a corporation as collateral security for a loan or other accommodation, its proceeds are considered to be received by the estate and are, therefore, included in the decedent's gross estate. In such a case, any related loan outstanding at the decedent's date of the death, plus interest accrued to that date, will be deducted in determining the decedent's taxable estate (discussed below).

| EXAMPLE 6.25 | At his date of death, Scott was the owner of a whole life insurance policy on his own life. His daughter, Rebecca, was the listed beneficiary at the time of his death, and the full policy proceeds of $300,000 were paid to Rebecca after Scott's death. Scott's gross estate will include the full death proceeds of $300,000 because Scott was the owner of the life insurance policy at the time of his death. |

If the proceeds of a life insurance policy made payable to the decedent's estate is considered community property under the local community property law and, as a result, one-half of the proceeds belongs to the decedent's spouse, then only one-half of the proceeds is included in the decedent's gross estate.

Quick Quiz 6.1

Highlight the answer to these questions:

1. A court award for wrongful death paid to the decedent's family will be included in the decedent's gross estate.
   a. True
   b. False

2. The value of the decedent's reversionary interest is calculated as of the moment immediately before his death or the alternate valuation date.
   a. True
   b. False

3. Proceeds of a life insurance policy on the life of the decedent will be included in the decedent's gross estate if, at the decedent's death, the decedent possessed any incidents of ownership in the policy.
   a. True
   b. False

4. A straight life annuity is included in a decedent's gross estate since the annuitant's interest terminates at his death.
   a. True
   b. False

False, False, True, False.

Incidents of Ownership

"Incidents of ownership" are not limited to the direct ownership of the life insurance policy in the technical legal sense. An incident of ownership is the right of the insured, or his estate, to enjoy any of the economic benefits of the policy. Thus, it includes, among others, the powers to change the beneficiary, surrender or cancel the life insurance policy, assign the life insurance policy, revoke an assignment, pledge the life insurance policy for a loan, or obtain from the insurer a loan against the surrender value of the policy.

A decedent is considered to have an incident of ownership in a life insurance policy on his life held in trust if the decedent has the power to change the beneficial ownership in the policy or its proceeds, or has the power to change the time or manner of enjoyment of the property for the trust beneficiaries even though the decedent may not have a beneficial interest in the trust.

EXAMPLE 6.26

Six years before her death, Roxanne transferred a paid-up whole life insurance policy on her life to her son, Daniel. At the time of the gift, Roxanne retained the right to change the beneficiary of the life insurance policy and, as such, was deemed to have an incident of ownership in the policy at her date of death. Accordingly, the full death benefit would be included in Roxanne's gross estate.

Recall that in some instances, the proceeds of a life insurance policy are included in a decedent's gross estate under a different section of the Internal Revenue Code. For example, if the decedent possessed incidents of ownership in a life insurance policy on his life but gratuitously transferred all rights in the life insurance policy within three years of his date of death, the proceeds would be included in his gross estate under Section 2035. Also, a decedent must include in his gross estate the value of rights in a life insurance policy on the life of another person.

PROPERTY FOR WHICH MARITAL DEDUCTION WAS PREVIOUSLY ALLOWED (IRC SECTION 2044)

A marital deduction will be allowed for property included in the gross estate of the first spouse to die and transferred to the surviving spouse if a QTIP election is properly made at the death of the first spouse. When a QTIP election is made, any property remaining at the death of the surviving spouse must be included in the surviving spouse's gross estate. This topic will be discussed in detail in Chapter 10.

VALUATION OF ASSETS AT DEATH

The valuation of property included in a decedent's gross estate is either the fair market value at the decedent's date of death, or if properly elected by the executor, the fair market value at the alternate valuation date (discussed below). Fair market value is the value that would be paid for the property in a transaction where there is a willing buyer and willing seller, where neither party is acting under compulsion, and where both parties have full knowledge of the facts. "Fair market value" is the value that the assets would trade at in a perfect world. Unfortunately, a perfect world does not exist. Sometimes it is difficult to ascertain the fair market value of property due to a lack of an established market or the lack of factual knowledge about the property.

HARD-TO-VALUE ASSETS

Hard-to-value assets such as real estate, art, jewelry, antiques, collectibles, and closely held business interests usually require an appraisal. Appraising the value of property is as much of an art as it is a science, and appraisers tend to specialize in valuing specific types of property. When closely held businesses are being appraised (discussed in detail below), the extent of the decedent's ownership interest is important, since minority and marketability discounts may apply.

Key Concepts

Underline/highlight the answers to these questions as you read:

1. Describe the valuation issues related to real estate, stocks, life insurance, and closely held businesses.

2. What is the alternate valuation date and why is it used?

Closely Held Businesses

Closely held businesses are difficult to value because of the unique characteristics they possess. Factors to be considered in valuing a closely held business include the following:

- Nature of the business,
- Economic outlook,
- Book value of stock,
- Financial condition of the business,
- Goodwill,
- Earnings capacity and the ability to pay dividends,
- Shares that have been sold previously.

The value of closely held businesses may be significantly reduced using various valuation discounts. These discounts are commonly associated with use of a family limited partnership, a family limited liability company, or some other closely held business.

Minority Discount

A **minority discount** is a reduction in the value of an asset caused by the transfer of a minority interest in a business. A minority interest is any interest that is not a controlling interest. Minority owners cannot manage the business or compel its sale or liquidation. Therefore, outside buyers would not be willing to pay the same proportional amount for a minority interest as they would for a majority or controlling interest. For transfer tax purposes, minority discounts (when available) often range between 15 percent to 50 percent.

Lack of Marketability Discount

A **lack of marketability discount** is a reduction in the value caused by the transfer of an asset that has an inherent lack of marketability. Interests in a closely held business and partnership interests are more difficult to sell than interests in more marketable assets such as publicly traded stock. Therefore, a discount is often allowed for the lack of marketability. Lack of marketability discounts typically range between 15 percent to 50 percent, and can be applied to both minority and majority interests. A lack of marketability discount can be used in combination with a minority discount to produce an even larger overall discount.

> Tom died owning a 3% interest in a closely held business. The business is valued at $500,000, and an appraiser applied a lack of marketability discount and a minority discount that totaled 40%. The value of the 3% interest included in Tom's gross estate is only $9,000 [$500,000 x 3% x (100% - 40%)].

EXAMPLE 6.27

Blockage Discount

A **blockage discount** is attributable to the value of large blocks of corporate stock that are listed on a public exchange. A discount may be available because a large block of stock is often less marketable than smaller amounts of stock. In theory, a large amount of stock included in the decedent's gross estate cannot be liquidated at one time without causing a decrease in the stock's market price. The actual amount of the discount would be based on the decrease in the realizable price below the current market price of the stock.

Key Person Discount

A discount may be allowed for a business in which a key person has died or becomes disabled, called a **key person discount**. The discount is based on the economic reality that the value of the stock of a closely held business will decline if a key person, such as the founder, dies or becomes disabled. The discount may be reduced by the value of key person life insurance proceeds payable to the corporation on the death of the key person.

FINANCIAL SECURITIES

Financial securities are priced by the market and appear to be easily valued. The fair market value of a financial security is not, however, its closing price on the date of the decedent's death. Rather, it is the average of the high and low trading price for the decedent's date of death or the alternate valuation date (discussed below). If the valuation date is a weekend, the valuation of the financial security is the average of the applicable values for the trading day before and the trading day after.

EXAMPLE 6.28

Rex died on Friday, June 11. His gross estate included 100 shares of XCD Corporation stock. On the date of Rex's death, the XCD Corporation stock closed at a price of $10, but had traded at a high price during the day of $11 and a low price of $8. The value of the 100 shares of XCD Corporation stock in Rex's gross estate is $950 [(($11 + $8) ÷ 2) x 100], the average of the high and low price for the date of death.

EXAMPLE 6.29

Diane died on Saturday, June 12. Her gross estate included 200 shares of Tel Corporation stock. Because Diane died on a Saturday and the stock is not traded on a Saturday, the average of the values as determined on the previous Friday and the subsequent Monday are used to value the stock. The following per share information was determined.

	HIGH	LOW	AVERAGE
Friday, June 11	$62.00	$61.00	$61.50
Monday, June 14	$63.00	$61.00	$62.00

The 200 shares of Tel Corporation stock will be included in Diane's gross estate at $12,350 [(($61.50 + $62.00) ÷ 2) x 200].

Accrued Interest

If the financial security included in the decedent's gross estate is a bond or any other type of interest bearing instrument, any interest accrued, but not paid to the decedent at the decedent's date of death, is added to the value of the instrument.

EXAMPLE 6.30

Rosie's gross estate included a semi-annual coupon bond. On the date of her death, the bond traded at a high price of $980 and a low price of $976. A coupon interest payment of $60 was also due to be paid six days after Rosie's death. $59 of the interest payment had accrued at the time of Rosie's death. The bond will be included in Rosie's gross estate at a value of $978 [($980 + $976) ÷ 2] plus the accrued interest of $59, for a total value related to the bond of $1,037 ($978 + $59).

Accrued Dividends

If the financial security included in a decedent's gross estate is a dividend paying stock, the value of any declared dividends at the decedent's date of death may also be included in the decedent's gross estate. The inclusion of the dividend, and its presentation in the gross estate, depends upon the decedent's date of death in relation to the dividend date of declaration, the X dividend date, the date of record, and the date of payment, as discussed below.

The **date of declaration** is the date the board of directors approves and declares that a dividend will be paid to the shareholders. The **X dividend date** is the date that the market price of the stock adjusts for the dividend (i.e., the market price is reduced approximately by the amount of the dividend). The **date of record** is the date that the company determines who owns stock in the company and is entitled to a dividend regardless of whether or not they own the stock as of the payment date. Shareholders who purchase stock between the date of record and the date of payment are not entitled to the dividend. The date of payment is the date the company pays the dividend to its shareholders.

If the date of death is on or after the date of declaration and before the X dividend date, there is no adjustment to the stock value and the value of the dividend is not included in the decedent's gross estate. If the date of death is on or after the X dividend date and before the date of record the dividend is added to the calculated stock value (the average of the high and the low for the valuation date). If the date of death is on or after the date of record and before the date of payment, the dividend is accrued and is separately stated within the decedent's gross estate. Note that the X dividend date may be the same as the date of record, in which case there is no adjustment to the stock value.

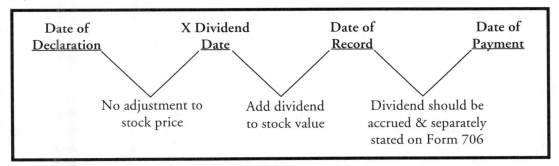

Date of Declaration	X Dividend Date	Date of Record	Date of Payment
No adjustment to stock price	Add dividend to stock value	Dividend should be accrued & separately stated on Form 706	

Financial Securities Not Traded on Valuation Date

If the stock is not traded on the decedent's date of death, the value of the stock according to the IRS Regulations should be the stock price following the decedent's date of death multiplied by the number of days from the stock trade before the date of death. Added to this is the stock price directly preceding the death multiplied by the number of days (trading days) between the death and the next trading day. This sum should be divided by the sum of the days before and after the death. Weekends, holidays, or other days that the market is closed are not included in the calculation.

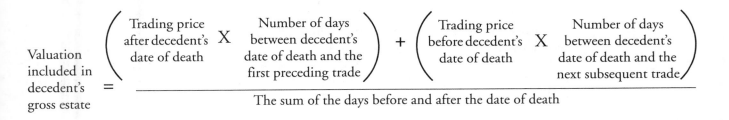

$$\text{Valuation included in decedent's gross estate} = \frac{\left(\begin{array}{c}\text{Trading price after decedent's date of death}\end{array} X \begin{array}{c}\text{Number of days between decedent's date of death and the first preceding trade}\end{array}\right) + \left(\begin{array}{c}\text{Trading price before decedent's date of death}\end{array} X \begin{array}{c}\text{Number of days between decedent's date of death and the next subsequent trade}\end{array}\right)}{\text{The sum of the days before and after the date of death}}$$

EXAMPLE 6.31

Unpopular Inc. stock does not trade on a regular basis. If Ashton dies on Thursday, May 6 and the most recent trades for Unpopular stock are:

Day of the week	Date	Price
Monday	5/3	$27
Wednesday	5/5	$25
Thursday	5/6	Date of Death
Monday	5/10	$28
Tuesday	5/11	$29

The date of death artificial valuation that will be included in Ashton's gross estate is $26, as calculated below.

$$\frac{(28 \times 1) + (25 \times 2)}{3 \text{ days}} = \frac{78}{3} = \$26$$

The stock price following the death should be multiplied by the number of days from the stock trade before the date of death (in this case, 1 day). Added to this is the stock price directly preceding the death, multiplied by the number of days (trading days) between the death and the next trading day (in this case, 2 days, Friday and Monday). This sum should be divided by the sum of the days before and after the death (2 + 1 = 3 days).

LIFE INSURANCE

The value of life insurance for gift tax purposes is the interpolated terminal reserve (which approximates the cash value of the policy) if the policy is in pay status, or the replacement cost of the policy if it is paid up. Alternatively, the value of life insurance included in the gross estate of an insured who owned or possessed incidents of ownership in a policy will be its face value (the death proceeds). If an annuity settlement option is chosen by the beneficiary, the amount includible in the decedent's gross estate will be the amount that would have been payable as a lump sum (generally the death proceeds).

THE ALTERNATE VALUATION DATE

Because death is presumed to be involuntary, the **alternate valuation date** is provided to give relief to a decedent who happened to die on a date where his gross estate had a high value due to temporary market conditions. The executor can make an election to value the estate on the date six months after the decedent's date of death, if such election will decrease both the value of the gross estate and the estate tax liability. Under this election, all assets are valued at the date six months after the decedent's date of death or the asset's date of disposition, if earlier than six months. The alternate valuation date initially applies to all assets in the gross estate, not just to specific assets.

EXHIBIT 6.5

To Qualify

1. The total value of the gross estate must decline after the date of death, and
2. The total estate tax must be less than the estate tax calculated using the date of death values.

Valuation if Properly Elected

1. All assets valued at the alternate valuation date
2. Except:
   - Assets distributed or sold after death but before the alternative valuation date, which are valued at the date of distribution or sale, and
   - Wasting assets (annutized annuities, patents, royalties, installment notes, lease income), which must be valued at the date of death.

There are several exceptions to using the alternate valuation date to value assets. Wasting assets are always valued at the decedent's date of death. Wasting assets include those assets whose value changes merely due to the passage of time, rather than market conditions. Annuities, patents, copyrights, and installment notes are examples of wasting assets which must be valued at the decedent's date of death. Additionally, assets disposed of between the decedent's date of death and the alternate valuation date will be valued as of their date of disposition.

Since the election to use the alternate valuation date creates a lower valuation in the decedent's gross estate, it also results in a lower income tax basis to the heirs of the estate. Consideration should be given to the marginal estate tax rate versus the heir's marginal income tax rate to determine the overall lowest tax cost. An assessment should also be made as to whether the beneficiary intends to sell or otherwise dispose of the asset some time in the near future so that the most appropriate income tax basis will be used.

To elect the alternate valuation date, an estate tax return must be filed, and both the value of the gross estate and the total estate tax liability must

Quick Quiz 6.2

Highlight the answer to these questions:

1. A minority interest is any interest that, in terms of voting, is not a controlling interest.
   a. True
   b. False

2. The executor can make an election to value the estate nine months after the date of death.
   a. True
   b. False

3. Assets disposed of between the date of death and the alternate valuation date are valued on the date of disposition if the alternate valuation date is properly elected.
   a. True
   b. False

True, False, True.

be lower than what the primary date of death valuation date would have yielded. The election to utilize the alternate valuation date is made on Form 706, but will not be valid if the return is filed more than one year after the time prescribed by law (including extensions) for filing the Form 706.

EXAMPLE 6.32

Riley died recently and left the assets shown below at their fair market value at his date of death (DOD) and at six months after his DOD:

Item	Value at DOD	Value Six Months after DOD
Land	$5,000,000	$4,500,000
Stock	$300,000	$310,000
Annuity	$100,000	$95,000
Condominium	$300,000	Sold 2 months after DOD for $295,000
Total	$5,700,000	$5,200,000

If Riley's executor properly elects the alternate valuation date, Riley's total estate will be $4,500,000 + $310,000 + $100,000 + $295,000 = $5,205,000. The land and stock are valued at the alternate valuation date, the annuity (a wasting asset) must be valued at Riley's DOD ($100,000), and the condominium will be valued as of the sale (disposition) date ($295,000).

One final point is worth making. Since most individuals will not incur an estate tax when they die, the election to use the alternative valuation date is not available to them. This is because the value in the estate is also the basis for heirs for income tax capital gains purposes, going forward.

DEDUCTIONS TO DETERMINE THE ADJUSTED GROSS ESTATE

To determine the **adjusted gross estate**, certain deductions are taken from the gross estate in recognition that the entire value of the gross estate will not be transferred to the heirs due to the presence of these costs. Under our transfer tax system, the estate will be subject to tax on the value of the property transferred to the surviving heirs.

The adjusted gross estate is determined by deducting the following items from the gross estate:

- Funeral expenses,
- Last medical expenses,
- Administrative expenses,
- Debts of the decedent,
- Losses during estate administration.

The application of the Qualified Family owned business deduction (which was repealed for tax years after 2003 but may still impact certain estates), Section 6166 Installment Payments of Estate Tax, and Section 2032A Special Use Valuation all depend upon the size of the adjusted gross estate. These provisions will be discussed at length later in the textbook.

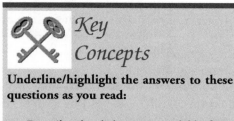

Key Concepts

Underline/highlight the answers to these questions as you read:

1. Describe the deductions available from the gross estate.

2. What expenses are deductible from the adjusted gross estate to determine the taxable estate?

THE ABBREVIATED ESTATE TAX FORMULA - DEDUCTIONS FROM THE GROSS ESTATE   **EXHIBIT 6.6**

(1)	Gross Estate		$	Gross Estate
	Less Deductions:			
(2)	Last Medical Expense	$		
(3)	Administrative Expenses	$		
(4)	Funeral Expenses	$		
(5)	Debts of Decedent	$		
(6)	Losses During Estate Administration	$	$	Deductions
(7)	Equals: Adjusted Gross Estate		$	Adjusted Gross Estate

Funeral Expenses
Reasonable expenses for the decedent's funeral, such as interment costs, the cost of the burial plot, grave marker, and transportation of the body to the place of burial are deductible from the gross estate to determine the adjusted gross estate. A reasonable expenditure for a tombstone, monument, or mausoleum, or for a burial lot, either for the decedent or his family, including an estimate of reasonable future care, may also be deductible from the gross estate. These funeral expenses must actually be incurred by the estate to be deducted.

Last Medical Expenses
Medical expenses related to the decedent's last illness are deductible from the decedent's gross estate provided the expenses are not included as a deduction on the decedent's final federal income tax return.

Administrative Expenses

Any expenses related to the administration of the estate are deductible from either the estate tax return (Form 706) or the estate's income tax return (Form 1041). The amounts deductible as administrative expenses are limited to expenses that are actually and necessarily incurred in the administration of the decedent's estate. Examples of these expenses include expenses related to the collection of the assets, payment of the debts, and the distribution of property to the heirs. More specifically, these expenses often include attorney and accountant fees for preparing the decedent's estate tax return and the estate's income tax return, the expenses related to retitling the assets through the probate process, and the executor's fee (often limited by state law). The costs of appraisals and any fees related to valuing the assets included in the gross estate and the debts deducted from the gross estate are also considered administrative expenses that are deductible from the gross estate in arriving at the adjusted gross estate. Any expenditures not essential to the proper settlement of the decedent's estate, but incurred for the individual benefit of any heirs or legatees, are not deductible.

Because the decedent's estate tax return is usually filed before the administration of the estate has been completed, executors may deduct an estimate of the future administrative expenses.

Debts

The value of the decedent's debts at his date of death are deductible from the decedent's gross estate in calculating the adjusted gross estate. Debts are any amount the decedent was obligated to pay the moment before his death, including any interest accrued up to the decedent's date of death. Debts generally include items such as outstanding mortgages, income tax due, gift tax payable, credit card balances, and other miscellaneous outstanding debts such as amounts due to retailers and other monthly service type providers (gas bills, electric bills, etc.). Liabilities imposed by law or arising out of torts are also deductible. Only those claims which are enforceable against the decedent's estate may be deducted. Only interest accrued to the date of the decedent's death is allowable even if the executor elects the alternate valuation date.

Losses During Estate Administration

Any losses to the estate during the period of administration, including casualty and theft losses, are deductible expenses. Losses can arise during the administration of an estate just as they can arise during an individual's life. For example, an estate can suffer a loss due to a fire, storm, shipwreck, casualty, or theft. The value of the loss is only deductible if the loss is not reimbursed by

Quick
Quiz 6.3

Highlight the answer to these questions:

1. Funeral expenses are allowed as funeral expense deductions even if they have not been incurred.
   a. True
   b. False

2. Administration expenses include appraisal and valuation fees necessary to determine the value of assets included in the gross estate for estate tax purposes.
   a. True
   b. False

3. Liabilities imposed by law or arising out of torts are not deductible.
   a. True
   b. False

4. The taxable estate of a decedent is the gross estate less the marital and charitable deductions.
   a. True
   b. False

False, True, False, False.

the decedent's insurance provider. If the loss is partially reimbursed, the excess of the loss over the reimbursement is a deduction from the gross estate to arrive at the adjusted gross estate.

To be deductible, the loss must occur during the administration of the estate. Any loss before the death of the decedent is accounted for on the decedent's final income tax return. Any loss with respect to an asset after its distribution to the heir is not deductible by the decedent's estate, but on the heir's income tax return.

No deduction is allowed under this section if the estate has waived its right to take the deduction on the estate tax return in order to permit its allowance on the estate's income tax return.

State Death Tax Deduction

A deduction for estate, inheritance, legacy, or succession taxes paid to any state, territory, or the District of Columbia is allowed for decedents dying after 2004. Prior to 2005, a credit against the estate tax was allowed. The credit for state death taxes reduced the total estate tax dollar for dollar for the state death tax paid. In contrast, the deduction for state death taxes only reduces the total taxable estate by the amount of the state death taxes paid, which reduces the total estate tax by an amount equal to the state death taxes multiplied by the estate's marginal estate tax rate. As such, the replacement of the credit for state death taxes with the deduction for state death taxes will increase the overall estate taxes due at the decedent's death.

The deduction can be claimed for payments that are anticipated, but not yet paid; however, the payments must be made within four years after the return is filed. Certain exceptions may apply if a section 6166 election is made (discussed in Chapter 13) to pay the federal estate tax in installments. The deduction is not subject to any dollar limits. If property is transferred to the state in lieu of cash the deduction is the lesser of the state inheritance tax liability discharged or the fair market value of the property on the date of transfer.

DEDUCTIONS TO DETERMINE THE TAXABLE ESTATE

THE ABBREVIATED ESTATE TAX FORMULA - ADJUSTED GROSS ESTATE THROUGH TAXABLE ESTATE

EXHIBIT 6.7

(7)	Equals: Adjusted Gross Estate		$	Adjusted Gross Estate
(8)	Less: Unlimited Charitable Deduction	$		
(9)	Less: Unlimited Marital Deduction	$	$	
(10)	Equals: Taxable Estate		$	Taxable Estate

THE CHARITABLE DEDUCTION

An unlimited charitable deduction is allowed for the value of assets included in the decedent's gross estate which are transferred to a charitable organization at the decedent's date of death. Chapter 9 is entirely devoted to the charitable deduction from the adjusted gross estate to determine the taxable estate.

THE UNLIMITED MARITAL DEDUCTION

An unlimited marital deduction is allowed for the value of assets included in the decedent's gross estate which are transferred to the decedent's surviving spouse. Chapter 10 is entirely devoted to the unlimited marital deduction, which is a deduction from the adjusted gross estate to determine the taxable estate.

THE TAXABLE ESTATE

The **taxable estate** is the adjusted gross estate less the unlimited charitable and marital deductions discussed above and in detail in Chapters 9 and 10 respectively. The taxable estate is not the final calculation in the calculation of the total estate tax. The total of all post-1976 taxable gifts are added to the taxable estate to determine the tentative tax base.

DETERMINING THE TENTATIVE TAX

Thus far in the estate tax calculation, most values have been based upon the fair market value of assets the decedent had an interest in at his death. However, the estate tax calculation and the gift tax calculation are based on a unified transfer schedule which taxes all transfers made over a decedent's lifetime and at death at the same tax rates. Accordingly, the total value of all post-1976 taxable gifts (valued as of the date of the gifts) must be added to the decedent's taxable estate.

| EXHIBIT 6.8 | THE ABBREVIATED ESTATE TAX FORMULA (TAXABLE ESTATE THROUGH TENTATIVE TAX BASE) |

(10)	Equals: Taxable Estate		$ _____	Taxable Estate
(11)	Add: Previous (post 1976) Taxable Gifts	$ _____	$ _____	
(12)	Equals: Tentative Tax Base	$ _____	$ _____	Tentative Tax Base

POST-1976 TAXABLE GIFTS

All taxable gifts after 1976 must be added to a decedent's taxable estate. These gifts are added back at the fair market value as of the date of the gift. These values can be directly determined from an individual's previously filed gift tax returns.

THE TENTATIVE TAX BASE

The tentative tax base is the amount used to determine the tentative tax, the total transfer (estate and gift) tax on all transfers during an individual's life and at the individual's death. The **tentative tax base** equals the sum of taxable estate plus the post-1976 taxable gifts.

THE TENTATIVE TAX

The **tentative tax** is the total transfer taxes, estate and gift, on all property transferred by the decedent during his life and at his death. It is determined by applying the tax rate from the unified tax rate schedule to the tentative tax base (the combined value of the taxable estate and post-1976 taxable gifts).

The tentative tax is then reduced by the total gift tax paid during the individual's life, or payable on gifts included in the tax base to give the decedent credit for the tax paid on the post-1976 taxable gifts added when determining the tentative tax base. The estate tax remaining after the reduction for the gift tax paid may be further reduced by certain available credits as discussed below.

TAX RATE SCHEDULE FOR GIFTS AND ESTATES (FOR 2007-2009)

EXHIBIT 6.9

Over $0 but not over $10,000	**18%** of such amount.
Over $10,000 but not over $20,000	$1,800 plus **20%** of the excess of such amount over $10,000
Over $20,000 but not over $40,000	$3,800 plus **22%** of the excess of such amount over $20,000
Over $40,000 but not over $60,000	$8,200 plus **24%** of the excess of such amount over $40,000
Over $60,000 but not over $80,000	$13,000 plus **26%** of the excess of such amount over $60,000
Over $80,000 but not over $100,000	$18,200 plus **28%** of the excess of such amount over $80,000
Over $100,000 but not over $150,000	$23,800 plus **30%** of the excess of such amount over $100,000
Over $150,000 but not over $250,000	$38,800 plus **32%** of the excess of such amount over $150,000
Over $250,000 but not over $500,000	$70,800 plus **34%** of the excess of such amount over $250,000
Over $500,000 but not over $750,000	$155,800 plus **37%** of the excess of such amount over $500,000
Over $750,000 but not over $1,000,000	$248,300 plus **39%** of the excess of such amount over $750,000
Over $1,000,000 but not over $1,250,000	$345,800 plus **41%** of the excess of such amount over $1,000,000
Over $1,250,000 but not over $1,500,000	$448,300 plus **43%** of the excess of such amount over $1,250,000
Over $1,500,000 but not over $2,000,000	$555,800 plus **45%** of the excess of such amount over $1,500,000
Over $2,000,000 but not over $3,500,000	$780,800 plus **45%** of the excess of such amount over $2,000,000
Over $3,500,000	$1,455,800 plus **45%** of the excess of such amount over $3,500,000

CREDITS FROM THE TENTATIVE TAX

The tentative tax less the gift tax paid during a decedent's life is further reduced by certain available credits such as the applicable estate tax credit (unified credit), the credit for tax on prior transfers, and the foreign death tax credit.

THE ABBREVIATED ESTATE TAX FORMULA - CREDITS

EXHIBIT 6.10

(13)	Tentative Tax		$ _____	Tentative Tax
	Less: Credits			
(14)	Previous Gift Tax Paid	$ _____		
(15)	Applicable Estate Tax Credit	$ _____		
(16)	Credit for Tax Paid on Prior Transfers	$ _____		
(17)	Foreign Death Tax Credit	$ _____	$ _____	Total Credits
(18)	Equals: Federal Estate Tax Liability		$ _____	Federal Estate Tax Liability

APPLICABLE ESTATE TAX CREDIT (PREVIOUSLY CALLED THE UNIFIED CREDIT)

As discussed in Chapter 5, the applicable estate tax credit equivalency amount will exclude up to $3,500,000 (for 2009) of cumulative taxable transfers during an individual's lifetime or at death from estate transfer tax. The applicable estate tax credit equivalency can be defined as the taxable fair market value of the property that can be transferred without creating an estate tax greater than the applicable estate tax credit. The applicable estate tax credit for 2009 is $1,455,800 ($780,800 + $675,000).

For tax years beginning before December 31, 2003, the credit available against lifetime transfers and the credit available against transfers at death was unified. An individual could transfer a statutorily determined amount without incurring transfer taxes either during life or at death. Accordingly, the credit was known as the unified credit. However, EGTRRA 2001 created different credit amounts applicable to transfers during life and transfers at death, thus the credit was no longer unified. EGTRRA 2001 increased the unified credit against estate taxes for years after 2003, while the unified credit against gift taxes for years after 2003 remains at the same amount. Since the credit amounts are no longer unified, the credit against gift taxes is referred to as the "applicable gift tax credit" and the credit against the estate tax is referred to as the "applicable estate tax credit." The following exhibit illustrates the differences in the applicable gift and estate tax credits.

| EXHIBIT 6.11 | APPLICABLE CREDIT AMOUNTS |

Year of Death	Applicable Estate Tax Credit	Applicable Estate Tax Credit Equivalency	Applicable Gift Tax Credit	Applicable Gift Tax Credit Equivalency
1997	$192,800	$600,000	$192,800	$600,000
1998	$202,050	$625,000	$202,050	$625,000
1999	$211,300	$650,000	$211,300	$650,000
2000	$220,550	$675,000	$220,550	$675,000
2001	$220,550	$675,000	$220,550	$675,000
2002	$345,800	$1,000,000	$345,800	$1,000,000
2003	$345,800	$1,000,000	$345,800	$1,000,000
2004*	$555,800	$1,500,000	$345,800	$1,000,000
2005	$555,800	$1,500,000	$345,800	$1,000,000
2006 - 2008	$780,800	$2,000,000	$345,800	$1,000,000
2009	$1,455,800	$3,500,000	$345,800	$1,000,000
2010	REPEALED	REPEALED	$345,800	$1,000,000
2011	$345,800	$1,000,000	$345,800	$1,000,000

*Note the change in the applicable estate tax credit amount but no corresponding change in the applicable gift tax credit amount.

CREDIT FOR TAX PAID ON PRIOR TRANSFERS

If property included in a decedent's gross estate was inherited from someone else within the recent past and estate tax was paid at that transfer, a credit is available for the estate taxes paid at that time. The credit is calculated using a percentage limitation based upon the length of time the decedent survived the transferor. The calculation of this credit is beyond the scope of this text, but generally the credit is calculated by multiplying the appropriate percentage from the following table by the attributable estate tax paid at the transferor's death.

CREDIT FOR TAX PAID ON PRIOR TRANSFERS

EXHIBIT 6.12

Years Between Deaths	Credit Percentage
More than 2, not more than 4	80%
More than 4, not more than 6	60%
More than 6, not more than 8	40%
More than 8, not more than 10	20%
More than 10	0%

FOREIGN DEATH TAX CREDIT

A credit is allowed against the calculation of the federal estate tax for any estate, inheritance, legacy, or succession taxes paid to a foreign country. The credit is allowed only for foreign death taxes paid (1) with respect to property situated within the country to which the tax is paid, (2) with respect to property included in the decedent's gross estate, and (3) on behalf of a decedent who was a citizen or resident of the United States at the time of his death. No credit is allowed for interest or penalties paid in connection with the payment of foreign death taxes.

Key Concepts

Underline/highlight the answers to these questions as you read:

1. Describe the credits available against the tentative estate tax.

2. Identify the payment and reporting requirements of the Form 706.

3. What penalties are imposed with regard to filing the Form 706 late?

ESTATE TAX LIABILITY

The federal **estate tax** liability is equal to the tentative tax less any applicable credits available to a decedent's estate.

EXHIBIT 6.13 **THE ABBREVIATED ESTATE TAX FORMULA - CREDITS**

(13)	Tentative Tax	$ _____	Tentative Tax
	Less: Credits	$ _____	
(18)	Equals: Federal Estate Tax Liability	$ _____	Federal Estate Tax Liability

The federal estate tax must be paid by the executor or administrator of a decedent's estate. The entire tax is payable by the estate regardless of the fact that the gross estate may consist, in part, of property which does not come within the possession of the executor or the administrator. If there is no executor or administrator, any person in actual or constructive possession of any property of the decedent is required to pay the entire tax to the extent of the value of the property in his possession. The executor or administrator will become personally liable to the United States if he pays any other estate debts before paying the debts due to the United States.

If the estate tax is not paid by the due date, then the spouse, transferee, trustee, surviving tenant, person in possession of the property by reason of the exercise, nonexercise, or release of a power of appointment, or beneficiary who receives or possesses on the date of the decedent's death, property included in the gross estate under Sections 2034 through 2042, is personally liable for the tax to the extent of the value, at the time of the decedent's death, of such property.

PAYING AND REPORTING ESTATE TAXES

FILING REQUIREMENTS

The federal estate tax return, Form 706, must be filed if a decedent's gross estate, plus adjusted taxable gifts, is greater than the applicable estate tax credit equivalency (also called the applicable estate tax exclusion amount) for the year of death. When required, Form 706 and the payment of any estate tax owed is due nine months after the decedent's date of death. The executor may request an extension to file the return for an additional six months by filing IRS Form 4768 within nine months after the decedent's date of death. The executor may also request an extension of time, not to exceed 12 months, to pay the estate tax due if the request is based upon reasonable cause. Any estate tax that cannot be paid at the original due date of the estate tax return will begin to accrue interest, and if an extension has not been granted, penalties will also accrue (as discussed below). Some examples follow that illustrate cases involving reasonable cause for granting an extension of time to pay.

EXAMPLE 6.33

An estate includes sufficient liquid assets to pay the estate tax when otherwise due. The liquid assets, however, are located in several jurisdictions and are not immediately subject to the control of the executor. Consequently, such assets cannot be readily marshalled by the executor, even with the exercise of due diligence so the executor does not have the funds necessary to pay the estate tax due.

An estate is primarily comprised of assets consisting of rights to receive payments in the future (i.e., annuities, royalties, contingent fees, or accounts receivable). These assets provide the executor with insufficient present cash to pay the estate tax when due and the estate cannot borrow against these assets except upon terms which would inflict loss upon the estate.

EXAMPLE 6.34

An estate includes a claim to substantial assets which cannot be collected without litigation. Consequently, the size of the gross estate is unascertainable as of the time the tax is otherwise due.

EXAMPLE 6.35

PENALTIES

If an executor does not request an extension of time to file, or an extension of time to pay, the estate may be subject to penalties. The penalty is a function of the estate tax due times a percentage based on the delay. The failure-to-file penalty is five percent per month up to a maximum penalty of 25 percent. If the failure-to-file is determined to be fraudulent, the penalty is increased to 15 percent per month up to a maximum of 75 percent. The failure-to-pay penalty is 0.5 percent per month up to a maximum penalty of 25 percent. If, in one month, both the failure-to-file penalty and the failure-to-pay penalty apply, the failure-to-file penalty is reduced by the failure-to-pay penalty. For purposes of this calculation, any fraction of a month counts as a full month. Note that the failure to pay and failure to file penalties for estate tax purposes match the rules imposed for income tax purposes.

The executor files the estate tax return 45 days after the due date and the executor had not requested an extension of time to file or pay. Along with the return she remits a check for $10,000, the balance of the estate tax due. Disregarding any interest which may be assessed, the combined total failure-to-file and failure-to-pay penalties equal $1,000.

EXAMPLE 6.36

The calculation is as follows:

Failure-to-pay penalty:		
[0.5% x $10,000 x 2 (two months, any fraction counts as a full month)]		$100
Plus: Failure-to-file penalty [5% x $10,000 x 2 months]	$1,000	
Less: Failure-to-pay penalty (they run concurrently)	($100)	$900
Total penalties (failure-to-file and failure-to-pay)		$1,000

As illustrated, the failure-to-file penalty of $1,000 is reduced by the failure-to-pay penalty of $100 creating a total failure-to-file penalty of $900. Adding the failure-to-pay penalty of $100 to the failure to file penalty creates a total penalty of $1,000 ($100 + $900).

ADJUSTED BASIS TO HEIRS AND LEGATEES

Generally when an heir receives property from a decedent, the adjusted basis of the property for income tax purposes is the property's fair market value as reported on the decedent's estate tax return. This can be either the fair market value at the decedent's date of death or the alternate valuation date (six months after the date of death) if it was selected. The new adjusted basis is referred to as a "step-to" fair market value basis for the heir because the heir "steps to" the new basis at the date of death or alternate valuation date, if applicable. There are several exceptions to the general rule which are discussed individually below.

The holding period of property acquired from a decedent is always deemed to be long-term (i.e., held for the required long-term holding period). This provision applies regardless of whether the property is disposed of at a gain or loss and regardless of decedent's holding period.

IRD ASSETS

Assets classified as income in respect of a decedent (IRD) assets do not qualify for the Section 1014 "step-to" basis adjustment. IRD assets are those resulting from income-tax deferral planning. When a taxpayer has the choice of either recognizing income or deferring that income into the future, an IRD asset is created. Common examples of IRD assets include qualified retirement plans, 401(k) and 403(b) plans, IRAs, annuities, savings bonds, and installment notes. The beneficiary of these assets will have an adjusted basis equal to the decedent's adjusted basis, if any, in the asset. Denying IRD assets a Section 1014 "step-to" basis adjustment ensures that the government will be able to collect the income tax due on the deferred income.

EXAMPLE 6.37

Over his lifetime, Reginald made regular contributions to his IRA, and always claimed an income tax deduction for the contributions. Reginald died this year when the IRA was worth $1,000,000, and the total value of his gross estate, including the IRA was $2,000,000. Since Reginald has an estate under the applicable exemption amount of $3,500,000 (2009), there will be no estate tax due. However, his heirs will have a basis in the IRA equal to Reginald's basis, since the IRA is an IRD asset. When they take distributions from the IRA, the heirs will have to pay income tax on these distributions. Had the step-to basis adjustment of Section 1014 applied, Reginald's heirs would not have had to pay income tax on the IRA accumulation, even though Reginald had constructive receipt over the contributions to the account, but chose to defer the taxes on that income.

HEIR DONOR

If an heir receives property from a decedent that was acquired by the decedent through a gift from the same heir within one year of the decedent's death, the heir/donor takes the decedent's basis (which will be the donor's basis). The heir/donor does not receive a step-to fair market value in the adjusted basis of the property.

Joey gives property to his son that at the date of gift has a fair market value of $7,000. No gift taxes were paid. Joey has an adjusted basis in the property of $2,300. Joey's son dies within one year of the date of the gift. Joey's son bequeathed the property back to Joey. Because Joey had gifted the property to his son and received it back as an inheritance within one year, Joey's adjusted basis in the property is $2,300 (his original adjusted basis).

SURVIVING OWNER

A decedent's share of property titled as joint tenancy with rights of survivorship will pass to the surviving property owners. After the decedent's death, the survivor determines his basis in the property by adding the value of the property included in the decedent's gross estate to his (the survivor's) original adjusted basis.

Michael and Jeff owned, as joint tenants with rights of survivorship, land that they purchased for $60,000. Jeff furnished two-thirds of the purchase price and Michael one-third. At the date of Jeff's death, the property had a fair market value of $100,000. Michael figures his new adjusted basis in the property as follows:

Interest Michael bought initially	$20,000
Interest Michael received @ Jeff's death (2/3 of $100,000)(Step-to fair market value)	$66,667
Michael's adjusted basis after Jeff's death	$86,667

COMMUNITY PROPERTY

As discussed in Chapter 3, community property is a form of property ownership between spouses in which each spouse is deemed to own a one-half interest in all of the property acquired during their marriage. Community property does not have an automatic right of survivorship at the death of one spouse. For a decedent who owns community property with his spouse, only one-half of the fair market value of the property is included in the decedent's gross estate.

An heir who receives a decedent's one-half of community property will receive the one-half interest with an adjusted basis equal to the fair market value at the decedent's date of death or the alternate valuation date, whichever is used on the decedent's estate tax return. The surviving spouse's one-half interest in community property will also receive a step-to fair market value at the decedent's date of death even though it was not included in the decedent's gross estate. This special treatment which gives a step-to fair market value adjusted basis to both halves of the property interest at the death of one spouse is only applicable to community property.

Community property receives an adjustment in adjusted basis to the fair market value on both spouses' shares at the death of the first spouse.

EXAMPLE 6.40

Ted and his wife, Alice, own a mountain retreat. Ted dies and leaves the property, which has a basis of $200,000 and a fair market value at Ted's date of death of $1,000,000, to Alice. If the property is community property, Alice's new adjusted basis in the property is $1,000,000. If the property is not a community-property state, Alice's new adjusted basis in the property is $600,000 (her original adjusted basis of $100,000 plus his one-half at the fair market value at his date of death of $500,000).

Quick Quiz 6.4

Highlight the answer to these questions:

1. The lifetime applicable estate tax credit amount excludes up to $1,455,800 (for 2009) of cumulative taxable transfers.
   a. True
   b. False

2. A foreign death tax credit is allowable for interest or penalties paid in connection with foreign death taxes.
   a. True
   b. False

3. An extension of time to pay tax at the request of the executor may be granted for a reasonable period of time, not to exceed 12 months.
   a. True
   b. False

4. The failure-to-pay penalty is reduced by the failure-to-file penalty giving the adjusted failure-to-pay penalty.
   a. True
   b. False.

False, False, True, False.

BASIS RULES FOR YEARS BEGINNING AFTER 2009 (EGTRRA 2001)

Beginning in 2010, after the estate and generation-skipping transfer taxes have been repealed, the rules providing for a step-to fair market value adjusted basis for property acquired from a decedent are repealed. Heirs of property transferred at the decedent's death will receive the property with a basis equal to the lesser of either the adjusted basis of the decedent, or the fair market value of the property on the decedent's date of death. In other words, the heir will receive a carryover basis, unless the fair market value is lower.

The executor may increase (i.e., step up) the adjusted basis in a selected number of assets transferred at the decedent's date of death. Generally, the executor of the decedent's estate is permitted to increase (i.e., step up) the basis of assets transferred by a total of $1.3 million, and the basis of property transferred to a surviving spouse by an additional $3 million, (for a total basis increase of $4.3 million for property transferred to a surviving spouse). An heir's basis in property can never be increased above the fair market value of the property at the decedent's date of death.

The cumulative example in Chapter 4 detailed the calculation of the probate estate. Continuing with that example, we will calculate the gross estate and the estate tax due after presenting some additional facts.

Cody and Reese were married years ago and had one child, Amber. Cody and his longtime friend, Kandi, were recently flying in Kandi's new plane. For a brief period, Kandi was distracted and lost control of the plane. Unfortunately, the plane crashed and Kandi died instantly and Cody died a few days later as a result of the injuries sustained during the crash. When Cody died, he and Reese owned the following property:

- Personal residence valued at $500,000 held tenancy by the entirety. The home had an outstanding mortgage of $200,000.
- Car 1 valued at $10,000 held fee simple by Cody.
- Car 2 valued at $15,000 held joint tenancy with rights of survivorship by Cody and Amber.
- Diamond ring valued at $50,000 held fee simple by Reese.
- Boat valued at $20,000 held tenancy in common by Cody and Amber (equal contribution).
- Life Insurance Policy 1 on Reese's life owned by Cody. The fair market value of the policy was $100,000 and the death benefit was $200,000. The beneficiary is Amber.
- Life Insurance Policy 2 on Cody's life, owned by Cody. The fair market value of the policy was $85,000 and the death benefit was $500,000. The only beneficiary is Kandi.
- IRA account valued at $3,500,000 owned by Cody with Amber as the beneficiary.
- Irrevocable Trust by Cody for the benefit of Amber created five years ago. The trust is valued at $500,000, and Amber is the beneficiary at Cody's death. There were no taxable gifts on the initial or subsequent transfers to the trust.

Note: Unless otherwise stated, assume equal contributions were made by all parties for jointly owned property.

The accident was found to be the fault of the plane manufacturer, therefore Cody's heirs received $100,000 for wrongful death and $500,000 for his pain and suffering. Cody's last medical expenses were $40,000, his funeral expenses were $30,000, the administrative fees for the estate were $100,000, and he had existing debts of $100,000. Cody's will left $100,000 to a qualifying charity and the remaining probate assets to Reese. His will states that debts and expenses will reduce the assets that will transfer to Reese. Assuming the executor forgot to file the estate tax return, and filed and paid 65 days late and that Cody did not make any transfers during his life, calculate Cody's gross estate, the estate tax due and any penalties (excluding interest) using the 2009 estate tax rates and available credits. The following charts are provided to assist in answering this problem. The solution follows.

GROSS ESTATE CALCULATION (COMPLETE THE LAST COLUMN)

Asset	Full Value	Cody's Interest	Probate Estate	Gross Estate
Home	500,000	250,000	0	
Car 1	10,000	10,000	10,000	
Car 2	15,000	7,500	0	
Diamond Ring	50,000	0	0	
Boat	20,000	10,000	10,000	
Life Insurance 1	100,000	100,000	100,000	
Life Insurance 2	500,000	500,000	500,000	
IRA	3,500,000	3,500,000	0	
Trust	500,000	0	0	
Wrongful Death	100,000	0	0	
Pain and Suffering	500,000	500,000	500,000	
Total	$5,795,000	$4,877,500	$1,120,000	

THE ABBREVIATED ESTATE TAX FORMULA (FILL IN THE APPROPRIATE AMOUNTS)

(1) Gross Estate

Less Deductions:

(2) Last Medical Expenses

(3) Administrative Costs

(4) Funeral Expenses

(5) Debts of the Decedent

(6) Losses During the Administration of the Estate

(7) Equals: Adjusted Gross Estate

(8) Less: Unlimited Charitable Deduction

(9) Less: Unlimited Marital Deduction

(10) Equals: Taxable Estate

(11) Add: Previous Taxable Gifts (post 1976)

(12) Equals: Tentative Tax Base

(13) Tentative Tax

Less: Allowable Credits

(14) Credit for Previous Gift Tax Paid

(15) Applicable Estate Tax Credit (Unified Credit)

(16) Credit for Tax Paid on Prior Transfers

(17) Foreign Death Tax Credit

(18) Equals: Federal Estate Tax Liability

PENALTIES (FILL IN THE APPROPRIATE AMOUNTS)

Failure-to-pay penalty: [0.5% x Penalty Tax x Months]		$
Plus: Failure-to-file penalty [5% x Penalty Tax x months]	$	
Less: Failure-to-pay penalty (Run concurrently)	$	$
Total penalties (Failure-to-file and failure-to-pay)		$

EXAMPLE SOLUTIONS

GROSS ESTATE

The gross estate is calculated as follows:

Note that the pain and suffering award is included in Cody's gross estate because it is personal to Cody, while the proceeds of wrongful death award are not included in Cody's gross estate because it is not personal to Cody.

Asset	Full Value	Cody's Interest	Probate Estate	Gross Estate
Home	500,000	250,000	0	250,000
Car 1	10,000	10,000	10,000	10,000
Car 2	15,000	7,500	0	7,500
Diamond Ring	50,000	0	0	0
Boat	20,000	10,000	10,000	10,000
Life Insurance 1	100,000	100,000	100,000	100,000
Life Insurance 2	500,000	500,000	500,000	500,000
IRA	3,500,000	3,500,000	0	3,500,000
Trust	500,000	0	0	0
Wrongful Death	100,000	0	0	0
Pain & Suffering	500,000	500,000	500,000	500,000
Total	**$5,795,000**	**$4,877,500**	**$1,120,000**	**$4,877,500**

Estate Tax Calculation

The estate tax is calculated as follows:

THE ABBREVIATED ESTATE TAX FORMULA

(1)	Gross Estate		$4,877,500	Gross Estate
	Less Deductions:			
(2)	Last Medical Expenses	$40,000		
(3)	Administrative Expenses	$100,000		
(4)	Funeral Expenses	$30,000		
(5)	Debts of the Decedent	$100,000		
(6)	Losses During the Administration of the Estate	$0	$270,000	Deductions
(7)	Equals: Adjusted Gross Estate		$4,607,500	Adjusted Gross Estate
(8)	Less: Charitable Deduction	$100,000		
(9)	Less: Marital Deduction	$1,000,000	$1,100,000	
(10)	Equals: Taxable Estate		$3,507,500	Taxable Estate
(11)	Add: Previous Taxable Gifts (post 1976)		$0	Post-1976 Gifts
(12)	Equals: Tentative Tax Base		$3,507,500	Tentative Tax Base
(13)	Tentative Tax		$1,459,175	Tentative Tax
	Less: Allowable Credits			
(14)	Credit for Previous Gift Tax Paid	$0		
(15)	Applicable Estate Tax Credit (Unified Credit)	$1,455,800		
(16)	Credit for Tax Paid on Prior Transfers	$0		
(17)	Foreign Death Tax Credit	$0	($1,455,800)	
(18)	Equals: Federal Estate Tax Liability		$3,375	Federal Estate Tax Liability

MARITAL DEDUCTION SUMMARY

Asset	Gross Estate	Available for Spouse	Available for Marital Deduction
Home	250,000	YES	250,000
Car 1	10,000	YES	10,000
Car 2	7,500	NO	0
Diamond Ring	0	-	0
Boat	10,000	YES	10,000
Life Insurance 1	100,000	YES	100,000
Life Insurance 2	500,000	YES	500,000
IRA	3,500,000	NO	0
Trust	0	-	0
Pain & Suffering	500,000	YES	500,000
Wrongful Death	0	-	0
Total	$4,877,500		$1,370,000

The marital deduction is determined by adding the assets that transfer to the spouse and subtracting from that amount the amounts that must be paid from the probate estate. The estate can only receive a marital deduction for the amount of assets the surviving spouse actually receives.

Amount available for marital deduction	$1,370,000
Less expenses paid from the amount available for the marital deduction:	
• Medical Expenses	40,000
• Administrative Expenses	100,000
• Funeral Expenses	30,000
• Debts	100,000
• Charitable contribution	100,000
Total Net Marital Deduction	$1,000,000

Failure-to-pay penalty:		
[0.5% x $3,375 x 3 months (Any fraction counts as a full month)]		$51
Plus: Failure-to-file penalty [5% x $3,375 x 3 months]	$507	
Less: Failure-to-pay penalty (Run concurrently)	($51)	$456
Total penalties (Failure-to-file and failure-to-pay)		$507

Generally, the failure-to-file penalty is reduced by the failure-to-pay penalty creating an adjusted failure-to-file penalty. Adding the failure-to-pay penalty (to the failure to file penalty) determines the total penalty of $507.

Key Terms

Adjusted Gross Estate - The adjusted gross estate is equal to the gross estate less any deductions for funeral expenses, last medical expenses, administrative expenses, debts, and losses during the administration of the estate.

Alternate Valuation Date - An alternate date, other than the date of death, to value a decedent's gross estate. The alternate valuation date is either six months after the date of death, or if the asset is disposed of within six months of the date of death, the asset's disposition date. Wasting assets do not qualify to use the alternative valuation date.

Blockage Discount - A reduction in the fair market value of a large block of stock because the transfer of a large block of stock is less marketable than other transfers of smaller amounts of stock.

Date of Declaration - The date a board of directors approves and declares a dividend to be paid to its shareholders.

Date of Record - The date that a dividend paying company determines the owners of its stock who are entitled to a dividend (regardless of whether or not the individual owns the stock as of the payment date).

Gross Estate - The gross estate consists of the fair market value of all of a decedent's interests owned at the decedent's date of death plus the fair market value of certain property interests the decedent transferred during his life, in which he retained some rights, powers, use, or possession.

Key Person Discount - A reduction in the fair market value of transferred stock due to an economic reality that the value of the stock will decline if a key person, such as the founder, dies or becomes disabled.

Lack of Marketability Discount - A reduction in the fair market value of a transferred asset because the interest is more difficult to sell to the public.

Minority Discount - A reduction in the fair market value of a transferred interest in property because the interest is not a controlling interest.

Power of Appointment - The power to name who will enjoy or own property.

Reversionary Interest - Interests that have been transferred and subsequently revert back to the transferor. Also, includes a possibility that the property transferred by the decedent may return to him or his estate and a possibility that property transferred by the decedent may become subject to a power of disposition by him.

Straight Single Life Annuity - An annuity for a term equal to the annuitant's life.

Survivorship Annuity - An annuity that provides payments to one person, and then provides payments to a second person upon the death of the first.

Key Terms

Taxable Estate - The adjusted gross estate less the available unlimited marital and unlimited charitable deductions.

Tentative Tax - The estate tax calculated on the tentative tax base.

Tentative Tax Base - The tentative tax base equals the taxable estate plus all post-1976 taxable gifts.

X Dividend Date - The date the market price of a stock adjusts for a declared dividend (i.e., the market price of the stock is reduced approximately by the amount of the dividend).

DISCUSSION QUESTIONS

1. List six assets included in a decedent's gross estate.

2. What is a revocable transfer?

3. If a decedent owns a life insurance policy on his own life, at what value is it included in his gross estate?

4. What is meant by "incidents of ownership" in a life insurance policy?

5. What is a straight single life annuity, and to what extent is its value included in a decedent annuitant's gross estate?

6. What is a general power of appointment?

7. How is real estate valued for purposes of inclusion in a decedent's gross estate?

8. How are publicly traded common stocks valued in a decedent's gross estate?

9. List three valuation discounts.

10. What are the requirements for an estate to elect the alternate valuation date?

11. List three available deductions from a decedent's gross estate.

12. How is the applicable estate tax credit related to the applicable estate tax credit equivalency?

13. Explain the availability of the credit for tax on prior transfers.

14. Under what circumstances may an estate take a credit for foreign death taxes paid?

15. When is a decedent's federal estate tax return due?

16. What is an heir's adjusted basis in property inherited before 2010?

17. How is the holding period of inherited property in the hands of the heir calculated?

1. Charles had been working with an estate planner for several years prior to his death. Accordingly, Charles made many transfers during his life in an attempt to reduce his potential estate tax burden, and Charles' executor, Tom, is thoroughly confused. Tom comes to you for clarification of which assets to include in Charles' gross estate. Which of the following transactions will not be included in Charles' gross estate?

    a. Charles gave $40,000 to each of his three grandchildren two years ago. No gift tax was due on the gifts.

    b. Charles purchased a life insurance policy on his life with a face value of $300,000. Charles transferred the policy to his son two years ago.

    c. Charles and his wife owned their personal residence valued at $250,000 as tenants by the entirety.

    d. After inheriting a mountain vacation home from his mother, Charles gifted the vacation home to his daughter to remove it from his gross estate. Charles continued to use the property as a weekend getaway and continued all maintenance on the property.

2. The gross estate of a decedent who died in the current year would not include which of the following items?

    a. A luxury sedan, valued at $60,000, driven every day by the decedent.

    b. Cash of $1,000,000 given to decedent's daughter two years ago. No gift tax was paid on the transfer.

    c. A bond given to decedent's cousin last year. Gift tax of $4,000 was paid on the transfer.

    d. A home which the decedent owned as tenants by the entirety with his wife.

3. Despite his efforts to transfer all of his property out of his estate during his life, Gordon died on January 16th still owning the following property:

	Adj. Basis	FMV
Personal Residence	$20,000	$320,000
Rental Property	$84,000	$80,000
Rental Income on above property (February payment)	$2,000	$2,000
Cancelled vacation cruise refund (check received 12/31 but not cashed)	$4,500	$4,500
Cash	$18,000	$18,000

What is the value of Gordon's gross estate?

   a. $124,500.
   b. $128,500.
   c. $422,500.
   d. $424,500.

4. In August of the current year, Jim died of lung cancer. Jim's son, Doug, has decided to prepare his father's estate tax return, but has come to you for clarification on whether the following list of items are included in Jim's gross estate. After reviewing the list, which item(s) will you tell Doug to exclude from Jim's gross estate?

   a. A life insurance policy on the life of Jim's wife owned by Jim.
   b. A check from Doctor's Hospital for the refund of medical expenses that Jim initially paid, but were subsequently paid for by Jim's health insurance company. The reimbursements were due to Jim before his death.
   c. A check from ABC Corporation for dividends in the amount of $15,000 declared September 23rd (the month after Jim's death).
   d. A payment of $500,000 from Mutual Life Insurance of America representing the proceeds of a life insurance policy owned by Jim.

5. To avoid inclusion in a power holder's gross estate, a power should limit the appointment of property to the power holder for the sole purpose of:

   a. Pleasure.
   b. Support.
   c. Wealth.
   d. Happiness.

6. Before her death, Alice loaned Jerry $400,000 in return for a note. The terms of the note directed Jerry to make monthly payments including interest at the applicable federal rate. If Alice dies before the note is repaid, which of the following affects the valuation for Alice's gross estate?

    1. Jerry's inability to make payments timely.

    2. The market rate of interest.

    3. The remaining term of the note.

    4. Alice forgives the note as a specific bequest in her will.

        a. 1 only.

        b. 1 and 2.

        c. 1, 2, and 3.

        d. 2, 3, and 4.

7. Gus dies owning several shares of an infrequently traded stock. If Gus dies on Wednesday, November 7th, and the stock has the following trading information:

        Monday, 11/5 $31
        Thursday, 11/8 $36
        Monday, 11/12 $28

What is the per share value of the stock on the federal estate tax return?

        a. $31.

        b. $33.

        c. $34.

        d. $36.

8. Of the following expenditures from an estate, which is not a deduction from the gross estate to arrive at the taxable estate?

        a. Payment to United Charitable Organization (a 501(c)(3)) to satisfy a specific bequest.

        b. Distribution of assets to spouse to satisfy specific bequests listed in will.

        c. Payment to Second USA Bank for a credit card balance.

        d. A payment to decedent's friend for $10,000 to satisfy a specific bequest.

9. When a U.S. citizen dies and bequeaths property to his U.S. citizen spouse, the marital deduction is limited to the following amount:

        a. $345,800.

        b. $780,800.

        c. $1,455,800.

        d. The marital deduction is unlimited.

10. After an extensive hospital stay, Daryl died of heart failure in August of the current year. In computing Daryl's taxable estate, which of the following is not deductible?

    a. Payment to Good Insurance representing the past due balance of Daryl's car insurance for the month July.

    b. Per the will, a payment to Daryl's friend John.

    c. Payment to Brian's Engraving for Daryl's tombstone.

    d. Payment to Howe & Dewey, LLP, the estate's attorneys.

11. Johnny died eight months ago and his executor is finalizing his estate tax return. The executor has determined that Johnny's gross estate includes $400,000 of real estate, $750,000 of cash and cash equivalents, and $300,000 of qualified retirement plans. The total gross estate is $1,450,000. As the executor reviews the deductions, which of the following will he deduct from the total gross estate to arrive at the adjusted gross estate on his Form 706?

    a. Income in Respect of Decedent (IRD).

    b. Unlimited charitable deduction.

    c. Unlimited marital deduction.

    d. Executor's fee.

12. Jude has begun some estate planning. What is the maximum amount of estate tax Jude can avoid by using the applicable estate tax credit during 2009?

    a. $780,800.

    b. $1,455,800.

    c. $2,000,000.

    d. $3,500,000.

13. If a decedent dies in 2009 with a taxable estate of $4,000,000 and has never used any of his applicable estate tax credit, what amount of the decedent's estate tax will be absorbed by the applicable estate tax credit amount in 2009?

    a. $780,800.

    b. $1,455,800.

    c. $2,000,000.

    d. $3,500,000.

14. An estate tax return must be filed for a U.S. resident or a U.S. citizen dying during 2009 if the total value of his gross estate plus post-1976 adjusted taxable gifts on his date of death is greater than:

    a. $345,800.

    b. $1,000,000.

    c. $1,455,800.

    d. $3,500,000.

15. If an estate pays the funeral expenses of the decedent, on which tax return are these expenses deducted?

      a. The decedent's final return (Form 1040).

      b. The decedent's estate tax return (Form 706).

      c. The income tax return of the decedent's estate (Form 1041).

      d. The surviving spouse's income tax return (Form 1040).

16. Christie's father has been diagnosed with cancer and has been given one year to live. In an attempt to avoid capital gains tax, Christie transfers her stock with an adjusted basis of $1,000 and a fair market value of $11,000 to her father. Christie's father dies seven months after the transfer when the fair market value of the stock was $12,000 and Christie's father's will leaves her everything, including the stock. Christie subsequently sells the stock for $19,000. What is Christie's capital gain on the transaction?

      a. $7,000.

      b. $10,000.

      c. $18,000.

      d. $19,000.

Quick Quiz Explanations

Quick Quiz 6.1
1. False. Wrongful death actions belong to the survivors, not the decedents and are not included in the decedent's gross estate.
2. False. The alternative valuation date is not available for reversionary interests.
3. True.
4. False. Since there is nothing left to transfer, a straight life annuity is excluded from the decedent's gross estate.

Quick Quiz 6.2
1. True.
2. False. If the alternative valuation date is selected, the assets must be valued six months (not 9 months) after death.
3. True.

Quick Quiz 6.3
1. False. To be deductible for estate tax purposes, funeral expenses must have actually been incurred and, if paid, are under funeral expenses. If unpaid, they are deductible as an estate debt.
2. True.
3. False. Debts, including liabilities arising out of tort litigation, are deductible from the gross estate.
4. False. The taxable estate also includes deductions for funeral expenses, final medical expenses, administrative expenses, debts, and losses during estate administration.

Quick Quiz 6.4
1. False. The lifetime applicable estate tax credit amount excludes up to $3,500,000 (2009) of cumulative taxable transfers.
2. False. A foreign death tax credit is allowed for foreign death taxes paid; it is not permitted for interest and penalties assessed on foreign death taxes.
3. True.
4. False. The failure to file penalty is reduced by the failure to pay penalty giving the adjusted failure-to-file penalty.

Transfers During Life & At Death

INTRODUCTION

Individuals engage in several types of asset transfers throughout their lives. These transfers include transfers to strangers, which are usually arm's-length transactions with the expectation of receiving consideration of equal value in return (e.g., sale or exchange). Lifetime transfers also include transfers to related parties and loved ones. These transfers may involve an exchange with a stranger, or alternatively, may be designed to benefit loved ones by transferring property to them gratuitously or at a reduced cost (e.g., gift, bargain sale, sales with death options).

LIFETIME TRANSFERS

Chapter 5 identifies the advantages of gifting property during life versus making bequests at death (see Exhibit 5.8, "Advantages of Lifetime Gifts vs. Bequests"). Unlike the discussion of gifts in Chapter 5, this chapter describes many transfers that do not involve gifts, but instead involve sales and other transfers (even between related parties and loved ones). When property is gifted, the fair market value of the property is removed from an individual's gross estate. The value of the property is also removed from the individual's gross estate when it is sold, but the sale does not directly reduce an individual's overall gross estate since the fair market value of the consideration received replaces the fair market value of the property transferred. While there is no immediate impact on the transferor's taxable estate when property is sold for full and adequate consideration, a significant estate planning benefit can be realized over time if the asset sold had a significant potential for appreciation and was replaced with an asset with a lower growth potential. Use of this type of planning allows senior family members to transfer the appreciation on assets out of their estates to junior family members.

Although a sale of property does not qualify for many of the advantages identified in Exhibit 7.1 (such as the annual exclusion, the support exclusion, and the qualified transfers exclusion), the sale of any asset may be advantageous for several reasons. First, when an asset is sold, it is removed from the transferor's gross estate and often replaced with cash or a receivable. Even though the gross estate is not immediately reduced by the transfer of the asset, any future appreciation of the value of the sold asset will be excluded from the transferor's gross estate. Second, any future income from the asset after the sale will be excluded from the transferor's gross estate. Finally, when an individual sells an asset during his life, he is subject to capital gains tax, currently a 15 percent tax, on the appreciation above his adjusted basis. The capital gain income tax, when paid, will also reduce the transferor's gross estate. The following chart summarizes the similarities and differences between all three techniques.

EXHIBIT 7.1	COMPARISON OF GIFTS/BEQUESTS AND SALES		
Transfer Type	**Gifts and Lifetime Transfers**	**Bequests at Death**	**Sales During Life**
Support	Excluded from Gross Estate	Included in Gross Estate	N/A
Qualified Transfers	Excluded from Gross Estate	Not Applicable	N/A
Annual Exclusion	Excluded from Gross Estate	Not Applicable	N/A
Future Appreciation	Excluded from Gross Estate*	Included in Gross Estate	Excluded from Gross Estate
Income on Transferred Assets	Excluded from Gross Estate	Included in Gross Estate	Excluded from Gross Estate
Gift Tax Paid	Excluded from Gross Estate**	Included in Gross Estate	N/A
Income (Capital Gains) Tax Paid	N/A	N/A	Excluded from Gross Estate
* Provided that the grantor does not retain an interest in the property under Sections 2036 - 2038. ** Unless the gift tax is paid within 3 years of death, in which case it is subject to the gross-up approach.			

ARM'S-LENGTH TRANSACTIONS

An arm's-length transaction is a transfer between unrelated parties in the form of a sale, an installment sale, or an exchange. Each of these transactions involves a transfer of property between individuals for valuable consideration based on the fair market value of the transferred property. These types of transfers have no impact on the transferor's gross estate or on the transferor's balance sheet until income tax is paid (since the seller must recognize gain on the transaction and pay income tax on the gain, the cash outflow for the tax payment reduces the seller's gross estate). While the relative liquidity of a transferor's total assets may change after the transfer, the total value of assets is theoretically equal to what it was prior to the transfer. Arm's-length transactions do not attempt to reduce the transferor's gross estate or to economically benefit the transferee. The buyer and the seller enter the transaction without passing property to the buyer at a reduced cost.

SALE

A **sale** is the direct transfer of property to another for money or property of equal fair market value. A sale does not directly affect the gross estate of the seller or the buyer, as each party to the sale has transferred one asset for another asset of equal value.

Jerry agrees to sell Claude his 47' yacht for $180,000 cash. Before the sale, Jerry's gross estate totaled $980,000, comprised of $800,000 of cash and the yacht with a fair market value of $180,000. Before the sale, Claude's gross estate totaled $1,400,000 of cash. After the sale, Jerry would have a gross estate with the same total of $980,000, but now it would be completely comprised of cash. Claude would have a gross estate with the same total of $1,400,000, but it would be comprised of $1,220,000 of cash and the 47' yacht with a fair market value of $180,000.

EXAMPLE 7.1

Estate planners can consider selling assets with high appreciation potential to younger family members. This shifts the future appreciation and replaces the transferred property with an asset that will have lower appreciation potential. This type of planning may be particularly appropriate for individuals who have already used their lifetime gift exemption, and wish to make a transfer that does not trigger the imposition of a gift tax.

Quick Quiz 7.1

Highlight the answer to these questions:

1. A sale is a mutual transfer between individuals of assets with equal fair market values.
   a. True
   b. False

2. A sale qualifies for the annual exclusion.
   a. True
   b. False

3. Individuals may enter into arm's-length transactions with loved ones.
   a. True
   b. False

True, False, True.

INSTALLMENT SALE

An **installment sale** is a sale of property in which the buyer makes a series of installment payments to the seller. The effect of this transaction is that the buyer pays the seller the purchase price of the property over a specified term plus interest at the current market rate. The installment payments are paid in cash over the term of the note, and at the seller's death any outstanding principal of the installment note, including any accrued interest, is included in the seller's gross estate. An installment sale, therefore, does not immediately reduce the fair market value of the seller's gross estate.

EXAMPLE 7.2

Jackson agreed to sell his vacation property to Barry for $250,000 payable over 10 years at $25,000 per year. Before the sale, Jackson's gross estate totaled $1,250,000 including cash of $1,000,000 and the value of the vacation home. Barry paid Jackson 4 installment payments, totaling $100,000, but still owed Jackson $150,000 of principal when Jackson died. Jackson consumed the interest payment received on the note, but saved the principal payments. Jackson's gross estate totals $1,250,000, but will be comprised of $1,100,000 of cash and $150,000 of a note receivable from Barry.

An installment sale may be entered into by a related buyer and seller with the intention of accomplishing a planning objective. The agreed upon sales price of the property in the installment sale may be the property's fair market value, but the interest rate charged on the note may not be commensurate with the true level of risk the seller is assuming with the note. The interest rate may be lower than the current market rate of interest or may even be equal to zero. In either case, the buyer benefits because of the lower interest payment required and the seller benefits because he will receive less interest income and will therefore reduce his gross estate by the interest income reduction.

| **EXAMPLE 7.3** | Carolyn owns a business with a fair market value of $200,000. Carolyn agrees to sell the property to her daughter, Janice, at the fair market value using an installment sale. Since Janice does not have a job, does not have a steady income, and recently filed for bankruptcy, the appropriate interest rate that should be charged in the note is 18 percent. However, Carolyn agrees to set the interest rate at four percent. Because the offered interest rate is lower than the fair market value interest rate, Janice will pay a lesser note payment and Carolyn will have less taxable interest income and thus a lower gross estate. (The IRS may challenge the transaction, however, as a gift/sale.) |

There is a practical limitation on this planning technique. The interest rate charged on the note may be below the prevailing market rate given the risk characteristics involved. However, the interest rate must be at least equal to the applicable federal rate in order to avoid gift loan treatment and adverse income tax consequences.

EXCHANGE

An **exchange** is a mutual transfer of assets with equal fair market values between individuals. Like the installment sale and the outright sale, an exchange will not directly impact a transferor's gross estate.

| **EXAMPLE 7.4** | Martin and Jesse each owned a car with a fair market value of $36,000, and the two agreed to an even exchange for each other's car. After the exchange of the cars, both Jesse and Martin would have gross estates equal to their gross estates before the exchange, only now their estates are comprised of different assets. |

TRANSFERS TO LOVED ONES

As used in this text, the term "loved ones" denotes both related parties (family members) and other intended beneficiaries who are not related parties. Transfers of assets to loved ones can be accomplished as an arm's-length transaction in the same way as transfers to strangers (through sale, installment sale, or exchange). There are additional transfer methods that are designed to benefit a transferee loved one that would not be used with an unrelated party. These include partial sale-gift transactions, outright gifts, gifts in trusts, transactions that use minority and liquidity discounts (usually gifts), and transfers that are not subject to gift tax rules. Each one of these transfers is examined separately below.

TRANSFERS NOT SUBJECT TO GIFT TAX

Chapter 5 covers transfers to loved ones that are not subject to gift tax. These transfer techniques include those used to satisfy legal support obligations, qualified transfers, and below-market rate loans. As you may recall from Chapter 5, transfers not subject to gift tax reduce an individual's gross estate without using the annual exclusion or the individual's applicable estate tax credit amount.

A grandparent pays medical or law school tuition for a grandchild. The payments are made directly to the institutions and are treated as qualified transfers not subject to gift tax. These tuition payments immediately reduce the grandparent's gross estate without using any of the grandparent's annual exclusion or applicable estate tax credit.	**EXAMPLE 7.5**

Dave's wife has a gross estate that falls below the applicable estate tax credit equivalency of $3,500,000 for 2009. Dave can give his wife an amount equal to the difference between his wife's gross estate and the applicable estate tax credit equivalency without incurring gift taxes, thus lowering Dave's gross estate without using any of his applicable estate tax credit amount. Dave's wife will be able to fully use her applicable estate tax credit amount in the event that she dies before Dave.	**EXAMPLE 7.6**

GIFTS OUTRIGHT AND IN TRUST

When an individual makes a gift, either outright or in trust, the gifted property is transferred to the donee or to the trustee of the trust. As discussed in Chapter 5, the donor of the property may be required to file a gift tax return, depending upon the value of the gifted property, and must also determine whether the gift qualifies as a present or future interest gift. Recall that the annual exclusion is available to offset the gift tax consequences of the transfer only if the gift is a gift of present interest.

Usually, outright gifts and gifts in trust are reserved for transfers to loved ones. Ideally these gifts are gifts of a present interest and qualify for the annual exclusion, reduce the transferor's gross estate (since the donor relinquishes all control), and remove future appreciation of the gifted property from the transferor's gross estate. Also, if gift tax is paid after full use of the applicable gift tax credit, the gift tax paid from the transferor's gross estate is removed if the transferor lives at least three years following the date of the gift.

EXAMPLE 7.7

In 2009, Felix started a company with 1,000 shares of stock. Felix's capital contribution was $1,000 or $1 per share. After his contribution, Felix immediately gifted 100 shares of the stock to his daughter, and filed a gift tax return showing the fair market value of the gift to be $100 (100 shares x $1). This gift is exempt from gift tax because it is a gift of a present interest and Felix can use his annual exclusion. (Note that if this was Felix's only gift this year, he would not be required to file a gift tax return, but he may choose to file return to begin the statute of limitations.) Two years later, in 2011, when Felix's company was worth $200,000 ($200 per share) Felix transferred 100 shares to his daughter, and filed a gift tax return valuing the transfer at the annual exclusion of $13,000 ($20,000 (100 x $200) less a minority discount of 35%). In 2013, after the three-year statute of limitations expired on both gifts, the company was sold for $5,000,000, or $5,000 per share. Felix has successfully transferred approximately $1,000,000 (200 shares x $5,000) to his daughter while only using his annual exclusion to make the gift. This example assumes the valuation was proper in 2009 and that the minority and market ability discount of 35% was appropriate.

As discussed in Chapter 5, when direct outright gifts are made, the value of the gifted property for gift tax purposes should be documented with a proper approval report if the gifted property is not cash, marketable securities, or if a valuation discount is used when valuing the property. Because the reported value on the gift tax return may be challenged by the IRS, the transferor should file a gift tax return to begin the running of the statute of limitations. Any increase in the fair market value of the property under audit by the IRS will subject the transferor to additional gift tax, potential tax penalties, and interest.

Key Concepts

Underline/highlight the answers to these questions as you read:

1. List three common examples of transfers not subject to gift tax.

2. What is the term of a private annuity?

3. What are the income tax consequences of a SCIN to the seller?

4. How is the buyer's adjusted basis determined in property acquired in a private annuity?

PARTIAL SALE-GIFT TRANSACTIONS

When an individual sells an asset for an amount less than the asset's fair market value, the seller is deemed to have made a gift to the buyer equal to the difference between the fair market value of the property and the actual sales price. These combination sale-gift transactions, also known as bargain sales, generally occur between family members since the seller will only realize a discounted price from the sale in an effort to transfer the property to a family member at a reduced cost. Usually the gift amount (the discount from fair market value) would not exceed the seller's (donor's) annual exclusion or remaining applicable gift tax credit amount.

With a bargain sale, the property is removed from the transferor's gross estate and is replaced by a reduced amount equal to the consideration paid by the buyer. Any appreciation or income on the property after the transaction is completed is attributable to the buyer/donee.

EXAMPLE 7.8

Larry owned an office building with a fair market value of $3,000,000. He wants to transfer the property to his son, Greg, but does not want to pay any gift tax on the transfer and wants to benefit Greg in the transfer. Larry agrees to sell the building to Greg for $1,987,000 (a $1,013,000 discount from the fair market value). The discount of $1,013,000 is treated as a present interest gift eligible for the annual exclusion, and a taxable gift of $1,000,000. Since Larry has not made any prior taxable transfers, the $1,000,000 taxable gift will be offset by Larry's applicable gift tax credit and no gift tax will be due. Greg will have purchased the building at a discount and all future appreciation and income from the property will be attributable to him.

FULL CONSIDERATION TRANSFERS/SALES

There are some transfers for full and adequate consideration (typically structured as a sale of property), intended to benefit transferee loved ones, that a transferor would not typically consider with an arm's-length transferee. These transfers include private annuities and self-cancelling installment notes (SCIN).

Private Annuities

A **private annuity**, unlike a commercial annuity, is a transaction between two (usually related) private parties. The seller/annuitant sells an asset to a buyer in exchange for an unsecured promise from the buyer to make fixed payments to the annuitant for the remainder of the annuitant's life. The promise must be unsecured to comply with the private annuity requirements found in the Treasury regulations. The annuity term is equal to the life expectancy of the seller/annuitant based on the annuitant's age at the date of sale. The interest rate used for determining the interest portion of each payment and the present value of the private annuity is the Section 7520 rate. While the life expectancy of the annuitant (as determined by the IRS mortality tables) is used for income tax and financial calculations, a private annuity requires payments to be made over the lifetime of the seller/annuitant which may fall short of or exceed the life expectancy found in the IRS mortality tables. By selling the asset as a private annuity, the annuitant defers the recognition of any capital gain over his remaining life expectancy, receives a constant stream of income for the remainder of his life, and removes the asset transferred and any of its subsequent appreciation from his gross estate.

Exhibit 7.2 illustrates the application of a private annuity with an individual whose life expectancy is 16 years as of the date of the sale. The annuity payment is calculated using a term of 16 years. If the seller outlives his life expectancy, the annuity payments continue until the seller's death (21 years after the sale is assumed in the exhibit). On the other hand, if the seller dies prior to the term of 16 years, the annuity payments terminate at the seller's death (seven years after the sale is assumed in the exhibit).

EXHIBIT 7.2 **PRIVATE ANNUITY GRAPHICAL ILLUSTRATION**

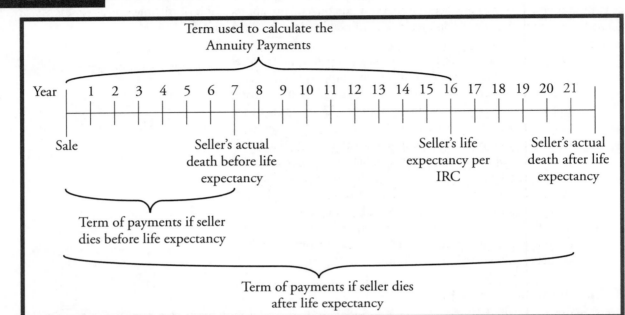

Gift and Estate Tax Consequences of Private Annuities

Provided the fair market value of the property transferred is equal to the present value of the life annuity, there is no taxable gift upon the sale of the property in exchange for the private annuity. Since the annuitant does not have any right to annuity payments after his death, the value of the private annuity is zero at the death of the annuitant and is not included in the seller/annuitant's gross estate. Any annuity payments received before the seller's death will be included in the seller's gross estate to the extent the funds were not consumed. This technique of transferring assets without triggering transfer tax is particularly effective when the actual life expectancy of the annuitant is substantially less than the table life expectancy. In this case, the annuitant is not expected to reach his life expectancy and the asset transferred in exchange for the private annuity plus its future appreciation is transferred to the buyer without the imposition of transfer taxes and without use of the applicable estate or gift tax credit amount. To prevent abuse in this planning area, Treasury Regulations prohibit the use of private annuities if the seller/annuitant is terminally ill. If, however, the annuitant survives for at least eighteen months after the date of the sale, it is presumed that he was not terminally ill as of the date of the sale.

Risks

A private annuity involves investment risks for both the seller/annuitant and the buyer. The annuitant is selling an asset in return for an unsecured promise to receive payments from the buyer. The seller bears the risk that the buyer will not make payments (default risk). Additionally, the annuitant has purchasing power risk, interest rate risk, and reinvestment risk due to the receipt of serial payments over a period of time. The buyer, on the other hand, bears the risk that the annuitant will substantially outlive his life expectancy, thus requiring the buyer to continue paying the annuitant until the annuitant's death. If this happens, the buyer will pay significantly more than he would have paid if he bought the property in an outright sale or for an installment note. The buyer also has business risk; the risk that the asset is not worth the value of the annuity.

Income Tax Issues
Annuitant
Each private annuity payment is split into three components (1) interest (at the Section 7520 interest rate in effect at the date of the sale), (2) capital gain, and (3) income-tax free return of capital (adjusted basis).

<table>
<tr><td>

Father, age 70, sells his business to his son. The fair market value of the business is $2,000,000 and father's adjusted basis is $1,200,000. The Section 7520 rate for the month of the sale is 6% and father's life expectancy according to the IRS life expectancy table is 16 years. What is the yearly payment from son to father? What amount of each payment is capital gain, ordinary income and return of capital?

</td><td>

EXAMPLE 7.9

</td></tr>
</table>

To calculate the answer, follow these steps:

1. Calculate the yearly payment using simple time value of money.
    N = 16
    PV = $2,000,000
    i = 6%
    FV = 0
    PMT_{OA} = $197,904.29

2. Multiply the yearly payment by the number of years the payments are expected to be made. This is the total payment expected to be made.
    $197,904.29 x 16 payments = $3,166,468.64

3. Divide the adjusted basis by the total expected payments. This is the exclusion ratio.

    $$\frac{\text{Adjusted Basis}}{\text{Total Expected Payment}} = \text{Exclusion Ratio}$$

    $$\frac{\$1,200,000}{\$3,166,468.64} = 37.9\%$$

4. Multiply the yearly payment by the exclusion ratio. This is the return of adjusted basis.
    Annual Payment x Exclusion Ratio = Return of Adjusted Basis
    $197,904.29 x 37.9% = $75,005.73

5. Subtract the adjusted basis from the current fair market value and divide by the number of expected payments. This is the yearly capital gain portion.

$2,000,000	Fair Market Value
- $1,200,000	Adjusted Basis
$800,000	Total Capital Gain
÷16	
$50,000	**Annual Capital Gain Recognized**

6. Subtract both the return of adjusted basis and the capital gain from the yearly annuity payment. This determines the interest portion.

$197,904.29	Yearly Annuity Payment
- $75,005.73	Return Basis Component
- $50,000.00	Capital Gain Component
$72,898.56	**Interest and Ordinary Income Component**

In this example, if the father died unexpectedly from a heart attack two years after the sale, he was able to transfer $2,000,000 of property out of his gross estate while only receiving payments of $395,808.58 ($197,904.29 x 2) from his son. If the property appreciated at a rate of 10% per year, the father transferred $2,420,000 in value ($2,000,000 at 10% appreciation per year for two years), received $395,808.58 in return and did not pay any transfer (gift or estate) taxes.

Financial Impact on the Buyer

The buyer makes the serial payment consisting of the interest and principal, interest payments are nondeductible for income tax purposes, and the buyer's adjusted basis in the property exchanged for the private annuity is equal to the total of all annuity payments actually paid. If the seller/annuitant dies shortly after the transfer, the buyer will have a low basis in the asset, which will require payment of capital gains tax if the asset is sold. The increase in capital gains tax, however, is more than offset by the estate tax savings.

Self-Cancelling Installment Notes (SCIN)

Another transfer device that can be used when the transferor is in poor health is the self-cancelling installment note (SCIN). The SCIN transaction involves a sale for the full fair market value of the property transferred over a term defined by the seller. The unique feature of a SCIN is that if the seller dies before all of the installment payments have been made, the note is cancelled and the buyer has no further obligation to pay. In this instance, the seller is taking the risk that he will die before receiving all payments under the SCIN and must be compensated for this risk. The buyer will pay a premium, called a SCIN premium, to compensate the seller for this risk. All else equal, therefore, the buyer will pay more for property sold by a SCIN than he will in a straight installment sale. Unlike the private annuity, where the seller cannot take a security interest in the underlying property, a SCIN can be secured.

Exhibit 7.3 illustrates the application of a SCIN with an individual whose life expectancy is 16 years from the date of the sale. The SCIN payment is determined using the IRC life expectancy factor, which is the maximum term of the SCIN. However, if the seller dies prior to his life expectancy (seven years as illustrated in the exhibit) the SCIN payments terminate at that point.

SCIN GRAPHICAL ILLUSTRATION

EXHIBIT 7.3

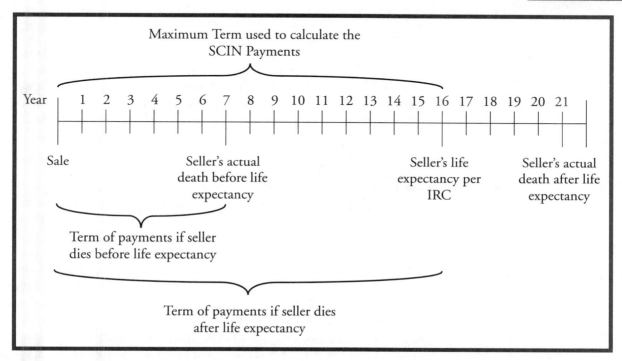

Gift and Estate Tax Consequences
The property transferred by a SCIN is removed from the seller's gross estate, but the payments received will, if not consumed, be included in the seller's gross estate. There is no gift involved in a SCIN provided the present value of the note less the SCIN premium is equal to the fair market value of the asset transferred, and the SCIN premium is appropriate for the mortality risk of the transferor and the value transferred. Like the private annuity, the SCIN is generally used when the transferor is in poor health and expected to die before the end of the defined SCIN term.

Income Tax Consequences - Buyer/Seller
A SCIN is classified for tax purposes as an installment sale. The buyer will make serial payments of interest and principal. Unlike the tax treatment that applies to private annuities, the interest paid by the buyer for a SCIN is deductible if permitted by the Code (i.e., business interest, qualified residence interest, or investment interest). In addition, the buyer's adjusted basis in the property, regardless of the number of installment payments made, is the agreed upon purchase price of the property which includes the full face value of the remaining note payments.

The seller receives the installment payments in three components (1) interest income, (2) capital gain, (3) return of adjusted basis, and also receives (4) the SCIN premium as either additional interest income or capital gain depending upon how the SCIN premium was calculated.

Risks

The seller of property under a SCIN undertakes default risk, interest rate risk, purchasing power risk, and reinvestment risk. The buyer's risk is that the transferor outlives the SCIN term, and thus the buyer pays more for the property, by an amount equal to the SCIN premium, than he would have paid under a normal installment sale. The buyer also has business risk (the risk the asset is not worth the value of the note).

SCIN vs. Private Annuity

Both the SCIN and the private annuity are full consideration sales between related parties entered into for the purpose of transferring property at a reduced cost to the buyer and reducing the seller's gross estate. As discussed above, each has its own advantages and disadvantages which may fit particular situations. For example, SCIN payments only continue until the death of the seller or the end of the SCIN term, whereas private annuity payments continue for the life of the seller. A seller who needs the income from the property to live on would probably use a private annuity for the added security of receiving payments over his lifetime.

Additionally, a private annuity does not allow the seller to keep a security interest in the property sold, but this is permitted with a SCIN. For a seller who is concerned about the default risk of the buyer, the use of a SCIN provides more security because the seller could reclaim the property sold in the event the buyer defaults.

From the buyer's perspective, a SCIN allows the buyer to deduct the portion of the SCIN payment attributable to interest if the property purchased is business, investment property, or a personal residence, whereas interest associated with a private annuity payments is nondeductible. A SCIN also provides the buyer an adjusted basis in the property purchased equal to the agreed upon purchase price of the property, but the adjusted basis for property acquired by private annuity is the sum of the annuity payments actually paid to the seller. Both of these differences will substantially affect the buyer's tax liability during the term of the payments and after the seller's death. Each individual situation, as well as the buyer's intentions, should be considered when arranging a transfer as either a private annuity or a SCIN.

EXHIBIT 7.4	SCIN VS. PRIVATE ANNUITY

	SCIN	Private Annuity
Term of Payment	Determined by Seller	Life of Annuitant
Deductibility of Interest	Depends on Property	None
Buyer's Adjusted Basis	Purchase Price of Property	Sum of Annuity Payments Paid
Seller May Keep Collateral Interest	Yes	No

Grantor Retained Annuity Trust (GRAT)

A Grantor Retained Annuity Trust (GRAT) is an irrevocable trust that pays a fixed annuity (income interest) to the grantor for a defined term and pays the remainder interest of the trust to a noncharitable beneficiary at the end of the GRAT term. The GRAT is funded by the grantor with a transfer of property, and the annuity can be a stated dollar amount, fixed fraction, or a percent of the initial fair market value of the property transferred to the GRAT. The following exhibit illustrates the formation and application of a GRAT:

FORMATION OF A GRAT

EXHIBIT 7.5

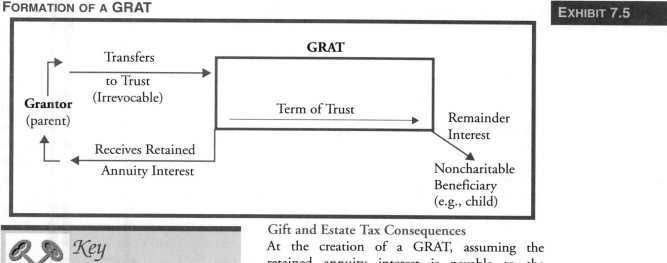

Gift and Estate Tax Consequences

At the creation of a GRAT, assuming the retained annuity interest is payable to the grantor, the annuity portion is not subject to gift tax. However, the present value of the expected future remainder interest is a gift of a future interest subject to gift tax. The value of the remainder interest is determined by subtracting the present value of the expected future annuity payments from the fair market value of the original transfer to the GRAT.

EXAMPLE 7.10

Mike, age 55, transfers a business with a fair market value of $3,000,000 to a GRAT with a term of 10 years. The Section 7520 interest rate at the date of transfer is 8% and Mike retains an annual annuity payment of $298,059 from the trust. The remainder beneficiary is Mike's son James. What is the taxable gift at the date of transfer?

N = 10 Years

PMT = $298,059

i = 8%

PV = $2,000,000

Fair Market Value of Asset	$3,000,000
Less PV of Annuity	$2,000,000
Taxable Gift	**$1,000,000**

Mike can use his applicable gift tax credit to transfer the asset to James, and if Mike outlives the GRAT term, the entire asset has transferred to James without being subject to transfer tax.

The term of the annuity is defined by the grantor. The longer the term, the higher the present value of the annuity payments and thus the lower the value of the remainder interest for gift tax purposes. However, if the grantor of the GRAT dies during the annuity term, the fair market value of the property within the GRAT, as of the grantor's date of death, is included in his gross estate under Section 2036. If this occurs, the grantor does not save any transfer tax.

Appreciating Property

An appropriate time to consider using a GRAT is when the transferor holds property that is expected to appreciate at a rate greater than the Section 7520 interest rate applicable to the GRAT. At the end of the GRAT term, (provided the grantor survives the annuity term) the property will transfer to the remaindermen. In this situation, the grantor will have transferred the appreciated remainder interest in the property at a gift tax cost calculated using the present value of the remainder interest at the date of transfer.

EXAMPLE 7.11	In 2009, Eric, age 55, transfers $2,000,000 to a 10-year GRAT. The remainderman is Eric's only child, Andrew. The Section 7520 rate is 5%. Eric retains an annual annuity payment of $129,505 yielding a present value of the retained interest of $1,000,000 and a future interest taxable gift of $1,000,000, against which Eric can use his applicable gift tax credit, and thus pay no gift tax.

PMT = $129,505

N = 10

i = 5%

PV = $1,000,000 - Present Value of Retained Annuity Interest

Value of Property Contributed to GRAT ($2,000,000) less Value of Retained Annuity Interest ($1,000,000) = Value of Future Remainder Interest ($1,000,000)

If the property transferred to the GRAT actually appreciates at 10% annually, the growth in excess of the Section 7520 rate, 5%, will be transferred to the remaindermen transfer tax free. The following chart illustrates the growth of the property and the amount that will transfer to the remainder beneficiary using assumptions.

Assuming that all works as planned, (Eric lives through the 10 years and annually consumes the $129,505 annuity) Eric will transfer to Andrew $3,123,509, the value of the asset at the end of the GRAT term, by simply using his applicable gift tax credit in 2009.

Year	Beginning Balance	+	10% Growth	-	Annuity Payment	=	Ending Balance
1	$2,000,000		$200,000		($129,505)		$2,070,495
2	$2,070,495		$207,050		($129,505)		$2,148,040
3	$2,148,040		$214,804		($129,505)		$2,233,338
4	$2,233,338		$223,334		($129,505)		$2,327,167
5	$2,327,167		$232,717		($129,505)		$2,430,379
6	$2,430,379		$243,038		($129,505)		$2,543,912
7	$2,543,912		$254,391		($129,505)		$2,668,798
8	$2,668,798		$266,880		($129,505)		$2,806,173
9	$2,806,173		$280,617		($129,505)		$2,957,285
10	$2,957,285		$295,729		($129,505)		$3,123,509

Note that Eric could have only transferred $1,000,000 to the GRAT, thus creating a zero value gift (the value of the annuity is $1,000,000, creating a remainder interest with a value of $0). At the end of the 10 year GRAT term the remainder value would be $529,766. This amount will be transferred with no transfer tax and without the use of the applicable gift tax credit.

Risk

Upon creation of the GRAT, the greatest risk is the grantor's failure to survive the GRAT term, causing the fair market value of the property transferred to the GRAT to be included in the grantor's gross estate. However, this risk is minimal because if this occurs (ignoring transactional costs) the grantor is no worse off than if he had not created the GRAT. Without the GRAT, the property would also have been included in his gross estate.

Income Tax Consequences

A GRAT is subject to the grantor trust rules for income tax purposes. There are no income tax consequences on the initial transfer to the GRAT because for income tax purposes, the grantor is still deemed to own all of the assets in the GRAT. However, all trust income flows through to the grantor annually, and is included in the grantor's income, without regard to the amount of the distributions made to the grantor. The grantor's usual objective in establishing a GRAT is to remove appreciation potential of the assets from his gross estate while minimizing transfer taxes. Income tax savings is not the motivation to establish GRAT.

Quick Quiz 7.2

Highlight the answer to these questions:

1. A SCIN payment terminates at the death of the buyer.
   a. True
   b. False

2. At the date a GRAT is funded, the value of the remainder interest is the excess of the contributions to the trust over the present value of the annuity stream.
   a. True
   b. False

3. At the end of the QPRT term, the annuitant must sell the home.
   a. True
   b. False

4. A family limited partnership utilizes lack of control and marketability discounts to transfer the partnership interests at a reduced transfer tax cost.
   a. True
   b. False

False, True, False, True.

Grantor Retained Unitrust (GRUT)

Another device similar to the GRAT is called a GRUT (**Grantor Retained Unitrust**). Instead of paying a fixed annuity, a GRUT pays a fixed percentage of the trust's assets each year as revalued on an annual basis. The GRUT is less suitable for hard to value assets (e.g. real estate, businesses) because the annual revaluation requirement is cumbersome. Also, if the asset is appreciating faster than the Section 7520 interest rate it causes the annual payment to the grantor to increase each year, which defeats the objective of lowering the grantor's gross estate. For these reasons, GRUTs are used less frequently than GRATs in estate plans.

Qualified Personal Residence Trust (QPRT)

A **Qualified Personal Residence Trust** (QPRT) is a special form of a GRAT. The grantor contributes a personal residence to a trust and instead of receiving an annuity in dollars, the grantor of the QPRT receives use of the personal residence as the annuity interest component.

At the end of the trust term, the residence passes to the remaindermen. If the grantor is still living, he may then lease, at a fair market value rent, the property from the remaindermen and continue to use it as his personal residence. If the grantor dies before the expiration of the trust term, the fair market value of the residence is included in the grantor's gross estate.

A QPRT may only be established with a personal residence of the grantor. No more than two QPRTs established by a single grantor may be in existence at one time. In the case of spouses who have a joint interest in a personal residence, they can transfer the property to the same or separate QPRTs. The use of separate trusts may be more appropriate if the life expectancy of each spouse is substantially different. If a residence transferred to a QPRT is sold, it can be replaced using the proceeds in the QPRT. The capital gain exclusion rules ($250,000 for single, $500,000 for married filing jointly) are applicable with regard to any income tax consequences. Care should be taken to draft the QPRT documents so that the grantor continues to qualify for the homestead exemption.

Gift and Estate Tax Consequences (QPRTs)

The original transfer of the residence is treated as a gift to the extent that the fair market value of the residence exceeds the present value of the grantor's retained interest (the use) as determined under Section 7520. This is an excellent transfer device when the personal residence is appreciating at a much greater rate than the Section 7520 interest rate and there is an intent to keep the property in the family for the long-term.

As in the case of the GRAT, if the grantor dies during the term of the QPRT, the full fair market value of the home will be included in the grantor's gross estate. However, if the grantor outlives the QPRT term, the personal residences will not be included in the decedent's gross estate.

Tangible Personal Property Trust (TPPT)

Tangible Personal Property Trusts (TPPTs) are very similar to QPRTs, with one exception – a TPPT is funded with personal property, not real property. TPPTs usually transfer artwork, antiques, and other items of personal property that have the potential to appreciate in value. The grantor retains the right to use the personal property as the "annuity" interest component of the trust. At the end of the trust term, the personal property transfers to the remainder beneficiary.

Gift and Estate Tax Consequences

The original transfer of the personal property to the trust is treated as a gift to the extent that the fair market value of the personal property exceeds the present value of the grantor's retained interest. Valuation of the retained interest, however, is difficult, and the IRS will scrutinize the transfer to a TPPT due to the difficulty of valuing the right to use a piece of tangible personal property.

As in the case of the QPRT, if the grantor dies during the term of the TPPT, the full fair market value of the trust property will be included in the grantor's gross estate. However, if the grantor outlives the trust term, the property will not be included in the grantor's gross estate.

FAMILY LIMITED PARTNERSHIPS (FLP)

A **family limited partnership** (FLP) is a limited partnership created under state law with the primary purpose of transferring assets to younger generations using valuation discounts.

Usually, one or more family members transfer highly appreciating property to a limited partnership in return for both the one percent general and the 99 percent limited partnership interests. In a limited partnership, the general partner has unlimited liability and the sole management rights of the partnership, while the limited partners are passive investors with limited liability and no management rights.

EXHIBIT 7.6 FAMILY LIMITED PARTNERSHIP

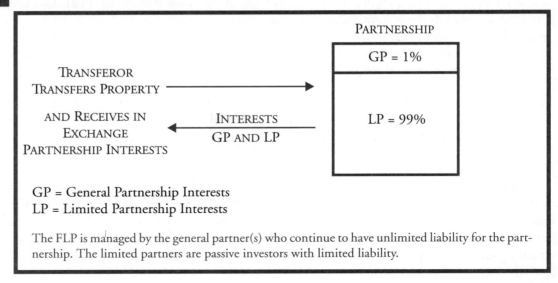

PARTNERSHIP

GP = 1%

TRANSFEROR
TRANSFERS PROPERTY

AND RECEIVES IN   INTERESTS   LP = 99%
EXCHANGE   GP AND LP
PARTNERSHIP INTERESTS

GP = General Partnership Interests
LP = Limited Partnership Interests

The FLP is managed by the general partner(s) who continue to have unlimited liability for the partnership. The limited partners are passive investors with limited liability.

Gift and Estate Tax Consequences

Upon creation of the partnership, there are neither income nor gift tax consequences because the entity created (the limited partnership and all of its interests, both general and limited) is owned by the same person, or persons, who owned the assets before the transfer.

Once the FLP is created, the owner of the general and limited partnership interests values the limited partnership interests. Since there are usually transfer restrictions on the limited partnership interests (limiting the marketability), and the limited partners have little control of the management of the partnership (lack of control), limited partnership interests are usually valued with a substantial discount. It is not uncommon for the value of such discounted interests to range between 20-40 percent less than similar proportional interests. The original transferor (grantor) then begins an annual gifting program using the discounts, the gift tax annual exclusion, and gift-splitting (where applicable) to transfer limited partnership interests to younger generation family members at reduced transfer costs.

EXAMPLE 7.12

In 2009, Adam, age 52, is married to Barb and they have three children and nine grandchildren. The three children are happily married and Adam and Barb think of their children's spouses as their own children. Adam transfers a 100% interest in a business with a fair market value of $3,200,000 to a family limited partnership. Adam receives back a general partnership interest of one percent and 162 units of limited partnership interests representing 99 percent, at $19,555 (($3,200,000 x 99%) / 162) per unit. Adam then transfers two limited partnership units to each child, spouse of child, and grandchild using a 33.5 percent discount, the annual exclusion, and the split gift election.

$19,555 x 0.665 (1.00 - 0.335) = $13,000 x 2 = $26,000 per donee x 15 donees (3 children, 3 spouses, 9 grandchildren) = 30 units valued at $586,650 (30 x $19,555) total, but discounted to represent $390,000 (30 x $13,000) and each under the annual exclusion amount. (Note that the actual numbers, if calculated, have a slight rounding error.)

In this scenario, Adam does not pay any transfer tax. It will take six years with this level of distribution for Adam to transfer his entire limited partnership interest under the annual exclusion to his children, their spouses, and his grandchildren.

Asset Control

One of the unique features of the FLP, and perhaps its most important non-tax benefit, is that the original owner/transferor can maintain control of the property transferred to the limited partnership by only retaining a small general partnership interest. If the FLP is funded with a business interest, the general partner could remain president of the business, direct the company's strategic plan, receive reasonable compensation and fringe benefits, hire and fire employees, receive executive perks, and generally control the limited partners' interests. As with all limited partnerships, the limited partners have no control over any of these enumerated management decisions.

The FLP is often undertaken as a series of transfers, including an initial nontaxable contribution of property to the partnership followed by annual exclusion gifts of limited partnership interests. While a general partner has control over partnership affairs, an individual who transfers his property to an FLP needs to be financially secure without the transferred property, both from a net worth and cash flow perspective.

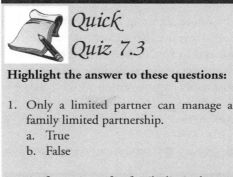

Quick Quiz 7.3

Highlight the answer to these questions:

1. Only a limited partner can manage a family limited partnership.
   a. True
   b. False

2. At formation of a family limited partnership, the founder is subject to gift tax on the transfer of the property interest to the family limited partnership.
   a. True
   b. False

False, False.

Asset Protection

The use of the FLP structure can also help protect family assets. By placing the assets in the FLP and only making gifts of limited partnership interests to heirs, judgments or liens entered against a donee (limited partner) will not jeopardize the assets of the partnership. A donee's creditor would not be able to force the donee to liquidate his interest, since the donee does not have the right to force the liquidation of a limited partnership interest.

Transferring limited partnership interests to children and children's spouses can also help protect assets from divorce claims. If the child and his spouse divorce, even if the divorced spouse received a limited partnership interest, he or she could not force distributions from the partnership, participate in management, require his or her interest to be redeemed, or force a liquidation of the partnership.

Design and Implementation

The creation of family limited partnerships and the use of discounts to transfer value at a lower gift tax cost has been regularly contested by the IRS. However, in several cases, the courts have ruled in favor of the taxpayer and upheld discounts on the valuation of limited partnership interests in the range of 10 percent to 40 percent, as long as the FLP was operated like a separate business. The IRS has won and the valuation discounts have not been allowed in cases where the family withdrew money from the business at leisure, shared checking accounts with the business, had the FLP pay medical or other ordinary living expenses for the family, and when other non-business transactions were prevalent within the FLP.

The estate planning benefits of the FLP are lost and expenses are increased (as the result of legal fees) when the IRS successfully contests the use of the FLP arrangement. To mitigate against this risk and to ensure the use of the favorable discounts, the FLP should possess economic substance by having its own checking accounts, tax identification number, payroll (including payment of reasonable compensation to the general partner if he is managing the business), and should not allow family members to withdraw funds at will, nor should the FLP pay for personal expenses of its owners.

| EXHIBIT 7.7 | SUMMARY CHARACTERISTICS OF FAMILY LIMITED PARTNERSHIPS (FLPs) |

Advantages	Disadvantages
• Control retained by senior family member • Valuation discounts • Annual exclusion gifts • Some creditor protection • Restrictions can be placed on transferability of limited partnership interests of junior family members	• Attorney setup fees • Appraisal fees • Operational requirements

SUMMARY

Whereas the SCIN and the private annuity are both sales transactions for adequate consideration and the retained interest trusts (GRAT/QPRT/TPPT) are partial gift/partial sale transactions, the FLP is often used to engage in a series of gifts. With each of the private annuity, SCIN, GRAT, or QPRT, the senior family member either needs or desires the income from or use of the transferred property. With the FLP, the transferor wants to retain control of the property temporarily and ultimately transfer the property under the annual exclusion gifting regime. In all cases, the transferor's intent is to reduce his gross estate and avoid and minimize transfer taxes. However, when transferring assets during life in order to reduce the gross estate, individuals must be aware of the impact that such transfers may have on certain government programs.

Medicare/Medicaid

Medicare is a federally funded and state-administered health insurance program primarily designed for individuals over the age of 65. Under certain circumstances, Medicaid provides limited long-term care benefits. Traditional Medicare will generally pay the full cost of nursing home stays for the first 20 days and can continue to pay the cost of the nursing home stay for the next 80 days, subject to a daily deductible of approximately $133.50 (for 2009). For individuals covered by the Medicare Managed Care plan, there is no deductible for days 21 through 100, but there are strict qualifying rules. Therefore, even under the best of circumstances, the maximum benefit will be for 100 days.

Medicaid is also a health insurance program sponsored by the federal government and administered by the states, but it is primarily intended to benefit certain low-income individuals and families. One of the primary benefits of Medicaid is that, unlike Medicare, the Medicaid program will pay for long-term care in a nursing home for persons who meet the qualifications. Note that Medicaid does not cover "custodial" stays in a nursing home, which often occur with diseases such as Alzheimer's or Parkinson's. Eligibility for Medicaid is subject to certain requirements, such as age; whether the applicant is pregnant, disabled, blind, or aged; the applicant's income and resources; and whether the applicant is a U.S. citizen or a lawfully admitted immigrant. The rules for counting income and resources vary from state to state and from group to group.

Because the Medicaid eligibility requirements are strict, particularly with respect to the applicant's income and resources, individuals often seek to plan for their Medicaid eligibility long before they need it. For example, in most states there is a Medicaid monthly income limit for an individual (although the states vary in amount). In addition, a Medicaid recipient cannot have countable resources in excess of the state mandated amount. (To determine the limits for any particular state, go to the state's website.) Countable resources include any assets that are available to the Medicaid recipient other than certain exempt assets. Thus, many individuals find themselves in the position of not having enough assets to pay for nursing home care, but also having too many assets to qualify for Medicaid.

However, because of the increasing frequency of people giving away their assets in order to try to qualify for Medicaid, the federal government has adopted a penalty test that imposes a period of ineligibility upon anyone who gives away their assets in order to qualify for the income or resource requirements of Medicaid. If an individual has transferred assets for less than fair market value, the state must withhold payment for nursing facility care (and certain other long-term care services) for a period of time referred to as the penalty period. States can "look back" to find transfers of all assets for 60 months prior to the date that the individual applies for Medicaid.

The length of the penalty period is determined by dividing the value of the transferred asset by the average monthly private-pay rate for nursing facility care in the State. For example, if an individual gave away assets worth $90,000, divided by a $3,000 average monthly private-pay rate, the result is a 30-month penalty period. There is no limit to the length of the penalty period.

For certain types of transfers, these penalties are not applied. The principal exceptions include transfers to a spouse, or to a third party for the sole benefit of the spouse; transfers by a spouse to a third party for the sole benefit of the spouse; transfers to certain disabled individuals, or to trusts established for those individuals; transfers for a purpose other than to qualify for Medicaid; and transfers where imposing a penalty would cause undue hardship.

TRANSFERS TO CHARITIES

Many of the transfers that can be made during life to non-family members (arm's-length) and to loved ones (arm's-length, full sales, partial sales, partial gifts, and full gifts) are presented above. Chapter 9 discusses another type of transfer during our lives - transfers to charitable organizations.

EXHIBIT 7.8 | **SUMMARY OF TRANSFERS DURING LIFE**

ARM'S-LENGTH TRANSACTIONS FOR FULL CONSIDERATION		
• Sale		
• Installment Sale		
• Exchanges		
TYPICAL TRANSFERS TO LOVED ONES		
Arm's-Length	**Full-Consideration**	**Retained Interest Gifts***
• Sale	• Private Annuities	• GRATs
• Installment Sale	• SCINs	• GRUTs
• Exchange		• QPRTs
		• TPPTs
		• Bargain Sale
Gifts	**Gifts With Use of Discounts**	**Transfers Resulting in No Tax**
• Outright	• Family Limited Partnership	• Qualified Transfers
• Gifts in Trust		• Payments for Support
		• Payments to Divorcing Spouses
		• Transfers in a Business Setting
		• Gifts to Spouses**
		• Annual Exclusion Gifts
TRANSFERS TO CHARITIES		
See Chapter 9		
• Outright Gifts		
• Charitable Annuities		
• Pooled Income Funds		
• Gifts in Trust		
• Charitable Remainder Trusts		
• CRATs		
• CRUTs		
• Charitable Lead Trusts		
• CLATs		
• CLUTs		

* The four devices below (GRATs, GRUTs, QPRTs, and TPPTs) are not actually sales in the traditional sense of a sale to a transferee. Rather the grantor is exchanging an asset put in trust for a stream of dollars or use with a present value less than the value of the transferred asset. That difference being the amount of the gift in present value terms. ** Gifts to spouses are subject to gift tax, but may be nontaxable due to the marital deduction.

Property can be transferred at death in one of three ways: (1) by will; (2) by contract (beneficiary designation); and (3) by operation of law (e.g., titling of property, use of trusts, intestacy). When an individual dies, all of his or her property must be transferred in some combination either to heirs, charities, or the government (taxes).

TRANSFERS BY WILL

A will is a legally enforceable document that transfers property to designated beneficiaries at death. To be effective, a will should meet the minimum requirements set forth under state law. A person who dies with a will is said to have died testate and is referred to as a testator. The will should direct the payment of expenses, debts, and taxes, but if such a determination is not made in the will, the decedent's state law of domicile will control. After the debts, expenses, and taxes have been paid, the remaining property is transferred to the beneficiaries, generally in the following order:

1. Personal property is transferred to legatees.
2. Real property is transferred to devisees.
3. Residuary legatees take anything remaining in the estate that has not been specifically disposed of by will.

Specific bequests (e.g., I leave my home at 321 Clover Street to my son Billie) may be of tangible or intangible personal property, real property, or cash. The residuary estate consists of what is left after all specific bequests have been satisfied. If the estate is not sufficient to discharge all of the decedent's bequests and the decedent has not expressed a preference, the order of disposition will be determined under decedent's state law of domicile. Otherwise, the residuary estate may be distributed under one of several methods to be chosen by the testator.

Universal/Residual Legatees

A universal legacy is created when the testator gives to one or several persons his entire estate (all of my estate to A). A residual legatee receives the balance of the estate after all specific bequests are satisfied. For example, if a decedent's will says "$100,000 to A, the balance of my estate to B," B is both a residual and universal legatee. A legacy may be general or specific. A general legacy may be a fraction or certain proportion of the estate or a fraction or certain proportion of the balance of the estate.

Per Stirpes/Per Capita

In the event a child named as a residual or universal legatee is dead, or disclaims his interest, and such pre-deceased child has children, those children may take by representation per stirpes (the children share their pre-deceased parent's interest) or per capita (the children become equal beneficiaries in the estate with no relation to the deceased child's interest).

EXAMPLE 7.13

Brandy has three children - Amber, Britney, and Charley. Each child has two children of their own. Assume Brandy dies and is survived only by Britney and Charley. If Amber's children inherit per stirpes then each of them will share Amber's 1/3 interest. If instead the children inherit per capita, then Amber's two children move into the same generation as Britney and Charley and each of them will receive 1/4 of Brandy's assets.

Disinheritance

A testator may attempt to disinherit specific people, or a class of people, by not listing them as legatees in the will. Simply not listing an heir in a will may not be sufficient to disinherit them if it appears to the court to be an oversight. In the United States, it is not possible to completely disinherit a surviving spouse, since he or she could exercise his or her right of election against the estate, and receive between one-third and one-half of the property under state law, unless the couple entered into a legally enforceable prenuptial agreement.

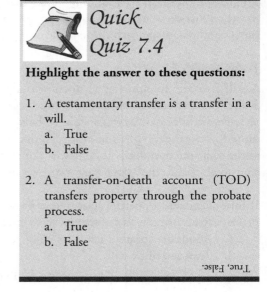

PROPERTY TRANSFERRED AT DEATH BY CONTRACT

There are a number of ways to transfer property at death by contract. These include use of life insurance, annuities, qualified plans, individual retirement plans (IRAs), transfer-on-death accounts (TODs), Totten Trusts, and payable on death bank accounts (PODs). The distinguishing feature in all of these types of transfers is that an agent (for example, a life insurance company) is directed to transfer or pay a named beneficiary upon the death of the principal. Quite commonly all that is necessary to have the agent pay the named beneficiary is for the beneficiary to present a certified death certificate to the agent.

TRANSFERS AT DEATH BY OPERATION OF LAW

The most common forms of transfer at death by operation of law include joint titling of property with a survivorship feature, intestacy, revocable trusts becoming irrevocable, and other trusts created under the trust law.

Titling

Two forms of titling that have survivorship features are joint tenancy with right of survivorship and tenancy by the entirety. The surviving joint owners of the property take the property outright after presenting a certified death certificate. The property is not transferred through the probate process, but is transferred to the joint owners by operation of law.

Trusts

An irrevocable trust will operate in accordance with the terms of its governing instrument and is not subject to the probate process. Some trusts are created by will (testamentary trusts), or are created (but not funded) prior to the grantor's death waiting for assets to be transferred to them pursuant to the terms of the grantor's will (standby trusts).

Care must be taken if assets under the will are to pour over to a preexisting trust or if non-will assets (e.g., those under contract) are to pour over to a testamentary trust (beneficiary of life insurance is the XYZ trust, a testamentary trust).

All assets transferred to a testamentary trust pursuant to the decedent's will are included in the decedent's probate estate. If the beneficiary of any assets that would normally pass by contract is the decedent's estate, then those assets will also be included in the probate estate.

Probate

As discussed in Chapter 4, transfers through probate are governed by either the intestacy laws (when the decedent dies without a will) or the decedent's will (in which case the decedent is said to have died testate). The intestacy rules apply when there is no will, the will is invalid in whole or in part, or the will does not dispose of all of the decedent's probate property. Intestate successors are commonly called heirs, testate successors are called legatees (for personal property transfers), and devisees (for real property transfers).

If intestacy rules apply, the state will commonly classify and prioritize heirs. The most common prioritization is (note that different states may have differing orders):
1. Surviving spouse
2. Descendents
3. Parents, siblings, and descendents of siblings
4. More remote ascendants (grandparents, aunts, uncles)
5. More remote collaterals (cousins, nieces, nephews)
6. Decedent's domiciliary state

Usually the most favored class takes to the exclusion of other classes and the nearest relative in the class takes to the exclusion of other more distant relatives in that same class. Persons of the same degree of distance share equally. Descendents of relatives who would take, but have predeceased the descendent, take according to state law. A renunciation or disclaimer by an heir may also lead to representation per stirpes.

CHARITABLE TRANSFERS AT DEATH

All property of the decedent at death must be included in the gross estate. However, there is an unlimited charitable estate tax deduction. There is no income tax deduction for assets left to a charity at death. Property can be left to charities by contract, through use of state titling laws, in trust laws, and by will. Property generally does not pass to charities by virtue of intestate laws except where there are no living relatives, and at that point the assets escheat (transfer) to the state (these rules may vary by state).

In the event a split interest charitable remainder trust (CRT) is established at death, the charitable estate tax deduction is equal to the fair market value of the property transferred to the CRT less the discounted present value of the retained interest (the annuity or unitrust). The annuitant could be the surviving spouse or some other person. If such property should also qualify for the unlimited marital deduction the surviving spouse must be the only noncharitable beneficiary (see Chapter 9 for full discussion on charitable transfers).

Key Terms

Exchange - A mutual transfer of assets with equal fair market values between individuals.

Family Limited Partnership (FLP) - A limited partnership created under state law with the primary purpose of transferring assets to younger generations using minority and marketability discounts to create reduced gift tax valuations.

Grantor Retained Annuity Trust (GRAT) - An irrevocable trust that pays a fixed annuity to the grantor (settlor) for some defined term, and pays the remainder interest of the trust to a noncharitable beneficiary.

Grantor Retained Unitrust (GRUT) - A irrevocable trust that annually pays a fixed percentage of the value of its assets (as revalued on an annual basis) to the grantor or (settlor) for some defined term, and pays the remainder interest of the trust to a noncharitable beneficiary.

Installment Sale - A sale of property that includes a note from the buyer to the seller. The buyer pays the seller the full valuable consideration of the property over a specified set of terms.

Private Annuity - The annuitant sells an asset to a buyer in exchange for an unsecured promise from the buyer to make fixed annual payments to the annuitant for the remainder of the annuitant's life.

Qualified Personal Residence Trust (QPRT) - A special form of a GRAT in which the grantor transfers his home to the QPRT and receives "use" of the personal residence as the annuity. The remainder interest of the trust passes to a noncharitable beneficiary.

Sale - The direct transfer of property to another for a note, money, or property of equal fair market value.

Self-Cancelling Installment Note (SCIN) - An installment sale that terminates at the earlier of the (1) death of the seller or (2) the term set forth in the installment note.

Tangible Personal Property Trusts (TPPT) - A special form of a GRAT in which the grantor transfers tangible personal property to the TPPT and receives "use" of the property as the annuity. The remainder interest transfers to a noncharitable beneficiary.

1. Explain how an intra-family sale of property can be an advantageous strategy for reducing an individual's gross estate.

2. List three of the major differences in the gross estate treatment of transfers during life and bequests at death.

3. List the transfer techniques most commonly used with loved ones.

4. What is the term of a private annuity?

5. What is the buyer's adjusted basis in property purchased through a private annuity?

6. What is the SCIN premium?

7. If the seller outlives the term of a SCIN, how is the buyer affected?

8. What is the buyer's adjusted basis in property purchased through a SCIN?

9. Explain the gift tax consequences of a SCIN and a private annuity.

10. What is a Grantor Retained Annuity Trust (GRAT)?

11. Explain the gift tax consequences of a GRAT.

12. How does a Grantor Retained Unitrust (GRUT) differ from a GRAT?

13. What is a Qualified Personal Residence Trust (QPRT)?

14. Explain the gift tax consequences of a QPRT.

15. What is the usual primary purpose of establishing a family limited partnership?

16. Discuss the discounts available when valuing the interests of a family limited partnership.

17. List the disadvantages of using a family limited partnership to transfer interest in property.

18. Which property transfers at death by contract law?

1. Which of the following statements regarding installment sales is correct?

    a. All payments received by the seller in an installment sale are considered interest income.

    b. At the death of the seller, the principal balance of the installment sale is included in the seller's gross estate.

    c. The present value of the expected remainder value of the property sold in an installment sale is subject to gift tax at the date of the transfer.

    d. An installment sale would never be used with a related party.

2. In 2009, Roxanne paid Badlaw University $12,000 for her nephew's tuition and gave her nephew $23,000 in cash. Roxanne is single and did not make any other gifts during the year. What is the amount of Roxanne's taxable gifts for the year?

    a. $0.

    b. $2,000.

    c. $10,000.

    d. $23,000.

3. During the year, Johnson created a trust for the benefit of his six children. The terms of the trust declare that his children can only access the trust's assets after the trust has been in existence for 15 years and the trust does not include a Crummey provision. If Johnson transfers $72,000 to the trust during the year, what is his total taxable gifts for the year?

    a. $0.

    b. $12,000.

    c. $60,000.

    d. $72,000.

4. Which of the following statements regarding private annuities is correct?

    a. If a seller dies before the end of the private annuity term, the buyer continues to pay the annuity to the seller's estate.

    b. A private annuity must include a risk premium to compensate the seller for the possibility of cancellation at the seller's death.

    c. A private annuity cannot give the seller a security interest in the property.

    d. With a private annuity, the buyer must make the annuity payments for the lesser of the term of the annuity or the life of the seller.

5. Perry's father sold the family business to him using a private annuity. The private annuity was structured such that Perry would pay his father $40,000 per year plus interest, for the remainder of his father's life. At the date of the sale, Perry's father's life expectancy was 20 years and Perry's father was in great health. After six years, Perry's father died of a heart attack and Perry sold the business for $2,000,000 six months after his father's death. What is Perry's capital gain/loss on the transaction?

    a. $240,000.

    b. $1,760,000.

    c. $1,960,000.

    d. $2,000,000.

6. Which of the following statements regarding self-cancelling installment notes (SCINs) is correct?

    a. If a seller outlives the SCIN term, the buyer continues to pay the SCIN payment until the seller's death.

    b. If the buyer dies before the end of the SCIN term or the death of the seller, his gross estate includes a debt equal to the present value of the remaining payments.

    c. A SCIN cannot give the seller a collateral interest in the property sold.

    d. If the seller dies before the end of the note term, the seller is deemed to have made a taxable gift to the buyer equal to the difference between the payments made and total principal payments on the SCIN.

7. Todd purchased his mother's home through use of a SCIN. Under the terms of the SCIN, Todd was to pay his mother $20,000, plus interest, and a SCIN premium, per year for 10 years. If Todd's mother died after 4 payments were made, what would be Todd's adjusted basis in the home?

    a. $0.

    b. $80,000.

    c. $160,000.

    d. $200,000.

8. Harry, age 60, owns 400 shares of ABC Corporation, which he expects to increase 300% over the next four years. Harry eventually wants to transfer the stock in ABC Corporation to his son, Billy, but Billy is currently incapable of managing the stock or the income from the stock. Harry expects Billy to be responsible in five years. Of the following, which transfer method would work best to remove the expected appreciation of the stock from Harry's gross estate and protect the property for Billy?

    a. Private annuity.

    b. SCIN.

    c. GRAT.

    d. QPRT.

9. Which of the following statements regarding a Grantor Retained Annuity Trust (GRAT) is correct?

    a. The remainder interest of a GRAT is payable to a noncharitable beneficiary.

    b. The term of the trust should be set equal to the life expectancy of the grantor.

    c. The remainder beneficiary is taxed on the income in the GRAT each year.

    d. At the end of the GRAT term, the property reverts to the grantor.

10. Dave transferred $1,500,000 to a GRAT naming his two children as the remainder beneficiaries while retaining an annuity valued at $500,000. If this is the only transfer Dave made during the year, what is Dave's total taxable gift for the year?

    a. $0.

    b. $987,000.

    c. $1,000,000.

    d. $1,487,000.

11. Of the following statements regarding a Qualified Personal Residence Trust (QPRT), which is true?

    a. At the end of the QPRT term, the residence reverts to the grantor.

    b. At creation of the QPRT, the grantor has a taxable gift to the remainder beneficiary eligible for the annual exclusion.

    c. At the end of the QPRT term, the grantor must begin paying rent to the remainder beneficiaries of the QPRT if he continues to live in the residence.

    d. A QPRT is ideal for a personal residence that is expected to appreciate at a lower rate than the Section 7520 rate.

12. In an effort to keep any of its future appreciation out of her gross estate, Mary, a 73-year-old widow, transferred her home into a Qualified Personal Residence Trust (QPRT) naming her only son as the remainder beneficiary. Which of the following statements regarding a QPRT is false?

    a. If Mary has a taxable gift at the date of formation of the trust, the gift is not eligible for the annual exclusion.

    b. If Mary outlives the term of the QPRT and continues to live in the house, she must pay her son rent.

    c. At the termination of the QPRT, the personal residence is distributed to Mary's son.

    d. If Mary dies during the term of the QPRT, her gross estate will include the value of her home at the date of the transfer to the QPRT.

13. Which of the following statements regarding Family Limited Partnerships (FLPs) is correct?

    a. The primary purpose of creating a FLP is to provide joint management of the property contributed to the FLP.

    b. At the creation of the FLP, the transferring individual will have a capital gain equal to the difference between the fair market value of the property transferred and his adjusted basis in the property.

    c. The limited partners in the FLP control all of the day-to-day functions of the FLP.

    d. Transfers of the limited partnership interests in the FLP are usually eligible for minority and lack of marketability valuation discounts.

14. Which of the following techniques will not help an individual lower his gross estate?

    a. Pay-on-Death Arrangement (POD).

    b. Grantor Retained Annuity Trust (GRAT).

    c. Sale.

    d. Self-Cancelling Installment Note (SCIN).

15. Which of the following does not transfer property at death by operation of law?

    a. Property owned JTWROS.

    b. Property owned tenancy in common.

    c. Intestacy.

    d. A revocable living trust.

16. Which of the following does not transfer property at death by contract?

    a. Tenancy by the entirety.

    b. IRAs.

    c. Life insurance.

    d. POD accounts.

Quick Quiz Explanations

Quick Quiz 7.1
1. True.
2. False. A sale is not a taxable gift and does not qualify for the gift tax annual exclusion.
3. True.

Quick Quiz 7.2
1. False. A SCIN payment terminates at the death of the seller, not at the death of the buyer.
2. True.
3. False. At the end of the QPRT term, the remainder beneficiary of the QPRT owns the home. There is no legal requirement that forces the sale of the home.
4. True.

Quick Quiz 7.3
1. False. Only a general partner can manage a family limited partnership.
2. False. There are no gift tax consequences on the formation of a family limited partnership. Gift tax consequences do result upon transfer of family limited partnership units to other individuals.

Quick Quiz 7.4
1. True.
2. False. A transfer on death account (TOD) is a probate avoidance device.

Trusts

INTRODUCTION

Trusts are used in estate planning to provide for the management of assets and flexibility in the operation of the plan. Most trusts, other than charitable trusts, provide great flexibility by allowing the trustee to make decisions based on criteria set forth in the trust document by the grantor. This flexibility can be particularly important when the trust arrangement will last for an extended period of time. Charitable trusts are often used in estate planning, but are relatively inflexible both in their creation and in their operation because the government dictates the provisions of the trust due to the income tax benefits accruing to the donor and granted by the government. Charitable trusts generate tax benefits for the grantor and are often used for both lifetime and testamentary planning purposes. The purpose of this chapter is to introduce the reader to trust concepts, describe how trusts work, and review the advantages, disadvantages, and uses of specific types of trusts commonly used in the estate planning process.

The basic structure of a trust is depicted by the following diagram:

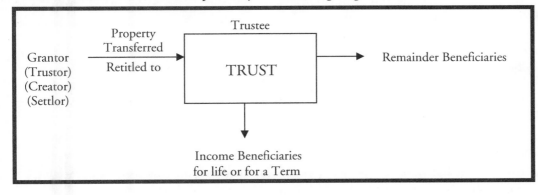

DEFINITIONS

A **trust** is a structure that vests legal title to assets in one party, the trustee, who manages those assets for the benefit of others, the beneficiaries of the trust. The beneficiaries hold the beneficial, or equitable, interest in the trust. By dividing the ownership rights into two parts (legal and equitable), a trust can be a useful tool in managing both the property and the tax consequences attached to the transfer of property.

To form a trust, a grantor of a trust transfers (retitles) money or other property to the trustee. The money or property transferred is referred to as the trust principal, corpus, res, or fund. The trust principal will be managed by the trustee to accomplish the grantor's objectives as expressed in the detailed provisions of the trust document.

PARTIES

The three parties to a trust agreement are the grantor, the trustee, and the beneficiaries.

GRANTOR (SETTLOR, CREATOR, TRUSTOR)

The **grantor** is the person who creates and initially funds the trust. In some instances, a grantor is referred to as a settlor, trustor, or creator. These names all have the same meaning. As the individual who creates the trust arrangement, the grantor establishes the terms and provisions of the trust and determines the scope and limits of the trustee's actions and discretion in managing the trust assets.

In sophisticated estate planning situations, a single trust may have multiple grantors. For example, many family members, and possibly many generations of family members, may contribute property to a dynasty trust (discussed in Chapter 13). While those individuals who become grantors of a trust after its creation are not usually permitted to change the terms of the trust, making transfers to an existing trust may be a cost effective way of arranging for property transfers if the existing trust arrangement satisfies some of their goals.

Key Concepts

Underline/highlight the answers to these questions as you read:

1. Identify the parties to a trust.

2. List the duties of a fiduciary.

3. Differentiate between an income beneficiary and a remainder beneficiary.

TRUSTEE

The **trustee** is the individual or entity responsible for managing the trust assets and carrying out the directions of the grantor that are formally expressed in the trust instrument. A trustee is said to be vested with legal title to the trust assets, but must, at all times, act in the best interest of trust beneficiaries. As such, the trustee is considered to be a **fiduciary**, a person who has a legal duty to act in the best interest of another as a result of holding a position of trust and confidence.

Other individuals and entities considered to be fiduciaries include executors and administrators of decedents' estates, as well as guardians of minors and incapacitated individuals.

The law imposes several duties to ensure that a fiduciary always acts in the best interests of those he is charged to protect. Among these duties are (1) the duty of loyalty and (2) the duty of care. A trustee must be loyal to the beneficiaries of a trust and must make decisions that are in the best interests of the beneficiaries (and consistent with the terms of the trust) even if those decisions result in a loss to the fiduciary. Furthermore, a trustee owes a duty of care to all beneficiaries, and therefore should make decisions only after engaging in a diligent investigation of the facts and thoughtful consideration of the impact on all of the beneficiaries.

These duties of loyalty and care can be summarized in a concept referred to as the Prudent Man Rule. The **Prudent Man Rule** states that the trustee, as a fiduciary, must act in the same manner that a prudent person would act if the prudent person was acting for his own benefit after considering all of the facts and circumstances surrounding the decision. Simply stated, the standard is a codification of the golden rule – do unto others as you would have them do unto you. Most states have adopted the Prudent Man Rule as a way of assessing trustee performance, and have codified this standard in the Prudent Investor Act. The Prudent Investor Act sets some practical limits on the nature and type of investments that trustees can purchase under the Prudent Man Rule.

One of the most important decisions a grantor makes when creating a trust is the appointment of the trustee. The grantor should appoint an individual or entity who will carry out the grantor's intent as expressed in the trust instrument. Sometimes, more than one trustee is appointed to create a system of checks and balances over trust operations. When only one trustee is in charge, it is difficult to challenge the decisions of the trustee when the trustee appears not to be operating under the Prudent Man Rule. Furthermore, care must be exercised when appointing a trustee who is either a current or potential beneficiary of the trust, or a person who can make discretionary distributions from the trust to benefit a person for whom he has a legal support obligation. In such cases, the trustee may be deemed to have a general power of appointment over the trust, requiring an inclusion of the fair market value of the trust assets in the trustee's gross estate should the trustee die while holding such power.

BENEFICIARY

The **beneficiary** is the person (or persons) who holds the beneficial title to the trust assets. While the beneficiary's name does not appear on the deed to the trust assets, the trustee must manage the assets in the best interests of the beneficiary.

A trust may have more than one type of beneficiary. Since most trusts are designed to terminate at some point in the future, the two most common types of beneficiaries are income and remainder beneficiaries.

The **income beneficiary** is the person or entity who has the right to current income or distributions from the trust or the current right to use the trust assets. When distributions are made during the term of the trust, the income beneficiary is generally the person who receives those distributions.

The **remainder beneficiary** is the individual or entity who is entitled to receive the assets that remain in the trust on the date of its termination.

Sometimes, the income and remainder beneficiaries of a trust are the same person (or persons).

EXAMPLE 8.1	Christopher is concerned about the ability of his son, Sampson, to manage money. Nevertheless, Christopher would like to begin to transfer assets to Sampson now to help minimize Christopher's future gross estate and the resulting estate tax liability. Christopher believes that as Sampson matures, he will become more responsible and therefore should be entitled to have access to the assets. To accomplish his goal, Christopher creates a trust, and begins to make annual transfers of property to the trust. The trust names Sampson as the income beneficiary and states that fifteen years from now, the trust will terminate and Sampson (or his issue, per stirpes) will receive the assets remaining in the trust at that time. Provided Sampson lives for the next 15 years, he is both the income and the remainder beneficiary of the trust.

In other situations, the income and remainder beneficiaries of the trust are different persons.

EXAMPLE 8.2	Henry and his wife, Sandra, have two children, Jennifer and Jackie. Jackie is a special needs child. Because Jackie is unable to completely support herself, Henry would like to ensure that she is provided for, but wants to protect his assets for the benefit of Jennifer and her children. Henry created a trust naming Jackie as the discretionary income beneficiary for her lifetime. The trustee, therefore, can make distributions for the benefit of Jackie or purchase assets for her use. At Jackie's death, any remaining assets of the trust will be distributed to Jennifer outright, or if Jennifer does not survive Jackie, to Jennifer's children in equal shares, per stirpes. The trust that Henry created names Jackie as the discretionary income beneficiary and Jennifer (or her issue) as the remainder beneficiary. Note that if the trust income exceeds Jackie's needs, as determined by the trustee, the excess may be retained by the trustee for the benefit of Jennifer, the remainder beneficiary.

It is also possible for a trust to have only income beneficiaries and no remainder beneficiaries.

EXAMPLE 8.3	Thomas has been working on his estate plan and has expressed an interest in establishing a dynasty trust for the benefit of his family. If the trust is created in a state that has abolished the rule against perpetuities (discussed below), or in an offshore jurisdiction, the trust will not terminate. Thomas creates a dynasty trust for the benefit of his descendents,

or for the benefit of his family based on degrees of consanguinity in the event of an indefinite failure of issue. Because the trust will never terminate, there are no remainder beneficiaries of the trust. All of the individuals who are entitled to benefit from the trust are considered income beneficiaries.

Traditionally, income beneficiaries are entitled to receive all of the income from the trust and the remainder beneficiaries are entitled to receive the principal of the trust. From a legal perspective each state determines the definition of income and principal for trusts established in that state, but generally the term "income" includes dividends and interest earned on trust investments, and "principal" includes the original trust principal plus all capital gains. Capital gains, or gains derived from the appreciation in value of trust property, are considered corpus of the trust and are retained in the trust for the benefit of the remainder beneficiaries. In most states, absent instructions contained in the trust document to the contrary, the income beneficiary will receive income and dividends and the trust will retain the capital gains for the benefit of the remaindermen.

When long-term trusts (such as dynasty trusts) are created, the income beneficiaries are not always permitted to receive a distribution of the trust income. It is more common for long-term trusts to give the trustee discretion as to the timing and amount of income distributions, and to include specific language in the trust instrument authorizing the trustee to purchase assets for the use of the beneficiaries of the trust. Allowing beneficiaries to use trust assets, instead of requiring distributions from the trust, often results in better estate planning from a multi-generational perspective.

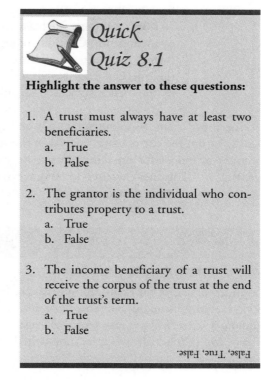

EXAMPLE 8.4

At his death, Gerald created a dynasty trust for the benefit of his family. The trust requires the trustee to distribute the income to his children, and when each child dies, to split up that child's share and distribute the income to the child's children. All of Gerald's children are independently wealthy and are renowned art collectors. When they receive the income distributions from the trust, they use the money to purchase art that is displayed in their homes and offices. When each of the children die, the fair market value of the art that they purchased will be included in their gross estates, and will be subject to estate tax.

EXAMPLE 8.5

Assume the same facts as above, except that Gerald's trust did not mandate the distribution of income to the children. Instead, the trustee used the income of the trust to purchase artwork that is displayed in the homes and offices of the children. When the children die, the fair market value of the artwork will not be included in their gross estates and will not be subject to estate tax, since the children did not own the artwork, and therefore have nothing to transfer through their estate at death. Gerald's grandchildren can now enjoy the art owned by the trust and exclude the value of the art from their gross estates as well. In such a case, the income earned by the trust is subject to income tax at the trust level.

As the above examples demonstrate, the ability to separate the ownership of assets (vested in the trustee) from the use of assets (vested in the trust beneficiaries) can, over time, save a significant amount of money for the family by avoiding the transfer tax as it would be applied to multiple generations. Trust beneficiaries do not have to own assets; it is better to give them the right to use trust assets as if they owned them.

WHY USE A TRUST?

MANAGEMENT

A principal reason for establishing a trust is to provide for the management of the trust property. Not everyone is adept at managing assets. A person not experienced in handling wealth may squander it or invest imprudently. A trust can be used to provide professional management of assets for individuals who are not suited, by training or experience, to manage assets for themselves.

EXAMPLE 8.6

Suzanne thinks of herself as the world's foremost expert in the fields of financial planning and money management. Her husband and children have relied on her to manage all of the family finances. Instead of leaving her property outright to her family when she dies, Suzanne can transfer the property into a trust, name professional money managers as trustees, and they will manage the money for her husband and children.

CREDITOR PROTECTION

When asked, most individuals would say they would rather receive an outright transfer of money than a transfer in trust. This is often based on the belief that with an outright transfer, they will have complete control over the assets and can use the assets in a way that will maximize their utility. If, however, an outright transfer of assets is made, the creditors of the recipient (judgment creditors or otherwise) will have access to those funds to satisfy outstanding obligations.

If property is placed in a trust with appropriate spendthrift protection provisions instead of being transferred outright, the creditors of the beneficiary will not be able to access the funds in the trust to satisfy outstanding creditor claims. A spendthrift clause, coupled with a provision that allows the trustee to make distributions solely on a discretionary basis, is a very strong and effective asset protection tool. The **spendthrift clause** simply states that the beneficiary may not anticipate distributions from the trust, and may not assign, pledge, hypothecate, or otherwise promise to give distributions from the trust to anyone and, if such a promise is made, it is void and may not be enforced against the trust. Most states enforce spendthrift clauses, since the property in trust never belonged to the beneficiary and the beneficiary cannot be sure that he will ever receive discretionary distributions from the trustee. In some states, claims for spousal or child support can be obtained from a trust despite the presence of a spendthrift clause.

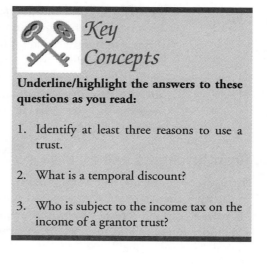

Key Concepts

Underline/highlight the answers to these questions as you read:

1. Identify at least three reasons to use a trust.

2. What is a temporal discount?

3. Who is subject to the income tax on the income of a grantor trust?

EXAMPLE 8.7

Pat, a registered nurse, always wanted her children to enter the medical profession. None of her children became physicians, but her grandson, Keegan, decided to go to medical school. Understanding the malpractice dilemma faced by physicians, Pat decided she wanted to protect any property that would pass during her lifetime, or at her death, to Keegan from Keegan's creditors. She created a trust that named Keegan as the discretionary income beneficiary for life and upon Keegan's death, would distribute the trust corpus to Keegan's children in equal shares, per stirpes. The trust included a spendthrift clause. If a malpractice claim is filed against Keegan, the assets in the trust will not be available to satisfy those claims. If the trust purchases assets for Keegan's use instead of making distributions to Keegan, those assets will also be protected. Note that if Pat had not used a trust, any assets that she transferred to Keegan directly would be subject to malpractice claims.

A spendthrift clause protects the trust assets from the claims of the beneficiary's creditors provided that the beneficiary did not create the trust for his own benefit. If the beneficiary is also the grantor of the trust, the trust is referred to as a **self-settled trust** and, as a general rule, spendthrift protection will not apply. While states allow protection when an individual creates a trust for another person, the assets of a self-settled trust are not protected. A few states, such as Alaska and Delaware, have changed their laws to allow the creation of a self-settled asset protection trust, but this protection is far from being the majority rule.

EXAMPLE 8.8

Jonathan decided that he needed to protect his assets from his potential creditors, and created a trust in the state of Texas. He transferred all of his assets to the trust and named himself as the discretionary beneficiary of the trust. The trust included a spendthrift clause. Despite the presence of a spendthrift clause, Jonathan's creditors will be able to gain access to the trust assets to settle any debts since the trust is a self-settled trust.

SPLIT INTERESTS IN PROPERTY

A trust is often used to take a single asset or property interest and divide it into different interests to satisfy a client's estate planning and wealth transfer objectives. As already illustrated in this chapter, a trust can create two or more separate property interests – an income interest and a remainder interest. This may be particularly important for clients who have most of their estate tied up in a very valuable asset that they do not want to sell and do not want to divide amongst their children.

EXAMPLE 8.9

William owns a farm that has been in his family for over 100 years. The farm is the primary asset in his estate and generates substantial income for William and his family. Some of William's children are interested in continuing the farming business, while others are pursing different careers. William and his wife, Marge, want to treat all of their children equally, meaning that they want each of their children to receive the same amount of money or property from their estate. If the children who want to run the farm receive the farmland, there will be no other assets to give to the other children. William can put the land into a trust that allows the trustee to lease the land to the children who will run the farm. He can name his other children as the income beneficiaries of the trust, so that they derive some value from William and Marge's estate for a period of time, after which the land will be distributed to the children running the farming operation. In this case, the single piece of farmland has been split into two separate pieces – an income interest and a remainder interest. The children who wish to continue the farming can do so, provided that they "pay" for the other children's interest in the land through the income of the farming operation. The children pursuing other opportunities will "cash-out" over time and will therefore be treated fairly in the eyes of William and Marge.

From a more sophisticated planning perspective, a split interest arrangement (i.e., a trust) can be used to create temporal discounts on the transfer of property. A temporal discount is a discount generated by the passage of time. By delaying a beneficiary's enjoyment of the property, it is possible to lower the value of a gift or estate transfer for tax purposes.

EXAMPLE 8.10

Mike recently transferred $1,000,000 to a trust. Mike retained the right to receive an annuity of $50,000 each year for 10 years. Upon termination of Mike's annuity income interest, the trust will terminate and the assets will be transferred to James and Allison. When Mike created the trust, he made a completed gift of the remainder interest in the trust to James and Allison. The present value of the $50,000 per year income stream that Mike will receive is $350,000, and therefore the remainder interest in the trust is $650,000 ($1,000,000 initial funding - $350,000 income interest retained). Since James and Allison had to wait to receive the gift (in this case, they had to wait 10 years), Mike was able to generate a $350,000 temporal discount on the transfer for gift tax purposes. Mike will have a taxable gift of $650,000 against which he could use his applicable gift tax credit.

AVOIDING PROBATE (LIVING TRUST)

Perhaps one of the most popular uses of a trust is to avoid probate. Probate is the process of collecting a decedent's property, paying off the decedent's debts and any taxes that may be due, and transferring (retitling) what is left to the decedent's heirs. In some states, probate is an expensive process, sometimes costing five to six percent of the value of the decedent's probate estate.

An alternative to the probate process is the use of a **revocable living trust**. All of an individual's property is transferred (retitled) to a revocable trust (a trust that the grantor can terminate at anytime) that is managed by the grantor and is for the benefit of the grantor during his lifetime. Upon the grantor's death, the trust becomes irrevocable and the property passes to the grantor's heirs under the terms of the trust. Since the probate court does not need to intervene and transfer the property (the property will transfer according to the trust document), probate costs and expenses are avoided on the trust property. It is important to note, however, that a revocable trust does not avoid estate taxes – it only avoids probate and probate fees and expenses. Because the grantor retained an interest in the trust, the full fair market value of the assets are included in his gross estate for estate tax purposes.

MINIMIZING TAXES

When used appropriately in the estate planning process, trusts can generate transfer and income tax savings. The tax savings result from (1) the transfer of future appreciation to the grantor's heir, (2) the minimization of transfer taxes on subsequent generations, (3) the reduction in the size of the grantor's gross estate, and (4) the reduction of income taxes for the donor of income produced on the transferred asset.

Once an irrevocable trust is established and funded, all future asset appreciation belongs to the beneficiaries of the trust. The appreciation and income occurring after the gift was made is not taxable to the grantor. Contrast this with a situation where the grantor retains the property throughout his lifetime and bequeaths the property to his heirs at death. In this case, all of the appreciation on the property is subject to estate tax because the appreciation occurred before the transfer of the property.

When a trust is established to last for multiple generations, transfer tax is minimized by preventing the property from being included in each beneficiary's gross estate. Since the gift and estate taxes are transfer taxes, not property taxes, and the property is not transferred, no transfer tax can result.

EXAMPLE 8.11

Brian created a generation-skipping transfer trust thirty years ago in a state that has abolished the rule against perpetuities. His only child, Michael, died this year. Despite the fact that Michael was the primary beneficiary of the trust and was permitted to use the trust's assets, none of the assets in the trust will be included in Michael's gross estate, since he did not own the assets. Michael's children will now be able to receive trust benefits and use the trust's assets. If, in contrast, Brian gave the assets transferred in trust directly to Michael, those assets would have been subject to estate tax, perhaps leaving only about half of the assets for Michael's children.

Finally, when a grantor trust is created (discussed below), the grantor is required to pay the income tax liability on the trust income. By paying the income tax liability, the grantor of the trust reduces his gross estate by the amount of the income taxes paid. In addition to reducing the size of the grantor's gross estate, the payment of the trust's income tax liability is not considered to be a taxable gift, since the payment requirement is imposed by tax law. Contrast this with a situation where an individual, without legal compulsion, agrees to pay the income tax liability of another. In this instance, the payment of the income tax liability would be considered a gift for gift tax purposes.

TRUST DURATION – THE RULE AGAINST PERPETUITIES

A potential problem with the use of trusts is that the property placed in trust may be removed from the stream of commerce for a very long period of time, and would therefore violate a common law dictate stating that any restraint on the alienation of property is void as a matter of law.

In the late 1500's, the Duke of Norfolk, whose oldest son and heir was non compos mentis (not competent), created a trust to protect the family property for his son. The Duke transferred all of his property to the trust, and prohibited the trustee from selling any of the property, thereby removing the property from commerce. This trust provision created controversy amongst many who did not believe that property should be encumbered with such restrictions. After many years of litigation, the Duke of Norfolk's case was resolved when Lord Chancellor Nottingham decided the case and issued what is now known as the **rule against perpetuities** (RAP). The RAP states that all interests in trust must vest, if at all, within lives in being, plus 21 years.

Key Concepts

Underline/highlight the answers to these questions as you read:

1. Which states have abolished the rule against perpetuities?

2. Identify the situations in which the grantor of an irrevocable trust must include the trust assets in his gross estate.

The RAP appears to be a simple rule, but it's interpretation has been far from easy. Since the Duke of Norfolk's case, numerous court decisions have further interpreted the rule. In addition, there are many treatises that have been written attempting to explain the purpose and application of the rule. From a practical perspective, the effect of the RAP was to place a limit on the amount of time that property could be held in trust. As the rule states, all interests in trust must vest, if at all, within lives in being (persons alive at the inception of the trust) plus 21 years. Note that it is possible to have a trust last longer than the RAP period, provided that all interests in the trust vest within the RAP period. For example, if all of the beneficiaries of the trust are given a testamentary general power of appointment over their portion of the trust assets during the perpetuities period, the trust will not have to terminate until 21 years after the last beneficiary holding the testamentary general power of appointment dies. The general power of appointment will cause the trust interest to vest in each beneficiary holding such power and will therefore meet the requirements of the RAP.

Due to the uncertainties associated with the length of the perpetuities period under the RAP, some states have adopted the uniform statutory rule against perpetuities. The uniform statutory rule against perpetuities sets the perpetuities period at 90 years, and creates a presumption that all interests that vest within that 90-year period are valid interests. The IRS recognizes the perpetuities period contained in the uniform statutory rule against perpetuities, provided that the perpetuities period is not defined in the governing instrument as the longer of the 90-year period or the RAP period.

Some states have taken a completely different approach. Alaska, Delaware, South Dakota, and several other states have abolished the RAP. In these states it is possible to create a trust that will have a perpetual duration. To address a common law issue concerning the alienation of property, however, most states that have abolished the RAP have also adopted legislation stating that the grantor of a perpetual trust may not include language in the trust prohibiting the trustee from selling the property. These laws are known as anti-alienation statutes. The replacement of the RAP with anti-alienation statutes seems to address the original issue brought forth in the Duke of Norfolk's case more appropriately. If alienation of property is the issue, the fatal flaw in the Duke's plan was not that he placed the property in trust, but rather that he prohibited the trustee from selling the property. As long as the trustee can freely dispose of the property (thereby keeping the property in the stream of commerce), it should not matter how long the trust holding the property can be in existence. The repeal of the RAP presents several attractive estate planning opportunities for clients with long-term wealth transfer goals.

Quick Quiz 8.3

Highlight the answer to these questions:

1. The uniform statutory rule against perpetuities set the perpetuities period at 90 years.
   a. True
   b. False

2. If a grantor retains the right to receive income from a trust, the value of the trust will be included in his gross estate.
   a. True
   b. False

3. If gift tax is paid on a transfer to a trust within three years of the decedent's date of death, the gift tax is included in the decedent's gross estate.
   a. True
   b. False

True, True, True.

ACCOUNTING AND INCOME TAXATION OF TRUSTS

INCOME TAXATION OF TRUSTS

Trusts are treated for income tax purposes as hybrid entities. All income a trust receives, whether from foreign or domestic sources, is taxable to the trust, to the beneficiary, or to the grantor of the trust unless specifically exempted by the Internal Revenue Code (IRC). To the extent that the income of the trust is distributed to the beneficiaries, the beneficiaries who receive the distributions will be subject to income tax on the income. In the absence of provisions to the contrary in the trust instrument, the trust is allowed to deduct distributions to beneficiaries from its taxable income, with a few modifications. Therefore, trusts can eliminate income by making distributions to beneficiaries.

The income taxation of trusts and estates is governed by Subchapter J of the Code, which creates a model whereby income tax liability is shared by the trust or estate and its beneficiaries. Under general rules of trust and estate income taxation, a trust or estate pays income tax on the amount of income it retains, and the beneficiaries pay income tax on the distributions of trust income that they receive. This approach ensures that trust income will not be subject to double taxation and places the burden of paying the income tax on the party receiving the income. Since trustees of a trust (or the executors/administrators of an estate) are often given the discretionary right to distribute income to the beneficiaries, the trustee or executor can avoid taxation at the trust level by passing all income through to the beneficiaries.

A special rule may apply to certain gains earned by a trust if the grantor makes a contribution of appreciated property to the trust. If the appreciated property is sold within two years of the date of transfer, an income tax is imposed on the trust equal to what the grantor would have paid if the gain had been included in his or her income for the year the sale occurred.

The income tax rate schedule that applies to estates and trusts is compressed when compared to individual tax rates. Once a trust or estate has $11,150 in taxable income it is subject to income tax at the highest marginal income tax rate for trusts and estates (See Exhibit 8.1).

In the past, some planners have tried to avoid the imposition of the harsh marginal income tax rate table for trusts by establishing a series of trusts, all of which will have income that is expected to remain in the lowest marginal tax bracket. To prevent this type of planning from occurring, the Internal Revenue Code treats a set of substantially similar trusts, created for the purpose of avoiding income tax at higher marginal rates, to be taxed as a single trust.

INCOME TAX RATE SCHEDULE FOR ESTATES AND TRUSTS (FOR 2009)

EXHIBIT 8.1

If taxable income is:	The tax is:
Not over $2,300	15% of taxable income
Over $2,300 but not over $5,350	$345 plus 25% of the excess of such amount over $2,300
Over $5,350 but not over $8,200	$1,107.50 plus 28% of the excess of such amount over $5,350
Over $8,200 but not over $11,150	$1,905.50 plus 33% of the excess of such amount over $8,200
Over $11,150	$2,879 plus 35% of the excess of such amount over $11,150

Simple and Complex Trusts

Simple trusts are trusts that mandate the annual distribution of all trust income. The beneficiaries of a simple trust pay all income tax on the income of the trust. The trust does not incur any income tax liability because it is able to fully deduct the amount distributed to the beneficiaries from the amount of income earned. If the trust incurred any capital gains, however, the trust would have tax liability if those gains are set aside for the remainder beneficiaries of the trust.

A simple trust has all of its income (but not necessarily any of its principal) distributed on an annual basis to its beneficiaries. The definition of income for this purpose is limited to interest and dividends earned on trust assets. To be classified as a simple trust, there cannot be any principal distributions or charitable gifts made during the year. Any trust that has a distribution of principal or makes charitable gifts will be treated as a complex trust for that year.

A complex trust, on the other hand, is a trust that is permitted to accumulate income, benefit a charity, or distribute principal. A simple trust becomes a complex trust in any year in which it distributes principal or benefits a charity. It then reverts back to a simple trust in subsequent years. If the complex trust accumulates income, it is taxed on that income at the trust income tax rates (see Exhibit 8.1). Each beneficiary of a complex trust is taxed on his pro rata share of the distribution deduction taken by the trust. The distribution deduction is the lesser of the amount actually distributed to the beneficiaries of the trust or distributable net income. Distributable net income, as calculated under Section 643(a), is an approximation of the actual economic benefit available to the income beneficiaries of the trust and is the maximum amount that can be taxed to the beneficiaries. Income distributed to the beneficiaries has the same character in the hands of the beneficiaries as it does in the hands of the trust (e.g., ordinary income, capital gain, etc.). Distributions in excess of distributable net income are generally treated as tax-free distributions of principal.

Simple and complex trusts are treated as separate taxable entities for income tax reporting purposes. Trusts are permitted to take many of the same deductions available to individuals, such as deductions for investment or business interest paid, taxes paid, depreciation and depletion, charitable contributions, and administration expenses necessary to maintain, preserve, and increase the income or principal of the trust. Due to their nature as pass-through entities, trusts are also permitted to deduct income distributed to the beneficiaries, referred to as the distribution deduction. Note that a simple trust that has only interest and dividend income, and distributes all of that income to the beneficiaries will not be subject to income tax due to the presence of the distribution deduction. Simple trusts that have realized income gains, and complex trusts, are typically subject to income taxation at the trust level. A simple trust is entitled to a personal exemption of $300, complex trusts are entitled to a personal exemption of $100, and estates are entitled to a personal exemption of $600. This means that the first $300 or $100 of trust income, or the first $600 of income for an estate is exempt from income taxation after the appropriate deductions are claimed.

Distributable Net Income
The determination of what constitutes income for trusts and estates as set forth in the Internal Revenue Code is complex. The concept of **distributable net income** (DNI) is used by the Code to ensure that income earned by a trust is subject to only one level *of* tax. DNI equals the total income of a trust *or* estate for the taxable year, after making the following adjustments:
1. Adding back the allowable deduction for income distributed to trust beneficiaries and the trust's personal exemption.
2. Excluding capital gains if they are not either,
   - Paid, credited, or required to be distributed to a beneficiary in the taxable year, or
   - Paid, permanently set aside, or used for charitable purposes.

3. Adding tax exempt interest, and, in the case of a foreign trust, foreign income reduced by the deductions allowed against that income, with a proportionate amount of tax-exempt or foreign income allocated to the charitable deduction if claimed by the trust.

Extraordinary dividends and taxable stock dividends are excluded from the DNI of a simple trust if the trustee allocates them in good faith to the corpus of the trust in accordance with the requirements of the governing instrument or state law, and does not distribute them to the beneficiaries.

As indicated above, capital gains are excluded from DNI unless they are distributed or required to be distributed to a beneficiary, or are paid or permanently set aside for the benefit of a charity. Unless the trust instrument or state law specifies otherwise, capital gains are usually considered to be a return to principal and are typically not available for distribution to the income beneficiaries. If a trust has capital gains and does not distribute those gains to the beneficiaries, however, the trust will be subject to some income tax for the year. If a trust distributes capital gains, then the beneficiary will pay income tax on the capital gains. In this scenario, the trust will not be liable for capital gains income taxation (capital gains will be included in DNI) since the gains are passed through to the beneficiary.

DNI is used in the income tax system for three purposes in income taxation:
1. to ensure that a trust or estate receives a deduction for income that it actually distributes to its beneficiaries,
2. to limit the beneficiary's exposure to income taxation on trust distributions, and
3. to maintain the character of the income that is distributed to the beneficiaries.

The trust's DNI (calculated in accordance with the rules set forth above) represents the maximum distribution deduction the trust may take for distributions of income to trust beneficiaries. The calculation of DNI ensures that the trust is not able to receive a distribution deduction for distributions of principal to the beneficiaries. Since DNI essentially equals trust income, the distribution deduction should be, and is, limited to this amount.

> The Jarvis Family Trust received $4,000 in taxable interest, $4,000 in tax-exempt interest, $12,000 in dividends, and $60,000 in capital gains during the current tax year. The trust is not required to distribute its income to its beneficiaries on an annual basis, and will therefore be considered a complex trust for income tax purposes. DNI for the year equals $20,000 ($4,000 in taxable interest, $4,000 in tax exempt interest, and $12,000 in dividends). Capital gains are not included in DNI since the trustee is not permitted to distribute principal to the beneficiaries, and there are no charitable beneficiaries of the trust. The maximum distribution deduction the trust is entitled to this year equals its DNI of $20,000.

EXAMPLE 8.12

EXAMPLE 8.13	Continuing our example, assume that the Jarvis Family Trust distributes all of its income to its beneficiaries. Ignoring other deductions and exemptions, the trust will have a total of $80,000 in income for the year (including capital gains). When the trust distributes $20,000 to the beneficiaries, it receives a distribution deduction of a like amount. The difference of $60,000 (representing capital gains in this example that are allocated to principal and retained by the trust) will be subject to tax at the trust level.

In the event that the trust document permits the trustee to distribute both income and principal to the beneficiaries, the trust's distribution deduction is limited to its DNI. Since principal is not included in income or DNI, it should not qualify the trust for a deduction for income tax purposes.

EXAMPLE 8.14	Continuing with our example above, assume that the Jarvis Family Trust gives the trustee the power to make both principal and income distributions, and the trustee distributes $100,000 to the beneficiaries in the current tax year. The beneficiaries will have a total of $80,000 of income potentially subject to tax, and the trust will receive a distribution deduction of $80,000. The remaining portion of the distribution, or $20,000 will be treated as a tax-free distribution of capital. Generally, capital gains are not included in DNI unless they are paid, credited, or required to be distributed to a beneficiary in the taxable year. Since the capital gains, as well as the interest and dividend income, are distributed to the beneficiaries, they are included in DNI. In this case, the beneficiaries will pay tax on all trust income for the current year, and the trust will not be liable for any tax because the trust is funneling the income through to the beneficiaries.

Another purpose of DNI is to ensure that the income distributed to the beneficiaries retains its character for income tax purposes. From the beneficiary's standpoint, this is important since different forms of income are subject to different levels of tax. For example, tax-exempt income and stock dividends are tax exempt when received by the beneficiaries, interest and non-qualified dividends are taxed at ordinary tax rates, and capital gains and qualified dividends are taxed at capital gains tax rates.

EXAMPLE 8.15	Continuing with our example above, when the Jarvis Family Trust distributes $100,000 to its beneficiaries this year, only $80,000 is potentially subject to taxation (which equals the trust's DNI for the current tax year). Of that $80,000, $4,000 is tax-exempt interest, which will not be subject to tax. Interest and dividends make up $12,000 of the DNI, which will be taxed accordingly, and the remaining $60,000 of DNI represents capital gain, which will be taxed at capital

gains rates (ordinary tax rate if the gain is a short-term gain, and a maximum of 15 percent if the gain is a long-term capital gain). The additional $20,000 distributed to the beneficiaries is a distribution of principal, and is therefore treated as a nontaxable return of capital.

GIFT TAX AS APPLIED TO TRUSTS

Whether or not a transfer to a trust will be taxable for gift tax purposes depends on the characteristics of the trust. If the trust is a revocable trust, a transfer to the trust will not be considered a completed gift for gift tax purposes, and therefore, will not be subject to gift tax. If the trust is an irrevocable trust, any transfer to the trust will be considered a taxable gift (unless the grantor retains some interest in the trust) subject to gift tax. When irrevocable trusts are created for charities, however, the unlimited gift tax charitable deduction is available to avoid gift tax on the portion of any transfer that is determined to be for the charity.

INCLUSION/EXCLUSION FROM GROSS ESTATE OF TRUST ASSETS

For estate tax purposes, the assets held by an irrevocable trust funded during a grantor's lifetime are generally excluded from the gross estate of the grantor. When a grantor funds an irrevocable trust for a noncharitable beneficiary, gift tax rules apply because the transfer is treated as a completed gift at that time. Therefore, the gift tax liability must be calculated, and to the extent that the gift liability exceeds the grantor's remaining applicable gift tax credit, gift tax must be paid. Since the taxable transfer occurs during the life of the grantor, the grantor no longer owns the property and therefore it is not included in the grantor's gross estate at his death.

There are some situations, however, where the value of the assets of an irrevocable trust funded during the grantor's life are included in the grantor's gross estate. The assets of an irrevocable trust are included in the grantor's gross estate if a grantor makes a transfer to an irrevocable trust, but retains (1) the right to receive income from the trust; (2) the right to use the trust assets; (3) the ability to exercise voting rights on stock transferred to the trust; (4) a reversionary interest with a value greater than five percent of the trust; (5) the right to terminate, alter, amend, or revoke the trust; or (6) the right to control beneficial enjoyment of the trust. To the extent that the grantor paid gift tax on the transfers made to the trust, and the value of the trust assets are included in his gross estate, the grantor's estate will receive a tax credit for the gift taxes actually paid.

EXAMPLE 8.16

Forty years ago, James purchased a tract of raw land several miles outside of a major city. Over the years, the city has expanded, and the land that James owns has appreciated in value. James transferred the land to a Charitable Remainder Unitrust (CRUT - discussed in Chapter 9), and retained the right to receive a 5% unitrust payout each year for his life, and named his local library (a qualified charity) as the remainder beneficiary of the trust. When James dies, the full value of the assets inside the CRUT will be included in his gross estate, since at the date of his death, he had a right to receive income from the trust. His estate will also be entitled to a charitable deduction for the same amount, since the trust terminates at James' death and all of the trust assets are transferred to charity. Note that the inclusion of the CRUT assets in his gross estate will not increase his estate tax liability due to the availability of the charitable deduction, but may have an impact on his ability to qualify for a Section 303 redemption, a Section 6166 deferral of estate tax, or a Section 2032A special use valuation (discussed in Chapter 12).

EXAMPLE 8.17

Thirty five years ago, Don purchased a beach house in Stone Harbor, NJ. Ten years ago, Don transferred the beach house to a qualified personal residence trust (QPRT), retaining the right to use the property for 20 years, with the remainder interest passing to his only daughter, Beth. Don passed away last month. The full fair market value of the beach house (the only asset of the QPRT) will be included in Don's gross estate, since at the time of his death, he had a retained right to use the property that had been transferred to the trust. To the extent that Don paid gift tax on the value of the remainder interest that was given to Beth, his estate will receive a credit for the deemed gift taxes paid (to avoid double transfer taxation as discussed in Chapter 6).

In the event a grantor makes a transfer to an irrevocable trust in which the grantor retains an interest, and the grantor releases his interest in the trust within three years of death, the three-year rule (IRC Section 2035) requires the full fair market value of the trust to be included in the grantor's gross estate.

EXAMPLE 8.18

Ellen created and funded an irrevocable trust five years ago for the benefit of her daughter, Marguerite. The purpose of the trust was to hold Ellen's extensive jewelry collection, and to avoid transfer tax on the subsequent appreciation of the jewelry. Upon funding the trust, Ellen paid a gift tax on the transfer. Ellen also reserved the right to occasionally use some of the jewelry that she had irrevocably transferred to the trust. When she attended an estate planning seminar last week, Ellen realized that her retained right to use the jewelry held in the trust would cause the fair market value of the trust assets to be included in her gross estate. Consequently, Ellen released her retained right to use any of the jewelry currently owned by the trust. If Ellen dies within three years of releasing her right to use the jewelry, the full fair market value of the trust assets will be included in her gross estate, and her estate will receive a credit for the gift taxes deemed paid on the transfer of the jewelry to the trust. If Ellen dies more than three years after the release of her right to use the jewelry, the fair market value of the trust assets will not be included in her gross estate.

EXAMPLE 8.19

Thirty five years ago, Don purchased a beach house in Stone Harbor, NJ. Ten years ago, Don transferred the beach house to a qualified personal residence trust (QPRT), retaining the right to use the property for 20 years, with the remainder passing to his only daughter, Beth. Assuming that Don is alive upon the expiration of his retained interest in the trust, the value of the trust assets will not be included in his gross estate. In this case, Don did not release his right to use the property; rather, his retained right expired due to the passage of time. Don does not have to satisfy the three-year rule, since he did not take any action to terminate his retained interest.

Quick Quiz 8.4

Highlight the answer to these questions:

1. Distributable net income (DNI) of a trust is the amount that must be distributed to the trust beneficiaries on an annual basis.
   a. True
   b. False

2. Assets transferred to a trust are excluded from the gross estate of the trust's grantor.
   a. True
   b. False

3. Gift tax paid on transfers to a trust within 3 years of the grantor's date of death will be included in the grantor's gross estate.
   a. True
   b. False

False, False, True.

As noted earlier, if a grantor makes a transfer to an irrevocable trust in which he does not retain an interest, there is no inclusion in the gross estate of the grantor. The lifetime gift to the trust will, however, be an adjusted taxable gift to the extent that the value of the transfer exceeds the allowable annual exclusion amount. As detailed in Chapter 6, if the gift to the trust was made within three years of the grantor's death, any gift taxes actually paid on the transfer will also be included in the grantor's gross estate.

EXAMPLE 8.20

Five years ago, Adam created and funded the Luckhardt Dynasty Trust, a perpetual trust for the benefit of his heirs. At the time the trust was created, Adam transferred $1,000,000 to the trust and allocated a portion of his generation-skipping transfer tax exemption (see Chapter 13) to the transfer. Since Adam had used his applicable gift tax credit and applicable annual exclusions in prior transfers to family members, the funding of the dynasty trust was a fully taxable event for gift tax purposes, and Adam paid $410,000 in gift taxes on the transfer. If Adam dies this year, there will not be anything included in his gross estate related to this transaction, since he died more than three years after the transfer. In funding the trust, however, Adam made an adjusted taxable gift of $1,000,000 (recall that no annual exclusions were used in making the transfer), which will be added back to his tentative taxable estate for purposes of calculating his estate tax, and his estate will be given a credit for the gift taxes deemed paid.

<table>
<tr><td>**EXAMPLE 8.21**</td><td>Assume the same facts as above, except that Adam created the Luckhardt Dynasty Trust two years before his death. Since Adam died within three years of making the transfer, the $410,000 in gift taxes paid will be included in his gross estate under the three-year rule and the $1,000,000 adjusted taxable gift will be added to his tentative taxable estate for purposes of calculating the estate tax. Adam's estate will also receive a credit for the gift taxes actually paid on all prior transfers, including this transfer to the Luckhardt Dynasty Trust.</td></tr>
</table>

In addition to income, gift, and estate taxes, a trust may be subject to generation-skipping transfer taxes (GSTT). Whenever a trust will include a skip person as a beneficiary, it is important to consider the GSTT ramifications, and, if appropriate, allocate a portion of the GST exemption to the trust to avoid a current or future GSTT. Refer to Chapter 13 on Generation-Skipping Transfer Taxes for more information on this subject.

EXHIBIT 8.2 **SUMMARY OF TAX ISSUES RELATED TO TRUSTS**

	Revocable Trusts	Irrevocable Trusts
Income Tax	Income is taxed to grantor.	• Income is taxed to beneficiaries if distributed. • Income is taxed to trust if retained (unless the trust is a grantor trust, in which case all income is taxed to the grantor).
Gift Tax	No gift tax consequences, since the grantor can take the property back.	• Treated as a completed gift and is subject to gift tax.
Estate Tax – Gross Estate	Full fair market value of trust assets included in the grantor's gross estate.	Not included in the gross estate of the grantor unless: • The grantor retained an interest as of the date of his death; • The grantor released an interest in the trust within 3 years of his death; or • The grantor did not retain an interest in the trust but funding the trust generated a gift tax within 3 years of the grantor's death.
Estate Tax – Adjusted Taxable Gift	No adjusted taxable gift.	• To the extent the gift to the trust exceeds the annual exclusion (if applicable), the adjusted taxable gift is added back to the tentative tax base for purposes of calculating the estate tax due.
Generation-Skipping Transfer Tax	GSTT is not an issue, since the trust assets are included in the grantor's estate.	• GSTT may be an issue, depending on the identification of the beneficiaries of the trust.

CLASSIFICATION OF TRUST ARRANGEMENTS

REVOCABLE TRUSTS

The grantor of a **revocable trust** typically retains the right to revoke the trust at any time prior to his incapacity or death. Revocable trusts are commonly used to avoid probate and to provide for management of the grantor's assets should he become incapacitated.

IRREVOCABLE TRUSTS

In contrast to the revocable trust, the grantor of an **irrevocable trust** cannot take back the property that was transferred to the trust. To achieve estate tax and gift tax planning objectives, a trust must be irrevocable, but not all irrevocable trusts are effective for estate tax purposes. If, for example, the grantor retains some right over the property transferred to the trust, the value of the trust assets may be included in his gross estate for estate tax purposes.

Key Concepts

Underline/highlight the answers to these questions as you read:

1. What is a funded trust?

2. Which type of trust can accumulate income?

INTER VIVOS TRUST

Any trust that is created during the lifetime of the grantor is referred to as an **inter vivos trust**. All revocable trusts are also inter vivos trusts. Irrevocable trusts can be either inter vivos trusts (if created during the grantor's lifetime) or testamentary trusts (if created by the grantor's will).

TESTAMENTARY TRUSTS

A trust created after the death of the grantor is referred to as a **testamentary trust.** Generally, the grantor leaves instructions in his will for the executor of the estate to create and fund a trust after the grantor's death. Two of the most common types of testamentary trusts are credit shelter (or bypass) trusts and marital deduction trusts (QTIP Trusts, General Power of Appointment Trusts, or Estate Trusts).

STANDBY TRUST

A **standby trust**, also known as a contingent trust, is a trust created during the grantor's lifetime that is either unfunded or minimally funded. The trust simply "stands" by and waits for a triggering event to activate it. The trust may be used during life, during times of incapacity, or at death to assist with estate administration.

POUROVER TRUST

A **pourover trust** is a trust that receives assets from another source, generally the grantor's estate at the grantor's death. The trust is generally unfunded or minimally funded until the assets "pour" into the trust.

GRANTOR TRUST

Grantor trusts can be revocable or irrevocable trusts. To qualify for grantor trust status, the trust must be an inter vivos trust. When a trust is characterized as a grantor trust, the grantor of the trust, not the trust itself or the trust beneficiaries, is responsible for paying the income tax attributable to the trust's income. Grantor trusts, particularly when combined with other planning tools, are very powerful estate planning vehicles. Grantor trusts are covered in more detail below.

FUNDED OR UNFUNDED

A trust can be either funded or unfunded. A funded trust is a trust that has received a transfer of property from the grantor. Technically, a trust is not considered to be in existence until it is funded. A properly drafted trust document is not enough – to come alive, the trust must have property transferred into it.

An unfunded trust is a trust that has been drafted, but not funded. In some instances, individuals wish to have a trust created so that it is available to receive money or property in the future. As discussed above, a standby trust can be used for this purpose.

SIMPLE OR COMPLEX

As previously stated, for income tax purposes, a trust can be either a simple trust or a complex trust. A **simple trust** is any trust that requires all of the trust income to be distributed on an annual basis to the beneficiaries, and does not have a charitable organization as one of its beneficiaries. A **complex trust** is any trust that does not meet the definition of a simple trust. That is, a complex trust is a trust that is either permitted to accumulate income, or a trust that may make distributions to a charitable organization.

SPECIFIC TRUSTS USED IN ESTATE PLANNING

INTER VIVOS REVOCABLE TRUSTS

Perhaps the most common type of trust created today is the revocable trust. A revocable trust must be created during the grantor's lifetime (once the grantor dies, he can no longer take action to revoke a trust), and is therefore a form of inter vivos trust. All revocable trusts are grantor trusts for federal income tax purposes, requiring the grantor of the trust to pay income tax on all of the trust income.

Probate Avoidance

Revocable trusts are effective probate avoidance devices. When an individual creates a revocable trust and transfers all of his property to the trust, the disposition of the trust property at the death of the grantor will be governed by the terms of the trust and will not become part of the grantor's probate estate. The grantor's will does not control the disposition of the property because the property is not included in the probate estate. A revocable trust becomes irrevocable upon the grantor's death.

The use of revocable trusts is important in states that have high probate costs. In some states, the cost of probating a decedent's will could range from five to six percent of the value of the probate estate. For individuals with large estates residing in a state where probate costs are high, the use of a revocable trust may be prudent. In

Key Concepts

Underline/highlight the answers to these questions as you read:

1. Identify the name of the trust in John F. Kennedy, Jr.'s will.

2. Indicate at least three benefits of using a revocable living trust.

3. What is the main goal of utilizing a testamentary bypass trust?

other states, probate costs are more reasonable, and therefore, a revocable trust may not be necessary as probate is not costly and perhaps not worth avoiding.

Privacy

Regardless of the costs associated with probating a decedent's will, the use of a revocable trust can provide a degree of privacy for the decedent and his family. To probate a will, the will must be submitted to the probate court (in some states, the probate court is referred to as the Surrogates Court or the Orphans Court), and the will is open for public inspection. The activities of the executor are supervised by the court, and a record of the decedent's property and debts is placed on file, along with the names of the individuals who will receive the property. As an alternative to this public airing of the decedent's assets and affairs, a revocable trust could be created in conjunction with the will. Any assets the grantor places into the revocable trust during his lifetime will pass according to the terms of the trust, and assets outside of the trust that are subject to probate at his death are transferred to the revocable trust in accordance with the directions contained in the decedent's will. While the will is a public document, the disposition of the assets under the terms of the trust document is a private matter. A good example of a will that pours over to a revocable trust is the will of John F. Kennedy, Jr. (see Exhibit 8.3). While

John F. Kennedy, Jr. included a few specific bequests in his will, the majority of his assets passed to a trust that governed the ultimate disposition of the property.

Discourages Will Contests

Another benefit associated with the use of a revocable trust is that will contests are discouraged. While state law differs in this area, it is more difficult for a decedent's beneficiaries and the heirs-at-law to contest the disposition of property through a revocable trust than through a will. As discussed in Chapter 4, the Uniform Probate Code gives any individual who can potentially benefit from a will contest the right to contest the will. Generally, this means that anyone whose share of the estate would be larger in the event that a will contest was successful can contest the will. Note that any heir-at-law who was not specifically provided for may be inclined to contest the will, since he has nothing to lose by doing so. Furthermore, all beneficiaries and heirs-at-law must be notified of the death of the decedent and the submission of the will for probate so that they have the opportunity to bring a will contest if desired. A revocable trust, in contrast, does not have any notice requirements, and the terms of the trust generally remain confidential and are not subject to public inspection. Heirs-at-law who are not named as beneficiaries of the revocable trust are generally not entitled to see the trust document, and if a contest is brought, a higher standard must be met to break the trust as compared with setting aside a will in a probate court. While a revocable trust does not provide complete protection against contests, it creates more obstacles for a potential claimant than a will contest.

Estate Taxes

Revocable trusts provide significant probate avoidance and privacy benefits, but are not effective for reducing taxes for estate planning purposes. Because the trust is revocable by the grantor, the grantor has not made a completed gift to the revocable trust for gift tax purposes. Therefore, no gift tax is due upon creation of the trust, but the entire value of the trust is included in the grantor's gross estate for estate tax purposes. Revocable trusts are probate-efficient but not estate tax-efficient devices. Many people mistakenly believe that once the trust is created and they have transferred their assets to the trust, they will avoid state and federal estate and inheritance taxes at their death. As stated, the establishment of the revocable trust will only shelter the assets from inclusion in the probate estate.

EXHIBIT 8.3

THE LAST WILL AND TESTAMENT OF JOHN F. KENNEDY, JR.

John F. Kennedy, Jr. planned to leave the bulk of his holdings to his wife, Caroline Bessette-Kennedy, or their children. But John and Caroline died together in a plane crash in July of 1999 without leaving any issue (children). Therefore, his property will go to the children of his sister, Caroline Kennedy Schlossberg. The bulk of his estate is left to the beneficiaries of a trust he established in 1983. Kennedy also left the scrimshaw set, or carved whale ivory set, once owned by his father to nephew John B.K. Schlossberg. Kennedy's cousin Timothy P. Shriver was named executor of the will. Kennedy's estate is reportedly worth $100 million.

I, JOHN F. KENNEDY, JR., of New York, New York, make this my last will, hereby revoking all earlier wills and codicils. I do not by this will exercise any power of appointment.

<u>FIRST:</u> I give all my tangible property (as distinguished from money, securities and the like), wherever located, other than my scrimshaw set previously owned by my father, to my wife, Carolyn Bessette-Kennedy, if she is living on the thirtieth day after my death, or if not, by right of representation to my then living issue, or if none, by right of representation to the then living issue of my sister, Caroline Kennedy Schlossberg, or if none, to my said sister, Caroline, if she is then living. If I am survived by issue, I leave this scrimshaw set to said wife, Carolyn, if she is then living, or if not, by right of representation, to my then living issue. If I am not survived by issue, I give said scrimshaw set to my nephew John B.K. Schlossberg, if he is then living, or if not, by right of representation to the then living issue of my said sister, Caroline, or if none, to my said sister Caroline, if she is then living. I hope that whoever receives my tangible personal property will dispose of certain items of it in accordance with my wishes, however made unknown, but I impose no trust, condition or enforceable obligation of any kind in this regard. <u>SECOND</u>: I give and devise all my interest in my cooperative apartment located at 20-26 Moore Street, Apartment 9E, in said New York, including all my shares therein and any proprietary leases with respect thereto, to my said wife, Carolyn, if she is living on the thirtieth day after my death.

<u>THIRD:</u> If no issue of mine survive me, I give and devise all my interests in real estate, wherever located, that I own as tenants in common with my said sister, Caroline, or as tenants in common with any of her issue, by right of representation to Caroline's issue who are living on the thirtieth day after my death, or if none, to my said sister Caroline, if she is then living. References in this Article THIRD to "real estate" include shares in cooperative apartments and proprietary leases with respect thereto.

<u>FOURTH:</u> I give and devise the residue of all the property, of whatever kind and wherever located, that I own at my death to the then trustees of the John F. Kennedy Jr. 1983 Trust established October 13, 1983 by me, as Donor, of which John T. Fallon, of Weston, Massachusetts, and I are currently the trustees (the "1983 Trust"), to be added to the principal of the 1983 Trust and administered in accordance with the provisions thereof, as amended by a First Amendment dated April 9, 1987 and by a Second Amendment and Complete Restatement dated earlier this day, and as from time to hereafter further amended whether before or after my death. I have provided in the 1983 Trust for my children and more remote issue and for the method of paying all federal and state taxes in the nature of estate, inheritance, succession and like taxes occasioned by my death.

<u>FIFTH:</u> I appoint my wife, Carolyn Bessette-Kennedy, as guardian of each child of our marriage during minority. No guardian appointed in this will or a codicil need furnish any surety on any official bond.

<u>SIXTH</u>: I name my cousin Anthony Stanislaus Radziwill as my executor; and if for any reason, he fails to qualify or ceases to serve in that capacity, I name my cousin Timothy P. Shriver as my executor in his place. References in this will or a codicil to my "executor" mean the one or more executors (or administrators with this will annexed) for the time being in office. No executor or a codicil need furnish any surety on any official bond. In any proceeding for the allowance of an account of my executor, I request the Court to dispense with the appointment of a guardian ad litem to represent any person or interest. I direct that in any proceeding relating to my estate, service of process upon any person under a disability shall not made when another person not under a disability is a party to the proceeding and has the same interest as the person under the disability.

<u>SEVENTH:</u> In addition to other powers, my executor shall have power from time to time at discretion and without license of court: To retain, and to invest and reinvest in, any kind or amount of property; to vote and exercise other rights of security holders; to make such elections for federal and state estate, gift, income and generation-skipping transfer tax purposes as my executor may deem advisable; to compromise or admit to arbitration any matters in dispute; to borrow money, and to sell, mortgage, pledge, exchange, lease and contract with respect to any real or personal property, all without notice to any beneficiary and in such manner, for such consideration and on such terms as to credit or otherwise as my executor may deem advisable, whether or not the effect thereof extends beyond the period settling my estate; and in distributing my estate, to allot property, whether real or personal, at then current values, in lieu of cash.

INTER VIVOS IRREVOCABLE TRUSTS

To achieve estate and gift tax benefits, a trust created during the grantor's lifetime must be irrevocable. When an inter vivos irrevocable trust is created, the grantor cannot take the property back after it has been transferred to the trustee. Consequently, a transfer of money or property to the trust is considered a completed gift to the beneficiaries of the trust, and gift tax may be due at that time.

Gift Tax

Most transfers to trusts are transfers of a future interest and are therefore not eligible for the annual gift tax exclusion. However, a transfer to a trust which requires the income of the trust to be paid to the income beneficiary each year will qualify as a gift of a present interest eligible for the annual exclusion to the extent of the present value of the income interest. Also, a transfer to a trust which includes a Crummey power will qualify as a present interest and will be eligible for the annual exclusion (discussed in detail below).

After the application of the annual exclusion, an individual's applicable gift tax credit will offset any gift tax liability, but once the credit has been exhausted, the individual will be required to pay gift tax on the transfer.

EXAMPLE 8.22	Jennifer created an irrevocable trust for the benefit of her son, Patrick, and funded it with a gift of $13,000. The trust requires the Trustee to distribute the income of the trust to Patrick on an annual basis. Upon Patrick's death, the principal of the trust will be distributed as directed by Patrick (Patrick has a testamentary general power of appointment). The value of Patrick's income interest, determined in accordance with IRS valuation requirements (see Chapter 7 for more information on using the Section 7520 interest rate) is $10,500. Therefore, $10,500 (a gift of a present interest) of the $13,000 gift will qualify for the gift tax annual exclusion, and the gift tax on the remaining $2,500 will first be offset by Jennifer's remaining applicable gift tax credit amount. To the extent that Jennifer has already used her applicable gift tax credit amount, the $2,500 future interest gift will result in the current requirement to pay gift tax.

Crummey Power

A Crummey power makes it possible to qualify a transfer to an irrevocable trust for the gift tax annual exclusion. A Crummey power (named for the taxpayer who first used the technique) allows the beneficiaries of the trust to withdraw any contribution made to the trust within a certain period of time (typically 30 days). Since this gives the beneficiary a general power of appointment over the property transferred to the trust (the general power is the right to reduce the contribution to the trust to the beneficiary's possession), the transfer to the trust is treated as a present interest transfer for gift tax purposes, and therefore qualifies for the gift tax annual exclusion.

Judy created a trust for the benefit of her son, Chris. Each year, Judy contributes $5,000 to the trust, and Chris has a right to withdraw the contribution for 30 days. The trust allows the trustee to accumulate income and principal, and make discretionary distributions to Chris. Since Chris has the right to withdraw the $5,000 contribution each year, the gift is a gift of a present interest and qualifies for the gift tax annual exclusion.

EXAMPLE 8.23

Qualifying a transfer to an irrevocable trust for the gift tax annual exclusion through the use of a Crummey power can create an estate tax problem for the beneficiary who has the Crummey demand right. Recall that the Crummey power is a general power of appointment, and the IRC requires property subject to a general power of appointment to be included in the power-holder's gross estate if the power holder dies while holding the power. Therefore, the grantor can qualify for the gift tax annual exclusion only if the beneficiary will be subject to estate tax on the property over which he held a withdrawal power.

In addition, if there are multiple beneficiaries of the trust and the power holder lapses the right to appoint the assets, then a taxable gift has occurred. The Code does, however, provide one exception known as the de minimis rule, or "5-and-5" power, which states that the only portion considered to be a taxable gift will be the lapsed general power of appointment which exceeds the greater of (1) $5,000 or (2) five percent of the trust corpus. When the annual exclusion was first granted, it was less than $5,000. Over time, the annual exclusion has increased because it is adjusted for inflation. The $5,000 associated with the "5-and-5" power, however, is not adjusted for inflation. As a result, the "5-and-5" power no longer necessarily shelters 100 percent of a contribution from gift tax. Therefore, whenever a trust that gives the beneficiaries the right to demand distribution of the grantor's contribution to the trust is created, the "5-and-5" power must be considered.

William created a Crummey trust this year for the benefit of his son, Gerald. Recently, William attended a seminar on financial planning and learned that he can give $13,000 a year to Gerald without gift tax consequences. When he created the trust, he made a gift of $13,000 to the trust, and Gerald had the right to withdraw the entire contribution so that it would qualify as an annual exclusion gift. Since the trust had no value until William transferred the $13,000 to the trustee, $5,000 (the greater of $5,000 or 5% of the trust assets) worth of Gerald's demand right (a general power of appointment) will lapse if Gerald does not make a withdrawal. This is the de minimis amount. The remaining $8,000 ($13,000 - $5,000) of the withdrawal right exceeds the de minimis amount, and although there are no gift tax consequences (because Gerald is the only beneficiary of the trust), estate tax consequences for Gerald may result if he dies holding the power.

EXAMPLE 8.24

EXAMPLE 8.25	Assume the same facts as above, except that William created the trust for Gerald's benefit 30 years ago. The current value of the trust is $650,000. This year, William transfers $13,000 to the trust and Gerald has the right to demand a distribution of that amount pursuant to the Crummey power. The entire $13,000 gift made to the trust is subject to a general power of appointment, but it will be ignored and lapse, since $13,000 is less than 5% of the value of the trust $32,500 ($650,000 x 5%). Therefore, there will be neither estate nor gift tax consequences to Gerald.
EXAMPLE 8.26	Patrick created a Crummey trust for the benefit of his daughters, Ellen, Anna, and Margaret. Each of the children has the right to withdraw, pursuant to the Crummey power, a proportionate share of the annual contribution. Patrick transferred $13,000 to the trust this year. Consequently, each of his children can withdraw $4,333 ($13,000 ÷ 3). Since the amount each daughter can withdraw is less than the greater of $5,000 or 5% of the trust corpus, the withdrawal rights will lapse and the children will not suffer any estate tax consequences as a result of holding the withdrawal right.

In addition, it is important that the beneficiary refrain from taking any action with respect to the lapsing power. If the beneficiary releases the power by telling the trustee that he will not exercise the right during the lapse period, it is possible for the IRS to argue that a lapse of the right never occurred, and therefore, there should be inclusion in the beneficiary's gross estate since the beneficiary held a general power of appointment and took action by releasing the right. Recall that the gross estate includes property over which the decedent exercised a power of appointment. Beneficiaries of Crummey trusts should not make an affirmative election to forgo the right to withdraw; the right to withdraw should be terminated by the passage of time, as set forth in the trust document, without the beneficiary's affirmative action.

While the "5-and-5" lapsing amount places a de minimis limitation on the amount that a beneficiary can appoint without being subject to tax, the gift tax annual exclusion also imposes a limitation. Only the first $13,000 in gifts to an individual will qualify for the gift tax annual exclusion. Any amount over the $13,000 threshold will create a taxable gift, and will result in either (1) a reduction in the grantor's applicable gift tax credit or (2) a requirement to pay gift taxes. Most individuals who create Crummey trusts limit the beneficiary's withdrawal right by stating that the beneficiary is not permitted to withdraw more than the annual exclusion amount.

EXAMPLE 8.27	David created a trust this year for the benefit of his son, Lewis. The trust gives Lewis an unlimited Crummey withdrawal right over the entire contribution made by David. This year, David makes a gift of $100,000 to the trust. Despite the fact that Lewis can withdraw the entire amount, only $13,000 of the gift will qualify for the gift tax annual

exclusion. The remaining $87,000 will be considered a taxable gift and will either deplete David's applicable gift tax credit or require him to pay gift tax. Furthermore, since the lapsing amount (as discussed above) this year is $5,000 (the trust had no other assets at the time the contribution was made), Lewis is deemed to have a general power of appointment over $95,000, which may result in estate tax consequences for Lewis. If David had limited Lewis' withdrawal right to the gift tax annual exclusion amount, the consequences would be exactly the same for David, but Lewis would be deemed to have a general power of appointment over only $8,000 as opposed to $95,000. This may have assisted in saving transfer taxes for the family over time.

There are three primary ways of dealing with the lapsing issue from an estate planning perspective. Some grantors will state that the withdrawal right of each of the beneficiaries shall be no more than the lesser of (1) the gift tax annual exclusion amount, or (2) the greater of $5,000 or five percent of the trust corpus. When this approach is taken, the general power of appointment held by the beneficiary will never exceed the lapsing amount, and therefore the beneficiary, provided that he allows the general power of appointment to lapse, will not be subject to any estate tax consequences. This is the simplest way of dealing with the lapsing issue, but may not be practical in some situations.

The second method of dealing with the lapsing issue is to create a hanging power. A hanging power states that, to the extent that a demand beneficiary has a right to withdraw that does not lapse (the portion of the gift tax annual exclusion amount over the "5-and-5" amount), the non-lapsing portion will hang over to a subsequent year, when it can lapse under the "5-and-5" standard.

EXAMPLE 8.28

Randy created a Crummey trust for the benefit of his son, Keegan. Randy contributes $13,000 annually at the beginning of each year. Keegan has a cumulative annual right of withdrawal over any property transferred to the trust during the year. The withdrawal right lapses at the end of each year to the extent of the greater of $5,000 or 5% of the trust property. Keegan does not make any withdrawals. Contributions to the trust and the hanging power are illustrated in the following table.

Year	Value of Trust at Beginning of Year	Contribution	Lapsing Amount (5/5 Lapse Rule)	Amount that "Hangs"	Cumulative Total Hanging Amount
1	$0.00	$13,000.00	$5,000.00	$8,000.00	$8,000.00
2	$14,300.00	$13,000.00	$5,000.00	$8,000.00	$16,000.00
3	$30,030.00	$13,000.00	$5,000.00	$8,000.00	$24,000.00
4	$47,333.00	$13,000.00	$5,000.00	$8,000.00	$32,000.00
5	$66,366.30	$13,000.00	$5,000.00	$8,000.00	$40,000.00
6	$87,302.93	-	$5,000.00	-	$35,000.00
7	$96,033.22	-	$5,000.00	-	$30,000.00
8	$105,636.55	-	$5,281.83	-	$24,718.17
9	$116,200.20	-	$5,810.01	-	$18,908.16
10	$127,820.22	-	$6,391.01	-	$12,517.15
11	$140,602.24	-	$7,030.11	-	$5,487.04
12	$154,662.47	-	$7,733.12	-	-

* Assume that the trust balance grows at a rate of 10% annually.

In this example, Randy makes contributions to the trust in Years 1 through 5. In Years 1 through 5, the contribution that Randy makes exceeds the de minimis amount, and therefore Keegan has a general power of appointment (withdrawal right) that "hangs over." During the funding period, the total amount that hangs over increases each year. Note that in Year 8, when the value of the trust exceeds $100,000, the amount that lapses moves from the $5,000 minimum amount to 5% of the value of the trust assets. After Year 5, Randy does not make any additional contributions to the trust, but the value of the trust continues to grow at a rate of 10% per year. Since there is a "hanging amount" from prior years, Keegan continues to have a withdrawal right each year equal to the lapsing amount. In Years 6 through 11, the lapsing amounts reduce the hanging withdrawal right until Year 11, when Keegan no longer has a right to withdraw any money from the trust. Provided Keegan lives until the hanging amount has been extinguished, he will not have to worry about estate tax consequences as a result of holding a withdrawal right over the annual contribution that Randy made to the trust. If Keegan dies before the hanging amount is used up, there will be an inclusion in his gross estate, since he held a general power of appointment over the property and not all of the general power lapsed prior to his death.

A third way of dealing with the lapsing issue is to give the demand beneficiary a continuing right to appoint a portion of the trust equal to the non-lapsing amount. This is a simpler solution than the hanging power, but will result in a small inclusion in the beneficiary's gross estate.

EXAMPLE 8.29

Assume the same facts as above. Instead of including a hanging power provision in the trust document, Randy gives Keegan a continuing power to appoint the amount in excess of the lapsing amount. In year 5, the last year that Randy made a contribution to the trust, the total withdrawal right that did not lapse was $40,000. This represents the amount of the general power of appointment that Keegan possessed that did not lapse under the "5-and-5" de minimis rule. When Keegan dies, his gross estate will include $40,000 since he had the continuing right to appoint that property. Note that the fair market value of the assets in the trust will not be included in his estate (assuming there were no other retained rights involved that would cause inclusion).

LIFE INSURANCE TRUSTS (ILITs)

A life insurance trust is an irrevocable inter vivos trust often referred to as an **irrevocable life insurance trust** (ILIT) or **wealth replacement trust** (WRT). Life insurance is often used to replace the wealth for a decedent's family that was lost through estate and inheritance taxation or charitable contributions at the decedent's death, and therefore may be referred to as a wealth replacement trust.

The purpose of an ILIT is to prevent an insured party from having incidents of ownership in the life insurance policy on his life. When a person owns a policy on his own life, the death benefit of that policy is included in his gross estate under Section 2042. Provided that an insured person did not own the policy or any incident of ownership over the policy within three years of his death, the death benefit of the policy is not subject to estate taxation.

> **Quick Quiz 8.6**
>
> **Highlight the answer to these questions:**
>
> 1. The most common use for an inter vivos revocable trust is to avoid federal estate taxes.
>   a. True
>   b. False
>
> 2. An ILIT is created to own the life insurance policy on the grantor's life and ensure inclusion in the decedent's gross estate.
>   a. True
>   b. False
>
> False, False.

When an ILIT is created, the grantor often wants to qualify the gifts to the ILIT for the gift tax annual exclusion so that his applicable gift tax credit amount will be available for other planning either during lifetime or at death. Since an ILIT is irrevocable, transfers to the ILIT are usually made subject to a Crummey withdrawal right on behalf of the beneficiaries. ILITs are discussed in depth in Chapter 11.

BYPASS (CREDIT SHELTER) TRUSTS

A **bypass (or credit shelter) trust**, also known as a "B Trust," is commonly used in estate planning. A bypass trust can be either an inter vivos (during lifetime) or a testamentary (at death) trust.

Testamentary Bypass Trust

The most common approach to using a bypass trust calls for the creation of the trust at the individual's death. Most couples who have over $3,500,000 and less than $7,000,000 in joint assets (in 2009) can completely avoid federal estate taxation by transferring $3,500,000 in property to a bypass trust at the death of the first spouse. While the $3,500,000 will be subject to estate tax (since it will not qualify for the marital deduction), the decedent's applicable estate tax credit will be available to completely offset estate tax up to $1,455,800 (the credit equivalency amount of $3,500,000 in taxable transfers).

Transferring property to a bypass trust does not deprive the surviving spouse from using the property. The bypass trust can be structured so that all of the income of the trust is payable to the surviving spouse. In addition, the trustee can be given the right to make discretionary distributions of principal for the surviving spouse's health, education, maintenance, and support (an ascertainable standard). Furthermore, the surviving spouse can be given the right to demand, on an annual basis, the greater of $5,000 or five percent of the trust corpus. While the surviving spouse will not have title to the property in the bypass trust, all of the property can be made available to the surviving spouse so that the surviving spouse can maintain his standard of living. Upon the surviving spouse's death, the assets in the bypass trust usually pass to the children (or some other noncharitable beneficiary), and are not included in the surviving spouse's gross estate for federal estate tax purposes (even with the powers given to the surviving spouse).

Inter Vivos Bypass Trust

While most individuals create a bypass trust at death, creating an inter vivos bypass trust can yield even bigger benefits. When all property transfers occur at the death of an individual, everything is potentially included in the gross estate and subject to estate tax. As discussed in Chapter 6, the applicable estate tax credit amount is not a static number (it increases over the period 2005-2009, disappears in 2010, and reappears in 2011, but is not indexed for inflation). Instead of waiting until death to create the trust, an individual can transfer $1,000,000 in assets (2009) to an inter vivos bypass trust and shield the transfer with the applicable gift tax credit amount. Once this is accomplished, all future growth and appreciation in the property that is transferred to the bypass trust escapes federal estate taxation at the decedent's death. While most people will not be interested in using this technique due to a loss of control over the assets transferred to the trust, very high net worth individuals should consider using their applicable gift tax credit amount during their lifetime to avoid subjecting the appreciation of the property to transfer tax.

| EXAMPLE 8.30 | Elizabeth is a very wealthy individual. She is 54 years old, is married to Philip, and has four children. She has never used any of her applicable gift tax credit amount for planning purposes. Elizabeth owns an asset that she believes will appreciate substantially in the future. The current value of the asset is $1,000,000, and she decides to transfer the asset to an inter vivos bypass trust. Once the asset is transferred, she will have used her applicable gift tax credit, and all future lifetime transfers will be subject to transfer tax (with the exception of annual exclusion gifts and qualified transfers). Elizabeth died at the age of 94. As she had expected, the asset |

she transferred to the bypass trust appreciated in value at an after-tax rate of return of 10%. The $1,000,000 transferred to the trust when she was 54 years old grew to $45,259,255 by the date of her death. By creating the bypass trust during her lifetime, $44,259,255 ($45,259,255 - $1,000,000) was transferred to Elizabeth's heirs without transfer tax consequences. Had Elizabeth held on to the asset and created a bypass trust at her death, her estate would have included the $45 million, and would have had to pay estate tax (at 2009 rates) of approximately $20,000,000. Her heirs would have received only half of the date of death value of the asset.

POWER OF APPOINTMENT TRUSTS

Power of appointment trusts are inter vivos or testamentary irrevocable trusts. As the name implies, the trust grants the beneficiary a power of appointment over the trust assets. The power of appointment can be a general power of appointment or a limited (special) power of appointment. However, the power must be a general power of appointment to qualify for the marital deduction.

Power of appointment trusts are frequently used in planning to take advantage of the unlimited estate tax marital deduction. A trust that grants a surviving spouse a power of appointment over the assets during lifetime may qualify for the marital deduction in the estate of the first spouse to die. A special type of power of appointment trust, called an **estate trust**, grants the surviving spouse a testamentary general power of appointment over the trust assets. More information on the requirements and uses of power of appointment trusts for marital deduction purposes can be found in Chapter 10.

Power of appointment trusts may also be used to avoid the generation-skipping transfer tax. By granting a non-skip person a general power of appointment over a trust that will distribute assets to a skip person, it is possible to change the identity of the transferor for tax purposes. Since the non-skip person will be required to include the value of the trust assets in his gross estate because of the general power of appointment, he will be considered the transferor for generation-skipping transfer tax purposes. This technique is useful for individuals who have already used their generation-skipping transfer exemption and desire to transfer more property to skip persons without generation-skipping transfer tax consequences. Note, however, that there are estate tax consequences for the non-skip holder of the general power of appointment. The generation-skipping transfer tax is fully discussed in Chapter 13.

QUALIFIED TERMINABLE INTEREST PROPERTY (QTIP) TRUSTS

A **QTIP trust**, which is typically created at the death of the first spouse to die, grants the surviving spouse a lifetime right to the income of the trust while transferring the remainder interest to individual(s) of the grantor's choosing. A QTIP trust qualifies for the unlimited marital deduction even though the spouse does not receive outright access to the assets. More information on QTIP trusts may be found in Chapter 10.

While most individuals create QTIP trusts after death, it is possible to create an inter vivos QTIP trust. While this type of planning is not common, it might be used under particular circumstances to equalize vastly disproportionate amounts of wealth between spouses.

GRANTOR RETAINED INCOME TRUSTS (GRITS)

Grantor Retained Income Trusts (GRITs) are trusts created by a person who keeps an income interest in the trust or a right to use trust assets. Generally, the grantor will transfer property to the trust, retain some form of income or use interest for a period of time, and upon termination of the trust, transfer the remainder interest to a third party. Since the third party does not receive the immediate right to possess or enjoy the property, a discount on the value of the remainder interest is available due to the passage of time (referred to as a temporal discount). Historically, individuals wishing to transfer business or property interest at a discount would transfer the interest to the GRIT and retain an income interest from the trust which would be valued using very aggressive income payment rates. The increased value of the income interest would reduce the value of the remainder interest and the transfer would be subject to less transfer tax. After the transfer, the trustee of the GRIT would reduce the income payout from the trust by investing in non-income-producing property. The grantor would benefit from the increased value of the income interest for transfer tax purposes, but would not actually receive any income from the trust. The enactment of the anti-freeze rules of Section 2701 eliminated a grantor's ability to benefit in this manner by placing requirements on the valuation of the income and remainder interests of trusts, and IRC Section 2702 specifically authorizes the four types of GRITs that may be established. These are Grantor Retained Annuity Trusts (GRATs), Grantor Retained Unitrusts (GRUTs), Qualified Personal Residence Trusts (QPRTs), and Tangible Personal Property Trusts (TPPTs).

GRANTOR RETAINED ANNUITY TRUSTS (GRATS)

Grantor Retained Annuity Trusts (GRATs) are a special type of GRIT created when the grantor funds a trust and retains a right to receive a fixed percentage of the initial contribution to the trust on an annual basis for a specified term of years. At the termination of the specified term of the trust, the assets remaining in the trust at that time pass to the remainder beneficiaries. GRATs are discussed in detail in Chapter 7.

| EXAMPLE 8.31 | Jonathan transfers $1,000,000 to a 10-year GRAT in which he retains the right to receive a 5% annuity interest. Jonathan named his son and daughter as the remainder beneficiaries of the trust. Each year during the 10-year period, Jonathan will receive a distribution of $50,000 ($1,000,000 x 5%). When the 10-year period expires, the trust will terminate, and the assets in the trust at that time will pass to his son and daughter. |

GRANTOR RETAINED UNITRUSTS (GRUTS)

As also detailed in Chapter 7, a Grantor Retained Unitrust (GRUT) is the second form of GRIT that is permissible under Chapter 14 of the Code. In substance, a GRUT has the same characteristics as a GRAT with one exception: the income stream received by the grantor is a fixed percentage of the annual value of the trust assets. Instead of fixing the dollar value of the distribution to the grantor, a GRUT provides a variable income stream that will increase as the value of the assets inside the trust increases, or decrease as the value of the assets in the trust decreases. GRUTs are not as effective as GRATs in transferring appreciation on a gift-tax free basis, since the appreciation is shared between the grantor and the remainder beneficiaries. The effects of a GRUT are generally contrary to the grantor's goals and are therefore created far less frequently than GRATs.

QUALIFIED PERSONAL RESIDENCE TRUSTS (QPRTs)

A Qualified Personal Residence Trust (QPRT), as detailed in Chapter 7, is a GRAT in which the grantor contributes a personal residence to the trust and the retained income interest is the grantor's right to "use" the personal residence.

TANGIBLE PERSONAL PROPERTY TRUSTS (TPPTs)

Tangible Personal Property Trusts (TPPTs) are very similar to QPRTs, with one exception – personal property, not real property, is used to fund them. Grantor's of TPPTs usually transfer artwork, antiques, jewelry, and other items of personal property that have the potential to appreciate in value. A temporal discount is available due to the delay in the remainder beneficiary's use or enjoyment of the asset. Valuation of the retained interest, however, is difficult and the IRS will scrutinize the TPPT due to the difficulty of valuing the right to use a piece of tangible personal property.

Key Concepts

Underline/highlight the answers to these questions as you read:

1. What type of property is contributed to a QPRT?

2. What type of property is contributed to a TPPT?

3. Identify the key differences between a Section 2503(b) trust and a Section 2503(c) trust.

DYNASTY TRUSTS

Dynasty trusts are arrangements designed to last for very long periods of time (preferably forever, if created in a state that has abolished the rule against perpetuities). The primary advantage achieved through use of a dynasty trust is an ability to avoid transfer taxation at the death of each generation of the family. To the extent that assets are kept in the trust and are not distributed to the beneficiaries, the value of the assets will not be included in the beneficiary's gross estate even if the beneficiary has the right to use the assets. Dynasty trusts are discussed above and are covered in more detail in Chapter 13.

GRANTOR TRUSTS

Grantor trusts are trusts governed under Sections 671 to 679 of the Internal Revenue Code. When a grantor trust is created, the grantor, not the trust or its beneficiaries, will be subject to income tax on the trust income.

Grantor trusts have many names (mostly used for marketing purposes), and include "Intentionally Defective Grantor Trust (IDGT)" (sometimes pronounced "I-dig-it" or "Id-It" depending on your location in the country), "Defective Trust," and "Intentionally Defective for

Income Tax Only Trust (IDIOT)." The term defective merely means that, for income tax purposes, there is a defective provision in the trust requiring the grantor to pay tax on the trust income. "Defective" in this context does not imply that the trust will not be effective for estate, gift, or generation-skipping transfer tax planning purposes.

The concept of a grantor trust can be confusing if you think of the federal tax system as one tax system. There are three separate tax systems in the United States: (1) an income tax system, (2) an estate and gift tax system, and, (3) a generation-skipping transfer tax system. Each of these systems is separate and distinct, and it is possible to make a transfer that is complete for one system but incomplete (or defective) for another system.

For example, if an individual creates an irrevocable trust and does not retain an interest in the trust, a completed gift has been made for gift and estate tax purposes. At the time a transfer is made to the trust, gift tax may be due but the fair market value of the property in the trust at the date of the grantor's death will not be included in his gross estate. That same trust could contain a provision that would make it incomplete (or defective) for income tax purposes (such as a right given to the grantor to substitute assets in the trust with other assets of equivalent value), thereby triggering grantor trust status and requiring the grantor to pay the income tax on the trust income.

Several grantor trusts have been discussed throughout this text, namely revocable living trusts, GRATs, GRUTs, QPRTs, and TPPTs, but other types of trusts may also include provisions which will make the trust a grantor trust.

The circumstances requiring the grantor to be treated as owner of the trust for income tax purposes include situations where:

1. The grantor has a reversionary interest in the trust that exceeds five percent of the value of the trust upon creation or upon an additional contribution;
2. The grantor or a non-adverse party can revoke the trust acting alone or with the consent of a non-adverse party;
   - Whereas an adverse party is a person having a substantial beneficial interest in the trust which would be adversely affected by the exercise or nonexercise of the trust power he/she possesses, a non-adverse party is a person who is not an adverse party (IRC Section 672). Note that in a grantor trust situation, if the grantor or a non-adverse party (i.e., a party that would be subject to the control of the grantor) has the power to revoke the trust, the power is imputed to the grantor, creating a

grantor trust. If the non-adverse party alone has the power to revoke, that power is attributed to the grantor, triggering grantor trust status.

3. The grantor or a non-adverse party (or both) can control the beneficial enjoyment of the trust;
4. The grantor retains certain administrative powers, including:
   - the right to purchase, exchange, deal with, or dispose of the principal or income of the trust for less than full and fair or adequate consideration;
   - the right to borrow principal or income without adequate security;
   - a power of administration exercisable in a nonfiduciary capacity by any person without the approval or consent of any person in a fiduciary capacity. (These powers include the power to vote stock of a corporation in which the grantor or the trust has a significant voting interest, the power to control investment of the trust funds, and the power to reacquire the trust corpus by substituting other property of equivalent value.);
5. The income of the trust, at the discretion of the grantor or a nonadverse party (or both), is or may be:
   - distributed to the grantor,
   - held or accumulated for future distribution to the grantor, or
   - applied to the payment of premiums on insurance policies on the life of the grantor or the grantor's spouse.
6. The income of the trust is distributed to the grantor's spouse, or held or applied for future distribution to the grantor's spouse, or applied to the payment of premiums on insurance policies on the life of the grantor's spouse.

A final grantor trust rule creates a trust where the beneficiary, not the grantor, becomes liable for payment of income tax on the trust income. Under this rule, if a person other than the grantor has the sole power to vest the principal or income of the trust in himself or herself, that person will be treated as owner of the principal, requiring the trust's income to be taxable to that individual. This type of trust is commonly referred to as a beneficiary defective trust, and is most commonly created when the trust grants the beneficiaries a Crummey right of withdrawal.

Recall that several of the powers listed above that create a grantor trust for income tax purposes may also run afoul of the retained interest rules for estate tax purposes, resulting in the fair market value of the trust assets being included in the gross estate of a decedent. When planning with grantor trusts, it is important to tread carefully and make sure that the grantor trust provisions employed do not trigger an estate tax inclusion for the client.

Incorporating a grantor trust power in a trust document that does not trigger inclusion in the gross estate for estate tax purposes, however, allows the grantor to make a series of tax-free gifts to the beneficiaries of the trust. Since the grantor will be responsible for paying the income tax on trust income, amounts that the trust or the beneficiaries would have otherwise had to spend to cover the tax liability will remain in the hands of the trust or its beneficiaries. The grantor, in paying the income tax, is paying an obligation imposed upon him or her by the Internal Revenue Code, and is therefore not deemed to be making a gift to the trust or its beneficiaries. In addition to making a gift-tax free indirect transfer to the trust beneficiaries, over time, as the grantor pays the income tax liability for the trust, he is also reducing the size of the taxable estate, saving, at the highest marginal estate tax rate, 45 percent in estate taxes.

<table>
<tr><td>

EXAMPLE 8.32

</td><td>

Randy created a trust several years ago. The trust's terms permit Randy to acquire trust property by substituting property of equal value, a power that makes the trust a grantor trust. This year the trust earned $100,000 in ordinary income, and had no capital gains. Randy is in the highest marginal ordinary income tax bracket, so he paid $35,000 in taxes on the trust income (35%). By paying the tax, Randy relieved the trust and the trust's beneficiaries of the $35,000 income tax liability (alternatively stated, Randy let the trust keep, for the benefit of the beneficiaries, the $35,000 it would have used to pay the income tax liability), and at the same time, removed $35,000 from Randy's gross estate. If Randy dies after making the income tax payment, he will save $15,750 in estate taxes (45 percent of the value removed from his gross estate), making the net cost of paying the income tax equal to $19,250. As illustrated, over time Randy can make a significant additional wealth transfer to the beneficiaries of the trust by paying the tax on trust income for them.

</td></tr>
</table>

TRUSTS FOR MINORS – SECTION 2503(b) AND SECTION 2503(c) TRUSTS

Strictly speaking (from a legal perspective), minors are not permitted to own property. Property that is transferred to a minor must be either held in trust for the benefit of the minor, or must be held in a custodial account (such as the Uniform Gift to Minors Act Account (UGMA) or Uniform Transfers to Minors Act Account (UTMA) as discussed in Chapter 5).

If property is transferred to a trust for the benefit of a minor, the minor will not be able to legally access those funds until the later of (1) the date the minor reaches the age of majority, or (2) the date set forth in the trust instrument. Since the minor cannot receive a present right to enjoy or use the property, any gift to a trust for the benefit of a minor would be considered a future interest gift. As previously stated, a future interest gift does not qualify for the gift tax annual exclusion. Consequently, any transfer to a trust for a minor (even those under $13,000 in value, the 2009 gift tax annual exclusion) would require the donor to use part of his applicable gift tax credit amount or, if the applicable gift tax credit has been previously used, pay gift tax.

The Code does provide two exceptions to this otherwise harsh result, thus allowing the transfer to a trust for the benefit of a minor to qualify for the annual exclusion. Section 2503 of the Code states that if property is transferred to a trust for the benefit of a minor that meets the requirements of Section 2503(b) or 2503(c), the transfer will be treated as a present interest gift that qualifies for the gift tax annual exclusion even though, absent these provisions, the gift tax annual exclusion would not apply. In enacting Section 2503 of the Code, Congress recognized that individuals may wish to make transfers to minors in a way that would not result in using their applicable gift tax credit amount.

2503(b) Trust

A **2503(b) trust** may hold property in trust for the lifetime of the beneficiary (or beneficiaries), but must make income distributions to the beneficiary (or beneficiaries) on an annual basis. This means, at a minimum, the interest and dividends received by the trust must be distributed. Once distributed, the income can be placed in a custodial account for the benefit of the child, or may be used for the child's benefit. Gifts made to a 2503(b) trust will partially qualify for the gift tax annual exclusion. The portion qualifying for the gift tax annual exclusion equals the present value of the income interest that the child will receive over the term of the trust.

2503(c) Trust

A **2503(c) trust**, unlike its counterpart the 2503(b) trust, allows income to be accumulated in the trust, and allows the grantor to qualify the entire gift to the trust up to the annual exclusion amount for the gift tax annual exclusion, but can have only one beneficiary. The trustee of the 2503(c) trust may, but is not required to, make principal and income distributions for the benefit of the child. In order to achieve these benefits, the trust must terminate when the child reaches age 21, or, at a minimum, the child must be given the right to receive the trust assets at age 21. A 2503(c) trust compares favorably with UGMA and UTMA accounts in states where a child would have access to custodial account funds at an age earlier than 21, but still places a substantial constraint on those who wish to avoid giving the minor a right to the property. Individuals who wish to fully utilize the gift tax annual exclusion for transfers to trusts for minors, and who wish to keep the property in trust after the child reaches age 21 without giving the child a right to access the funds should consider the creation of a standard Crummey trust.

CRUMMEY TRUSTS

Crummey trusts, as discussed above, are trust agreements that allow the beneficiary to withdraw the contribution made by the grantor to the trust. These trusts are named for the taxpayer who successfully litigated a case in the tax court that held that the grant of the withdrawal right transforms a future interest gift in trust to a present interest gift that qualifies for the gift tax annual exclusion. The withdrawal right is generally limited to the gift tax annual exclusion amount. In granting the beneficiary a withdrawal right, however, a general power of appointment is conferred, and it is important to consider the lapsing issues under the "5-and-5" power created by the withdrawal right (discussed above).

Crummey trusts are often used as alternatives to Section 2503(c) trusts when the grantor wishes to keep the property in trust after the beneficiary reaches age 21. Crummey trusts are frequently associated with irrevocable life insurance trusts, since the grantor of an ILIT often wishes to make transfers to the trust without using any of his applicable gift tax credit amount.

CHARITABLE TRUSTS

Charitably inclined individuals frequently use trusts to accomplish two objectives: (1) transfer assets to charity in a tax efficient manner, and (2) assist in estate planning by transferring assets to noncharitable beneficiaries. A full discussion of charitable trusts is included in Chapter 9, but a brief review of the available types of charitable trusts follows.

Charitable Remainder Trusts (CRTs) are created when the grantor transfers assets to a trust, retains an annuity or unitrust interest for a period of time or for his life, and the remainder value passes to a qualified charity. CRTs are often used to transform illiquid assets into a cash flow stream in a tax efficient manner while at the same time accomplishing the grantor's charitable objectives.

Charitable Lead Trusts (CLTs) are created when the grantor transfers assets to a trust, gives an income stream (which must be an annuity or unitrust interest to qualify for the income tax charitable deduction) to a charity for a fixed period of time followed by a transfer of the remainder interest in the trust to a third party or, possibly, back to the grantor. If a third party is named as remainder beneficiary of the trust, use of a CLT can achieve significant wealth transfer goals.

Private foundations may be structured as either corporations or trusts, but most family foundations use the trust form. A private foundation manages a family's social capital, and makes a distribution of at least five percent of its assets each year to charitable organizations or charitable causes. Private foundations are often coordinated with other charitable techniques, such as charitable remainder trusts and charitable lead trusts, to maximize the tax and charitable benefits available to the grantor.

TOTTEN TRUSTS

As detailed in Chapter 4, **totten trusts** are not really trusts, but rather bank accounts that include payable on death beneficiary clauses (PODs). A bank account with a payable on death clause is transferred to the named beneficiary upon the death of the owner and escapes probate.

BLIND TRUSTS

A **blind trust** is a revocable trust arrangement whereby an individual transfers property to the trust for management purposes when self-management of the assets might be deemed to be a conflict of interest. Blind trusts are commonly used by high ranking political officials to provide management of their assets during their term in office. For example, an individual who is elected as President of the United States has loftier concerns than asset management, and the decisions he makes as President may impact the price of securities owned in his personal portfolio. To avoid any appearance of impropriety, and to ensure that presidential decisions are made objectively, the President will transfer all of his assets to a blind trust before entering office, and the trustee manages those assets. Upon leaving office, the blind trust typically terminates and any assets revert to the grantor of the trust.

Key Terms

2503(b) Trust - A trust for the benefit of a minor designed to qualify the present value of the income interest of the trust for the annual exclusion. A 2503(b) trust must pay its income annually to the minor, but may hold the trust property for the minor's lifetime.

2503(c) Trust - A trust for the benefit of a minor designed to qualify the contribution to the trust for the annual exclusion. A 2503(c) trust must give the minor the right to receive the trust assets when he reaches age 21, but is not required to pay the income to the minor at any earlier time.

Beneficiary - The person(s) entitled to receive the death benefit of a life insurance policy at the insured's death. Also, the person(s) who hold(s) the beneficial title to a trust's assets.

Blind Trust - A revocable trust arrangement whereby an individual transfers property to the trust for management purposes when self-management of the assets might be deemed to be a conflict of interest.

Bypass Trust (also known as a Credit Shelter Trust or B Trust) - A trust created to ensure that an individual makes use of his applicable estate tax credit.

Charitable Lead Trust (CLT) – A trust in which a charitable organization receives the income interest and a noncharitable beneficiary (usually a family member) receives the remainder interest.

Charitable Remainder Trust (CRT) – A trust in which a noncharitable beneficiary receives the income interest and a charitable organization receives the remainder interest.

Complex Trust - A trust that does not meet the definition of a simple trust.

Distributable Net Income (DNI) - A tax concept that allocates taxable income between the trust and beneficiaries to ensure the trust income is subject to only one level of tax.

Estate Trust - A trust which grants the surviving spouse a testamentary general power of appointment over the trust assets. Because of the spouse's general power of appointment over the trust's assets, the fair market value of the trust will be eligible for the unlimited marital deduction at the death of the first-to-die spouse.

Grantor - The person who creates and initially funds a trust. The grantor is also known as the settlor or creator.

Grantor Retained Income Trust (GRIT) - A trust in which the grantor retains an income or use interest in the trust.

Income Beneficiary - The person or entity who has the current right to income from a trust, or the right to use the trust assets.

Inter Vivos Trust - A trust that is created during the grantor's lifetime.

Key Terms

Irrevocable Life Insurance Trust (ILIT) - An irrevocable trust that owns and holds life insurance on its grantor's life. An ILIT is also known as a wealth replacement trust (WRT).

Irrevocable Trust - A trust created by a grantor that cannot be revoked. The grantor cannot take back the property that was transferred to the trust.

Pourover Trust - A trust that receives assets that "pour" into it from another source, generally the grantor's estate at the grantor's death.

Prudent Man Rule - A rule which requires a trustee, as a fiduciary, to act in the same manner that a prudent person would act if the prudent person were acting for his own benefit.

QTIP Trust - A trust that grants the surviving spouse a lifetime right to the income of the trust while transferring the remainder interest to individual(s) of the grantor's choosing, typically created at the death of the first spouse to die.

Remainder Beneficiary - The individual or entity entitled to receive the assets that remain in the trust at the date of the trust's termination.

Revocable Living Trust - A revocable trust that is managed by the grantor and is for the benefit of the grantor during his lifetime. The property transferred to the trust avoids the individual's probate estate, but is included in the individual's gross estate.

Revocable Trust - A trust created where the grantor of the trust retains the right to revoke the trust at any time prior to his incapacity or death.

Rule Against Perpetuities (RAP) - A common law rule which requires that all interests in a trust must vest, if at all, within lives in being plus 21 years.

Self-Settled Trust - A trust where the beneficiary is also the grantor of the trust.

Simple Trust - A trust that requires all of the trust income to be distributed on an annual basis to the beneficiaries and does not have a charitable organization as one of its beneficiaries.

Spendthrift Clause - A clause in a trust document which does not allow the beneficiary to anticipate distributions from the trust, assign, pledge, hypothecate, or otherwise promise to give distributions from the trust to anyone. If such a promise is made, it is void and may not be enforced against the trust.

Standby Trust - A trust created during the grantor's lifetime that is either unfunded or minimally funded. A standby trust is also known as a contingent trust.

Key Terms

Testamentary Trust - A trust created after the death of the grantor. The grantor's will generally includes all of the trust provisions.

Totten Trust - Not a trust, but rather a bank account with a beneficiary clause.

Trust - A structure that vests legal title (the legal interest) to assets in one party, the trustee, who manages those assets for the benefit of the beneficiaries (who hold the equitable title) of the trust.

Trustee - The individual or entity responsible for managing the trust assets and carrying out the directions of the grantor that are formally expressed in the trust instrument.

Wealth Replacement Trust (WRT) - An irrevocable trust that owns and holds life insurance on its grantor's life. A WRT is also known as an Irrevocable Life Insurance Trust (ILIT).

DISCUSSION QUESTIONS

1. Why are trusts used in estate planning?

2. What is a trust?

3. List the common parties of a trust.

4. Who is the fiduciary of a trust?

5. Explain the legal duties imposed on a fiduciary.

6. Describe the two most common types of beneficiaries.

7. List three reasons the use of a trust is beneficial to an estate plan.

8. What is a spendthrift clause and why is it included in a trust?

9. How can the creation of a trust reduce estate taxes?

10. What is the effect of the rule against perpetuities?

11. Under what circumstances will the fair market value of the assets of an irrevocable trust be included in the grantor's gross estate?

12. What are the most common reasons for using a revocable trust?

13. How is a testamentary trust created?

14. Explain the differences between an unfunded trust and a funded trust.

15. At the death of the grantor of a revocable trust, what controls the disposition of the trust's property?

16. Describe a Crummey provision and explain why a trust would contain a Crummey provision.

17. List and explain the three methods used to prevent estate tax consequences from the lapsing of a general power of appointment created by a Crummey power.

18. What is the purpose of an Irrevocable Life Insurance Trust (ILIT) and why is it created?

19. Under what circumstances will the death benefit of a life insurance policy owned by an ILIT be included in the insured's gross estate?

20. In the ideal estate plan, what amount would be transferred to a testamentary bypass trust?

21. List the various forms of Grantor Retained Income Trusts (GRITs).

22. What is the primary reason to use a GRAT for estate planning purposes?

23. List the primary difference between a GRAT and a GRUT.

24. How is a GRAT more effective in reducing the grantor's gross estate than a GRUT?

25. Discuss the consequences of a grantor dying during the term of a TPPT.

26. What is a dynasty trust and what is its primary purpose?

27. Who is subject to the income tax on the income of a grantor trust?

28. What is the primary purpose of using a 2503(b) or 2503(c) trust?

29. List the requirements of a 2503(b) trust.

30. Describe a Totten Trust and its benefits.

MULTIPLE-CHOICE PROBLEMS

1. Which of the following is not a party to a trust?

    a. Trustee.
    b. Income beneficiary.
    c. Grantor.
    d. Principal.

2. Which of the following statements concerning trust formation is correct?

    a. The trustee of the trust will receive the trust corpus after paying the income to the income beneficiary.
    b. The remainder beneficiary of a trust receives an annuity payment each year.
    c. The grantor of a trust contributes property to a trust which will be managed by the trustee.
    d. The income beneficiary of a trust always receives the trust property at the termination of the trust.

3. A trustee is subject to which of the following?

    a. Prudent Man Rule.
    b. Trustee's Ethical Code.
    c. Uniform Trustee Provisions.
    d. Fiduciary Responsibilities Doctrine.

4. Which of the following statements concerning trusts is correct?

    a. A trust can have several beneficiaries, including different classes and individuals.
    b. When a grantor contributes property to a trust, he must recognize any unrealized capital gain or loss he has in the contributed property.
    c. A trust can only have one trustee.
    d. The gift of a remainder interest in a trust is a gift of a present interest.

5. All of the following statements concerning the income beneficiary of a trust are correct, EXCEPT?

    a. An income interest in a trust can be given to the beneficiary, while also naming the same individual as the remainder beneficiary of the trust.

    b. A decedent will commonly create a testamentary trust that names his wife as the income beneficiary of his property for the rest of her life and his children as the remainder beneficiaries.

    c. A dynasty trust only has income beneficiaries. The trust property will never vest with a remainder beneficiary.

    d. When the property is paid to the remainder beneficiary at the termination of a trust, if the income beneficiary is a different individual than the remainder beneficiary, the income beneficiary is treated as having made a taxable gift to the remainder beneficiary.

6. Your son has been studying trusts in his financial planning class. He has come to you for more information. Of the following statements listed below, which do you tell him?

    a. Of the many reasons people create trusts, one reason is to provide for asset management.

    b. Testamentary trusts are created during the grantor's life.

    c. The property within a revocable living trust is not included in decedent's probate or gross estate.

    d. The grantor of a trust must include the full fair market value of any property transferred to a trust within three years of his death in his gross estate.

7. Of the following statements regarding trusts, which is false?

    a. A trust can provide asset protection for a beneficiary.

    b. A trust can provide the grantor with a yearly payment.

    c. Property held within a trust will avoid probate.

    d. Income within a trust is not taxed until the beneficiary receives a distribution.

8. A spendthrift clause:

    a. Requires the fiduciary of a trust to make small distributions.

    b. Protects the trust assets from the claims of the beneficiary's creditors.

    c. Eliminates the problems associated with multiple beneficiaries.

    d. Prevents the lapse of a general power of appointment and its subsequent estate tax consequences.

9. Of the following, which does not reduce a grantor's federal gross estate?

   a. A contribution of highly appreciative property to an irrevocable trust.

   b. A contribution of high income, zero growth property to an irrevocable trust.

   c. The creation of a grantor trust that requires the grantor to pay income tax on the trust's income.

   d. A contribution of depreciable personal property to a revocable living trust.

10. Which of the following situations would not cause the inclusion of an irrevocable trust in a grantor's gross estate?

    a. The grantor has retained the right to receive the income from the irrevocable trust.

    b. The grantor has retained the right to use the assets contributed to the irrevocable trust for the remainder of his life.

    c. The grantor retains an annuity from the irrevocable trust for a term of years less than his life expectancy.

    d. The grantor retains the right to revoke the trust.

11. Marcia created an irrevocable trust with no retained powers in 2007 with a contribution of $600,000. She named her only daughter as the sole income and remainder beneficiary and paid gift tax at the date of the transfer of $25,000. In 2009, Marcia died of lung cancer. The fair market value of the property in the irrevocable trust was $3,000,000 at the date of her death. What amount of the trust is included in Marcia's gross estate?

    a. $0.

    b. $600,000.

    c. $625,000.

    d. $3,000,000.

12. Stephanie contributed $450,000 to a revocable living trust in 2005. She named herself as the income beneficiary and her only son as the remainder beneficiary. The term of the trust was equal to Stephanie's life expectancy. Stephanie died in 2009, when the fair market value of the trust's assets is $2,000,000. How much is included in Stephanie's probate estate related to the revocable living trust?

    a. $0.

    b. $345,800.

    c. $450,000.

    d. $2,000,000.

13. Phil contributed $300,000 to an irrevocable trust and did not retain any right to the trust's assets. The income beneficiary of the irrevocable trust was Phil's nephew, and the remainder beneficiary of the irrevocable trust was Phil's niece. At the time of the transfer, Phil paid gift tax of $20,000. Phil died two years later, when the value of the irrevocable trust was $1,200,000. With regard to the transfer to the irrevocable trust, how much is included in Phil's gross estate?

    a. $0.

    b. $20,000.

    c. $300,000.

    d. $1,200,000.

14. Of the following, which is not a characteristic of a revocable trust?

    a. The grantor can take the property back from the trust.

    b. The income of the trust is always payable to the grantor.

    c. At the grantor's date of death, the fair market value of the trust's assets are included in his federal gross estate.

    d. At the grantor's date of death, the fair market value of the trust's assets are included in his probate estate.

15. A trust created in the will of a decedent is a:

    a. Standby trust.

    b. Testamentary trust.

    c. Trust by will.

    d. Decedent's trust.

16. Justin's grandfather contributed $350,000 to a simple irrevocable trust naming Justin as the income beneficiary and his brother, Ryan, as the remainder beneficiary. At the time of the transfer Justin's grandfather paid $12,000 of gift tax. This year, the trust generated $14,000 of taxable dividend income and $3,000 of capital gains. What amount of taxable income will Justin include on his federal Form 1040 from this trust this year?

    a. $0.

    b. $3,000.

    c. $12,000.

    d. $14,000.

17. Of the following statements, which is not a typical advantage of using a revocable trust?

    a. Privacy.

    b. Estate tax reduction.

    c. Probate avoidance.

    d. Reversion of the trust's assets to the grantor.

18. A trust created to receive an amount equal to the decedent's remaining applicable estate tax credit equivalency at the decedent's date of death is a:

    a. Standby trust.

    b. Pourover trust.

    c. Bypass trust.

    d. Revocable trust.

19. In 1999, Maria funded a bypass trust with $675,000, the applicable estate tax credit equivalency at the time. At Maria's death in 2009, her will included a testamentary bypass trust and a residual bequest to her U.S. citizen husband. If Maria's net worth at her death was $4,000,000, how much will be transferred to the bypass trust to maximize its benefits?

    a. $0.

    b. $2,000,000.

    c. $2,825,000.

    d. $4,000,000.

20. Of the following statements regarding an Irrevocable Life Insurance Trust (ILIT), which of the following is true?

    a. A contribution to an ILIT that includes a Crummey power is eligible for the gift tax annual exclusion.

    b. Contributions to an ILIT are not taxable gifts until the insured dies and the transfer is deemed complete.

    c. ILITs are designed so the insured retains ownership of the life insurance policy.

    d. The grantor of an ILIT is deemed the owner of the life insurance policy to the extent he remains the insured of the life insurance policy.

21. Which of the following is not a correct statement regarding a power of appointment trust?

    a. The trust will qualify for the unlimited marital deduction if the surviving spouse is given a general power of appointment over the trust's assets.

    b. Powers of appointment trusts are irrevocable trusts that can be created either during lifetime or at death.

    c. A general power of appointment trust qualifies the grantor's contributions for the gift tax annual exclusion if the beneficiary is allowed to take withdrawals at his discretion.

    d. A special power of appointment trust that limits the surviving spouse's right to an ascertainable standard qualifies the trust for the unlimited marital deduction.

22. Maureen created a Qualified Personal Residence Trust (QPRT) in 1997. The annuity term of the QPRT is ending this year. If Maureen continues to live in the house after this year, how is Maureen's estate planning affected?

    a. The QPRT is automatically null, and the home reverts to Maureen.

    b. Maureen must begin to pay the remainder beneficiary of the QPRT a fair market value rent.

    c. Maureen's probate estate will now include the value of the home at her date of death.

    d. Maureen's gross estate will now include the fair market value of the home at her date of death.

23. Of the following statements regarding Tangible Personal Property Trusts (TPPTs), which is true?

    a. A TPPT is designed to utilize temporal discounts to transfer tangible personal property at a reduced gift tax cost.

    b. Only easy-to-value personal property may be included in a TPPT.

    c. Property which is expected to depreciate in value should be transferred to a TPPT.

    d. A TPPT is designed to utilize minority and lack of marketability discounts to transfer property at a reduced gift tax cost.

24. Which of the following statements regarding 2503(b) trusts is correct?

    a. The trustee has full discretion to make principal distributions to the beneficiary.

    b. All income of a 2503(b) trust must be paid to the beneficiary at least annually.

    c. When the beneficiary reaches the age of majority, the principal of a 2503(b) trust must be paid to the beneficiary.

    d. No portion of a contribution to a 2503(b) trust qualifies for the annual exclusion.

25. The main difference between a 2503(b) and a 2503(c) trust is:

    a. The 2503(b) trust requires the trustee to accumulate income, whereas the 2503(c) trust requires the trustee to distribute all income.

    b. The 2503(c) trust only allows distributions for the health, education, maintenance, and support of the beneficiary.

    c. The 2503(c) trust must terminate, or the beneficiary must have the right to receive the trust's assets, when the beneficiary reaches age 21. A 2503(b) trust may hold property for the lifetime of the beneficiary.

    d. The trustee of a 2503(b) trust must distribute the principal of the trust within five years of the beneficiary reaching the age of majority. With a 2503(c) trust the trustee must distribute the principal of the trust at the death of the beneficiary.

Quick Quiz Explanations

Quick Quiz 8.1

1. False. A trust may have only one beneficiary. Two beneficiaries are not required.
2. True.
3. False. The income beneficiary is entitled to receive the income, or current distributions from the trust. The remainder beneficiary receives the corpus of the trust at the end of the trust's term.

Quick Quiz 8.2

1. False. One of the classic reasons for using a trust is to protect assets from the claims of the beneficiaries' creditors.
2. False. A spendthrift clause provides asset protection by legally restricting a beneficiary's ability to anticipate distributions from the trust. A properly constructed spendthrift clause will prevent creditors from being able to access trust assets unless they are distributed to the beneficiary.
3. True.
4. False. Since transfers to a revocable living trust are revocable, the property in the trust is included in the grantor's gross estate pursuant to the retained interest rule (Section 2038).

Quick Quiz 8.3

1. True.
2. True.
3. True.

Quick Quiz 8.4

1. False. DNI is a tax concept that maintains the character of the income that is distributed to the beneficiaries, and limits the beneficiary's exposure to income taxation on trust distribution. It is not necessarily required to be distributed to the trust beneficiaries.
2. False. Assets transferred to a trust are only excluded from the gross estate of the grantor if the trust is irrevocable and the grantor has not retained any interest in the trust that would require inclusion in the gross estate under the retained interest rules (Sections 2036-2038).
3. True.

Quick Quiz 8.5

1. False. Revocable trusts allow the grantor to take back the property that was transferred to the trust.
2. True.
3. False. A trust that requires all income to be distributed on an annual basis is a simple, not complex, trust.

Quick Quiz Explanations

Quick Quiz 8.6

1. False. Revocable trusts cannot avoid estate taxes due to the grantor's retained right to revoke the transfer. The most common use for inter vivos revocable trusts is to avoid probate, not estate tax.
2. False. ILITs are used to exclude life insurance from a decedent's gross estate.

Quick Quiz 8.7

1. True.
2. False. The fair market value of the remainder interest in a GRAT is subject to gift tax when the GRAT is created.
3. True.

Charitable Giving

INTRODUCTION

Charitable giving is a way of life in America. In 2001, a national poll indicated that 89 percent of American households donated money to charity, and 83.9 million Americans donated over 15.5 billion hours of their time to charity in 2000. The most frequent contributors to charity include college graduates, retirees, and other households with incomes over $100,000. The Giving USA Foundation estimated that charitable giving in the United States in 2007 amounted to $306.39 billion, exceeding $300 billion for the first time in history.

Gifts to charity can be made during life (inter vivos) or at death (causa mortis). A donor needs to consider charitable objectives and the desired timing of the gift, in addition to the tax consequences of making a charitable donation. The character of the property given, the type of charity, the timing of the contribution, and, for inter vivos giving, the taxpayer's adjusted gross income (AGI) are all factors that can affect the tax consequences of charitable donations.

GENERAL ISSUES REGARDING CHARITABLE CONTRIBUTIONS AND TAXATION

Charitable deductions of any size are not taxable gifts. In addition, direct gifts to charities made during life usually generate a current income tax deduction for the donor. Under certain conditions, even a remainder interest given to a charity will generate a current income tax deduction for the donor. All bequests made at death to qualified charities are deducted from the decedent's adjusted gross estate to arrive at the taxable estate. The deduction is unlimited but is only available for those assets included in the decedent's gross estate. If a donor makes a gift to a charity of a complete interest in property and has no other gifts that year, no gift tax return is required. However, a gift tax return will be required for any split interest gift involving a qualifying charity and any other donee or where the donor is required to file a gift tax return as a result of noncharitable gifts made during the year.

Under certain conditions, the value of an otherwise lifetime gift to charity may be included in the decedent's gross estate. However, such an amount will also be deducted from the adjusted gross estate to arrive at the taxable estate. A common example is where the decedent had assigned the ownership of a life insurance policy to a qualified charity and the decedent died within three years of the assignment. Because the assignment was made within three years of the decedent's death, the death benefit must be included in the decedent's gross estate, but will also be eligible as a deduction from the adjusted gross estate to arrive at the taxable estate. There are some potentially unfortunate consequences from this type of a transaction which will be covered in Chapter 12, Post Mortem Elections. Other examples of this inclusion and deduction is when the donor retains a general power of appointment over property that upon his death passes to a qualified charity, and also when a donor creates a charitable remainder trust and possesses the right to receive income payments (at death) from the trust when he/she dies.

QUALIFYING ORGANIZATIONS

The Internal Revenue Code (Section 170(c)) defines which organizations will qualify for charitable status. They include:

Key Concepts

Underline/highlight the answers to these questions as you read:

1. Identify the types of organizations that qualify for charitable status per the IRC.

2. List three examples of qualifying charities.

3. Which websites are available to provide more information on specific charitable organizations?

1. A state, a possession of the United States, or any political subdivision (contribution must be solely for public purposes).
2. A corporation, trust, or community chest, fund, or foundation that is organized in the U.S. and is operated exclusively for:
    a. religious, charitable, scientific, literary, or educational purposes;
    b. fostering national or international amateur sports competition;
    c. preventing cruelty to animals or children.
3. A post or organization of war veterans organized in the United States.
4. A domestic fraternal society, order, or association, operating under the lodge system, but only if the contribution is to be used for the purposes listed in 2 above.
5. A cemetery company (not deductible if the donation is limited to the maintenance of a specific cemetery plot).

| EXHIBIT 9.1 | CHARITABLE ORGANIZATIONS |

Charities that would generally qualify under this definition include:	Charities that generally do NOT qualify under this definition include:
• Churches, temples, synagogues • Public parks • Colleges and universities • United Way • Boy Scouts and Girl Scouts of America • Salvation Army • American Heart Association • American Society for Prevention of Cruelty to Animals	• Foreign organizations • For-profit groups • Homeowners' associations • Political groups • Labor unions • Chambers of commerce • Social clubs • Individuals • Civic groups

There are three easy ways to determine if an organization qualifies as a charitable organization. IRS Publication 78, Cumulative List of Organizations, lists the qualifying charitable organizations and is updated annually, with cumulative supplements issued quarterly (weekly changes are published in the Internal Revenue Bulletins). The IRS website (www.irs.gov) also lists the charitable organizations, and Guidestar, the National Database of Nonprofit Organizations (www.guidestar.org) allows you to verify the organization's status as well as view the organization's informational tax return, Form 990.

EXAMPLE 9.1

Question: If an organization tells you that your contribution is tax deductible when, in fact, it is not, can you still take a deduction?

Answer: No. The burden is on the taxpayer to verify a qualifying organization's charitable status.

TYPES OF CHARITABLE ORGANIZATIONS

Charitable organizations can be categorized as public charities, private operating foundations, or private nonoperating foundations. The classification of the organization will affect the amount of income tax deduction allowed for the charitable contribution.

Public charities are those that receive broad support from the general public. Specifically, an organization must meet two tests. The first test, under Section 509(a)(2)(A) of the IRC, states that more than one-third of the organization's support must be from a combination of gifts, grants, contributions, membership fees, and gross receipts from sales in an activity which is not an unrelated trade or business. The second test, under Section 509(a)(2)(B), requires that not more than one-third of an organization's support can come from the sum of gross investment income plus unrelated business taxable income (reduced by related taxes).

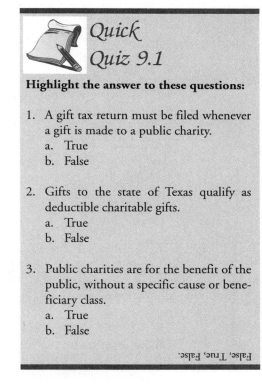

Quick Quiz 9.1

Highlight the answer to these questions:

1. A gift tax return must be filed whenever a gift is made to a public charity.
   a. True
   b. False

2. Gifts to the state of Texas qualify as deductible charitable gifts.
   a. True
   b. False

3. Public charities are for the benefit of the public, without a specific cause or beneficiary class.
   a. True
   b. False

False, True, False.

If an organization does not meet the two tests described above, it is considered to be a private foundation. **Private foundations** generally receive their support from a single individual or family and can be classified as either operating or nonoperating. **Private operating foundations** are those that spend at least 85 percent of their adjusted net income (or minimum investment return, if less) on activities engaged in for the active conduct of an exempt purpose. In addition, an assets test, endowment test, or support test must be met. (Although beyond the scope of this text, more information on this topic can be found in IRC Code Section 509.) If a private foundation does not meet the tests to be classified as operating, then it is deemed to be a **private nonoperating foundation**. Most family established foundations are private, nonoperating foundations.

CHARITABLE GIFTS DURING LIFE

Generally, any gift to a charity of money, property (including tangible, intangible, or real), or any right with value will qualify as a charitable contribution, and thus its value may be deductible for federal income tax purposes. While generally neither gifts of a partial interest nor services are deductible for federal income tax purposes, any out of pocket expenses directly related to a charitable activity are deductible for federal income tax purposes.

GIFTS OF CASH

Individuals may deduct cash contributions made to qualified charitable organizations subject to some limitations. The value of the cash contribution is reduced by any tangible benefit received by the donor from the donation.

Key Concepts

Underline/highlight the answers to these questions as you read:

1. Under what circumstance is only 80% of a contribution deductible?

2. Which expenses can be deducted in relation to gifts of services?

3. Identify the requirements of a contribution acknowledgement for contributions in excess of $250.

4. What IRS form is used to report noncash contributions in excess of $500?

EXAMPLE 9.2

Larry purchased a $150 per couple ticket to a fund raising dinner for the benefit of the local ballet company. The dinner served had a fair market value of $25 per person. Larry took his girlfriend Camille to the dinner. Larry's charitable deduction is $100 [$150 FMV - (2 x $25)].

For cash contributions to college and universities where the donor receives the right to purchase tickets to athletic events, 80 percent of the contribution will be allowed as a charitable contribution.

EXAMPLE 9.3

Mr. Crimson donates $1,000 to the Tide Pride fund at his college alma mater. In exchange, Mr. Crimson receives the right to purchase football tickets. Mr. Crimson's charitable deduction will be $800 ($1,000 x 80%).

If a taxpayer receives an item of low (de minimis) value that has the organization's name or logo on it, then the contribution is deductible in full.

EXAMPLE 9.4

Sally makes a donation of $50 to her local public radio station. In return, Sally receives a mug with the station's call letters on it. Sally does not have to reduce the donation by the value of the mug—the entire $50 donation will qualify as a charitable contribution.

GIFTS OF SERVICES

When donating services to a charitable organization, only the unreimbursed out-of-pocket expenses directly connected with the services are deductible. The value of the service itself is nondeductible.

EXAMPLES OF DEDUCTIBLE OUT-OF-POCKET EXPENSES

EXHIBIT 9.2

- Car expenses - direct expenses such as gas and oil (not depreciation or insurance), or alternatively the standard mileage deduction at 14 cents per mile can be taken.
- Support for foster children in excess of payments received, if no profit motive exists.
- Travel and transportation expenses incurred in connection with attending a convention on behalf of a qualified organization.
- Uniforms required to be worn while performing a charitable service.

EXAMPLE 9.5

Mary volunteers as an aide at the local hospital. She is required to wear a special pink uniform. If she buys the uniform, the cost of her uniform is deductible as a charitable contribution.

EXAMPLE 9.6

Sarah delivers Meals on Wheels to the elderly in her community. She drives 2000 miles a year performing this service. Out-of-pocket expenses incurred in connection with the mileage include $167 in gas, $80 pro rata share of insurance, and a $25 parking fine. Sarah's maximum deduction is $280 (14 cents x 2000 miles). Actual expenses would only be $167, since the insurance and parking fine are not considered to be out-of-pocket charitable expenses.

Question: What if Sarah paid for the parking and avoided the fine?

Answer: She would consider the actual cost of parking as a charitable contribution.

GIFTS OF PROPERTY

Generally, the income tax charitable deduction for donated property is the fair market value of the property at the date of the contribution, subject to AGI limitations. However, the taxpayer needs to consider the specific type of property (ordinary income, capital gain, or Section 1231) contributed to determine the deductible amount of the charitable contribution.

An easy way to determine the type of property donated is to determine the income tax consequences if that donated property would have been sold. If the result of the sale is ordinary income or short-term capital gain, then such property is ordinary income property. Alternatively, if the sale of the property would have resulted in long-term capital gain or Section 1231 gain, then such property is capital gain property. A detailed discussion of the deductible amounts related to each type of property follows.

Ordinary Income Property

Ordinary income property is property that, if sold, would result in recognition of ordinary income. Examples include inventory, capital assets held one year or less, and works of art created by the donor. The deduction for donated ordinary income property is equal to the fair market value of the property reduced by any ordinary income that would have resulted from its sale. As a result, the deductible amount is usually the adjusted basis of the property. In the event the fair market value is less than the adjusted basis (no ordinary income would result from this sale), the deduction is equal to the fair market value of the property itself.

EXAMPLE 9.7

Robert donates a sculpture he created (adjusted basis $100, fair market value $500), painting supplies from his crafts store (adjusted basis $200, fair market value $100), and some Mackie Corporation stock which he has held less than one year (adjusted basis $1,500, fair market value $2,000) to the local art museum. Given this information, his charitable deduction would be:

Sculpture	$100	The deduction for a work of art created by the donor is limited to adjusted basis.
Painting Supplies	$100	When the fair market value of the ordinary income property is less than the adjusted basis, the charitable deduction is limited to the fair market value.
Stock	$1,500	The deduction for a short-term capital asset is limited to its adjusted basis.
TOTAL	$1,700	

Capital Gain Property

Property that, if sold, would result in either capital gain or Section 1231 gain is considered to be **capital gain property**. A capital asset includes intangible property (e.g., stocks and bonds), tangible property (automobile), and real property. Section 1231 property is commercial in nature or used to generate income, must be held long term (greater than one year), and is eligible for depreciation. There is a special requirement for tangible property put to an unrelated use that is discussed further below. Otherwise, subject to the following two exceptions listed below, the charitable deduction for capital gain property is the property's fair market value.

EXAMPLE 9.8

Assume the Mackie Corporation stock described in the example above was held long-term by Robert and donated to Robert's church. The charitable deduction in such a case would be $2,000, the fair market value of the stock.

Donation to a Private Nonoperating Foundation

There are two exceptions to the general rule which provides for a fair market value deduction for capital gain property. First, when capital gain property is donated to a private nonoperating foundation, the deduction is limited to the adjusted basis of the property if the taxpayer elects to use the 30 percent AGI ceiling. If he/she chooses to use the 20 percent AGI ceiling for current year deductions, then fair market value at the time of donation can be the charitable contribution.

<table>
<tr><td>Robert donates the Mackie Corporation stock (held long-term) to Delle Foundation (a private nonoperating foundation, whose purpose is to promote medical research in the area of relieving stress for people who work with Type A individuals). Robert's charitable donation is limited to the adjusted basis of the stock, $1,500, because the donation is to a private nonoperating foundation.</td><td>**EXAMPLE 9.9**</td></tr>
</table>

Donation of Property for Unrelated Use

The second exception to the fair market value deduction for capital gain property applies to donations of **tangible property** (property that is not realty, is not permanently affixed to the land, has physical substance, and is capital in nature) put to an unrelated use. This includes art, jewelry, automobiles, books, etc. that are not created by the donor. When tangible property is donated to a public charity and is used in a manner that is unrelated to the exempt purpose of the charity, the deduction is limited to the donor's adjusted basis of the property. If the donation is made to a governmental entity, the donated property must be used exclusively for public purposes, or it will be considered "unrelated use" property. The assumption underlying this rule is that if the donated property is unrelated to the mission of the charity, the charity will sell the donated property shortly after the date of donation so the appropriate value of the charitable deduction would be the lesser of fair market value or the donor's adjusted basis. Furnishings that are contributed to a charity and are used in the offices that carry out the charitable objective are considered related use property.

<table>
<tr><td>Paul has a valuable coin collection he has been managing for over 30 years. Paul has been a savvy investor, and the collection has a fair market value well in excess of Paul's adjusted basis. If Paul contributes the coin collection to the local museum, whose intent is to display the coin collection, Paul will have a charitable deduction equal to the fair market value of the coin collection. If, however, Paul contributes the coin collection to his church, it is hard to imagine a situation where the coin collection could be used for religious purposes. In this case, Paul's deduction would be limited to the lesser of the fair market value of the collection, or his adjusted basis in the coin collection. Even if the church sold the coin collection and used the proceeds for religious purposes, it would still be considered an unrelated use, and Paul's charitable deduction in this case would be limited to his adjusted basis in the coin collection.</td><td>**EXAMPLE 9.10**</td></tr>
</table>

The taxpayer must establish or be able to reasonably anticipate at the time of the donation that the property will not be put to an unrelated use. If one of these two requirements is met, the property is considered related use even if the charitable organization later sells or exchanges the property. No recapture provision at the lesser value would apply.

To ensure the availability of a charitable deduction equal to the fair market value of the donated property, a taxpayer may create a contract with the charitable organization requiring the charity to put the donated tangible property to a related use.

<table>
<tr><td>

EXAMPLE 9.11

</td><td>

Michael owns artwork with an adjusted basis of $100 and a fair market value of $100,000. He donates the artwork to Loyal University and contractually requires the university to display the artwork in the art department for 2 years for the educational purpose of art students. Because the artwork will be put to a related use of Loyal University, Michael will be able to deduct the fair market value of $100,000 (subject to AGI limitations).

</td></tr>
<tr><td>

EXAMPLE 9.12

</td><td>

Question: If a taxpayer is holding property that has depreciated relative to its adjusted basis, is it better for the taxpayer to donate the property to a charitable organization, or sell it first and donate the proceeds from the sale?

Answer: Sell the property and donate the proceeds of the sale, otherwise the taxpayer will lose the capital loss deduction.

</td></tr>
</table>

CONTRIBUTION BASE (ADJUSTED GROSS INCOME) LIMITATIONS

Depending upon the classification of the charitable organization and the type of donated property, the IRC (Section 170(b)) prescribes an adjusted gross income (AGI) limitation for contributions. The income deduction limitation for individual contributions is either 20 percent, 30 percent, or 50 percent of the donor's contribution base, depending on the classification of the charitable organization and the type of property contributed. Overall, the total deductible contributions for the tax year cannot exceed 50 percent of the donor's contribution base. A donor's contribution base is his/her AGI, not taking into account net operating loss carrybacks. Since most taxpayers do not have net operating loss carrybacks, when discussing the charitable deduction limitations in this chapter, we use AGI.

50 Percent Organizations
50 percent organizations include:
- Public charities (including churches, schools, hospitals),
- Private operating foundations, and
- Private nonoperating foundations that distribute their contributions to either public charities or private operating foundations within two and one-half months of their tax year-end (referred to as a pass-through private foundation).

If the donee organization is a 50 percent charity, then a donor can deduct charitable contributions to these charities up to a limit of 50 percent of his AGI. An exception exists for contributions of appreciated capital gain property, which are limited to 30 percent of AGI. Taxpayers are permitted to avoid the 30 percent ceiling on this type of property by electing to use the adjusted basis to determine the amount of the deduction instead of the fair market value. The contribution would then be subject to a 50 percent of AGI ceiling. In other words, for a contribution of appreciated property, a taxpayer has the choice of a deduction equal to the fair market value with a 30 percent of AGI limitation or a deduction equal to the adjusted basis with a 50 percent of AGI limitation.

30 Percent Organizations

Contributions to private nonoperating foundations that do not qualify as 50 percent organizations (i.e., those private foundations that do not distribute its income by the 15th day of the 3rd month of the organization's tax year-end) are subject to either a 20 percent or 30 percent of AGI limitation, depending on the type of property contributed. Contributions of cash and ordinary income property are subject to a 30 percent of AGI limitation, whereas contributions of long-term capital gain property are subject to a 20 percent of AGI limitation. The taxpayer can make an election of whether to use fair market value (where the 20 percent AGI threshold usually applies) or their adjusted basis (to benefit from the 30 percent AGI threshold).

Special Rules and Carryforward of Disallowed Contributions

If a taxpayer makes donations to both 30 percent and 50 percent organizations during a year, the 50 percent donations are considered first. Any charitable contribution deductions disallowed because of the AGI limitations may be carried over for five years and are used in a first-in-first-out order. The carryover amounts retain their classifications as 20 percent, 30 percent, or 50 percent donations.

CHARITABLE CONTRIBUTION DEDUCTIONS (PERCENT OF TAXPAYER'S AGI)　　　**EXHIBIT 9.3**

Type of Property Donated	Valuation for Purposes of Charitable Deduction	Ceiling for Public Charities, Private Operating Foundations and Certain Private Nonoperating Foundations	Ceiling for Other Private Nonoperating Foundations (PNOF)	
Cash	Fair Market Value	50%	30%	
Ordinary Income Property and Short-term Capital Gain Property	Lesser of the adjusted basis or the fair market value	50%	30%	
Long-term Capital Gain property:				
- Intangible	Fair market value	30%*	Adjusted Basis	20%**
- Tangible Personalty	Fair market value -- (a) related use	30%*		20%
	Adjusted basis -- (b) unrelated use	50%		
- Real Property	Fair market value	30%*		20%

*Taxpayer has the option to use the adjusted basis and the 50% of AGI ceiling for regular charities.
**Certain contributions of qualified appreciated stock may use the fair market value.

Choosing the Adjusted Basis Over the Fair Market Value (Special Election)

The determination of whether to select the adjusted basis as the charitable deduction for each contribution instead of the fair market value should be made with great care. The factors to consider include:

- The donor's current AGI and the projected AGI for the next 5 years;
- The fair market value of the donated property;
- The adjusted basis of the donated property; and
- The time value of money.

EXAMPLE 9.13

Suppose Jerry makes the following charitable contributions:

Type of Property	Basis	FMV	Donee
Stock (LT)	$35,000	$40,000	University
Stock (ST)	$10,000	$12,000	United Way

LT = Long-term   ST = Short-term

Jerry's AGI is $100,000. His charitable contribution income tax deduction, not using the alternative adjusted basis/50% election is:

Type of Property	Adjusted Basis or FMV	Deduction	5-Year Carryover
Stock (LT)	$40,000 (FMV) limited to 30% of AGI	$30,000	$10,000
Stock (ST)	$10,000 (adjusted basis) limited to 50% of AGI	$10,000	$0
Total deductible contributions		$40,000	$10,000

Jerry's total deduction for the year is $40,000 which does not, in total, exceed 50% of Jerry's AGI or $50,000. Jerry would have a charitable contributions carryover of $10,000 that must be used within 5 years.

If Jerry had elected to use the adjusted basis for the long-term stock with a 50% of AGI ceiling, his deduction would be as follows:

Type of Property	Adjusted Basis or FMV	Deduction	5-Year Carryover
Stock (LT)	$35,000 (adjusted basis) limited to 50% of AGI	$35,000	$0
Stock (ST)	$10,000 (adjusted basis) limited to 50% of AGI	$10,000	$0
Total deductible contributions		$45,000	$0

Under these circumstances, Jerry would have a current $45,000 charitable contribution deduction. Since Jerry deducted the full adjusted basis of both assets in the first year, there is no carryover contribution for use in future years. Jerry would have to consider a number of factors to decide which option to take - the time value of money, his projected AGI over the next five years (will he be able to use the carryover?), and his immediate cash needs.

EXAMPLE 9.14

Merrily has an AGI of $50,000 consisting entirely of taxable bond interest. She has a rare antique that her father bequeathed to her. Her adjusted basis in the antique is $200,000, and the antique has a fair market value of $1,000,000. Assuming that her AGI will remain at $50,000 for the next six years, which tax election (adjusted basis or fair market value) creates better tax benefits for her if she donates the antique to a museum in 2009?

Tax Year	AGI	Deductible Amount	
		Adjusted Basis (subject to 50% of AGI)	FMV (subject to 30% of AGI)
2009	$50,000	$25,000	$15,000
2010	$50,000	$25,000	$15,000
2011	$50,000	$25,000	$15,000
2012	$50,000	$25,000	$15,000
2013	$50,000	$25,000	$15,000
2014	$50,000	$25,000	$15,000
TOTALS	$300,000	$150,000	$90,000

Because of the five year carry forward limit and the difference in AGI limitations, Merrily has a greater total deduction by electing to deduct the adjusted basis rather than the fair market value of the antique. By electing to deduct the adjusted basis of the antique, she can deduct 50% of AGI up to the adjusted basis of the antique rather than being limited to 30% of AGI up to the fair market value. Recognize that even with the election to deduct the property based upon the adjusted basis, Merrily will not be able to receive cumulative deductions equal to her adjusted basis in the antique, let alone the full fair market value, because of the AGI limitations.

The situation would obviously be quite different if Merrily's adjusted basis in the antique was substantially lower, or alternatively, if Merrily were to have, and expect to continue to have, a much higher AGI.

EXAMPLE 9.15

Assume instead Merrily has an AGI of $400,000 and donates the same antique with an adjusted basis of $200,000, and a fair market value of $1,000,000. Assuming that her AGI remains at $400,000 for the next 6 years, which tax election (adjusted basis or fair market value) creates better tax benefits for her?

		Deductible Amount	
Tax Year	**AGI**	**Adjusted Basis** (subject to 50% of AGI)	**FMV** (subject to 30% of AGI)
2009	$400,000	$200,000	$120,000
2010	$400,000	0	$120,000
2011	$400,000	0	$120,000
2012	$400,000	0	$120,000
2013	$400,000	0	$120,000
2014	$400,000	0	$120,000
TOTALS	$2,400,000	$200,000	$720,000

Obviously, even though the deduction is limited to 30% of her AGI each year, Merrily should elect to deduct the fair market value of the antique as her charitable deduction as it produces a much greater overall deduction.

VALUATION, RECORD KEEPING, AND REPORTING

Determining the fair market value of donated property can be difficult. The fair market value of any property is the price at which a fully informed, willing seller and a fully informed, willing buyer will complete a transaction. IRS Publication 561, *Determining the Value of Donated Property*, as well as some third party publications, such as "blue books," may offer assistance in valuation. A qualified appraisal will also provide the determination of value, but the IRS only requires an appraisal for property donated with a value in excess of $5,000. The additional cost for the appraisal is a miscellaneous itemized deduction subject to the two percent of AGI floor.

When a taxpayer makes any charitable contribution in the form of cash or a canceled check, a detailed receipt (indicating the donee's name, the date, and the amount of contribution) should be retained by the taxpayer as supporting documentation.

Contemporaneous written acknowledgment by the donee organization is required when an individual contributes cash or property valued at $250 or more per donation. This is not aggregated. For instance, if a church-member gave $200 each week to the church as a charitable contribution over the course of the year, no written acknowledgement is required since each donation was less than $250. For donations over $250, the acknowledgment must include:

- The amount of cash or a description (but not value) of the property;

- Whether any goods or services were given in consideration of the donated property; and

- A good faith estimate of the value of the goods and services provided in consideration of the donated property.

If the value of a donated item is $5,000 or less, but more than $500, the donor must provide information on how and when the property was acquired, as well as its adjusted basis. This information, along with the donee's name and address, and the date of the contribution, must be provided on Form 8283, *Noncash Charitable Contributions*. Form 8283 must also be filed whenever the aggregate total of all non-cash contributions exceeds $500. Form 8283 must be filed with the donor's income tax return for the year in which the property was contributed and the deduction is first claimed.

If a donated item is valued at more than $5,000, and the item is neither cash nor a publicly traded security, then the donor must obtain a qualified appraisal on the property and the appraisal must be attached to the donor's tax return. If the donated property is a non-publicly traded stock, the donor is required to obtain an appraisal if the value is more than $10,000. The IRS maintains a list of approved appraisers, although the use of an approved appraiser does not guarantee that the IRS will not challenge the valuation.

EXAMPLE 9.16

Question: Are appraisal fees deductible for federal income tax purposes as part of the charitable contribution?

Answer: No. However, appraisal fees can be deducted for federal income tax purposes as a miscellaneous itemized deduction subject to the 2% of AGI floor.

EXHIBIT 9.4 **CHARITABLE CONTRIBUTIONS/REPORTING**

Amount or Value of Donation	Cash	Property
Under $250	Canceled check	Receipt with donee name, date, description of property
$250-$500	Contemporaneous acknowledgment from donee organization	Contemporaneous acknowledgment from donee organization
Over $500, but no more than $5,000	Same as above	Same as above plus maintain records of how and when property was acquired, its adjusted basis and file Form 8283
Over $5,000 ($10,000 for non-publicly traded stock)	Same as above	Same as above plus must obtain qualified appraisal and attach appraisal to the return

When taxpayers donate art work that has been appraised at $50,000 or more, taxpayers may request a statement of value from the IRS. The statement of value can only be requested <u>after</u> the donation has been made, and the taxpayer is required to file the statement with the income tax return, whether the taxpayer agrees with the value or not. A minimum fee of $2,500 is imposed by the IRS for the statement of value with an additional $250 fee for each additional item over three. The statement of the value can provide the donor with a level of assurance at the time of filing that his deduction will not be subsequently disallowed or limited by the IRS.

OTHER OUTRIGHT GIFTS TO CHARITY

BARGAIN SALES OF PROPERTY TO CHARITIES

Recall (from Chapter 7) that a person may sell property at a price below its fair market value to benefit a related party. Persons may also sell property to a charity at a price below its fair market value. When a bargain sale to charity occurs, the transaction is split into two elements, a sale element and a charitable contribution element. The adjusted basis of the property is allocated pro rata between the sale element and the charitable contribution element.

EXAMPLE 9.17

Donor sells real estate at a fair market value of $100,000 and with an adjusted basis of $100,000 to a charity for $60,000 cash. The transaction is split into two: a sale of $60,000 (less pro rata allocation of the property's adjusted basis, or

$60,000 = no gain or loss) and a charitable contribution equal to the bargain on the sale of $40,000.

BARGAIN SALES OF APPRECIATED PROPERTY TO CHARITIES

When a bargain sale of appreciated property to a charity occurs, the capital gain portion of the sale element should be considered for income taxation purposes. The capital gain portion is calculated as follows:

$$\text{Sale Component} - \left[\frac{\text{Sale Component}}{\text{Fair Market Value}} \times \text{Donor's Adjusted Basis} \right] = \text{Capital Gain}$$

EXAMPLE 9.18

Referring to the last example and considering instead that the donor's adjusted basis of the property was $30,000, what is the result of the sale of $100,000 property to a charity for $60,000? The sale component of $60,000 is reduced by the proportional basis of $18,000 (60% x $30,000), creating a capital gain of $42,000 ($60,000 - $18,000). The charitable deduction remains, as in the last example, at $40,000.

CHARITABLE GIFT ANNUITIES

With the dramatic increase in individual retirement life expectancy, charities have been promoting charitable gift annuities. Donations can come in a variety of forms, including cash, securities, or property subject to the gift acceptance policy of the charity. This transaction involves an inter vivos transfer of property to a charity in exchange for the charity's promise to pay an annuity either to the donor, the donor and his spouse, or to another person. The charity keeps the principal, but is obliged to provide lifetime income to the annuitant.

The annuity paid to the donor is dependent upon the age of the donor (annuitant), or donors (annuitants) in the case of a joint life annuity. An older donor will receive a greater annuity percentage payout due to reduced life expectancy, but in either case the present value of the annuity will be less than the value of the property contributed to the charity in return for the annuity. For example, a charity that receives property from a 60 year old in exchange for an annuity may only pay the annuitant a 5.7 percent annuity, whereas an 82 year old transferring the same property will receive an 8.5 percent annuity from the same charity. The value of the property contributed less the present value of the annuity equals the charitable income tax deduction in the year of the transfer. The single life rate

Key Concepts

Underline/highlight the answers to these questions as you read:

1. How is a bargain sale of appreciated property to a charity treated for income tax purposes?

2. Why are charities promoting charitable gift annuities now more than in the past?

3. How is the value of a gift of encumbered property calculated?

guidelines provided by the American Council on Gift Annuities (effective February 1, 2009 through June 30, 2009) are as follows:

Age	Annuity Rate
60	5.0%
65	5.3%
70	5.7%
75	6.3%
80	7.1%
85	8.1%
90+	9.5%

The charitable annuity can be created to provide either an immediate or a deferred benefit annuity. If the annuity is a single-life contract that is paid to the donor, the donor receives a charitable income tax deduction in the year of the transfer and removes the value of the asset from his gross estate. In the case of an annuity payable to another person, the donor receives a charitable income tax deduction equal to the present value of the remainder interest, the value of the property may not be included in his gross estate, and the donor has made a potentially taxable gift (equal to the present value of the annuity) to the person who receives the annuity.

Unlike transfers to qualified charitable remainder trusts (CRATs, CRUTs, and Pooled Income Funds - discussed below), an income tax liability may arise on the transfer of appreciated property in exchange for an annuity. Similarly, the bargain sale rules apply.

Benefits of charitable gift annuities to the donor include:
- simplicity,
- low (or no) cost,
- guaranteed fixed income for life,
- provides an income tax charitable deduction to the donor,
- annuity payments have a tax-free recovery of capital components,
- principal is removed from donor's estate.

Donor transfers property to XYZ charity in exchange for a
life annuity to begin immediately. Information regarding the
assets and transfer is as follows:

EXAMPLE 9.19

Date of Transfer	July 1, 2009
Fair market value of property	$200,000
Adjusted basis	$80,000
Annuity amount paid monthly	$719.78 (beginning August 1, 2009)
Section 7520 discount rate	9% (0.75%/month)
Table life expectancy	20 years
(Table V Reg 1.72-9)	
Present value of annuity payments	$80,000 (N = 240, i =.75, PMT$_{OA}$ = $719.78)

The donor must split the transaction into two elements (1)
the sale element and (2) the charitable gift component.

	Sale Component		Charitable Contribution Component
	$80,000	(PV of the annuity)	$120,000 ($200,000 - $80,000)
Pro rata adjusted basis	- $32,000	($80,000 x ($80,000/$200,000))	
Capital gain portion	$48,000		

Over the life of the annuity the donor will collect:

240 monthly payments x $719.78 = $172,747.20 total
amount received.

Broken down as:		
Return of Capital	$32,000.00	
Capital gain amount	$48,000.00	
Ordinary income	$92,747.20	(interest component)
Total Amount Received	$172,747.20	

Each payment, as described in the previous example, will consist of three components: ordinary
income to the extent of interest, capital gain, and return of capital (exactly as a purchased
annuity). Once the sum of the return of capital components equals the purchase amount, any
remaining payments are taxable since the return of capital component cannot exceed basis.

EXAMPLE 9.20

In 2009, the donor in the above example would have received five payments of $719.78. The ordinary income component would be calculated using an amortization table or calculator as follows:

Initial annuity obligation	$80,000.00	
End of year obligation	- $79,392.05	(N = 5, i =.75, PV = $80,000, PMT$_{OA}$ = ($719.78))
Principal reduction	$607.95	
Total annuity payments	$3,598.90	($719.78 x 5)
Less principal reduction	- $607.95	
Equals interest earned	$2,990.95	Ordinary Income (taxable)
Principal reduction		$607.95
Less basis recovery	(40% x $607.95)	- $243.18
Capital gain component	(60% x $607.95)	$364.77

CHARITABLE ANNUITY OF ENCUMBERED PROPERTIES (MORTGAGED)

A donor may transfer encumbered property directly to a charity in exchange for the charity's payment of an annuity to the donor. The annuity payments are a general obligation of the charity. As discussed above, a charitable annuity is treated as a bargain sale transaction. If the property is encumbered by a mortgage, the donor may be relieved of the obligation to pay the mortgage and receive a periodic annuity from the charity.

Calculation of the Donation

The donation equals the fair market value of the property minus the principal of the mortgage and the present value of annuity. The annuity is valued using Section 7520 interest rate (which is 120 percent of the federal midterm rate). A higher rate is more advantageous from the donor's perspective, since the charitable income tax deduction consists of the value of the contribution less the mortgage principal and the present value of the annuity stream.

Income Tax Consequences

Each benefit component (the relief of the mortgage and the annuity) receives a proportionate allocation of basis, potential capital gain, and ordinary income. Any capital gain and the ordinary income related to the mortgage must be recognized in the year of the transfer. The donor can avoid recognizing the ordinary income and capital gain associated with the annuity in the year of transfer if (1) the annuity is non-assignable to the charity, and (2) the donor or the donor and his designated survivor's trust are the only annuitants. Under these conditions, the annuitant will recognize return of capital, ordinary income, and capital gain ratably over the life of the annuity (life expectancy of donor, Table V of Treasury Regulation 1.72-9).

EXAMPLE 9.21

Colin donates a building with a fair market value of $800,000, an adjusted basis of $250,000, and a mortgage of $200,000 to a charitable organization. In return for the donation, Colin receives an annuity for the remainder of his life of $32,000 per year from the charity.

Fair market value	$800,000
Adjusted basis	$250,000
Mortgage	$200,000
Annuity (annual)	$32,000
Section 7520 discount rate	10%
Life expectancy of donee	20 years

Step #1 - Calculate the present value of the annuity.

PMT_{OA}	$32,000
i	10%
N	20
PV	$272,434

Step #2 - Calculate charitable donation.

Fair market value of property - Principal of mortgage - Present value of annuity = Charitable Donation

$800,000 - $200,000 - $272,434 = $327,566

Step #3 - Calculate total capital gain.

Fair market value of property - Charitable donation - Adjusted basis = Capital gain

$800,000 - $327,566 - $250,000 = $222,434

Step #4 - Allocate capital gain between relief of debt and annuity.

Present value of annuity	$272,434	57.66%
Relief of debt	$200,000	42.34%
	$472,434	

57.66% x $222,434 = $128,255
42.34% x $222,434 = $94,179

Reconcile:

Donation	$327,566
Relief of debt capital gain	$94,179
Capital gain attributable to annuity	$128,255
Return of capital	$250,000
Total Value	$800,000

Colin would be required to recognize $94,179 of capital gain in the year of the donation related to the relief of debt. Colin would also recognize capital gain of $128,255 and interest income ratably over the life of the annuity.

GIFTS OF LIFE INSURANCE TO CHARITIES

Life insurance may be donated to charities and has certain advantages over other property. Assuming the policy is a permanent life insurance policy, the death benefit will be payable to the charitable organization at the insured's death as long as the premiums, which are generally paid on an installment basis, are paid. The amount of the gift can be leveraged if the insured dies prior to full life expectancy (i.e., the death benefit far exceeds the premiums paid plus an investment return).

Death proceeds from life insurance are received tax free to a charity and are received without delay of probate or other administrative processes by simply providing the insurer with a certified death certificate. Use of life insurance on charitable giving is particularly valuable if the donor anticipates that a will contest would void the charitable gift.

A gift of life insurance to a charity is valued according to general gift tax rules (fair market value at the date of gift). When life insurance is sold, any gain is ordinary gain, so a gift of life insurance is a gift of ordinary income property.

Therefore, the charitable deduction is equal to the lesser of the donor's adjusted basis or the fair market value of the life insurance policy. See Chapter 11 for a complete, detailed discussion of gifts of life insurance.

GROUP TERM LIFE INSURANCE

Life insurance premiums paid by an employer for a group term life insurance policy (up to a face value of $50,000) are excluded from an employee's gross income. Any group term life insurance coverage in excess of $50,000 paid for by an employer will create taxable income based on the table life insurance rates under Section 72 (Table 1 found in Treasury Regulation 1.79-3). An employee can avoid such income inclusion by irrevocably naming a charitable beneficiary for any amount of employer provided life insurance in excess of $50,000.

CHARITABLE GIFTS OF A SPLIT INTEREST

A lifetime charitable gift may produce an income tax deduction, but if a charitable gift is made at an individual's death, no income tax deduction is available. However, there may be estate tax benefits. The date of the gift is determined by the date of irrevocability. If an individual makes a charitable gift at his death, the value of the asset is included in his gross estate, but the value of the asset is fully deducted from the adjusted gross estate (using the unlimited charitable deduction) to arrive at the taxable estate.

A charitable trust can be a useful vehicle for a donor who wants to make a donation to charity, but does not want to give an undivided interest to the charity. For example, a donor who owns appreciated stock, real property, or a business, and needs the income from the property for living or retirement expenses, but wishes that the ultimate ownership of the property will transfer to charity at a later date. Conversely, the donor might not currently need the income from the asset, but would like the stock, or other asset, to pass to a spouse or a child at the donor's death. A charitable donation of a split interest can provide a solution to these two scenarios and fulfill the donor's objective. The advantages of charitable trusts created during life are that the donor gets a charitable income tax deduction at the time of the transfer, retains some right to enjoy the property, and reduces his taxable estate. To receive the current income tax deduction at the creation of a charitable trust, the trust must be in the precise form of one of the following:

Key Concepts

Underline/highlight the answers to these questions as you read:

1. Identify three types of charitable trusts.

2. Why is a pooled income fund more advantageous than a CRAT for a small donor?

3. How is the value of the annuity interest of a CRAT calculated for gift tax purposes?

4. Who receives the annuity payment in a CLAT?

- Pooled Income Fund
- Charitable Remainder Trust (Annuity or Unitrust)
- Charitable Lead Trust (Annuity or Unitrust)

IRC Section 664 delineates the requirements for charitable remainder annuity trusts and charitable remainder unitrusts. When the donor transfers property to an irrevocable charitable remainder trust, the trust provides an income interest (minimum rate of return of 5%) for the donor for some specified period of time, and at the end of that period, the trust corpus is paid to the named charity. In this case, the donor receives a charitable income tax deduction equal to the value of the remainder interest in the year the property is placed in the trust. Upon the death of the donor, the full fair market value of the trust property is included in the donor's gross estate, but is offset by the unlimited charitable deduction equal to the full fair market value of the property.

POOLED INCOME FUNDS (PIF)

Pooled income funds are analogous to a mutual fund provided by a charity. All donor contributions are pooled into a trust created and maintained by a single charity, and each donor receives an allocable share of the trust's income for life. No defined term trusts are allowed. The income stream can fluctuate based upon the underlying performance of the pooled income fund. Pooled income funds are also not permitted to invest in tax-exempt securities. As with the remainder trusts described in detail below, the donor receives a current income tax deduction for the present value of the remainder interest. Pooled income funds are advantageous for a small donor because the individual can receive the benefits of gifting the remainder interest in property without the legal expense of creating an individual annuity trust. Furthermore, the pooling of funds creates additional investment diversification and protection.

Unlike CRATs and CRUTs, pooled income funds are subject to substantiation rules. The charity must provide written acknowledgment of the transfer of cash or property, state whether any goods or services were given to the donor in exchange, and indicate the donor's income interest in the fund.

CHARITABLE REMAINDER ANNUITY TRUST (CRAT)

A **charitable remainder annuity trust (CRAT)** is less flexible than a CRUT. CRATs provide a fixed annuity to the donor for an amount that is at least five percent (but not more than 50 percent for transfers after June 18, 1997) of the initial net fair market value of the property contributed to the trust. Even if the principal must be invaded, the annuity must be paid at least annually to the donor. The term of the annuity may be for life, or if for a certain number of years, must be no more than twenty years. The remainder interest is paid to a named charity, and once a CRAT is established, additional principal contributions are not allowed. The trustee of a CRAT can be given the right, known as a **sprinkling provision**, to make distributions to the income beneficiaries as he desires. Even though the trust is irrevocable, the donor does not have to notify the charity of its beneficial status, and the donor may reserve the right to change the designated remainder charitable beneficiary to another qualifying charitable organization without affecting the trust or its charitable status. Like charitable gift annuities, tax relief is greater for CRATs in a higher interest rate environment.

CHARITABLE REMAINDER UNITRUST (CRUT)

A **charitable remainder unitrust (CRUT)** provides more flexibility than a CRAT. The yearly pay out is a fixed percentage, or fraction, that is at least five percent (but not more than 50 percent for transfers after June 18, 1997) of the annual net fair market value of the assets. To determine the yearly cash payment, the assets are revalued annually. Unlike the CRAT, the CRUT annuity payments may be limited to the income earned by the trust, with a catch up provision if the income later exceeds the current percentage payout. For example, if in Year 1 the annuity payout should be $5,000 but the trust's income was only $4,500, the trust document could be written to limit the annuity payment to the income, $4,500. If trust income is greater than $5,000 in a subsequent year, the $500 deficiency from Year 1 can be paid at that time. A CRUT which includes such language is often referred to as a **NIMCRUT,** a Net Income With Make-Up Trust. NIMCRUTs work well with deferred annuities since the trustee can trigger annuitization. Unlike a CRAT, the settlor of a CRUT may make additional principal contributions after the trust is established. The trustee of a CRUT can also be given a sprinkling provision to make distributions to the income beneficiaries as he desires. Other variations include NICRUTs and FlipCRUTs. NICRUTs pay the lesser of the percentage payout stipulated in the trust or the actual income generated. FlipCRUTs are unitrusts that start off as NIMCRUTs, but upon a triggering event they "flip" to a standard CRUT. After the flip, the makeup provision is lost. A FlipCRUT can be funded with a non-productive asset, such as raw land, that is anticipated to be sold. FlipCRUTs have strict standards. For instance, during the NIMCRUT phase, 90 percent of assets must consist of non-tradeable or fixed assets.

When drafting remainder trusts, care must be exercised in granting the trustee latitude in choosing investments. Treasury Regulation Section 1.664-1(a)(3) prohibits the trust from restricting the trustee in such a manner that endangers the trustee's ability to generate a reasonable amount of income. Restricting the investment of the trust to tax-exempt securities might violate these regulations. Several revenue procedures issued by the IRS provide sample trust provisions which state that nothing in the trust may restrict the trustee from an investment strategy that results in realization of a reasonable amount of income or gain. Inclusion of a similar provision in a charitable remainder trust is advisable.

SUMMARY OF CHARACTERISTICS OF CHARITABLE REMAINDER TRUSTS

EXHIBIT 9.5

	CRAT	CRUT	Pooled Income Funds (PIF)
Income Tax Deduction	Total value of property less present value of retained annuity payments	Total value of property less present value of retained unitrust payments	Total value of property less present value of retained income interest
Income Recipient	Noncharitable beneficiary (usually donor)	Noncharitable beneficiary (usually donor)	Noncharitable beneficiary (usually donor)
Income	At least 5% and no more than 50% of <u>initial</u> fair market value of assets paid at least annually for life or term ≤20 years (similar to fixed annuity)	At least 5% and no more than 50% of <u>current</u> fair market value of assets (revalued annually) paid at least annually for life or term ≤ 20 years (similar to variable annuity)	Trust rate of return for year
Remainderman	Qualified Charity	Qualified Charity	Qualified Charity
Additional Contributions Permissible	No	Yes	Yes
Sprinkling Provisions	Yes	Yes	No
When Income is Insufficient for Payment	Must invade corpus	Can pay up to income earned and make up deficiency in subsequent year	N/A
Can Invest in Tax - Exempt Securities	Yes	Yes	No

CALCULATION OF THE GIFT AND REMAINDER INTEREST

Charitable Remainder Annuity Trust (CRAT)

The calculation of the income (the annuity payment) and remainder interest of a charitable remainder annuity trust is fairly straightforward. The value of the income interest is derived by multiplying the annual annuity by a factor from the IRS Valuation Table S based on the Section 7520 rate (published monthly by the IRS) and the age of the annuitant at the date of the transfer. The income interest is then subtracted from the fair market value of the property contributed to the trust (at the contribution date) to determine the value of the remainder interest. As stated earlier, the value of the remainder interest qualifies as a current income tax deduction for the donor.

EXAMPLE 9.22	John, age 65, funds a Charitable Remainder Annuity Trust (CRAT) with $500,000 in cash and securities. In exchange, the trust provides for an annual annuity to John of 7% of the initial fair market value of the assets. Assume a Section 7520 rate of 10%.

Income interest = 7.1213 (from Table S utilizing John's age and the 10% Section 7520 rate) x $35,000 (the annuity) = $249,245.50

Remainder interest = $500,000 - $249,245.50 (the income interest) = $250,754.50

The implicit life expectancy is approximately 14 years ($500,000/$35,000).

Subject to AGI limitations, John can deduct $250,754.50 in the year of the transfer as a charitable income tax deduction. If his charitable deduction is limited due to the AGI limitations, he may utilize the five-year carryover.

CRATs must meet a five percent probability test. Actuarily, the income beneficiary must have a five percent or less chance of outliving trust assets to qualify for a charitable deduction.

Charitable Remainder Unitrust (CRUT)

Calculating the value of the remainder interest of a CRUT is more complex and beyond the scope of this text. IRS Publication 1458 provides the factors for valuing remainder interests in CRUTs, and further guidance is given in Treasury Regulation Section 1.664-4. The income tax deduction for a CRUT is usually determined using professional software, but the charitable income tax deduction will be less than the CRAT because of the flexibility available with the use of the CRUT.

CRATs vs. CRUTs

EXHIBIT 9.6

ADVANTAGES	
CRATs	**CRUTs**
• Protects against declining balances	• Inflation protection
• Provides a certain and fixed income stream	• Can make subsequent contributions

DISADVANTAGES	
CRATs	**CRUTs**
• No inflation protection	• Require annual revaluation
• Income stream percentage may be limited by 5% probability test	• Have principal erosion risk

A CRT AND LIFE INSURANCE FOR WEALTH REPLACEMENT

For an inter vivos CRAT or CRUT, the disenfranchised parties, if any, would be the natural heirs of the donor (usually the donor's children). In such cases, the income tax savings created by the charitable deduction, in real dollar terms, can be used to purchase life insurance which will serve as a wealth replacement asset for the asset which was transferred to the charity.

EXAMPLE 9.23

In the above example, the charitable deduction was $250,754.50 (the remainder interest). Assume that John's marginal total state and federal income tax rate is 40%. The total amount of tax savings is $100,302 ($250,754.50 x 40%). This tax savings could be used to fund a wealth replacement asset (life insurance policy on the donor). Assuming a rate of return of 9% (variable universal life insurance) for a period of 20 years (the assumed table life expectancy for a 65 year old) the cash value ignoring any insurance costs would be $562,132.

NON-TRUST SPLIT INTEREST CHARITABLE GIFTS

The most common forms of split interest charitable gifts are CRATs, CRUTs, and PIFs. An infrequently used split interest technique involves the transfer of a remainder interest in a personal residence or farm. The donor can donate the underlying ownership of the property to a charity, but reserve the right to enjoy the property for the remainder of his life or for a term of years. This is similar to a QPRT, but a charity is the remainder beneficiary instead of a loved one. As with the charitable trusts, the current income tax charitable contribution deduction is equal to the present value of the remainder interest. An added benefit is the removal of the asset (and all of its administrative burdens) from the probate estate of the owner.

The Treasury Regulations give guidance to determine whether property is considered a personal residence or a farm. A personal residence does not have to be the taxpayer's principal residence, but the taxpayer must have used the property as a personal residence (not rental property). Accordingly, a taxpayer's vacation home would qualify as a personal residence, as well as stock owned in a cooperative housing corporation where the taxpayer has a personal residence. Farms include any land (and improvements) used by the taxpayer (or tenant) in producing crops, fruits, other agricultural products, or for raising livestock. When determining the value of the remainder interest of a farm, any depreciation or depletion must be taken into account.

EXAMPLE 9.24

Question: How would appreciation, availability of the personal residence capital gain exclusion, and the health of the donor be factors in deciding to gift a remainder interest in a personal residence to a charity?

Answer: If the Section 7520 interest rate at the date of the transfer is less than the expected appreciation rate, the gift is beneficial. The personal residence capital gain exclusion can be used to offset any capital gain. The donor should be in good health.

Quick Quiz 9.4

Highlight the answer to these questions:

1. Charitable bequests in a will do not produce any income tax benefits.
   a. True
   b. False

2. A pooled income fund is analogous to a mutual fund provided by a charity.
   a. True
   b. False

3. A CRAT provides an annuity to the grantor for a term defined by the grantor.
   a. True
   b. False

4. A CLAT provides an annuity to a charity for a term defined by the grantor.
   a. True
   b. False

True, True, True, True.

CHARITABLE LEAD TRUSTS

Another split interest vehicle available for charitable donors is the **Charitable Lead Trust (CLT)**. The charitable organization receives the income interest during the term of the trust and a noncharitable beneficiary (usually a family member) receives the remainder interest. This vehicle is often used by high net worth individuals who do not need the current income from a particular asset or set of assets. It is most advantageous to fund a charitable lead trust with highly appreciating assets since future appreciation is effectively removed from the estate. The trust is often structured to obtain an income tax deduction equal to the full fair market value of the property transferred while the remainder interest is valued at zero to eliminate any taxable gift. Unlike charitable remainder trusts, charitable lead trusts are not tax exempt entities and not covered under Section 664.

The charitable lead trust, which may take the form of annuity or unitrust (CLAT or CLUT), is an irrevocable trust, and if the grantor (donor) drafts the trust document to treat the trust as a grantor trust then the grantor will receive an income tax deduction at the inception of the trust. However, when the CLT qualifies the grantor for an income tax deduction (referred to as a qualified charitable lead trust), the grantor must subsequently recognize all income of the CLAT or CLUT. If an income tax deduction is desired, the trust must be designed as a grantor trust. The remainderman (noncharitable beneficiary) may either be the donor, in which case the grantor trust status is certain, or another family member (non-spouse) in which case there is a taxable gift equal to the fair market value of the remainder interest. Alternatively, a grantor may create a nonqualified CLT (any CLT which is not considered a grantor trust for income tax purposes), in which case the grantor will not receive a charitable income tax deduction and will not be required to include the income of the CLT on his own tax return. CLATs are particularly appealing in a low interest rate environment, since effectively they increase the value of the income interest which reduces the value of the remainder (taxable) interest.

TESTAMENTARY GIVING TO CHARITIES

As discussed in Chapter 6, a deduction is allowed from the gross estate for bequests to qualified charities. Generally, these are the same charities that qualify for an income tax charitable deduction with the exception of cemeteries. In addition, some foreign charities, which are not eligible for an income tax charitable deduction, are permitted donees for the estate tax charitable transfer deduction.

The methods of charitable transfers at death (testamentary) include the following:
1. A specific bequest or device.
2. A general legacy of a particular percentage or dollar amount of a decedent's gross estate.
3. A residuary bequest.
4. A remainder interest in property - personal residence or farm.
5. A split interest in a charitable trust, income or remainder interest.

Requirements must be met to qualify for the estate tax charitable deduction. First, the bequest must be mandatory. If the decedent qualifies the charitable transfer upon some contingency, an estate tax charitable deduction is disallowed unless the possibility that the transfer will not occur is very remote. Second, the amount of the bequest must be ascertainable at the date of the decedent's death, and the asset must be included in the decedent's gross estate. The courts have disallowed estate tax charitable deductions where the executor was given the power to determine the amount of the contribution. In one case, the executor was given the power to make a bequest to the decedent's household employee, with the remainder going to a charity. The remainder amount was ruled to be uncertain and the estate tax charitable deduction was denied, since the value of the estate tax charitable deduction was dependent upon how much the executor decided to give to the employee.

A transfer to a testamentary trust created for the purpose of providing scholarship funds qualifies as a deductible charitable transfer for the estate tax calculation, however the wording of the trust instrument must be precise. An estate tax charitable deduction was disallowed in a case where the scholarship funds were limited to individuals with the same surname as the decedent. The IRS interpreted the language to be a requirement and disallowed the estate tax charitable deduction. In similar cases, estate tax charitable deductions have been allowed when the surname parameter was explicitly stated as a preference and not a requirement.

Some items are more beneficial (valuable) if given at death, rather than during the donor's life. An example would be a political figure who was contemplating contributing his personal papers to a museum. If he gives the papers during life, his income tax deduction is limited to his adjusted basis, which would be very low. If he waits and transfers his papers by will, the deduction from the gross estate will be the substantially higher (provided the papers appreciated in value) fair market value of the papers. Alternatively, the decedent could bequeath the papers to a noncharitable beneficiary who would then have the increased adjusted basis in the papers due to the "step-to" fair market value. The heir could then donate the papers to charity to receive a substantial income tax deduction.

As discussed in Chapter 2, a disclaimer clause in a will can provide that if an heir disclaims an interest in an asset, the asset will transfer to a specified charity. In such a case, the value of the asset that actually transfers to the charity will qualify for the unlimited estate tax charitable deduction.

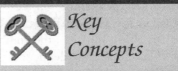

Key Concepts

Underline/highlight the answers to these questions as you read:

1. List the requirements for a testamentary transfer to charity to qualify for the unlimited estate tax charitable deduction.

2. Identify the charitable transfers methods used at death.

3. How often must the value of the assets in a CRUT be determined?

4. Which IRC Section provides the directions to reform a disqualified split interest?

TANGIBLE PROPERTY

As detailed above, when tangible property is donated to a charity and the charity does not use the property for a related use, the charitable deduction is generally equal to the donor's adjusted basis. However, the taxpayer may contractually require the charity to put the donated property to a related use so that the taxpayer is able to deduct the fair market value of the property as opposed to the adjusted basis.

Recall Example 9.10 about the coin collector who donated his valuable coin collection to a museum and was able to deduct the fair market value of the coin collection. If the same contribution had been made to a university, and the donor contractually required the university (donee) to place the coin collection in the library for a period of two years for the purposes of students studying old coins (a related educational use), the deduction would also be equal to the fair market value of the coin collection. However, if the coin collection had been donated to the university so the university could sell the coin collection, the donor's deduction would only be the adjusted basis of the coin collection (the period of two years used in this example is not precise but goes to the facts and circumstances to establish related use).

COMMUNITY PROPERTY

If community property is donated to a charity and the donor, or donors, retain an interest in the property, care must be exercised to avoid unwanted taxable results. For example, a transfer to a charitable remainder trust may be contemplated and funded using community property, but if the trust benefits only one spouse, the donee spouse has made a gift to the other spouse. If separate property is used to fund a trust that benefits both spouses, then a gift has occurred from the donee spouse to the other spouse. While there is no federal gift tax due because of the unlimited marital deduction, there may be a gift tax imposed by certain states that do not have an unlimited marital deduction for state estate tax and/or state inheritance tax.

CHOOSING BETWEEN THE CRAT OR THE CRUT

If the client's primary objective is to maximize the income payments to the noncharitable beneficiaries, a CRUT is generally preferable to a CRAT, particularly if the trust assets are expected to appreciate. However, due to the guaranteed income payment from the CRAT, the

Quick Quiz 9.5

Highlight the answer to these questions:

1. A bequest to a charitable organization based on a contingency is not eligible for the charitable deduction.
   a. True
   b. False

2. A will cannot create a CRAT.
   a. True
   b. False

3. The remainderman of a pooled income fund is the grantor.
   a. True
   b. False

4. Tax-exempt securities are prohibited investments for CRUTs.
   a. True
   b. False

True, False, False, False.

noncharitable beneficiary would receive more from a CRAT than a CRUT if the value of the trust assets decline.

The CRAT has a significant cost advantage over a CRUT holding the same property if the underlying trust assets are not readily marketable and require a qualified annual appraisal. This is because the CRAT only requires one valuation at the funding of the trust and a CRUT requires yearly valuations. Yearly appraisals for property that is not readily marketable can be very expensive.

<table>
<tr><td>**EXAMPLE 9.25**</td><td colspan="2">A 60 year-old individual with property valued at $1,000,000 and with a $0 adjusted basis contributes property to a CRAT retaining a 6% annuity interest. The IRS factor rate for the date of the transfer is 9%.</td></tr>
</table>

$1,000,000	Fair market value
$0	Adjusted basis
6%	Annuity percentage (chosen by donor)
60	Age (single life annuity)
$60,000	Amount of annuity
8.3031	Factor (Table S at 9%) - Based on date of transfer
$498,186	PV of annuity
$501,814	Charitable remainder = FMV of trust - PV of annuity

As calculated here, the donor would receive an annuity of $60,000 (6% of the initial contribution) for the remainder of his life (single life annuity), and in the year of the contribution of the property, a charitable contribution deduction equal to $501,814.

To illustrate the effects of the grantor's choice of annuity, listed below are several annuity options at 7%, 8%, 9%, and 10%, and the corresponding charitable contribution of each.

Assumed Annuity Percentage	6%	7%	8%	9%	10%
	$60,000	$70,000	$80,000	$90,000	$100,000
Factor	8.3031	8.3031	8.3031	8.3031	8.3031
PV of Annuity	$498,186	$581,217	$664,248	$747,279	$830,310
Charitable Deduction	$501,814	$418,783	$335,752	$252,721	$169,690

The alternative to creating the CRAT could have been to sell the property, pay capital gains tax on its appreciation, and then reinvest the proceeds in a commercial annuity (9% for the date of the annuity). The following calculation illustrates this scenario:

$1,000,000		
X	85%	15% Federal Capital Gains Tax
$850,000		
X	9%	Factor Rate at Date of the Annuity
$76,500		Annuity

The individual would receive a $76,500 annuity for the remainder of his life but would not receive any charitable deduction. Contrast this with an 8% CRAT (as detailed above) which pays the individual an $80,000 annuity and allows the individual to take a charitable contribution of $335,752. There may also be a reduction for state tax on capital gains.

REFORMATION OF DISQUALIFIED SPLIT INTERESTS

Unfortunately, advisors who create CRATs, CRUTs, CLATs, and CLUTs do not always fully comply with the specific requirements necessary for a donor to receive a charitable deduction. It also happens that a split gift interest is inadvertently created under certain conditions such as an election to take against the will.

It would be a harsh result indeed if due to a minor drafting flaw, oversight, or unexpected minor noncharitable beneficiary interest, the entire charitable deduction was disallowed. Section 2055(e)(3) of the Code outlines the procedure to correct the error to reduce this harsh treatment. The reformation must be commenced prior to the due date of the estate tax return or the trust's income tax return if no estate tax return is required. The details of the information are beyond the scope of this text.

Key Terms

Capital Gain Property - Property that, when sold, results in either capital gain or Section 1231 gain.

Charitable Lead Trust - A trust in which a charitable organization receives the income interest and a noncharitable beneficiary (usually a family member) receives the remainder interest.

Charitable Remainder Annuity Trusts (CRAT) - A trust that provides a fixed annuity to the donor (usually for life) for an amount that is greater than or equal to 5% of the initial net fair market value of the property contributed to the trust. The remainder interest of the trust passes to a named charitable organization.

Charitable Remainder Unitrust (CRUT) - A trust that provides a payment to the donor (usually for life) equal to a fixed percentage of the trust assets as valued annually. The remainder interest of the trust passes to a named charitable organization.

Ordinary Income Property - Property that, when sold, results in recognition of ordinary income.

Pooled Income Funds (PIF) - Donor contributions are pooled in a trust created and maintained by the charity. Each donor receives an allocable share of the income from the trust for his life.

Private Foundation - A charitable organization that receives its support from a single individual or family. It can be either a private operating foundation or a private nonoperating foundation.

Private Nonoperating Foundation - A charitable organization (private foundation) that does NOT spend at least 85% of its adjusted net income (or minimum investment return, if less) on activities engaged in for the active conduct of the exempt purpose.

Private Operating Foundation - A charitable organization (private foundation) that spends at least 85% of its adjusted net income (or minimum investment return, if less), on activities engaged in for the active conduct of the exempt purpose.

Public Charities - Charitable organizations that receive broad support from the general public.

Sprinkling Provision - The trustee's right to make distributions to the trust beneficiaries at his discretion.

Tangible Property - Property that is not realty and may be touched.

DISCUSSION QUESTIONS

1. What factors must an individual consider before making a charitable gift?

2. Define "charitable organization" as detailed in the Internal Revenue Code.

3. Identify three ways to verify a charitable organization's qualifying status.

4. How does a private operating foundation differ from a private nonoperating foundation?

5. List at least three examples of deductible out-of-pocket expenses related to donating services to a charitable organization.

6. If ordinary income property is contributed to a charitable organization, what is the maximum deductible amount?

7. What does it mean for a charity to be a "50% organization?"

8. List the factors a donee must consider when electing to deduct the adjusted basis of donated property as opposed to electing to deduct the fair market value of the property.

9. If an individual donates property with a fair market value of $750, what information must the donor provide to the IRS and on what tax form is the information provided?

10. Why would a donor request a statement of value from the IRS?

11. If a charitable annuity pays the annuity to the donor, how is the value of the donor's charitable income tax deduction calculated?

12. Under what circumstances may the donor of encumbered property, donated in return for a charitable annuity, avoid recognizing the ordinary income and capital gain associated with the annuity in the year of the transfer?

13. Which charitable trusts provide the donor with an income tax deduction in the year the property is transferred to the trust?

14. Explain how a pooled income fund benefits a donor.

15. How is a Charitable Remainder Annuity Trust (CRAT) less flexible than a Charitable Remainder Unitrust (CRUT)?

16. If an individual donates the underlying ownership interest of his personal residence to a charity, but retains the right to live in the residence for the remainder of his life, how is the donor's charitable deduction calculated?

17. When a donor creates and funds a CLAT under the grantor trust provisions, how is the income of the trust treated for income tax purposes each year?

18. Under what circumstances is a testamentary charitable transfer deductible from a decedent's adjusted gross estate?

19. How may a testamentary charitable transfer be more beneficial to a donor than an inter vivos charitable transfer?

MULTIPLE-CHOICE PROBLEMS

1. Which of the following statements is not true?

    a. A charitable gift during life can reduce estate taxes.

    b. A charitable gift during life can reduce income taxes.

    c. Only a full, outright donation of property will qualify as a deductible charitable contribution.

    d. The donor of a charitable gift may be required to file a gift tax return including the charitable contribution.

2. Which of the following does not qualify as a charitable organization?

    a. The state of Kentucky.

    b. The city of Los Angeles.

    c. A cemetery company organized to maintain cemetery plots in a county.

    d. Republican National Committee.

3. Terrence contributed $15,000 to a foreign charitable organization. At the time of the contribution, the organization told him that his contribution was tax deductible for income tax purposes. Ignoring any income limitations, how much of the $15,000 contribution is deductible?

    a. $0.

    b. $7,500.

    c. $10,000.

    d. $15,000.

4. The Organization to Prevent Cruelty to Animals receives contributions from the general public to fund programs to prevent cruelty to animals. Of its total support during the year, 75% of the funds are from contributions from supporting individuals. What type of charity is The Organization to Prevent Cruelty to Animals?

    a. Public Charity.

    b. Private Foundation.

    c. Private Operating Foundation.

    d. Public Nonoperating Charity.

5. Which of the following statements is not correct?

    a. An organization that spends less than 85% of its adjusted net income on activities engaged in for the active conduct of its exempt purpose is a public charity.

    b. Public charities receive broad support from the general public.

    c. An organization that is not a public charity and spends 90% of its adjusted net income on activities engaged in for the active conduct of its exempt purpose is a private operating foundation.

    d. A public charity can receive up to 33% of its support from its gross investment income and its unrelated business taxable income.

6. Cathy and Mark paid $400 for two tickets to the United Church's annual gala ball. The church determined that the fair market value of each ticket was $100. How much can Cathy and Mark deduct on their income tax return?

    a. $0.

    b. $100.

    c. $200.

    d. $400.

7. Doug graduated from the University of Pittsburgh. Each year, season tickets are sold only to those who make a contribution to the university of $1,000 or more. If Doug contributes $1,000, so that he meets the requirements to purchase season tickets, how much is his deductible contribution for the year?

    a. $0.

    b. $800.

    c. $900.

    d. $1000.

8. Connie cooks and delivers meals for the homeless and the elderly at Thanksgiving. Connie spends $200 on food, she drives 300 miles, and she spends 15 hours of her time (valued at $10/hour) completing the charitable service each year. Of these expenses, how much will Connie deduct on her income tax return for the year?

    a. $0.

    b. $200.

    c. $242.

    d. $392.

9. Chris donated one of his original creation paintings to his alma mater, Backwoods University. His adjusted basis in the artwork was $400 and the fair market value was $150. Chris also contributed 100 shares of XYZ corporation that had an adjusted basis of $50 and a fair market value equal to $1,000 (held long-term). Ignoring the AGI limitations, what is the maximum amount Chris can deduct in relation to these donations?

    a. $200.
    b. $1,150.
    c. $1,300.
    d. $1,400.

10. Maggie contributed $10,000 to a private nonoperating foundation that has never made any distributions. Maggie also contributed $15,000 to a private operating foundation. Maggie's AGI for the tax year was $100,000. What is Maggie's charitable contribution deduction for the year?

    a. $10,500.
    b. $25,000.
    c. $50,000.
    d. $100,000.

11. Which of the following is not an issue when considering whether to deduct the adjusted basis or the fair market value of contributed property?

    a. The current market rate of interest.
    b. The donor's current and projected adjusted gross income for the 5 years after the contribution.
    c. The fair market value of the donated property.
    d. The capital gains rate in effect at the time of the transfer.

12. Robin contributed $100 to the United Way and $300 to the Church of Good People. Which of the following statements concerning her contribution to the charitable organizations is correct?

    a. Robin must file IRS Form 8283.
    b. Both the United Way and the Church of Good People are required to send a confirmation of the contribution to Robin.
    c. Only the United Way is required to send a confirmation of the contribution to Robin.
    d. Only the Church of Good People is required to send a confirmation of the contribution to Robin.

13. Which of the following contributions would require the taxpayer to obtain a statement of value from the IRS?

    a. The taxpayer is never required to obtain a statement of value.

    b. Taxpayer donates art work valued at $150,000 to a private nonoperating foundation.

    c. Taxpayer donates art work valued at $10,000 to a public charity.

    d. Taxpayer donates art work valued at $15,000 to a public charity.

14. Denis sold a parcel of land to a qualified charitable organization for $10,000. The parcel of land had a fair market value of $100,000 and an adjusted basis of $50,000. What taxable gain must Denis recognize at the time of the contribution?

    a. $0.

    b. $5,000.

    c. $50,000.

    d. $90,000.

15. Michael transfers $100,000 of stock to a charitable organization in return for a life annuity on his life valued at $43,000. With regards to this transfer, how much is Michael's charitable deduction?

    a. $0.

    b. $43,000.

    c. $57,000.

    d. $100,000.

16. Which of the following statements regarding life insurance is true?

    a. When an individual designates a charitable organization as the beneficiary of his life insurance policy, the individual can deduct the face value of the policy as a charitable contribution on his income tax return.

    b. If an individual designates a charitable organization as the beneficiary of his life insurance policy, but retains the right to change the beneficiary designation, the death proceeds of the life insurance policy will be included in his gross estate.

    c. If an individual designates a charitable organization as the beneficiary of his life insurance policy, and then dies without changing the beneficiary designation, the death proceeds of the life insurance policy will be included in his taxable estate.

    d. Transferring ownership of a life insurance policy to a charitable organization does not qualify for an income tax charitable deduction.

17. Four years ago, Walter created a charitable remainder trust with himself as the income beneficiary and a charity as the remainder beneficiary. In the current year, Walter would like to make an additional contribution to the trust. Which of the following charitable trusts would allow Walter to make an additional contribution during the year?

    a. CRAT.

    b. CRUT.

    c. CRET.

    d. CRIT.

18. Gillian transfers property to a revocable trust naming herself as the income beneficiary and the United Way as the remainder beneficiary. What type of trust has Gillian created?

    a. Revocable living trust.

    b. CRAT.

    c. CRUT.

    d. Pooled income fund.

19. Todd irrevocably transfers property to a trust over which he retains an annuity payment each year equal to 6% of the initial fair market value of the property transferred to the trust. Todd designates the United Way as the remainder beneficiary. Which of the following statements concerning this transfer is true?

    a. Todd can make an additional contribution to the trust in subsequent years.

    b. Todd must inform the United Way of their right to the remainder of the trust's assets.

    c. Todd will receive an income tax charitable deduction on his income tax return for the year in which the trust is formed.

    d. The United Way can force Todd to transfer the present value of their interest to them immediately.

20. Which of the following statements concerning a pooled income fund is correct?

    a. A pooled income fund is created for each individual.

    b. The pooled income fund is managed by its contributors.

    c. Pooled income funds invest strictly in tax-exempt securities.

    d. The income of a pooled income fund is paid to the contributors.

Quick Quiz Explanations

Quick Quiz 9.1

1. False. Gifts made to public charities, regardless of size, do not require the filing of a gift tax return.
2. True.
3. False. Public charities are often organized to benefit specific causes or beneficiary classes. Charities are classified as public charities based on their source of funding, not their charitable objectives.

Quick Quiz 9.2

1. False. When a product is donated, the lower of the donor's adjusted basis or the fair market value of the property is allowed as a deduction. While the value of services donated to a charity are not deductible, any costs incurred in performing those services (such as the cost of uniforms, mileage expenses, parking fees, and the like) that are not reimbursed may be claimed as a charitable deduction.
2. False. Gifts of services provide great value to charitable organizations, but do not qualify the donor for a tax deduction.
3. False. In some cases, electing to deduct cost basis may be more advantageous to a taxpayer. Since the value of gifts to charities may only be carried forward five years under the deduction limitations, when a donor has low income relative to the size of the gift, electing to deduct cost basis and moving to the 50% deduction limitation may maximize tax benefits. (See Examples 9.14 and 9.15)
4. False. The taxpayer has the burden of proving the value of the deduction for tax purposes.

Quick Quiz 9.3

1. True.
2. True.
3. True.

Quick Quiz 9.4

1. True.
2. True.
3. True.
4. True.

Quick Quiz 9.5

1. True.
2. False. Charitable Remainder Trusts (CRTs), in the form of CRATs and CRUTs, may be created during life or on a testamentary basis (by instructing the executor of the estate to create the trust after the testator's death).
3. False. The remainderman of a Pooled Income Fund (PIF) is the charity that sponsors and manages the fund. The grantor is only entitled to a pro-rata portion of the income generated by the pool of assets during his or her life.
4. False. Tax-exempt securities are permissible investments for CRTs. PIFs, however, may not invest in tax exempt securities.

The Unlimited Marital Deduction

THE MARITAL DEDUCTION DEFINED

THE SINGLE ECONOMIC UNIT

Historically, the amount of property that an individual could leave to his spouse without transfer tax consequences was limited. Prior to 1981, for example, only one-half of a deceased spouse's estate could qualify for the marital deduction.

Under current law, an individual is permitted to leave an unlimited amount of property to his spouse at his death without incurring any estate tax. This approach is consistent with the gift tax rules, which allow an individual to make outright lifetime gifts of an unlimited amount of property to a spouse without paying any gift taxes. The theory behind the **unlimited marital deduction** is that a married couple should be treated as a single economic unit for estate tax purposes. To the extent that property is consumed by either spouse during their lifetime, it should not be subject to gift or estate tax. Only the property owned by either spouse that remains after the death of the surviving spouse (or, in the eyes of the law, the termination of the economic unit), and that passes to some other party, should be subject to estate tax. Therefore, property that passes from one spouse to another is usually not subject to estate tax at the death of the first spouse, but if the surviving spouse does not consume the property before his or her death, the property will be subject to estate tax in the surviving spouse's estate.

BENEFITS OF THE UNLIMITED MARITAL DEDUCTION

1. Defers estate taxes until the death of the surviving spouse.
2. May fund the applicable estate tax credit of the surviving spouse.
3. Ensures the surviving spouse has sufficient assets to support his lifestyle.

ADVANTAGES OF THE UNLIMITED MARITAL DEDUCTION

Use of the unlimited marital deduction can result in several benefits. First, using the marital deduction defers the payment of estate tax until the death of the surviving spouse. In some high-net worth planning situations, it may make sense to incur estate tax at the first death to increase the total tax savings for the family, but the temporary repeal of the estate tax under EGTRRA 2001 actually encourages deferral.

EXAMPLE 10.1

An elderly, married individual dies in early 2009 when the applicable estate tax credit equivalency is $3,500,000. The combined estate of the decedent and his surviving spouse is $7,000,000 (for purposes of this example, all assets are in the name of the decedent), and the surviving spouse is expected to die before 2010. If the decedent transfers $3,500,000 to a bypass trust (B Trust) at his death, and leaves $3,500,000 to his surviving spouse, use of the marital deduction will result in lower taxes for the family. As the applicable estate tax credit equivalency rises to $3,500,000 in 2009, followed by the temporary repeal of the estate tax in 2010, what would have otherwise been a taxable joint estate may escape estate taxation altogether by deferring estate tax currently and taking advantage of the applicable estate tax credit.

A second advantage of the unlimited marital deduction is an opportunity to fund the applicable estate or gift tax credit of the surviving spouse. When one spouse is wealthy, and the other is not (the term wealthy, as used here, implies that a person has sufficient assets to fully use the applicable credit amount), assets can be transferred to the surviving spouse during life or upon the death of the wealthy spouse, so that the non-wealthy spouse can make full use of his/her own applicable estate or gift tax credit. This benefit is also illustrated in the example above. Since the surviving spouse had no assets, the applicable estate tax credit belonging to the second spouse would have been wasted if the decedent had not transferred sufficient property to the surviving spouse so that she could fully utilize the credit. Finally, and probably most importantly, the use of the marital deduction to transfer assets to the surviving spouse helps ensure that the surviving spouse will have sufficient assets to maintain his lifestyle after the death of the first spouse.

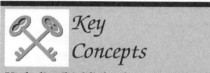

Key Concepts

Underline/highlight the answers to these questions as you read:

1. Identify the advantages of the unlimited marital deduction.

2. List the requirements of the unlimited marital deduction.

3. What are the consequences of utilizing the unlimited marital deduction for the first-to-die spouse?

REQUIREMENTS OF THE UNLIMITED MARITAL DEDUCTION

In order to claim a marital deduction, the decedent must have been married as of the date of his death and the surviving spouse must receive property through the estate. As such, property left to a divorced spouse will not qualify for the marital deduction. If, however, the couple is separated but not yet divorced, property passing to the separated spouse will qualify for the unlimited marital deduction.

LIMITATIONS OF THE UNLIMITED MARITAL DEDUCTION

To prevent abuse, the unlimited marital deduction is limited in two ways: (1) the property passing to the spouse must qualify for the marital deduction, and (2) only the net value of qualifying property that is left to a surviving spouse can be included as the marital deduction. These qualification rules are discussed below. The term "net value" for marital deduction purposes equals the gross value of the qualifying property left to the surviving spouse less any taxes, debts, or estate administration expenses payable out of the spousal interest. If an individual gives his executor the authority to pay expenses and taxes out of the marital share, the marital deduction must be reduced by that amount even if the executor chooses not to use the marital share to pay for those expenses. The purpose of this rule is to prevent individuals who allocate taxes, debts, and administration expenses to the marital share from qualifying for the marital deduction for the taxes, debts, and expenses they incurred during lifetime or during the administration of their estate.

Quick Quiz 10.1

Highlight the answer to these questions:

1. Unless the inherited property has been consumed, a second-to-die spouse must include the property in his gross estate if the first-to-die spouse elected the marital deduction on the property.
   a. True
   b. False

2. Transfers to a divorced spouse qualify for the unlimited marital deduction. The only requirement is that the individuals were married within the last three years.
   a. True
   b. False

3. Use of the marital deduction will defer the payment of estate tax on property transferred to the surviving spouse until the surviving spouse's death.
   a. True
   b. False

True, False, True.

EXAMPLE 10.2

Derek died in 2009 with an estate valued at $4,500,000. Derek's will creates a credit shelter trust at his death and leaves all of his property in excess of the applicable estate tax credit equivalency amount to his wife, Cheryl. The apportionment clause in the will allocates all debts to the marital share. Derek's debts were $250,000. The first $3,500,000 in Derek's estate will pass to the credit shelter trust, leaving only $1,000,000 for Cheryl. Since debts must be paid out of the property passing to Cheryl, Derek's estate will qualify for a marital deduction of $750,000 ($1,000,000 spousal share less $250,000 of debts equals the net value of qualifying property left to the surviving spouse).

Note that the marital deduction does not avoid estate taxes; it merely postpones them. If a transfer of property to a surviving spouse qualifies for the marital deduction, the value of that property will be included in the surviving spouse's gross estate if the property has not been ultimately consumed by the surviving spouse. While the marital deduction may look enticing, care should be exercised in planning to prevent over-utilization of the marital deduction and an increase in the total estate taxes paid by a married couple.

If property is not transferred to the surviving spouse outright, special qualification rules must be met for such property to qualify for the marital deduction. There are primarily three ways to leave property to a spouse and qualify for the marital deduction. These three ways are summarized in the following chart and are discussed throughout this chapter:

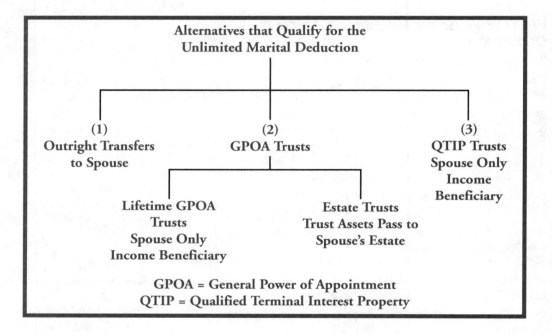

QUALIFICATION FOR THE MARITAL DEDUCTION

For a transfer to qualify for the estate tax marital deduction, the property interest must meet three requirements. First, the property must be included in the decedent's gross estate. Second, the property must be transferred to the surviving spouse. Third, the interest must not be a terminable interest unless it meets one of the exceptions to the terminable interest rule.

If the surviving spouse is not a U.S. citizen, additional requirements must be met in order to qualify for the unlimited marital deduction. The special rules that apply to noncitizen spouses will be addressed later in this chapter.

INCLUSION IN THE DECEDENT'S GROSS ESTATE

A general principal of taxation is that an individual cannot deduct something that is not first brought into the tax base. For example, an attorney who volunteers legal services to a charity cannot take a charitable deduction for the value of his time because he never reported the value of his time as taxable income. Likewise, if property is not included in the gross estate of the decedent, the decedent will not be permitted to deduct the value of that property from the gross estate as a marital deduction.

Key Concepts

Underline/highlight the answers to these questions as you read:

1. Identify the property transfers that qualify for the unlimited marital deduction.

2. What is the terminable interest rule and what is its impact on the marital deduction?

3. Identify the rules related to the survivorship clause and the time allowed to qualify the property transferred for the unlimited marital deduction.

EXAMPLE 10.3

Sal and Norma were married for 51 years when Sal died. Many years ago, Norma purchased a life insurance policy on Sal's life. Norma was the named owner and beneficiary of the policy, and made all of the premium payments. Upon Sal's death, Norma collected the $1,000,000 death benefit from the insurance company. Sal's estate will not be entitled to a marital deduction for the $1,000,000 of insurance proceeds because the insurance proceeds were not included in his gross estate as the policy was owned by Norma.

EXAMPLE 10.4

Assume the same scenario as above, except that Sal created and funded an Irrevocable Life Insurance Trust (ILIT) that purchased a policy on his life. The ILIT was properly drafted and administered, and, as a result, the death benefit received by the ILIT was not included in Sal's gross estate. Even though Norma is the primary beneficiary of the ILIT and will receive all of the trust income for the rest of her life under the terms of the trust, the death benefit will not qualify for the marital deduction since it was not included in Sal's gross estate.

PROPERTY TRANSFERRED TO A SURVIVING SPOUSE

In order to qualify for the unlimited marital deduction, the property must pass from the decedent to, and for the benefit of, the surviving spouse. If the property passes from someone other than the decedent to the surviving spouse, or if the property passed by the decedent goes to someone who is not his surviving spouse, the marital deduction will not be available. If the decedent leaves property to his surviving spouse as trustee for some other individual, the surviving spouse does not have a beneficial interest in the property and the transfer will not qualify for the marital deduction.

| EXAMPLE 10.5 | George died last month, leaving behind his wife, Laura, and two minor children. George's will creates a credit shelter trust for the benefit of his two minor children, and names Laura as the trustee of the trust. While Laura has legal title to the property inside the trust, she does not have beneficial title to the property, and therefore the money and property passing to the credit shelter trust do not qualify for the unlimited marital deduction. |

Generally, property that is included in the decedent's gross estate and is transferred to the surviving spouse by any means will meet the "transferred to" requirement for the marital deduction, even if the decedent is not the person transferring the property.

| EXAMPLE 10.6 | Shortly before his death, Henry was estranged but not divorced from his wife, Eleanor. Henry wrote a will leaving all of his property to his children, Richard, John, and Jeffrey, including specific language disinheriting Eleanor. After Henry's death, Eleanor elected against his will, and was awarded one-half of Henry's estate, which represented her "elective" or "statutory" share. Despite the fact that Henry tried to disinherit Eleanor, property in his gross estate passes to his surviving spouse, and therefore the property included in the gross estate that passes to Eleanor qualifies for the marital deduction. |

| EXAMPLE 10.7 | Charlie owned a beach house that he transferred to his wife, Jane, retaining the right to use the home for the rest of his life. Charlie recently died, and the full fair market value of the beach home was included in his gross estate since he had retained the right to use the property. Since Jane received the house, the fair market value of the house qualifies for the marital deduction. |

EXAMPLE 10.8

Lewis gave his son, David, a general power of appointment over farmland located in Long Island, New York. The power of appointment states that David can appoint the property to anyone he wishes, including himself, either during lifetime or at death. In the event that David does not exercise the power, the property will be transferred to David's spouse or, if David's spouse predeceases him, to David's children, per stirpes. David died last month and had never exercised the power during lifetime or through his will. Since David had a general power of appointment over the property the full fair market value of the property is required to be included in David's estate. Since the property is transferred to David's spouse at death, the value of the property qualifies for the unlimited marital deduction.

EXAMPLE 10.9

Ed wrote his will at the height of the last bull market cycle. Since he was feeling wealthy and generous, he decided to leave $3,000,000 of his $6,000,000 estate directly to his children, with the remainder to his wife, Peggy. After the will was written, the stock market crashed and when Ed died last month, his estate was only worth $2,900,000. As a result, under the terms of the will, Ed's children will receive the entire estate and Peggy will receive nothing. The children decide to disclaim $2,000,000 of the property that would pass to them so that it will pass under the terms of the will to Peggy. The $2,000,000 disclaimed by the children qualifies for the unlimited marital deduction.

THE TERMINABLE INTEREST RULE

The **terminable interest rule** is based on the premise that a marital deduction should only be permitted when property passing from the decedent spouse to a surviving spouse will be included in the surviving spouse's gross estate. The current unlimited marital deduction allows individuals to defer estate tax at the death of the first-to-die spouse but not avoid it entirely. As a general rule, any property left by a decedent directly to his surviving spouse that is held until the surviving spouse's death is included in the surviving spouse's gross estate.

There are situations, however, where property left to the surviving spouse will not be included in the surviving spouse's gross estate. For example, if the decedent leaves property in trust for the benefit of the surviving spouse, and the trust gives the spouse the right to receive all income, the right to receive distributions for health, education, maintenance, and support, and the right to demand the greater of $5,000 or five percent of the trust corpus each year, the spouse will not have a sufficient ownership interest in the property to require an inclusion in her estate. The terminable interest rule is designed to prevent the use of the unlimited marital deduction in circumstances where the surviving spouse will not have to include in his gross estate the value of property passing from the deceased spouse.

Terminable Interest Defined

A terminable interest is any interest in property passing from a decedent to his surviving spouse where the surviving spouse's interest in that property will terminate at some point in the future. To be classified as a terminable interest, it does not matter how the interest terminates – whether by passage of time or upon the occurrence or non-occurrence of some contingency. All that matters is that the interest will terminate. If a contingency is attached to property resulting in a termination of the surviving spouse's interest, it will be considered a terminable interest if the contingency might occur.

EXAMPLE 10.10	Jennifer, a famous musician, recently passed away leaving all of her property to her husband, Eric. In addition to Jennifer's tangible personal property, Eric inherited ownership of the copyrights on Jennifer's musical compositions. Copyrights protect property for a limited period of time, and, therefore, expire with the passage of time. The copyrights that Jennifer left to Eric are terminable interest property (but see Example 10.13).
EXAMPLE 10.11	Ken recently died. Ten years before his death, he retired from his tenured faculty position at Home State University. Home State University's benefit package included a pension plan that provided a lifetime income for Ken, and a 50% survivor annuity for his wife, Liz, should Ken die before her. Liz is now entitled to receive 50% of the retirement income that Ken was receiving before his death for the rest of her life. Because the survivor annuity will terminate upon Liz's death, the annuity interest that Liz received from Ken's estate is a terminable interest (but see Example 10.14).
EXAMPLE 10.12	Steve's will left his condo to his wife, subject to the condition that if his wife does not survive his sister, his sister will get the property. At the time of Steve's death, his sister had terminal cancer with two weeks to live, and his wife was very healthy. Shortly after Steve's death, his sister passed away. Despite the fact that it was unlikely that Steve's wife would predecease his sister, it was possible that his wife would predecease his sister, and therefore the bequest of the condo, subject to the survival contingency, is a terminable interest.

The Terminable Interest Rule and the Unlimited Marital Deduction

A terminable interest, alone, will not prevent the use of the unlimited marital deduction for the transfer. The marital deduction will not be available if the following three criteria are met:

1. a terminable interest is transferred to a surviving spouse, **and**
2. another interest in the same property passes from the decedent to someone other than the surviving spouse (a third party) for less than full and adequate consideration in money or money's worth, **and**
3. the third party may possess or use any part of the property after the interest of the surviving spouse terminates.

Recall the facts from the Jennifer and Eric example (Example 10.10), above. When Jennifer died, she left all of her property to Eric. While the copyrights to her musical compositions were terminable interests, no person other than Eric had any interest in the property, since all rights under the copyrights were given to Eric. If Eric dies before the copyrights expire, the value of the copyrights will be included in his gross estate. Consequently, the transfer of the copyrights to Eric will qualify for the unlimited marital deduction.

EXAMPLE 10.13

Recall the facts from the Ken and Liz example (Example 10.11), above. When Ken died, Liz received an annuity that paid 50% of Ken's pension benefit to her for the rest of her life. As noted above, the annuity Liz received was a terminable interest. Since no one other than Liz has an interest in the annuity and since no person can possess any part of the property after Liz's interest expires (since the annuity payments terminate at Liz's death), the full value of the annuity Liz receives will qualify for the unlimited marital deduction.

EXAMPLE 10.14

Andy's will gave his wife the right to use his beach house for life, and stated that the beach house would be transferred to his children at her death. The transfer to Andy's wife is a terminable interest. Andy's children received an interest in the property (remainder interest) that allows them to possess or use the property after the surviving spouse's death. Consequently, the value of the transfer to the surviving spouse (the right to use the property for the rest of her life) is a terminable interest that will not qualify for the unlimited marital deduction.

EXAMPLE 10.15

Andy gave his beach house to his children, subject to the condition that he and his wife could use the house for the rest of their lives. When Andy died, the full fair market value of the house was included in his estate. Andy's wife still has the right to use the house for the rest of her life,

EXAMPLE 10.16

which has been valued at 40% of the value of the house. Since Andy's children received an interest in the property that allows them to possess or use the property after his wife's death, the value of the life estate given to Andy's wife does not qualify for the unlimited marital deduction.

EXAMPLE 10.17

Assume the same facts as above, except that Andy sold, at fair market value, the remainder interest in his beach house to his children, subject to the condition that he and his wife could use the beach house for the remainder of their lives. At Andy's death, the full fair market value of the house is included in his estate due to the retained interest. Because his children paid for their remainder interest in the house, the terminable interest given to his wife will qualify for the unlimited marital deduction since the children did not receive their interest for less than full or fair consideration.

The terminable interest rule has one additional caveat. If the deceased spouse's will directs his executor to use property included in the gross estate to purchase terminable interest property for the surviving spouse, the unlimited marital deduction is not available for that property.

EXAMPLE 10.18

Fred and Betty have been married for 40 years. Fred has always taken care of the family finances, and was not sure if Betty would be able to handle them if he died first. Fred included a provision in his will directing his executor to purchase a life annuity for Betty so that she would not run out of money during her lifetime. The value of the annuity that is transferred to Betty through Fred's estate is a terminable interest that does not qualify for the unlimited marital deduction.

EXAMPLE 10.19

Assume the same facts as above, except that, instead of having his executor purchase an annuity after his death, Fred purchases a deferred annuity contract naming Betty as the beneficiary. When Fred dies, Betty will receive an income stream for life. The value of the annuity is included in Fred's gross estate, it is a terminable interest (it will end at Betty's death), and it will qualify for the unlimited marital deduction because no one other than the surviving spouse received an interest in the annuity for less than adequate consideration allowing them to enjoy the property after Betty's interest expires.

Exceptions to the Terminable Interest Rule

The terminable interest rule prevents terminable interest transfers to the surviving spouse from qualifying for the marital deduction when another party receives an interest in (usually ownership of the property after the surviving spouse's death) the same property for less than adequate consideration. There are, however, several exceptions to the terminable interest rule. The exceptions include:

1. A survival contingency of no more than six months.
2. A terminable interest, either outright or in trust, over which the surviving spouse has a general power of appointment.
3. A Qualified Terminable Interest Property (QTIP) Trust.
4. A Charitable Remainder Trust (CRT) where a spouse is the only noncharitable beneficiary.

In planning large estates, contingency clauses are often used to ensure that the combined estates of a married couple make full use of their available applicable estate tax credits and to provide for the orderly disposition of the client's wealth.

Survivorship Clause

As discussed in Chapter 2, a **survivorship clause** included in a will creates a terminable interest. In such a situation, if the surviving spouse does not survive for the stated number of months, his interest terminates. Recall that in classifying a terminable interest, there only has to be the possibility that the interest passing to the surviving spouse will terminate – certainty is not required.

Quick Quiz 10.2

Highlight the answer to these questions:

1. A transfer to a surviving spouse as trustee of a trust for the benefit of her children will qualify for the unlimited marital deduction.
   a. True
   b. False

2. A terminable interest is any interest in property passing from the decedent to his surviving spouse where the surviving spouse's interest in that property will terminate at some point in the future.
   a. True
   b. False

3. Only a terminable interest that terminates at a certain period of time will qualify for the marital deduction.
   a. True
   b. False

4. A terminable interest in a general power of appointment trust will qualify for the unlimited marital deduction.
   a. True
   b. False

False, True, False, True.

While a survivorship clause creates a terminable interest that under the general rules would not qualify for the unlimited marital deduction, an important exception applies. Provided that (1) the survivorship clause does not require the surviving spouse to survive for more than six months after the decedent's death, and (2) the surviving spouse actually does survive the stated period, the transfer of property to the surviving spouse will qualify for the marital deduction. If the survival clause requires the spouse to survive for a period of more than six months after the decedent's death to inherit under the will, any transfers subject to the survival clause that pass to the surviving spouse will not qualify for the unlimited marital deduction.

EXAMPLE 10.20

Gary's will creates a credit shelter trust at his death and directs his executor to fund the credit shelter trust with the maximum amount that can be transferred without increasing his federal estate tax liability. The remainder of Gary's gross estate is left to his wife provided that she survives him for five months, and, if she does not survive him, the property is transferred to The Gary Foundation. While the survival contingency creates the possibility of a terminable interest, it is not longer than six months, and therefore, if the property actually transfers to his wife, the bequest to Gary's wife qualifies for the marital deduction.

EXAMPLE 10.21

Wally's will leaves all of his property to his wife if she survives him for nine months, and if she does not survive him, the property is transferred to his children, per stirpes. Since Wally's will creates the possibility of a terminable interest for his spouse and the survival contingency is more than six months, the transfer to his spouse will not qualify for the marital deduction. Even if Wally's wife survives him by nine months and takes all of the property, the marital deduction will not apply.

Quick Quiz 10.3

Highlight the answer to these questions:

1. If the deceased spouse's will directs his executor to use property in the estate to purchase an annuity for the surviving spouse, the unlimited marital deduction is not available for that property.
   a. True
   b. False

2. If a will includes a survival contingency longer than 6 months, the unlimited marital deduction will not apply to the transfer.
   a. True
   b. False

3. If a survival clause requires the surviving spouse to outlive the decedent by more than 8 months, the property will not qualify for the marital deduction, even if the surviving spouse lives for 20 years after the death of the decedent.
   a. True
   b. False

True, True, True.

General Power of Appointment (GPOA)

The second exception to the terminable interest rule deals with terminable interests coupled with the surviving spouse having a general power of appointment. Once the surviving spouse has a general power of appointment over the property, the property will be included in the surviving spouse's gross estate under IRC Section 2042. Therefore, even though a terminable interest is created, the inclusion in the surviving spouse's gross estate due to the general power of appointment will allow the transfer to qualify for the marital deduction in the first spouse's gross estate. Typically, these transfers are completed by use of trust vehicles. The use of General Power of Appointment Trusts is discussed later in this chapter.

Qualified Terminable Interest Property (QTIP) Trust

The third exception to the terminable interest rule involves the use of a Qualified Terminable Interest Property Trust (QTIP Trust), which is discussed later in this chapter.

Charitable Remainder Trust (CRT)

The fourth exception to the terminable interest rule applies when a spouse is named as the only noncharitable income beneficiary of a Charitable Remainder Trust (CRT). (A full discussion of CRTs is included in Chapter 9.)

A Charitable Remainder Trust is structured to provide an income stream from the trust to the grantor or the grantor's designee, followed by a transfer of the remainder interest in the trust to a qualified charity when the income interest expires. The income stream can be structured as either an annuity interest or a unitrust interest. An annuity interest is a right to receive a fixed percentage of the initial contribution to the trust for the entire term of the income interest. Charitable Remainder Trusts that create an income stream in the form of an annuity are referred to as Charitable Remainder Annuity Trusts (CRATs).

John created a Charitable Remainder Annuity Trust (CRAT), naming his wife, Patty, as the income beneficiary for her lifetime, and the McFadden Foundation, a qualified charity, as the remainder beneficiary. John funded the CRAT with $1,000,000 in highly appreciated stock, and set the income payout rate at 5%. Each year until her death, Patty will receive $50,000 from the CRAT. When Patty dies, the trust will terminate and the remaining principal will be distributed to The McFadden Foundation. Note that John did not incur any gift tax in forming the CRAT, since he gave the income interest to his spouse, which qualifies for the gift tax marital deduction. The remainder interest that passes to the charity will qualify for the gift tax charitable deduction.

A unitrust interest is created by granting the income beneficiary a right to receive an income stream equal to a fixed percentage of the value of the trust assets as determined each year. When a unitrust income stream is used, the CRT is referred to as a Charitable Remainder Unitrust (CRUT).

Randy created a Charitable Remainder Unitrust (CRUT) naming his wife, Kelly, as the income beneficiary for her lifetime, and The Jarvis Foundation, a qualified charity, as the remainder beneficiary. Randy funded the CRUT with $1,000,000 in highly appreciated stock, and set the income payout rate at 5%. In the first year of the trust's existence, Kelly will receive $50,000 from the CRUT ($1,000,000 x 5%). If, in year two, the value of the trust assets rises to $1,100,000, Kelly will receive an income distribution of $55,000 ($1,100,000 x 5%). If, in year three, the value of the trust assets falls to $950,000, Kelly will receive an income distribution of $47,500 ($950,000 x 5%). When Kelly dies, the trust will terminate and the remaining principal will be distributed to The Jarvis Foundation. Note that

Randy did not incur any gift tax in forming the CRUT, since he gave the income interest to his spouse, which qualifies for the gift tax marital deduction. The remainder interest that passes to the charity will qualify for the gift tax charitable deduction.

In both of the examples above, the grantor of the CRT created an interest for his spouse during his lifetime. It is also possible to create a testamentary CRT by placing instructions in a will directing the executor of the estate to create and fund a CRT at the grantor's death. The spouse can be named as the income beneficiary of this testamentary CRT as well, but if the spouse is named as beneficiary of a testamentary CRT, a terminable interest is created since the spouse will only receive the income interest and, after the spouse's interest expires, a charity receives the remainder interest. Without a special exception to the marital deduction rules, the ability to treat the property as qualified terminable interest property would not be available to qualify the spouse's interest for the marital deduction since the CRT will only pay an annuity or unitrust amount, which is not the same as the requirement of distributing all income to the spouse when the QTIP election is made (discussed below). Congress recognized that some individuals might want to use a CRT in their estate plan to benefit both their surviving spouse and a charity, so they enacted a special provision in the IRC Section 2056 stating that when a spouse is named as the only noncharitable income beneficiary of a charitable remainder trust, despite the fact that the CRT income interest is a terminable interest, it will qualify for the marital deduction.

The CRT exception is consistent with the theory underlying the marital deduction and the terminable interest rule. Recall that the terminable interest rule was enacted to ensure that the property passing to the surviving spouse would be subject to tax either in the estate of the first-to-die spouse or in the estate of the surviving spouse. If a CRT is created, the remainder interest in the trust is permanently set aside for a qualified charity. As such, the remainder interest would not be taxed in either estate under normal estate tax principles since it qualifies for the charitable deduction. While the spouse will receive a terminable interest in the trust, the fact that a charity receives an interest in the trust after the spouse's term expires exempts the remaining value from estate tax. Therefore, allowing an income interest in a CRT to qualify for the marital deduction is consistent with the philosophy of treating the two spouses as a single economic unit, and allows property to pass to qualified charities without estate tax consequences.

OUTRIGHT BEQUESTS TO THE SPOUSE

The simplest way to qualify the transfer of property for the unlimited marital deduction is to transfer property directly to the surviving spouse. Many individuals prefer this method, since the surviving spouse has complete control over the property during his lifetime. To the extent that the surviving spouse does not consume the property received from the decedent, that property will be included and taxed in the surviving spouse's gross estate. Therefore, all outright transfers of property to the surviving spouse will qualify for the estate tax marital deduction. Standard "I Love You" wills make direct transfers of all of the decedent's property to his surviving spouse. In addition, any property which is jointly titled between the decedent and his spouse with a survivorship feature will, upon transfer to the surviving spouse, qualify for the unlimited marital deduction.

LIMITING A DIRECT TRANSFER

While an outright transfer to the surviving spouse is simple and provides the surviving spouse with complete control over the property, it may be more appropriate to limit the surviving spouse's control over the property through the use of a trust. In situations where the surviving spouse is not capable of managing assets or may need protection from current and future creditors, a transfer in trust should be considered. Furthermore, if the deceased spouse would like to protect his property for his children and is concerned that the surviving spouse may remarry (making his assets available to the surviving spouse's new husband or wife), a trust may be preferred. Once a transfer to the surviving spouse is accomplished through the use of a trust, a terminable interest results, potentially disqualifying the transfer for the marital deduction. There are two types of trusts, General Power of Appointment Trusts and QTIP Trusts, which can be created to protect property for a decedent's heirs and still qualify for the unlimited marital deduction. These trusts are addressed below.

GENERAL POWER OF APPOINTMENT (GPOA) TRUSTS

A **General Power of Appointment (GPOA) Trust**, also known as an "A Trust," creates a terminable interest for a surviving spouse that will nevertheless require the unconsumed assets to be included in the surviving spouse's gross estate and thus qualify the transfer of the property to the trust for the unlimited marital deduction.

QUALIFYING A GPOA TRUST FOR THE MARITAL DEDUCTION

To qualify for the marital deduction, the trust must grant to the surviving spouse a power to appoint the trust property to himself, his estate, his creditors, or the creditors of his estate. Possession of one or more of these rights requires the fair market value of the trust assets to be included in the surviving spouse's gross estate. Note that it is not necessary to give the surviving spouse the right to appoint the property to all of these individuals or entities – the right to appoint the property to one of them is sufficient. The power of appointment can be exercisable during the surviving spouse's lifetime, or only at the surviving spouse's death, or both during the surviving spouse's lifetime and at his death. Any such trust must meet the following additional requirements to qualify for the unlimited marital deduction:

1. The surviving spouse, and only the spouse, must be entitled to receive all of the income from the trust at least annually;
2. The general power of appointment granted to the surviving spouse must be exercisable by the surviving spouse alone; and
3. No person other than the surviving spouse may appoint any part of the property to anyone other than the surviving spouse during the life of the surviving spouse.

> **EXAMPLE 10.24**
>
> Lee died last month. His will created a credit shelter trust to hold that portion of his gross estate that could be transferred without increasing his federal estate tax liability, and a trust for the benefit of his wife, Betty, to hold the remaining assets in his gross estate. The trust for Betty states that she is entitled to receive all of the income from the trust on a quarterly basis and that Betty has the right to appoint the principal of

the trust during her lifetime or at her death to any of Betty and Lee's heirs or to her estate. In addition, Lee gave his brother a power of appointment over Betty's trust, allowing him to appoint the principal of the trust to Betty and Lee's issue solely to cover educational expenses. Since someone other than the surviving spouse can appoint property to someone other than the surviving spouse, the transfer in trust for Betty will not qualify for the unlimited marital deduction.

Estate Trusts

A general power of appointment trust that only grants the surviving spouse the power to appoint the property to his estate is referred to as an **estate trust**. Unlike a normal power of appointment trust, an estate trust does not require the annual distribution of income to the surviving spouse. Rather, an estate trust permits the trustee to distribute all, none, or some income to the spouse. Note, however, that if income is accumulated in an estate trust, such accumulated income is included in the surviving spouse's gross estate in addition to the original principal of the trust.

For the trust to qualify, no one other than the surviving spouse can have a beneficial interest in the trust. Upon the surviving spouse's death, the trusts assets must pass to the spouse's estate. Estate trusts are useful for passing non-income producing property since there is no statutory requirement for the trust to produce income. The trustee controls the trust assets during the spouse's lifetime.

While an estate trust offers more creditor protection over assets during the surviving spouse's lifetime and allows for a more flexible disposition scheme (due to the ability to accumulate income), it is not the best option to use in all states. Some states may impose an inheritance tax on assets passing through an estate trust, and thus include those assets in the probate estate of the surviving spouse (thereby subjecting the assets of the trust to the creditors of the surviving spouse's estate), but will not subject a regular general power of appointment trust to inheritance tax or consider it part of the probate estate. A clear understanding of both the state and federal tax, transfer rules, and probate will allow a planner to structure the estate plan in the most effective way for the client.

QUALIFIED TERMINABLE INTEREST PROPERTY (QTIP) TRUSTS

In considering what transfers should be allowed to qualify for the unlimited marital deduction, Congress recognized that in certain circumstances, an individual may wish to qualify assets for the marital deduction while still retaining control over the ultimate disposition of those assets. All of the marital deduction techniques discussed to this point grant the surviving spouse the right to determine who ultimately receives the property. Use of a **Qualified Terminable Interest Property (QTIP) Trust**, also known as a "C Trust," allows a decedent to qualify a transfer for the marital deduction at his death yet still control the ultimate disposition of the property.

Key Concepts

Underline/highlight the answers to these questions as you read:

1. Describe the use of a QTIP Trust and its impact on the unlimited marital deduction.

2. Identify the requirements for a QDOT to qualify for the unlimited marital deduction.

A QTIP Trust holds property for the benefit of a surviving spouse and makes income distributions to the surviving spouse at least annually. At the surviving spouse's death, the trust property will transfer to the remainder beneficiary as determined by the grantor of the QTIP Trust, the first-to-die spouse. To qualify a trust as a QTIP Trust, the executor of the decedent's estate must make an election on the estate tax return to qualify the trust for the marital deduction. The election defers any estate tax on the property until the death of the surviving spouse. Even though it is a terminable interest, the QTIP Trust will qualify for the unlimited marital deduction since the surviving spouse will be required to include in his gross estate the fair market value, at the surviving spouse's date of death, of the assets in the trust. Despite the fact that the assets are taxed in the surviving spouse's gross estate, the assets will pass according to the terms of the trust created by the first-to-die spouse.

QUALIFYING AS A QTIP TRUST

In order to qualify as a QTIP Trust, the following requirements must be met:

1. The property transferred to the trust must qualify for the unlimited marital deduction. Consequently, it must be included the gross estate of the first-to-die spouse and must be transferred to the surviving spouse (in this case, in trust).
2. The surviving spouse is entitled to all of the trust income for her life and that income must be paid at least annually. If the trust earns income during the surviving spouse's lifetime that is not distributed as of the date of the surviving spouse's death, the trust must distribute this income to the surviving spouse's estate (this is referred to as "stub income").
3. The surviving spouse must have the authority to compel the trustee to sell non-income producing investments and reinvest those proceeds in income-producing investments.
4. During the surviving spouse's lifetime, no one can have the right to appoint the property to anyone other than the surviving spouse.

5. The transferor or his executor must file an election to treat the trust as a QTIP Trust on the transferor's gift tax return (Form 709) or the decedent's federal estate tax return (Form 706).

THE QTIP TRUST AS A LIFETIME TRANSFER DEVICE

Most QTIP elections are made at the death of the first spouse. However, it is possible to make lifetime transfers to a QTIP Trust. An example of an application of a lifetime QTIP Trust is the transfer from a wealthy spouse to a spouse whose gross estate does not equal the applicable estate tax credit equivalency ($3,500,000 for 2009) of an amount in trust sufficient to fully use the spouse's applicable estate tax credit equivalency in the event the less wealthy spouse dies first. If the QTIP Trust meets all of the qualifications listed above, the current transfer to the trust would qualify for the gift tax unlimited marital deduction, and at the death of the donee spouse, the trust property will transfer to the remainder beneficiary as designated by the donor spouse. Such a transfer assures that the assets are transferred to the party or parties chosen by the more wealthy spouse, but makes use of the applicable estate tax credit equivalency of both spouses.

ESTATE TAXES

Upon the death of the surviving spouse, the executor of the surviving spouse's estate may require the trustee of the QTIP Trust to pay, out of the trust assets, any estate taxes attributable to the inclusion of the trust assets in the surviving spouse's gross estate. This provision is included in the law to prevent one spouse from forcing the other spouse to pay estate taxes attributable to his assets.

EXAMPLE 10.25

Jim died leaving behind his wife, Carolyn, and their children, Jake and Hank. After Jim's death, Carolyn remarried and had children with her new husband. Jim's will created a QTIP Trust at his death that met all of the requirements for the marital deduction. The QTIP Trust requires all of the income to be paid to Carolyn during her lifetime and at her death, and when the trust terminates, distributes all of its assets to Hank and Jake, per stirpes. Upon Carolyn's death, Hank and Jake will receive the trust assets, less the estate tax attributable to those assets. If the QTIP Trust was not required to pay the estate taxes on the trust property, Carolyn's estate would have to pay those taxes, resulting in a reduction of the amount of property that can pass to her heirs, which may or may not include Jake, Hank, and her other children.

The surviving spouse can waive, in his will, the requirement that the QTIP Trust pay the estate taxes attributable to the QTIP Trust property. If the beneficiaries of both spouse's estates are the same, for example, it may be more appropriate for each spouse to waive his right to have the QTIP Trust pay estate taxes on trust property, since the property in the QTIP Trust may not be considered part of the probate estate and may result in providing additional creditor protection for the beneficiaries.

PLANNING FOR THE NONCITIZEN SPOUSE

The unlimited estate tax marital deduction is not available for an outright bequest to a surviving spouse if the surviving spouse is not a U.S. citizen. For noncitizen spouses, there is a special annual exclusion amount of $133,000 (2009) available for lifetime transfers by a citizen spouse to a noncitizen spouse. As discussed above, Congress allows an unlimited marital deduction in the estate of the first-to-die spouse on the assumption that the property that has not been consumed will be subject to estate tax at the surviving spouse's death. If the surviving spouse is not a U.S. citizen, he could, after receiving the decedent's property, return to his country of origin with the property in hand. When this non-U.S. citizen spouse dies, the U.S. would not have jurisdiction over either the surviving spouse or the property, and therefore would not be able to collect the estate tax on the transfer of property at the surviving spouse's death. To prevent this from happening, special rules apply to transfers to non-U.S. citizen spouses.

> John, a U.S. citizen, recently died leaving behind his wife, Margaret, a citizen of the United Kingdom, and his children. John's will leaves all of his property to Margaret. If the marital deduction applied to the transfer of John's property to Margaret, and Margaret returned to England after John's death with the property, the U.S. would not be able to tax the remaining property at Margaret's death. Therefore, the unlimited marital deduction is not available for John's estate.

EXAMPLE 10.26

One remedy to this problem is having the non-U.S. citizen surviving spouse become a U.S. citizen before the due date of estate tax return and maintain residency in the United States following the death of the decedent-spouse. If both of these conditions are met, the transfer to the surviving spouse will qualify for the unlimited estate tax marital deduction. Upon the death of the surviving spouse, the U.S. will be able to collect an estate tax on the value of the remaining assets.

QUALIFIED DOMESTIC TRUST

For individuals who do not wish to obtain U.S. citizenship, the citizen-spouse, or the executor of the citizen-spouse's estate, can create a **Qualified Domestic Trust (QDOT)**. A QDOT will allow the U.S. government to subject remaining assets to estate taxation upon the death of the noncitizen surviving spouse by maintaining jurisdiction over those assets. In order to qualify the QDOT for the unlimited marital deduction, the following requirements must be met:

1. at least one of the QDOT trustees must be a U.S. citizen or a U.S. domestic corporation;
2. the trust must prohibit a distribution of principal unless the U.S. citizen trustee has the right to withhold estate tax on the distribution;
3. the trustee must keep a sufficient amount of the trust assets in the United States to ensure the payment of federal estate taxes, or the trustee must have a minimum net worth sufficient to assure the payment of estate taxes upon the death of the noncitizen surviving spouse; and
4. the executor of the citizen-spouse's estate must elect to have the marital deduction apply to the trust.

If all of the requirements listed above are met, the transfer of property into the QDOT will qualify for the marital deduction in the citizen-spouse's estate, and the principal remaining in the QDOT at the date of the surviving spouse's death will be subject to estate tax. The surviving spouse is entitled to receive all of the income of the QDOT for life, but if the principal of the trust is distributed to the surviving spouse during lifetime, the distribution will be subject to estate tax. The estate taxes payable on lifetime or testamentary distributions of principal are equal to the amount of estate tax that would have been imposed had the property been taxed in the citizen-spouse's gross estate. All income distributions, as well as distributions of principal on account of hardships, to the noncitizen surviving spouse are not subject to estate tax. However, all distributions of income from the QDOT to the surviving spouse are subject to ordinary income tax.

ALTERNATIVES TO QUALIFICATION

At first glance, the unlimited marital deduction appears to be a planning panacea – once you qualify for the marital deduction, there is no estate tax on the value of the property at the death of the first spouse. Remember, however, that the marital deduction is only a deferral device; it is available in the first spouse's estate only if the assets transferred will be available to be taxed in the surviving spouse's gross estate.

OVERQUALIFICATION

In estate planning, it is important to avoid qualifying too many assets for the marital deduction. In 2009, an individual can pass up to $3,500,000 of assets to a non-spouse during lifetime or at death without triggering federal transfer tax. When an individual leaves his entire estate to the surviving spouse, the applicable estate tax credit equivalency ($3,500,000 in 2009) is lost and cannot be retrieved. When too many assets pass to a surviving spouse, resulting in an increase in overall estate taxes for the family when the surviving spouse dies, the unlimited marital deduction is said to be **overqualified**.

Key Concepts

Underline/highlight the answers to these questions as you read:

1. Describe overqualification and underqualification.

2. What is a bypass trust and why is it created?

3. Describe a disclaimer and its applications.

4. What are the estate tax consequences of an ILIT?

Vic and Valerie had been married for 35 years at the date of Vic's death in 2009. Vic and Valerie have three children. Valerie is the daughter of a southern business tycoon and has significant assets totalling $1,000,000 in her own name. In addition, Valerie expects to receive a substantial inheritance from her parents of $2,000,000. Vic's will leaves all of his assets, $4,000,000, to Valerie, and, if Valerie predeceased him, the assets are split between his children, in equal shares, per stirpes (typically referred to as an "I Love You" will). Assume funeral and administrative expenses are $100,000 for the first spouse to die, and $400,000 for the second spouse to die. Since Vic left all of his assets to Valerie outright, his entire estate qualifies for the marital deduction. Vic will not be able to use his applicable estate tax credit, since none of his property is passing to his children or anyone other than his wife. Vic's estate is overqualified for the marital deduction. Furthermore, Vic's assets will be added to Valerie's and will likely be subject to estate tax at the highest marginal rate at Valerie's death.

EXAMPLE 10.27

Given the above information, the estate tax calculation for Vic's Estate follows:

Vic's Gross Estate	$4,000,000
- Funeral & Admin Expenses (assumed)	($100,000)
- Debts	($0)
- Taxes due at death	($0)
Adjusted Gross Estate	$3,900,000
- Marital Deduction	($3,900,000)
- Charitable Deduction	($0)
Taxable Estate	$0
+ Post'76 Gifts	$0
Tentative Tax Base	**$0**
Tentative Estate Tax	$0
-Applicable Estate Tax Credit	($0)
Total Estate Tax Liability	**$0**

At Valerie's subsequent death in 2009, her estate tax calculation follows (assuming no growth in the value of the assets between deaths):

Valerie's Assets	$3,000,000
Assets from Vic's Estate	$3,900,000
- Funeral & Admin Expenses (assumed)	($400,000)
- Debts	($0)
- Taxes due at death	($0)
Adjusted Gross Estate	$6,500,000
- Marital Deduction	($0)
- Charitable Deduction	($0)
Taxable Estate	$6,500,000
+ Post'76 Gifts	$0
Tentative Tax Base	**$6,500,000**
Tentative Estate Tax	$2,805,800
-Applicable Estate Tax Credit	($1,455,800)
Total Estate Tax Liability	**$1,350,000**

As Example 10.29 will detail, if Vic had left $3,500,000 in a bypass trust for the benefit of Valerie, he would have been able to use his applicable estate tax credit amount. Furthermore, Valerie's gross estate would not include the $3,500,000 in the bypass trust, resulting in an overall estate tax savings for Vic and Valerie.

UNDERQUALIFICATION

In contrast, the unlimited marital deduction can also be **underqualified**. Underqualification means that too much of the decedent's property was subject to estate tax at the death of the first spouse due to a failure to make adequate use of the unlimited marital deduction.

Patty and John had been married for 40 years at the date of John's death. Patty and John have three children. The value of Patty's gross estate is $450,000, and the value of John's gross estate is $4,000,000. John's will leaves $3,750,000 to a bypass trust for the benefit of Patty and their children, and the rest of his estate outright to Patty. Since John's estate exceeds the applicable estate credit equivalency amount of $3,500,000 (2009), estate tax will be due on the $250,000 ($3,750,000 - $3,500,000) excess. John has underqualified the marital deduction in his estate. If John had left $3,500,000 to the bypass trust and $500,000 (the $250,000 she was already receiving plus an additional $250,000 that was originally going to the bypass trust) to Patty, his estate would not have a federal estate tax liability, and since Patty's gross estate will be less than $3,500,000 (her assets of $450,000 plus the $500,000 she received from John's estate, assuming there is no growth in the value of the assets), Patty's estate would not have a federal estate tax liability either. John's underqualification of the marital deduction causes $250,000 of assets to be subject to estate tax that would have passed tax free to the children at Patty's death had the appropriate marital deduction been used.

BYPASS TRUST

A **bypass trust** (sometimes referred to as a **credit shelter trust** or "B Trust") is used to ensure that an individual can make full use of his applicable estate tax credit amount. Instead of overqualifying the marital deduction by leaving all property to the surviving spouse, a bypass trust is created to receive property with a fair market value equal to the decedent's remaining applicable estate tax credit equivalency ($3,500,000 in 2009) from the decedent's gross estate, while the remainder of the property passes to the surviving spouse (either outright, or through the use of a GPOA Trust or QTIP Trust). The portion of the gross estate that funds the bypass trust will be subject to federal estate tax, but the applicable estate tax credit will be available, eliminating any estate tax liability. As long as any remaining property passing to the surviving spouse qualifies for the estate tax marital deduction, no estate tax will be payable at the death of the first spouse.

For the Benefit of the Surviving Spouse

Many individuals wish to leave as much property to their surviving spouse as possible and may be uncomfortable with using a bypass trust since the assets in the trust will not be transferred to the spouse. While the surviving spouse will not own the assets transferred to the bypass trust, the trust may be established for the surviving spouse's lifetime benefit, followed by a remainder interest to the children (or other beneficiaries named in the trust). Typically, a bypass trust gives the surviving spouse the right to receive the trust income (by including a mandatory distribution clause or leaving the distribution to the discretion of the trustee). Furthermore, the trustee can be given the right to distribute the principal to the surviving spouse (or any other beneficiary) on a discretionary basis, or subject to an ascertainable standard. (If the trust document is written to allow distributions at the discretion of the trustee, the surviving spouse should not be the trustee to avoid the appearance of a conflict of interest, and the inclusion of the trust assets in the surviving spouse's estate.) An **ascertainable standard** allows distributions of any amount for the recipient's health, education, maintenance, or support. In addition, the surviving spouse can be given a right to demand the greater of (1) $5,000 or (2) five percent of the trust corpus on an annual basis. While these rights provide the surviving spouse with significant access to the trust assets during his lifetime, none of these rights are sufficient to constitute ownership of trust assets or require the surviving spouse to include the fair market value of the bypass trust's asset in his gross estate. Bypass planning is important for any client where the combined estates of the husband and wife exceed the applicable estate tax credit equivalency.

EXAMPLE 10.29	Recall the Vic and Valerie example (Example 10.27). Instead of leaving all of his assets to Valerie, Vic's will could have created a bypass trust at his death, and funded it with $3,500,000 of his assets. The $3,500,000 transferred to the bypass trust would not qualify for the marital deduction and would be subject to estate tax at Vic's death. Vic's applicable estate tax credit would shield this amount from estate tax, and since all of his other assets are passing to Valerie ($400,000), those transfers would qualify for the marital deduction. Vic would have no estate tax liability at his death. The bypass trust created under Vic's will could provide for Valerie, giving her (a) income from the trust, (b) distributions for health, education, maintenance, and support, and (c) the right to demand the greater of $5,000 or 5% of the trust corpus on an annual basis without causing an inclusion of the trust assets in Valerie's gross estate. At Valerie's death, the assets remaining in the bypass trust would pass to the children free of estate tax.

The estate tax calculation for Vic's Estate follows:

Vic's Gross Estate	$4,000,000
- Funeral & Admin Expenses (assumed)	($100,000)
- Debts	(0)
- Taxes due at death	(0)
Adjusted Gross Estate	$3,900,000
- Marital Deduction	($400,000)
- Charitable Deduction	(0)
Taxable Estate	$3,500,000
+ Post'76 Gifts	0
Tentative Tax Base	**$3,500,000**
Tentative Estate Tax	$1,455,800
- Applicable Estate Tax Credit	**($1,455,800)**
Total Estate Tax Liability	**$0**

Since Vic's tax base equals his applicable estate tax credit equivalency amount, he will not have to pay any tax on the assets used to fund the bypass trust. At Valerie's subsequent death later in 2009, her estate tax calculation follows (assuming no growth in the value of the assets between deaths):

	Current Example	Previous Example	Savings
Valerie's Gross Estate	$3,000,000	$3,000,000	0
Assets from Vic's Estate	$400,000	$3,900,000	($3,500,000)
- Funeral & Admin Expenses (assumed)	($400,000)	($400,000)	0
- Debts	(0)	(0)	0
- Taxes due at death	(0)	(0)	0
Adjusted Gross Estate (AGE)	$3,000,000	$6,500,000	($3,500,000)
- Marital Deduction	(0)	(0)	0
- Charitable Deduction	(0)	(0)	0
Taxable Estate	$3,000,000	$6,500,000	($3,500,000)
+ Post'76 Gifts	0	0	0
Tentative Tax Base	**$3,000,000**	**$6,500,000**	**($3,500,000)**
Tentative Estate Tax	$1,230,800	$2,805,800	($1,350,000)
- Applicable Credit	($1,230,800)	($1,455,800)	0
Total Estate Tax Liability	**$0**	**$1,350,000**	**($1,350,000)** [1]

[1] The reason that the savings is $1,350,000 and not the difference between $2,805,800 and $1,230,800 or $1,575,000 is because Valerie did not use up her entire credit of $1,455,800, thus the difference of $225,000.

Note that compared with Example 10.27, Valerie's tentative taxable estate is reduced by $3,500,000, representing the amount that Vic transferred to the bypass trust at his death. Since the assets transferred to the bypass trust at Vic's death were subject to estate tax (and covered by his applicable estate tax credit), they are not included in Valerie's gross estate in the current example. If those assets were included in Valerie's gross estate, those assets would be taxed twice, which would be inconsistent with the premise of treating a married couple as one economic unit. As this example illustrates, use of a bypass trust at the death of the first spouse saves estate taxes on $3,500,000 of property if Valerie dies in 2009 (a tax savings of $1,350,000 or 0.45 x $3,000,000).

Graphically, the estate plan (for the current example) would look like this:

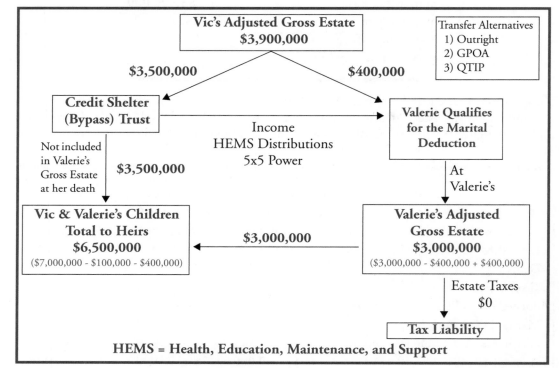

HEMS = Health, Education, Maintenance, and Support

COMMON TRUST ARRANGEMENTS

A common testamentary trust arrangement includes the transfer of the remaining applicable estate tax credit equivalency to a bypass trust, also known as a B Trust, the transfer of a certain amount to a General Power of Appointment Trust, also known as an A Trust, and the transfer of the remaining balance to a QTIP Trust, known as a C Trust. The arrangement is often referred to as an **ABC Trust arrangement**.

With such an arrangement, a decedent can accomplish several objectives. First, the decedent can guarantee the full use of his applicable estate tax credit equivalency with the transfer to the B Trust. The decedent can also provide the necessary funds to his surviving spouse in several ways. The A Trust allows the spouse to receive income distributions as well as appoint the principal to herself. The B and C Trusts allow income distributions to the surviving spouse as well as the ability for the surviving spouse to receive principal distributions from the B and C Trusts for health, education, maintenance and support. In addition, the A Trust and C Trust qualify the transfers for the unlimited marital deduction. However, a key difference between the A and the C Trust is the selection of the ultimate beneficiaries of the trust property. Because the surviving spouse will have a GPOA over the trust property of the A Trust, the surviving spouse can choose the ultimate beneficiary of the trust property, whereas the decedent (grantor) will choose the remainder beneficiary of the C Trust.

Most often the ABC Trust arrangement is used in situations where the decedent and the surviving spouse's heirs are different individuals, as in the case of blended families. The ABC arrangement allows the decedent to provide support to his surviving spouse while maintaining control over the ultimate disposition of the C Trust property.

<table>
<tr><td>

Betty and Bill were married for ten years before Bill's death. Betty and Bill had three children together. Prior to his marriage to Betty, Bill had a child with his former wife. At Bill's death, his gross estate had a fair market value of $4,700,000 and Bill had not made any lifetime transfers. Bill's will included the common ABC Trust arrangement. The will directed $3,500,000 to the B Trust (bypass) for the equal remainder benefit of each of Bill's children (all four). The remainder of $1,200,000 ($4,700,000 - $3,500,000) was divided between the A Trust (Power of Appointment Trust), $600,000, which gave Betty a GPOA over the trust assets and the C Trust (QTIP trust), $600,000, with the remainder beneficiary designated as Bill's child from his previous marriage. Betty would be the income beneficiary of each of the A, B, and C Trusts for her life. With this arrangement, Bill's executor would make the QTIP election on the C Trust to qualify it for the unlimited marital deduction. The A Trust would qualify for the unlimited marital deduction because of the general power of appointment, and the assets transferring to the B Trust, would create an estate tax that would be offset by Bill's applicable estate tax credit. Thus, at Bill's death, no estate tax would be due. Furthermore, Betty would appoint the A Trust assets to their three children at her death, and Bill's child will receive the assets of the C Trust at Betty's death. The arrangement allowed Bill to be certain that his child from his former marriage would receive a pro rata allocation of his assets while providing his surviving spouse income and the ability to use the assets in case of need.

</td><td>

EXAMPLE 10.30

</td></tr>
</table>

DISCLAIMERS

Despite the tax savings that can be generated by using a bypass trust, many individuals are still uncomfortable with the prospect of keeping property away from their spouses. A disclaimer allows the surviving spouse to make a determination of how much property is needed after the first spouse dies.

A qualified disclaimer allows an individual to refuse property from the estate of a decedent. The disclaimer can include a particular asset, amount, fraction of an interest or all property the heir is entitled to receive. When a disclaimer is used, the property will pass to the next person eligible to receive it under the disclaimer clause of the decedent's will or, if no one is listed, under the state intestacy statute. As discussed in Chapter 2, to be valid, a disclaimer must be executed in writing within nine months of the decedent's death and the disclaimant must not have received any benefit from the disclaimed property.

Disclaimers and Bypass Trusts

An individual who is uncomfortable placing a large amount of money in a bypass trust could leave all of his property to the surviving spouse but include a provision in the will stating that if the surviving spouse disclaims any or all of the bequest, the disclaimed property will be placed in a bypass trust, thus giving the surviving spouse an income interest in the trust as noted above. Upon the death of the first spouse, the surviving spouse can assess his financial situation and to the extent that he does not need to receive the property directly, can disclaim his interest in the marital bequest in whole or in part. Once the disclaimer is made, the bequest will not qualify for the marital deduction, but it will qualify as a transfer offset by the applicable estate tax credit. Disclaiming the interest will allow the surviving spouse to prevent the property from being included in his gross estate, even though the surviving spouse will receive an interest in the bypass trust. Note that the property will pass to a trust benefiting the spouse as opposed to passing outright to some other beneficiary.

This result may seem surprising. Usually, for a disclaimer to be valid, the disclaimant cannot receive an interest in the disclaimed property. In this situation, the surviving spouse disclaims a bequest but nevertheless receives an interest in the trust that is created as a result of the disclaimer. There is a special exception in the law that allows a surviving spouse to execute a qualified disclaimer, yet receive a benefit from the property disclaimed if that property is transferred into a trust in which the surviving spouse receives an income interest, without requiring the value of the trust to be included in the surviving spouse's estate at his death. Anyone other than a surviving spouse executing a similar disclaimer would be deemed to have retained a lifetime right to the income from the property, thereby requiring the property to be included in the gross estate (IRC Section 2036).

IRREVOCABLE LIFE INSURANCE TRUST (ILIT)

Provided that a client is comfortable with limiting the amount of property that is transferred outright to a spouse, a myriad of planning options emerge. One of the most powerful is the use of an Irrevocable Life Insurance Trust (ILIT) to provide for the surviving spouse, prevent property from being included in the gross estate of either spouse, and protect assets from the claims of the beneficiaries' creditors (discussed in detail in Chapter 11).

A properly drafted ILIT can accomplish all of these objectives. By allowing the trustee of the ILIT to apply for and purchase a life insurance policy on the life of the insured/grantor of the ILIT, the insured will possess no incidents of ownership in the policy thereby keeping the policy out of his gross estate. The grantor of the ILIT can then name his spouse as the primary beneficiary of the trust, granting the surviving spouse:

1. the right to income;
2. the right to receive distributions for health, education, maintenance, and support; and
3. the right to demand up to $5,000 or five percent of the trust corpus each year without subjecting the principal of the ILIT to estate taxation in the surviving spouse's gross estate.

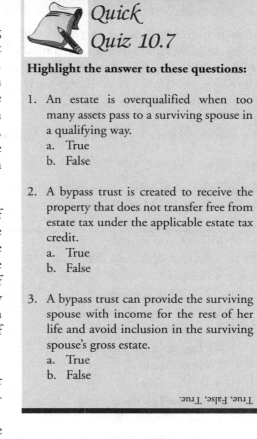

Since no estate tax inclusion results, the marital deduction is unnecessary. At the death of the surviving spouse, the ILIT can continue in existence for the benefit of the children, protecting the assets from the claims of the children's creditors, or can terminate and distribute any remaining principal to the children.

As use of an ILIT and bypass trust illustrates, certain structures can be created that allow the surviving spouse to receive benefits, even though the unlimited estate tax marital deduction does not apply to the transaction. When using these techniques, the transaction does not have to meet the requirements associated with qualifying for the unlimited marital deduction.

Mike has an estate valued at $8,000,000. In addition, there is a fully paid-up life insurance policy on Mike's life that has a $1,500,000 death benefit. Mike is married to Mary and has two children. Mike is expected to die before Mary, who is substantially younger than him. Mike and Mary have asked you to help them with their estate planning and would like you to consider the following three alternative scenarios:

Assume for each scenario funeral and administrative expenses of $100,000.

SCENARIO 1

Assume that all of Mike's assets, including the death benefit on the life insurance policy he owns on his life, pass to Mary. When Mike dies in early 2009, the estate tax calculation is as follows:

Mike's Gross Estate	$9,500,000	$8 million + $1.5 million
- Funeral & Admin Expenses	($100,000)	
- Debts	(0)	
- Taxes due at death	(0)	
Adjusted Gross Estate	$9,400,000	
- Marital Deduction	($9,400,000)	
- Charitable Deduction	(0)	
Taxable Estate	$0	
+ Post'76 Gifts	0	
Tentative Tax Base	**$0**	
Tentative Estate Tax	$0	
- Applicable Estate Tax Credit	(0)	
Total Estate Tax Liability	**$0**	

Mike's gross estate includes the $8,000,000 in assets that he held at the date of his death, plus the $1,500,000 death benefit from the life insurance policy Mike owned on his life at the time of his death. Since all of Mike's assets, including the death benefit on the life insurance policy, pass to Mary, his estate qualifies for a $9,400,000 marital deduction, resulting in a taxable estate of $0. Note that Mike has not made use of his applicable estate tax credit. Assuming that Mary dies later in the year (2009), and that Mary's only assets are those that she inherited from Mike and that the value of the assets that she inherited did not change, Mary's estate tax calculation would be as follows:

Mary's Gross Estate	$0
Assets from Mike's Estate	$9,400,000
- Funeral & Admin Expenses	($100,000)
- Debts	(0)
- Taxes due at death	(0)
Adjusted Gross Estate	$9,300,000
- Marital Deduction	(0)
- Charitable Deduction	(0)
Taxable Estate	$9,300,000
+ Post'76 Gifts	0
Tentative Tax Base	**$9,300,000**
Tentative Estate Tax	$4,065,800
- Applicable Estate Tax Credit	($1,455,800)
Total Estate Tax Liability	**$2,610,000**

The net result of Scenario 1 is that Mike and Mary pay total federal estate taxes of $2,610,000 on the $9,500,000 estate, or approximately 27 percent of the gross estate in estate taxes. Mike and Mary's heirs receive $6,690,000 ($9,500,000 - $100,000 - $100,000 - $2,610,000) assuming that there is no additional tax levied by their state of residence. The cost of poor planning was $1,575,000 calculated as Mike's applicable estate tax credit equivalency that went unused multiplied by the marginal estate tax rate of 45 percent ($3,500,000 x 0.45 = $1,575,000) for the year of Mary's death.

SCENARIO 2

Mike creates an ILIT to own the life insurance on his life. For this scenario assume that Mike was able to fund the ILIT using annual exclusion gifts subject to a Crummey right of withdrawal. In this case, the $1,500,000 death benefit is excluded from Mike's gross estate because he did not possess at his death (or in the three years immediately preceeding his death) any incident of ownership in the life insurance policy. Instead, the life insurance policy was owned by the trustee of the ILIT. The results of the estate planning of Scenario 2 are as follows:

At Mike's death, the $1,500,000 life insurance proceeds are paid to the ILIT. The trust grants Mary the right to receive the trust income and the right to principal distributions for her health, education, maintenance, and support. Effectively, all of these assets are available for Mary in the event she will need them during her lifetime. At Mary's death, any amounts remaining in the ILIT are split equally among Mike and Mary's children. Mike's estate tax calculation is as follows:

Mike's Gross Estate	$8,000,000	(assets)
- Funeral & Admin Expenses	($100,000)	
- Debts	(0)	
- Taxes due at death	(0)	
Adjusted Gross Estate	$7,900,000	
- Marital Deduction	($7,900,000)	
- Charitable Deduction	(0)	
Taxable Estate	$0	
+ Post'76 Gifts	0	
Tentative Tax Base	**$0**	
Tentative Estate Tax	$0	
- Applicable Estate Tax Credit	(0)	
Total Estate Tax Liability	**$0**	

Note that Mike's gross estate is $1,500,000 less than it was in Scenario 1 due to the exclusion of the life insurance proceeds. However, again, Mike has failed to utilize his applicable estate tax credit in his estate planning process. Assuming that Mary dies later this year (2009), and assuming that the assets that Mike bequeathed to Mary remained at the same value and that these are the only assets included in Mary's gross estate, Mary's estate tax calculation would be as follows:

Mary's Gross Estate	$0
Assets from Mike's Estate	$7,900,000
- Funeral & Admin Expenses	($100,000)
- Debts	(0)
- Taxes due at death	(0)
Adjusted Gross Estate	$7,800,000
- Marital Deduction	(0)
- Charitable Deduction	(0)
Tentative Tax Base	$7,800,000
+ Post'76 Gifts	0
Tentative Tax Base	**$7,800,000**
Tentative Estate Tax	$3,390,800
- Applicable Estate Tax Credit	($1,455,800)
Total Estate Tax Liability	**$1,935,000**

Note that moving the life insurance to the ILIT saves the family $675,000 (0.45 x $1,500,000) in taxes ($2,610,000 from Scenario 1, less $1,935,000 from Scenario 2). The total estate tax, as a percentage of the gross assets transferred, is approximately 20 percent, and Mike and Mary's children will receive $7,365,000 ($9,500,000 - $100,000 - $100,000 - $1,935,000). While the results of Scenario 2 are certainly better than the results of Scenario 1, additional planning can further reduce Mike and Mary's estate taxes.

SCENARIO 3

Assume that Mike moves the life insurance policy into an ILIT so that the death benefit will remain outside of his estate and that he makes full use of his applicable estate tax credit. For this scenario, assume that Mike was able to fund the ILIT using annual exclusion gifts subject to a Crummey right of withdrawal. In this case, the $1,500,000 death benefit will be excluded from Mike's gross estate because he did not own, at his death (or in the three years immediately preceeding his death), any incident of ownership in the life insurance policy. Instead, the life insurance policy was owned by the trustee of the ILIT.

At Mike's death, the $1,500,000 life insurance proceeds are paid to the ILIT. The trust grants Mary the right to receive the trust income and the right to principal distributions for her health, education, maintenance, and support. Effectively, all of these assets are available for Mary in the event that she needs them during her lifetime. At Mary's death, any amounts remaining in the trust are split equally among Mike and Mary's children.

Mike's will directs his executor to create a bypass trust and to fund it with the maximum amount that can be transferred without increasing Mike's estate tax. Since Mike has not made any taxable transfers during his lifetime, the full applicable estate tax credit equivalency of $3,500,000 is available. Therefore, Mike's executor transfers $3,500,000 in assets to the bypass trust. During her lifetime, Mary will have the right to receive the trust income and the right to receive distributions of principal for her health, education, maintenance, and support. Similar to the ILIT, the assets of the bypass trust are available to Mary should she need them during her lifetime. At Mary's death, any amounts remaining in the bypass trust are split equally among Mike and Mary's children.

Mike's estate tax calculation follows:

Mike's Gross Estate	$8,000,000
- Funeral & Admin Expenses	($100,000)
- Debts	(0)
- Taxes due at death	(0)
Adjusted Gross Estate	$7,900,000
- Marital Deduction	($4,400,000)
- Charitable Deduction	(0)
Taxable Estate	$3,500,000
+ Post'76 Gifts	0
Tentative Tax Base	**$3,500,000**
Tentative Estate Tax	$1,455,800
- Applicable Estate Tax Credit	($1,455,800)
Total Estate Tax Liability	**$0**

Unlike Scenario 1 or Scenario 2, Mike has made full use of his applicable estate tax credit equivalency ($3,500,000 in 2009) to reduce the overall estate taxes paid by Mike and Mary. Assuming that the assets that Mike bequeathed to Mary are the only assets included in Mary's gross estate, and they did not appreciate or depreciate and that Mary died later in 2009, Mary's estate tax calculation would be as follows:

Mary's Gross Estate	$0
Assets from Mike's Estate	$4,400,000
- Funeral & Admin Expenses	($100,000)
- Debts	(0)
- Taxes due at death	(0)
Adjusted Gross Estate (AGE)	$4,300,000
- Marital Deduction	(0)
- Charitable Deduction	(0)
Taxable Estate	$4,300,000
+ Post'76 Gifts	0
Tentative Tax Base	**$4,300,000**
Tentative Estate Tax	$1,815,800
- Applicable Estate Tax Credit	($1,455,800)
Total Estate Tax Liability	**$360,000**

By using both the ILIT and his applicable estate tax credit, Mike has been able to reduce the estate taxes paid on the property from $2,610,000 (Scenario 1) to $360,000 (Scenario 3), a savings of $2,250,000. The percentage of the assets utilized to pay estate taxes is approximately 3.8 percent. The additional amount that the heirs received is due solely to the estate tax savings resulting from the use of the ILIT and the bypass trust. As these scenarios illustrate, good estate planning can save large amounts of transfer tax dollars.

Reconciliation of Net to Heirs		Change in Net to Heirs Scenario 1 to 3	
Total Estate	$9,500,00	Scenario 3	$8,940,000
Less Funeral	$200,000	Scenario 1	$6,690,000
	$9,300,000	Savings	$2,250,000
Estate Taxes	$360,000	From ILIT	$675,000
Net to Heirs	$8,940,000	From Bypass Trust	$1,575,000
		Total Savings	$2,250,000

Reconciliation of Scenario 1 to 3 Estate Tax		
Estate Tax Scenario 1	$2,610,000	
Savings from ILIT	($675,000)	($1,500,000 X 0.45)
Savings from Bypass Trust	($1,575,000)	($3,500,000 X 0.45)
Estate Tax Scenario 3	$360,000	

Alternative Approach to Reconciliation	
Mike's Total Assets	$9,500,000
Funeral Expenses for Mike	($100,000)
Funeral Expenses for Mary	($100,000)
Life Insurance Proceeds	($1,500,000)
Applicable Estate Tax Credit Equivalence for Mike	($3,500,000)
Applicable Estate Tax Credit Equivalence for Mary	($3,500,000)
Net Assets	$800,000
45% Marginal Estate Tax Rate	45%
Total Estate Tax Due	$360,000

Key Terms

ABC Trust Arrangement - A common trust arrangement that utilizes a bypass trust (the B Trust), a GPOA Trust (the A Trust), and a QTIP Trust (the C Trust) to provide the necessary support to a surviving spouse while maximizing the use of the decedent's applicable estate tax credit and providing the decedent the ability to determine the ultimate beneficiary of most of his assets at the death of the surviving spouse.

Ascertainable Standard - An objective standard for allowing distributions defined in the Internal Revenue Code as distributions for health, education, maintenance, or support (HEMS).

Bypass Trust (also known as a Credit Shelter Trust or B Trust) - A trust created to ensure that an individual makes use of his applicable estate tax credit.

Estate Trust - A trust which grants the surviving spouse a testamentary general power of appointment over the trust assets. Because of the spouse's general power of appointment over the trust's assets, the fair market value of the trust will be eligible for the unlimited marital deduction at the death of the first-to-die spouse.

General Power of Appointment Trust (A Trust) - An irrevocable trust that can be created either during an individual's lifetime or at an individual's death that gives the agent the right to appoint the settlor's assets.

Overqualified - A decedent's taxable base is less than the applicable estate tax credit equivalency because too many assets have passed to a surviving spouse.

Qualified Domestic Trust (QDOT) - A trust created for the benefit of a noncitizen spouse which has enough transfer stipulations to allow the U.S. government to subject assets remaining at the death of the noncitizen surviving spouse, as well as distributions of principal, to estate taxation. Assets transferred to a QDOT qualify for the unlimited marital deduction.

Qualified Terminable Interest Property Trust (QTIP Trust or C Trust) - A trust which allows a decedent to qualify a transfer for the marital deduction at his death yet still control the ultimate disposition of the property.

Survivorship Clause - A clause included in a will requiring that the legatee survive for a specific period in order to inherit under the will. The bequest will qualify for the marital deduction if the property transfers to the surviving spouse and the time period of the survivorship clause is six months or less.

Terminable Interest - An interest that terminates at some point.

Underqualified - When too much of a decedent's property is subject to estate tax at the death of the first spouse due to improper use of the unlimited marital deduction.

Unlimited Marital Deduction - Because a married couple is viewed as one single economic unit for estate and gift tax purposes, an individual receives a deduction from his gross gifts or from the adjusted gross estate for transfers to a spouse. Hence, transfers to a spouse are not subject to estate or gift tax.

1. Explain the theory behind the unlimited marital deduction.

2. List three benefits of the unlimited marital deduction.

3. Discuss the following statement: "The use of the unlimited marital deduction does not avoid estate tax, it merely postpones it."

4. List the three most common methods of leaving property to a spouse and qualifying the transfer for the marital deduction.

5. What are the three requirements for a transfer of property to qualify for the unlimited marital deduction?

6. Define terminable interest.

7. List the exceptions to the terminable interest rule.

8. Identify the requirements necessary for a General Power of Appointment (GPOA) Trust to qualify for the unlimited marital deduction.

9. Identify the requirements necessary for a QTIP Trust to qualify for the unlimited marital deduction.

10. Discuss the alternatives available for paying the estate taxes incurred at the death of the surviving spouse attributable to the QTIP Trust property.

11. Identify the requirements necessary for a Qualified Domestic Trust (QDOT) to qualify for the unlimited marital deduction.

12. How is a bypass trust used in estate planning?

13. What is a qualified disclaimer and how is it used?

1. When a U.S. citizen dies and bequeaths property to his U.S. citizen spouse, the marital deductions is limited to the following amount:

    a. $0.

    b. $1,455,800.

    c. $3,500,000.

    d. The marital deduction is unlimited.

2. Jeremy and Rosa were married forty years ago after meeting on the beaches of Cozumel. Rosa moved to the U.S. with Jeremy, but she never applied for U.S. citizenship. If Jeremy is concerned about utilizing the marital deduction for the fair market value of the property he bequeaths to Rosa, which of the following techniques could he use?

    a. Qualified Terminable Interest Trust (QTIP).

    b. Section 2503(b) Trust.

    c. Section 2503(c) Trust.

    d. Qualified Domestic Trust (QDOT).

3. When a U.S. citizen married to a resident alien dies, what is the maximum value of a specific, outright bequest of property that can qualify for the unlimited marital deduction?

    a. $0.

    b. $1,455,800.

    c. $3,500,000.

    d. The marital deduction is unlimited.

4. An executor may elect the unlimited marital deduction for which of the following transfers?

    1. Decedent's will directs the creation of a CRAT and the decedent's nonresident alien spouse is the income beneficiary. The trustee of the CRAT is a citizen of the United Kingdom.

    2. Bequest to U.S. citizen spouse of the right to use property for the remainder of her life. Executor has elected QTIP on the property.

    3. A payment of $650,000 to fulfill a specific bequest to decedent's U.S. citizen spouse. Decedent's spouse became a U.S. citizen two months before the filing of the decedent's estate tax return.

    4. A payment of $250,000 to fulfill a specific bequest to decedent's resident alien spouse.

    a. 2 only.

    b. 2 and 3.

    c. 3 and 4.

    d. 1, 2, and 3.

5. Juan's will creates a General Power of Appointment Trust (GPOA Trust) that distributes income to his wife annually for life and gives his wife a general power of appointment over the assets in the trust. Which of the following statements is true regarding a GPOA Trust?

    a. The GPOA Trust only qualifies for the unlimited marital deduction if the trustee agrees to make distributions of principal to Juan's wife.

    b. The unlimited marital deduction cannot be elected over the property transferred to the trust because Juan's wife cannot appoint assets to herself, her creditors, or to anyone on her behalf.

    c. The unlimited marital deduction is not available because Juan's wife does not have the current right to the assets in the trust.

    d. The GPOA Trust automatically qualifies for the unlimited marital deduction because Juan's wife has a general power of appointment over the trust's assets.

6. If a decedent bequeaths the outright ownership of his house to his children subject to his wife's right to live in that house for the remainder of her life, which of the following statements is correct?

    a. If the wife disclaims her interest in the house, the house is not included in the decedent's taxable estate.

    b. If the children disclaim their interest in the house, the house will automatically transfer to the decedent's spouse as the life estate beneficiary.

    c. If the decedent's wife is a resident alien of the U.S., a QTIP election over the property will allow a marital deduction equal to the fair market value of the property.

    d. If the executor makes a QTIP election on the house, the house is not included in the decedent's taxable estate.

7. Which of the following is not a benefit of the unlimited marital deduction?

    a. The estate tax on property can be deferred until the death of the second-to-die spouse.

    b. The unlimited marital deduction can fund the applicable estate tax credit of the surviving spouse.

    c. The use of the unlimited marital deduction can shelter the future appreciation of an asset from estate taxes at the death of the second-to-die spouse.

    d. The unlimited marital deduction can ensure the surviving spouse has sufficient assets to support her lifestyle.

8. Of Pablo's $10,000,000 federal gross estate, his will includes one specific bequest of $7,500,000 to his wife, Ariana, and directs the debts and other expenses of $1,000,000 to be payable from the residuary of the estate. The residuary heirs are Pablo's children. What is the amount of the marital deduction included on Pablo's federal estate tax return?

    a. $0.

    b. $6,500,000.

    c. $8,500,000.

    d. $7,500,000.

9. Given only the following information, which would qualify for the estate tax unlimited marital deduction?

    a. Property transferring to a surviving spouse as beneficiary of an irrevocable trust created six years ago. At the time of the trust's creation, the gift was complete, but the decedent did not pay any gift tax as the only beneficiary of the trust was the decedent's spouse.

    b. A bequest of 2,000 shares of Holiday Incorporated stock to a surviving spouse. The surviving spouse is a U.S. citizen.

    c. The bequest of the life estate interest in a home to the surviving spouse. The decedent bequeathed the remainder interest to his children.

    d. A bequest of property with a fair market value of $10,000 to a surviving spouse. The surviving spouse disclaims the interest and the property transfers to the decedent's residual heirs, his children.

10. Jeff died in the current year. He had inherited the following property from his wife in 1992:

Asset	Fair Market Value at Wife's Date of Death	Fair Market Value at Jeff's Date of Death
Life Estate* in Home	$240,000	$600,000
Cash	$450,000	$250,000
1991 Chevrolet	$14,000	Sold in 1996
IRA	$380,000	$500,000

*No QTIP election.

Considering only the property listed above, what is the value of the property included in Jeff's gross estate?

    a. $250,000.

    b. $704,000.

    c. $750,000.

    d. $1,350,000.

11. Which of the following property interests qualifies for the unlimited marital deduction?

a. John dies and leaves his vacation home to his wife as trustee of a testamentary trust created for the sole benefit of his two children.

b. The executor of John's estate made the QTIP election for the bequest of a life estate interest in his personal residence to Deborah, John's wife.

c. John bequeaths his interest in community property to his wife subject to his wife surviving him by more than 8 months.

d. At John's death, his will created a trust for the benefit of his wife. The trust document gives his wife the authority to appoint assets to herself, her creditors, and her heirs with the approval of John's brother, Colin.

12. Which of the following is not a requirement for a GPOA Trust to be eligible for the unlimited marital deduction?

a. No person, other than the surviving spouse, may appoint any part of the trust property to anyone other than the surviving spouse.

b. The general power of appointment granted to the surviving spouse must be exercisable by the surviving spouse alone.

c. The surviving spouse's right to the trust property must be limited to an ascertainable standard, such as health, education, maintenance, and support.

d. The surviving spouse must be entitled to receive all of the income from the trust, at least annually.

13. Which of the following statements is true?

a. An estate is described as overqualified when, due to a failure to make proper use of the marital deduction, too much of the property is subject to estate tax at the death of the first spouse.

b. An estate is described as underqualified when, due to a failure to make proper use of the marital deduction, not enough property is subject to estate tax at the death of the first spouse.

c. A bypass trust aids in guaranteeing the full use of an individual's applicable estate tax credit.

d. An estate that does not take advantage of its available applicable estate tax credit is transferring assets at the lowest possible cost.

14. Which of the following statements regarding bypass trusts is false?

    a. A bypass trust can give the surviving spouse the right to distributions of principal for an ascertainable standard without causing inclusion of the trust's assets in the surviving spouse's gross estate.

    b. A surviving spouse can demand the greater of $5,000 or 5% of the trust's principal each year without causing inclusion of the trust's assets in her gross estate.

    c. Distributions of trust income to the surviving spouse will not create an ownership interest in the trust's assets.

    d. The right to appoint the assets of the trust to herself, her creditors, or anyone she desires will not create an interest which will cause inclusion of the trust's assets in the surviving spouse's gross estate.

15. Jimmy and Rebecca have been married for 35 years. Jimmy had a net worth of $4,000,000 when he died in 2009. Which of the following scenarios would incur the lowest overall (at Jimmy's death and Rebecca's death) estate taxes assuming the property transfers at equal value at the death of both individuals and utilizing 2009 estate tax rates?

    a. Jimmy's will directs that all of his property is transferred to Rebecca.

    b. In his will, Jimmy funds a trust with $3,500,000 for the benefit of his two children. Rebecca will receive an annual income distribution from the trust. All other assets will transfer to Rebecca.

    c. At Jimmy's death, specific bequests totalling $275,000 are transferred per the direction of the will to individual's other than Rebecca. The remainder of the assets are transferred to a trust with the income payable to Rebecca for her life and the remainder interest payable to the children at Rebecca's death. Jimmy's executor elected to treat this as a QTIP trust.

    d. Jimmy's will directs the transfer of $345,800 to his two children and the remainder of his assets to his wife, Rebecca.

16. Which of the following allows an individual to refuse property from the estate of a decedent?

    a. Bypass trust.

    b. Exclusionary clause.

    c. Disclaimer.

    d. Rejection.

17. Within how many months must an heir file a qualified disclaimer for it to be valid?

    a. 6 months.

    b. 9 months.

    c. 12 months.

    d. 15 months.

18. Janice died in 2009. She had been married to Thomas for 17 years, and the two had amassed a community property estate of $9,000,000. Janice's will directs three specific bequests to her mother, brother, and father of $350,000, $225,000, and $100,000, respectively and creates a bypass trust to receive property equal to any remaining applicable estate tax credit available after her specific bequests. The bypass trust gives Thomas the right to income for his life and the remainder of the trust to her two sons and leaves the residual of the estate to Thomas. Janice's will directs the residual to be used to pay the estate taxes. What is the marital deduction on Janice's federal estate tax return?

    a. $675,000.

    b. $1,000,000.

    c. $2,825,000.

    d. $3,500,000.

Quick Quiz Explanations

Quick Quiz 10.1

1. True.
2. False. Transfers to a divorced spouse never qualify for the unlimited marital deduction.
3. True.

Quick Quiz 10.2

1. False. A transfer of property to a surviving spouse as trustee for the benefit of the children will not qualify for the marital deduction. As trustee, the surviving spouse will have a fiduciary duty to the trust beneficiaries, and while he will hold legal title to the trust assets, beneficial title belongs to the beneficiaries. As such, the trust property will not be included in the surviving spouse's estate, and the transfer will not qualify for the marital deduction.
2. True.
3. False. Generally, terminable interests to not qualify for the marital deduction. There are four primary exceptions to this rule: (1) six month survival contingencies; (2) terminable interests over which the surviving spouse has a general power of appointment; (3) QTIP Trusts; and (4) CRTs where the only non-charitable beneficiary is the surviving spouse. To qualify for the marital deduction, one of these four exceptions must be met. The period of time in which a terminable interest terminates is irrelevant.
4. True.

Quick Quiz 10.3

1. True.
2. True.
3. True.

Quick Quiz 10.4

1. True.
2. False. To qualify the trust as a QTIP trust, and obtain a marital deduction in the estate of the first spouse to die, the executor must elect to treat the trust as a QTIP trust, which requires the surviving spouse to include the remaining assets of the QTIP trust in his or her estate when the surviving spouse dies. Despite the terminable interest held by the spouse in the QTIP, the full fair market value of the remaining assets will be included in the surviving spouse's estate at death.
3. True.
4. False. A QTIP election cannot be made to qualify a transfer to a non-U.S. citizen spouse for the unlimited marital deduction. Deferral of estate taxes can be achieved, however, through use of a Qualified Domestic Trust (QDOT) for the benefit of the surviving non-citizen spouse.

Quick Quiz Explanations

Quick Quiz 10.5

1. True.
2. True.
3. True.

Quick Quiz 10.6

1. False. To be valid, a disclaimer must be made within nine months of the decedent's death.
2. False. When an individual disclaims property, the property will pass in accordance with the terms of the decedent's will, by intestacy, or to the successor beneficiary in a transfer by contract scenario. The disclaimant may not direct the disposition of the property.
3. True.

Quick Quiz 10.7

1. True.
2. False. Bypass trusts are used to hold property that will transfer free of estate tax through use of the applicable estate tax credit.
3. True.

Life Insurance in Estate Planning

INTRODUCTION

One of the great uncertainties in life is that, usually, one does not know exactly when he or she will die. At any point in time, individuals may want to achieve goals and objectives that require financial resources beyond those that they have already accumulated. Life insurance is a tool that can be used to ensure that a person will have the capital to fund all of his important goals, even if he dies before acquiring sufficient resources to fund those goals himself. Viewed in this context, life insurance is a hedge against the untimely death of the income earner and the resulting shortfall of resources that may result from early death.

Many misconceptions surround the use of life insurance and some individuals engaged in the financial and estate planning process do not fully comprehend the need for life insurance protection. For persons who have modest estates and who have achieved most of their goals during their lifetime (for example, retiring the mortgage on a principal residence, funding their children's education, and saving for an adequate retirement income), large amounts of life insurance may not be necessary. Most individuals, however, should consider using life insurance in their estate plans. For individuals with estates in excess of the applicable estate tax credit equivalency amount ($3,500,000 for 2009), and for individuals who have not accumulated sufficient financial resources to fund all of their estate planning goals, life insurance is an essential part of the estate planning process because it provides liquidity in a timely manner.

OBJECTIVE OF LIFE INSURANCE

Depending upon the goals and current financial situation of the client, life insurance can be used to provide for several client objectives. Common objectives that can be served by using life insurance include protecting the income stream of the client's family, providing liquidity at the insured's death, providing a source of retirement income, funding the children's education, and creating or sustaining family wealth. Keep in mind that while there are no absolutes in financial planning, the general rule with regard to ownership of life insurance is that if the purpose of the life insurance is to provide estate liquidity and benefits to heirs, the insured should not own the policies. If on the other hand, life insurance is intended to be used during the insured's life for education or retirement (by accessing policy cash values), the insured will need to own the policy, thus causing inclusion of any death benefit in the insured's estate at death.

PROTECT INCOME STREAM FOR BENEFICIARIES

One of the most important issues that an individual faces in the estate planning process is ensuring that surviving family members have an adequate income stream to maintain their standard of living. This need is particularly acute for young individuals who have not had time to accumulate a significant estate and for individuals who are the sole breadwinner of their family.

Several issues should be considered when funding this goal of income stream protection. The most obvious is the need to replace the lost income stream due to the death of one spouse. Even where both spouses are working, the loss of one income stream can present a significant financial hardship on the family. Expenses beyond normal recurring expenses may be incurred by the surviving spouse, particularly when children are still at home, since the decedent's domestic services will no longer be available to the family. In determining the appropriate dollar amount of life insurance to carry, clients should consider the amount of income needed on an inflation-adjusted basis to allow the surviving spouse and any dependent children to maintain their current standard of living.

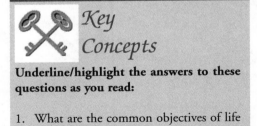

Key Concepts

Underline/highlight the answers to these questions as you read:

1. What are the common objectives of life insurance?

2. Identify the four main types of life insurance policies and their characteristics.

3. Identify and define the parties to a life insurance contract.

The amount of life insurance necessary to adequately insure a person may be determined by using a needs analysis, a human value method, or a capitalized income model. The needs approach and human value approach are covered in insurance textbooks. The capitalized income approach is fairly straightforward and may be calculated as follows.

$$\text{Life insurance needed} = \frac{\text{Gross income - Adjustments}}{\text{Riskless rate adjusted for inflation}}$$

EXAMPLE 11.1

Jack, age 40, makes $100,000 per year of which 30% goes to taxes and Jack personally consumes 20% of the remainder. Jack is married to Jill, age 40, who has no investment experience. They have three small children. The current and projected long-term Treasury Bond is returning 6% and inflation is projected to be 2.5%.

$$\frac{\$100{,}000 - 30\% \; (\$100{,}000) - 20\% \; (\$70{,}000)}{(1.06/1.025) - 1} = \frac{\$56{,}000}{0.03415 \; \text{(rounded)}} = \$1{,}639{,}824$$

The amount of life insurance needed to fully insure Jack's life is estimated to be $1,639,824 producing perpetual income at the riskless rate of $93,389 in the initial year following death. Jill would then spend ($56,000 x 1.025%) $57,400 in the first year and reinvest the $40,989 back into principal leaving her with a riskless inflation adjusted annuity equal to $56,000 (as indexed for inflation).

The amount of annual income the family needs may include allowances for day-to-day spending, maintaining mortgage payments and real estate taxes on family residences, credit card and consumer loan payments, and primary and secondary school tuition payments for the children. Note that some of these expenses could be relieved at the death of the first spouse by ensuring that the death benefit is sufficiently large to allow the payment of the decedent's outstanding debts.

EXAMPLE 11.2

David, a 42 year old father of three, recently died. He was married to Martha, age 39. All of his children are under age 18. Upon the birth of their third child, David and Martha purchased a new home. The home was worth $350,000 when David died, and the outstanding mortgage balance was $225,000. Monthly payments on the mortgage were $1,900. As part of his estate plan, David purchased a life insurance policy to ensure his family would have enough money in the event of his untimely death. David purchased enough insurance so that if he died, the mortgage on the house could be paid off in full. As a result of the mortgage being paid off, Martha's monthly expenses have declined by $1,900.

One benefit of paying off outstanding debts at the death of the first spouse is that the surviving spouse will not have the burden of servicing the outstanding debt. This strategy may be particularly helpful if the surviving spouse is not skilled at managing finances.

A SOURCE OF FUNDS FOR EDUCATION

One of the family objectives most frequently cited in the financial planning process is a desire to assist children in obtaining a college education. The extent of desired funding for this goal may differ from client to client, but it is not uncommon for parents to want to provide their children with a college education.

Assuming that the client will live beyond the children's graduation from college, a funding plan can be established that will call for saving a specific amount on a monthly or annual basis. Since most individuals do not initially have the resources to set aside a lump sum to cover the total for educational costs, the untimely death of the client may result in a shortfall in educational funding. Life insurance can be used in the estate planning process to ensure that the desired level of funding for education will be available. This illustrates the need to coordinate estate planning with the traditional lifetime financial planning needs of the client.

PROVIDE LIQUIDITY AT DEATH

One of the classic reasons for using life insurance in an estate plan is to create immediate liquidity at the decedent's estate. If the decedent was the primary breadwinner of the family, this is particularly important to the survivors.

Depending upon the structure of the estate plan, there may be a time delay in transferring assets to the family members. For example, if the decedent's property is being transferred via the probate process, months may pass before the probate property is made available to the family. During this period, the family will need money to pay the mortgage, buy clothes for the children, pay school tuition, and possibly, if the surviving spouse is not working, provide for living expenses. The funeral expenses of the decedent must be paid (usually before the funeral), as well as any outstanding medical and hospital bills incurred during the decedent's last illness. It may be either desired or advantageous to provide sufficient liquidity at death to pay off all outstanding liabilities, such as the mortgage on the residence, credit card debt, and consumer loans. When these debts are extinguished quickly after the decedent's death, the administration of the estate often moves faster and the surviving spouse is not burdened with the monthly task of servicing the debt, allowing him to focus on caring for the family.

For individuals with large estates, or closely held businesses, liquidity may be necessary to provide the funds for the payment of estate and inheritance taxes. Federal estate taxes are due nine months after a person's death. Most states have a similar time frame for the payment of state estate or inheritance tax. Because the federal tax, if due, tends to be large, it is not always easy to pay that tax from the decedent's assets without having to sell assets. Unless the decedent had a very liquid estate, the estate may sell some assets to generate the cash necessary to pay the estate tax. In the case of a closely held business owner, this could be fatal. If the business is sold quickly in a "fire-sale" fashion, the family may realize far less than the fair market value of the business. An effective solution to this problem is to purchase life insurance coverage sufficient to cover not only the debts of the decedent and the cash flow needs of the family immediately after death, but also any expected estate taxes that will be due within nine months. If the individual has partners, he may wish to have a buy-sell agreement with the partners that is funded with insurance. A buy-sell agreement allows the parties to require the surviving partners to buy out the deceased partner's share and is generally funded with life insurance. Ensuring that the cash is available to cover all of these expenses will allow a more orderly administration of the estate and a more efficient disposition of the decedent's assets. Insurance to be used for paying estate taxes is usually placed in an irrevocable life insurance trust (ILIT) so that transfer taxes are avoided on the proceeds. ILIT's are discussed at length below.

A SOURCE FOR RETIREMENT INCOME

After the income stream for survivors, educational needs of children, and liquidity needs of the estate are provided for, there may still be a need for additional income for the surviving spouse. Life insurance can provide a lump sum dollar amount at death that will satisfy the needed income for the surviving spouse.

In constructing a financial plan for a client, a central issue typically addressed is providing for an adequate retirement income for the client and his spouse. Usually, a plan is established where the client saves a specific dollar amount on a weekly, monthly, or annual basis that will, when combined with future investment earnings, provide for the desired level of retirement income. If an individual dies before this goal is fully funded, a shortfall may result for the surviving spouse. Life insurance can provide a lump sum that can be set aside to make up for the loss of annual contributions by the deceased spouse, providing financial security for the surviving spouse.

If life insurance is purchased to fund the client's financial and estate planning objectives, it may also be useful for funding retirement needs even if a death does not occur before retirement. When a cash-value life insurance policy is purchased, and the premium is paid on a regular basis, the life insurance cash value will grow over time. If by the time the client retires, the mortgage on the home has been paid off, the children's education has been paid for, and an adequate retirement income has been funded, the death benefit of the life insurance policy may be more than necessary to fund remaining liquidity needs. In this case, the owner of the policy could take tax-free distributions of his adjusted basis in the life insurance policy and take loans from the cash value of the life insurance policy to supplement retirement income. If the client's estate will not have significant liquidity needs at death, the policy could be surrendered. The surrender of a life insurance policy will subject any gain in excess of the adjusted basis in the policy to ordinary income taxation, but the proceeds could be used to supplement retirement income.

Keep in mind, however, if the client wants control over loans or access to cash values during life to fund education or retirement needs, the client must own the life insurance policy. For the estate planning purposes of income replacement for survivors and estate liquidity, the client generally will not want ownership of the life insurance policy because such ownership will cause inclusion of the proceeds in the decedent's gross estate.

CREATE OR SUSTAIN FAMILY WEALTH

Some individuals have estate planning objectives that go beyond providing for their individual needs and the needs of their children. Individuals who tend to think of wealth maximization for the family in the long-run may wish to create pools of capital that can be used by future family members such as grandchildren, great-grandchildren, and so on. Some common examples of planning techniques for these individuals include the use of dynasty trusts, Generation-Skipping Trusts, and foundations (all of these techniques are covered elsewhere in this book). A significant amount of capital may be needed to ensure that these arrangements can be created to benefit future generations of the family.

Life insurance may be the ideal funding arrangement for individuals with these types of goals. Even if an individual has not yet accumulated a large net worth, long-range goals could be funded appropriately as long as there is sufficient income to pay the life insurance premiums. When the client dies, the life insurance company will pay the death benefit to the accumulation vehicle (usually a trust) and the client's long-range objectives will be satisfied. Some individuals feel that life insurance is the best way to fund these vehicles, since all of the client's assets, aside from those used to pay the life insurance premiums, are available for use of the client and his or her family during their lifetime, and the life insurance death benefit will "create" the wealth necessary to satisfy the long-run client objectives at death.

Life insurance also presents an opportunity for wealthy individuals and families to sustain family wealth. For example, assume that as part of his estate planning, a grandparent created a dynasty trust for his family. Throughout the lifetime of the beneficiaries, the dynasty trustee distributes some of the income and assets of the trust to the family members. If the trustee had purchased a life insurance policy on the life of each beneficiary of the trust, upon the death of each beneficiary the trust would receive a capital infusion that may partially or wholly reimburse the trust for the distributions made to that beneficiary during his lifetime. When used in this way, life insurance ensures that current generations of the family enjoy the family's accumulated wealth without depriving that wealth from future generations of the family.

<table>
<tr><td>EXHIBIT 11.1</td><td></td></tr>
</table>

OBJECTIVES OF LIFE INSURANCE

- Protect income stream for beneficiaries.
- Source of funds for education.
- Provide liquidity at death.
- Source for retirement income.
- Create or sustain family wealth.

TYPES OF LIFE INSURANCE

Several types of life insurance policies exist in the market today. Many contracts have unique features that may prove valuable in a given planning situation. It is important to remember, however, that life insurance is not a one-size-fits-all product. What works for one client's plan may not be the best solution for another client. The planner should always try to fit the characteristics of the contract to the planning issues being addressed. The basic types of life insurance are summarized below.

TERM INSURANCE

A **term insurance policy** is a life insurance contract that states if the insured dies within the term of the contract, the insurance company will pay the stated death benefit. The premium on a term insurance policy reflects the actuarial risk that the insured will die during the term of the contract. Some commentators refer to the premium on a term insurance policy as the "pure cost of life insurance protection" since none of the premium dollars are allocated to a savings account (as is the case in universal life, whole life, and variable universal life insurance policies).

The premium on a term insurance policy will be lower than the alternative permanent policies available, since there is no cash accumulation account to be funded. This may be advantageous in certain circumstances. For example, a young individual who has not had time to accumulate much wealth may need a large amount of life insurance protection to provide an income stream for the surviving spouse, pay off the mortgage on the principal residence, pay for children's education, and so on. Because the individual is young, however, the pure cost of insurance is low, which allows him or her to purchase the necessary coverage at a relatively reasonable cost. As the client's income increases and the needs being funded by the life insurance become more permanent (for example, liquidity to pay death taxes), the term insurance contract may be converted to a permanent type of policy.

One point of caution should be noted, however. Many individuals have been taught that "buying term and investing the difference" is always an optimal strategy. This is not the case. When an individual has a permanent need for life insurance protection, buying term and investing the difference can be a disaster. As the individual gets older, the pure cost of the insurance protection (the premium on a term policy) increases exponentially. At advanced ages, the annual cost of the insurance policy may be prohibitive and if the premium is not paid, the policy will lapse. With life expectancies increasing, this may prove to be a significant problem. When choosing the most appropriate policy, consider the use of permanent insurance for permanent needs.

Term insurance is appropriate for funding temporary needs. For example, a young couple who wishes to ensure that there will be sufficient money to send the children to college in the event of their premature death could purchase a term insurance policy to cover this need (perhaps a 30 year level term insurance contract). Once the children graduate from college, the need for the insurance disappears and the policy can be cancelled. Term insurance may also be useful as a hedge when engaging in sophisticated estate planning involving the use of GRATs, GRUTs, QPRTs, and other transfers that may result in estate tax inclusion. All of these techniques pose a risk of estate tax inclusion for a period of time and term insurance can be purchased to cover the estate taxes due in the event that the insured dies before the transfers are complete for estate planning purposes.

UNIVERSAL LIFE

Universal life insurance is, in essence, a term insurance policy with a cash accumulation account attached to it. One of the advantages of universal life insurance is that the premium is flexible – if the owner of the policy has extra income in a particular year, he can make additional contributions to the policy. If money is tight in another year, no premium has to be paid as long as there is enough in the cash accumulation account to pay that year's premium. All of the premiums paid go into the cash accumulation account, and each month or year the insurance company will take the pure cost of insurance protection out of the cash value. As long as there is sufficient money in the cash account to pay the current year premium, the policy remains in force. The money inside of the cash accumulation account grows on a tax-deferred basis depending on the investment returns.

Like a term insurance policy, the pure cost to maintain the policy increases as the insured's age increases. The insurer typically does not guarantee that the universal life policy will remain in force as long as a certain premium is paid. Instead, the policy will remain in force only as long as there is enough cash in the accumulation account to pay the increasing pure insurance premium. This type of policy is probably best suited to cover temporary needs and a permanent type of life insurance protection should be used when the client's need for life insurance is permanent.

VARIABLE UNIVERSAL LIFE

Variable universal life insurance policies are simply universal life insurance policies (described above) with one added feature – the insured can choose how to invest the cash in the cash accumulation account. Usually, the insurer will offer several different investment choices in the form of mutual funds including equity funds, bond funds, and money market funds. Variable universal life insurance policies do not provide guarantees like whole life policies do, and will remain in force only as long as there is sufficient value in the investment account to pay the annual pure insurance premium. Variable universal life insurance policies are a good option for younger clients with a higher risk tolerance for investments, since the accumulation of funds inside of the policy over the long-run can be significant.

WHOLE LIFE

Whole life insurance provides guarantees from the insurer that are not found in term insurance and universal life insurance contracts. As long as the insured pays a stated premium each year, the insurer guarantees that the life insurance policy will remain in force. Part of each premium is allocated to a cash savings account that will grow over time. The cash that is accumulating in the contract is used to pay the higher costs of life insurance protection when the insured reaches advanced ages. Even if the cash account runs out, the life insurance is guaranteed to remain in force provided that the insured pays the premium. Whole life insurance policies are useful when the client wants such guarantees, and for middle-aged and older clients who are obtaining life insurance protection. The cash value of a whole life policy is invested by the insurer and usually has a minimum guaranteed return.

SECOND-TO-DIE

A second-to-die policy has two insureds, and may be issued as a permanent (cash value) policy, or a term policy. The advantage of a second-to-die policy is that one of the parties (usually spouses) may be uninsurable, but the insurance company will still issue the policy since the policy pays the death benefit at the death of the second spouse. Usually the objective of second-to-die insurance is to provide estate liquidity to pay estate taxes at the death of the second spouse. Consequently, a second-to-die policy is usually owned by an irrevocable life insurance trust (ILIT).

EXHIBIT 11.2

TYPES OF LIFE INSURANCE

- Term
- Universal Life
- Variable Universal Life
- Whole Life
- Second-to-Die

PARTIES TO A LIFE INSURANCE POLICY

Before examining the tax consequences of holding life insurance, it is important to distinguish between the owner of the policy, the insured of the policy, and the beneficiary of the policy. It is possible that different people will occupy each of these positions for a single life insurance policy. The tax ramifications of policy ownership are often dependent on the identification of the parties to the life insurance policy.

OWNER

The **owner** of the policy is the person who has title to the contract. The owner may or may not be the insured, and may or may not be the beneficiary. The owner is the person who can exercise control over the economic rights of the policy. For example, the owner can borrow from the cash value of the policy, can pledge the policy for a loan, and can increase or decrease the premium payments made on the policy (depending upon the type of policy and the current funding status).

INSURED

The **insured** is the person whose life is covered by the contract. When the insured dies, the life insurance company will pay the death benefit to the beneficiary named in the policy.

BENEFICIARY

The **beneficiary** is the person entitled to receive the death benefit once the insured dies. The owner of the life insurance policy can designate the beneficiary on a form provided by the life insurance company. In the event that no beneficiary is named, the owner of the policy will receive the death benefit. In the event that the owner of the policy was also the insured, the owner's estate will receive the death benefit. It is always advantageous to make sure that beneficiary designations are on file with the insurance company and that the appropriate party is named as the beneficiary. When there is a named beneficiary for the life insurance policy, the death benefit will avoid probate and will generally avoid income taxation.

EXHIBIT 11.3

PARTIES TO A LIFE INSURANCE POLICY

Owner - the person who has title to the policy.

Insured - the person whose life is covered by the policy.

Beneficiary - the person entitled to receive the death benefit once the insured dies.

INCOME TAX TREATMENT OF LIFE INSURANCE

GENERAL

Internal Revenue Code (IRC) Section 61(a)(10) states that "income from life insurance and endowment contracts" is subject to income tax. For federal income tax purposes, any accretion to wealth constitutes taxable income and a life insurance contract results in an accretion to wealth for the beneficiary of the policy. Absent a provision to the contrary, therefore, the death benefit of a life insurance contract would be taxable to the beneficiary of the policy.

Luckily, Section 101(a) of the Code gives us an exception that states "Except as otherwise provided...gross income does not include amounts received (whether in a single sum or otherwise) under a life insurance contract, if such amounts are paid by reason of the death of the insured." Therefore, as a general rule, the death benefit paid on a life insurance policy will escape income taxation in the hands of the beneficiary. The transfer-for-value rule is the only exception to this general rule.

TRANSFER FOR VALUE

While the death benefit on a life insurance policy is not typically subject to income taxation, the death benefit in excess of the transferee's adjusted basis will be subject to income tax if the life insurance policy is transferred for valuable consideration.

Referred to as the **transfer-for-value rule**, the condition that subjects the policy death benefit subject to tax is a transfer for value. The life insurance policy must be exchanged for valuable consideration in order for the transfer-for-value rule to apply. Consider the following examples:

> ### Key Concepts
>
> **Underline/highlight the answers to these questions as you read:**
>
> 1. What is the general rule regarding the income tax treatment of life insurance?
>
> 2. What is the transfer-for-value rule?
>
> 3. What are the settlement options available to beneficiaries of a life insurance policy?

EXAMPLE 11.3

Five years ago, John purchased a life insurance policy on his life and named himself as the owner and beneficiary of the policy. He recently learned that the death benefit will be subject to estate taxation, since he is both the insured and the owner of the policy. To avoid estate taxation of the death benefit, John gave the policy to his wife, Patty, who is now listed as the sole owner and beneficiary of the contract. When John dies, Patty will not have to pay income tax on the death benefit because John made a gratuitous transfer of the policy to Patty; he did not give her the policy in return for valuable consideration.

EXAMPLE 11.4

Jessie has had a very bad year. His wife, Nellie, left him and took everything he owned except for a life insurance policy he has on Nellie's life. The life insurance policy has a cash value of $50,000 and a death benefit of $500,000. Jessie owes Margie, the meanest banker in town, $200,000. Jessie has considered filing for bankruptcy. During a recent meeting, Margie discovered that Jessie had the insurance policy and offered to forgive the debt he owed her in exchange for the policy. Margie's reasoning was that the $50,000 cash value was better than nothing and she might hang on to the policy until Nellie died to receive the death benefit. Jessie happily agreed to the exchange. This is an example of a transfer for value because the policy was exchanged for extinguishment of debt. Margie will have an adjusted basis in the policy of $200,000 (the amount of debt forgiven). If she were to cash in the policy today she would have a $150,000 loss and if she waits until the death benefit is paid she will have a taxable gain of $300,000.

EXAMPLE 11.5

John, Randy, Tom, and Keegan are partners in the XYZ partnership. They decide to enter into a cross-purchase buy-sell agreement to ensure that their families will receive full value for their partnership interest when they die. Under a cross-purchase agreement, they will each have to purchase a policy on everyone else's life, requiring a total of 12 life insurance policies. To simplify the arrangement, they decide to create a trust that will hold one life insurance policy on each partner's life. As each partner dies, the trust will purchase the interest with the life insurance proceeds. When the first partner dies, everything works as planned, with one exception. A transfer for value has occurred, since the ownership of the remaining three policies on the lives of the survivors has shifted from 4 partners to three. Initially, each partner owned (indirectly) 25% of each policy, but after the first death, each of the surviving partners owns 33% of each policy. This was not a gratuitous transfer, but rather a transfer for valuable consideration because there was an economic reason behind the buy-sell agreement.

Even if the transfer-for-value rule applies, certain exceptions to the rule will prevent the death benefit in the policy from being subject to income tax. Alternatively stated, if an exception to the transfer-for-value rule applies, we go back to the general rule that states that the death benefit paid by reason of the insured's death is not subject to income tax. IRC Section 101(a)(2) states that the transfer-for-value rule will not apply when there is a transfer of a life insurance policy to any of the following individuals:

1. the insured,
2. a partner of the insured,
3. a partnership in which the insured is a partner,
4. a corporation in which the insured is a shareholder or officer,
5. a transferee who takes the transferor's basis in the contract.

Therefore, when planning a transaction that could be considered a transfer for value, it is important to structure the transaction so that it meets an exception to the transfer-for-value rule so that the death benefit will not be subject to income taxation. Consider the following examples:

EXAMPLE 11.6

Randy is a key employee at a large international manufacturing company. The company purchased a life insurance policy on Randy's life several years ago to provide compensation to the company for the loss of Randy's services in the event of his early death. Randy is retiring this month and the company no longer needs the life insurance policy on Randy's life. Randy, however, could use the policy for estate planning purposes. The value of the policy is $65,000. If Randy purchases the policy from the company for $65,000, a transfer for value has occurred, but the death benefit will not be subject to income tax because the life insurance policy was transferred for valuable consideration to the insured.

EXAMPLE 11.7

Assume the same facts as above, except that instead of purchasing the policy himself, Randy has the trustee of an irrevocable grantor trust (of which he is the grantor) purchase the policy for $65,000. Randy does this to ensure that the death benefit will not be subject to estate tax at his death. The transaction constitutes a transfer of a life insurance policy for valuable consideration, but the death benefit will not be subject to income tax because the transferee (the irrevocable grantor trust) is considered to be the same as the transferor. This result is attained because, for income tax purposes, Randy is considered to be the owner of the assets inside of the irrevocable grantor trust he created and therefore the sale is treated in the same manner as a sale of the policy to the insured.

EXAMPLE 11.8

Recall the XYZ Partnership example stated above, where John, Randy, Tom, and Keegan enter into a trusted cross-purchase buy-sell agreement. While a transfer for value occurs at the death of the first partner, the death benefits on the remaining three life insurance policies held by the trust will not be subject to income taxation because the transfer was to a partner of the insured, (an exception to the transfer-for-value rule). Note that if XYZ was a corporation, no exception to the transfer-for-value rule would apply, since the transfer is not made to a corporation in which the insured was a shareholder or officer, but was made to the remaining shareholders.

John, Randy, Tom, and Keegan are all equal shareholders in the XYZ Corporation. The shareholders decide to enter into an entity-type buy-sell agreement where the corporation agrees to purchase the shares of a deceased shareholder. The corporation will fund the buy-sell agreement with life insurance. Keegan owns several life insurance policies on his own life and the total death benefit is significantly higher than what is necessary to satisfy his estate planning goals. Keegan sells one of his life insurance policies to the corporation at fair market value. While a transfer for value has occurred, the corporation will not have to pay income tax on the death benefit in excess of basis since the transferee was a corporation in which the insured was a shareholder or officer.

EXAMPLE 11.9

The transfer-for-value rule can be a serious trap for the unwary. It is important to consider the income tax implications of any transfer of life insurance that is not considered a gratuitous transfer <u>before</u> entering into such a transaction. The "transfer-for-value rule" subjecting the death benefit to income taxation cannot be avoided by having the parties cancel the transaction at a later time.

SETTLEMENT OR CASH SURRENDER

When the insured dies, the beneficiary can choose to receive the policy benefits in one of several different ways, referred to as **settlement options**, assuming the owner had not previously established an irrevocable settlement option. One option, of course, is a **lump sum death benefit**. (As previously stated, the death benefit itself is exempt from income tax provided that there has been no transfer of the policy for valuable consideration.) As an alternative, the beneficiary can choose to keep the life insurance proceeds on deposit at the insurer and receive the interest that accrues on the balance on a regular basis. Some life insurance policies offer various annuity options as well.

While the death benefit on the policy is typically income-tax free, any interest accumulated on the death benefit is subject to ordinary income tax. If a beneficiary elects, for example, to leave the death benefit on deposit with the insurance company and receive distributions of the interest

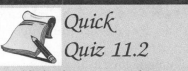

Quick Quiz 11.2

Highlight the answer to these questions:

1. The transfer-for-value rule subjecting the death benefit to income taxation can be avoided by having the parties cancel the transaction at a later point in time.
   a. True
   b. False

2. The owner of a life insurance policy can select the settlement option that will be payable to the beneficiary.
   a. True
   b. False

3. If the death benefit of a life insurance policy payable to a beneficiary is left on deposit with the insurance company, the beneficiary will receive tax-exempt interest on the policy proceeds.
   a. True
   b. False

4. The surrender value of a term life insurance policy increases each year the premium is paid.
   a. True
   b. False

False, True, False, False.

credited to the death benefit, the interest payments will be taxed as ordinary income. If an annuity option is chosen, the rules under Section 72 of the IRC (the exclusion ratio) are used to determine what portion of each payment is treated as a nontaxable return of adjusted basis, and what portion is taxable income. The income tax implications should be considered by the owner or by the beneficiary when selecting a particular settlement option.

Even if a beneficiary elects to take a lump sum distribution, part of the distribution will be subject to income tax. The life insurance policy matures on the date the insured dies and the death benefit becomes payable on that date. To collect the death benefit, the beneficiary of the policy must notify the insurance company of the insured's death, provide proof of death (usually a certified copy of the death certificate), and comply with the insurance company's requests for information. The insurance company could pay quickly or the claim could take some time. It is not unusual for several months to pass before the beneficiary receives the payment for the death benefit especially if the cause of death is suspect. Interest on the death benefit accrues, however, from the date of the insured's death. Therefore, when the beneficiary receives the death benefit, he will also receive fully taxable interest on the death benefit that accrued from the time of the decedent's death to the date the insurance company actually paid the claim.

Instead of waiting for the life insurance policy to mature, the owner of the policy could surrender it and receive the "surrender value" of the contract. The **surrender value** is generally the cash value of the contract less a surrender charge which is governed by the contract or by state law. If the owner of the policy surrenders it to the insurance company and receives an amount that is greater than his adjusted basis in the policy, the difference between the amount received and the owner's adjusted basis is considered taxable income. In this instance, the policy benefit was not paid by reason of the death of the insured, and therefore did not qualify for the income tax exclusion offered in the IRC. Any amount received in excess of the owner's adjusted basis in the policy will be taxed as ordinary income.

POLICY DIVIDENDS

Policy dividends issued on a life insurance policy are not like cash dividends issued on stock. When a corporation distributes a cash dividend to its shareholders, the dividend represents a distribution of the earnings and profits of the corporation and is fully subject to income tax. A dividend on a life insurance policy, however, is not treated as a distribution of profits, but rather as a return of the policy owner's adjusted basis.

In pricing a life insurance policy, actuaries assume that the pool of individuals being insured will experience a specified rate of mortality. If, on average, the individuals in the pool live longer than the actuaries estimate, the insurance company imposed a higher than appropriate mortality charge when issuing the policy. To compensate a policy holder for this overcharge, the insurance company issues a policy dividend which returns the overcharge to the policy owner. Consequently, since the policy owner is receiving a return of his adjusted basis in the contract, no taxable income is recognized. Note, however, that the issuance of a policy dividend decreases the policyholder's adjusted basis in the contract, and, if the contract is surrendered at a later time, a greater gain in the policy may result, increasing the ordinary income tax due at that time.

Some individuals choose to keep policy dividends on deposit with the insurer, in return for which the insurer pays interest on the balance. The interest earnings on the dividends are taxable to the owner of the policy even if the interest is not distributed to the owner on an annual basis. The individual may also choose to purchase additional life insurance with the policy dividends. In such a case, the individual's adjusted basis would be reduced by the dividend payment and then subsequently increased by the additional purchase. The net effect to the owner's adjusted basis would be zero, or in other words the owner's adjusted basis would not change.

LOANS

One of the benefits of using a cash value life insurance policy in an estate plan is that the cash value of the policy is available through loans to the policy owner if needed. The owner of the policy can borrow from the cash value of the policy at a favorable interest rate specified in the contract.

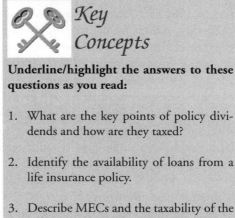

Key Concepts

Underline/highlight the answers to these questions as you read:

1. What are the key points of policy dividends and how are they taxed?

2. Identify the availability of loans from a life insurance policy.

3. Describe MECs and the taxability of the policy.

4. What are the rules for policy exchanges under Section 1035?

5. What are the rules associated with accelerated death benefits?

Unlike other loans the owner may be able to obtain, the loan from the life insurance policy need not be paid back. If the loan is not paid back, interest will accrue at the specified rate until the death of the insured.

Generally, no income tax consequences result from taking a loan from the policy cash value. It may appear that the owner of the policy has constructive receipt over the cash value and that by exercising the borrowing privilege he is withdrawing part of the growth in the policy. However, while constructive receipt of income results in immediate taxation of income, in the case of a life insurance policy loan a substantial risk of forfeiture exists. When the policy owner takes a loan from the policy, the outstanding loan balance plus the accumulated interest due will reduce the death benefit payable from the policy dollar for dollar. The substantial risk of forfeiture prevents the owner of the life insurance policy from being taxed on the income until the policy lapses.

If the life insurance policy **lapses**, the gain in the policy will include the outstanding loan, and will be subject to ordinary income tax. From a planning perspective, individuals usually do not take policy loans unless (1) they expect to repay them, or (2) if the loan will not be repaid, the policy will remain in force until the death of the insured.

These rules only apply when the contract meets the definition of life insurance as provided by the Internal Revenue Code. If the contract is funded in a way that violates the definition of life insurance, it is considered a **modified endowment contract (MEC)** and will lose some of its tax deferral features.

MECs

Prior to 1986, life insurance contracts were sometimes used as tax-deferral investment vehicles. While the product purchased was called life insurance, the contract was being used merely to defer taxable income to another tax year. To illustrate, assume that Harry has received a large inheritance from the estate of his uncle and is 10 years away from retirement. Harry would like to invest the proceeds, but would like to avoid paying income tax on the investment income until after retirement, when he will be in a lower income tax bracket. Since the rules governing retirement plan contributions limit the amount that can be contributed on an annual basis, it would not be possible to put the entire inheritance into retirement planning vehicles. Instead, Harry purchases a single-premium life insurance policy with his inheritance and invests the cash value of the policy in several mutual funds offered by the insurer. Over the last 10 years of Harry's working life, none of the gains will be subject to income tax since they are inside the income-tax free life insurance contract. When Harry retires, he can begin to take policy loans from the contract, paying no income tax on the distributions. If the policy ever lapses, Harry will have to pay income tax on the gain, but the tax would have been deferred for many years to a time when he will be in a lower tax bracket. Harry never intended to use the life insurance policy as life insurance, but rather as a tax-free/tax-deferred investment accumulation device.

In 1986, Congress defined life insurance for federal income tax purposes. In doing so, Congress focused on the funding of the contract. Since most of the abusive uses of life insurance involve situations where all of the premium is paid in the first few years of the contract's existence, a policy that has its premium payments front-loaded will not be eligible to receive the tax benefits traditionally associated with life insurance. In particular, if the owner of the policy attempts to borrow from the policy cash value, the loan will be considered a taxable distribution to the policy holder to the extent of any gain in the contract. The death benefit received by the beneficiary will continue to be income-tax free to the extent that the policy has not been transferred for value.

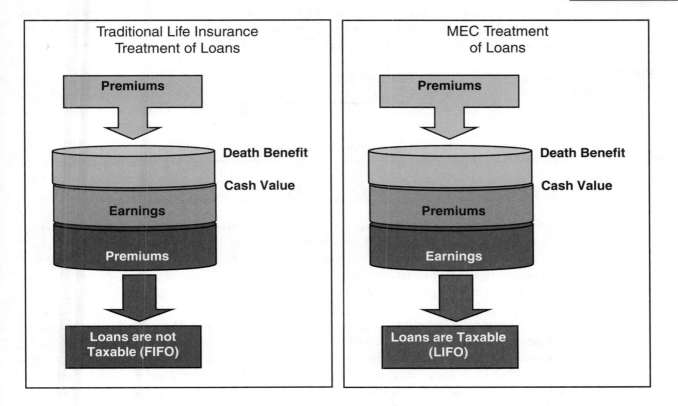

Patrick purchased a single premium life insurance policy on his life 10 years ago for $100,000 (thus a MEC). The current value of the policy is $275,000. Patrick needs some cash to put a down payment on a vacation home, so he borrows $50,000 from the policy. The gain inherent in the policy is $175,000 ($275,000 - $100,000), and, therefore, the $50,000 loan will be treated as a 100% taxable distribution to Patrick. If Patrick dies next year, the beneficiary of the policy will receive the net death benefit free of federal income tax.

EXAMPLE 11.10

In adopting the MEC rules, Congress set forth two tests that determine whether a life insurance policy will be considered a modified endowment contract. These tests, the corridor test and the premiums paid test, are more appropriately covered in an insurance course. If the policy is paid up before it is seven years old, it will generally be treated as a modified endowment contract and the owner of the contract will not enjoy the lifetime tax benefits associated with traditional life insurance policies because the policy has been deemed an investment rather than insurance. MEC status only affects loans, not the taxation of proceeds at death.

POLICY EXCHANGES 1035

IRC **Section 1035** allows the owner of a life insurance contract to exchange the contract for another life insurance contract, an endowment contract, or an annuity contract on the same insured without causing any gain in the policy to be subject to income tax. In order to qualify for this favorable tax treatment, the existing policy must be exchanged directly for the new policy.

EXHIBIT 11.5 **EXCHANGE TREATMENT FOR LIFE INSURANCE AND ANNUITIES**

	EXCHANGE FROM	
EXCHANGE TO	Life Insurance	Annuity
Life Insurance	OK	Taxable Event
Annuity	OK	OK

To the extent that the owner receives cash or other property in the exchange (referred to as "boot" for income tax purposes), gain in the policy is taxable to the extent of boot received. If, at the time of the exchange, the owner of the policy had an outstanding policy loan, and the policy loan was extinguished as a result of the exchange, the principal amount of the outstanding loan will be treated as boot and will therefore be subject to income taxation.

When a life insurance contract is exchanged under Section 1035, the owner's adjusted basis in the new policy is equal to his adjusted basis in the old policy plus any consideration paid for the issuance of the new policy. The carryover basis rules apply to this transaction. Normally, however, basis will not be an issue with life insurance policies unless (1) the policy is a modified endowment contract and the owner is taking a distribution or borrowing money from the policy, or (2) the policy is surrendered before the death of the insured triggering income taxation on the policy gain.

There are a few additional rules that are important to note when considering a 1035 exchange. First, two individual life insurance policies cannot be exchanged for one joint life policy insuring both lives. Second, Section 1035 does not apply to an exchange of life insurance if the insured is not a United States citizen.

ACCELERATED DEATH BENEFITS

Some life insurance companies allow insureds who are terminally or chronically ill to receive an **accelerated death benefit** under the contract. Essentially, the owner surrenders the life insurance contract in return for a payment that is less than the death benefit (and greater than the cash value) and the proceeds are typically used to pay for the medical care of the insured. Recall that only amounts received under a life insurance contract by reason of the death of the insured are exempt from income tax (IRC Section 101(a)). Absent some other statutory provision, receipt of an accelerated death benefit would trigger taxable income for the owner of the policy.

The Code (Section 101(g)) states, however, that amounts received under a life insurance contract on the life of an insured individual who is chronically or terminally ill may be excluded from gross income. For individuals who are chronically ill, however, the nontaxable portion is limited to the amounts incurred by the payee (that are not reimbursed by insurance) for qualified long-term care services provided for the insured.

A **chronically ill individual** is a person who is not terminally ill but has been certified by a licensed health care provider as being unable to perform, without assistance, at least two activities of daily living for at least 90 days, or a person with a similar level of disability. Activities of daily living, as defined in IRC (Section 7702(B)(c)(2)(B)), are (1) eating, (2) toileting, (3) transferring, (4) bathing, (5) dressing, and (6) continence.

A **terminally ill individual** is a person who has been certified by a licensed health care provider as having a condition or illness that can reasonably be expected to result in death within 24 months. (IRC Section101(g)(4)(A)).

The income tax exclusion found in IRC Section 101(g) also applies to sales of life insurance by chronically or terminally ill individuals to **qualified viatical settlement providers** or companies that purchase life insurance policies from terminally and chronically ill individuals. Prior to accepting an accelerated death benefit from the life insurance company, it would be wise to determine if selling the policy to a qualified viatical settlement provider would provide more income for the owner.

While these rules were enacted in order to provide a source of funds for chronically and terminally ill individuals to pay for medical expenses, they can be used effectively for estate planning purposes as well. This is particularly true when the insured is the owner of the life insurance policy and is in a high estate tax bracket, as illustrated in the next example.

Quick Quiz 11.3

Highlight the answer to these questions:

1. Dividends issued on life insurance policies are distributions of the earnings and profits of the insurance company.
   a. True
   b. False

2. The beneficiary of a life insurance policy can take a loan for an amount up to the cash value of the life insurance policy.
   a. True
   b. False

3. If a life insurance policy is determined to be a MEC, any loans against the policy are taxable to the extent that the owner has gain in the policy.
   a. True
   b. False

4. IRC Section 1035 allows the owner of a life insurance contract to exchange the contract for another life insurance contract, an endowment contract, or an annuity contract on the same insured without any tax consequences.
   a. True
   b. False

5. Surrender payments from a life insurance contract to an insured individual who is chronically or terminally ill may be excluded from gross income.
   a. True
   b. False

False, False, True, True, True.

EXAMPLE 11.11

Elizabeth is a 92 year old widowed great-great grandmother, and has recently been diagnosed as terminally ill. Her physicians expect her to live no more than six months. She has 6 children, 18 grandchildren, and 36 great-grandchildren. Elizabeth owns a life insurance policy on her life with a death benefit of $1,000,000. Her gross estate (including the life insurance death benefit) is expected to be over $10,000,000. If Elizabeth dies owning the life insurance policy, the $1,000,000 death benefit will generate a $450,000 federal estate tax (in 2009), leaving only $550,000 for her heirs. Instead, Elizabeth could sell the life insurance policy to a viatical settlement provider and receive $800,000. If Elizabeth used the proceeds to make annual exclusion gifts to her descendents (a total of 60 people), she could immediately remove $780,000 from her estate. Her heirs would be better off by $230,000 ($780,000 - $550,000). If she lived to January 1st of next year, she could give the rest away as annual exclusion gifts. As a result of this planning, Elizabeth's family receives more, and the federal government receives less, of her accumulated wealth.

GIFT TAX TREATMENT OF LIFE INSURANCE

In estate and financial planning, life insurance is often gifted directly or indirectly to individual family members or charities. An understanding of the gift tax treatment of life insurance is important when planning for these transfers.

A life insurance policy is a unique form of property because several parties can hold an interest in the policy. While the insured is alive, the owner of the policy can exercise all of the economic rights over the policy, such as borrowing from the policy cash value or pledging the policy as collateral for a loan. Once the insured dies, the death benefit is paid to the beneficiary named on the policy, which may or may not be the policy owner. These different economic interests may be gifted or transferred to different individuals, but often with gift tax consequences. If the owner of the policy is also the insured, estate tax consequences may result. This section reviews the common types of transfers of life insurance that may trigger gift tax liability.

Key Concepts

Underline/highlight the answers to these questions as you read:

1. Describe the gift tax treatment of life insurance policies.

2. What are the benefits, particularly in terms of income tax, of donating a life insurance policy to charity?

CHANGING THE BENEFICIARY ON THE LIFE INSURANCE POLICY

The individual, trust, or entity that owns a life insurance policy will also often be named as the beneficiary of the policy. Some individuals mistakenly believe that by filing a change of beneficiary form with the life insurance company, ownership of the policy has been transferred.

If a change of beneficiary is made, a completed gift does not occur for federal gift tax purposes. When the insured dies, whoever is named as the beneficiary of the policy will receive the death benefit, but until the insured's death, the original owner may still exercise all economic rights over the policy, including the right to change the beneficiary in the future. Even if an irrevocable beneficiary designation is made with the insurer, the owner of the policy will still be able to exercise all economic rights over the policy until the insured's death, except to name a different beneficiary, and therefore a completed gift has not been made.

Planners should tread cautiously when changing the beneficiary of a life insurance policy without transferring ownership. If the insured is also the owner of the policy, the IRC (Section 2042) will require the death benefit to be included in his federal gross estate and any beneficiary can be named on the policy without triggering a gift tax. If the owner is not the insured, however, and the owner designates a third party as the beneficiary of the policy, a completed gift is made when the insured dies. The value of the gift is the death benefit of the policy. This unintended consequence may result in serious gift tax problems for the owner of the policy.

> Ken and Greg are brothers. Greg purchased a $1,000,000 life insurance contract on Ken's life, and was initially designated as both the owner and the beneficiary of the policy. Both brothers have enjoyed financial success in their careers. Jodie, Ken and Greg's sister, has recently fallen on hard times and Greg decides to name Jodie as the beneficiary of the life insurance policy he owns on Ken's life. No taxable gift occurred at the time the beneficiary was changed. One year after the beneficiary change became effective, Ken unexpectedly died, and the insurance company paid the $1,000,000 death benefit to Jodie. Because Greg owned the policy, and the death benefit was paid to Jodie, Greg will be deemed to have made a $1,000,000 gift to Jodie for federal gift tax purposes. The gift to Jodie will qualify for the annual gift tax exclusion ($13,000), but this will be a small consolation for Greg, who has now used up almost all of his applicable gift tax credit amount. (Recall that during the EGTRRA estate tax phase-out period, the maximum amount of lifetime gifts that can be made by each individual before paying gift tax remains at $1,000,000 even though the amount that can be transferred at death increases over the same period.)

EXAMPLE 11.12

The same result would occur if a husband was to transfer a policy to his wife while remaining the insured, and the wife names the daughter as the beneficiary. This is referred to in the profession as the "unholy trinity."

OUTRIGHT GIFT OF A LIFE INSURANCE POLICY

When the owner of a life insurance policy transfers ownership of the policy to another by gift, a gift tax may result. To transfer the ownership of the policy, appropriate change of owner forms must be filed with the life insurance company that issues the contract; as discussed earlier, a mere change of beneficiary is not sufficient. If ownership is formally transferred, the gift of the policy will be considered a present interest gift and will qualify for the gift tax annual exclusion. If the value of the policy is less than the gift tax annual exclusion, there will be no gift tax consequence and a gift tax return does not need to be filed. If the value of the policy exceeds the gift tax annual exclusion, however, a taxable gift results, requiring the donor to allocate a portion of his applicable gift tax credit amount to the transaction or, if the applicable gift tax credit has already been used up, pay gift tax on the transfer.

For gift tax purposes, the value of the policy depends on whether the policy is still in premium pay status or is already paid up.

A life insurance policy is in **premium pay status** if premiums are currently being paid on the policy. For a policy in pay status, the value for gift tax purposes is the sum of the policy's interpolated terminal reserve plus any unearned premium. The insurance company that issued the policy will provide this value upon request. When requesting a value from the insurance company, it is important to make sure that the value of the policy is calculated as of the date of the gift.

A **paid-up policy** is either a policy where premiums are no longer necessary to keep the policy in force, or a policy that cannot accept additional premiums without causing the policy to become a modified endowment policy. The gift tax value of a paid-up policy is the replacement cost of the policy, which equals the present cost charged by the insurance company to issue a similar contract.

There is one exception to the valuation rule for gifts of life insurance policies: If a physician has determined that the insured has a physical condition that is terminal, the value of the policy will be the death benefit, discounted for the predicted life expectancy of the insured. When the insured is known to have a terminal condition, the normal actuarial tables cannot be used to approximate the value of the policy.

| EXAMPLE 11.13 | Assume the same facts as Example 11.12. Here, instead of simply naming Jodie as the beneficiary of the policy, Greg formally transferred ownership and filed the appropriate forms with the insurer. At the time Greg transferred ownership, Ken had not been diagnosed as terminally ill, and the policy was in pay status. The insurance company reported that the interpolated terminal reserve plus unearned premium on the policy as of the date of the gift was $10,500. Upon transfer of ownership, Greg made a completed gift of a present interest to Jodie that will qualify for the gift tax annual exclusion. Since the value of the policy was less than the annual exclusion amount ($13,000 for 2009), Greg will not have to pay any gift tax and will not have to file a gift tax |

return with the IRS. When Ken dies, Greg will not be deemed to have made a gift of the death benefit to Jodie, since Jodie is the owner of the policy.

GIFTS OF PREMIUMS

Sometimes, it may make sense to have a single individual or entity own and be the beneficiary of a life insurance policy, but perhaps that person or entity does not have sufficient resources to make the premium payments. In many planning situations, for example, life insurance on the lives of senior generation family members may be owned by junior generation family members or by an entity created for their benefit. Family wealth typically resides with the senior generation family members. A simple way to resolve this problem involves a cash gift made to the junior family members or entity equal to the premium due on the policy. The junior member would then pay the premium. The cash gift is considered a gift for gift tax purposes, so, ideally the premium is less than the annual exclusion.

When life insurance policies are owned outright by individuals, gifts of cash that qualify for the gift tax annual exclusion can be made to the policy owner at the time the premium is due. If a trust is the owner of the life insurance policy, a gift of the premium to the trust that includes a **Crummey provision** (a general power of appointment over the contribution to the trust given to the beneficiaries of the trust) will qualify such gift for the gift tax annual exclusion. A more detailed review of life insurance trusts will be addressed later in this chapter.

GIFTS OF LIFE INSURANCE TO CHARITIES

Life insurance is often the object of charitable gifts. An individual with charitable intent may find that a gift of excess life insurance to a charitable organization can generate current tax benefits. Some individuals with modest means may want to make a sizable gift to charity and may use life insurance as a way of creating a legacy for a specific charitable cause. Other clients may anticipate a will contest after their death and would like to ensure that a certain amount of money will be transferred to a charitable organization. A successful will contest could have the effect of disinheriting a charitable beneficiary, but the death benefit paid to a charitable beneficiary of a life insurance policy are not usually successfully challenged by disgruntled heirs.

Life insurance is generally considered ordinary income property. Thus, gifting life insurance policies to a charity will follow the income tax charitable deduction rules for ordinary income property. The deduction for donated ordinary income property is equal to the fair market value of the property reduced by any ordinary income that would have resulted from its sale. The net deduction is usually the adjusted basis of the property. In the event the fair market value is less than the adjusted basis (no ordinary income would result from this sale), the deduction is equal to the fair market value of the property itself. If the policy is "paid up" (i.e., no premiums remain to be paid), the fair market value is equal to the policy's replacement value. If premiums remain unpaid on the policy, the fair market value is the policy's interpolated terminal reserve value. If the donor continues to pay the premiums on any policy donated to a charity, those premium payments are an additional tax-deductible charitable gift.

The income tax charitable deduction for a gift of an existing life insurance policy is limited to 50 percent of the donor's contribution base (which is adjusted gross income not taking into consideration net operating loss carrybacks) if the policy is given to a public charity and 30 percent of the donor's contribution base if the policy is given to a private charity. Simply naming the charity as the beneficiary or making the charity the irrevocable beneficiary of the policy is not sufficient to generate a current income tax deduction, since the owner (not the charity) will be able to exercise economic rights over the policy and could possibly prevent the charity from receiving anything. The ownership of the policy must be transferred to the charity if the donor wishes to qualify the gift for the income tax charitable deduction.

A potential estate tax issue arises when the owner/insured transfers a life insurance policy to a charity and dies within three years of the transfer. While the charity is the owner and beneficiary of the policy, the insured had incidents of ownership in the policy within three years of death, requiring an inclusion of the death benefit in the insured's gross estate. When this occurs, the entire death benefit would qualify for the estate tax unlimited charitable deduction, resulting in no additional estate tax. Note, however, that if the insured/decedent was also a business owner and was planning on a Section 303 redemption, a Section 6166 deferral of estate taxes, or a Section 2032A Special Use Valuation, the inclusion of the death benefit in the gross estate may prevent use of these favorable elections.

If the donor/insured lives for more than three years after the transfer, the death benefit proceeds on the policy are removed from his gross estate. The three-year rule of the IRC (Section 2035) is discussed in more detail in the next section. The gift of the policy to the charity will not be considered an adjusted taxable gift, since the annual exclusion and the gift tax charitable deduction apply to the transfer.

After a life insurance policy is given to a charity, the donor typically continues to make the premium payments on the policy. The amount of the premium payment will be deductible as a charitable gift, subject to the 30 percent of adjusted gross income limitation if the recipient is a public charity and 20 percent if the recipient is a private charity. If the donor would like to qualify for the higher 50 percent of adjusted gross income limitation, he could make a gift of cash to the charity and allow the charity to pay the premium on the policy directly.

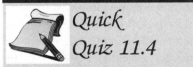

Quick Quiz 11.4

Highlight the answer to these questions:

1. When the owner of a life insurance policy designates the beneficiary of the policy, he has made a taxable gift equal to the present value of the expected future death benefit to the beneficiary.
    a. True
    b. False

2. For gift tax purposes, the value of a life insurance policy in pay status is the replacement cost of the policy plus the present value of any outstanding premiums.
    a. True
    b. False

3. When a life insurance policy is donated to a charity, the donor may deduct the fair market value of the policy as a charitable deduction on his income tax return (subject to income limitations).
    a. True
    b. False

False, False, True.

FEDERAL ESTATE TAX TREATMENT OF LIFE INSURANCE

LIFE INSURANCE ON SOMEONE ELSE'S LIFE

When an individual dies owning a life insurance policy on the life of another person, the value of the life insurance policy will be included in his gross estate (IRC Section 2033). The value of the policy will generally be the interpolated terminal reserve plus any unearned premium.

> Ted recently died. One of his assets was a life insurance policy on the life of Ted's friend Ron, who is still living. The interpolated terminal reserve plus unearned premium of the policy on Ron's life was $26,000 as of the date of Ted's death. Therefore, $26,000 will be included in Ted's gross estate.

EXAMPLE 11.14

LIFE INSURANCE ON THE INSURED/ DECEDENT'S LIFE

The IRC (Section 2042) states that if a decedent owns a life insurance policy on his own life, or possesses any incidents of ownership in the policy on the date of his death, the policy death benefit will be included in his gross estate. While the beneficiary will receive the death benefit free of income tax (as set forth in IRC Section 101), the insured will have to include the death benefit proceeds of the policy in his gross estate.

Key Concepts

Underline/highlight the answers to these questions as you read:

1. When would a life insurance policy be included in the gross estate?

> Barbara recently died. She owned a life insurance policy on her own life in the amount of $1,000,000. Barbara's sister, Rita, was named as the beneficiary. Rita received the death benefit income-tax free, but because Barbara owned the policy, the full death benefit is included in her gross estate.

EXAMPLE 11.15

An **incident of ownership in a life insurance policy** is the ability to exercise any economic right in the policy. Incidents of ownership include, but are not limited to, the right to borrow from the cash value in the policy, the right to assign the policy for a loan, and the right to change the beneficiary of the policy. The right to pay the premiums on a life insurance policy is not considered an incident of ownership in the policy. If an insured/decedent possessed any incident of ownership in a life insurance policy on his life at the time of death, the policy death benefit will be included in his gross estate.

> Last year, Jim transferred ownership of the life insurance policy on his life to his son, Chris. Jim frequently invests in real estate ventures and occasionally needs a quick source of cash. Therefore, he retained the right to borrow against the cash value of the policy he transferred to Chris. Jim recently died and as of the date of his death, he still had the right to bor-

EXAMPLE 11.16

row from the cash value of the policy. The full policy death benefit will be included in Jim's gross estate.

EXAMPLE 11.17

Five years ago, Jim transferred complete ownership of his life insurance policy (insuring Jim) to his son, Chris. The value of the policy as of the date of the transfer was less than the gift tax annual exclusion amount. Jim recently died. At the time of his death, Jim did not possess any incident of ownership over the policy and therefore the death benefit will not be included in his gross estate.

THE THREE-YEAR LOOK BACK RULE

The death benefit on a life insurance policy once owned by the decedent may be included in his gross estate even if he does not own an interest in the policy as of the date of his death. IRC Section 2035 gives us the **three-year rule**, which states that if an individual gratuitously transfers ownership (or any incident of ownership) of a life insurance policy on his life within three years of death, the death benefit of the policy is included in his gross estate.

The three-year rule applies when the insured gifts a policy or incidents of ownership in a policy on his life within three years of his death. If the owner of the policy is not the insured and the owner gives the policy to another party, the three-year rule does not apply. The gift of the policy will, however, be subject to gift tax. To the extent that the value of the policy exceeds the annual exclusion, it will be considered an adjusted taxable gift and will therefore be added back to the taxable estate for purposes of calculating any estate tax due.

EXAMPLE 11.18

Two years ago, Roger gifted a life insurance policy he owned on the life of Connie to their son, Glen. The value of the policy at the time of the gift was $59,000. The transfer of the life insurance policy was a present interest gift qualifying for the gift tax annual exclusion. The adjusted taxable gift that Roger made was therefore $46,000 ($59,000-$13,000). Roger allocated part of his applicable gift tax credit to the transfer, and therefore paid no gift tax. Roger died this year, and was survived by Connie and Glen. The value of the policy is not included in his gross estate, because the policy insured Connie, not Roger, and therefore the three-year rule does not apply. The adjusted taxable gift of $46,000 will, however, be added back to Roger's taxable estate to determine how much estate tax he must pay. [Note that if Roger had paid gift tax on the transfer of the policy, in addition to the inclusion of the adjusted taxable gift in his gross estate, the gift tax paid would be added back into his gross estate because Roger died within three years of making the gift.]

Quick Quiz 11.5

Highlight the answer to these questions:

1. Life insurance proceeds payable to the estate of a decedent are included in the decedent's federal gross estate.
   a. True
   b. False

2. The owner of a life insurance policy will include the value of the life insurance policy in his federal gross estate if he dies before the insured.
   a. True
   b. False

3. The three-year rule does not apply to the sale of a life insurance policy.
   a. True
   b. False

4. The three-year rule requires inclusion of the death benefit of any life insurance policy transferred within three years of the death of the insured in the insured/owner's federal gross estate.
   a. True
   b. False

True, True, True, True.

Note that the three-year rule applies only to gratuitous transfers (gifts) of life insurance policies or incidents of ownership in life insurance policies. It does not apply to a sale of a life insurance policy. Of course, if a life insurance policy is sold for valuable consideration, the transfer-for-value rule applies, causing the death benefit to be subject to income taxation in the hands of the beneficiary. By taking advantage of the exceptions to the transfer-for-value rule, it may be possible to remove the death benefit of a policy owned by the insured from his gross estate. For planning purposes, the following exceptions to the transfer-for-value rule are relevant in this context: a transfer to (1) a partner of the insured, (2) a partnership in which the insured is a partner, (3) a corporation in which the insured is a shareholder or officer, and (4) a transferee who takes the transferor's basis. A sale of a life insurance policy from the insured to any of these individuals or entities will avoid both the transfer-for-value rule and the three-year rule.

From a planning point of view, if a client is healthy and is not at an advanced age the risk of dying within three years of transfer is generally small. In the case of a party who is insurable, the planner must weigh the cost of creating a new policy (generally expensive for permanent policies but inexpensive for term) with the risk of the three-year look back rule.

John owns a cash value life insurance policy with a death benefit of $1,000,000 on his life that was purchased several years ago to pay off his mortgage and put his children through college in the event of his early death. The cash value of the policy is $65,000. His mortgage is paid off and all of the children have completed both college and graduate school. After retiring from his position as head of security of a national pharmaceutical firm, John created a security consulting partnership with a former colleague, Randy. Randy and John have just entered into a cross-purchase buy-sell agreement requiring the surviving partner to purchase a deceased partner's interest. Randy purchased John's life insurance policy for $65,000, and will use the death benefit to fund his obligations under the buy-sell agreement.

EXAMPLE 11.19

Because Randy is John's partner, the sale of the policy meets an exception to the transfer-for-value rule. Since the policy was not gifted to Randy, the three-year rule does not apply, and the death benefit will be immediately removed from John's estate.

EXAMPLE 11.20

Many years ago, Sam purchased a life insurance policy on his own life. Never envisioning that he would have a taxable estate, he owned the policy and named his wife, Ellen, as the beneficiary. Business has been very kind to Sam and he would be subject to the highest marginal estate tax bracket if he died today. The policy has a value of $83,000 and a death benefit of $1,000,000. Sam created an irrevocable trust that qualifies as a grantor trust for income tax purposes. The trust purchased the life insurance policy from Sam. If Sam dies immediately following the sale, the death benefit will be excluded from his estate, because the three-year rule only applies to gratuitious transfers of life insurance. The trust will also receive the death benefit income-tax free, and the transfer-for-value rule does not apply since all transactions between a grantor trust and the grantor are ignored for income tax purposes. Because the grantor trust is irrevocable and Sam has not retained any rights that would cause inclusion, the value of the trust will not be included in Sam's gross estate.

CREATION OF A LIFE INSURANCE TRUST (ILIT)

Life insurance death benefits are exempt from income taxes (provided there has been no transfer for value), but are subject to estate taxes if the policy is owned by the insured. This can pose a significant tax problem in estate planning. One solution to this problem is to have a trust own the life insurance policy so that the insurance proceeds will not be subject to estate tax at the insured's death. These trusts are often referred to as irrevocable life insurance trusts (ILITs) or Wealth Replacement Trusts (WRTs).

The concept of the ILIT is relatively simple. Instead of having the insured own the life insurance policy on his own life, thus causing estate tax inclusion, the insured can create a separate trust whose trustee will own and have all incidents of ownership in the life insurance policy. The insured avoids inclusion of the policy proceeds in his gross estate since he neither owns the policy nor has any incident of ownership over the policy. If the trust owns the policy, the proceeds will not be included in the insured's gross estate even though the insured created the trust and set forth the terms for distribution of trust assets (the death benefit on the life insurance policy) to the beneficiaries.

UTILIZING THE ANNUAL EXCLUSION

An ILIT can get a bit complex when we consider the funding of the life insurance premiums. Typically, the insured/grantor of the trust will make annual gifts to the trust so that the trustee can pay the premiums on the life insurance policy. Generally, all gifts to irrevocable trusts are considered future interest gifts and therefore do not qualify for the gift tax annual exclusion. However, the future interest characterization of the gift can be transformed into a present interest by the inclusion of a Crummey provision in the trust document. A Crummey provision states that the annual contribution made to the trust may be withdrawn by the beneficiaries for a

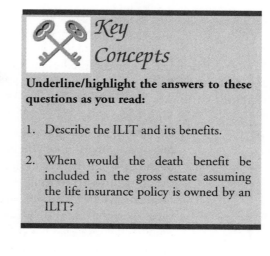

Key Concepts

Underline/highlight the answers to these questions as you read:

1. Describe the ILIT and its benefits.

2. When would the death benefit be included in the gross estate assuming the life insurance policy is owned by an ILIT?

specified period (usually 30 days) after the contribution is made. The trustee must give the beneficiaries notice of their right to withdraw their pro rata share of the annual contribution. Because the beneficiaries have the right to reduce the contribution to the trust to their possession, and use the funds in any way they see fit, the future interest gift in trust is transformed into a present interest gift that qualifies for the gift tax annual exclusion. To the extent that the gift to the trust does not exceed the gift tax annual exclusion multiplied by the number of beneficiaries of the trust, the donor will not have to use up any of his applicable gift tax credit when funding the trust.

Crummey Powers

As discussed previously, a Crummey power allows the beneficiary of a trust to withdraw the annual contribution. In other words, the beneficiary has a right to appoint the annual contribution to himself. Whenever an individual has the right to appoint property to himself, he possesses a general power of appointment. General powers of appointment are usually included in the gross estate of the person holding the power if the power holder dies while holding the power. While the Crummey power allows the donor to make a transfer under the annual exclusion rather than utilize his applicable gift tax credit, a beneficiary who holds a Crummey power may, as a result of that power, be required to include part of the trust assets in his gross estate.

If an individual has a general power of appointment over the annual contribution made to the trust, and the value of the general power of appointment does not exceed the greater of (1) $5,000, or (2) five percent of the trust corpus, the general power of appointment is ignored, and the beneficiary will not trigger gift tax if there is more than one party to the trust. This exception is often referred to as the **"5-and-5" rule**. Technically, a general power of appointment lapses to the extent that its value does not exceed $5,000 or five percent of the trust corpus in order to maximize the tax benefits of Crummey trusts, therefore, the contribution made to the trust should not exceed (1) $5,000 per beneficiary or (2) five percent of the trust corpus times the number of beneficiaries. When this convention is followed, the grantor will qualify gifts made to the trust for the gift tax annual exclusion and the beneficiaries will not have any inclusion in their gross estates by reason of possessing a general power of appointment over the contribution made to the trust, as long as the power lapses before the power holder dies.

Once the beneficiary's withdrawal right from the trust exceeds the greater of $5,000 or five percent of the trust corpus, there will be estate tax consequences for the beneficiary who dies after the Crummey power lapses.

<table>
<tr><td>EXAMPLE 11.21</td><td>Pat created an irrevocable life insurance trust with Crummey demand rights to hold a policy on his life. The beneficiaries of the trust are his four children. Pat transferred $16,000 to the trust this year to fund the annual premium. The trustee notified each of the beneficiaries (or their guardians) of their right to withdraw their pro rata share of the contribution, $4,000. Because each beneficiary's Crummey power (general power of appointment) is less than $5,000, there will be no inclusion in any of the beneficiary's estates as a result of the Crummey power if a beneficiary dies after the Crummey power lapses.</td></tr>
<tr><td>EXAMPLE 11.22</td><td>Fifteen years ago, Pat created an irrevocable life insurance trust, with Crummey demand rights, to hold a policy on his life. The current value of the trust is $150,000. The beneficiaries of the trust are his four children. This year, Pat transferred $25,000 to the trust to pay the annual premium on the life insurance policy. Upon receiving the contribution, the trustee notified the beneficiaries of their right to withdraw $6,250 each from the trust. While the Crummey demand right (general power of appointment) exceeds the $5,000 limit, no beneficiary has the right to withdraw more than 5% of the trust corpus ($7,500). Therefore there will be no inclusion in the beneficiary's gross estates if a beneficiary dies after the Crummey power lapses.</td></tr>
</table>

OTHER OBJECTIVES

While the primary purpose of an ILIT is to exclude the death benefit of a life insurance policy from an insured's federal gross estate, the trust can be used for other estate planning objectives as well. First, the trust document will govern the disposition of the property. Instead of leaving a large death benefit to a family member, the trust will provide for management and conservation of the funds for the benefit of the family members. Second, the trust provides a degree of asset protection for the insured and the insured's family. During the insured's lifetime, the cash value of the policy is protected from the insured's creditors. After the insured's death, to the extent that the death benefit remains in the trust and is managed for the benefit of the beneficiaries, the funds are protected from the claims of the beneficiary's creditors.

Life Insurance Proceeds Made Available to the Executor of the Insured's Estate

Since the objective of a life insurance trust is typically to provide liquidity for the estate while keeping the policy death benefit out of the insured's estate, it is important to avoid situations that will trigger inclusion by having incidents of ownership. Recall that the IRC requires the death benefit of a life insurance policy on the insured to be included in the insured's gross estate when:

1. The insured owns the policy at any time within the three year period before his death;

2. When the insured possesses any incident of ownership over the policy at any time within the three year period before his death; and

3. When the proceeds of the policy are made available to the executor.

Proceeds of the policy are deemed to be made available to the executor of the insured's estate when the proceeds are required to be or may be used by the executor to pay the insured's estate taxes or administration expenses. A life insurance trust that mandates the payment of the insured's estate taxes, for example, will cause the death benefit of the policy owned by the ILIT to be included in the insured's gross estate, thereby defeating the purpose of the life insurance trust. It is important in drafting a life insurance trust to ensure that the trust does not require the trustee to pay estate taxes or administration expenses of the estate.

Quick Quiz 11.6

Highlight the answer to these questions:

1. By creating an ILIT, the insured eliminates any risk created by the three-year rule.
   a. True
   b. False

2. Irrevocable life insurance trusts are primarily designed to ensure that the death benefit is excludable from the insured's federal gross estate.
   a. True
   b. False

False, True.

EXAMPLE 11.23

John, a personal injury attorney, drafted an ILIT to hold a new life insurance policy on his life for the benefit of his wife, Patty, and their children. John was not experienced in drafting estate planning documents, but became aware of the desirability of excluding the death benefit on life insurance policies from estate taxation. In drafting the ILIT, John copied the trustee powers section from a revocable trust form that he had in his forms library. Like most revocable trusts, the trustee was given the power to pay estate taxes and administration expenses of the grantor (in this case, the grantor is also the insured). Upon John's death, the death benefit will be considered available to the executor and the full death benefit will be taxed in John's estate.

Providing Liquidity to the Estate

Two provisions are commonly found in life insurance trusts that allow the trust to provide the needed liquidity for the insured's estate while, at the same time, preventing the policy death benefit from being subject to estate tax. These provisions include:

1. Giving the trustee of the life insurance trust the right to purchase assets from the estate of the insured; and
2. Giving the trustee of the life insurance trust the right to loan money to the estate of the insured.

Frequently, estates have little or no liquidity, and if forced to liquidate, such liquidation would cause a substantial loss. Both of these provisions require the estate to trade something of value (assets or a promissory note) in return for access to the policy death benefit and are therefore considered to be arm's-length transactions. The life insurance trust should not require the trustee to purchase assets or make a loan to the estate and the decedent's will should not require the estate to sell assets to the life insurance trust or borrow money from the trust. The reason for this is that any such requirement may be construed as the insured or his estate having an incidents of ownership in such a policy thus causing the proceeds to be included in the gross estate. After the death of the insured, the executor of the insured's estate and the trustee of the life insurance trust should determine whether or not a sale of assets or a loan should be made.

| EXAMPLE 11.24 | Tom, a tax attorney, drafted an ILIT to hold a new life insurance policy on his life for the benefit of his wife and children. The life insurance trust gave the trustee the authority to purchase assets from his estate and the authority to make loans to his estate, but specifically prohibited the trustee from directly paying estate taxes or administration expenses of Tom's estate. Upon Tom's death, the proceeds of the life insurance policy will not be deemed to be available to the executor and will therefore be excluded from his taxable estate. |

It is not uncommon to encounter situations where the beneficiary of a life insurance policy on the decedent's life or the trustee of an ILIT holding a life insurance policy on the decedent's life is also the executor of the decedent's estate. If the executor receives the policy death benefit in an individual capacity and there is no express or implied requirement for the executor, as an individual, to use the death benefit to pay estate taxes or administration expenses, the death benefit will not be deemed "payable to the executor," and will not be included in the insured's estate.

| EXAMPLE 11.25 | Keegan is the original owner and beneficiary of a life insurance policy on the life of his father, Randy. There is no express or implied agreement that Keegan will use the proceeds of the policy to pay estate taxes or administration expenses of Randy's estate. Randy's will names Keegan as the executor of his estate. When Randy dies, the death benefit on the life insurance policy paid to Keegan will not be considered "payable to the executor" and will not be included in Randy's estate. |

Likewise, if the trustee of an ILIT holding a life insurance policy on the life of the insured is also executor of the insured's estate, the policy proceeds are not deemed to be "payable to the executor" solely because the executor is also serving as trustee. The terms of the ILIT must make the policy proceeds available for the payment of estate taxes and/or administration expenses of the insured to trigger estate tax inclusion.

EXAMPLE 11.26

Lewis is the executor of David's (his father's) estate. Lewis is also the trustee of an ILIT that David created for estate liquidity purposes. The ILIT allows Lewis, as trustee, to purchase assets from David's estate, or to loan money to David's estate. The ILIT prohibits Lewis, as trustee, from directly paying estate taxes and administration expenses in David's estate. The proceeds will not be considered to be "payable to the executor" despite the fact that Lewis is serving both as trustee and executor, and will therefore not be subject to estate taxation.

The purpose of the ILIT is to remove the proceeds of life insurance from the insured's estate, provide estate liquidity at death, and to avoid inclusion of the proceeds in the surviving spouse's estate while making the income from such trust available to the surviving spouse and providing the trustee with the power to invade the corpus for health, education, or maintenance of any beneficiary (a limited power of appointment subject to an ascertainable standard).

VISUAL DEPICTION OF AN IRREVOCABLE LIFE INSURANCE TRUST (ILIT)

EXHIBIT 11.6

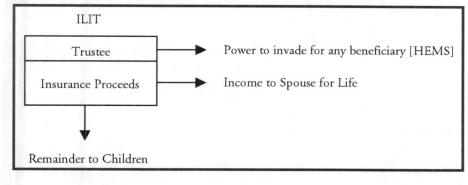

Key Terms

5-and-5 Rule - When an individual has a general power of appointment over the annual contribution made to the trust and the value of the general power of appointment does not exceed the greater of (1) $5,000 or (2) 5% of the trust corpus.

Accelerated Death Benefit - A reduced payment of the death benefit of a life insurance policy paid to the insured during the insured's lifetime in return for a surrender of the life insurance contract.

Beneficiary - The person(s) entitled to receive the death benefit of a life insurance policy at the insured's death. Also, the person(s) who hold(s) the beneficial title to a trust's assets.

Chronically Ill Individual - A person who has been certified by a licensed health care provider as being unable to perform, without assistance, at least two activities of daily living for at least 90 days, or a person with a similar level of disability.

Crummey Provision - The explicit right of a trust beneficiary to withdraw some or all of any contribution to a trust for a limited period of time after the contribution. A Crummey provision converts what otherwise would have been a gift of a future interest (not eligible for the annual exclusion) to a gift of a present interest, eligible for the annual exclusion.

Incident of Ownership in a Life Insurance Policy - The ability to exercise any economic right in a life insurance policy.

Insured - The person whose life is covered by the life insurance contract.

Lapse - When a power or right ends because of time or circumstance.

Lump Sum Death Benefit - A single payment of a life insurance death benefit to a beneficiary.

Modified Endowment Contract (MEC) - A life insurance policy that appears to function like an investment contract because the policy is paid up in just a few payments. MECs function like other life insurance policies except for the tax treatment of loans from the policy.

Owner - The person who holds title to a life insurance contract.

Paid-Up Policy - A life insurance policy where no more premium payments are necessary to keep the life insurance policy in force, or a life insurance policy that cannot accept additional premiums without causing the life insurance policy to become a modified endowment contract.

Policy Dividends - Refunds of overcharged premiums to life insurance policy owners. The payments are treated as a return of the policy owner's adjusted basis.

Premium Pay Status - Premiums are currently being paid on the life insurance policy.

Key Terms

Qualified Viatical Settlement Provider - A state licensed business that is regularly engaged in the business of buying life insurance policies from the policy owners.

Section 1035 Exchange - A tax-free exchange of a life insurance contract for another life insurance contract, a modified endowment contract, or an annuity contract on the same insured.

Settlement Options - The beneficiary's available options when receiving the death benefit, usually either lump sum or annuity.

Surrender Value - The cash value of the life insurance policy less a surrender charge which is governed by the policy or state law.

Term Insurance Policy - A life insurance contract which states if the insured dies within the term of the contract, the insurance company will pay a stated death benefit.

Terminally Ill Individual - A person who has been certified by a licensed health care provider as having a condition or illness that can reasonably be expected to result in death within 24 months.

Three-Year Rule - If an individual gratuitously transfers ownership of a life insurance policy on his life, or any incident of ownership in a policy on his life within three years of his date of death, the death benefit of the policy is included in his federal gross estate.

Transfer for Value - A transfer of an asset by means of a sale, exchange or any transfer which includes valuable consideration. If a life insurance policy is transferred for value, the death benefit in excess of the transferor's adjusted basis will be subject to income tax, unless the transfer meets certain exceptions.

Universal Life Insurance - A term insurance policy with a cash accumulation account attached to it.

Variable Universal Life Insurance - A universal life insurance policy with investment options available for the cash accumulation account.

Whole Life Insurance - A permanent insurance policy which guarantees that the policy will remain in force as long as the premium is paid. The policy has a cash account attached to it which grows tax deferred.

1.   List the five most common objectives of using life insurance in an estate plan.

2.   When selecting the amount of life insurance needed to protect the income stream of beneficiaries, what should be considered?

3.   What is the advantage of paying off debt at the death of the first spouse?

4.   How is life insurance included in a plan for funding college education?

5.   Why is liquidity an issue when a decedent's assets pass through the probate process?

6.   Why is liquidity an issue for a large estate?

7.   How can life insurance provide financial security for a surviving spouse in retirement?

8.   How can life insurance fund retirement needs while the insured is still alive?

9.   List the basic types of life insurance.

10. Define a term life insurance policy.

11. Why is the premium on a term insurance policy lower than the premium on a permanent policy?

12. Why is the strategy of "buy term and invest the difference" not an optimal strategy for people who have a permanent need for life insurance protection?

13. How is a term insurance policy used when an estate plan includes a GRAT?

14. How does a universal life insurance policy differ from a term life insurance policy?

15. What guarantee does the insurer give the insured under a whole life insurance policy?

16. How is the cash value of a whole life insurance policy invested?

17. In general, how does a variable universal life insurance policy differ from a universal life insurance policy?

18. Identify the parties to a life insurance policy.

19. In the event that a life insurance policy does not have a named beneficiary, who receives the death benefit?

20. Briefly describe the transfer-for-value rule.

21. List the exceptions to the transfer-for-value rule.

22. List the settlement options available for life insurance policies.

23. Discuss the tax consequences to a beneficiary who chooses to leave the life insurance proceeds on deposit at the insurer.

24. How is the surrender value of a life insurance policy calculated?

25. If an owner elects to receive the surrender value of the life insurance policy, why might it be taxable?

26. How do dividends from corporations differ from dividends on a life insurance policy?

27. List some of the advantages and disadvantages of taking a loan from a life insurance policy.

28. The designated beneficiary of a life insurance policy will receive the death benefit of the policy at the death of the insured. Why is the designation of the beneficiary not a completed gift for federal gift tax purposes?

29. In general, how is the value of a life insurance policy in pay status determined for federal gift tax purposes?

30. In general, how is the value of a paid-up life insurance policy determined for federal gift tax purposes?

31. How can the owner of a life insurance policy receive a current income tax deduction for the value of the life insurance policy?

32. If the owner of a life insurance policy gifts ownership of the policy to charity, what is the effect of the owner continuing to pay the premiums?

33. Define "incident of ownership" in a life insurance policy and give an example.

34. With regards to the federal estate tax and life insurance, what is the three-year rule?

35. What provision allows the gift of premium payments to an ILIT to be eligible for the annual exclusion?

1. Jack purchased a life insurance policy on his own life and never designated a beneficiary. In this case, the life insurance policy death benefit is:

    a. Included in Jack's federal gross estate if Jack dies within three years of the initial premium payment.

    b. Included in Jack's federal gross estate if Jack paid the premiums until his death.

    c. Never included in Jack's federal gross estate.

    d. Always included in Jack's federal gross estate.

2. Colleen transferred ownership of a whole life insurance policy on her life to an Irrevocable Life Insurance Trust (ILIT) six years ago and retained the right to borrow against the policy. When Colleen dies, the proceeds of the life insurance policy are:

    a. Included in Colleen's federal gross estate if she has any outstanding loans against the life insurance policy.

    b. Included in Colleen's federal gross estate if Colleen continued paying the policy premiums after the life insurance policy was transferred to the ILIT.

    c. Never included in Colleen's federal gross estate.

    d. Always included in Colleen's federal gross estate.

3. Carol and Joe, unrelated business partners, began operating a drug store in southern Florida. They funded a buy/sell agreement with a cross-purchase life insurance arrangement. Carol purchased a life insurance policy with Joe as the insured, and Joe purchased a life insurance policy with Carol as the insured. If Carol dies, which of the following is/are true?

    1. The death benefit of the life insurance policy on Carol's life, owned by Joe, is excluded from Carol's federal gross estate.

    2. The death benefit of the life insurance policy on Carol's life, owned by Joe, is included in Carol's federal gross estate if Carol own's 50% or more of the stock of the drug store.

    3. The value of the life insurance policy on Joe's life, owned by Carol, is included in Carol's federal gross estate.

    4. The death benefit of the life insurance policy on Carol's life, owned by Joe, is included in Carol's federal gross estate.

    a. 1 only.

    b. 1 and 3.

    c. 1, 2, and 3.

    d. 1, 2, 3, and 4.

4. Many individuals who have been diagnosed with terminal illnesses sell their life insurance policies to viatical settlement providers. Which of the following statements is true regarding the transfer of a policy from an individual with a terminal illness to a viatical settlement provider?

    a. If the individual dies within three years of the transfer, the full proceeds of the insurance policy are included in his federal gross estate.

    b. The individual is subject to capital gain taxes on the difference between his adjusted basis in the life insurance policy and the amount paid to him by the viatical settlement provider.

    c. Regardless of when the individual dies, the payment from the viatical settlement company is excluded from income tax.

    d. If the individual lives for more than one year after the transfer, the individual will be subject to income tax on the payment from the viatical provider.

5. Last year, Jerry gave a life insurance policy with a $400,000 death benefit to his son, Brad. At the time of the gift, the value of the life insurance policy was $50,000 and Jerry had to pay $5,000 in federal gift tax. Jerry unexpectedly died this year. What amount will be included in Jerry's federal gross estate related to this life insurance policy?

    a. $5,000.

    b. $400,000.

    c. $405,000.

    d. $455,000.

6. Four years ago, Marvin gave a life insurance policy with a $750,000 death benefit to his daughter, Marsha. At the time of the gift, the value of the life insurance policy was $65,000, and Marvin paid $10,000 in federal gift tax. Marvin unexpectedly died this year. What amount will be included in Marvin's federal gross estate related to this life insurance policy?

    a. $0.

    b. $10,000.

    c. $65,000.

    d. $750,000.

7. Louie gave a $1,000,000 life insurance policy on his own life to his brother. At the date of the gift, the life insurance policy was valued at $200,000. Which of the following statements regarding the gift of this life insurance policy is correct?

   a. If Louie dies two years after this gift, his federal gross estate will include $200,000.

   b. If Louie dies four years after this gift, his federal gross estate will include $200,000.

   c. If Louie dies two years after this gift, his federal gross estate will include $1,000,000.

   d. If Louie dies four years after this gift, his federal gross estate will include $1,000,000.

8. As part of his employee benefit package, Larry's employer provided him with a $50,000 term life insurance policy. Larry named his wife, Cynthia, as the sole beneficiary of the life insurance policy. Which of the following statements is true with regard to this life insurance policy?

   a. Because the term insurance policy is part of a group term life insurance policy, the death benefit payable to Cynthia is considered taxable income.

   b. At Larry's death, the death benefit payable to Cynthia will be included in Larry's federal gross estate.

   c. Larry cannot change the beneficiary of the life insurance policy without Cynthia's prior written approval.

   d. If Cynthia dies before Larry, her federal gross estate will include the life insurance policy death benefit.

9. James owned a life insurance policy with his brother, Fred, as the insured. When James died, his will specifically bequeathed the policy to his sister, Lolita. Which of the following statements regarding the value of the life insurance policy to include in James' federal gross estate is not true?

   a. If the life insurance policy is a term life insurance policy, the value is the unused premium.

   b. If a new life insurance policy is involved, the net premium paid is the value.

   c. If the life insurance policy is a whole life policy in pay status, the value is equal to the unearned premium plus the interpolated terminal reserve.

   d. If the life insurance policy is a paid-up or single premium life insurance policy, its value is its replacement cost.

10. Which of the following is not a reason for using life insurance in an estate plan?

    a. The proceeds of the life insurance policy can be used to create liquidity for the decedent's estate.

    b. The proceeds of the life insurance policy can be used to eliminate any debt for the decedent's surviving spouse.

    c. The insured can borrow the death benefit from the life insurance policy to fund his retirement.

    d. Expected future education expenses can be funded with the death benefit of the life insurance policy.

11. Which of the following statements regarding term life insurance is correct?

    a. The premium on a term life insurance policy reflects the actuarial risk that the insured will die during the term of the contract.

    b. The cash accumulation account of a term life insurance policy is invested in the bond portfolios of the insurer.

    c. The cash accumulation account of a term life insurance policy is invested in individual stocks selected by the insured.

    d. The premium of a term life insurance policy will decrease as the pure cost of life insurance increases.

12. Travis, 28, and his wife, 26, have recently moved into a new home. They financed $350,000 of the $500,000 purchase price and utilized all of their savings to pay the down payment of $150,000. Travis' wife stays at home with their 3-year old son, Alex, and is expecting a baby in two months. Which of the following statements is not correct?

    a. Travis should consider a 30 year term life insurance policy on his life which could fund his children's educational needs if he should die during the term.

    b. A universal life insurance policy would provide Travis with the insurance protection of a term life insurance policy and would also provide him with a tax-deferred savings mechanism.

    c. A whole life insurance policy would provide Travis with the least expensive temporary life insurance needed to eliminate the mortgage at his death.

    d. Travis should consider a whole life insurance policy on his life which could fund his children's educational needs or pay off the mortgage if he dies while those needs exist, and which could also provide Travis with a source of funds if he lives through his retirement.

13. Mary selected her son as the beneficiary of a whole life insurance policy on her life. Which of the following statements concerning this beneficiary designation is incorrect?

    a. Mary could have chosen her son and her daughter as co-beneficiaries.

    b. If Mary lists her nephew as the contingent beneficiary of the whole life insurance policy, her nephew will collect the death benefit if her son dies before Mary.

    c. If Mary entered an irrevocable beneficiary designation, she is the complete owner of the life insurance policy and can amend the irrevocable beneficiary designation at anytime.

    d. At Mary's death, her son will receive the death benefit of the life insurance policy.

14. Which of the following statements regarding universal life insurance policies is true?

    a. As long as the premium of a universal life insurance policy is paid, the insurer guarantees that the life insurance policy will remain in force.

    b. A universal life insurance policy will be cancelled if the pure cost of insurance protection increases and the cash accumulation account does not have the funds to pay the additional cost.

    c. Funds within the cash accumulation account of a universal life insurance policy cannot be used to pay the policy premium.

    d. A universal life insurance policy allows the insured to select the cash accumulation account investments.

15. Raphael is the owner of a variable life insurance policy on his life. His wife, Isabel is the designated beneficiary. Which of the following statements is correct?

    a. If Isabel dies before Raphael, Isabel must include the value of the life insurance policy in her federal gross estate.

    b. At Raphael's death, the variable life insurance policy death benefit will be paid to Isabel.

    c. When the beneficiary of a life insurance policy is the wife of the insured/owner, the death benefit payable to the wife is included in the insured's probate estate.

    d. As beneficiary, Isabel can borrow against the death benefit during Raphael's life.

16. Jason is the owner of a paid-up whole life insurance policy on his own life. Which of the following is not true?

    a. Jason has title to the whole life insurance contract.

    b. Jason can borrow against the cash value of the whole life insurance policy.

    c. The death benefit of the whole life insurance policy will be included in Jason's federal gross estate.

    d. If Jason gifts the whole life insurance policy to his son, the value for gift tax purposes is the sum of the policy's interpolated terminal reserve plus any unearned premium.

17. Jim purchased a yacht from Ronald for $200,000 seven years ago. The terms of the sale included a note of $50,000 and cash for the remaining amount. Ronald had a zero basis in the yacht. Immediately after purchasing the yacht, Jim's business began to fail and Jim could no longer make the payments. In exchange for the note, Jim gave Ronald a life insurance policy on his life with a face value of $50,000. This year, Jim died and Ronald received the death benefit as the designated beneficiary of the policy. How much of this death benefit is taxable to Ronald?

    a. $0.
    b. $50,000.
    c. $150,000.
    d. $200,000.

18. In which of the following situations would the death benefit of a life insurance policy be taxable, partially or wholly?

    a. Deborah, as designated beneficiary, received the $80,000 death benefit of Larry's life insurance policy. Larry had purchased the policy for $35,000 from his employer when he retired in 1997.

    b. Clean-it, LLC, received the $100,000 death benefit of David's life insurance policy. In 1990, David, the owner of 50% of the stock of Clean-it, LLC sold the policy to Clean-it for $12,000 as part of an entity-type buy-sell agreement.

    c. Weakam, Ullo, and Evans, LLP, received the $1,000,000 death benefit of a life insurance policy on Randy Evans, one of the managing partners. Randy had sold the policy to Weakam, Ullo, and Evans, LLP in 1945 when the business was just starting out as part of an entity-type buy-sell agreement.

    d. Adam sold a $100,000 death benefit life insurance policy to Dawson for $35,000 as part of cross-purchase buy-sell agreement. Dawson and Adam were the only two shareholders of Cupper Corporation and each owned a policy on the other.

19. Pamela's dad, Tim, died on August 10 of this year. Six years ago, Tim had gifted ownership of a paid-up $1,000,000 whole life insurance policy on his life with a replacement value of $150,000 and an adjusted basis of $100,000 to Pamela. If Pamela, as designated beneficiary, receives the death benefit of the life insurance policy this year, how much will be taxable to her?

    a. $0.
    b. $50,000.
    c. $100,000.
    d. $1,000,000.

20. Jerry is the owner, the insured, and the beneficiary of a whole life insurance policy. Which of the following situations regarding this scenario is incorrect?

    a. When Jerry dies, his federal gross estate will include the death benefit of the life insurance policy.

    b. When Jerry dies, his probate estate will include the death benefit of the life insurance policy.

    c. Jerry's estate will include the death benefit in its taxable income.

    d. If Jerry designates a new beneficiary before he dies, and the beneficiary is alive at the time of Jerry's death, the death benefit will be excluded from his probate estate.

21. Which of the following is not a valid settlement option for the designated beneficiary of a life insurance policy?

    a. A lump sum payment of the death benefit.

    b. Individual Retirement Account Rollover.

    c. Life Annuity.

    d. Term Annuity.

22. Jackie's father died last month and she is the listed beneficiary on his insurance policy. Jackie has contacted the insurer and has requested a lump sum payment of the death benefit of the life insurance policy. Which of the following statements regarding this lump sum payment is true?

    a. When Jackie receives the lump sum payment of the death benefit from the insurer, part of the payment will be taxable.

    b. Because Jackie has elected a lump sum payment of the death benefit, she will actually receive a payment less than the face value of the policy.

    c. Had Jackie elected the life annuity, each payment would have been excluded from her gross income.

    d. Jackie could have elected to leave the death benefit on deposit with the insurer and continue the tax-deferred growth of the policy.

23. Who has the right to surrender a life insurance policy for its cash surrender value?

    a. The insured of the life insurance policy.

    b. The owner of the life insurance policy.

    c. The beneficiary of the life insurance policy.

    d. The insurer of the life insurance policy.

24. At age 69, John, a widower, needs more than his pension and Social Security income to pay his living and medical expenses. His children do not have the resources to help him and he has already liquidated his individual retirement accounts. Which of the following is true if John decides to surrender his whole life insurance policy to the insurer?

    a. John would receive the present value (using the actuarial factors according to John's life expectancy) of the life insurance policy death benefit.

    b. Any amount of surrender value paid to John would reduce the death benefit payable to the listed beneficiary of the policy dollar-for-dollar.

    c. To surrender the life insurance policy, John must receive the approval of the listed beneficiary of the life insurance policy.

    d. The surrender value of the policy would be paid to John and the life insurance contract would be cancelled.

25. Gayle is the owner and insured on a $1,000,000 face value life insurance policy in pay status. Gayle's adjusted basis in the life insurance contract is $250,000. If Gayle gifts this life insurance policy to her daughter and listed beneficiary, Celeste, which of the following statements is correct?

    a. After the date of the gift, any dividends paid on the life insurance policy will be taxable to Gayle.

    b. Celeste can amend the beneficiary designation of the life insurance policy to include her son, Matt, as a co-beneficiary.

    c. If Celeste dies before Gayle, Celeste's probate estate will include the replacement value of the life insurance policy.

    d. If Gayle dies within 3 years of the gift of the life insurance policy to Celeste, the death benefit will be included in Gayle's probate estate.

26. The owner of a life insurance policy has decided to surrender the life insurance policy to the insurer. Since inception of the life insurance contract, the owner has paid premiums of $100,000 and received cash policy dividends equal to $20,000. If at the surrender date, the owner receives a cash payment of $140,000 from the insurer, what is his gain/loss subject to income tax on the life insurance policy?

    a. $0.

    b. $20,000.

    c. $40,000.

    d. $60,000.

27. Mr. Fahey, age 71, has been paying the premium on a whole life insurance policy for the past 30 years. The policy has a $1,000,000 death benefit and has built up a cash value of $250,000. Mr. Fahey's adjusted basis in the life insurance policy is $200,000. Which of the following statements is not correct?

    a.   If the insurer pays Mr. Fahey a life insurance policy dividend of $3,000, his adjusted basis in the whole life insurance policy will increase to $203,000.

    b.   If the insurer pays Mr. Fahey a life insurance policy dividend of $4,000, his adjusted basis in the whole life insurance policy will decrease to $196,000.

    c.   The cash surrender value of Mr. Fahey's whole life insurance policy would be equal to the cash value of the policy less a life insurance policy surrender charge.

    d.   Mr. Fahey can take a loan from the cash value of the life insurance policy without suffering any income tax consequences.

28. Which of the following statements is true?

    a.   Life insurance policy dividends are taxable as dividend income.

    b.   Life insurance policy dividends kept on deposit with the insurer will generate tax-deferred interest income.

    c.   If a life insurance policy lapses, any outstanding loans will be required to be repaid to the insurer immediately at the lapse.

    d.   If a life insurance policy owner takes a loan from the policy, the death benefit of the policy will be reduced by any outstanding loans plus the accumulated interest due on the loan at the death of the insured.

29. Warren purchased a single premium life insurance policy on his life 15 years ago for $65,000. The current value of the policy is $155,000. Which of the following statements regarding Warren's life insurance policy is true?

    a.   If Warren takes a loan of $140,000 against the cash surrender value of the life insurance policy, he will have long-term capital gain of $65,000.

    b.   If Warren takes a loan of $65,000 against the cash surrender value of the life insurance policy, he will not have any capital gain.

    c.   If Warren takes a loan of $75,000 against the cash surrender value of the life insurance policy, he will recognize $10,000 of long-term capital gain.

    d.   If Warren takes a loan of $155,000 against the cash surrender value of the life insurance policy, he will recognize $90,000 of long-term capital gain.

30. Twelve years ago, Paul purchased a single premium $1,000,000 life insurance policy on his own life for $150,000 and named his daughter as the sole beneficiary. Paul gifted ownership of the policy to Holly this year when the value of the life insurance policy was $200,000. Paul paid $15,000 of gift tax on the transaction. At Paul's death, how much of the death benefit that Holly receives will be subject to income tax?

    a. $0.
    b. $785,000.
    c. $800,000.
    d. $1,000,000.

31. The owner of a whole life insurance policy would like to exchange his life insurance policy for an annuity on his life. Currently, the value of the life insurance policy is $150,000, excluding a $50,000 loan the owner has against the life insurance policy, and the owner's adjusted basis in the policy is $65,000. Which of the following statements is true?

    a. If the owner exchanges the life insurance policy for an annuity, the owner must recognize a $135,000 capital gain on the exchange.
    b. The owner's basis in the annuity after the exchange will be $115,000.
    c. The exchange will be considered a transfer for valuable consideration.
    d. If the annuity has a death benefit, the beneficiary will have to include the death benefit in her taxable income at the owner's death.

32. Sally was recently diagnosed with stage four lung cancer. Her doctors have given her 9 months to live. She has many medical expenses and needs money. If Sally sells a whole life insurance policy, with a $1,000,000 face value and a $250,000 adjusted basis to a viatical settlement provider for $350,000, how much capital gain will Sally have to recognize for income tax purposes on the sale?

    a. $0.
    b. $250,000.
    c. $350,000.
    d. $1,000,000.

33. In an attempt to exclude the death benefit of a paid up $500,000 face value whole life insurance policy from his gross estate, Jerry gifted the policy to his daughter. Six months prior to the gift, Jerry had been diagnosed with a terminal illness and given a 12 month life expectancy by his doctor. What is the gift tax value of the gift of this policy?

    a. The replacement cost of the life insurance policy.
    b. The life insurance policy's interpolated terminal reserve plus any unearned premium.
    c. $500,000 discounted for Jerry's six month life expectancy.
    d. The cash surrender value of the life insurance policy.

34. In an attempt to exclude the death benefit of a paid up $500,000 face value whole life insurance policy from his gross estate, Jerry gifted the policy to his daughter. Six months prior to the gift, Jerry had been diagnosed with a terminal illness and given a 12 month life expectancy by his doctor. Jerry died 4 years after the gift of the life insurance policy. What amount is included in his federal gross estate related to this whole life insurance policy?

    a. $0.
    b. $250,000.
    c. $500,000.
    d. $500,000 discounted for Jerry's six month life expectancy.

35. Which of the following is not considered an incident of ownership?

    a. The right to change the beneficiary of a life insurance policy.
    b. The insured making cash gifts to the owners of the life insurance policy of the premium amount.
    c. The right to take loans against the cash value of the life insurance policy.
    d. A provision in an ILIT that directs the trust to pay the federal estate taxes of the insured.

Quick Quiz Explanations

Quick Quiz 11.1

1. True.
2. False. A whole life insurance policy will pay the stated death benefit if the insured dies while the policy is in force. It also creates a cash value pool that can be used to pay for future increases in mortality charges. Whole life insurance policies provide guarantees that if the stated premium is paid, the policy will remain in force until the insured dies.
3. True.
4. True.
5. True.

Quick Quiz 11.2

1. False. The transfer-for-value rule imposes income tax on the death benefit of a life insurance policy that has been transferred for valuable consideration once the transfer for value occurs. Subsequently cancelling the transfer for value will not invalidate this tax result.
2. True.
3. False. While the death benefit on a life insurance policy is typically received income-tax free, interest earnings on death benefits remaining on deposit with the life insurance company are subject to income tax.
4. False. The surrender value of a term insurance policy is merely the unearned premium on the policy, which is reduced to zero each year. Therefore, there is no accumulation of surrender value from year to year in a term insurance policy.

Quick Quiz 11.3

1. False. Unlike corporate dividends, which represent a distribution of earnings and profits that are subject to tax, dividends on a life insurance policy represent a return of part of the insured's capital, and are therefore not subject to income tax.
2. False. If a loan is taken for the full cash value, the policy will lapse since there will be no cash left to cover policy expenses. Each insurance contract has rules governing the amount of loans that may be taken against the cash value of the policy.
3. True.
4. True.
5. True.

Quick Quiz Explanations

Quick Quiz 11.4

1. False. Naming a beneficiary on a life insurance policy is not considered a completed gift, since the owner has the right to change the beneficiary. As such, no gift tax would be due upon changing the beneficiary of a life insurance policy.
2. False. The gift-tax value of a life insurance policy in pay status is the interpolated terminal reserve plus the unearned premium. If the policy was paid up, its value for gift tax purposes would be the replacement cost.
3. True.

Quick Quiz 11.5

1. True.
2. True.
3. True.
4. True.

Quick Quiz 11.6

1. False. Creation of an ILIT does not eliminate the estate inclusion risk associated with the three year rule. If the insured gratuitously transfers his or her life insurance policy to the ILIT, and dies within three years, the three-year rule of Section 2035 will require the death benefit to be included in the insured's gross estate. If, however, an ILIT is created, and the ILIT applies for and purchases a policy in the life of the grantor (so that the grantor never possesses any incidents of ownership in the policy), the ILIT can be used to keep the death benefit out of the grantor's estate.
2. True.

12

Special Elections & Post Mortem Planning

INTRODUCTION

While proper financial and estate planning can result in an estate plan that minimizes transfer taxes and is tailored to a client's needs, changes to the client's circumstances often occur after the plan has been adopted. Even individuals who periodically revise and update their estate plan may end up with planning that does not necessarily fit their needs when they die. After the death of the client, there are several issues that need to be addressed, as well as techniques that are available to the executor to modify the lifetime planning completed by the decedent so as to better reflect the needs of the decedent's family. This chapter reviews common estate issues that arise when an individual dies, as well as the tools available to modify the decedent's pre-death estate plan.

LIQUIDITY NEEDS

Access to readily available cash is vitally important in the administration of a decedent's estate. Having sufficient liquid resources available to cover estate and inheritance taxes, medical expenses, funeral expenses, administration costs, and the needs of the surviving family members during the estate administration process is paramount. Since most individuals do not regularly maintain sufficient cash and liquid assets in their investment and banking portfolios to cover all of these costs and expenses, life insurance is often used to provide the needed liquidity. As discussed in prior chapters, an ideal way to hold life insurance is in an irrevocable life insurance trust (ILIT) so that the dollar amount of the death benefit of the policy is not included in the decedent's gross estate.

LAST MEDICAL COSTS

Most of an individual's lifetime medical expenses are incurred within the last three months of life. As people age and medical needs increase, this reality becomes more evident. Many medical costs are covered by insurance (private health insurance, Medicare, Medicare supplement, and retiree health insurance), but those costs not covered by insurance become a debt of the estate. In the administration of a decedent's probate estate, medical costs will be paid before any distributions are made to beneficiaries, and could in extreme circumstances, deplete the entire estate. Maintaining proper medical insurance coverage until death helps minimize estate costs (by transferring the payment responsibility to the insurance company) and may help preserve the assets of the estate for the heirs. Medical expense insurance eases the liquidity needs of the estate by providing an outside source of funding for these expenses.

FUNERAL COSTS

Funerals can be expensive and prices are continuing to increase. A burial of a decedent's remains costs on average $6,000 to $12,000, depending upon the level of service selected and the cost of materials used. Cremations can also be expensive, but are typically less expensive than a burial. In either case, these costs must usually be paid shortly after the decedent's death and prior to the service being rendered. If the decedent did not have sufficient funds on hand at death to cover the expenses, life insurance proceeds are often used to cover these expenses since insurance death claims are usually paid shortly after the decedent's death. Often, a family member advances a deposit for the funeral service, or pays for the entire service and is reimbursed by the estate when the estate generates sufficient liquidity to repay the loan.

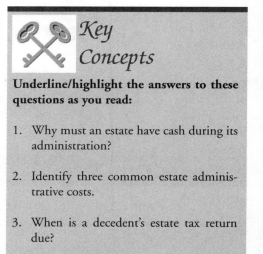

Key Concepts

Underline/highlight the answers to these questions as you read:

1. Why must an estate have cash during its administration?

2. Identify three common estate administrative costs.

3. When is a decedent's estate tax return due?

An alternative to having the estate pay for the funeral expenses is to have the decedent pre-arrange and pre-fund the funeral during his life. This can be accomplished either formally (by making arrangements with a funeral director and paying for the services in advance) or informally (by leaving instructions for the heirs along with sufficient cash to cover the expenses). If a funeral is pre-arranged and pre-funded, these administrative burdens are relieved and the estate's liquidity needs decrease.

TRANSITION OR ADJUSTMENT PERIOD COSTS

A decedent's surviving family members will need cash to cover their living and other normal expenses, often referred to as transition or adjustment period costs, during the estate administration process. This is particularly true when a person dies unexpectedly, when the decedent is young, or when the surviving spouse and the dependent children do not have independent sources of funds.

To the extent that the decedent held cash accounts as joint tenancy with rights of survivorship with his surviving spouse, the surviving spouse should be able to immediately access those funds to cover living expenses. If all of the liquid accounts were titled solely in the name of the decedent, the funds are first frozen by the financial institution and then transferred to the estate upon presentation of the death certificate.

In determining the appropriate amount of life insurance to place on a person's life, transition and adjustment expenses should be considered. Including these expenses in the plan for a working individual is even more important, since a significant source of income for the family disappears when the decedent dies. Estate administration can extend from approximately nine months to several years depending upon the size and complexity of the estate, and longer periods of estate administration will increase the liquidity needs for the decedent. Without proper planning for transition expenses, the surviving spouse and dependent heirs may not have access to any of the estate's funds during this administration period.

ADMINISTRATIVE COSTS

Administration costs for the estate include executor's and attorney's fees, fees for preparation of the estate and inheritance tax returns, and fees for appraisal reports and the opinions of experts. For complex estates, these costs can be substantial and must normally be paid as incurred. Consequently, the estate will need to have a liquid source of funds to cover these expenses.

Planning to provide liquidity is even more important for a decedent's estate that consists of a large number or percentage of hard to value assets. Assets that are difficult to value include artwork, jewelry, antiques, commercial real estate, and closely held business interests. All of these types of assets must be appraised to justify the value included in the gross estate. Appraisals can be complex and expensive, and often involve the time of experts, which is also typically expensive. Factoring these costs into the liquidity needs of large estates is an important consideration for a financial planner.

INCOME, ESTATE, AND GENERATION-SKIPPING TRANSFER TAXES

Taxes are a fact of both life and death. Federal estate taxes and generation-skipping transfer taxes occasioned by the decedent's death are due

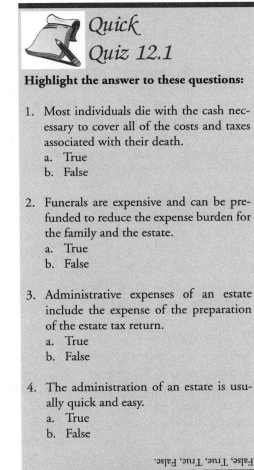

nine months after the decedent's date of death. Most states impose a similar time frame for payment of state inheritance and estate taxes. Any gift taxes generated by the decedent's gifts prior to death will be due April 15th of the year following the decedent's death, and income taxes on income generated by the estate will be due on an annual basis during the estate administration. Having a source of funds to pay these taxes is critical in the estate administration process. In some special circumstances, it may be possible to defer payment of some of these taxes, but that deferral is not without cost. Once the taxes are due, interest begins to accrue if the tax is not paid in full by the due date of the tax return.

LIQUIDITY SOURCES AND IMPLICATIONS

SALE OF ASSETS

One way to generate liquidity to pay estate taxes and administration expenses is to sell some of the decedent's assets. If the assets are liquid, or easy to sell, this approach can be effective. While a sale may require much effort from the executor or administrator (and may therefore increase the administration expenses), assets that are easy to liquidate (such as stocks and bonds) can generally be sold at fair market value.

Selling assets is not an attractive alternative when a significant portion of the decedent's gross estate consists of hard-to-value assets (such as artwork and jewelry, business interests, or real estate). Not only is it difficult to determine the fair market value of these assets, but it is also very difficult to find a buyer who is willing to pay fair market value shortly after the decedent's death. When these types of assets need to be liquidated to pay the estate taxes and the administration expenses, they are often sold for less than fair market value, resulting in a loss for the heirs. Whenever a taxable estate includes illiquid assets, other methods of generating liquidity should be considered.

Key Concepts

Underline/highlight the answers to these questions as you read:

1. Identify three ways an executor can generate liquidity for an estate.

2. Identify the parties involved in a split-dollar life insurance arrangement.

3. How much of a stock redemption must the executor complete to receive the special capital gains treatment of Section 303?

4. Is the interest on a loan used to pay estate taxes deductible?

LIFE INSURANCE

Using life insurance to generate estate liquidity matches the need for funds at death with the availability of funds. When an insured decedent dies and incurs estate taxes and administration expenses, the life insurance policy will mature, making a large amount of cash available to cover those expenses. One disadvantage to life insurance is that if the decedent owns the policy, the death benefit will be included in the gross estate. The traditional technique used to avoid estate taxation of the death benefit is the use of an irrevocable life insurance trust (ILIT). Some business owners and corporate executives may also use a split-dollar life insurance arrangement.

Irrevocable Life Insurance Trust (ILIT)

An **irrevocable life insurance trust (ILIT)** is an irrevocable trust that is funded by the grantor and which owns life insurance on the grantor's life. Typically, the grantor makes annual contributions to the trust to pay the life insurance policy premium and the beneficiaries of the trust are given a Crummey power over the annual contribution to qualify the gifts for the gift tax annual exclusion. Once the grantor dies, the trustee collects the life insurance death benefit proceeds and uses or distributes them in accordance with the terms of the trust document.

As discussed in Chapter 6, when using an ILIT, it is important to avoid estate tax rules (under Section 2042) which require the life insurance policy death benefit to be included in the insured's gross estate. The requirements state that the death benefit of a life insurance policy is included in the decedent's gross estate if (1) the decedent owned the policy at the time of his death, (2) the death benefits are made available to the executor or the estate, or (3) the decedent had any incident of ownership in the policy at the time of his death. A grantor should also be concerned with the three-year lookback rule (IRC Section 2035) which states that if the decedent transferred the life insurance policy or any incident of ownership in the life insurance policy within three years of his death, the full death benefit is subject to estate taxation. An often overlooked application of this rule states that if the death benefit is made available to the executor of the estate for the purpose of paying death taxes, the full death benefit is subject to estate taxation. In other words, if an ILIT allows the trustee to pay the estate taxes and administration expenses of the decedent's estate, or gives the executor of the estate the right to demand a distribution from the ILIT for that purpose, the death benefit will be subject to estate tax even though the policy was not owned by the decedent.

There are two ways to address this issue. Instead of making the proceeds available to the estate, the ILIT could give the trustee the discretion to make loans (bearing an adequate interest rate and backed up with security) to the decedent's estate, or to purchase property from the decedent's estate. The decedent's will should contain similar language allowing the executor or administrator of the estate to sell assets to any party, including the ILIT, or to borrow money from any source, including the ILIT. Since the decedent's estate and the ILIT created by the decedent are two separate entities, as long as an arm's-length transaction is entered into to provide liquidity for the estate, the proceeds of the life insurance policy are not deemed to be made available to the estate, thereby escaping inclusion in the decedent's gross estate.

Split-Dollar Life Insurance Arrangements

Split-dollar life insurance is not a type of life insurance, but rather a form of ownership for a life insurance policy. When a split-dollar arrangement is created, two parties have an ownership interest in one life insurance policy. One party typically owns the death benefit protection, while another party owns the cash value. Split-dollar arrangements are often established to allow executives and business owners the opportunity to purchase life insurance at a reduced out of pocket cost. In an employer-employee context, a traditional split-dollar arrangement would provide death benefit protection to the employee while the employer would have an interest in the policy cash value to the extent of its share of the premium payments. The employee would typically pay the portion of the premium reflecting the pure cost of insurance protection, and the employer would pay the portion of the premium reflecting the increase in the cash value of the policy. A reverse split-dollar plan is an arrangement where the employee owns the cash value, and the employer owns the pure death benefit protection provided by the policy.

When a split-dollar arrangement is established, the employee often transfers his portion of the policy (typically the pure death benefit protection) to an ILIT so that the death benefit received will be excluded from his gross estate. To the extent that an ILIT is used to hold a portion of the policy, the issues discussed above are relevant. If the insured owns a portion of the policy directly, that portion of the death benefit will be included in his gross estate, and can therefore be used to pay estate taxes and administration expenses.

TAX-ADVANTAGED ACCOUNTS

Some individuals have large accumulations in their tax-advantaged accounts (qualified plans, individual retirement accounts) and believe that these accounts will provide the liquidity needed to pay the estate taxes and the administration expenses at their death. This is particularly true for those individuals whose estates consist primarily of qualified plans and IRAs. While it is possible for the estate to access these types of accounts to generate cash needed by the estate, pension plans and IRAs are not the most efficient source of funds for estate liquidity purposes.

Perhaps the most important feature of a tax-advantaged account is that it provides deferral of income tax. Assets placed in a tax-deferred account do not incur income tax on income as it is earned, but rather defer that income to a future tax year (presumably when the client retires). If the client died after making a deferral decision, but before he took the money out of the tax-deferred account, and could receive a step-up in basis on the deferred account at his death, the income that was transferred to the deferred account will forever escape income taxation. To combat this potential for abuse, Congress created the Income in Respect of a Decedent (IRD) rules.

The IRD rules state that when an individual has chosen to defer income during his lifetime, the value of those deferrals at death will not qualify for a step-up in basis. Instead, whoever receives the decedent's income tax-deferred accounts must pay income tax on the distributions received from the accounts. However, if the IRD causes the estate to be subject to estate tax (because it is included in the decedent's gross estate), the beneficiary of the tax-advantaged account will be eligible for a deduction in the form of a miscellaneous itemized deduction not subject to the 2% of AGI floor. The amount of the deduction is equal to the estate tax attributable to the net IRD.

If the executor or administrator of the decedent's estate takes a distribution from a tax-advantaged account to pay the estate taxes and administration expenses, the distribution is taxable income to the estate. The executor can take a distribution equal to the amount necessary to pay the estate taxes and the administration expenses plus the income tax liability generated by the distribution, but this may result in a significant reduction in the amount of assets available for the heirs.

For individuals whose gross estate consists primarily of tax-advantaged accounts and who are insurable, a better approach may be to take distributions from the qualified plan or IRA during their lifetime and transfer the funds to an ILIT holding a life insurance policy. The ILIT can be used to provide liquidity for the estate. This approach will minimize the distributions from the tax-advantaged plan necessary to cover the estate's liquidity needs, and allow those plans to achieve further income tax deferral by stretching out the distributions after the decedent's death over the lifetime of the beneficiaries.

CORPORATE REDEMPTION FROM CLOSELY HELD BUSINESSES

Owners of closely held and family C corporations have yet another source of funds to cover estate liquidity needs – the corporation itself. A corporate redemption of some or all of the decedent's stock at death can transform an illiquid asset (a closely held business interest) into a liquid asset (cash).

A corporate redemption is a sale of company stock from a shareholder back to the issuing corporation. Federal tax law requires all partial redemptions of corporate stock to be treated as a dividend distribution unless an exception can be found in the Code. Despite the fact that stock is sold to the corporation, the entire amount distributed to the shareholder is generally treated as a dividend distribution subject to ordinary income tax. Usually, the sale of an asset results in a capital gain, which allows the seller to take into consideration his adjusted basis when determining the amount subject to the capital gains tax, but corporate redemptions do not allow the shareholder to take his or her basis into account, subjecting the entire distribution to dividend tax treatment.

A major exception to the treatment of a partial redemption as a dividend distribution is found in IRC Section 303. IRC Section 303 states that the estate of a deceased shareholder may redeem enough shares to cover the death taxes (federal and state estate, inheritance, and generation-skipping transfer taxes), funeral expenses, and administrative expenses of the decedent, and the shares redeemed for this purpose will qualify for capital gains tax treatment. The imposition of Section 303 will usually result in the avoidance of income tax on the redemption, since the redemption occurs after death, and at death, the decedent's estate receives a step up in the adjusted basis of the shares equal to their fair market value at the decedent's date of death. If the redemption occurs shortly after death, Section 303 redemption essentially allows the estate of a deceased shareholder to receive cash from the corporation in a tax-free exchange, and allows the corporation to reduce its earnings and profits (the accumulated earnings of the corporation that are typically subject to dividend taxation when distributed) which also benefits the surviving shareholders.

To qualify for a Section 303 redemption, more than 35 percent of the decedent's adjusted gross estate must consist of the closely held business interest. In the event that the decedent owned interests in several closely held businesses, the fair market value of all of the closely held business interests can be aggregated to meet the 35 percent test provided that the decedent owned at least 20 percent of each company's outstanding stock. In addition, the shareholder redeemed must be responsible for the payment of the estate taxes, administration expenses, and funeral expenses.

> **EXAMPLE 12.1**
>
> Roger died last month, leaving an adjusted gross estate valued at $2,000,000. One of the assets in his estate was an interest in a closely held business valued at $800,000. The tax apportionment clause of Roger's will allocated all taxes and expenses to his residuary estate, which will be distributed to his three children in equal shares. Roger's will also included a specific bequest of the closely held business stock to his son. Roger's son received the entire interest in the closely held business, but would not be responsible for paying the estate taxes and administration expenses for the estate (all three children are responsible, per the will), and therefore Roger's estate will not qualify for a Section 303 redemption.

EXAMPLE 12.2

Don died last month, leaving an adjusted gross estate of $2,000,000 including a closely held interest in a C corporation valued at $900,000. Don's will leaves all of his property with the exception of his closely held business interest to two of his children in equal shares. The business interest, as part of Don's residuary estate, will pass to his third child. According to the tax apportionment clause in the will, all estate taxes and administration expenses are allocated to the residuary estate. Since Don's third child will receive only the net value of the closely held business after the estate taxes and administration expenses have been paid, Don's third child is responsible for the payment of estate taxes and administration expenses. Don's estate will qualify for a Section 303 redemption, since more than 35% of his adjusted gross estate ($2,000,000 x 35% = $700,000) consists of the closely held C corporation stock.

Quick Quiz 12.2

Highlight the answer to these questions

1. Selling an estate's assets is the best way to generate the cash necessary to cover the administration expenses of the estate.
   a. True
   b. False

2. Estate planning should always ensure that the decedent owns his life insurance policy.
   a. True
   b. False

3. Distributions from qualified plans are subject to ordinary income tax.
   a. True
   b. False

4. An estate may not take a loan to pay its estate tax.
   a. True
   b. False

False, False, True, False.

When a Section 303 redemption is used, only the amount necessary to cover estate taxes, administration expenses, and funeral expenses of the decedent may be redeemed at favorable capital gains tax rates. To the extent that the estate redeems an amount in excess of the taxes and expenses of the estate, the redemption must meet the Code requirements to achieve capital gains tax treatment (i.e., there must be a complete redemption, or a substantially disproportionate redemption) or the excess amount will be treated as a dividend distribution to the estate, subject to dividend income tax (15% for 2009).

DISTRIBUTION OF ASSETS

In some cases, the executor or administrator of an estate will distribute the estate's assets in lieu of a cash payment to creditors and those providing estate administration services. However this is not be possible for the payment of taxes – both the federal and state governments require a cash payment within nine months of the decedent's date of death.

When an asset is distributed in lieu of a cash payment, the estate must recognize any gain on the asset to the extent that the fair market value of the asset at the date of distribution exceeds the estate's adjusted basis in the asset (generally the fair market value at the decedent's date of death). If the payment requires the recipient to report income upon receipt (payment for performance of services), the recipient will have to pay income tax on the fair market value of the asset at the time of distribution.

LOANS FOR PAYMENTS OF TAXES AND OTHER COSTS

If liquidity is needed and all else fails, the estate may borrow money to cover the estate taxes and administration expenses of the decedent. If there is not an adequate source of funds available (such as from a life insurance policy), borrowing to cover taxes and expenses may be the most prudent approach.

Borrowing to cover taxes and administration expenses is an attractive alternative for several reasons. First, borrowing may prevent the need for a fire-sale of the assets, thereby protecting the value of the estate for the heirs and giving the executor or administrator more time to find a purchaser willing to pay the true fair market value of the assets. Second, the interest incurred on the note is a tax-deductible expense for the estate. Particularly for estates that have significant amounts of taxable income, the interest deduction may offset taxable income at the high estate income tax rates (due to the compressed rate brackets for estates and trusts).

INCOME TAX ISSUES ON DECEDENT'S FINAL RETURN

After an individual dies, a final income tax return (Form 1040) must be prepared and filed. The final return will include all of the decedent's taxable income and deductions until the date of his death. At the decedent's death, the decedent's estate is created and the estate will pay income tax on the income it receives to the extent that income is not distributed to the decedent's heirs.

JOINT OR SEPARATE FINAL RETURN

For the year of the decedent's death, if the decedent was married and is survived by a spouse, the decedent's final income tax return may be filed as married filing separately or married filing jointly. Generally, it is more advantageous to file as married filing jointly due to the more favorable tax rate schedules and the income splitting benefits of joint returns. However, if the surviving spouse has concerns about a joint filing, or if the executor determines that filing separately would make more economic sense, separate returns are permitted.

The surviving spouse may file as a qualified widow(er) for two years following the decedent's death and enjoy the lower tax rates applicable to joint returns provided that (1) the surviving spouse has not remarried, and (2) the surviving

> **Key Concepts**
>
> Underline/highlight the answers to these questions as you read:
>
> 1. Identify the requirements for a surviving spouse to file as a qualifying widow.
>
> 2. Which expenses can be deducted on the estate tax return or the decedent's final income tax return?
>
> 3. What is the threshold for deducting medical expenses on the decedent's final income tax return?

spouse is maintaining a home for one or more dependent children. (Note that if the surviving spouse remarries, he will be entitled to the married filing jointly lower rates if the new couple files their income tax returns as married filing jointly.)

PASSIVE LOSSES

If the decedent had income tax losses from prior tax years that were suspended due to the application of the passive activity loss rules, those losses can be claimed on the decedent's final income tax return. To the extent that the decedent had passive loss carryforwards, it may be more advantageous to file the final return as married filing jointly due to the possibility of offsetting not only the decedent's taxable income, but also the spouse's taxable income with the passive loss carryforwards.

EXPENSE ELECTIONS

Certain expenses can be claimed either on the decedent's final income tax return (Form 1040) or on the estate tax return (Form 706).

The executor or administrator of the estate may elect to deduct unpaid medical expenses as of the date of the decedent's death either on the decedent's final income tax return or on the estate tax return. Of course, the executor cannot elect to deduct the same expenses on both returns. As a general rule, if the decedent's estate is not subject to estate tax (either because the taxable estate is less than the applicable estate tax credit amount or estate taxes have been avoided through use of the unlimited marital or unlimited charitable deduction), the expenses should be deducted from the decedent's final income tax return. Medical expenses are deductible on the final income tax return only to the extent that they exceed 7.5 percent (or 10 percent if the decedent was subject to the alternative minimum tax) of the decedent's adjusted gross income in the year of death. If the election is made to include the medical expenses on the final income tax return, the nondeductible portion (the amount equal to 7.5

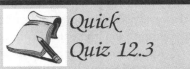

percent (or 10 percent) of the decedent's adjusted gross income) is not permitted to be deducted on the estate tax return. When a decedent has a taxable estate, it is usually more advantageous to deduct the medical expenses from the estate tax return, since the lowest estate tax rate is higher than the highest income tax rate, and will generate a bigger tax benefit and there is no AGI floor for estate tax purposes, allowing the entire amount of the medical expenses to be deductible. The executor may elect to deduct a portion of the medical expenses on the decedent's estate tax return, and the remaining portion of the medical expenses on the decedent's final income tax return if this yields a better overall tax result.

INCOME TAX ISSUES REGARDING THE ESTATE FIDUCIARY INCOME TAX RETURN (FORM 1041)

SELECTION OF TAX YEAR

Since an estate is not a natural person, it is not required to use a calendar year for tax purposes. The executor can elect to have the estate's tax year-end on the last day of any month during the year. When the executor elects to have the estate's tax year-end on the last day of any month other than December, the estate is said to have a fiscal year for tax purposes.

Whether a fiscal year is elected by the executor often depends upon the timing of the receipt of estate income. By electing a fiscal year, it is possible to control the timing of income recognition, thereby minimizing the income tax the estate has to pay on its income by keeping the income in a lower tax bracket.

EXPENSE ELECTIONS

Expenses of administering the decedent's estate and any casualty losses suffered during estate administration may be deducted on either the fiduciary income tax return for the estate (Form 1041), or the decedent's estate tax return (Form 706), but not both. The executor may elect to deduct some of the expenses on the income tax return and some of the expenses on the estate tax return if this yields a better overall tax result.

Like the deduction for medical expenses, to the extent that the decedent's estate is subject to estate taxes, it is usually better to deduct the administrative expenses or the casualty loses on the decedent's estate tax return, since the lowest estate tax rate is higher than the highest income tax rate. In the event that the estate is not subject to federal estate taxes (i.e., the tentative tax is less than the applicable estate tax credit amount, or estate taxes have been avoided through use of the unlimited marital or unlimited charitable deduction), an income tax deduction should be claimed.

> ### Key Concepts
>
> **Underline/highlight the answers to these questions as you read:**
>
> 1. Identify a reason an executor may choose a fiscal year-end for the income tax purposes of the estate.
>
> 2. Why would an executor choose to waive his executor's fee?
>
> 3. How would the marginal income tax bracket of the heirs affect an executor's decision to make distributions to the heirs?

WAIVER OF EXECUTOR'S FEES

Executor's fees are deductible either on the fiduciary income tax return (Form 1041) or on the estate tax return (Form 706), but not on both. Executor's fees are taxable income to the recipient and will require the recipient to pay income, and potentially, self-employment taxes on the amount received. (If paid to a professional executor or administrator, self-employment tax also applies to such fees. For a nonprofessional executor or administrator (a person serving in such capacity in an isolated instance, such as a friend or relative of the decedent), self-employment tax only applies if a trade or business is included in the estate's assets, the executor actively participates in the business, and the fees are related to operation of the business.

In many cases, the executor of the estate is also an heir of the estate. No income tax consequences are triggered when an heir receives a distribution from an estate. Therefore, an executor who is also an heir of the estate should consider whether or not he would like to waive the executor's commission. If the executor decides to waive the commission, a waiver should be executed early in the estate administration process to prevent the IRS from arguing that the executor had constructive receipt of the executor's fee and thus taxable income.

For relatively small estates, a waiver of the executor's fee usually makes financial sense. If the total value of the estate is less than the applicable estate tax credit equivalency amount, a deduction for the executor's fee will not reduce the estate taxes due (no estate taxes will be due). By waiving the fee, the executor will avoid the recognition of taxable ordinary income (potentially subject to self-employment tax as discussed previously) on the distribution and will receive the inheritance free of income taxes. An exception to this rule may apply when the estate is in a high income tax bracket, the executor is in a lower income tax bracket, and the executor's earnings already exceed the Social Security taxable wage base. In this circumstance, it is necessary to calculate the benefits of the executor taking the fee as compared with receiving an inheritance and choose the course that results in the greatest overall tax savings.

For larger estates, taking an executor's fee may produce a more attractive tax benefit, since estate tax rates are higher than income tax rates. This may not be true for estates that are subject to the lower marginal tax rates or in situations where the executor will have to pay self-employment taxes on the income. Again, a mathematical calculation will be necessary to determine what course of action is most appropriate.

In situations where there are multiple beneficiaries of an estate and the executor is also a beneficiary, waiving the executor's fee may result in the executor receiving less, not more, of the property. This can happen when all of the beneficiaries share the estate equally. If the executor waives the fee, the amount that would have been paid to the executor is split up among all of the heirs. In this circumstance, the executor may be better off by taking a fee, even if it creates taxable income. Receiving an executor's fee, however, may create a conflict between the executor and the other heirs who may feel that the executor is taking part of their inheritance. To avoid this type of conflict, as discussed in Chapter 2, a will should include a discussion of the executor selection and the determination of the executor's fee.

SUMMARY OF ALTERNATIVE TAX DEDUCTIONS

EXHIBIT 12.1

	Decedent's Income Tax Return 1040	Estate Income Tax Return 1041	Estate Tax Return 706	Notes
Unpaid Medical Expenses	Yes	No	Yes	Not both, but may split > 7.5% AGI (10% if AMT Taxpayer)
Casualty Losses	Yes During Life	Yes After Death	Yes After Death	Not both, but may split >10% AGI if occurred before death
Executor Fees (Taxable income to the Executor)	No	Yes	Yes	May be waived for better tax result

U.S. SAVINGS BONDS AND INCOME IN RESPECT OF DECEDENT (IRD) ASSETS

U.S. savings bonds are income in respect of decedent assets. IRD assets do not receive a step to fair market value in basis at the owner's date of death. U.S. savings bonds are treated in this way because usually income tax is not paid on the interest as it accrues – it is paid when the owner redeems the bond. If the estate redeems the bond, the estate will have to pay income tax on the interest income or, if circumstances dictate, distribute the income to the heirs and allow them to pay the income tax. In either case, whoever receives the income may receive a corresponding IRD deduction (a deduction equal to the estate tax attributable to the value of the IRD asset). Other IRD assets include qualified plan accounts, IRAs, annuitized annuities, installment notes, accrued dividends, accrued rent, and wages owed to the decedent at the time of his death.

If the decedent has made any charitable bequests in his will, it may be wise to satisfy those bequests with any U.S. savings bonds or IRD assets held by the estate. While the charity will recognize income upon the receipt of the asset, no income tax will be paid because charitable organizations are exempt from income tax.

Quick Quiz 12.4

Highlight the answer to these questions:

1. An executor must file a fiduciary income tax return for the estate on a calendar year basis.
   a. True
   b. False

2. An executor may choose to waive his executor's fee.
   a. True
   b. False

3. A casualty loss may be deducted on the fiduciary income tax return or on the estate tax return.
   a. True
   b. False

4. U.S. savings bonds do not receive a step-to fair market value at the decedent's date of death, and when redeemed all of the interest will be subject to ordinary income tax.
   a. True
   b. False

False, True, True, True.

EXHIBIT 12.2 PARTIAL LIST OF IRD ASSETS

- Qualified Plans
- IRAs
- U.S. Savings Bonds
- Installment Notes
- Annuitized Annuities
- Accrued Dividends
- Accrued Wages

DISTRIBUTIONS AND TAX BRACKET ANALYSIS

During the administration of an estate, it is important to keep the marginal estate and income tax bracket of the estate and the marginal income tax bracket of the heirs in mind. In most cases, the estate will be in a higher marginal tax bracket due to the compressed rate brackets that apply to trusts and estates (see Exhibit 8.1 in Chapter 8 for the trust and estate income tax rates).

If the estate is in a higher marginal tax bracket than the heirs, the executor should consider distributing the income of the estate to the heirs (in the manner provided for in the decedent's will). The income will then pass through to the heirs and they will pay income tax on that income at their lower income tax rates.

If the heirs are in the same tax bracket as the estate, or in a higher tax bracket, distribution of income will not be necessary for income tax savings and the executor may wish to hold the income to ensure that the estate has sufficient liquidity to meet its needs. To the extent that the estate is holding assets that have appreciated from the date of the decedent's death and the heirs are in a higher income tax bracket than the estate, it may be wise to consider selling the assets prior to making distributions to the heirs so that the overall income tax liability is minimized. In such a case, the estate would pay the tax on the gain rather than the heirs.

Key Concepts

Underline/highlight the answers to these questions as you read:

1. How does a couple make the election to split gifts for the tax year?

2. What is the "fair market value" of an asset?

3. Identify the qualification requirements to utilize Section 6166.

4. Identify the qualification requirements of a special use valuation.

5. How does the availability of a QTIP election benefit the decedent?

GIFT TAX ISSUES

ELECTION TO SPLIT GIFTS FOR YEAR OF DEATH

Many individuals use lifetime gifting as a key component of their estate planning strategy. By giving away assets during their lifetime, not only will the asset be removed from their gross estate (at least the portion that qualifies for the gift tax annual exclusion), the future appreciation of the asset will be transferred to the donee as well. Once an individual begins gifting property, annual gifts usually continue until the individual's death. When a couple decides to begin gifting property to their heirs, they will first make use of the annual exclusion, and only after the annual exclusion has been used will they make transfers subject to gift tax. One of the ways a married couple can make full use of their annual exclusions is to elect to split gifts of separate property made during the year. The gift-splitting election treats a gift of separate property as being made one-half from each spouse, thereby allowing use of each spouse's annual exclusion for the gift. The election is made on each spouse's annual gift tax return, requires each spouse to sign the other's gift tax return, and applies to all gifts made by either spouse during the year.

If a decedent made gifts during the last tax year before his death, those gifts must be reported on a timely filed gift tax return. The decedent will not, however, be available to sign the gift tax return for gift-splitting purposes with his spouse. The IRC allows a surviving spouse, however, to elect gift-splitting on the gifts made by the decedent in the decedent's final tax year. This can be a valuable planning tool and can help preserve the decedent's applicable estate tax credit amount for testamentary transfers from his estate.

> | |
> |---|
> | Michael has a wife and two children. Michael's daughter, Maureen, graduated from college in May and began a career as an elementary school teacher. Michael decided to reward Maureen for her hard work and he purchased a new car for her that cost $21,000. The funding for the car came from Michael's separate (not marital) assets. Since the gift exceeded the gift tax annual exclusion amount ($13,000), the excess ($8,000) would have reduced Michael's applicable gift tax credit amount by the corresponding gift tax. If Michael's wife, Diane, elects to split gifts with Michael for Michael's final tax year, the $21,000 gift to Maureen will be treated as if one-half was made by Michael and one-half was made by Diane. Under the gift-splitting election, neither party gave Maureen an amount in excess of the gift tax annual exclusion. Michael's applicable gift tax credit amount will not be reduced as a result of the gift, and as a result, more property can pass to Michael's heirs without being subjected to gift or estate tax. |

EXAMPLE 12.3

VALUATION OF ASSETS

As discussed in Chapter 6, a decedent's assets are included in his gross estate at their fair market value. Fair market value is the value that would be paid for the property in an arm's-length transaction where there is a willing buyer and willing seller, where neither party is acting under compulsion, and where both parties have full knowledge of the facts. "Fair Market Value" is the value that the asset would trade at in the ideal world.

Small estates will be encouraged to overstate the value of its assets, while large estates will tend to understate the value of its assets. A small estate (one that does not have to pay estate tax), may benefit by assigning higher values to its assets, since the value of the assets included in the gross estate receive a step-up in basis for the heirs. The heirs of a small estate will have a smaller taxable capital gain for income tax purposes to the extent that the adjusted basis of the assets is higher. Larger estates (estates that have to pay estate taxes) would rather undervalue the assets and save on estate taxes, even if this means that the heirs will have higher capital gains taxes to pay. Larger estates have a tendency to do this because estate tax rates are significantly higher than capital gains rates. The IRS scrutinizes estate tax returns for exaggerations or minimizations in asset valuation.

SELECTION OF VALUATION DATE

Generally, the value of property included in a decedent's gross estate is determined as of the date of the decedent's death. However, forcing the valuation date to be the date of the decedent's death may result in a hardship for some estates. This is particularly true when the estate consists primarily of illiquid assets and the value of those assets depreciates, instead of appreciates, during the estate administration process. In this circumstance, the executor or administrator of the estate can elect on the estate tax return (Form 706) to use the alternative valuation date for estate tax purposes.

ALTERNATE VALUATION DATE

If the executor or administrator elects to value the estate's assets on the **alternate valuation date**, the fair market value of the assets six months after the decedent's date of death is included in the gross estate. In order to elect the alternate valuation date, both of the following conditions must be met: (1) the value of the assets included in the gross estate six months after decedent's date of death must be lower than the value of the assets on the date of death, and (2) there must be a reduction in the total estate tax due as a result of the election.

Note that the impact of these two requirements is to prevent small estates (estates that do not have an estate tax liability) from electing the alternate valuation date to increase the value of the assets included in the gross estate, thereby increasing the step-up in basis for the heirs. If an additional step-up in basis could be achieved with no estate tax cost, income tax savings would result for the beneficiaries of the estate due to the decreased capital gain.

Estates that are subject to the estate tax would not elect the alternative valuation date if the election would result in an increase in estate taxes, since the estate tax is more expensive than the capital gains tax. From a practical standpoint, therefore, the alternate valuation date election is available only for estates subject to estate tax, and only when estate tax savings can result.

ALTERNATE VALUATION DATE (AVD)

EXHIBIT 12.3

To Qualify
1. The total value of the gross estate must depreciate after the date of death; and
2. The total estate tax must be less than the estate tax calculated using the date of death values.

Valuation if properly elected
1. All assets valued at the alternate valuation date
2. Except:
   - Assets distributed before 6 months which are valued at the date of distribution or sale; and
   - Wasting assets (annuitized annuities, patents, royalties, installment notes, lease income) which must be valued at the date of death.

INSTALLMENT PAYMENTS OF ESTATE TAX (SECTION 6166)

Closely held business owners often face a severe liquidity problem at death. Their largest and most valuable asset is usually their business interest. The inclusion of the value of the business interest in the decedent's gross estate may result in a large estate tax liability that is due nine months after the date of death, but it is often difficult to liquidate the business interest in such a short period of time, or it may be imprudent to liquidate the business interest if, as a result, the owner group or family will lose control.

To help closely held business owners resolve this problem, Congress enacted Section 6166 of the Internal Revenue Code, which allows for the deferral of estate taxes attributable to the closely held business interest. When the executor of the estate elects to make installment payments of estate tax under Section 6166, it is possible to extend the payment of estate taxes attributable to the closely held business over a 14-year period. The first four years of payments are interest-only, followed by 10 payments that amortize the estate tax liability over the payment period (although may be paid over a shorter period). If the family of the decedent wishes to keep the business interest, an installment payment of estate taxes will allow the estate taxes to be paid with the ongoing earnings of the business, thereby relieving the estate of the obligation to pay a large amount of cash for taxes shortly after the decedent's death.

To qualify for a Section 6166 deferral of estate tax, three requirements must be met: (1) the value of the business interest must exceed 35 percent of the value of the decedent's adjusted gross estate, (2) the business interest must be a closely held business (a sole proprietorship; a partnership if at least 20 percent of the total capital interest is included in the decedent's gross estate; a partnership with 45 or fewer partners; a corporation if at least 20 percent of the voting stock is included in the decedent's gross estate; a corporation with 45 or fewer shareholders), and (3) the entity must have been actively engaged in the conduct of a trade or a business at the date of the decedent's death.

The interest paid on the deferred tax is two percent on the tentative tax generated on $1,330,000 (indexed annually for inflation) plus the applicable estate tax credit equivalency amount for the year of death, less the applicable estate tax credit for the year of death. For 2009, the two percent rate would apply to the tentative tax generated on $4,830,000 [$1,330,000 (indexed number for 2009) + $3,500,000 (applicable estate tax credit equivalency amount for 2009)] less $1,455,800 (applicable estate tax credit for 2009), or the estate tax due of $598,500 [$4,830,000 generates an estate tax of $2,054,300 less $1,455,800]. If the amount of estate tax attributable to the closely held business is less than the amount computed above, the two percent portion applies to the lesser amount. If the balance of the unpaid estate taxes exceeds this amount, the excess is subject to an interest rate equal to 45 percent of the regular underpayment rate (as imposed by IRC Section 6601(a)).

Neither the two percent interest nor the interest on the excess portion are deductible on the decedent's estate tax return.

SPECIAL USE VALUATION (SECTION 2032A)

Generally, fair market value implies the value of a property in its highest and best use. Over the years, the highest and best use of a particular piece of property may change. For example, 50 years ago, the use of property outside of a city for farming purposes may have been the highest and best use of the land, but as the city expands, the highest and best use of the property may shift from farming activities to a residential subdivision or office complex. For estate tax purposes, the fair market value (i.e., the highest and best use value) of the property must be included in the gross estate; the value of the land in its current use does not matter. If an individual is using a piece of real property as a farm or in another trade or business that is not employing the property at its highest and best use, the value of the property may be higher than the value of the property in its current use. This may create an estate tax that could be much larger than an estate tax based on the value of the property utilizing its current use value. As a result, the farming operation or business enterprise may not be able to continue, since the real estate it is using must be sold to pay the estate taxes it has generated. To help provide relief in cases such as this, Congress enacted the Special Use Valuation provisions under Section 2032A of the IRC. If special use valuation is elected, the value included in the decedent's gross estate will be the current use value of the property, subject to a limitation that the highest and best use value cannot be reduced by more than $1,000,000 in 2009.

In order to qualify for special use valuation, the following conditions must be met: (1) the decedent was at the time of his death a citizen or resident of the U.S., (2) the property must be used in a farming operation or trade or business that was actively managed by the decedent or the decedent's family for five out of the eight years immediately preceding the decedent's death, (3) the value of the real and personal property used in a qualifying manner must equal or exceed 50 percent of the decedent's gross estate (as adjusted only for secured mortgages for property included in the gross estate), (4) the value of the real property used in a qualifying manner must equal or exceed 25 percent of the value of the gross estate (as adjusted only for secured mortgages for property included in the gross estate), (5) the qualifying property must be located in the U.S. and must pass to qualifying heirs (a member of the decedent's family who acquires the property from the decedent) who must actively participate in the farming activity or trade or business, and (6) the executor must file the election with the estate tax return, complete with a recapture agreement.

Subsequent to the transfer of the property to the qualifying heirs, the qualifying heirs must continue to use the property in its qualified use, as stated in the election included with the estate tax return, for a period of at least 10 years following the decedent's death. If the heirs stop using the property in a qualifying manner, or the property is sold during the 10-year period following the decedent's death, an additional tax is imposed. The amount that is imposed is the lesser of (1) the estate tax savings from special use valuation, or (2) an amount equal to the proceeds from the sale of the property less the special use valuation amount.

While special use valuation is available to business owners and farmers, it is rarely used. The qualification requirements are strict, and even if they can be met, the ongoing requirements necessary to avoid recapture of the estate tax savings place real restrictions on the heir's use of the property. When possible, it is usually more advantageous to use other estate planning techniques to deal with the property than attempt to maintain qualification for special use valuation over long periods of time.

INSTALLMENT PAYMENT OF ESTATE TAX
IRC SECTION 6166

- 14 annual installments
  - Payments 0 - 4: Interest-only payments
  - Payments 5 - 14: Interest and Estate Tax
  - 2% interest on first $598,500 (2009) of estate tax due attributable to the closely held business
- Eligibility
  - Value of closely held business interest > 35% of the AGE
  - If more than one business, they can be aggregated if the AGE includes ≥ 20% of the capital interest in the closely held business
    - if corporation with ≤45 shareholders, or
    - if partnership with ≤45 partners
- Closely held business actively engaged in trade or business

SPECIAL USE VALUATION
IRC SECTION 2032A

- Reduce the fair market value of real property up to $1,000,000 (2009)
- Eligibility
  - Business real property must be used in farm or business activity managed by the decedent or the decedent's family for 5 out of the 8 years prior to the decedent's death
  - Value of business real and personal property must be ≥ 50% of the GE as adjusted
  - Values of business real property must be ≥ 25% of the GE as adjusted
  - Real property must pass to qualifying heirs
  - Executor must file election with the estate tax return
  - Heirs must use property in business for at least 10 years

DISCLAIMERS

As discussed in Chapter 2, a **disclaimer** is an irrevocable and unqualified refusal to accept a gift or bequest. To be considered qualified for estate tax purposes, the disclaimer must meet the following requirements: (1) the disclaimer must be in writing, (2) the disclaimer must be made within nine months of the date on which the transfer creating the interest was made or the day on which the disclaiming party reaches the age of 21, (3) the disclaimant cannot specify the party to whom the property will be transferred as a result of the disclaimer, and (4) the disclaimant cannot accept any interest or benefit in the property prior to disclaiming. The availability of a disclaimer exists because an individual cannot be forced to accept a gift or bequest. By executing a qualified disclaimer, the disclaimant can prevent the property from being transferred to him.

By the Surviving Spouse

A special rule exists for surviving spouses. A surviving spouse may disclaim a bequest yet still receive benefits in the disclaimed property. Use of this provision adds flexibility to an estate plan by allowing the surviving spouse to make determinations regarding the size of the deceased spouse's taxable estate after the decedent has died.

> Philip died leaving his entire $4.5 million dollar estate to his wife, Elizabeth. Philip's will states that if Elizabeth disclaims any portion of the property left to her, that property is transferred to a bypass trust that makes income distributions to Elizabeth and allows principal distributions for Elizabeth's health, education, maintenance, and support (an ascertainable standard), with the remainder of the trust transferred to the children at Elizabeth's death. Elizabeth has a sizable estate of her own, and together Philip and Elizabeth have four children. If Elizabeth disclaims the amount that can pass through Philip's estate without triggering a federal estate tax, the disclaimer will be a qualified disclaimer even though Elizabeth will receive benefits from the disclaimed property. In this case Elizabeth would disclaim the amount necessary to create a $3,500,000 (2009) taxable estate. This amount would pass to the bypass trust.

EXAMPLE 12.4

In Favor of Surviving Spouse

In some situations, disclaimers are used to transfer property to the surviving spouse. This situation occurs when the property passing to the surviving spouse is insufficient, and the other heirs of the estate (usually the children) want to sufficiently provide for their surviving parent. To the extent that a disclaimer is executed and, as a result, property passes to the surviving spouse, the property passing as a result of the disclaimer will qualify for the estate tax marital deduction and will not be construed as a gift from the disclaimant to the spouse.

> At the time David wrote his will, the market was strong, and his net worth was high. He left a substantial portion of his estate directly to his children in the form of specific bequests, with the remainder to his wife, Lisa. In the event that any of his children predeceased him, the child's share would be transferred first to Lisa in the form of a QTIP trust, and, upon Lisa's death, to the child's issue, per stirpes. Unfortunately, David's portfolio declined in value very quickly as the stock market declined, and David died without changing his will. If the terms of his will are strictly adhered to, his children will receive all of his estate, and his wife, Lisa, will receive nothing. Since the children do not want to leave their mother destitute, they decide to disclaim a portion of their inheritance (in aggregate, an amount equal to the excess over what can be transferred through David's estate without triggering any estate tax liability). All of the requirements for a

EXAMPLE 12.5

qualified disclaimer are met, and the property passes to Lisa in the form of a QTIP trust. Since the property passed to the surviving spouse in a qualified way, David's estate would be entitled to a marital deduction for a like amount.

In Favor of Charities

If a disclaimer is executed and, as a result, the property is transferred to a charity under the terms of the decedent's will, the charitable transfer will qualify for the unlimited charitable deduction in the transferor's estate.

By Others Ignoring the Marital Deduction

In the event that an individual disclaims property and the property does not pass to the surviving spouse or a qualified charity, no estate tax savings will result in the transferor's estate. Overall family transfer tax savings may result, however, by preventing the inclusion of that property in the gross estate of a family member who does not need to receive it.

| EXAMPLE 12.6 | Lewis, a widower, died recently. He left his entire estate to his children, per stirpes. Isaac, Lewis' youngest child, is independently wealth and would prefer not to receive the inheritance from his father's estate. Lewis is not otherwise using his generation-skipping transfer tax exemption on any lifetime or death-time transfers. Isaac disclaims, and the property passes to his children (under the terms of Lewis' will and not under direction by Isaac), and the executor of Lewis' estate elects to allocate Lewis' generation-skipping transfer tax exemption to the transfer. While there will be no estate tax savings (or additional transfer tax cost) in Lewis' estate, when Isaac dies, none of the property will be subject to estate tax, since he does not own it. Transfer tax savings result for the next generation. |

Powers of Appointment

If the disclaimant has the authority to designate the recipient of the property as occurs with a general power of appointment, a qualified disclaimer of the bequest cannot be made. When such a situation exists, the original beneficiary has been granted a power of appointment over the property. The power of appointment will be considered a general power of appointment, since the original beneficiary would receive the property if he does not specify that the property will be transferred elsewhere. Consequently, the value of the property subject to the general power of appointment is subject to transfer tax in the hands of the beneficiary. While it is possible to plan for future disclaimers by having the decedent include a disclaimer clause in his will, naming the appropriate parties as alternate takers, care should be taken to avoid granting a general power of appointment, since this will result in transfer tax consequences for the beneficiary.

QUALIFIED TERMINABLE INTEREST PROPERTY (QTIP) ELECTION

One form of marital deduction transfer involves the use of the qualified terminable interest property (QTIP) election, which is discussed in depth in Chapter 10. While an individual can express a desire that his executor elect to qualify certain transfers for the unlimited estate tax marital deduction by making a QTIP election, the ultimate decision of whether to make the election, rests with the executor or administrator of the estate. The determination as to how much property should be qualified for the election is also made by the executor or administrator of the estate. As such, the QTIP election is a post mortem planning device, since the decisions are made after the decedent's death.

As discussed above, it is possible to allow the surviving spouse to determine the value that will qualify for the unlimited estate tax marital deduction by leaving property to the surviving spouse and allowing the surviving spouse to disclaim all or a portion of that property. This planning relies, however, on the judgment of the surviving spouse. If the surviving spouse is not versed in the intricacies of estate planning, or is not in the best position to make a decision due to the emotional stress caused by loss of a spouse, the anticipated estate planning benefits could be lost.

Use of a QTIP election can assist in meeting the objectives of the decedent. First, an independent party, the executor, is able to make a decision concerning the amount of property that will qualify for the marital deduction. The surviving spouse is relieved of this burden (unless, of course, the surviving spouse is also the executor of the estate), and the decision likely considers the interests of all of the beneficiaries of the estate (not just the surviving spouse). Furthermore, if a spousal disclaimer plan is used, the spouse has only nine months to make the disclaimer decision. The executor does not have to make the QTIP election until the due date of the estate tax return, including extensions. Since the executor can file for an automatic six month extension for the estate tax return, the executor has a total of 15 months (nine months for normal due date, plus a six month extension of time to file) to determine the applicability of the QTIP election. This may be particularly important if the surviving spouse is in ill health. If the surviving spouse

Quick Quiz 12.5

Highlight the answer to these questions:

1. A couple who elects to split gifts must agree to split all gifts made during the year.
   a. True
   b. False

2. A decedent's assets are included in his gross estate at the fair market value at his date of death or the alternate valuation date.
   a. True
   b. False

3. Section 2032A allows the executor to extend the payment of the estate tax over a maximum of 14 years.
   a. True
   b. False

4. To reap the full benefits of special use valuation, the heirs of the property must use the property in the same use as the decedent for at least ten years after the decedent's date of death.
   a. True
   b. False

5. A disclaimer must be filed within six months of the decedent's date of death.
   a. True
   b. False

True, True, False, True, False.

dies during the 15 month period after the first spouse's death, the executor can consider the overall tax impact on both estates before making the QTIP election.

QUALIFIED DOMESTIC TRUST (QDOT)

In the case of a noncitizen surviving spouse, a Qualified Domestic Trust (QDOT) can be created to qualify the estate for the marital deduction properly passing to the noncitizen spouse. QDOTs are discussed in detail in Chapter 10.

GENERATION-SKIPPING TRANSFER TAX ELECTIONS

The executor will also elect any allocation of the generation-skipping transfer tax (GSTT) exemption and if appropriate, a Reverse QTIP election so that the decedent remains the transferor of this QTIP property for GSTT purposes after the death of the surviving spouse, even though the property is included in the surviving spouse's gross estate for estate tax purposes (see Chapter 10 and Chapter 13).

Key Terms

Alternate Valuation Date - An alternate date, other than the date of death, to value a decedent's gross estate. The alternate valuation date is either six months after the date of death, or if the asset is disposed of within six months of the date of death, the asset's disposition date.

Disclaimer - An heir or legatee's refusal to accept a gift or bequest. The disclaimer allows assets to pass to other heirs or legatees without additional transfer tax.

Irrevocable Life Insurance Trust (ILIT) - An irrevocable trust that owns and holds life insurance on its grantor's life. An ILIT is also known as a wealth replacement trust (WRT).

Split-Dollar Life Insurance - A single life insurance policy in which two parties have an ownership interest. One party typically owns the death benefit, while the other party owns the cash value.

1. Why is it important for an estate to have cash?

2. How can an individual potentially reduce the medical expenses to be paid by his estate?

3. How can an individual reduce the funeral expenses that his estate will have to pay?

4. List three common administration costs of an estate.

5. Why should selling an estate's assets to generate the liquidity necessary for the estate taxes generally be the last option?

6. List three methods that an executor can use to reduce the liquidity requirements of an estate.

7. How can an ILIT be used to generate liquidity for an estate without requiring the value of the ILIT to be included in the decedent's gross estate?

8. Even if qualified plans are payable to the decedent's estate, why should the executor seek alternative means of meeting the cash requirements of the estate before taking distributions from the qualified plans?

9. Explain the tax benefit allowed by a Section 303 stock redemption.

10. What requirements must an estate meet to benefit from Section 303 stock redemption?

11. List two reasons why borrowing cash is an attractive option for the executor of an illiquid estate.

12. In the year of a decedent's death, what are his surviving spouse's filing status options?

13. What requirements must be met for a surviving spouse to file as a qualifying widow/widower?

14. Unpaid medical expenses of a decedent are deducted on which form, the estate tax return or the final income tax return?

15. When is the tax year-end of an estate for income tax purposes?

16. When would an executor choose to deduct an estate's administrative fees on the fiduciary income tax return?

17. Why might an executor choose to waive his executor's fee?

18. Why do small estates generally overvalue the fair market value of assets in the gross estate?

19. What are the two requirements for electing the alternate valuation date?

20. List the three requirements necessary for an estate to elect Section 6166.

21. Explain why the government would allow an estate to utilize the special use valuation as a property's fair market value in the gross estate.

22. Why is the special use valuation rarely used?

MULTIPLE-CHOICE PROBLEMS

1. Which of the following is not a typical reason an estate will have liquidity concerns?

    a. To meet specific bequests.

    b. To pay taxes.

    c. To pay life insurance premiums on the decedent's life.

    d. To pay funeral and administrative expenses and the executor's fee.

2. Which of the following estates will most likely have the greatest liquidity problem?

    a. An estate with $4,000,000 of marketable securities.

    b. An estate comprised of rental real estate and marketable securities totalling $2,000,000.

    c. An estate consisting of a closely held business interest valued at $3,000,000, several pieces of art work valued at $400,000, and $500,000 of cash.

    d. An estate comprised of a closely held business interest valued at $4,000,000, and cash of $100,000.

3. The executor of an estate liquidated assets to generate the cash necessary to pay the estate taxes. Of the following assets, which is the least likely to generate income tax consequences upon its sale?

    a. Real estate sold within three months of the decedent's date of death.

    b. Publicly traded securities sold two weeks after the decedent's date of death.

    c. The redemption of the stock of a closely held business. The redemption qualified for Section 303 treatment.

    d. Publicly traded securities sold eight months after the decedent's date of death.

4. Which of the following statements regarding selling an estate's assets to generate cash is not correct?

    a. The estate may have income tax consequences.

    b. The assets may not be sold at full, realizable fair market value.

    c. Any losses on the sale of the assets are deductible as losses on the estate tax return.

    d. Any selling expenses are deductible on the estate tax return.

5. In 2005, Amy funded an Irrevocable Life Insurance Trust (ILIT) naming her children as the beneficiaries. Amy contributed cash each year to the trust to pay the life insurance policy premiums. In 2009, Amy died in a car accident, and the policy death benefit of $1,000,000 was paid to the ILIT. Which of the following statements regarding this ILIT and Amy's estate is false?

    a. The ILIT will be included in Amy's gross estate because Amy had made a contribution to the trust within three years of her death.

    b. If Amy's executor can demand a distribution from the ILIT to pay Amy's estate taxes, the value of the ILIT will be included in Amy's gross estate.

    c. Amy's executor can sell the assets from Amy's estate to the ILIT without causing the value of the ILIT to be included in Amy's gross estate.

    d. If Amy had released her right to revoke the ILIT in 2007, the value of the ILIT would be included in Amy's gross estate.

6. Josh was a majority owner in a closely held business. He had an adjusted basis in his interest of $400,000, and at his death this year, the fair market value reported on his estate tax return was $6,000,000. Like most majority owner's in closely held businesses, Josh did not have much liquidity in his estate and his executor was forced to redeem some of his interest in the business. If Josh's executor redeemed 30% of Josh's interest for $2,500,000 to pay the estate tax and administration fees, how much is subject to capital gains tax?

    a. $0.
    b. $700,000.
    c. $2,100,000.
    d. $2,500,000.

7. Which of the following statements concerning an illiquid estate is true?

    a. If the executor of an illiquid estate takes a loan to pay estate taxes, and pledges the estate's assets as security for the loan, the interest on the loan is deductible.

    b. When an executor sells an estate's assets eight months after the decedent's date of death, any gain or loss is included in the fair market value of the asset in the decedent's gross estate.

    c. An heir who agrees to take an in-kind distribution, instead of a cash distribution, from the estate, will take the property with an adjusted basis equal to the decedent's adjusted basis immediately before his death.

    d. Real property valued under the Special Use Valuation rules can be sold after four years for an unrelated use without suffering recapture.

8. Which of the following is not a benefit of taking a loan to pay estate taxes and administration fees?

    a. The interest on the loan is deductible for income tax purposes.

    b. The executor of the estate will have more time to sell the estate's assets.

    c. The estate's assets will not be sold in a fire-sale fashion.

    d. The principal of the loan is a debt on the estate tax return.

9. Mary Jane's husband died in October of 2009. Which filing status will Mary Jane use on her 2009 income tax return?

    a. Single.

    b. Head of household.

    c. Married filing jointly.

    d. Qualifying widow.

10. Mary Jane's husband died in October of 2009. Mary Jane has a one year old dependent child and has not remarried. Which filing status will Mary Jane use on her 2012 income tax return?

    a. Single.

    b. Head of household.

    c. Married filing jointly.

    d. Qualifying widow.

11. The executor of an estate makes many elections before he files an estate tax return. Which of the following is not an available election for the executor?

    a. Utilizing the annual exclusion against the testamentary transfers.

    b. Selection of the tax year-end.

    c. Electing QTIP on certain property passing to the surviving spouse.

    d. Deducting the expenses of administering the decedent's estate on the estate's income tax return.

12. Before his death in 2009, Melvin incurred $65,000 in medical bills. Melvin's taxable estate at his death was $675,000 and his adjusted gross income for 2009 was $100,000. How much of Melvin's medical expenses will be deducted on his estate tax return?

    a. $0.

    b. $57,500.

    c. $65,000.

    d. $100,000.

13. In which of the following cases will Robert, the executor of his father's estate, not waive his executor's fee?

    a. Robert is a 35% taxpayer and his father's estate is a 20% taxpayer.

    b. Robert is the only heir of his father's estate.

    c. Robert and his mother are the only heirs to his father's estate. Neither Robert's father or his mother are very wealthy and his mother has very expensive prescription costs. Robert is a financial planner in the 35% marginal tax bracket.

    d. Robert is also one of three beneficiaries of his father's estate. The beneficiaries will share the residual of the estate equally.

14. Which of the following is not a requirement of using the special use valuation of property?

    a. The property must be used in a farming operation or a trade or business that was actively managed by the decedent or the decedent's family for 5 out of the 8 years immediately preceding the decedent's death.

    b. The value of the real and personal property used in a qualifying manner must equal or exceed 50 percent of the decedent's gross estate as adjusted.

    c. The value of the real property used in a qualifying manner must equal or exceed 75 percent of the value of the decedent's gross estate as adjusted.

    d. The qualifying property must pass to qualifying heirs who must actively participate in the farming activity or trade or business.

15. Joseph died this year. His will specifically bequeaths $1,000,000 to his son, Kevin and bequeaths the residual of his estate to his wife, Martha. At the time Joseph had written his will, his net worth was in excess of $4,000,000, but at his death his net worth had plummeted to $1,050,000. Because Kevin's mother would only receive $50,000 ($1,050,000-$1,000,000) of his father's assets, Kevin fully disclaimed his bequest three months after his father's death. How much will Kevin have to report as a taxable gift because of this disclaimer?

    a. $0.

    b. $38,000.

    c. $50,000.

    d. $1,000,000.

Quick Quiz Explanations

Quick Quiz 12.1

1. False. Most individuals do not have sufficient liquidity at death to cover expenses, taxes, and provide for surviving family members.
2. True.
3. True.
4. False. Typically administration of an estate takes at least 9 months, and can go on for several years for large estates.

Quick Quiz 12.2

1. False. Selling assets often results in realizing less than the fair market value of the property. Generally, other ways of generating liquidity should be considered.
2. False. Generally, a life insurance policy should be held in an ILIT to avoid estate taxation at the decedent's death.
3. True.
4. False. Borrowing money is a common way of generating liquidity for an estate.

Quick Quiz 12.3

1. False. For the year of the husband's death, a surviving spouse may file married filing jointly or married filing separately.
2. True.
3. False. When medical expenses are deducted on the estate tax return, no percentage limitations apply.

Quick Quiz 12.4

1. False. Fiduciary income tax returns may be filed on a fiscal year basis.
2. True.
3. True.
4. True.

Quick Quiz 12.5

1. True.
2. True.
3. False. Section 2032A allows the executor to include property in the gross estate at its current use value as opposed to its fair market value. Section 6166 allows the executor to extend the payment of estate taxes over a maximum of 14 years.
4. True.
5. False. A disclaimer must be filed within 9 months of the decedent's death in order to be effective.

Generation-Skipping Transfers

13

INTRODUCTION

In addition to the estate and gift tax systems, a third, separate, transfer tax system exists known as the generation-skipping transfer tax system (GSTT). The GSTT is an excise tax, imposed in addition to any gift or estate tax, on the transfer of property to a donee other than a spouse who is two or more generations younger than the donor.

The first GSTT was enacted by The Tax Reform Act of 1976 to remedy what Congress perceived as an abusive use of trusts to benefit several generations while avoiding estate and gift taxes. The 1976 GSTT was extremely complex, and it was widely criticized as conceptually flawed, unworkable, and ineffective. As a result, the 1976 GSTT was retroactively repealed by The Tax Reform Act of 1986 and replaced by a new GSTT system. The Economic Growth and Tax Relief and Reconciliation Act of 2001 (EGTRRA 2001) phases in a repeal of the GSTT over 10 years. Similar to the repeal of the estate tax system, if no new legislation makes the repeal permanent, the repeal of the GSTT falls under a sunset provision that will bring the GSTT system back in 2011 under the law in effect prior to EGTRRA 2001.

Unlike the estate tax system, which is a progressive tax, the GSTT rate is a flat tax rate equal to the maximum estate tax rate (45% in 2009) in effect at the time of the generation-skipping transfer (GST). This difference in the GSTT system coupled with the ability to elect the use of the GST exemption (discussed below) causes the calculation of GSTT to be different than the estate and gift tax calculations. The GSTT calculation is also discussed below.

Like the estate and gift tax systems, the GSTT system has an annual exclusion ($13,000 in 2009), a lifetime exemption ($3,500,000 in 2009), and an exemption for qualified transfers. The following exhibit identifies the similarities and differences among the GSTT, estate tax, and gift tax regimes that are covered throughout this chapter.

EXHIBIT 13.1 COMPARISON OF THE GIFT, ESTATE, AND GSTT TAX SYSTEMS

FEATURES	GIFT TAX TRANSFERS	ESTATE TAX TRANSFERS	GENERATION-SKIPPING TRANSFER TAX	
			GIFTS	BEQUESTS
Applies to	Lifetime Transfers	Transfers at Death	Lifetime Transfers to Skip Persons	Transfers at Death to Skip Persons
Calculation of Transfer Includes	Value of Lifetime Transfers, plus any GSTT Paid	Value of Transfers at Death, plus any GSTT Paid	Value of Lifetime Transfers to Skip Persons	Value of Transfers at Death to Skip Persons
Annual Exclusion (2009)	$13,000	N/A	$13,000	N/A
Lifetime Exemption (2009)	$1,000,000 Cannot allocate	$3,500,000 Note: Includes Gift Transfers	$3,500,000 Can Allocate	$3,500,000 Note: Includes GST Gifts
Nature of Tax Rate	Progressive	Progressive	Highest Gift Tax Rate (Flat) 45% for 2009	Highest Estate Tax Rate (Flat) 45% for 2009
Annual Exclusion Available for Transfers under Crummey Power	Yes	N/A	Yes for Outright Transfers Possible for Transfers in Trust (See Annual Exclusions)	N/A

N/A = Not applicable

PARTIES INVOLVED IN GENERATION-SKIPPING TRANSFERS

When discussing generation-skipping transfers, it is important to understand how each individual involved in the transaction is associated with the transfer and their impact on the GSTT system. Accordingly, the parties involved are specifically defined for GSTT purposes.

TRANSFEROR

Whether or not a transfer is subject to GSTT depends on whether the transferor is two or more generations older than the transferee. Thus, in order to determine the GSTT consequences of a particular transfer, one must first identify the transferor. When property is transferred during life and is subject to gift tax, the transferor is the donor. When the property is transferred at death and is subject to estate tax, the transferor is the decedent. If the property is subject to estate tax or gift tax at some future time, usually a new transferor is determined.

EXAMPLE 13.1

Theresa creates an irrevocable trust with income for life to her daughter, Catherine. When Catherine dies, the remainder will transfer to her daughter, Haley. If Catherine was given a general power of appointment over the trust assets, then the trust assets would be included in Catherine's gross estate when Catherine dies. Since the trust is an irrevocable trust, Theresa's transfer to create the trust was subject to gift tax. Therefore, Theresa is the original transferor of the trust assets for GSTT purposes. However, upon Catherine's death, Catherine becomes the transferor of the trust assets because the assets are included in Catherine's gross estate (due to the general power of appointment she held at her death) and subject to estate tax.

TRANSFEREE

The transferee is the individual who receives the property. For GSTT purposes, individuals are categorized into two groups: (1) non-skip persons and (2) skip persons. Broadly defined, non-skip persons are those individuals to whom transfers do not result in generation-skipping transfer tax consequences, whereas skip persons are those individuals to whom the same transfers would result in GSTT consequences.

Skip Person

A skip person, or the person to whom a transfer may result in a generation-skipping transfer tax, is broadly defined as a transferee who is two or more generations younger than the transferor. When determining whether an individual is a skip person, the Code treats lineal and non-lineal descendents differently.

Key Concepts

Underline/highlight the answers to these questions as you read:

1. Describe who is a skip person and who is not a skip person for both lineal and nonlineal descendents.

2. Explain the predeceased ancestor exception.

The IRC defines a skip person as any one of the following:
1. Any lineal descendent of the transferor's grandparent (or the transferor's spouse's grandparent) who is two or more generations younger than the transferor. (Certain exclusions may apply and are discussed below.)
2. Any person who is not a lineal descendent (as described in #1 above), is not the spouse of the transferor, and is more than 37½ years younger than the transferor.

For the purpose of applying these rules, any spouse or former spouse of a transferor and all charitable organizations are always considered to be in the same generation as the transferor. Also, adopted relatives are considered the same as blood relatives.

Lineal Descendents

To determine if an individual is considered a lineal descendent, consider the family tree below. The tree only considers those individuals who are descendents of the transferor's grandparent, and for purposes of lineal descendents, age is irrelevant. Exhibit 13.2 illustrates those individuals who are skip persons (two or more generations younger than the transferor) in relation to the transferor; the 1st cousins twice removed and 1st cousins thrice removed, the grand and great-grand niece and nephew and the grand and great-grandchild. Note that the adopted great-grand niece/nephew is considered to be in the same category as a nonadopted great-grand niece/nephew. Also, spouses of each of these individuals would be placed in the same category as their spouse.

EXHIBIT 13.2 **TABLE OF CONSANGUINITY (LINEAL DESCENDENTS)**

		Transferor's Grandparent		
Aunt/Uncle		Transferor's Parent		Aunt/Uncle
Cousin	Sibling	**TRANSFEROR**	Sibling	Cousin
1st Cousin Once Removed	Niece/Nephew	Child	Niece/Nephew	1st Cousin Once Removed
1st Cousin Twice Removed	Grandniece/nephew	Grandchild	Grandniece/nephew	1st Cousin Twice Removed
1st Cousin Thrice Removed	Adopted Great-Grand niece/nephew	Great-Grandchild	Great-Grand niece/nephew	1st Cousin Thrice Removed

All listed individuals are in the lineal line and follow the lineal rules.
Circled individuals are skip persons based on lineal lines.

Unrelated and Non-Lineal Descendents for GSTT Purposes

Unrelated individuals are those individuals who are not related to the transferor. Non-lineal descendents, for GSTT purposes, are relatives who are more distant than the lineal descendents of the transferor's grandparents. To determine whether unrelated individuals or nonlineal descendents are skip persons, the individual's age is the only relevant factor; where the individual falls in relation to the transferor's family tree is irrelevant.

Transferor's Great Grandparent

Great Aunt/Uncle	Transferor's Grandparent	Great Aunt/Uncle
1st Cousin Once Removed	Transferor's Parents	1st Cousin Once Removed
2nd Cousin	Transferor	2nd Cousin
2nd Cousin Once Removed		2nd Cousin Once Removed
2nd Cousin Twice Removed		2nd Cousin Twice Removed

Persons identified in blue are not considered part of the lineal line and follow the unrelated party rules. Whether the individuals in blue are skip individuals will depend on age.

A generation is defined as a 25 year time period. Exhibit 13.4 illustrates an 80-year-old transferor. His generation would include all individuals 12½ years older than him and 12½ years younger than him. The next generation includes all individuals born within the next 25 years below the first 12½ years. Therefore, all individuals between the ages 67½ and 42½ would be one generation below the transferor. Since neighbor is 67 (13 years younger than transferor), neighbor is one generation below transferor. Friend, age 55, also falls one generation below transferor. Individuals between the ages of 42½ and 17½ are two generations below transferor, and are therefore skip individuals. Thus, both neighbor's son and friend's son are skip persons, and any transfer from transferor to neighbor's son and/or friend's son are generation-skipping transfers.

If transferor had a child the same age as neighbor's son, the child would not be considered a skip person because the child is a lineal descendent. As detailed above, lineal descendents are deemed skip persons based on the transferor's family tree. Therefore, transferor may have a child the same age as neighbor's son, and transferor's child would not be a skip person even though neighbor's son would be a skip person.

EXHIBIT 13.4   UNRELATED PERSONS AND NONLINEAL DESCENDENTS

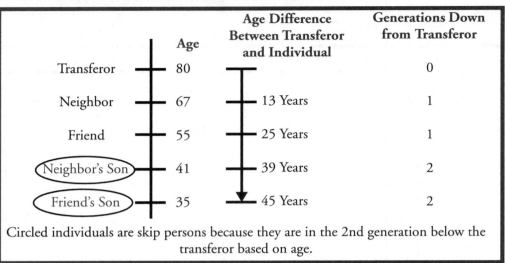

	Age	Age Difference Between Transferor and Individual	Generations Down from Transferor
Transferor	80		0
Neighbor	67	13 Years	1
Friend	55	25 Years	1
Neighbor's Son	41	39 Years	2
Friend's Son	35	45 Years	2

Circled individuals are skip persons because they are in the 2nd generation below the transferor based on age.

Trusts

A trust may also be considered a skip person (1) if all interests in the trust are held by skip persons, or (2) if the trust distributions can only be made to skip persons. For purposes of the first definition, a person is deemed to have an interest in a trust if he has the present right to receive income or principal distributions from the trust.

EXAMPLE 13.2

Anthony recently established an irrevocable trust for his grandson, Allen. The trust will pay income to Allen for his life, and at Allen's death the remaining trust assets will be distributed to Allen's children. Since Allen and his children are all skip persons and they are the only individuals that can receive distributions, the trust is also a skip person.

EXAMPLE 13.3

Beau created an irrevocable trust to pay income to his daughter, Joann, and his grandson, David. In this instance the trust is not a skip person because Joann, who is not a skip person holds a present right to receive distribution from the trust. Remember that if you have one person holding an interest in the trust that is not a skip person then the trust will NOT be a skip person for GSTT purposes until the last non-skip beneficiary's interest expires.

As mentioned, charitable organizations are considered to be in the same generation as the transferor. If a charitable organization holds an interest in a trust, then the trust cannot be a skip person. For this purpose, a charitable organization is deemed to have an interest in a trust (1) if it has a present, nondiscretionary right to receive income or principal, or (2) if the organization is the remainder beneficiary of a qualified charitable remainder trust or pooled income fund (as defined in Chapter 9).

Brett decided to participate in a pooled income fund benefiting his local church (a qualified charitable organization). Brett's grandson, Blake, will receive an annuity for his life, and the remainder will be paid to the church. Because of its remainder interest, the church has an interest in the pooled income fund and the pooled income fund is not considered a skip person since the charity is deemed to be in the same generation as the transferor.

EXAMPLE 13.4

Brett decided to create a charitable remainder trust naming his grandson, Blake, as the income beneficiary and giving the trustee the discretion to select the remainder charitable beneficiary. Because a specific charitable organization has not been declared, no charitable organization has an interest in the trust. Therefore, the trust would be considered a skip person.

EXAMPLE 13.5

Predeceased Ancestor Exception

If a child of the transferor is deceased at the time of a transfer, then that child's descendents move up one generation when determining if the transfer is a GST. As a result, certain transfers that, absent this rule, would be GSTs, will not be treated as GSTs.

Terrell gave $100,000 to his grandson, Willie. At the time the gift is made, Terrell's child, Charlotte, who is also Willie's mother, is deceased. For GSTT purposes, Willie is treated as being in Charlotte's generation (i.e., Willie is treated as being Terrell's child rather than Terrell's grandchild) and the $100,000 gift from Terrell to Willie is not a GST.

EXAMPLE 13.6

Margaret establishes an irrevocable trust for the benefit of her granddaughter, Sally. The trust instrument provides that Sally is to receive all of the trust's annual income until she reaches age 35, at which time the trust will terminate and distribute its principal to Sally. At the time Margaret establishes the trust, Margaret's child, Maxwell, who is also Sally's father, is dead. Therefore, for GSTT purposes, Sally is treated as Margaret's daughter rather than granddaughter, and neither the initial transfer to the trust nor any distributions from the trust to Sally are GSTs.

EXAMPLE 13.7

Assume the same facts as the above example, except that Celeste, Maxwell's surviving spouse, is the income beneficiary of the trust for her life. Upon Celeste's death, the trust will terminate and distribute its principal to Sally. Because Maxwell was dead at the time the trust was created, the termination of Celeste's interest in the trust will not be a GST.

EXAMPLE 13.8

EXAMPLE 13.9

Assume the same facts as the above example, except that Maxwell was living at the time the trust was created, but died before Celeste's interest in the trust terminated. Because Maxwell was alive at the time the trust was created, the termination of Celeste's interest in the trust at Celeste's death will be a GST.

The predeceased ancestor exception may also apply to transfers made to the transferor's grandniece(s) and/or grandnephew(s) if, at the time of the transfer, the transferor has no living lineal descendents.

The predeceased ancestor exception only applies if there is a death in an intervening generation. The exception will not apply to a "deemed death" for transfer purposes such as when an intervening generation executes a qualified disclaimer.

Non-Skip Person

A non-skip person is any person or trust that is not a skip person. Therefore, any lineal descendent less than two generations below the transferor (based on the family tree) are non-skip persons and non-lineal descendents and unrelated parties that are not more than 37½ years younger than the transferor are non-skip persons. Also, a transferor's spouse, or former spouse, is always considered a non-skip person because they are considered to be in the same generation as the spouse.

A trust is a non-skip person if any non-skip person holds an interest in the trust. Also, if no person has an interest in the trust, but a distribution may be made to a non-skip person, the trust is a non-skip person. Refer to Exhibits 13.2, 13.3, and 13.4 for a visual depiction of who is a skip person and who is a non-skip person.

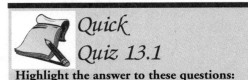

Quick Quiz 13.1

Highlight the answer to these questions:

1. Anyone who is less than two generations younger than the transferor is a skip person.
   a. True
   b. False

2. If a parent disclaims the property bequeathed to them, then the predeceased parent rule will apply if the assets are transferred to the children instead.
   a. True
   b. False

False, False.

QUALIFIED DISCLAIMERS

As discussed in prior chapters, qualified disclaimers allow property to pass to someone other than the primary beneficiary named in the decedent's will or under the state's intestacy laws. When the heir of an estate executes a qualified disclaimer, he is deemed, for estate tax purposes, to predecease the decedent. The property the disclaimant would have received will be transferred to the alternate beneficiary named under the will or, if there is no will, to the decedent's other heirs according to state intestacy law. Use of a qualified disclaimer prevents the property passing from the decedent, being included in the disclaimant's gross estate.

A qualified disclaimer by a parent cannot be used to avoid GSTT. The predeceased parent exception to the generation-skipping transfer tax applies only when the parent actually dies, thus "presumed death" for estate tax purposes will not suffice.

EXAMPLE 13.10

Morris recently died, leaving his entire estate to his son, Junior, and daughter, Barbara, in equal shares, per stirpes. Barbara has been very successful in her career and has accumulated substantial personal wealth. If Barbara disclaims her inheritance from Morris, the property she would have received from the estate will be transferred to her children (grandchildren of Morris). For estate tax purposes, Barbara is deemed to predecease Morris, allowing her children to take her share without any adverse gift tax imposed on Barbara. Since Barbara has not actually died, however, the transfer of property from Morris' estate to the grandchildren is a GST and will be subject to GSTT. Morris' executor can allocate part of Morris' GST exemption (if any remains) to the transfer to offset the GSTT due.

TYPES OF TAXABLE TRANSFERS

GSTT applies to three types of taxable transfers: (1) direct skips, (2) taxable distributions, and (3) taxable terminations. The amount of GSTT due on a taxable transfer, and the person liable for the tax, depends on the classification of the taxable transfer as a direct skip, a taxable distribution, or a taxable termination. Thus, it is important to understand the differences between these taxable transfers and to identify how and when each type may occur.

DIRECT SKIP

Definition

A **direct skip** is an outright transfer of property to a skip person that is subject to estate or gift tax. An outright gift to a grandchild or a trust that is a skip person during life or at death is a direct skip.

EXAMPLE 13.11

Clyde's great-grandson, Brandon, wanted a new car for his 16th birthday. Clyde bought him a brand new red convertible and parked it in the driveway on Brandon's birthday. Since Clyde gave Brandon an outright gift, and Brandon is a skip person, the gift is a direct skip. Note that even though Brandon is more than two generations below Clyde, the transfer is only taxed once because transfers to direct skips are only subject to GSTT once regardless of the number of generations skipped.

Taxation Issues on Direct Skips

The GSTT on a direct skip is imposed on the value received by the transferee. The transferor is liable for the GSTT on a direct skip, unless the direct skip is made from a trust. In the trust instance, the trustee is liable for the GSTT. Unless the transferor's will or the applicable trust document directs otherwise by specific reference to the GSTT, the property transferred in a GST is charged with any GSTT imposed on the transfer.

Key Concepts

Underline/highlight the answers to these questions as you read:

1. What are direct skips, taxable terminations, and taxable distributions?

2. Who is liable for the GSTT on a direct skip, taxable termination, and taxable distribution?

TAXABLE TERMINATION

Definition

A **taxable termination** is any termination of a trust interest unless at the termination of the trust, the trust property transferred is subject to (1) federal estate or gift tax, (2) a non-skip person receives an interest in the property transferred out of the trust, or (3) the distribution from the trust will never be made to a skip person.

EXAMPLE 13.12

Mike established an irrevocable trust to benefit his son, Adam. The trust will pay income to Adam for his life and the remainder will transfer to Adam's children at Adam's death. When Adam dies, a taxable termination has occurred because skip persons, Adam's children, receive an interest in the trust at its termination.

Taxation of Taxable Terminations

The taxable amount of a taxable termination equals the value of the trust property transferred less any expenses, indebtedness, and taxes attributable to the taxable termination. The trustee is responsible for paying (from the trust) the GSTT on a taxable termination.

TAXABLE DISTRIBUTION

Definition

A **taxable distribution** is any distribution from a trust to a skip person that is not a taxable termination or a direct skip.

EXAMPLE 13.13

Bobby established a revocable trust under which the trust income is payable to Bobby's child, Carolyn, for life. When Bobby's grandchild, Alex, attains 35 years of age, Alex is to receive one-half of the principal. The remaining one-half of the principal is to be distributed to Alex on Carolyn's death. Assume that Carolyn survives until Alex attains the age of 35. When the trustee distributes one-half of the principal to Alex on his 35th birthday, the distribution is a taxable distribution because it is a distribution to a skip person and is neither a taxable termination nor a direct skip.

Taxation of Taxable Distributions

The amount received by the transferee in a taxable distribution, reduced by any expenses incurred by the transferee in connection with the GSTT, is the taxable amount of the distribution. Unlike direct skips and taxable terminations, the transferee is liable for the GSTT on a taxable distribution. Therefore, if the trust pays the GSTT instead of the transferee, another taxable distribution occurs for an amount equal to the GSTT paid because the transferee was responsible for the tax, and the payment by the trust is considered a gift from the trust to the transferee. The GSTT rules dictate that the additional distribution for the taxes paid is treated as being made on the last day of the calendar year in which the original taxable distribution occurred. This occurs even if the actual tax payment occurs in a subsequent calendar year.

Angie established an irrevocable trust under which the trust income is payable to Angie's daughter, Maria, for life. When Angie's grandson, Wade, turns 25 years old, Wade is to receive net $1,000,000 of principal and the trustee is directed to pay all taxes associated with the transfer. The remaining principal will be distributed to Wade on Maria's death. When the trustee distributes the $1,000,000 of principal to Wade on his 25th birthday, Wade is liable for the GSTT on the distribution. Since the trust must pay the tax of $450,000 (45% of $1,000,000) there is deemed to be another GST for the taxes paid by the trustee, thus resulting in more tax due, which when paid by the trustee results in another taxable distribution. In total, the trust will have to pay out $1,818,182 ($1,000,000 x (1/(1 - 0.45)) in order to give Wade a net sum of $1,000,000.

EXAMPLE 13.14

EXCEPTIONS, EXCLUSIONS, AND EXEMPTION

Like the gift and estate tax systems, the GSTT System also has exceptions, exclusions, and exemptions.

EXCEPTIONS

The original GSTT system was retroactively repealed in 1986 and was replaced with a new GSTT system. Therefore, the current GSTT only applies to transfers made after the date of enactment, October 22, 1986, although certain transfers made between September 25, 1985 and October 23, 1986 are subject to GSTT. Transfers between these dates will not be subject to GSTT if:

- The transfer was to an irrevocable trust that was in existence on or before September 25, 1985, to the extent no additions were made to the trust after September 25, 1985.

- The transfer was pursuant to certain wills and revocable trusts executed before October 22, 1986 and the decedent died before January 1, 1987.

- The transfer was from a person who was suffering from a mental disability and as such could not change the disposition of his property beginning October 22, 1986 and continuing until the date of his death.

Specifically, the exception applies to trusts that were grandfathered at the time and trusts where the grantor was unable to change the trust due to mental capacity.

EXCLUSIONS

The GSTT system has both an exclusion available for qualified transfers and an annual exclusion of $13,000.

Medical and Educational Payments - Qualified Transfers

The direct payment of tuition to a qualified educational institution (see Chapter 5) or the direct payment of qualified medical expenses (see Chapter 5) to a medical care provider on behalf of a skip person is not subject to GSTT. The exclusion from GSTT also applies if the payments are made from a trust.

EXAMPLE 13.15	Tony established a trust for the benefit of his grandchildren. The trust instrument authorizes the trustee to pay tuition and medical expenses for any grandchild. If the trustee makes a tuition payment to a qualified educational organiza-

tion for one of the grandchildren the distribution from the trust is not subject to GSTT because it is a qualified transfer.

Annual Exclusion

Similar to the gift tax system, an annual exclusion of $13,000 per donee per donor for present interest gifts is available for GSTs. The application of the GST annual exclusion depends on the type of transfer. For transfers that constitute direct skips, the application of the annual exclusion is applied in the same manner as the annual exclusion for gift tax (as discussed in Chapter 5). Thus, a direct skip is a nontaxable gift for GSTT purposes to the extent the transfer is excluded from taxable gifts under the annual gift tax exclusion.

EXAMPLE 13.16

Last Christmas, Claude gave his grandson Darryl $13,000 outright. As discussed in Chapter 5, $13,000 is the gift tax annual exclusion, resulting in a nontaxable transfer for gift tax purposes. For GSTT purposes, the gift is also a nontaxable gift because the gift is not taxable under the gift tax system.

EXAMPLE 13.17

Assume in the example above that Claude gave his grandson Darryl $20,000 outright. Again, the $13,000 would be excluded from gift tax and GSTT. The remaining $7,000 would be subject to both gift tax and GSTT.

For gifts in trust, the gift tax annual exclusion and the GST annual exclusion differ. To qualify a gift in trust for the gift tax annual exclusion, the beneficiaries of the trust must have a present interest in the trust (which is often accomplished by giving the beneficiaries a Crummey power over the contributions made to the trust). Transfers to a trust deemed a skip person are nontaxable gifts for GSTT purposes only to the extent the transfer is equal to or less than the annual exclusion and the following requirements are met:

1. The beneficiaries are given a Crummey power over the contribution to the trust;
2. The trust assets can only be distributed for the benefit of the beneficiary during the beneficiary's lifetime; and
3. If the trust does not terminate before the beneficiary's death, the assets must be included in the beneficiary's gross estate.

EXAMPLE 13.18

Assume the same facts as above except that instead of giving Darryl the money outright, Claude established an irrevocable trust for Darryl with a contribution of $13,000. The trust requires the income to be distributed to Darryl for his life and the remainder to be distributed to Darryl when he attains the age of 30. The trust also gives Darryl a Crummey power. If Darryl dies before attaining the age of 30, his estate will receive the remainder of the trust. Since the trust only pays to Darryl, a skip person, and all benefits must be paid to him or his estate, the $13,000 transfer will qualify for the GST and gift tax annual exclusion and thus is a nontaxable gift for both gift tax and GSTT purposes.

Split Gifts

Gift splitting (discussed in Chapter 5), also applies to transfers subject to GSTT. Gift splitting enables a spouse to treat gifts of separate property as being made one-half from each spouse, allowing each spouse to use the other's annual exclusion. This enables an individual to transfer $26,000 (the combined annual exclusion for the two spouses) to an individual without incurring gift tax or GSTT. When an individual elects on the gift tax return (Form 709) to split gifts for gift tax purposes, any GSTs are also deemed split gifts.

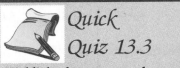
EXAMPLE 13.19

Harry gives $20,000 to his grandson and $20,000 to his granddaughter in a calendar year. Katie, Harry's wife, consents to have the gifts treated as made one-half by her for gift tax purposes (a split gift election). As a result, Katie is also treated as the transferor for GSTT purposes of one-half of the gifts (i.e., Katie is treated as the transferor of $10,000 to the grandson and $10,000 to the granddaughter). While these gifts are made to a skip person, the GSTT annual exclusion applies to these transfers, eliminating the GSTT.

EXEMPTION

Every individual is allowed a GST exemption equal to the applicable estate tax credit equivalency, currently $3,500,000 (2009). Unlike the gift and estate tax system, the same exemption applies to assets transferred during life or at death.

Allocation Rules

The applicable gift, estate, and GST tax credit equivalency is applied automatically to transfers until it is depleted. Since it is possible that a transferor may wish to save his or her GSTT credit for other transfers, the law permits the transferor to opt out of the automatic allocation provisions by including an election statement on the transferor's gift or estate tax return.

The transferor or his executor may affirmatively allocate the GST exemption any time between the date of the transfer and the due date, including extensions, of the transferor's federal estate tax return. If an estate tax return is not required and the automatic allocation provisions do not apply, the GST exemption must be allocated before what would have been the due date of the estate tax return, including extensions. When the GST exemption is allocated on a timely filed gift tax return, the allocation is effective as of the date of the transfer. An allocation after the due date is considered a late allocation and will require the use of the GST exemption for the property's fair market value at the date of the late allocation.

Allocation of the Exemption for Direct Skips During Life

If a direct skip occurs during a transferor's lifetime, the transferor's GST exemption that has not been used is automatically allocated to the direct skip. If the transferor does not want to use his GST exemption, the transferor must (1) describe on a timely filed federal gift and GSTT return (Form 709) the transfer and the extent to which the automatic allocation does not apply, or (2) timely file the federal gift and GSTT return (Form 709) with the payment of the GSTT due without the automatic allocation.

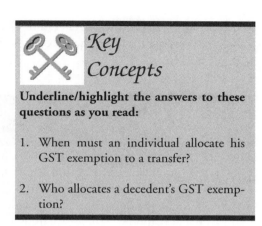

Key Concepts

Underline/highlight the answers to these questions as you read:

1. When must an individual allocate his GST exemption to a transfer?

2. Who allocates a decedent's GST exemption?

Allocation of the GST Exemption for Taxable Terminations and Taxable Distributions

If any GST exemption remains after the allocation to any direct skips, the exemption is allocated pro rata to any taxable terminations or taxable distributions from the decedent. The allocation, included on the transferor's gift tax return, must detail the name of the trust, the amount of the allocation, the value of the trust's assets at the date of the allocation, and the inclusion ratio (discussed below) of the trust after the allocation.

When an individual allocates the GST exemption to a trust in excess of the amount necessary to create a zero inclusion ratio (discussed below), the allocation of the excess exemption amount is void and available for subsequent allocation. However, in the case of a Charitable Lead Annuity Trust (CLAT), an allocation of GST exemption in excess of the amount necessary to obtain a zero inclusion ratio for the trust is not void and may not be restored to the transferor. As a result, an excess allocation of GST exemption to a CLAT wastes the transferor's GST exemption.

The **Estate Tax Inclusion Period (ETIP)** rule prevents a grantor from allocating any of his GST exemption to a transfer that would result in estate tax inclusion for the grantor if he died after the transfer. This rule prevents the grantor from allocating his GST exemption to the remainder interest in GRATs, GRUTs, QPRTs, and CLATs prior to the expiration of the retained interest term.

Allocation of the GST Exemption for Transfers at Death

When an individual dies with unused GST exemption, the executor of his estate allocates the GST exemption on the decedent's federal estate tax return (Form 706). This allocation may be for a testamentary GST or a late allocation to a lifetime transfer. In either case, the allocation is effective once the federal estate tax return (Form 706) is filed.

As with the allocation of the GST exemption to lifetime transfers in trust, the allocation at death must identify the name of the trust, the allocation to the trust, the fair market value of the trust's assets at the date of the allocation, and the trust's inclusion ratio after the allocation. Any allocation for a trust that will not be a GST trust is void and the GST exemption is available for subsequent allocation.

When an individual makes a generation-skipping transfer in the year of his death, the executor will be responsible for filing the decedent's gift tax return and allocating any GST exemption on that gift tax return.

APPLICABLE RATE, INCLUSION RATIO, AND APPLICABLE FRACTION

After it has been determined that a GST has occurred (whether a direct skip, taxable termination, or taxable distribution) the value of the GST is then multiplied by the **applicable rate**. The applicable rate is the maximum estate tax rate in effect at the time of the GST (45% for 2009) times the **inclusion ratio**, which is the difference between the applicable fraction (defined below) and one. The calculation and examples are provided below.

The applicable fraction is calculated by dividing the applicable GST exemption allocated to the transfer by the value of the transfer reduced by any federal estate tax or state death tax incurred by reason of the GST that is chargeable to the trust and is actually recovered from the trust, the amount of any charitable deduction allowed, and the value of the transfer that is a nontaxable gift (i.e., annual exclusion and qualified transfers).

The inclusion ratio is then determined by subtracting the applicable fraction from one. The inclusion ratio is then multiplied by the maximum transfer rate (45% for 2009) to calculate the applicable rate which is multiplied by the value of the GST to determine the GSTT due.

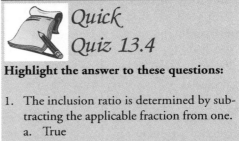

Quick Quiz 13.4

Highlight the answer to these questions:

1. The inclusion ratio is determined by subtracting the applicable fraction from one.
   a. True
   b. False

2. The 2009 lifetime GST exemption is $1,455,800.
   a. True
   b. False

True, False.

EXHIBIT 13.5   THE APPLICABLE FRACTION FORMULA

$$\text{Applicable Fraction} = \frac{\text{GST Exemption Allocated}}{\text{Value of Property Transferred} - \text{Death Taxes} - \text{Charitable Deductions} - \text{Nontaxable Gift Portion}}$$

Inclusion Ratio = 1 − Applicable Fraction

Applicable Rate = Inclusion Ratio × Maximum Transfer Tax Rate

---

In 2009, Cindy gave her granddaughter Marsha $3,513,000 outright. Cindy allocated her entire GST exemption to the transfer. As the calculation below illustrates, the transfer is subject to both gift tax and GSTT. Notice, however, there is no GSTT consequence because of the GST lifetime exemption of $3,500,000 for 2009 and the annual exclusion of $13,000. A gift tax consequence remains because the applicable gift tax credit equivalency is only $1,000,000 for 2009.

EXAMPLE 13.20

GSTT Calculation

		Notes:
Applicable Fraction (AF)	1.00	$3,500,000/($3,513,000 - $13,000)
Inclusion Ratio (IR)	0.00	1- AF
Applicable Rate	0.00	IR x Max Transfer Rate

GST	$3,513,000
Less: Annual Exclusion	($13,000)
Taxable GST	$3,500,000
Times: Applicable rate	0%
GSTT	**$0**

While the above formula is the appropriate calculation utilizing the applicable rate, the following calculation can be used for simple GSTT calculations involving direct skips.

GST	$3,513,000
Less: Annual Exclusion	($13,000)
Less: GST Exemption	($3,500,000)
Taxable GST	$0
Times: GSTT Rate	45%
GSTT	**$0**

Gift Tax Calculation

Gift	$3,513,000	
Plus GSTT Paid	$0	The GSTT paid is considered a gift.
Less: Annual Exclusions	($13,000)	
Less: Qualified Transfers	$0	
Less: Marital Deductions	$0	
Equals: Total Taxable Gifts	$3,500,000	
Add: Previous Taxable Gifts (post 1976)	$0	
Equals: Tentative Tax Base (TTB)	$3,500,000	
Tentative Tax (TT)	$1,455,800	
Less: Gift Tax Deemed Paid	$0	
Less: Applicable Gift Tax Credit	($345,800)	
Equals: Gift Tax Liability	**$1,110,000**	

EXAMPLE 13.21	Assume the same facts as the example above except that Cindy gave her granddaughter Marsha $4,013,000 outright. Under this scenario, there is both a gift tax consequence and a GSTT consequence. To gift $4,013,000, Cindy has to pay $5,674,250 ($4,013,000 gift + $225,000 of GSTT + $1,436,250 of gift tax).

GSTT Calculation

		Notes:
Applicable Fraction (AF)	0.875	$3,500,000/($4,013,000 - $13,000)
Inclusion Ratio (IR)	0.125	1- AF
Applicable Rate	0.05625	IR x Max Transfer Rate

GST	$4,013,000
Less: Annual Exclusion	$13,000
Taxable GST	$4,000,000
Times Applicable rate	0.05625
GSTT	**$225,000**

The following calculation can also be used for this simple GSTT calculation.

GST	$4,013,000
Less: Annual Exclusion	($13,000)
Less: GST Exemption	($3,500,000)
Taxable GST	$500,000
Times: GSTT Rate	45%
GSTT	**$225,000**

Gift Tax Calculation

Gift	$4,013,000	
Plus GSTT Paid	$225,000	Any GSTT Paid is part of the gift
Less: Annual Exclusions	($13,000)	
Less: Qualified Transfers	$0	
Less: Marital Deductions	$0	
Equals: Total Taxable Gifts	$4,225,000	
Add: Previous Taxable Gifts (post 1976)	$0	
Equals: Tentative Tax Base	$4,225,000	
Tentative Tax	$1,782,050	$1,455,800 + (0.45 x $725,000)
Less: Gift Tax Deemed Paid	$0	
Less: Applicable Gift Tax Credit	($345,800)	
Equals: Gift Tax Liability	**$1,436,250**	

GENERATION-SKIPPING TRANSFER TAX AND QTIPS

The election of the GST exemption may be complicated by the QTIP election when the fair market value of the decedent's transfers in a QTIP Trust to the surviving spouse is greater than the applicable estate tax credit equivalency. To remedy this situation, a Reverse QTIP election can be made. A Reverse QTIP election is a QTIP election that is made for estate tax purposes but not for GSTT purposes. Thus, the assets would qualify for the unlimited marital deduction for estate tax purposes (requiring all of the unused assets in the QTIP Trust at the surviving spouse's death to be included in his or her estate) while using the GST exemption of the first spouse to die to avoid future imposition of the GSTT. Since a partial Reverse QTIP election is not permitted, an executor may wish to create two QTIP Trusts for the same spouse and make a Reverse QTIP election for one of them so as to accomplish two goals: (1) elimination of estate tax at the death of the first spouse, and (2) full use of the decedent's GST exemption.

EXAMPLE 13.22

Decedent, age 60 has a gross estate in 2009 of $8,000,000 and wishes to leave $3,500,000 to a credit shelter trust. The income and remainder beneficiaries are his son, age 34, and his daughter, age 25, from his previous marriage. The balance of the estate, $4,500,000, will pass to a QTIP Trust. The income beneficiary of the QTIP Trust is his current spouse Joy, age 28, a known spendthrift, and the remainder beneficiary is Jordan, the decedent's newborn grandchild.

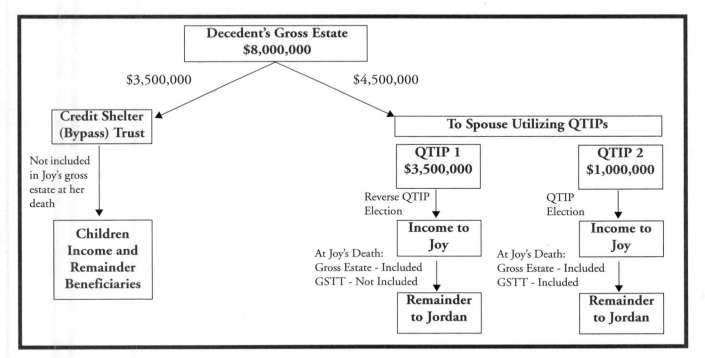

To eliminate any estate tax due and to fully use the decedent's GST exemption of $3,500,000, the executor would elect to treat property equal to $4,500,000 as QTIP in two QTIP Trusts, "QTIP 1" and "QTIP 2." The executor would than make a Reverse QTIP election for GSTT purposes for QTIP 1 using the decedent's GST exemption. At the death of the surviving spouse, Joy, the assets in QTIP 1 and 2 would be included in Joy's gross estate for estate tax purposes, but only QTIP 2 would be included in her gross estate for GSTT purposes. (As noted earlier, partial Reverse QTIP elections are not permitted necessitating the use of the two trusts.) At Joy's death, she can use her GST exemption for QTIP 2.

FILING REQUIREMENT AND RETURNS

Inter vivos direct skips are reported on Form 709, United States Gift and Generation-Skipping Transfer Tax Return, which is due on or before April 15 of the year following the calendar year in which the direct skip occurs. Direct skip transfers at death are reported on Schedule R or R-1 of Form 706, which is due nine months after the transferor's date of death.

Taxable distributions are reported on Forms 706-GS(D-1) and 706-GS(D), and taxable terminations are reported on Form 706-GS(T). Form 706-GS(D-1) is filed by the trustee of any trust that makes a taxable distribution. Anyone who receives a taxable distribution from a trust must file Form 706-GS(D). Forms 706-GS(D-1) and 706-GS(D) are due on or before April 15 of the year following the calendar year in which the taxable distribution is made.

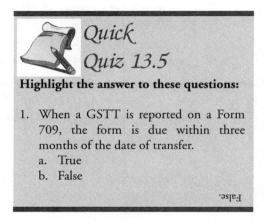

The trustee of any trust that has a taxable termination must file Form 706-GS(T) for the tax year in which the termination occurred. Form 706-GS(T) is due on or before April 15 of the year following the calendar year in which the taxable termination occurs.

EXHIBIT 13.6

Key Points

- Designed to tax large transfers between skipped generations (i.e., grandparent to grandchild).
- It is separate from, and additional to, the gift and estate tax systems.

Transfers Subject to GSTT

- Direct skips.
- Taxable termination.
- Taxable distribution.

GSTT Rate

- The GSTT rate is the highest marginal rate for the unified gift and estate tax rates (45% for 2009).
- Any GSTT paid will be added to the fair market value of the gift to determine total taxable gifts for the federal gift tax.

Exceptions to GSTT

- GSTT annual exclusion is $13,000 per donee per donor, gift splitting is available if both spouses elect.
- Crummey power can qualify a gift in trust for the GSTT annual exclusion if additional requirements are met.
- Indexed, but $13,000 for 2009.
- The predeceased parent rule applies for direct skips to lineal descendents and collateral heirs if the decedent does not have any direct lineal descendents (children, grandchildren). Use of a disclaimer will not invoke the predeceased parent exception.
- Lifetime exemption available during life or at death equal to the applicable estate tax equivalency of $3,500,000 for 2009.
- Qualified transfers are excluded.

AN OVERVIEW OF GENERATION-SKIPPING TRUSTS

Property transferred to a member of the next generation, and then later transferred to that person's heirs, is generally taxed twice, once each time the property is transferred. Over the years, estate planners have devised techniques to minimize transfer taxation by failing to give some generations an ownership interest in property. The generation-skipping trust has been used in estate planning to pass property ultimately to a generation at least two levels younger than the grantor of the trust while allowing the intervening generation some income benefits from the property on an estate tax-free basis.

Use of a generation-skipping trust allows the planner to split legal ownership of assets (ownership is held by the trust) from the use of assets (the beneficiaries of the trust may use the trust assets). If the beneficiaries do not have legal title to the trust assets when they die, the beneficiary cannot transfer anything in the trust at his death, and therefore no part of the trust will be included in the beneficiary's gross estate. Using a generation-skipping trust to avoid estate tax inclusion for descendents of the grantor can substantially increase the wealth that is transferred to future generations of the family because the estate tax paid at each generation is eliminated.

INTRODUCTION TO DYNASTY TRUSTS

Dynasty trusts are generation-skipping trusts created in perpetuity. Once created, a dynasty trust provides for trust beneficiaries, but avoids transfer taxation in the beneficiary's estate by restricting ownership of trust assets. When properly drafted, a dynasty trust will not vest ownership of trust property in any individual beneficiary. If a beneficiary is not deemed to own the trust assets, those assets cannot be included in the beneficiary's gross estate at death. Each time a property "vests" it is drastically reduced when it passes to the next generation, since estate taxes are payable from the property. According to Jesse Dukeminier, Maxwell Professor of Law at the University of California Los Angeles School of Law, a nationally recognized expert on the Rule Against Perpetuities, "A dynasty trust, free of estate, gift, and GST taxes for its duration, is a most valuable device for protecting the settlor's descendents from federal transfer taxes for a very long time. A $1,000,000 dynasty trust should be considered by every millionaire with descendents" because the long-term wealth accumulation potential of these trusts is significant. Assuming the trust will last for 120 years, if $1,000,000 is transferred to the trust shielded by the grantor's GST exemption, at an eight percent compounded growth rate per year, the value of the

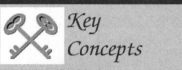

Key Concepts

Underline/highlight the answers to these questions as you read:

1. What was the original purpose of the Rule Against Perpetuities?

2. How are dynasty trusts taxed for income tax purposes?

3. How are the assets of a dynasty trust protected from the claims of a beneficiary's creditors?

4. Identify several types of dynasty trusts.

trust at termination will be \$10,252,992,943. The value of the same property with no trust arrangement (subject to transfer taxes every 30 years at 55%) would be \$420,436,792.

THE RULE AGAINST PERPETUITIES

At common law, any restraint on the alienation of property was considered void. As a result, trusts could not be created because they had the potential of restraining the disposition of property. Common law judges sought to ensure that property could be used in its most productive use and believed that allowing individuals to retain the right to use property led to inefficiency.

The Duke of Norfolk's case changed the rules. The Duke of Norfolk's case involved a situation where the Duke, whose oldest son and heir was "non compos mentis" (i.e., incompetent), attempted to transfer all of his property to a trust. Under the terms of the trust, the trustee was prohibited from selling the property, but could manage it for the benefit of the Duke's heirs in perpetuity. After about a century of litigation, including a review by the English House of Lords, Lord Chancellor Nottingham articulated "the Rule Against Perpetuities," which states "No interest [in real or personal property] is good unless it must vest, if at all, not later than twenty-one years after some life in being at the creation of the interest." The Rule Against Perpetuities was interpreted to mean that an interest in trust must terminate within lives in being plus 21 years in order to be valid. Note that this does not mean that a trust must terminate within lives in being plus 21 years, but rather that the interest vests, resulting in a termination of the trust no later than the expiration of all life estates vesting within the perpetuities period.

In its common law form, the Rule Against Perpetuities has created a tremendous amount of confusion. Volumes have been written trying to interpret its exact application, and many variations and interpretations have been set forth. Much of the confusion has been clarified by modern statutes setting forth the rules of construction for interpreting the Rule Against Perpetuities.

Some states have adopted The Uniform Statutory Rule Against Perpetuities (USRAP). Under USRAP, an interest in trust will be valid if it (1) will vest or terminate within lives in being plus 21 years (the common law Rule Against Perpetuities), or (2) the interest vests or terminates within 90 years of the creation of the trust. USRAP Section 1(e) prohibits a settlor from creating a trust for the longer of the common law perpetuities period or the 90-year period provided for in USRAP. The IRS and Treasury have accepted the 90-year perpetuities period provided for in USRAP, but conditioned their acceptance upon the condition that a trust settlor cannot create the trust with language which defines the trust duration as the longer of the common law perpetuities period or the 90-year perpetuities period.

A growing trend among the states is to abolish the Rule Against Perpetuities. The purpose of the Rule Against Perpetuities was to (1) ensure that property is freely alienable, and (2) prevent the dead hand from controlling the lives of the living. To address these concerns, states that have abolished the Rule Against Perpetuities typically require the property transferred in trust to be freely alienable by the trustee. Since most dynasty trusts use powers of appointment and/or give the trustee the discretionary power to terminate the trust upon changes in law or taxation, the influence of the dead hand is minimized, thereby addressing the second purpose of the Rule Against Perpetuities. Many states have abolished the Rule Against Perpetuities, but three states,

Delaware, Alaska, and South Dakota, do not assess a state tax on trust income. As a result, Delaware, Alaska, and South Dakota are the states where most individuals create dynasty trusts.

TAXATION OF DYNASTY TRUSTS

Once established, a dynasty trust, which is a complex trust, pays tax on its income to the extent that the income is not distributed to the beneficiaries.

Trust situs for income tax purposes is not always the same as trust situs for perpetuity purposes. If the grantor trust rules apply, the trust may be subject to taxation in the state where the grantor is domiciled. This result typically occurs when the dynasty trust has been set up as an **Intentionally Defective Grantor Trust (IDGT)**, a trust which gives the grantor sufficient control to be considered the owner for income tax purposes, but not so much control to require the trust property to be included in the transferor's gross estate. The grantor must be aware of potential income tax issues upon creation and during administration of the trust.

To achieve transfer tax objectives, the dynasty trust must have a zero inclusion ratio for GSTT purposes. Property in the dynasty trust will not be included in the estate of the beneficiaries of the trust, thereby avoiding estate taxation. A zero inclusion ratio for GST purposes results in a GSTT rate of zero.

BASIC STRUCTURE AND TYPES OF DYNASTY TRUSTS

Dynasty trusts are usually set up as family trusts that grant the trustee discretion to pay income and corpus among members of the family (usually defined as the lineal descendents of the grantor). The grantor usually funds the trust with personal (not real) property.

The trust document usually designates the state whose laws will govern the validity and construction of the trust, and will name the individual or corporation who will serve as trustee. It is not usually necessary for the grantor to reside in the state in which the trust is governed. In many instances, it is desirable to have the grantor be a resident of another state, since some states do not tax the trust income of non-residents. If the trustee maintains a place of business within the selected state, and the assets of the trust are administered in that state, a substantial relationship is established that is usually sufficient to guarantee that the trust will be enforced. For long-term trusts, like dynasty trusts, it is usually wise to allow the trustee to change the situs of the trust in the event of adverse legal or tax changes.

Unless the trust has a corporate fiduciary, it is usually wise to name two independent trustees. Some individuals include a clause that sets an age at which individual trustees (with the exception of family members) must resign and transfer trusteeship to others. Dynasty trusts typically name two or more "Trust Protectors," who are individuals that are not beneficiaries of the trust with the authority to remove the trustee. The grantor should never serve as trustee or trust protector of a dynasty trust.

Due to their very long duration, the trust instrument often gives the trustee the authority to terminate the trust in whole or in part if it is appropriate to do so. This may be necessary due to a change in tax law that makes the trust a hindrance, rather than a benefit.

A possible alternative to termination of the trust is making another dynasty trust the discretionary beneficiary of the trust assets. In this instance, the trustee will be able to pay over all of the trust assets to another trust upon the occurrence of adverse events.

The trustee is typically empowered to purchase assets for the beneficiary's personal use. If the trustee exercises this option, the assets are protected from the claims of the beneficiary's creditors, and will not be included in the beneficiary's estate for federal estate tax purposes. The purchase of assets inside of the trust can also protect those assets from the claims of a beneficiary's spouse, and in this way the trust can be used as an alternative to a premarital agreement. A beneficiary's spouse will generally not be able to demand assets held by the trust in the event of divorce. If a beneficiary is given the use of an asset owned by the trust, such as a piece of artwork, trust documents usually require the beneficiary to purchase an insurance policy on the property to reimburse the trust in the event of the asset's destruction.

Note that the right to use assets cannot extend to the grantor of the trust. If the grantor receives income from, or use of assets held by the trust, the assets will be included in the grantor's gross estate, even if the grantor had no legal entitlement to such income or use.

Usually, the trust is drafted to require that beneficiaries pay for their own consumable and wasting assets, such as vacations, food, and transportation. Assets purchased inside the trust are typically permanent assets that tend to appreciate over time.

The trustee should be required to refuse contributions to the trust not shielded by the grantor's GST exemption.

DYNASTY TRUSTS & BUSINESS SUCCESSION PLANNING

A dynasty trust can be used to acquire and hold closely held or family business stock. Once the stock is in the trust, the family can maintain control of the business for multiple generations, and avoid transfer taxation on the value of the business as long as the trust holds the interest. If the trust is used to hold family business interests, the trustee should be given the authority to split the trust into sub-trusts, with the beneficiary of the sub-trust holding the business interest named as investment trustee of the sub-trust. As noted above, use of a dynasty trust provides creditor protection, avoidance of transfer taxation at each generational level on the value of the business, as well as protection from the claims of a divorcing spouse.

TYPES OF DYNASTY TRUSTS

Pot Trusts

A **pot trust** is created as a single trust and remains a single trust during the period of its administration. These trusts are easily administered and the trustee has the flexibility to treat all beneficiaries equally, as opposed to basing beneficial interest in the trust on degree of relationship to the grantor (which is the result when a per stirpital trust is created).

Disadvantages of the pot trust include (1) the fact that "equal" treatment may lead to conflict between or within various generations of the family, and (2) this structure does not encourage beneficiaries to make additional contributions to the trust, since all trust assets benefit all individuals with an interest in the trust, including remote relatives (cousins many times removed). Significant benefits can be achieved if several generations of family members make contributions to the trust, shielded by their GST exemption. Successive generations may be hesitant to do so, however, unless the contributions they make will directly benefit their heirs.

Generational Sub-Trusts

Another common structure for dynasty trusts is a series of generational sub-trusts within the larger family trust. A sub-trust is created on the birth of the first member in a generation, or at the death of the surviving member of a generation.

Generational sub-trusts can avoid potential conflict between siblings or conflict between or within various generations of the family. As the number of sub-trusts rise, however, trust administration expenses increase.

Generational sub-trusts may encourage additional contributions, since the contributors know that the contributions will be earmarked for a specific branch of the family.

FUNDING THE TRUST

A dynasty trust is typically funded with cash or personal property. Due to the anti-alienation provisions enacted by states that have abolished the Rule Against Perpetuities, real property should not be placed in the trust. Instead, real property can be placed inside of a limited liability company (or family limited partnership), followed by a transfer of the limited liability company (or family limited partnership) interest to the dynasty trust. When selecting assets to transfer to a dynasty trust, highly appreciating assets are preferred if the GST exemption is going to be applied.

The trust can also be funded with a life insurance policy. Life insurance is an ideal asset for a dynasty trust since, during the accumulation phase, the growth in the cash value is shielded from income taxation. Furthermore, life insurance can be used to leverage the value of the trust, which can be particularly attractive with a GST trust. For example, if the settlor is age 50 and a standard risk, a $1,000,000 premium can purchase $6,500,000 worth of life insurance; if the settlor is age 60, the trustee can buy a policy paying $4,000,000. If the spouses are younger, for example, age 35, the trustee could buy, with a single premium payment of $2,000,000, a policy paying $62,000,000 on the death of the second to die.

Even if life insurance is not used, the value of the trust can grow significantly over time. If a $1,000,000 trust is invested in common stocks, which appreciate in value at the same rate stocks have appreciated over the 20th century, the original trust corpus of $1,000,000 will grow to over $200,000,000 in 100 years (or, inflation adjusted, to $10,000,000). If the settlor and spouse have created a life insurance trust, a $10,000,000 death benefit may grow to $2,000,000,000 upon the termination of the trust (or, adjusted for inflation, to $100,000,000).

GENERAL DRAFTING ISSUES FOR DYNASTY TRUSTS

Powers of Appointment

Whenever a long-term trust is created, flexibility becomes important because over time, tax laws, family situations, and economic environments change. To create flexibility, the trust document may grant certain beneficiaries the authority to change the dispositive provisions of the trust to better reflect current circumstances through the use of a power of appointment.

If a power of appointment is granted to a beneficiary of the trust, it should be a limited power of appointment to ensure that the trust assets are not included in the beneficiary's estate. A limited power of appointment can be very broad, and can give the holder the authority to appoint the trust assets to anyone in the world other than himself, his creditors, his estate, or the creditors of his estate. Instead of granting a power to a single individual, the trust document may grant a power to a committee of the heirs, who, by majority vote, may determine those matters specified in the power.

For tax purposes, a limitation is applied to powers of appointment. If the trust is set up as a perpetual trust, the donee of a special power of appointment cannot exercise the power after the common law perpetuities period has expired if the donee wants to continue to use the transfer tax exemption. This rule is commonly referred to as "The Delaware Tax Trap." The flexibility lost by use of a power of appointment can be offset by creating discretionary powers in trustees after the expiration of the perpetuities period.

Termination of the Trust

Typically, dynasty trusts are structured to terminate upon the death of the last lineal descendent of the grantor.

If a generational sub-trust approach is used, the trust should provide an allocation formula for distribution of the assets of a trust for the benefit of a family line with no living issue. The distribution among the remaining sub-trusts can be pro rata, based upon degree of relationship, or can be structured as an equal distribution.

In the event that all beneficiaries die with no lineal descendents, and all collateral branches of the family have been provided for, it is generally advisable to name a charity as the final repository of the principal. If the family also has a private foundation, the private foundation may be the ultimate beneficiary. If a private family foundation will not be used, the grantor should specify

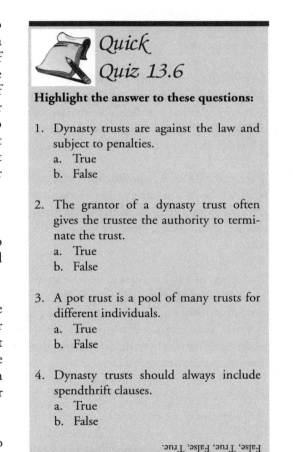

Quick Quiz 13.6

Highlight the answer to these questions:

1. Dynasty trusts are against the law and subject to penalties.
   a. True
   b. False

2. The grantor of a dynasty trust often gives the trustee the authority to terminate the trust.
   a. True
   b. False

3. A pot trust is a pool of many trusts for different individuals.
   a. True
   b. False

4. Dynasty trusts should always include spendthrift clauses.
   a. True
   b. False

False, True, False, True.

which charities should receive the funds, and should grant the trustee the right to distribute those funds to charities with like goals and objectives in the event the charity named is no longer in existence at the time of the termination of the trust.

Dynasty trusts often give the trustee or a committee of the heirs the authority to terminate the trust, if desirable, due to size (the trust is too small to justify administration expenses), tax reasons, or otherwise. When a termination provision is included in the document, it is often coordinated with powers of appointment granted to trust beneficiaries.

Broad Investment Powers

The trustee should be granted broad investment powers, including, if applicable, (1) the ability to invest in international securities, (2) a waiver of diversification requirements, especially if the trust will be used to hold family business interests, and (3) the ability to consider other trusts or resources in establishing the investment goals of the trust.

Spendthrift Clause as a Protective Provision

A spendthrift clause should always be included in a dynasty trust to prevent the garnishment of trust proceeds.

Definitions of Terms Used in the Trust Document

While certain terms are taken for granted in casual discussion, it is important to define those terms in a dynasty trust. The dynasty trust is designed to last for a very long time, and the common use of various terms changes over time. To ensure that the intent of the grantor is followed, the trust instrument should define important terms.

The term "ISSUE" should be specifically defined in the trust. The grantor should consider whether he wants issue to include illegitimate or adopted children, children conceived by artificial insemination after the death of the grantor or one of the beneficiaries, and, with modern technology, whether clones of beneficiaries will be eligible for distributions from the trust.

The term "SPOUSE" should also be specifically defined in the trust. Spouse should be defined to take into consideration divorce and remarriage without impacting the spendthrift clause. Some trust documents define "spouse" as the person to whom the beneficiaries are married from time to time. This implies that the only time an in-law is entitled to distributions from the trust is when he is married to the heir. Once the marriage terminates, for whatever reason, the in-law's interest in the trust terminates.

SUMMARY OF DYNASTY TRUSTS

Dynasty trusts are perhaps the ultimate tool in transfer tax planning, since they allow assets to pass from one generation to the next without the imposition of gift, estate, or GSTT. Dynasty trusts are not for everyone, however. Many individuals do not wish to tie up their property for long periods of time and would rather allow their heirs to have outright access to the property even if it will require paying more in transfer taxes. Like any other estate planning tool, a dynasty trust must be consistent with the goals and objectives of the client to be effective.

Key Terms

Applicable Rate - The maximum estate tax rate in effect at the date of the GST multiplied by the "inclusion ratio."

Direct Skip - A transfer of property or an interest in property to a skip person that is subject to estate or gift tax in the hands of the transferor.

Dynasty Trust - Generation-skipping trust created in perpetuity. Once created, a dynasty trust provides for trust beneficiaries, but avoids transfer taxation in the beneficiaries' gross estates by restricting ownership of trust assets.

Estate Tax Inclusion Period (ETIP) - The period during which, should the transferor or the transferor's spouse die, the fair market value of the transferred property would be included in the gross estate of the transferor or the transferor's spouse.

Generational Sub-Trust - Trust created on the birth of the first member in a generation, or at the death of the surviving member of a generation. A sub-trust can avoid potential conflict between siblings or conflict between or within various generations of the family.

Inclusion Ratio - Ratio determined by subtracting the applicable fraction from one.

Intentionally Defective Grantor Trust (IDGT) - A trust which gives the grantor sufficient control to be considered the owner for income tax purposes, but not so much control to require the trust property to be included in the transferor's gross estate.

Pot Trust - A trust created as a single trust and remains a single trust during the period of its administration. The trustee has the flexibility to treat all beneficiaries equally, as opposed to basing beneficial interest in the trust on the degree of relationship to the grantor.

Taxable Distribution - Any distribution from a trust to a skip person other than a taxable termination or a direct skip.

Taxable Termination - The termination of an interest in property held in trust *unless*: (1) a transfer subject to federal estate or gift tax occurs with respect to the property held in the trust at the time of the termination; (2) immediately thereafter a non-skip person has an interest in the property; or (3) *no* distributions may be made at any time thereafter to a skip person.

1.   Define skip person.

2.   To which type of transfers does the GSTT apply?

3.   Who is liable for the GSTT on a direct skip?

4.   Define taxable distribution.

5.   Who is liable for the GSTT on a taxable distribution?

6.   List the characteristics of a termination of an interest in property held in trust that does not create a taxable termination.

7.   Who is liable for the GSTT on a taxable termination?

8.   What is the GSTT rate?

9.   How much can an individual transfer to a skip person during his lifetime, or at his death, without incurring any GSTT?

10.   When must the allocation of the GST exemption take place?

11.   Explain the predeceased ancestor exception.

12.   What is a qualified transfer and what are its GSTT implications?

13.   What is the estate tax inclusion period?

14.   How are lifetime direct skips reported to the IRS?

15.   What are the benefits of using a generation-skipping trust?

16.   What is the Uniform Statutory Rule Against Perpetuities?

17.   Who pays the income tax on the income generated within a dynasty trust?

18.   Why should a dynasty trust give some beneficiaries a limited power of appointment?

1. To which of the following transfers does the GSTT not apply?

    a. A taxable termination.

    b. A taxable distribution.

    c. A direct skip.

    d. A skip-over.

2. Robin transfers to her son, Gerry; $40,000 to her niece, Bernadette; and pays Hollowpoint Medical Hospital $50,000 for her granddaughter, Jill's, medical expenses. Which of these transfers is subject to GSTT?

    a. None of the listed transfers will be subject to GSTT.

    b. The transfer to Jill.

    c. The transfers to Bernadette and Jill.

    d. The transfers to Bernadette, Gerry, and Jill.

3. Amy, a 46-year-old divorced mother of 3, has owned her own automotive repair center for 15 years. She would like to provide income to her assistant, JoAnn, and her other friends. Amy established a trust naming JoAnn, age 67, as the initial income beneficiary for her life. At JoAnn's death, Walt, a 59-year-old mechanic who has worked for Amy, will receive the income for the remainder of his lifetime. At Walt's death, the remainder interest will be divided equally between Amy's sons, Paul, John, and Donald. When will this trust be subjected to GSTT?

    a. At the date of creation of the trust.

    b. At JoAnn's death.

    c. At Walt's death.

    d. Never.

4. Mel has never made any gifts subject to GSTT. He is single and would like to transfer as much as he possibly can during the year to his grandchild without triggering any GSTT. How much can Mel transfer to his grandchild this year and meet his goal?

    a. $0.

    b. $13,000.

    c. $1,013,000.

    d. $3,513,000.

5. David, age 78, retired from his 40-year career at BBB Corporation last year. As part of an overall estate plan, David has begun establishing many different trusts. Of the following list of beneficiaries listed in David's trusts, who would be a skip person for purposes of the GSTT?

    a. Jenna, age 31, David's wife.

    b. Tiffany, age 22, David's girlfriend.

    c. Peter, age 25, David's grandson, whose mother is living, but whose father, (David's son) is deceased.

    d. Bill, David's 81-year-old lifelong neighbor.

6. Which of the following statements concerning the GSTT is not correct?

    a. Each individual can exclude up to $3,500,000 of transfers from GSTT.

    b. The GSTT is applied to a gift after the application of the annual exclusion.

    c. Gifts that are subject to GSTT can be split.

    d. The GSTT only applies to transfers in trust.

7. Many grandparents name their grandchildren as the beneficiaries of their life insurance policies. How should the life insurance policies for the benefit of grandchildren be held?

    a. A revocable life insurance trust should be established and funded with a transfer of the life insurance policy.

    b. The grandparent should be the owner with the grandchild as the listed beneficiary.

    c. An irrevocable life insurance trust should be created for the benefit of the grandchild.

    d. The ownership of the policy should be transferred to the grandchild.

8. Byron, age 65, gave $30,000 each to his son, his daughter, his six-year-old niece, his 21-year-old female neighbor, and his wife. Which of the transfers would be subject to GSTT?

    a. The transfer to his wife.

    b. The transfer to his neighbor.

    c. The transfer to his niece and the neighbor.

    d. The transfer to his niece, his neighbor, and his daughter.

9. Justin transfers $200,000 in 2009 to an irrevocable trust providing that income is to be accumulated for 22 years. At the end of 22 years, the accumulated income is to be distributed to Justin's child, Chip, and the trust principal is to be paid to Justin's grandchild, Beau. Justin allocates $80,000 of his GST exemption to the trust on a timely filed gift tax return. What is the GSTT rate applicable to the trust?

   a. 19.40%.

   b. 27.00%.

   c. 40.00%.

   d. 60.00%.

10. Upon what form is a lifetime GST reported?

    a. Form 1040.

    b. Form 709.

    c. Form 706.

    d. Form 1041.

11. Upon what form is a testamentary transfer subject to GSTT reported?

    a. Form 1040.

    b. Form 706.

    c. Form 1041.

    d. Form 709.

12. Which of the following statements regarding dynasty trusts is not true?

    a. A dynasty trust will not vest its ownership in each generation of beneficiaries.

    b. Alaska has laws that favor the creation of dynasty trusts.

    c. The income of a dynasty trust is always taxed at the trust level since ownership does not vest in the beneficiaries.

    d. A dynasty trust can give a beneficiary a limited power of appointment without causing inclusion of the trust's assets in the beneficiary's gross estate.

Quick Quiz Explanations

Quick Quiz 13.1

1. False. While a person two or more generations below the transferor is generally considered a skip person, exceptions such as the predeceased ancestor exception may change this result.
2. False. While the impact of executing a disclaimer is to allow property to pass as if the disclaimant had predeceased the transferor, since the disclaimant has not actually died, the disclaimer is ignored for generation-skipping transfer tax purposes.

Quick Quiz 13.2

1. False. A taxable termination occurs when the last non-skip beneficiary dies, or when the trust actually terminates. Usually, distributions from a trust to a skip person are considered to be taxable distributions.
2. False. When a taxable termination occurs, the trustee pays the GSTT due from the trust assets. The beneficiaries of the trust are not directly liable for paying the GSTT.

Quick Quiz 13.3

1. False. The GSTT applies to some transfers made before October 22, 1986 if specific requirements imposed by law have not been met.
2. True.
3. True.

Quick Quiz 13.4

1. True.
2. False. The lifetime exemption amount for the GSTT is $3,500,000 (2009).

Quick Quiz 13.5

1. False. Form 709, the Federal Gift and Generation-Skipping Transfer Tax Return, is due on or before April 15th of the year following the calendar year in which the direct skip occurs.

Quick Quiz 13.6

1. False. Dynasty trusts are legitimate planning vehicles used to avoid the imposition of future transfer taxes.
2. True.
3. False. A pot trust is a dynasty trust that keeps all of its assets in one account, which can be contrasted with a separate share trust, which has an account for each beneficiary.
4. True.

Basic Estate Plan

14

THE ESTATE PLANNING PROCESS

Chapter 1 introduced the six basic steps in the estate planning process. As you may recall, they are:

1. Establish the client/planner relationship.
2. Gather client information, including the client's current financial statements, and establish the client's transfer objectives, including family and charitable objectives.
3. Determine the client's financial status.
4. Develop a comprehensive plan of transfers consistent with all information and objectives.
5. Implement the estate plan.
6. Review the estate plan periodically and update the plan when necessary (especially for changes in family situations).

The first two steps, (1) establishing the client/planner relationship, and (2) gathering client information and establishing goals, were discussed in Chapter 1. The remaining steps are discussed in this chapter.

DETERMINE THE CLIENT'S FINANCIAL SITUATION

Once the client and family information is collected, the planner can begin to determine the financial situation of the client. The planner should define any areas of concern, including liquidity issues, potential excessive taxes or costs, and other situational needs, such as disability of an identified heir or blended family. The planner should also estimate the current value of the estate and liquidity needs now and at five-year intervals forward for the full life expectancy of the transferor, including estate transfer costs. Based on the client's objectives and priorities, the planner should make realistic judgments regarding the feasibility of meeting those objectives.

DEVELOP THE ESTATE PLAN

When contemplating the design of a simple estate plan, the following steps should be considered:

1. Identify the potential inheriting parties in terms of assets, competence, and relation to the transferor.
2. Identify all property interests in terms of value and property ownership type.
   - Identify any existing beneficiary designations.
   - Identify joint property owners and percentage of contribution to original purchase price of property.
   - Verify how life insurance is owned.
3. Have all documents prepared - will, durable power of attorney for both property and health care, and advance medical directives.
   - Identify legatees.
   - Identify property transferring to trusts.
4. Review any inter vivos trusts.
   - Identify property transferring to a trust or from a trust and its beneficiaries.
5. Verify use of the applicable estate tax credit.
6. Optimize use of the unlimited marital deduction.
7. Select use of the unlimited charitable deduction.

While the development of the estate plan should be specific to the client, common planning techniques are generally used for particular parties. The more common parties and devices used with each are discussed below. In addition, an estate planning checklist is provided below. This list is not exhaustive and should only be used by the planner to develop their own check list to use when creating the estate plan.

Spouse

Of course, if the individual is not married, step six, optimizing the use of the unlimited marital deduction, will be eliminated. However, if the individual is married, the surviving spouse's needs and desires (which will vary in each individual case) must be considered in the estate planning process. Ideally, a plan would transfer sufficient assets to non-spouse heirs to utilize the applicable estate tax credit and transfer the remainder of the estate's assets to the surviving spouse to qualify for the unlimited marital deduction.

An individual could choose to leave all of his property to his surviving spouse outright and allow the surviving spouse to disclaim the undesired property interest(s). The individual's will would contain a provision to direct the disclaimed property to children or other heirs thus fulfilling the use of the applicable estate tax credit and covering any needs and desires of the surviving spouse. However, this method does not guarantee use of the applicable estate tax credit, as the surviving spouse may not choose to disclaim a proper amount. Therefore, many individuals choose to use one of the following transfer methods which qualify for the unlimited marital deduction: (1) GPOA Trust, or (2) QTIP Trust. Any combination of these methods, coupled with outright transfers, may also be used, as in the case of the ABC Trust arrangement discussed in Chapter 10. The ABC Trust arrangement is frequently used in blended family situations to maximize the use of the unlimited marital deduction, the applicable estate tax credit, and to give the testator the power to control the ultimate disposition of his property.

Noncitizen Spouse
Recall that transfers to a surviving spouse who is not a U.S. citizen do not qualify for the unlimited marital deduction. So, in the case of an individual who would like to qualify transfers to his noncitizen spouse for the unlimited marital deduction, the individual will have to either use a QDOT or have his surviving spouse become a U.S. citizen.

Children
When an individual has children, one must consider an individual's desires to transfer assets to his children, regardless of the reasons. Most often, when property is transferred to, or for the benefit of minor children, the transfer is made in trust, which provides for the management and protection of the funds. If an individual dies with adult children, he may still consider the use of a trust, but in either case, the individual may also transfer assets outright to his children.

If a trust is desired, a bypass trust may be appropriate. If the child is a minor, the 2503(b) or (c) trust, or a Crummey trust, can be used to maximize the use of the annual exclusion. If the client desires to give property outright to a minor child, particular attention should be given to state law to determine the ability of minors to own property. Custodial accounts under UGMA or UTMA may also be appropriate.

Grandchildren
Grandchildren present additional opportunities to transfer wealth through a gifting program, but they also increase the risk of inadvertent tax consequences because of the GSTT system. The planner should determine if a lifetime gifting program is appropriate for the client to make use of the GST annual exclusion of $13,000 and qualified transfer exclusions. In addition, a Reverse QTIP election may be considered to make use of the GST exemption of $3,500,000.

Trusts
Trusts should be used in two distinct situations - when there is a split interest in property (i.e., income interest to spouse with remainder interest to children) and when the individual has any reservations about the heir's ability to manage, control, or preserve the assets.

Irrevocable Life Insurance Trust
As discussed throughout this text, an insured should not possess any incidents of ownership in the life insurance policies on his life unless the insured intends to use the cash value of the policy during his life for other financial planning purposes (e.g., educational funding or retirement funding). If the proceeds of the life insurance policy will be income replacement for the insured's beneficiaries, or will be used to pay estate taxes, the insured should not own the policy. As you may recall, such an arrangement may be accomplished either through the purchase of a new policy by the beneficiaries or by the trustee of an irrevocable life insurance trust (ILIT), or, alternatively, if a policy is already in existence, the policy may be assigned (transferred) to a named beneficiary or to the trustee of an ILIT.

The general problem with direct beneficiary ownership is that there is no assurance of management, no creditor protection, and it is difficult to accomplish a split asset arrangement. If there is a single mature beneficiary, direct ownership or assignment may be cost effective, but whenever there is a need for a split interest (see Exhibit 14.1), an ILIT is recommended.

EXHIBIT 14.1 **VISUAL DEPICTION OF AN ILIT**

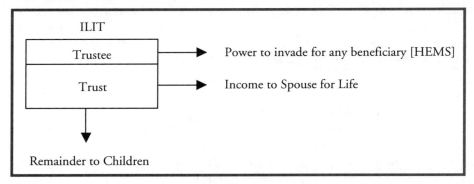

For example, suppose that the client did not know while planning the estate whether the spouse would need the income from the life insurance policy. It would seem prudent to set up the life insurance within an ILIT with the trust provisions calling for income to the spouse for life (note this does not utilize the marital deduction nor does it cause the insurance to be included in either spouse's gross estate) and the remainder to the insured's children. The trustee may also be given the power to invade for health, education, maintenance, or support (HEMS) for any beneficiary of the trust. A spouse, upon the death of the first-to-die spouse, may disclaim the income interest while continuing to enjoy the discretionary power of the trustee to invade for HEMS if the surviving spouse needed such invasion. In other words, the use of an ILIT allows the surviving spouse to decide if she needs the income from the life insurance policy, or whether it should transfer directly to the children at the death of the first-to-die spouse.

Applicable Estate Tax Credit

To satisfy the utilization of the credit equivalency ($3,500,000 for 2009), the testator could make lifetime taxable gifts of $1,000,000, the applicable gift tax credit equivalency, and then specifically bequeath $1,000,000, the remaining amount of the applicable estate tax credit equivalency at his death, directly to his children. The advantage of such an arrangement is that any future appreciation of the assets gifted during life is completely removed from the transferor's gross estate. The disadvantage created when the appreciation is removed from transferor's gross estate is (1) that the transferor loses control of the property transferred, and (2) such transfers may adversely affect the recipient (recipient may not be capable of handling wealth).

Alternatively, an amount equal to the applicable estate tax credit equivalency can be transferred at the transferor's death directly to his children. However, if the surviving spouse has a need to use some or all of the assets, such an arrangement will not be appropriate because the surviving spouse will not have a right to the assets.

Once again, the formation of a bypass trust (credit equivalency trust) will provide the transferor and his heirs' flexibility. The ILIT and the bypass trust are quite similar. Generally, the only difference is that the assets in the bypass trust are included in the gross estate of the decedent, but the proceeds from the insurance policy owned by the ILIT are not included in the decedent's gross estate.

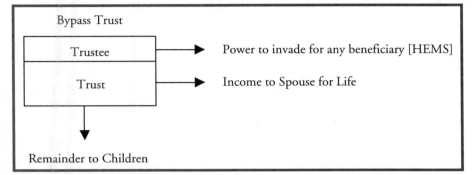

Optimize Use of the Unlimited Marital Deduction

As previously discussed, there are several qualifying ways to leave assets to a surviving spouse and eliminate the estate tax at the death of the first spouse. The decision between transferring property to a GPOA Trust or the QTIP Trust is dependent upon the testator's desire to retain control of the ultimate remainderman of the property. Generally, the GPOA Trust gives the surviving spouse a general power of appointment over the trust assets which gives the surviving spouse the power to name the ultimate remainder beneficiary of the property after her death. If the testator desires to retain control of the ultimate disposition of the property, perhaps in the case of different beneficiaries than the surviving spouse, a QTIP Trust is used. The QTIP Trust gives the testator the ability to preselect the ultimate remainder beneficiary of the trust property. Also, as noted above, the combination of these trusts is quite often used with the ABC Trust arrangement.

Quite a few things can derail an otherwise good plan. For example, any assets that qualify for the unlimited marital deduction at the death of the first-to-die spouse will be included in the surviving spouse's gross estate to the extent that they are not consumed. Therefore, if the surviving spouse dies soon after his spouse, there may be a bunching of assets and some form of estate equalization would possibly have been more advantageous if such bunching causes the marginal estate tax bracket to rise.

The usual objective is to treat spouses as one economic unit and push as many assets to lower generations without transfer taxes. This is accomplished through transfers for support, utilizing qualified transfers, utilizing annual exclusion gifts, utilizing the applicable credit during life or at death, electing to split gifts, and utilizing the GST exemption.

Select Use of Charitable Deduction

If the desire is to transfer assets to qualifying charities, it is usually wise to consider transferring tax-advantaged funds (IRAs, annuities) to these charities because these funds do not receive a step-to fair market value in adjusted basis at the decedent's death and are considered taxable income eligible for the Income in Respect of the Decedent deduction to taxable recipients. The charitable organization, as a tax exempt organization, would receive the assets income-tax free. After the charitable aspirations are satisfied, the remaining assets are distributed to the spouse and the remaining heirs.

Gifting Program

If the client has substantial assets, a lifetime gifting program may be considered to make use of the annual exclusion of $13,000. Depending on the number of descendents and the number of years in which the donor can utilize the plan, a substantial amount of wealth can be transferred. If the donor is married, a split gift election should also be considered to make use of the non-donor spouse's annual exclusion. Qualified transfers during life to education and medical institutions may also be considered especially in the case of gifts to grandchildren to avoid the GSTT.

IMPLEMENT THE PLAN

Once the plan has been designed, the planner should present the plan to the client, ensure the client understands all aspects of the plan, and following their approval, assist in implementing the plan. Unlike other areas of estate planning, the implementation generally involves a substantial amount of initial work, and very little subsequent work. The creation of the trusts and estate planning documents, the retitling of the assets and the selection of the beneficiaries are completed during implementation. Unless changes are needed, very little work is done until the client's death unless the planner's assistance is required in the interim.

The financial planner's involvement in the actual implementation of the plan will vary depending on the financial planner's education, experience, and comfort level. In the case of an experienced financial planner specializing in estate planning, much of the plan implementation may be done with the assistance of or by the planner. The planner may draft the estate planning documents if the planner is also an attorney, or seek the assistance of an attorney to draft these documents. (Generally, planners work closely with a particular firm or designated attorneys.) The planner may also sell (if properly licensed) the client the necessary insurance policies, execute the required investments, secure the necessary beneficiary designation forms, and help the client change title to property if needed. If trusts are used, the planner may continue to work with the client to ensure appropriate investments are made, Crummey provisions are handled appropriately, and tax returns are filed.

Alternatively, if the planner is not experienced in the estate planning field, he may outsource much of the work to other professionals. In this case, he may truly act as the team captain giving the client instructions on people to see and things to do and leave a majority of the work to the client and other professionals. The extent of the planner's involvement and the client's expectations of the planner should be detailed in the client engagement letter.

MONITOR THE PLAN

The estate plan should be reviewed periodically and updated when necessary. Typically, changes to the estate plan will occur when there has been a change in the family situation, usually a death, marriage, divorce, birth, or adoption. Good estate plans are created such that they anticipate some changes in family situations, for example births of children or grandchildren, but all changes cannot be foreseen. In addition, changes in the client's financial situation may also change the need for lifetime gifting programs and estate planning devices. The planner may wish to provide the client with specific situations in which they should return to update their estate plan, particularly marriages and divorces, moving from one state to another, or threshold changes in net worth. Because clients may forget to tell the planner of substantial changes over the years, the planner should meet with the client at least every five years to ensure necessary changes are addressed.

EXHIBIT 14.3 **ESTATE PLAN CHECKLIST**

❏ Yes	❏ No	Is the will properly prepared and updated?

If no, why: _____

❏ Yes	❏ No	Have appropriate provisions been implemented to account for all children?

If no, why: _____

❏ Yes	❏ No	Have disinherited heirs been addressed in the will?

If no, why: _____

❏ Yes	❏ No	Have the executor and successor executors been named and notified?

If no, why: _____

❏ Yes	❏ No	Have the trustee and successor trustees been named and notified?

If no, why: _____

❏ Yes	❏ No	Have guardians and successor guardians for children been named and notified?

If no, why: _____

❏ Yes	❏ No	If desired, have appropriate steps been taken to avoid probate (e.g., revocable living trusts, titling, designated beneficiaries)?

If no, why: _____

❏ Yes	❏ No	Will the appropriate property interests be transferred to the proper heirs?

If no, why: _____

❏ Yes	❏ No	Is the general power of attorney and/or power of attorney for health care properly prepared and updated?

If no, why: _____

❏ Yes	❏ No	Is the Living Will properly prepared and updated?

If no, why: _____

❏ Yes	❏ No	Have all beneficiary designations for life insurance, retirement accounts, etc. been changed?

If no, why: _____

❏ Yes	❏ No	Have all life insurance policies been transferred from the estate (unless the cash value is needed by the insured to pay for education or retirement)?

If no, why: _____

❏ Yes	❏ No	If an ILIT is used, does the trustee have the power to (but is not required to) loan money to and purchase assets from the estate?

If no, why: _____

❑ Yes	❑ No	Will the applicable estate tax credit be fully utilized?

If no, why: _____

❑ Yes	❑ No	Will the unlimited marital deduction be properly utilized?

If no, why: _____

❑ Yes	❑ No	Will the client make optimal use of annual exclusion gifts and qualified transfers during life?

If no, why: _____

❑ Yes	❑ No	If the client is married, will the client make appropriate use of gift-splitting?

If no, why: _____

❑ Yes	❑ No	If the client is married and the assets owned by each spouse are disproportionate, have appropriate measures been taken to ensure that the applicable estate tax credit of both spouses is utilized?

If no, why: _____

❑ Yes	❑ No	If the client is married to a non U.S. Citizen, has appropriate planning been utilized?

If no, why: _____

❑ Yes	❑ No	Have charitable intentions and desires been fulfilled?

If no, why: _____

❑ Yes	❑ No	If appropriate, has the use of a Family Limited Partnership, QPRT, or GRAT been implemented?

If no, why: _____

❑ Yes	❑ No	Do trusts include appropriate Crummey provisions?

If no, why: _____

EXHIBIT 14.4 **POST MORTEM CHECKLIST**

❏ Yes	❏ No	Has the appropriate valuation date been selected (date of death or alternate valuation date)?

If no, why: _____

❏ Yes	❏ No	Have appropriate disclaimers been used?

If no, why: _____

❏ Yes	❏ No	Have appropriate expense allocations been made between the Forms 1040, 1041, and 706?

If no, why: _____

❏ Yes	❏ No	Have appropriate Section 303 redemptions been completed?

If no, why: _____

❏ Yes	❏ No	If appropriate, was the Section 6166 election to pay by installments made?

If no, why: _____

❏ Yes	❏ No	Have appropriate 2032A special use elections been made?

If no, why: _____

❏ Yes	❏ No	Have appropriate QTIP elections been made?

If no, why: _____

❏ Yes	❏ No	Have appropriate Reverse QTIP elections for GSTT purposes been made?

If no, why: _____

❏ Yes	❏ No	If the decedent was married to a non U.S. Citizen, has a QDOT been utilized?

If no, why: _____

❏ Yes	❏ No	If needed, were extensions to file tax returns filed with the IRS?

If no, why: _____

❏ Yes	❏ No	Have all necessary income, gift, estate, and fiduciary tax returns been prepared, reviewed, and filed?

If no, why: _____

❏ Yes	❏ No	Has the probate process been completed and assets distributed?

If no, why: _____

COMPREHENSIVE CASE EXAMPLE

The following case illustrates the basic estate planning concepts and calculations discussed throughout the text.

GAIL AND TONY BACKGROUND

Gail and Tony have been married for 42 years. Gail is currently in good health, but due to a severe heart attack last year, Tony is only expected to live a few more years. They have the following children and grandchildren:

CHILDREN	AGES	GRANDCHILDREN
Shami	39	2 children
Lisa	36	5 children
Mary	30	4 children
Monica	29	3 children
Rick	25	No children

All of their daughters are healthy, employed, and married. Rick, their only son, is single and does not have any children.

Tony and Gail own Tony's Video and Games, a family-owned video and game store that has been very popular. Tony wants to sell half of the business to his key employee, Hari, and he wants to sell the other half to his oldest daughter, Shami, the CFO of the store.

Tony's grandson Philip, Monica's youngest child, was born with a serious physical disability. To provide additional support for Philip, Tony created an irrevocable trust with a $2,500,000 transfer five years ago. The trust meets the requirements of 2503(b). At the time of the transfer, the GST exemption was $2,000,000, the GST rate was 45 percent, and the annual exclusion was $12,000.

Tony has made the following additional lifetime transfers:
* Four years ago, Tony gave each of his five children $200,000 (assume the annual exclusion was $12,000) of his separate property.
* Two years ago, Tony gave each of his five children $100,000 of his separate property. The annual exclusion at that time was $12,000.

Gail has never made any taxable gifts during her lifetime nor has she agreed to split any of Tony's separate property gifts.

Tony and Gail each have a simple will which leaves most probate assets to each other and also includes a six-month survivorship clause. Each will also declares that debts are to be paid from the residual estate, and taxes are to be paid by the children's share of the estate.

Tony and Gail estimate the following at each of their deaths:
1. The last illness and funeral expenses are expected to be $250,000 per person.
2. Estate administration expenses are estimated at $200,000 per person.

WILL

Selected clauses from Tony's Statutory Last Will and Testament:

I, Tony, being of sound mind and wishing to make proper disposition of my property in the event of my death, do declare this to be my Last Will and Testament. I revoke all of my prior wills and codicils.

1. I have been married but once, and then to Gail with whom I am presently living. Out of my marriage to Gail, five children were born, namely Shami, Lisa, Mary, Monica, and Rick. I have adopted no one nor has anyone adopted me.

2. I give my deferred annuity to David's Charity, a qualified charitable organization.

3. I leave Auto 1 to my favorite grandchild, Don.

4. I give the residual of my estate to Gail, my wife.

5. In the event that Gail predeceases me or fails to survive me for more than six months from the date of my death, I give any interest of my estate determined to be payable to her to my children in equal and 1/5 shares.

6. In the event that any of the named legatees should predecease me, die within six months from the date of my death, disclaim, or otherwise fail to accept any property bequeathed to him or her and said legatee has no descendents, his or her share of all of my property of which I die possessed shall be paid equally among their surviving named legatees.

7. I name my best friend Gary to serve as the executor of my succession with full seizin and without bond.

8. I direct that the expenses of my last illness, funeral, and the administration of my estate shall be paid by my executor as soon as practicable after my death and allocated against the residual estate.

9. Since I have made numerous lifetime gifts to my children, all inheritance, estate, succession, transfer, and other taxes (including interest and penalties thereon) payable by reason of my death shall be allocated to the children's share, regardless of whether my spouse survives me.

STATEMENT OF FINANCIAL POSITION (TONY & GAIL)

ASSETS		LIABILITIES AND NET WORTH	
Cash/Cash Equivalents		**Liabilities**	
JT Cash	$100,000	Current Liabilities	
Total Cash/Cash Equiv.	**$100,000**	W Credit card 1	$1,000
		W Credit card 2	15,000
Invested Assets		**Total Current Liabilities**	**$16,000**
JT Tony's Video and Games	$5,000,000		
W Gail's Portfolio	500,000	**Long-Term Liabilities**	
H Deferred Annuity	233,047	JT Mortgage - Primary	$258,630
H 401(k) Plan	600,000	JT Mortgage - vacation 1	369,428
H Profit Sharing Plan	526,382	JT Mortgage - vacation 2	687,444
H Tony's Portfolio	4,000,000	**Total Long-Term Liabilities**	**$1,315,502**
JT Commercial Property A	1,500,000		
Total Investments	**$12,359,429**		
		Total Liabilities	**$1,331,502**
Personal Use Assets			
JT Primary Residence	$1,300,000		
JT Vacation Home 1	800,000		
JT Vacation Home 2	700,000		
JT Personal Property	875,000	**Net Worth**	**$15,087,927**
H Auto 1	80,000		
H Auto 2	55,000		
W Auto 3	40,000		
W Yacht	110,000		
Total Personal Use	**$3,960,000**		
Total Assets	**$16,419,429**	**Total Liabilities and Net Worth**	**$16,419,429**

Notes to Financial Statements:
1. Assets are stated at fair market value (rounded to even dollars).
2. Liabilities are stated at principal only (rounded to even dollars).
3. The adjusted basis of Tony's Video and Games is $1,000,000.
4. The 401(k) and the Profit Sharing Plan have the children designated as equal beneficiaries (with the consent of Gail). Tony has never designated a beneficiary of the deferred annuity. No other item has designated beneficiaries or automatic survivorship features unless specifically indicated.
5. Property Ownership:
   - JT - Joint tenancy with right of survivorship. Gail and Tony are joint tenants of all property owned JT.
   - H - Husband separate.
   - W - Wife separate.

ESTATE PLAN EXERCISE

Assuming the given facts and that Tony died today, answer the following questions: (For simplicity, assume the 2009 estate and gift tax rates apply to all transfers. Further, assume all exclusions are the same as 2009 unless otherwise stated.)

1. Calculate the gift tax and GSTT consequences of the gift to Philip made five years ago.

2. Calculate the annual exclusion and gift tax due on the gifts made four years ago.

3. Calculate the annual exclusion and gift tax due on the gifts made two years ago.

4. Calculate the total of the assets that will pass through Tony's Probate Estate assuming he died in 2009.

5. Calculate the estate tax due at Tony's death assuming he died in 2009. Assume $0 state death tax credit, $0 credit for prior transfers and $0 foreign death tax credit. (Hint: Use the layout provided in your book.)

6. Assume that Tony did not die today. Discuss possible options for the transfer of Tony's Video and Games from Tony and Gail to Hari and Shami.

7. What trust options would you recommend as part of Tony and Gail's overall estate plan?

8. What additional planning advice would you give Tony and Gail regarding their estate plan that has not been addressed?

ESTATE PLAN SOLUTIONS

The following are model solutions to the estate planning exercise. Note numbers are rounded for presentation but unrounded numbers were used for calculations.

1. Calculate the gift tax and GSTT consequences of the gift to Philip.
    The GSTT and gift tax consequences are calculated as follows:

GSTT Calculation

		Notes:
Applicable Fraction (AF)	0.8039	2,000,000/2,488,000
Inclusion Ratio (IR)	0.1961	1- AF
Applicable Rate	0.0883	IR x Max Transfer Rate
GST	$2,500,000	
Less: Annual Exclusion	($12,000)	
Taxable GST	$2,488,000	
Times Applicable rate	8.83%	(rounded)
GSTT	**$219,600**	

Transfers to a 2503 (b) trust are eligible for the annual exclusion
Numbers are rounded for convenience, but unrounded numbers were used throughout the calculation

Since the entire 2008 GST Exemption is used the problem could be calculated as follows:

GST	$2,500,000	
Less: Annual Exclusion	($12,000)	
Less: Applicable GST Exemption	($2,000,000)	
Taxable GST	$488,000	
Times Tax Rate	45%	
GSTT	**$219,600**	Same tax as calculated above.

Gift Tax Calculation

		Notes:
Total Gifts	$2,500,000	Gift to Philip
Plus GSTT Tax Paid	$219,600	GSTT paid is part of the gift.
Less: Annual Exclusions	($12,000)	
Less: Qualified Transfers	$0	
Less: Marital Deductions	$0	
Equals: Total Taxable Gifts	$2,707,600	
Add: Previous Taxable Gifts (post-1976)	$0	
Equals: Tentative Tax Base	$2,707,600	
Tentative Tax	$1,099,220	[$780,800 + 0.45($707,600)]
Less: Gift Tax Previously Paid	$0	
Less: Applicable Gift Tax Credit	($345,800)	
Equals: Gift Tax Liability	**$753,420**	

2. Calculate the annual exclusion and gift tax due on the gifts made four years ago.

The gift tax consequences are calculated as follows:

		Notes:
Total Gifts	$1,000,000	$200,000 to 5 children
Less: Annual Exclusions	($60,000)	$12,000 to 5 children - Gail did not gift split
Less: Qualified Transfers	$0	
Less: Marital Deductions	$0	
Equals: Total Taxable Gifts	$940,000	
Add: Previous Taxable Gifts (post-1976)	$2,707,600	
Equals: Tentative Tax Base	$3,647,600	
Tentative Tax	$1,522,220	[$780,800 + 0.45($1,647,600)]
Less: Gift Tax Previously Paid	($753,420)	
Less: Applicable Gift Tax Credit	($345,800)	
Equals: Gift Tax Liability	**$423,000**	(also 45% of $940,000)

3. Calculate the annual exclusion and gift tax due on the gifts made two years ago.

The gift tax consequences are calculated as follows:

		Notes:
Total Gifts	$500,000	$100,000 to 5 children
Less: Annual Exclusions	($60,000)	$12,000 to 5 children - Gail did not gift split
Less: Qualified Transfers	$0	
Less: Marital Deductions	$0	
Equals: Total Taxable Gifts	$440,000	
Add: Previous Taxable Gifts (post-1976)	$3,647,600	
Equals: Tentative Tax Base	$4,087,600	
Tentative Tax	$1,720,220	[$780,800 + 0.45($2,087,600)]
Less: Gift Tax Previously Paid	($1,176,420)	
Less: Applicable Gift Tax Credit	($345,800)	
Equals: Gift Tax Liability	**$198,000**	(also 45% of $440,000)

4. Calculate the total value of the assets that will pass through Tony's Probate Estate, assuming he died in 2009.

The total value of the assets that will pass through probate is calculated as follows:

Asset	Owned	Full Value	Tony's Interest	Probate Estate	Gross Estate	Marital Deduction
Cash	JT with Spouse	$100,000	$50,000	$0	$50,000	$50,000
Tony's Video and Games	JT with Spouse	$5,000,000	$2,500,000	$0	$2,500,000	$2,500,000
Gail's Portfolio	Wife only	$500,000	$0	$0	$0	$0
Deferred Annuity	Husband only	$233,047	$233,047	$233,047	$233,047	$0
401(k) Plan	Husband only	$600,000	$600,000	$0	$600,000	$0
Profit Sharing Plan	Husband only	$526,382	$526,382	$0	$526,382	$0
Tony's Portfolio	Husband only	$4,000,000	$4,000,000	$4,000,000	$4,000,000	$4,000,000
Commercial Property A	JT with Spouse	$1,500,000	$750,000	$0	$750,000	$750,000
Primary Residence	JT with Spouse	$1,300,000	$650,000	$0	$650,000	$650,000
Vacation Home 1	JT with Spouse	$800,000	$400,000	$0	$400,000	$400,000
Vacation Home 2	JT with Spouse	$700,000	$350,000	$0	$350,000	$350,000
Personal Property	JT with Spouse	$875,000	$437,500	$0	$437,500	$437,500
Auto 1	Husband only	$80,000	$80,000	$80,000	$80,000	$0
Auto 2	Husband only	$55,000	$55,000	$55,000	$55,000	$55,000
Auto 3	Wife only	$40,000	$0	$0	$0	$0
Yacht	Wife only	$110,000	$0	$0	$0	$0
Gift Tax Paid within 3 years	Husband only	$198,000	$198,000	$0	$198,000	$0
Total		**$16,617,429**	**$10,829,929**	**$4,368,047**	**$10,829,929**	**$9,192,500**

Reconciliation of Gross Estate to Marital Deduction:

Tony's Gross Estate		$10,829,929
Less Gross Estate Items:		
To Charity per Will	$233,047	
401(k) to Notes to F/S Named Beneficiary	$600,000	
Profit Sharing Plan to Children Named Beneficiary	$526,382	
Auto per Will	$80,000	
Gift Tax Gross Up for Gifts Made within 3 Years	$198,000	
		$ 1,637,429
Marital Deduction		**$9,192,500**

Expenses Allocated to the Marital Portion:

Qualified Marital Deducation		$9,192,500
Less Expenses:		
Last Illness and Funeral Expense	$250,000	
Estate Administration Expenses	$200,000	
Debt on Property Received by Gail	$657,751	
		$1,107,751
Net Marital Deduction		**$8,084,749**

5. Calculate the estate tax due at Tony's death assuming he died in 2009. (Hint: Use the layout provided in Chapter 6.)

The estate tax is calculated as follows. The answer provided for question #4 details the determination of the available amount for the marital deduction, the net amount passing to the spouse.

Gross Estate		$10,829,929
Less Deductions:		
Last Medical/Funeral	$250,000	
Administrative Costs	$200,000	
Debts	$657,751	
Losses During Estate Administration	$0	$1,107,751
Equals: Adjusted Gross Estate		$11,937,680
Less: Charitable Deduction	($233,047)	
Less: Marital Deduction	($8,084,749)	($8,317,796)
Equals: Taxable Estate		$3,619,884
Add: Previous Taxable Gifts (post-1976)		$4,087,600
Equals: Tentative Tax Base		$7,707,484
Tentative Tax [780,800 = 0.45(3,491,982)]		$3,349,168
Less: Credits		
Previous Gift Tax Paid	($1,374,420)	
Applicable Estate Tax Credit	($1,455,800)	
State Death Tax Paid	$0	
Prior Transfer Credit	$0	
Foreign Death Tax Credit	$0	
Total Tax Credit		($2,830,220)
Equals: Federal Estate Tax Liability (Refund)		**$518,948**

6. Assume that Tony did not die today. Discuss possible options for the transfer of Tony's Video and Games from Tony and Gail to Hari and Shami.

Because Tony's Video and Games is titled joint tenancy between Tony and Gail, both should agree on a plan to transfer the business. Nonetheless, if they could agree to transfer 50% of the business to Hari, the only real options would be either an outright sale or an installment sale. Since Hari is not a relative, neither Tony nor Gail would have any desire to transfer any of the business interest to Hari at less than its fair market value. In fact, if they sold the business to Hari via an installment sale, a market rate of interest would be charged. Of course, Tony and Gail will be subjected to capital gains taxes on the sales price above their adjusted basis of $1,000,000.

Tony may decide to sell the business through a direct sale to Shami also, but more likely Tony will transfer his interest in the other 50 percent to Shami utilizing either a SCIN or private annuity. Either of these options may create the possibility that a portion of the business may transfer to Shami for an amount less than fair market value because Tony, as the facts tell us, is in poor health and for both transfer devices the required installment payments cease at Tony's death. Gail would most likely transfer her interest in the business to

Shami through a direct sale or installment sale as Gail is in good health. If Gail sold her interest to Shami through the SCIN, Shami would likely overpay for the asset (compared to current fair market value) by an amount equal to the SCIN premium. If Gail utilized an installment sale, she could charge Shami the IRS imputed interest rate.

The options detailed above are not all inclusive, but are meant to be illustrative of a few various options.

7. What trust options would you recommend as part of Tony and Gail's overall estate plan?

Tony and Gail should consider using each of the following trusts:
- Revocable Living Trusts - to avoid assets transferring through probate.
- QPRT - to potentially transfer the vacation homes at a reduced transfer tax cost.
- GRAT - to potentially transfer any property to heirs at a reduced transfer tax cost.
  - ILITs - to create additional funds at either Tony's or Gail's death through the payment of the death benefit.

Again, these options are illustrative, as the expense of creating and maintaining a trust should be weighed against the client's needs.

8. What additional planning advice would you give Tony and Gail regarding their estate plan that has not been addressed?

For all clients, planning advice should be customized to the client and their circumstances. Below are just a few recommendations that could be made, although additional information may be needed.

- Begin utilizing the annual exclusion. Gail should agree to split Tony's gifts. If Tony and Gail utilized their annual exclusions each year together they could transfer $130,000 ($26,000 x 5) to their children, an additional $364,000 ($26,000 x 14) to their grandchildren, and an additional $104,000 ($26,000 x 4) to their sons-in-law, completely transfer tax free each year.
- Consider the availability of any qualified transfers (education or medical) - especially for Philip - to transfer additional assets without transfer tax costs.
- Create TOD and POD accounts to avoid probate.
- Ensure Will, Living Wills/Advance Medical Directives, and any Powers of Attorney are complete and up-to-date.
- Designating Gail as the beneficiary of the 401(k) and the profit sharing plan as Gail may be able to roll the assets into her own IRA and further delay the recognition of any income tax on the assets.

Topic List

The following is the topic list for the CFP® Certification Examination.

ESTATE PLANNING

CHARACTERISTICS AND CONSEQUENCES OF PROPERTY TITLING
A. Community Property vs. Non-Community Property
B. Sole Ownership
C. Joint Tenancy with Right of Survivorship (JTWROS)
D. Tenancy by the Entirety
E. Tenancy in Common
F. Trust Ownership

METHODS OF PROPERTY TRANSFER AT DEATH
A. Transfers Through the Probate Process
   1) Testamentary Distribution
   2) Intestate Succession
   3) Advantages and Disadvantages of Probate
   4) Assets Subject to Probate Estate
   5) Probate Avoidance Strategies
   6) Ancillary Probate Administration
B. Transfers by Operation of Law
C. Transfers through Trusts
D. Transfers by Contract

ESTATE PLANNING DOCUMENTS
A. Wills
   1) Legal Requirements
   2) Types of Wills
   3) Modifying or Revoking a Will
   4) Avoiding Will Contests
B. Powers of Attorney
C. Trusts
D. Marital Property Agreements
E. Buy-Sell Agreements

GIFTING STRATEGIES

A. Inter Vivos Gifting
B. Gift-Giving Techniques and Strategies
C. Appropriate Gift Property
D. Strategies for Closely-Held Business Owners
E. Gift of Present and Future Interests
F. Gifts to Non-Citizen Spouses
G. Tax Implications
   1) Income
   2) Gift
   3) Estate
   4) Generation-Skipping Transfer Tax (GSTT)

GIFT TAX COMPLIANCE AND TAX CALCULATION

A. Gift Tax Filing Requirements
B. Calculation
   1) Annual Exclusion
   2) Applicable Credit Amount
   3) Gift Splitting
   4) Prior Taxable Gifts
   5) Education and Medical Exclusions
   6) Marital and Charitable Deductions
   7) Tax Liability

INCAPACITY PLANNING

A. Definition of Incapacity
B. Powers of Attorney
   1) For Health Care Decisions
   2) For Asset Management
   3) Durable Feature
   4) Springing Power
   5) General or Limited Powers
C. Advance Medical Directives (e.g., Living Wills)
D. Guardianship and Conservatorship
E. Revocable Living Trust
F. Medicaid Planning
G. Special Needs Trust

ESTATE TAX COMPLIANCE AND TAX CALCULATION

A. Estate Tax Filing Requirements
B. The Gross Estate
   1) Inclusions
   2) Exclusions
C. Deductions
D. Adjusted Gross Estate
E. Deductions from the Adjusted Gross Estate
F. Taxable Estate
G. Adjusted Taxable Gifts
H. Tentative Tax Base
I. Tentative Tax Calculation

J. Credits
   1) Gift Tax Payable
   2) Applicable Credit Amount
   3) Prior Transfer Credit

SOURCES FOR ESTATE LIQUIDITY

A. Sale of Assets
B. Life Insurance
C. Loan

POWERS OF APPOINTMENT

A. Use and Purpose
B. General and Special (Limited) Powers
   1) 5-and-5 Power
   2) Crummey Powers
   3) Distributions for an Ascertainable Standard
   4) Lapse of Power
C. Tax Implications

TYPES, FEATURES, AND TAXATION OF TRUSTS

A. Classification
   1) Simple and Complex
   2) Revocable and Irrevocable
   3) Inter Vivos and Testamentary
B. Types and Basic Provisions
   1) Totten Trust
   2) Spendthrift Trust
   3) Bypass Trust
   4) Marital Trust
   5) Qualified Terminable Interest Property (QTIP) Trust
   6) Pour-Over Trust
   7) Section 2503(b) Trust
   8) Section 2503(c) Trust
   9) Sprinkling Provision
C. Trust Beneficiaries: Income and Remainder
D. Rule Against Perpetuities
E. Estate and Gift Taxation

QUALIFIED INTEREST TRUSTS

A. Grantor Retained Annuity Trusts (GRATs)
B. Grantor Retained Unitrusts (GRUTs)
C. Qualified Personal Residence Trusts (QPRTs or House-GRITs)
D. Valuation of Qualified Interests

CHARITABLE TRANSFERS

A. Outright Gifts
B. Charitable Remainder Trusts
   1) Unitrusts (CRUTs)

2)   Annuity Trusts (CRATs)
C.   Charitable Lead Trusts
     1)   Unitrusts (CLUTs)
     2)   Annuity Trusts (CLATs)
D.   Charitable Gift Annuities
E.   Pooled Income Funds
F.   Private Foundations
G.   Donor Advised Funds
H.   Estate and Gift Taxation

USE OF LIFE INSURANCE IN ESTATE PLANNING
A.   Incidents of Ownership
B.   Ownership and Beneficiary Considerations
C.   Irrevocable Life Insurance Trust (ILIT)
D.   Estate and Gift Taxation

VALUATION ISSUES
A.   Estate Freezes
     1)   Corporate and Partnership Recapitalizations (Section 2701)
     2)   Transfers in Trust
B.   Valuation Discounts for Business Interests
     1)   Minority Discounts
     2)   Marketability Discounts
     3)   Blockage Discounts
     4)   Key Person Discount
C.   Valuation Techniques and the Federal Gross Estate

MARITAL DEDUCTION
A.   Requirements
B.   Qualifying Transfers
C.   Terminable Interest Rule and Exceptions
D.   Qualified Domestic Trust (QDOT)

DEFERRAL AND MINIMIZATION OF ESTATE TAXES
A.   Exclusion of Property from the Gross Estate
B.   Lifetime Gifting Strategies
C.   Marital Deduction and Bypass Trust Planning
D.   Inter Vivos and Testamentary Charitable Gifts

INTRA-FAMILY AND OTHER BUSINESS TRANSFER TECHNIQUES
A.   Characteristics
B.   Techniques
     1)   Buy-Sell Agreement
     2)   Installment Note
     3)   Self-Canceling Installment Note (SCIN)
     4)   Private Annuity
     5)   Transfers in Trust
     6)   Intra-Family Loan

     7)   Bargain Sale
     8)   Gift or Sale Leaseback
     9)   Intentionally Defective Grantor Trust
     10)   Family Limited Partnership (FLP) or Limited Liability Company (LLC)
C.   Federal Income, Gift, Estate, and Generation-Skipping Transfer Tax Implications

GENERATION-SKIPPING TRANSFER TAX (GSTT)
A.   Identify Transfers Subject to the GSTT
     1)   Direct Skips
     2)   Taxable Distributions
     3)   Taxable Terminations
B.   Exemptions and Exclusions from the GSTT
     1)   The GSTT Exemption
     2)   Qualifying Annual Exclusion Gifts and Direct Transfers

FIDUCIARIES
A.   Types of Fiduciaries
     1)   Executor/Personal Representative
     2)   Trustee
     3)   Guardian
B.   Duties of Fiduciaries
C.   Breach of Fiduciary Duties

INCOME IN RESPECT OF A DECEDENT (IRD)
A.   Assets Qualifying as IRD
B.   Calculation for IRD Deduction
C.   Income Tax Treatment

POST MORTEM ESTATE PLANNING TECHNIQUES
A.   Alternate Valuation Date
B.   Qualified Disclaimer
C.   Deferral of Estate Tax (Section 6166)
D.   Corporate Stock Redemption (Section 303)
E.   Special Use Valuation (Section 2032A)

ESTATE PLANNING FOR NONTRADITIONAL RELATIONSHIPS
A.   Children of Another Relationship
B.   Cohabitation
C.   Adoption
D.   Same-Sex Relationships

Glossary

Abatement – The reduction in assets transferring to a legatee because the estate has insufficient assets to satisfy all of the legatees.

ABC Trust Arrangement – A common trust arrangement that utilizes a bypass trust (the B Trust), a GPOA Trust (the A Trust), and a QTIP Trust (the C Trust) to provide the necessary support to a surviving spouse while maximizing the use of the decedent's applicable estate tax credit and providing the decedent the ability to determine the ultimate beneficiary of most of his assets at the death of the surviving spouse.

Accelerated Death Benefit – A reduced payment of the death benefit of a life insurance policy paid to the insured during the insured's lifetime in return for a surrender of the life insurance contract.

Actual Contribution Rule – The value of a decedent's joint interest in property is based on the actual percentage of the original purchase price contributed by the decedent – not the decedent's ownership percentage.

Ademption – Extinction of a legacy because an asset, specifically bequeathed to a legatee, has been disposed of prior to death.

Adjusted Gross Estate – The adjusted gross estate is equal to the gross estate less any deductions for funeral expenses, last medical expenses, administrative expenses, debts, and losses during the administration of the estate.

Administrator – A person, usually a relative of the deceased, appointed by the probate court to oversee the probate process when an executor is not named in the will.

Advance Medical Directive/Living Will – Legal document expressing an individual's last wishes regarding life sustaining treatment.

Alternate Valuation Date – An alternate date, other than the date of death, to value a decedent's gross estate. The alternate valuation date is either six months after the date of death, or if the asset is disposed of within six months of the date of death, the asset's disposition date. Wasting assets do not qualify to use the alternative valuation date.

Ancillary Probate – Concurrent second probate process conducted in a non–domiciliary state in which the decedent owns property, which often requires the service of an attorney from that state, and separate court fees.

Annual Exclusion – An exclusion from gift taxes for present interest transfers less than or equal to $13,000 per year per donee.

Applicable Rate – The maximum estate tax rate in effect at the date of the GST multiplied by the "inclusion ratio."

Appointment of Executor Clause – A clause in a will that identifies the executor and any successor executor. This clause may also define the extent of the executor's powers and may grant specific or general powers.

Ascertainable Standard – An objective standard for allowing distributions defined in the Internal Revenue Code as distributions for health, education, maintenance, or support (HEMS).

Attestation Clause – Witness clause stating that the testator is of sound mind and that he signed the document in the witness' presence.

Attorney in Fact – Agent or power holder of a power of attorney.

Beneficiary – The person(s) entitled to receive the death benefit of a life insurance policy at the insured's death. Also, the person(s) who hold(s) the beneficial title to a trust's assets.

Bequest Clause – Directs the distribution of property, whether cash, tangible property, intangible property, or real property.

Blind Trust – A revocable trust arrangement whereby an individual transfers property to the trust for management purposes when self–management of the assets might be deemed to be a conflict of interest.

Blockage Discount – A reduction in the fair market value of a large block of stock because the transfer of a large block of stock is less marketable than other transfers of smaller amounts of stock.

Bypass Trust (also known as a Credit Shelter Trust or B Trust) – A trust created to ensure that an individual makes use of his applicable estate tax credit.

Capital Gain Property – Property that, when sold, results in either capital gain or Section 1231 gain.

Charitable Lead Trust (CLT) – A trust in which a charitable organization receives the income interest and a noncharitable beneficiary (usually a family member) receives the remainder interest.

Charitable Remainder Annuity Trusts (CRAT) – A trust that provides a fixed annuity to the donor (usually for life) for an amount that is greater than or equal to 5% of the initial net fair market value of the property contributed to the trust. The remainder interest of the trust passes to a named charitable organization.

Charitable Remainder Trust (CRT) – A trust in which a noncharitable beneficiary receives the income interest and a charitable organization receives the remainder interest.

Charitable Remainder Unitrust (CRUT) – A trust that provides a payment to the donor (usually for life) equal to a fixed percentage of the trust assets as valued annually. The remainder interest of the trust passes to a named charitable organization.

Chronically Ill Individual – A person who has been certified by a licensed health care provider as being unable to perform, without assistance, at least two activities of daily living for at least 90 days, or a person with a similar level of disability.

Codicil – A document that amends a will. A codicil is prepared subsequent to and separate from the will to modify or explain the will.

Community Property – A regime in which married individuals own an equal undivided interest in all of the property accumulated, utilizing either spouse's earnings, during the marriage.

Complex Trust – A trust that does not meet the definition of a simple trust.

Consideration – Payment or transfer of property in return for other property.

Contingent Legatee Clause – A clause in a will that names a secondary person to inherit if the original legatee is dead or disclaims the property.

Crummey Provision – The explicit right of a trust beneficiary to withdraw some or all of any contribution to a trust for a limited period of time after the contribution. A Crummey provision converts what otherwise would have been a gift of a future interest (not eligible for the annual exclusion) to a gift of a present interest, eligible for the annual exclusion.

Date of Declaration – The date a board of directors approves and declares a dividend to be paid to its shareholders.

Date of Record – The date that a dividend paying company determines the owners of its stock who are entitled to a dividend (regardless of whether or not the individual owns the stock as of the payment date).

Declaration Clause – A clause in a will which states this is the last will and testament of the testator.

Direct Gift – A direct payment of cash or transfer of property to a donee.

Direct Skip – A transfer of property or an interest in property to a skip person that is subject to estate or gift tax in the hands of the transferor.

Disclaimer – An heir or legatee's refusal to accept a gift or bequest. The disclaimer allows assets to pass to other heirs or legatees without additional transfer tax.

Distributable Net Income (DNI) – A tax concept that allocates taxable income between the trust and beneficiaries to ensure the trust income is subject to only one level of tax.

Domicile – Where a person lives, the location of their home.

Donee – The person who receives the gift.

Donor – The person who gives the gift.

Durable Feature – Allows a power of attorney to survive incapacity and/or disability.

Durable Power of Attorney Issued Either for Health Care or for Property – A written document enabling one individual, the principal, to designate another person(s) to act as his "attorney–in–fact." A durable power of attorney survives the incapacity and/or disability of the principal.

Dynasty Trust – Generation–skipping trust created in perpetuity. Once created, a dynasty trust provides for trust beneficiaries, but avoids transfer taxation in the beneficiaries' gross estates by restricting ownership of trust assets.

Economic Growth and Tax Relief Reconciliation Act of 2001 (EGTRRA 2001) – Tax act signed by President George W. Bush in June of 2001. The act phases in a repeal of the estate and generation–skipping transfer tax. It also creates separate applicable credits for gift tax and estate tax.

Effective Transfer – A transfer of a person's assets to the person or charitable institution intended by that person.

Efficient Transfer – A transfer that occurs when transfer costs are minimized consistent with the greatest assurance of effectiveness.

Equitable Ownership – Possession of the economic right to property.

Estate Administration or Succession – The passing of property at death to surviving heirs/legatees.

Estate Planning – The process of accumulation, management, conservation, and transfer of wealth considering legal, tax, and personal objectives.

Estate Tax Inclusion Period (ETIP) – The period during which, should the transferor or the transferor's spouse die, the fair market value of the transferred property would be included in the gross estate of the transferor or the transferor's spouse.

Estate Trust – A trust which grants the surviving spouse a testamentary general power of appointment over the trust assets. Because of the spouse's general power of appointment over the trust's assets, the fair market value of the trust will be eligible for the unlimited marital deduction at the death of the first–to–die spouse.

Exchange – A mutual transfer of assets with equal fair market values between individuals.

Executor – Estate representative designated in the will by the decedent. An executor may serve without bond if the bond is waived by the decedent.

F

Family Limited Partnership (FLP) – A limited partnership created under state law with the primary purpose of transferring assets to younger generations using minority and marketability discounts to create reduced gift tax valuations.

Fee Simple – The complete individual ownership of property with all the rights associated with outright ownership.

Felonious Homicide Statutes – Statute that prevents heirs who feloniously participated in the decedent's death from inheriting via the will or state intestacy laws.

5–and–5 Rule – When an individual has a general power of appointment over the annual contribution made to the trust and the value of the general power of appointment does not exceed the greater of (1) $5,000 or (2) 5% of the trust corpus.

Forced Heirship – A state requirement that a certain portion of the decedent's estate be transferred to a spouse and, in some instances, children.

Future Interest – An interest which is limited in some way by a future date or time. A gift of a future interest does not qualify for the annual exclusion.

G

General Power of Appointment Trust (A Trust) – An irrevocable trust that can be created either during an individual's lifetime or at an individual's death that gives the agent the right to appoint the settlor's assets.

Generational Sub–Trust – Trust created on the birth of the first member in a generation, or at the death of the surviving member of a generation. A sub–trust can avoid potential conflict between siblings or conflict between or within various generations of the family.

Gift – A voluntary transfer, without full consideration, of property from one person (a donor) to another person (a donee) or entity.

Grantor – The person who creates and initially funds a trust. The grantor is also known as the settlor or creator.

Grantor Retained Annuity Trust (GRAT) – An irrevocable trust that pays a fixed annuity to the grantor (settlor) for some defined term, and pays the remainder interest of the trust to a non-charitable beneficiary.

Grantor Retained Income Trust (GRIT) – A trust in which the grantor retains an income or use interest in the trust.

Grantor Retained Unitrust (GRUT) – A irrevocable trust that annually pays a fixed percentage of the value of its assets (as revalued on an annual basis) to the grantor or (settlor) for some defined term, and pays the remainder interest of the trust to a noncharitable beneficiary.

Gross Estate – The gross estate consists of the fair market value of all of a decedent's interests owned at the decedent's date of death plus the fair market value of certain property interest the decedent transferred during his life, in which he retained some rights, powers, use, or possession.

Guardianship Clause – A clause in a will which allows the testator to identify an individual(s) to raise any minor children.

Heir – One who inherits under state law.

Holographic Will – Handwritten will.

Incident of Ownership in a Life Insurance Policy – The ability to exercise any economic right in a life insurance policy.

Inclusion Ratio – Ratio determined by subtracting the applicable fraction from one.

Income Beneficiary – The person or entity who has the current right to income from a trust, or the right to use the trust assets.

Incomplete Transfer – Any transfers that include a revocable beneficiary designation or a transfer to a revocable trust. Incomplete transfers are not considered gifts for gift tax purposes.

Indirect Gift – A payment, or transfer, to a third party on behalf of a donor for the benefit of the donee.

Installment Sale – A sale of property that includes a note from the buyer to the seller. The buyer pays the seller the full valuable consideration of the property over a specified set of terms.

Insured – The person whose life is covered by the life insurance contract.

Intangible Personal Property – Property that cannot truly be touched such as stocks, bonds, patents, and copyrights.

Intentionally Defective Grantor Trust (IDGT) – A trust which gives the grantor sufficient control to be considered the owner for income tax purposes, but not so much control to require the trust property to be included in the transferor's gross estate.

Inter Vivos Trust – A trust that is created during the grantor's lifetime.

Intestacy – To die without a valid will or to die with a will that does not distribute all property.

Introductory Clause – A clause in a will which identifies the testator.

Irrevocable Life Insurance Trust (ILIT) – An irrevocable trust that owns and holds life insurance on its grantor's life. An ILIT is also known as a wealth replacement trust (WRT).

Irrevocable Trust – A trust created by a grantor that cannot be revoked. The grantor cannot take back the property that was transferred to the trust.

Joint Tenancy (with Right of Survivorship) – An undivided interest in property held by two or more related or unrelated persons, generally includes a right of survivorship.

Joint Will – One will executed by two or more individuals jointly that transfers their common interest in property.

Key Person Discount – A reduction in the fair market value of transferred stock due to an economic reality that the value of the stock will decline if a key person, such as the founder, dies or becomes disabled.

L

Lack of Marketability Discount – A reduction in the fair market value of a transferred asset because the interest is more difficult to sell to the public.

Lapse – When a power or right ends because of time or circumstance.

Legal Ownership – Possession of legal title to the property.

Legatee – One who inherits under the will.

Letters of Administration – A legal document that affirms the power of the administrator to act as the agent of the probate court.

Letters Testamentary – A legal document that affirms the power of the executor to act as the agent of the probate court.

Life Estate – An interest in property that ceases upon the death of the owner of a life interest or estate and provides a right to the income or the right to use property or both.

Living Will/Advance Medical Directive – Legal document expressing an individual's last wishes regarding life sustaining treatment.

Lump Sum Death Benefit – A single payment of a life insurance death benefit to a beneficiary.

M

Minority Discount – A reduction in the fair market value of a transferred interest in property because the interest is not a controlling interest.

Modified Endowment Contract (MEC) – A life insurance policy that appears to function like an investment contract because the policy is paid up in just a few payments. MECs function like other life insurance policies except for the tax treatment of loans from the policy.

Mutual Will – Two or more identical wills that leave all assets to the reciprocal party.

N

Net Gift – A gift that requires the donee to pay the gift tax. The gift tax is based on the value of the transfer less the gift tax.

No–Contest Clause – A clause in a will that discourages heirs from contesting the will by substantially decreasing or eliminating bequests to them if they file a formal legal contest to the will.

Nuncupative Will – Oral will consisting of dying declarations.

O

Ordinary Income Property – Property that, when sold, results in recognition of ordinary income.

Overqualified – A decedent's taxable base is less than the applicable estate tax credit equivalency because too many assets have passed to a surviving spouse.

Owner – The person who holds title to a life insurance contract.

Paid-Up Policy – A life insurance policy where no more premium payments are necessary to keep the life insurance policy in force, or a life insurance policy that cannot accept additional premiums without causing the life insurance policy to become a modified endowment contract.

Pay-on-Death Account (POD) – A bank account utilizing a beneficiary designation.

Per Capita – Sometimes called "by the head" allows the deceased person's heirs to move into the generational slot of the deceased heir and inherit accordingly.

Per Stirpes – Sometimes called "taking by representation" directs that the deceased person's designated share of an estate is transferred to his heirs.

Policy Dividends – Refunds of overcharged premiums to life insurance policy owners. The payments are treated as a return of the policy owner's adjusted basis.

Pooled Income Funds (PIF) – Donor contributions are pooled in a trust created and maintained by the charity. Each donor receives an allocable share of the income from the trust for his life.

Pot Trust – A trust created as a single trust and remains a single trust during the period of its administration. The trustee has the flexibility to treat all beneficiaries equally, as opposed to basing beneficial interest in the trust on the degree of relationship to the grantor.

Pourover Trust – A trust that receives assets that "pour" into it from another source, generally the grantor's estate at the grantor's death.

Power of Appointment – The power to name who will enjoy or own property.

Power of Attorney – Legal document that authorizes an agent to act on a principal's behalf.

Premium Pay Status – Premiums are currently being paid on the life insurance policy.

Present Interest – An unrestricted right to the immediate use of property. A present interest gift qualifies for the annual exclusion.

Principal – The grantor giver of a power of attorney.

Private Annuity – The annuitant sells an asset to a buyer in exchange for an unsecured promise from the buyer to make fixed annual payments to the annuitant for the remainder of the annuitant's life.

Private Foundation – A charitable organization that receives its support from a single individual or family. It can be either a private operating foundation or a private nonoperating foundation.

Private Nonoperating Foundation – A charitable organization (private foundation) that does NOT spend at least 85% of its adjusted net income (or minimum investment return, if less) on activities engaged in for the active conduct of the exempt purpose.

Private Operating Foundation – A charitable organization (private foundation) that spends at least 85% of its adjusted net income (or minimum investment return, if less), on activities engaged in for the active conduct of the exempt purpose.

Probate Process – The legal proceeding that serves to prove the validity of existing wills, supervise the orderly distribution of decedent's assets to the heirs, and protect creditors by ensuring that valid debts of the estate are paid.

Prudent Man Rule – A rule which requires a trustee, as a fiduciary, to act in the same manner that a prudent person would act if the prudent person were acting for his own benefit.

Public Charities – Charitable organizations that receive broad support from the general public.

QTIP Trust – A trust that grants the surviving spouse a lifetime right to the income of the trust while transferring the remainder interest to individual(s) of the grantor's choosing, typically created at the death of the first spouse to die.

Qualified Domestic Trust (QDOT) – A trust created for the benefit of a noncitizen spouse which has enough transfer stipulations to allow the U.S. Government to subject assets remaining at the death of the noncitizen surviving spouse, as well as distributions of principal, to estate taxation. Assets transferred to a QDOT qualify for the unlimited marital deduction.

Qualified Personal Residence Trust (QPRT) – A special form of a GRAT in which the grantor transfers his home to the QPRT and receives "use" of the personal residence as the annuity. The remainder interest of the trust passes to a noncharitable beneficiary.

Qualified Terminable Interest Property Trust (QTIP Trust or C Trust) – A trust which allows a decedent to qualify a transfer for the marital deduction at his death yet still control the ultimate disposition of the property.

Qualified Transfers – A payment made directly to a qualified educational institution for tuition, excluding room and board, or a payment made directly to a medical institution for the qualified medical expenses of someone else. Qualified transfers are excluded from gift tax.

Qualified Viatical Settlement Provider – A state licensed business that is regularly engaged in the business of buying life insurance policies from the policy owners.

Quasi–Community Property – Property that would be community property had the married couple been living in the community-property state at the time of acquisition (applies to married couples who move from a common law (separate property) state to a community-property state).

Real Property – Property that is land and buildings attached to the land.

Reciprocal Will – Two or more identical wills that leave all assets to the reciprocal party.

Remainder Beneficiary – The individual or entity entitled to receive the assets that remain in the trust at the date of the trust's termination.

Residence Domiciliary – An individual's legal state of residence.

Residuary Clause – A clause in a will which directs the transfer of the balance of any assets not previously bequeathed or distributed.

Reversionary Interest – Interests that have been transferred and subsequently revert back to the transferor. Also, includes a possibility that the property transferred by the decedent may return to him or his estate and a possibility that property transferred by the decedent may become subject to a power of disposition by him.

Revocable Living Trust – A revocable trust that is managed by the grantor and is for the benefit of the grantor during his lifetime. The property transferred to the trust avoids the individual's probate estate, but is included in the individual's gross estate.

Revocable Trust – A trust created where the grantor of the trust retains the right to revoke the trust at any time prior to his incapacity or death.

Rule Against Perpetuities (RAP) – A common law rule which requires that all interests in a trust must vest, if at all, within lives in being plus 21 years.

Sale – The direct transfer of property to another for a note, money, or property of equal fair market value.

Section 1035 Exchange – A tax–free exchange of a life insurance contract for another life insurance contract, a modified endowment contract, or an annuity contract on the same insured.

Self Proving Clause – A clause in a will which involves the notary signing a notarized declaration that he/she witnessed the testator and witnesses sign the will.

Self–Cancelling Installment Note (SCIN) – An installment sale that terminates at the earlier of the (1) death of the seller or (2) the term set forth in the installment note.

Self–Settled Trust – A trust where the beneficiary is also the grantor of the trust.

Settlement Options – The beneficiary's available options when receiving the death benefit, usually either lump sum or annuity.

Side Instruction Letter – Also known as a personal instruction letter, details the testator's wishes regarding the disposition of tangible possessions (household goods), the disposition of the decedent's body, and funeral arrangements. A side instruction letter is not legally binding, but generally followed.

Simple Trust – A trust that requires all of the trust income to be distributed on an annual basis to the beneficiaries and does not have a charitable organization as one of its beneficiaries.

Simultaneous Death Clause – A clause in a will that establishes a presumption of which person died first in simultaneous death situations.

Situs – The place, generally referring to the state, where property is located.

Sound Mind – A person's mental capacity.

Spendthrift Clause – A clause in a trust document which does not allow the beneficiary to anticipate distributions from the trust, assign, pledge, hypothecate, or otherwise promise to give distributions from the trust to anyone. If such a promise is made, it is void and may not be enforced against the trust.

Split Gift Election – An election available to a donor of separate property which allows him to utilize his spouse's annual exclusion and transfer up $26,000 per year per donee without incurring gift tax.

Split–Dollar Life Insurance – A single life insurance policy in which two parties have an ownership interest. One party typically owns the death benefit, while the other party owns the cash value.

Springing Power – The agent's power "springs" into existence upon some defined event or determination.

Sprinkling Provision – The trustee's right to make distributions to the trust beneficiaries at his discretion.

Standby Trust – A trust created during the grantor's lifetime that is either unfunded or minimally funded. A standby trust is also known as a contingent trust.

Statutory Will – A will meeting state statutes generally drawn up by an attorney and signed in the presence of witnesses.

Straight Single Life Annuity – An annuity for a term equal to the annuitant's life.

Surety Bond – A bond posted by the administrator or the executor of the estate to protect creditors, heirs, and legatees from losses created by the administrator or executor.

Surrender Value – The cash value of the life insurance policy less a surrender charge which is governed by the policy or state law.

Survivorship Annuity – An annuity that provides payments to one person, and then provides payments to a second person upon the death of the first.

Survivorship Clause – A clause included in a will requiring that the legatee survive for a specific period in order to inherit under the will. The bequest will qualify for the marital deduction if the property transfers to the surviving spouse and the time period of the survivorship clause is six months or less.

Sweetheart Will – Two wills executed by spouses that leave all assets to the other spouse.

T

Tangible Personal Property – Property that is not realty and may be touched.

Tangible Personal Property Trusts (TPPT) – A special form of a GRAT in which the grantor transfers tangible personal property to the TPPT and receives "use" of the property as the annuity. The remainder interest transfers to a noncharitable beneficiary.

Tangible Property – Property that is not realty and may be touched.

Taxable Distribution – Any distribution from a trust to a skip person other than a taxable termination or a direct skip.

Taxable Estate – The adjusted gross estate less the available unlimited marital and unlimited charitable deductions.

Taxable Termination – The termination of an interest in property held in trust unless: (1) a transfer subject to federal estate or gift tax occurs with respect to the property held in the trust at the time of the termination; (2) immediately thereafter a non–skip person has an interest in the property; or (3) no distributions may be made at any time thereafter to a skip person.

Tax–Appointment Clause – A clause in a will directing which assets will bear the payment of any debts and estate taxes.

Tenancy by the Entirety – A JTWROS that can only occur between a husband and wife.

Tenancy in Common – An undivided interest in property held by two or more related or unrelated persons.

Tentative Tax – The estate tax calculated on the tentative tax base.

Tentative Tax Base – The tentative tax base equals the taxable estate plus all post–1976 taxable gifts.

Term Insurance Policy – A life insurance contract which states if the insured dies within the term of the contract, the insurance company will pay a stated death benefit.

Term Interest – An interest in property that ceases after a defined period of time.

Terminable Interest – An interest that terminates at some point.

Terminally Ill Individual – A person who has been certified by a licensed health care provider as having a condition or illness that can reasonably be expected to result in death within 24 months.

Testamentary Trust – A trust created after the death of the grantor. The grantor's will generally includes all of the trust provisions.

Testate – When a decedent dies with a valid will.

Testator – Writer of a will.

Three–Year Rule – If an individual gratuitously transfers ownership of a life insurance policy on his life, or any incident of ownership in a policy on his life within three years of his date of death, the death benefit of the policy is included in his federal gross estate.

Totten Trust – Not a trust, but rather a bank account with a beneficiary clause.

Transfer Costs – Includes the gift and estate taxes and the costs of avoiding taxes, such as the cost of documents, planning, trusts, and other professional fees.

Transfer for Value – A transfer of an asset by means of a sale, exchange or any transfer which includes valuable consideration. If a life insurance policy is transferred for value, the death benefit in excess of the transferor's adjusted basis will be subject to income tax, unless the transfer meets certain exceptions.

Transfer–on–Death Account (TOD) – An investment account utilizing a beneficiary designation.

Trust – A structure that vests legal title (the legal interest) to assets in one party, the trustee, who manages those assets for the benefit of the beneficiaries (who hold the equitable title) of the trust.

Trustee – The individual or entity responsible for managing the trust assets and carrying out the directions of the grantor that are formally expressed in the trust instrument.

2503(b) Trust – A trust for the benefit of a minor designed to qualify the present value of the income interest of the trust for the annual exclusion. A 2503(b) trust must pay its income annually to the minor, but may hold the trust property for the minor's lifetime.

2503(c) Trust – A trust for the benefit of a minor designed to qualify the contribution to the trust for the annual exclusion. A 2503(c) trust must give the minor the right to receive the trust assets when he reaches age 21, but is not required to pay the income to the minor at any earlier time.

Unauthorized Practice of Law – The proffering of legal advice or services by one who is not a licensed attorney.

Underqualified – When too much of a decedent's property was subject to estate tax at the death of the first spouse due to improper use of the unlimited marital deduction.

Universal Life Insurance – A term insurance policy with a cash accumulation account attached to it.

Unlimited Marital Deduction – Because a married couple is viewed as one single economic unit for estate and gift tax purposes, an individual receives a deduction from his gross gifts or from the adjusted gross estate for transfers to a spouse. Hence, transfers to a spouse are not subject to estate or gift tax.

Usufruct – A Louisiana device similar to a life estate which provides the holder with the right to use property and/or the right to income from the particular property.

Variable Universal Life Insurance – A universal life insurance policy with investment options available for the cash accumulation account.

Wealth Replacement Trust (WRT) – An irrevocable trust that owns and holds life insurance on its grantor's life. A WRT is also known as an Irrevocable Life Insurance Trust (ILIT).

Whole Life Insurance – A permanent insurance policy which guarantees that the policy will remain in force as long as the premium is paid. The policy has a cash account attached to it which grows tax deferred.

Will – A legal document that provides the testator, or will maker, the opportunity to control the distribution of property, appoint an executor and avoid the state's intestacy law distribution scheme.

X Dividend Date – The date the market price of a stock adjusts for a declared dividend (i.e., the market price of the stock is reduced approximately by the amount of the dividend).

Index